THE COMPLETE BOOK OF

TRACTORS & TRUCKS

Fordson
Fordson

THE COMPLETE BOOK OF TRACTORS & TRUCKS

JOHN CARROLL & PETER J. DAVIES

HERMES HOUSE

This edition is published by Hermes House

Hermes House is an imprint of Anness Publishing Ltd
Hermes House, 88–89 Blackfriars Road, London SE1 8HA
tel. 020 7401 2077; fax 020 7633 9499; info@anness.com

A CIP catalogue record for this book is available from the British Library.

Publisher: Joanna Lorenz
Project Editor : Felicity Forster
Designer: Michael Morey
Jacket Design : Nigel Partridge
Picture Researcher(Tractors) : John Bolt
Editorial Reader: Joy Wotton
Production controller : Ben Worley

Previously published as The CompleteBooks of Tractors & Trucks

1 3 5 7 9 10 8 6 4 2

Notes

Where possible, weights are quoted in units appropriate to the manufacturer's country of origin. A UK 'imperial' ton is 2240lbs or 1016kgs. A US 'short ton is 2000lbs or 907kgs. A metric tonne is 2204lbs or 1000kgs

Contents

K790 JYC
640 NEW HOLLAND

J. PARRISH & SON
ERF
J. PARRISH & SON
SHEFFORD
BEDS.
816325
M223 DEG

General Introduction

Before the invention of the steam and diesel engines, the dual problems of farming the land and transporting heavy objects from one place to another have been solved by the use of animals such as oxen, horses, camels and elephants. In the last hundred years, however, there have been very rapid changes in the ways we haul and carry: tractors have become an essential agricultural tool used primarily for pulling farm implements, while trucks are now road vehicles employed to carry all kinds of heavy loads, from food, logs, cement and fuel to everyday garbage.

This book is divided into two halves, focusing on each of these important transport vehicles in turn. Within each half there are sections on the history and development of the vehicles, and an A–Z guide to the principal manufacturers.

The World of Tractors follows the history and development of the tractor, as well as the history of many of the great pioneers and inventors who contributed to its spectacular success. The *A–Z of Tractors* is an international sweep of farm machinery from around the world, including historical examples as well as lesser-known makes.

The World of Trucks charts the evolution of the truck, including sections on specialized vehicles such as fire trucks, logging trucks, mobile cranes and military trucks. The *A–Z of Trucks* features all the major manufacturers from around the world, including histories of the major companies and the decisions that shaped their successes and failures.

NEW HOLLAND
7740
NEW HOLLAND

TWX 84

6950
JOHN DEERE

MM
MINNEAPOLIS-MOLINE
G1050

TRACTORS

LANZ

The World of Tractors

Tractors are an everyday sight and are taken for granted as an essential farming tool. However tractors were not always so ubiquitous and the complete mechanization of farming has only been achieved recently. In some cases the mechanization of farming did not take place until the years after World War II. The United States, with its huge prairies to cultivate, pioneered the tractor and subsequent developments such as the combine harvester, with other nations – such as Great Britain – close behind. This section charts the development and history of the tractor as we now know it and the history of a number of the men whose efforts speeded up the development of farming machinery.

■ OPPOSITE *A 1923 12hp Lanz. Through use of a simple and reliable design Lanz became the predominant tractor maker in Germany.*

■ LEFT *At the beginning of the 1900s Case diversified into the manufacture of gasoline tractors after the success of its threshing machines.*

The Mechanization of Farming

The mechanization of agriculture is often considered to have begun with the 18th-century inventions of Jethro Tull's mechanical seed drill of 1701 and Andrew Meikle's threshing machine, patented in 1788, but these inventions built on far older technology. Carvings excavated at the Babylonian city of Ur show that wheeled carts were in use as early as 4000 BC. They are also known to have been used in India shortly afterwards. Knowledge of this invention spread so that by 2000 BC the use of wheels had reached Persia, and then Europe by about 1400 BC. Initially the wheels were fixed to an axle and the whole assembly rotated, but this was later refined so that just the wheels rotated. Many kinds of animals were used to pull carts, including oxen, water buffalo, donkeys, horses, camels, elephants and even slaves. Tracks, and then roads, suitable for use by primitive vehicles were built. The next development of equivalent importance was the mechanical means of propulsion.

THE AGE OF STEAM

Experimentation with steam power began as early as the first century AD, when Hero of Alexandria, a Greek mathematician and inventor, developed the aeolipile, a primitive form of steam engine. It consisted of a hollow sphere that was filled with water and heated so that the expulsion of a jet of steam through a nozzle produced thrust. This device was a major step towards self-propelled machines. In the 15th century Leonardo da Vinci worked on designs for mechanisms that would convert reciprocating movement into rotary movement, to enable a wheel to be driven. He also considered the workings of what is now known as a differential, by which two wheels on a common axle could describe curves of different radii at differing speeds.

In 1599 Simon Stevin (1548–1620) built a sail-rigged and tiller-steered cart and recorded some wind-powered journeys along flat Dutch beaches. At around the same time an Italian physicist, Giambattista della Porta (1535–1615) began experimentation with steam pressure. He constructed a steam pump that was capable of raising water and realized that there must be a way to harness this idea to

■ ABOVE *Once the technology of steam engines was proven it was developed rapidly for agricultural use. Buffalo-Pitts of New York made this 16hp machine in 1901.*

■ RIGHT *Early tractors, using engines other than steam for propulsion, adopted a steam engine configuration as shown by this 1903 10–22hp two-cylinder Ivel.*

■ ABOVE *Minneapolis Threshing Machine were among early manufacturers of steam traction engines and threshing machines dating back to 1874. This is a 45hp model of 1907.*

■ LEFT *This working machine is a Corn Maiden, a Ruston steam traction engine that was manufactured in Lincoln, England in 1918.*

■ RIGHT *Large steam traction engines were suited to the cultivation of the Midwest United States. This is a 25hp machine made by Reeves in 1906.*

■ FAR RIGHT *Case manufactured its first steam engine in 1876 and continued making them until the 1920s. This is a 110hp model manufactured in 1913.*

provide a means of propulsion. One of della Porta's pupils, Solomon de Caus, was intent on trying out the idea of steam propulsion in France but was incarcerated in an asylum at the instigation of members of the French clergy who disapproved of such experimentation. Another Italian, Giovanni Branca, combined della Porta's and de Caus's ideas and built a steam turbine. Steam from the boiler escaped through a nozzle into the perforated rim of a wheel and so turned it. Branca coupled this through a gear to a grinding machine and published an account of his experiments in 1629. Meanwhile another Jesuit, Jean de Hautefeuille (1647–1724), was experimenting with an internal combustion engine of sorts that used small amounts of gunpowder as the fuel.

A piston and cylinder were first employed in connection with steam by a French physicist, Denis Papin (1647–1712). In 1690 he designed a machine that used water vapour to move the piston inside the cylinder. The water within the cylinder was heated externally; as it vaporized it moved the piston upwards, then as it cooled the vapour condensed and the piston moved downwards through gravity. By 1707 the device was working well enough to power an engine in a boat. Unfortunately the local boatmen who had watched Papin testing his machine saw it as a threat to their livelihood and destroyed both the engine and the craft.

The first commercially successful atmospheric steam engine is acknowledged to have been the machine patented in 1698.

■ RIGHT *Case steam engine production peaked in 1912 as the company began to manufacture gasoline engined tractors. This is a 1916 65hp steam engine.*

■ LEFT *Horses were the primary source of power until widespread acceptance of the tractor. Many early adverts suggested that, unlike horses, tractors only "ate" when hungry.*

■ TOP RIGHT *The large machine such as this 1912 locomotive-style 18hp Avery would be superseded by smaller, more compact, machines in a decade.*

■ BOTTOM RIGHT *Nichols, Shepard and Co made this 20–70hp steam engine but later were one of the four companies that merged to form Oliver Farm Equipment in 1929.*

An English military engineer, Captain Thomas Savery (1650–1715), designed and built a pistonless mechanism for raising water, which became known as "The Miner's Friend".

Worthwhile experiments with steam power continued and led to the manufacture of workable engines. Amongst the early machines was the steam pump invented by Thomas Newcomen (1663–1729), that combined ideas from both Papin and Savery. Newcomen constructed a more efficient and less dangerous atmospheric steam engine and he formed a partnership with Savery, who possessed a general patent for such devices. The first practical engine was built in 1712. The pair refined the low-pressure atmospheric steam engine to the degree that most mines in Britain were using one by 1725. Across the Atlantic, the first low-pressure steam engine was installed in a copper mine in Belleville, New Jersey in 1753.

Meanwhile, Nicholas Cugnot (1725–1804), a French army engineer, built a steam-powered artillery carriage in 1769. This vehicle was the first machine designed especially for haulage and it could be said that this was when the era of mechanically propelled transport began. Cugnot's invention established Paris as the birthplace of the automobile in all its forms. His machine was a rudimentary three-wheeled vehicle, capable of speeds of up to 6.5kph/ 4mph. It was demonstrated on the streets of Paris, when it carried four people. The potential of Cugnot's invention was not perceived immediately and lack of support prevented its further development.

Technological advances specifically for agricultural purposes included Jethro Tull's seed drill and Andrew Meikle's invention of

■ BELOW *The mechanization of farming began with developments such as Jethro Tull's version of the plough (Figure 1) as well as rolling (Figure 7) and harrowing (Figure 6).*

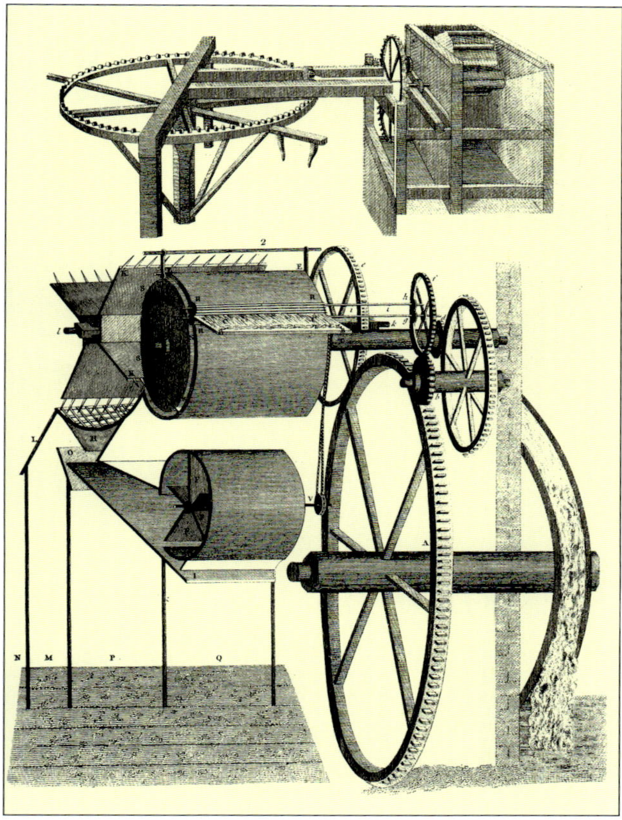

the mechanical thresher. Jethro Tull (1674–1741) devised a workable horse-drawn seed drill which dropped seed in rows. Andrew Meikle was a millwright from Dunbar in Scotland who, in the 1780s, developed a threshing machine for removing the husks from grain. Henceforward, after centuries in which farming techniques had changed little, the pace of development increased dramatically.

■ ABOVE RIGHT TOP *This illustration from 1756 shows the horse-drawn hoe-plough developed by Jethro Tull in the late 17th century.*

■ ABOVE RIGHT BOTTOM *Abbe Soumille's 18th-century seed drill which still relied on the power of human muscle.*

■ ABOVE *An 1811 engraving of Andrew Meikle's threshing machines. The top one is powered by a horse while the later one used a waterwheel.*

■ RIGHT *Threshers were further developed, as shown by this Oliver Red River Special of 1948 threshing in Illinois.*

Steam Power to Gasoline Engines

■ BELOW *From 1876 Case manufactured in excess of 35,000 steam engines before shifting its entire production to gasoline tractors during the 1920s.*

In Britain in the 1780s and '90s, William Murdock (1754–1839) and Richard Trevithick (1771–1833) experimented with steam-powered vehicles using steam at above atmospheric pressure. A Welsh inventor, Oliver Evans (1755–1819), who had emigrated to America and lived in Maryland, produced an elementary steam wagon in 1772. In 1787 he was granted the right to manufacture steam wagons in the State of Maryland. His wagons never went into production but he did build a steam-powered amphibious dredging machine in 1804, which he engineered to be driven under its own power from its place of manufacture to the River Schuylkill, where it was launched for its voyage to Delaware. In 1788 a vehicle of a similar configuration, known as The Fourness, had been assembled in Britain.

In America in 1793 Eli Whitney patented the steam-powered cotton gin, which mechanized the cleaning of cotton fibre. This made cotton a commercial commodity in the eastern states, assisted by the growing transport network – including transcontinental railroads – around the United

■ ABOVE *Steam engines worked in pairs and pulled a large plough backwards and forwards across a field by means of the cable on the drum under the boiler.*

■ LEFT *The angled lugs arranged at intervals around the circumference of the driven wheels were intended to aid traction in wet and heavy soils.*

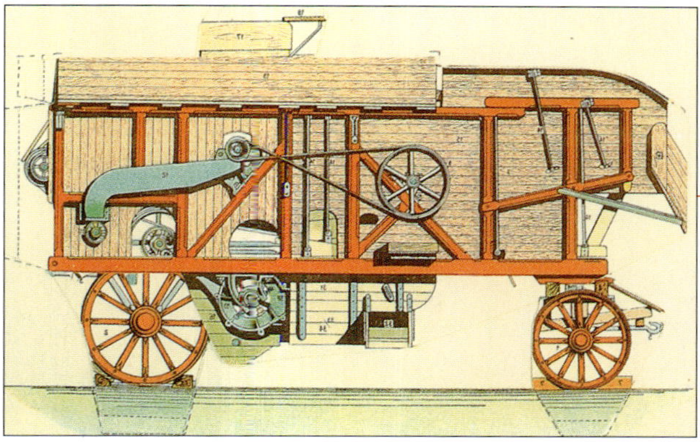

■ **ABOVE LEFT** ***By the late 19th century, threshers were portable and powered by a steam engine. This later one has pneumatic tyres.***

■ **ABOVE RIGHT** ***A portable threshing machine from around 1895. It had wooden-spoked wheels and was belt-driven by the steam engine that towed it.***

■ **BELOW** ***Despite such mechanization, threshing was still a complex and labour intensive process as this vintage thresher shows.***

States. Thomas Blanchard, from Springfield, Massachusetts produced a steam carriage in 1825 and a year later, in New Hampshire, Samuel Morey patented a two-stroke gasoline and vapour engine – this was America's first internal combustion engine.

Early farm implements were drawn by horses but in order to make them more productive it was clear that there was a need for an independent mechanical source of power. The advent of road travel and the railway locomotive again focused attention on the possibilities of steam-powered machinery that was independent of both roads and rails. Gradually the technology began to diversify: the steam traction engine became more refined and a practical proposition for farm use, while experiments proceeded with the gasoline-powered, internal combustion engine. American steam pioneers included Sylvester Roper of Roxbury, Massachusetts, John A. Reed from New York City, Frank Curtis from Massachusetts and the Canadian Henry Seth Taylor. Generally speaking at this time, the steam traction engine was reserved for providing power for driving equipment such as threshing machines.

New inventions took place throughout the 19th century, and these transformed farming practice. Cyrus McCormick's reaper of 1831

■ LEFT *The Princess Mary is an English Fowler ploughing engine of the sort designed to work in a pair. The cable is clearly evident on the drum.*

■ ABOVE RIGHT *Charles W. Hart and Charles H. Parr began pioneering work on gasoline tractors in the late 1800s in Wisconsin. They began the manufacture of machines such as this one in Iowa in 1900.*

was to revolutionize grain-harvesting. In 1837, John Deere developed a self-scouring steel plough especially suited to heavy prairie soils: farmers no longer had to stop constantly to clean their ploughs. In 1842, in Rochester, Wisconsin, Jerome Case perfected a machine that was both a thresher and a fanning mill. In 1859 oil was discovered in Pennsylvania and kerosene and gasoline were distilled from it. Kerosene was immediately a popular choice as a fuel oil because it was cheap.

In the closing years of the 19th century, vehicles powered by internal combustion engines started to make an appearance and names like Nikolaus Otto, Karl Benz, Gottlieb Daimler, Wilhelm Maybach, Albert De Dion, Clement Panhard and Armand Peugeot became prominent in Europe as a result of their efforts. Of these, it is the first who made the greatest mark as he patented the four-stroke gas-powered engine. When Otto's patents expired in 1890 the age of the internal combustion engine dawned. It was but a short step to the development of a practical agricultural tractor.

Companies specializing in agricultural equipment were active around the globe. In 1870 Braud was founded in France to manufacture threshing machines. In 1884 Giovanni Landini started a new company in Italy to manufacture agricultural implements, that went on to become a major tractor maker. In the United States in 1895 the New Holland Machine Company was founded in Pennsylvania and specialized in agricultural equipment. The J. I. Case Threshing Company had been formed in 1863 to build steam tractors. Its first experimental tractor appeared in 1892, powered by a balanced gas engine devised by an engineer called William Paterson. The machine was not as successful as its designers had hoped, however, and it never went into commercial production. Case continued to build large steam engines. John Charter built gas engines in Stirling, Illinois

■ BELOW *An English Fowler steam ploughing engine, no 15516, built in 1920 in Leeds, Yorkshire.*

■ BELOW *An illustration of an earlier Fowler ploughing engine from c1862. The flywheel for the steam engine is located on the side of the boiler and the governor towards the rear.*

and manufactured a tractor by fitting one of his engines to the chassis and wheels of a steam traction engine. The resultant hybrid machine was put to work on a wheat farm in South Dakota in 1889. It was a success and Charter is known to have built several more machines to a similar specification.

By 1892 a number of other fledgling manufacturers were starting to produce tractors powered by internal combustion engines. In Iowa, John Froëlich built a machine powered by a Van Duzen single-cylinder engine, and formed the Waterloo Gasoline Traction Engine Company. The company later dropped the word "Traction" from its name and manufactured only stationary engines until it introduced another tractor in 1916, the Waterloo Boy, the first successful gasoline tractor.

The Huber Company of Marion, Ohio had some early success: it purchased the Van Duzen Engine Company and built 30 tractors. Two other companies, Deering and McCormick, were building self-propelled mowers at this time; they were later to unite to become International Harvester. It was clear that the speed of mechanization of American farming was increasing. The name "tractor" was coined in 1906 by Hart-Parr, which had made its first gasoline tractor in Charles City, Iowa in 1902, and merged with Oliver in 1929.

■ ABOVE RIGHT *Before ploughing engines worked in pairs the concept of drawing the plough backwards and forwards relied on an anchor and pulley wheel.*

■ BELOW LEFT *A Fowler ploughing engine demonstrating drawing a five furrow anti-balance plough across the field.*

■ BELOW RIGHT *A mid-19th century illustration of a Garret and Sons steam engine ploughing across a field in England.*

The Beginnings of Mass Production

The contrasting economic conditions facing farming on either side of the Atlantic prior to World War I meant that America was where the majority of tractor production took place. Because of the differing sizes of farms on the two continents, designs that were specific to American prairie cultivation began to emerge and machines designed for drawbar towing of implements, especially ploughs, were experimented with.

The International Harvester Corporation was formed in 1902 through the merger of McCormick and Deering. Along with other companies, such as Avery, Russell, Buffalo-Pitts and Case, they built experimental machines at the beginning of the 20th century. Case built one in 1911 and by 1913 the company was offering a viable gasoline-powered tractor. Another early tractor was manufactured by two engineers, Charles Hart and Charles Parr. Although this first model was heavy and ungainly, they quickly went on to produce more practical machines, including the 12-27 Oil King. By 1905 the company was running the first factory in the United States dedicated solely to the manufacture of tractors. Many early tractors were massive machines styled after steam engines, because their

■ ABOVE *The increasing mechanization in farming inevitably led to mass production as demand for machines grew. This is a 1930 Case corn planter.*

■ LEFT *International Harvester was among the first makers of gasoline tractors and made more than 600 of these Type A Mogul tractors between 1907 and 1911. This is a 1908 model.*

■ ABOVE LEFT ***Huber Manufacturing of Marion, Ohio started by manufacturing steam engines but moved into gasoline tractor manufacture in 1911. By 1925 its Super Four model was rated at 18–36hp.***

■ ABOVE RIGHT ***Henry Ford designed the Fordson tractor in an attempt to do for farmers what the mass-produced Model T car had done for motorists in general.***

makers assumed that the new gasoline-powered machines would simply replace steam engines as a source of power and perhaps did not envisage the much wider role that tractors would come to play in farming. The trend to smaller tractors started in the second decade of the 20th century. Among the pioneers who made small tractors were the Bull Tractor Company with a three-wheeled machine, Farmer Boy, Steel King, Happy Farmer, Allis-Chalmers and Case. The latter manufactured the 10-20 in 1915.

As early as 1912, the Heer Engine Company of Portsmouth, Ohio produced a four-wheel-drive tractor. The Wallis Tractor Company produced a frameless model known as the Cub in 1913 while, six years earlier, the Ford Motor Company had built the prototype of what was intended to become the world's first mass-produced agricultural machine. The company did not actually start mass production of its first tractor, the Fordson Model F, until 1917. The frameless design, light weight and automobile-style method of production meant that the Ford Motor Company was soon among the industry leaders in tractor manufacture.

Many early tractors were built with two-cylinder engines as their source of power but even this allowed for a variety of configurations, including horizontally opposed cylinders, vertical and horizontal twins and the design of crankshafts, which varied as engineers sought to make engines as powerful and reliable as possible. John Deere's two-cylinder machines earned their "Johnny Popper" nickname from

■ RIGHT ***Case continued to produce threshing machines alongside tractors after its first prototype gasoline model was completed in 1892.***

■ LEFT *Henry Ford was unable to call his tractors Fords because the name was coined by a rival manufacturer. His 1917 Fordson was, however, far more successful than its rival.*

the distinctive exhaust note created by a crankshaft on which the con rods were offset by 180 degrees. The theory behind the offset crankshaft was that it would eliminate much of the engine's vibration. J. I. Case favoured the horizontally opposed twin in an attempt to minimize vibrations.

The popularity of tractors soared and, while a handful of only six tractor makers were recorded in the United States in 1905, there were in excess of 160 operating by 1920. Many of these companies were not realistic long-term propositions and others were bankrupted by the Wall Street Crash, while a number of companies all but disappeared in mergers.

In Britain, Hornsby of Lincoln was building tractors by the 1890s. Its first model, the Hornsby-Akroyd Patent Safety Oil Traction Engine, was completed in 1896. It weighed 8.5 tons and was powered by an oil-burning Stuart and Binney engine that was noted for its reliability. The engine was started by means of a blowlamp that created a hot spot in the cylinder head and so allowed the single-cylinder engine to fire up without the need for an electric starting mechanism. Hornsby used a 20hp engine with a horizontal cylinder for its tractor and constructed four of these machines. One of them was exhibited at the Royal Show in 1897 and was awarded the Silver Medal of the Royal Agricultural Society of England. In September of that year a landowner called Mr Locke-King bought one of the tractors: this was the first recorded sale of a tractor in Britain. The Hornsby Company supplied various machines to the British War Office with a view to military contracts, and experimented extensively with crawler tracks. The patents that it took out for these tracks were later sold to the Holt concern in the United States.

Petter's of Yeovil and Albone and Saunderson of Bedford both built tractor-type machines. Dan Albone was a bicycle manufacturer with

■ BELOW *The Hart-Parr 28–50 was a four-cylinder tractor of a basic design that endured in two- and four-cylinder types until Hart-Parr merged into the Oliver Farm Equipment company.*

■ ABOVE *In 1917 the 8–16 Junior was introduced by International Harvester in response to the demand for smaller and cheaper tractors, and asserted IH's position as a tractor maker.*

no experience of the steam propulsion industry, so he approached the idea of the tractor from a different viewpoint. He combined ideas from the automobile industry with those of agriculture and built a tractor named after the River Ivel.

Albone's machine was a compact three-wheeled design, which was practical and suited to a variety of farm tasks. It was a success and went into production; some machines were exported and the company would no doubt have become a major force in the industry had it not been for Albone's death in 1906. The company ceased production in 1916.

Herbert Saunderson was a blacksmith who went to Canada where he became involved with farm machinery and the Massey-Harris Company. He returned to Britain as that company's agent and imported its products. Later he branched out into tractor manufacture on his own account. Initially Saunderson built a three-wheeled machine because Albone's Ivel was attracting considerable attention at the time. Later, in 1908, a four-wheeled machine was constructed and the company grew to be the largest manufacturer and exporter of tractors outside the United States. A later model was the Saunderson Universal Model G. When World War I started, Saunderson was the only company in Britain large enough to meet the increasing demand for tractors. In the mid-1920s Saunderson sold his business to Crossley.

■ RIGHT *Avery manufactured gasoline tractors in Peoria, Illinois after switching from steam. Its largest machine was the four cylinder 40–80, one of a range of five models in 1919.*

■ LEFT *The Waterloo Boy Model N was the first tractor tested by the University of Nebraska in what became the noted Nebraska tractor tests. The company was later acquired by John Deere and helped to establish that company as a tractor maker.*

Other manufacturers were also developing tractors at this time, including Ransome's of Ipswich. Petter produced its Patent Agricultural Tractor in 1903. Marshall and Daimler built machines and looked for export sales. To this end a Marshall tractor was exhibited in Winnipeg, Canada in 1908.

In 1910 Werkhuizen Leon Claeys, founded in 1906, built its factory in Zedelgem, Belgium, to manufacture harvesting machinery. There were other, similar, tentative steps being made in numerous European countries. However, because labour was more plentiful and cheaper in Europe than in the United States, technological innovation was slower as it was not such an economic necessity. In Germany, Adolf Altona built a tractor powered by a single-cylinder engine that featured chain drive to the wheels. This machine was not wholly successful but considerable progress was made in Europe as a result of Rudolph Diesel's experiments with engines.

Diesel (1858–1913), sponsored by Krupp in Berlin, created a low-cost reliable engine that ultimately bore his name; it operated by compression-ignition and ran on heavy oil. Diesel experimented in France, England and Germany and found widespread acceptance of his engines throughout the world. He disappeared off a British cross-channel steamer during the night of 29 September 1913 and is believed to have committed suicide.

Deutz introduced a tractor and motor plough of what was considered to be an advanced design in 1907. Deutsche Kraftplug, Hanomag, Pohl and Lanz were four other German companies involved in the manufacture of tractors and powered agricultural machinery.

In France, De Souza and Gougis were two of the manufacturers that entered tractors in a tractor trial held at the National Agricultural College at Grignon, near Paris, where tractors undertook a variety of voluntary and

■ BELOW *While a number of tractor makers relied on an in-line four-cylinder engine configuration for their tractors Case persevered with Crossmotor models such as this 15–27 model of 1921.*

■ RIGHT *The merger of McCormick and Deering in 1902 led to the production of Mogul and Titan tractors for respective dealers of each make. This is a 1919 22hp Titan.*

compulsory tests. Elsewhere in Europe, progress was also being made. Munktell in Sweden made a tractor in 1913 and in Italy Pavesi made the Tipo B. In 1910, Giovanni Landini manufactured the first tractor with a fixed-mounted "hot-bulb" engine. In Russia an engineering company produced three designs prior to World War I.

Experimentation with tractors, crawler tracks and agricultural machinery continued until the outbreak of World War I. Farming had been depressed during this time, but the war demanded a huge jump in productivity. The British wartime government instituted policies to encourage increased domestic food production, including speeding up the rate of mechanization in an attempt to increase productivity and reduce the labour needed. A number of tractor producers had gone over to war-related work – Ruston Hornsby of Lincoln was involved with tank experimentation – but Saunderson tractors were in production and Weeks-Dungey entered the market in 1915.

Importing tractors from the United States was seen as a quick way to increase their numbers on British farms. The International Harvester Corporation marketed the models from its range that it considered to be most suited to British farming conditions: the Titan 10-20 and the Mogul 8-16. The Big Bull was marketed as the Whiting-Bull and a Parret model was renamed the Clydesdale. Another import was the Waterloo Boy, sold in Britain as the Overtime by the Overtime Farm Tractor Company. The Austin Motor Company offered a Peoria model and marketed it in Britain as the Model 1 Culti-Tractor. The war was to have far-reaching effects on both the economics of farming and on the production of tractors.

■ RIGHT *Advance-Rumely of LaPorte, Indiana was founded in 1915 and was one of the early tractor makers that was later absorbed into the Allis-Chalmers Company.*

McCORMICK-DEERING

The Evolution of the Tractor

By the end of World War I, the tractor was generally accepted as being a practical agricultural machine: Britain and the United States were exporting machines around the globe to countries as distant as Russia, South America and Australia. Henry Ford's mass-produced Fordson tractors, launched in 1917, established themselves commercially; they were initially manufactured in the United States for sale in Britain and beyond. The end of the war brought irreversible socio-economic changes and this meant that agriculture became increasingly mechanized as the 20th century progressed.

The Post-War Boom in Tractor Production

A period of prosperity followed World War I and in this boom the number of tractor manufacturers around the world quickly increased, while the tractor market shifted significantly. Acceptance of the fact that smaller tractors were practical changed the emphasis of the industry and threatened some of the established companies. Many of the new concerns were small companies with limited chances of success, especially when mass-produced machines, such as the Fordson, were gaining sales everywhere. Ford's tractor sold in vast numbers, achieving 75 per cent of total tractor sales in America. It was cheap to produce, so a greater number of farmers could afford it. Many small manufacturers struggled against this, producing insignificant numbers of various machines. They experimented and innovated but their products were never realistic long-term propositions.

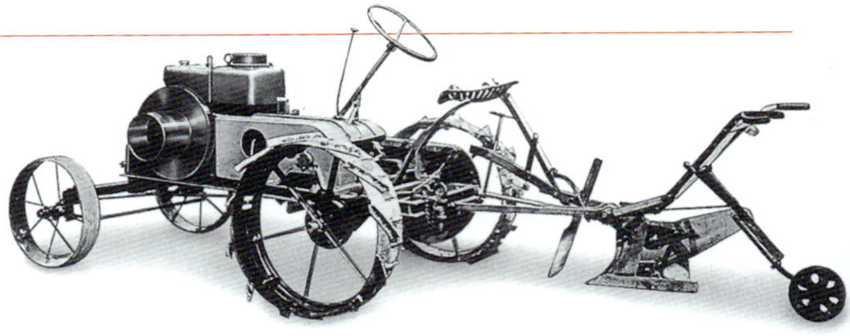

■ ABOVE *Diesel engines became popular in European tractors after World War I. This 1930 Fendt Dieselross has a 1000cc Deutz single cylinder diesel engine.*

By 1921 there were an estimated 186 tractor companies in business in the United States and production totalled 70,000 machines. There were also tractor producers in most European countries by the 1920s, including Breda, Pavesi, Fiat, Bubba and Landini in Italy, Steyr in Austria, Hofherr and Schrantz (HSCS) in Hungary, Hurliman and Burer in Switzerland and Kommunar in the USSR. Tractor makers in Australia included Ronaldson and Tippet. In the United States some of the small new companies included Bates, Ebert-Duryea,

■ LEFT *Taken in 1993 this photograph shows Jessica Godwin at 101 years of age, reunited with Fordson tractor number one made in 1917 when she was 25.*

■ ABOVE *This 1928 Deutz tractor is fitted with a side mower, powered by a single cylinder engine of 800cc/50cu in displacement. It runs on benzine fuel.*

Fagiol, Kardell, Lang, Michigan and Utility. A representative European product of the period was the Glasgow tractor, named after the city in which it was built between 1919 and 1924. It was produced by the DL Company, that had taken over the lease of a former munitions factory after the Armistice. The Glasgow was a three-wheeled machine, arranged with two wheels at the front and a single driven wheel at the rear to eliminate the need for a differential. The design was typical of a number of budget tractors built by small companies in both the United States and Europe.

Despite the influx of new manufacturers, the American tractor market soon developed into a competition for sales between Fordson, International Harvester, Case and John Deere. Fordson cut its prices to keep sales up, and in order to compete with the International Harvester Corporation offered a free plough with each tractor it sold. Having cleared all its outstanding stock with this marketing ploy, the

■ RIGHT *Large machines such as the Advance-Rumely Oil Pull 16–30 Model H became outdated during the 1920s, and were superseded by lighter, more compact, tractors.*

■ RIGHT *John Deere's Model D debuted in 1924 and production lasted until 1953, during which time more than 160,000 were manufactured. The GP was developed alongside the Model D intended for specific row crop cultivation.*

company was able to introduce its 15-30 and 10-20 models in 1921 and 1923 respectively, following these with the first proper row crop tractor in 1924. Called the Farmall, it was designed to be suitable for cultivation as it could be driven safely along rows of cotton, corn and other growing crops.

From then on the rival manufacturers used innovation as a way of staying ahead of the competition. Allis-Chalmers, Case, International Harvester, John Deere, Massey-Harris and Minneapolis-Moline all sought to offer more advanced tractors to their customers in order to win sales. For example, following Ford and International Harvester, Case introduced a cast frame tractor and although the engine ran across the frame, the model proved popular. Not to be outdone, John Deere offered its own interpretation of the cast frame tractor with the Model D of 1924. It was powered by a two-cylinder kerosene engine and had two forward gears and one reverse.

In Britain, the car maker Austin manufactured a tractor powered by one of its car engines. It sold well despite competition from the Fordson and stayed in production for several years. Ruston of Lincoln and Vickers from Newcastle-upon-Tyne manufactured tractors and Clayton made a crawler tractor

■ ABOVE *Steam engines such as this Fowler ploughing engine of 1920 were gradually replaced by tractors that towed ploughs from the rear drawbar.*

■ LEFT *As well as towing farm implements the tractor was eminently suited to the belt driving of machinery, as this John Deere illustrates. Tractors were rated with both drawbar and belt hp.*

■ RIGHT *In communist and Eastern Bloc countries tractor production was carried out under the auspices of the State, as seen here in the Polish Ursus tractor factory.*

■ RIGHT *As a result of the pioneering work by Henry Ford, tractor production was soon carried out on assembly lines. This method of production spread to all manufacturers, including Ursus.*

■ FAR RIGHT *Centralized production and farming were among the cornerstones of Soviet policy and reached Poland in the aftermath of World War II.*

■ ABOVE *The German manufacturer, Lanz introduced the Bulldog tractor in 1921.*

but, as in America, the other manufacturers were continually competing against the volume, price and quality of the Fordson tractor. The 1929 transfer of all Ford tractor manufacturing to Cork in Ireland showed that there was, by now, much in common between the tractor industries on each side of the Atlantic. Five years earlier the low-priced Fordson Model F tractor had gone on sale in Germany, meaning that German manufacturers also had to compete with Ford. Despite the similarities in worldwide tractor manufacturing there were still differences: one was in the different types of fuel employed by Ford and the Germans.

German manufacturers such as Stock and Hanomag publicly compared the Fordson's fuel consumption unfavourably with that of their own machines that used diesel fuel. Lanz introduced its Feldank tractor, that was capable of running on low-grade fuel through use of a semi-diesel engine. The Lanz company later introduced the Bulldog which the company became noted for. The first Bulldog models were basic and in many ways not as advanced as the Fordson. The Lanz HL model had no reverse gear, and power came from a single horizontal cylinder, two-stroke, semi-diesel engine that produced 12hp.

The Nebraska Tractor Tests

■ BELOW *The purpose of the Nebraska tractor tests was to give an independent evaluation of the abilities and power outputs of tractors such as this Allis-Chalmers.*

The purpose of tractor trials was to evaluate tractor performance and allow realistic comparisons to be made between the various models and makes. The Canadian Winnipeg Trials of 1908 were a success and became a regular event, continuing until 1912. A small tractor trial was held in Britain in 1910 while in the United States trials were held in Nebraska. The Nebraska Tractor Tests became established as a yardstick for determining the relative capabilities of tractors, preventing their manufacturers from claiming unlikely abilities and inflated levels of performance.

The tests were instituted as a result of a member of the Nebraska State Legislature acquiring both Ford and Bull tractors. Ford tractors were made by a Minneapolis company which had formed the Ford Tractor Company using the name of one of their engineers, and had nothing to do with the famous Henry Ford. The tractor did not amount to much and the eminent Nebraskan customer, Wilmot F. Crozier of Polk County, was less than satisfied with it, as he was with the Bull tractor that he had also purchased. Consequently, he sponsored a bill to make tractor testing mandatory in the state.

■ BELOW *A 1948 John Deere Model, a version of the model introduced in 1934 which achieved 18.72 drawbar and 24.71 belt hp.*

Starting in 1920 a series of tests was undertaken to examine horsepower, fuel consumption, and engine efficiency. There were also practical tests that gauged the tractor's abilities with implements on a drawbar. The tests were carried out at the State University in Lincoln, Nebraska. The law decreed that manufacturers must print all or none of the test results in their publicity material, ensuring that no one could publish the praise and delete the criticism. The Nebraska tests were noted for their fairness and authority and this led to their general acceptance far beyond the boundaries of the state.

The results of Nebraska Test Number 266 serve as an example to show the quality of the data supplied. A Massey-Harris Pacemaker made by Massey-Harris Company of Racine,

■ RIGHT *The Minneapolis-Moline U Models such as this 1942 UTS were introduced in 1938 and were rated at 30.86 drawbar and 38.12 belt hp in Nebraska tests.*

Wisconsin was tested between 10–19 August 1936. The tractor's equipment included a four-cylinder I-head Massey-Harris engine run at 1200rpm, with 9.84cm/3.875in bore and 13.3cm/5.25in stroke. It had an American Bosch U4 magneto, Kingston carburettor and a Handy governor. The tractor weighed 1837kg/4050lb. The Test H Data was as follows: in gear two a speed of 2.28kph/3.67mph was achieved, as was a load of 750kg/1658lb. The rated load was 16.21 drawbar hp and fuel economy equated to 6.65hp hours per gallon of distillate fuel. A maximum drawbar pull was achieved at 2.4mph in low gear with 1305kg/2878lb load. Fuel economy at the Test C maximum load of 27.52 belt hp was 10.39hp hours per gallon and the Test D rated load of 26.69 belt hp yielded 10.27hp hours per gallon. The standardized data meant that the results for each tractor were directly comparable.

■ LEFT *The belt drive pulley is seen here adjacent to the steering wheel on this International Harvester Corporation 8–16 Junior Model.*

■ BELOW *The horsepower rating was 8 drawbar hp and 16hp at the belt, hence the 8–16 designation.*

Tractor trials were instituted at Rocquencourt, France in the spring of 1920. These tested both domestic and imported models as part of a government drive to mechanize farming in France. In the autumn of the same year further trials were held at Chartres and 116 tractors were entered, coming from 46 manufacturers from around the world. In Britain, tractor trials were inaugurated at Benson, Oxfordshire in 1930.

The first running of the event attracted a variety of interest from English and American tractor manufacturers, including Ford, whose Fordson tractors were at this time being made in Ireland. The British manufacturers who submitted machines included AEC Limited, Marshalls, Vickers, McClaren and Roadless. Tractors came from further afield too: an HSCS tractor manufactured in Hungary competed in the Benson trials.

The Advent of Pneumatic Tyres

One of the first men to experiment with pneumatic tyres was Charles Goodyear, a resident of Woburn, Massachusetts. In 1839 he purchased the patent rights to a sulphur treatment process that helped him in his development of vulcanization, which made rubber both elastic and non-sticking, thus rendering it suitable for use in pneumatic tyres. Goodyear died in 1860, leaving a rich legacy to the auto industry, but also thousands of dollars of debt incurred in the widespread promotion of his product. The first car built by Alexander Winton in 1896 ran on pneumatic tyres made by Benjamin Franklin Goodrich. These were the first pneumatic tyres manufactured in the United States. Eight years earlier, in Ireland, the pneumatic tyre had been rediscovered by John B. Dunlop. The pneumatic agricultural tyre was the next major advance in improved tractor technology. The lack of practical pneumatic tyres had, until the early 1930s, hampered the universal use of tractors: while those with lugged metal wheels suitable for ploughing could not be used on surfaced public roads, solid tyres suitable for road use were inadequate in wet fields. Solid lugged wheels were also unsuitable for cultivation purposes, as they caused too much

■ ABOVE *This Farmall F-12 of the mid-1930s still has the old steel rimmed wheels that were in use before the advent of pneumatic tyres for tractors.*

■ LEFT *Pneumatic tyres were initially made available as an option in place of steel wheels, but soon became ubiquitous. They are fitted to this 1934 Farmall F-20.*

■ RIGHT *Like everything else connected with farming pneumatic tyres have become sophisticated, and various types and sizes are in use on this Massey Ferguson 6160 tractor and 139 baler.*

damage to the roots of crops. In the United States, Goodrich experimented with a zero-pressure tyre while Firestone explored the use of modified aircraft tyres. These had moulded, angled lugs and were inflated to around 15psi, giving them enough flexibility to cope with uneven surfaces. In 1932 Allis-Chalmers Model U tractors fitted with aircraft-type tyres inflated to 15psi were successfully tested on a dairy farm in Waukesha, Wisconsin. The company used the new tyres on a tractor with a four-speed transmission capable of working at ploughing speeds and also achieved 24kph/15mph on the road. It advertised this achievement widely in the farming press, but also hired racing drivers to display its new tractors with pneumatic tyres at speed, and unveiled a "hot rod" tractor at the Milwaukee State Fair of 1933. The tractor was shown working with a plough then a local racing driver, Frank Brisco, took it to 57kph/35.4mph on a race track. This created a sensation and Allis-Chalmers capitalized on the success by starting a tractor racing team. Valuable publicity was generated and by 1937 around 50 per cent of new tractors sold in the United States were fitted with pneumatic tyres.

■ RIGHT *While Allis-Chalmers was the first to promote pneumatic tyres for tractors, other manufacturers quickly followed. Shown here is the Case 1938 Model R.*

■ BELOW *The advent of four-wheel drive and high-speed tractors has placed greater emphasis on the performance of pneumatic tyres, both in the field and on the road.*

Scientific tests on tractors fitted with pneumatic tyres showed that fuel economy improved. University of Iowa tests showed that although rubber tyres added around $200 to the price of a tractor it took as little as 500 hours' work to recover this additional outlay. Rubber tyres enhanced a tractor's versatility, making it more suited to road use, and before long manufacturers offered higher top gear ratios to allow faster highway travel.

The Slide into Depression and World War II

The Wall Street Crash of 1929 and the economics of production and competition meant that the 1930s started on a different note to the previous decade. Gone was the optimism, and with it the numerous small tractor manufacturers with only a partially proven product. Only a few large companies remained producing fully workable tractors, whose new models reflected the increasing use of engineering technology. These included simple refinements such as the oil bath air filter, that gave engines a longer life when used in dusty conditions. Alongside these developments were improvements in vehicle lighting and fuel-refining techniques that enabled improvements in the efficiency and workability of tractors to be achieved. The Depression only slowed innovation rather than eliminating it, and it did not entirely deter new manufacturers from entering the market. In some countries the tractor-making companies had to take their chances in a competitive capitalist market, while in others there was less competition. In the USSR, created as a result of the Russian Revolution of 1917, tractor production continued under the auspices of the State.

■ ABOVE *As the tractor became more accepted and affordable it was not uncommon to see it being used with horses, as with this John Deere during harvesting.*

■ BELOW *The Depression reached its depths in 1932 but tractors were still being produced, as evidenced by this 1932 McCormick-Deering 10–20.*

Charles Deere Wiman, a great-grandson of John Deere, had taken over direction of the John Deere Company in 1928. Through the Great Depression, despite losses in the first three years of that decade, the company made a decision to support its debtor farmers as long as was necessary. The John Deere Company was fortunate that it had sufficient capital to be able to do this and was no doubt aware that it needed farmers to buy tractors as much as farmers depended on the machines.

During the worst of the Depression the total tractor production for 1932 was in the region of 20,000 and by 1933 only nine principal American manufacturers remained in the tractor business. These were Allis-Chalmers, Case, Caterpillar, Cleveland Tractor, International Harvester, John Deere, Massey, Minneapolis-Moline and Oliver. The Depression affected Europe equally badly but the major companies survived. In the years to come after World War II the tractor market would be divided between these makes, although mergers and amalgamations within the industry meant that numerous small tractor

■ LEFT *Despite worsening economic conditions International Harvester produced the 10–20 model while McCormick-Deering developed the similarly powered Farmall.*

■ RIGHT *The World War would necessitate intensified production of tractors in order to increase agricultural production.*

■ LEFT *Changing economic conditions caused Henry Ford to abandon tractor production in the United States in 1929 and transfer to Ireland, then England.*

■ RIGHT *Lanz tractors such as this 1923 12hp model, were basic and lacked reverse gears – the engine was simply run backwards to change direction.*

■ LEFT *The English Rushton tractor of the 1930s was closely modelled on the Fordson. This is a 14–20 four-cylinder model.*

makers, as well as makers of agricultural implements and specialized equipment, would eventually become constituent parts of the handful of global corporations manufacturing agricultural machinery. The tractor industry has, throughout its history, been characterized by takeovers and mergers of both fledgling and established companies in the race for sales and technological advances.

Around the globe, in the shorter term, technological progress was made. In 1940 New Holland changed owners and, following a

■ BELOW *In the late 1920s Caterpillar introduced a series of smaller crawler machines aimed at farmers. This one is haymaking in England in the 1930s.*

■ LEFT *The Lanz Bulldog concept proved popular in Europe to the extent that it was manufactured by numerous other companies.*

■ BELOW *During World War II British women took over men's jobs. These women are using a Fordson tractor and reaper for haymaking.*

company reorganization, began production of the first successful automatic pick-up hay baler. A year earlier Harry Ferguson and Henry Ford had made an agreement to produce tractors together and the result was the Model 9N. The 9N was virtually a new design although it had some similarities with the Fergusons of the mid-1930s manufactured by David Brown.

When World War II broke out in Europe on 3 September 1939, there were three major tractor producers in business in Britain: Fordson, Marshall and David Brown. It was immediately clear that once again a larger number of tractors would be required if farmers were to be able to feed the nation through the oncoming war. It was also apparent that tractors (like much other war material) would have to be imported from the United States, initially as ordinary purchases and later by means of the lend-lease scheme. This meant that the major American tractor manufacturers would be supplying their products in considerable numbers. Allis-Chalmers, Case, John Deere, Caterpillar, Minneapolis-Moline, Massey-Harris, Oliver, International Harvester and Ford machines were all imported. Ford also continued production at its British factory and the machines were redesigned to use less metal, and painted to make them less obvious in fields. Two years later, in December 1941, America entered the war, with the Japanese airstrike on Pearl Harbor in Hawaii. The might of American industry was now dedicated to winning the war, but the wartime exports had popularized American tractor brands far beyond their place of manufacture.

■ RIGHT *Hanomag was one of the German tractor-making companies that thrived during the 1930s with the production of both wheeled and tracked diesel engined machines.*

■ BELOW *Tractors found a wartime role on airfields. Here, a Fordson is seen towing a bomb trolley for the RAF Lancaster bomber seen behind its returning crew.*

■ LEFT *A 1934 MTZ 320 Deutz diesel tractor. Deutz, like Hanomag, specialized in diesel and semi-diesel engined tractor manufacture, as these engine types were favoured in parts of Europe.*

■ RIGHT *In the aftermath of World War I few tractor manufacturers existed in France although the likes of Latil, Renault and Austin did produce tractors there.*

■ LEFT *An earlier example of the Deutz diesel engined tractor which found favour in Europe prior to the outbreak of World War II. Steel wheels are indicative of the basic design.*

■ RIGHT *Before World War II, tractors were more stylishly advanced in America where, by 1934, the Model A was in production.*

Shortages caused by the war led to the modification of designs. The numerous Japanese conquests in the Far East resulted in a rubber shortage, for example, which meant that steel wheels came back into use. Pre-war designs became standardized and remained in production throughout the war period, with only minor and necessary changes being made. The changes could wait but the war years allowed the manufacturers to assist the war effort and plan for the post-war decades. John Deere's factories, for example, produced a wide range of war-related products, ranging from tank transmissions to mobile laundry units, but throughout this period, John Deere nonetheless maintained its emphasis on product design, and developed a strong position for the post-war market through the efforts of Charles Wiman and the wartime president, Burton Peek.

International Harvester and White manufactured half-tracks that were to provide the basis for a variety of special vehicles, including armoured personnel carriers, mortar carriers, self-propelled gun mounts and anti-aircraft gun platforms. Vast numbers were supplied under the lend-lease scheme to Britain, Canada and Russia, and many of the machines produced by International Harvester went abroad in this manner. Massey-Harris made approximately 2,500 tanks for the US army. Case made 15,000 tractors specifically for the military out of a total of 75,000 made for the war effort. Case employees assisted the war effort in another way: volunteers from the factory formed the 518th Ordnance Company Heavy Maintenance US Army.

■ BELOW *Although this is an early Fordson, steel wheels became common again during World War II due to rubber shortages caused by Japanese conquests.*

690
MASSEY FERGUSON
MF

The Innovators

The development of the tractor and other farming machinery was given additional impetus as a result of the efforts of numerous individuals in different countries. John Deere developed a steel plough suited for prairie use; later Henry Ford brought the capabilities of mass production to tractor manufacture; Messrs Holt and Best developed successful crawler technology; Jerome Case developed a workable thresher, and Cyrus McCormick a reaper. Adolphe Kégresse developed light crawlers with rubber tracks and later Harry Ferguson developed the three-point linkage for attaching implements to tractors. The sum of these men's efforts has led to the production of the technologically advanced tractors of today.

JOHN DEERE (1804–1886)

The story of John Deere, who developed the world's first commercially successful, self-scouring steel plough, closely parallels the settlement and development of the midwestern United States, an area that the homesteaders of the 19th century considered the golden land of promise.

John Deere was born in Rutland, Vermont on 7 February 1804. He spent his boyhood and young adulthood in Middlebury, Vermont where he received a common school education and served a four-year apprenticeship learning the blacksmith's trade. In 1825, he began his career as a journeyman blacksmith and soon became noted for his careful workmanship and ingenuity. His highly polished hay forks and shovels, especially, were in great demand throughout western Vermont, but business conditions in the state became depressed in the mid-1830s, and the future looked gloomy for the ambitious young blacksmith. Many natives of Vermont emigrated to the West, and the tales of golden opportunity that filtered back to Vermont so stirred John Deere's enthusiasm that he decided to dispose of his business and join the pioneers. He left his wife and family,

■ ABOVE *John Deere the blacksmith from Vermont, United States whose company is now the only tractor-making one to still have its founder's full name as its brand name.*

■ LEFT *John Deere developed the self-scouring plough and his successors developed tractors such as the GP models of the 1920s, seen here being used in the construction of a haystack.*

■ ABOVE LEFT *John Deere became a "full-line" agricultural product manufacturer, making ploughs as well as harvesting machinery. Recently the company has considerably diversified.*

■ ABOVE RIGHT *Row crop tricycle tractors, high crop clearance models and other specialist machines have long been produced by John Deere, enabling the company to stay at the forefront of agriculture.*

who were to join him later, and set out with a bundle of tools and a small amount of cash. After travelling many weeks by canal boat, lake boat and stagecoach, he reached the village of Grand Detour, Illinois, a place named after a river meander, that had been settled by pioneers from his native Vermont. The need for a blacksmith was so great that within a short time of his arrival in 1836 he had built a forge and was busy serving the community. There was a lot of general blacksmithing work to be done shoeing horses, and repairing ploughs and other equipment for the pioneer farmers. From them he learned of the serious problem they encountered in trying to farm the fertile but heavy soil of the Midwest. The cast-iron ploughs they had brought with them were designed for the light, sandy New England soil. The rich midwestern soil clung to the plough bottoms and every few steps it was necessary to scrape the soil from the plough. This made ploughing a slow and laborious task. Many pioneers were discouraged and were considering moving on, or heading back east.

John Deere studied the problem and became convinced that a plough with a highly polished and properly shaped mouldboard and share ought to scour itself as it turned the furrow

■ RIGHT *John Deere became involved in the tractor-making business after acquiring the Waterloo Boy company in 1918. It then had to catch up with established makers such as Ford.*

■ LEFT *A photo that illustrates how far John Deere harvesting technology has come in the course of a century, from binder to combine harvester: a Sidehill 6600 model.*

slice. In an attempt to provide a practical solution to the problem he fabricated a plough incorporating these new ideas in 1837, using the steel from a broken saw blade.

The new plough was successfully tested on the farm of Lewis Crandall near Grand Detour. Deere's steel plough proved to be exactly what the pioneer farmers needed for successful farming in what was then termed "the West", though his contribution to the growth of American agriculture would in due course far exceed the development of a successful design for a steel plough.

As a result of economic constraints, including those of labour and manufacturing costs, it was the practice of the day for blacksmiths to make tools to order for customers. John Deere's bold initiative was to manufacture his ploughs before he had orders for them. He would produce a stock of ploughs and then take them into the country areas to be sold. This was a wholly new approach to manufacturing and selling in the pioneer days, and one that quickly spread the word of John Deere's self-polishing ploughs.

Despite this innovative approach, there were many problems involved in attempting to operate a manufacturing business on the frontier including a lack of banks, a poor transport network and, worst of all, a scarcity of steel.

■ BELOW *A pneumatic tyred John Deere seed drill behind a row crop tricycle tractor. It is planting four rows at once.*

As a result, John Deere's first ploughs had to be produced with whatever pieces of steel he could locate. In 1843, he arranged for a shipment of special rolled steel from England. It had to be shipped across the Atlantic by steamship, up the Mississippi and Illinois Rivers by packet boat, and overland by wagon 65km/40 miles to Deere's infant factory in Grand Detour. In 1846, the first slab of cast plough steel ever rolled in the United States was made for John Deere and shipped from Pittsburgh to Moline, Illinois, where it was ready for use in the factory Deere opened there in 1848, to take advantage of the water power and easy transport offered by the

■ RIGHT *More than 150 years after John Deere developed the self-scouring plough that helped make cultivation of the prairies possible, his name is still prominent on the sides of tractors such as this.*

Mississippi River. Within ten years of developing his prototype, John Deere was producing 1,000 ploughs a year. In the early years of his business, Deere laid down several precepts that have been followed faithfully ever since by the company he founded. Among them was an insistence on high standards of quality. John Deere vowed, "I will never put my name on a plough that does not have in it the best that is in me." In 1868, Deere's business was incorporated under the name Deere & Company. The following year John Deere's son, Charles, who was later to succeed him as president, was elected vice-president and treasurer. One of his early partners chided him for constantly making changes in design, saying it was unnecessary because the farmers had to take whatever they produced. Deere's viewpoint was more far-sighted: if he did not improve and refine products, somebody else would. As a result the John Deere Company has continued to place a strong emphasis on product improvement, and consistently devotes a higher share of its income to research and development than many competitors. Its role as a significant force in the tractor industry began when it purchased the Waterloo Gasoline Engine Company in 1918, and produced its Model D in 1924.

■ RIGHT *Charles Deere, the son of John Deere, became vice-president and Treasurer of the company and later succeeded his father as president of the company.*

■ FAR RIGHT *One of the innovations successfully employed by John Deere's successors was that of styling tractors. Henry Dreyfuss styled the range in the 1930s and this design continued into the 1950s.*

Jerome Increase Case (1819–1891)

Jerome Increase Case founded the J. I. Case Company in Racine, Wisconsin in 1842 and soon gained recognition as the first builder of a steam engine for agricultural use. During his tenure as president of the company, it manufactured more threshing machines and steam engines than any other company in history. In addition to his innate talents as an inventor and manufacturer, Case also took an interest in politics and finance. He was made mayor of Racine, serving for three terms, and he was also returned as state senator for the Racine area for two terms. He was the incorporator and president of the Manufacturer's National Bank of Racine and founder of the First National Bank of Burlington (Wisconsin). Case also founded the Wisconsin Academy of Science, Arts and Letters, was president of the Racine County Agricultural Society and president of the Wisconsin Agricultural Society. He was often referred to in manufacturing and agricultural circles as the "Threshing Machine King". Case received a different kind of recognition as the owner of "Jay-Eye-See" (the phonetic rendering of his initials) – a black gelding racehorse acknowledged as the world's all-time champion trotter-pacer.

■ ABOVE *The company founded by J. I. Case became noted for the manufacture of threshing machines and later steam traction engines. Mass tractor manufacture was not started until 1911.*

■ LEFT *The company found itself in the doldrums in the mid-1930s and the sales people believed they could only sell the CC models, such as this, if IH dealers had sold all their F-12 models.*

■ ABOVE *The Case LA was a redesigned version of the Model L tractor. Its more rounded lines reflected the increasing emphasis on the appearance of tractors.*

At an early age, Jerome Case is said to have been inspired by an article in an agricultural newspaper about a new machine that would thresh wheat. For the farmer of the early 19th century, little had changed since biblical times: he cut wheat with a scythe, threshed it by hand with a flail and winnowed the grain from the chaff by tossing it in the air. It was back-breaking and time-consuming work. Each worker could thresh only six or seven bushels a day, thereby creating a bottleneck that prevented farmers from expanding the size and productivity of their holdings. Manpower in this period in the United States was relatively scarce. In 1820, the year after Case's birth, the population was about 5.5 million, although this figure did not include slaves. The further west one travelled the fewer people there were, so that farmers on the frontiers could count on little more than their own families as their workforce, which was one reason why farm families tended to be large. Case was born and lived during a pivotal period for Americans, when the technological achievements of the Industrial Revolution were underpinning the expansion of the United States. He was to become a part of this process, along with other innovators such as Cyrus McCormick and Eli Whitney whose inventions transformed American agriculture. By applying ingenuity and technology to farming, these men so raised production levels that North America would become the breadbasket of the world.

Case began his business by refining a crude threshing machine in Rochester, Wisconsin; soon afterwards he moved to Racine to take advantage of the area's plentiful supply of water to power his machines. By 1847 he had constructed the three-storey premises which

■ LEFT *Case introduced the row crop Model CC tractor in 1930. The machines were painted grey, and had a distinctive side steering arm which was variously nicknamed the "chicken perch" and the "fence cutter".*

■ RIGHT *Case introduced a bright new hue for its tractors in 1939 with the R-series of tractors. The new colour was called Flambeau Red and was one of a number of refinements to the range.*

became the centre of his agricultural machinery business. At this time a horse-driven J. I. Case threshing machine retailed at between $290 and $350.

Case's business prospered to the extent that by 1848 it became, and remains, the largest employer in Racine. As the business grew, Case continued to develop his threshing machines. In 1852 he wrote to his wife after demonstrating one of them to a group of farmers, "All were united in saying that if the machine could thrash 200 bushels in a day it could not be equalled by any in the country." In the afternoon of the demonstration he hitched up the horses and, in half a day, "thrashed and cleaned 177 bushels of wheat".

By 1862 Case's threshers were much improved and a system known as the "Mounted Woodbury" was employed to power them. Horses were hitched in pairs to long levers that looked like huge spokes on a horizontally positioned wheel. The driver stood on a central platform to drive the horses and the power they generated was carried through a set of gears to long rods that drove the gears of the thresher. One machine so equipped was the Sweepstakes thresher – the first of Cases's named threshers – a machine capable of threshing up to 300 bushels a day.

■ ABOVE *The VA series of tractors, still in Flambeau Red, were introduced by Case in 1942 with the intention of increasing profitability by manufacturing more parts in-house.*

■ BELOW *Although J. I. Case built his business on threshers it is unlikely that he envisaged that machines such as this, seen here harvesting maize in Zambia, would bear his name.*

In 1863 Jerome Case formed a partnership, J. I. Case and Company, with Massena Erskine, Robert Baker and Stephen Bull. Two years later the firm adopted Old Abe as its mascot. Old Abe was a bald eagle that had been the mascot of Company C of the 8th Wisconsin Regiment during the American Civil War. In this year the Eclipse thresher was introduced. This was a further improved version of the earlier models, designed to provide a cleaner separation of grain and straw and cope with larger capacities of wheat.

Steam power was the next major innovation to be embraced by J. I. Case and Company. The first Case steam engine was constructed in 1869 and was the first of approximately 36,000 to be built. The early models were stationary engines, mounted on a chassis and pulled by horses. The engine was used simply to provide power for belt-driven implements such as threshers. By 1876 the company was building self-propelled steam traction engines, one of which won a Gold Medal for Excellence at the Centennial Exposition in Philadelphia. In this year the company sold 75 steam engines and in the following year increased this figure to 109.

In 1878 steam engine sales more than doubled and in that year Case's first export sale was made at the Paris Exposition.

In 1880 the J. I. Case and Company partnership was dissolved and the J. I. Case Threshing Machine Company was incorporated in its place. Refinements to the line of threshers were being made continually and in 1880 the much refined Agitator thresher was introduced, using an improved method of horse propulsion, namely the "Dingee Sweep" horse power. The company diversified into the manufacture of steam engines to power sawmills.

A story from 1884 gives an indication of Jerome Case's character. The company had sold a thresher to a Minnesota farmer and it was in need of repairs which the local dealer and a mechanic were unable to carry out. Jerome Case himself travelled to the farm to inspect the disabled thresher. A crowd, surprised by his visit and the distance he had travelled, watched as he attempted to repair the machine. He was unable to remedy the fault and was so concerned that a defective machine had left his factory that he burned the thresher to the ground. The following day a brand new Case thresher was delivered to the farm.

■ ABOVE *A Case tractor collecting mown grass for silage on an English farm. Case acquired the noted English tractor maker David Brown during 1972.*

■ BELOW *The Case DEX was especially manufactured for the British tractor market. As with the LA the final drive was by means of enclosed chains instead of gears.*

In 1885 Case, by now the largest steam engine maker in the world, looked towards the growing South American market and appointed a distributor for its west coast. This was followed by the opening of a Buenos Aires office in 1890. Jerome Case died in 1891 and his brother-in-law, Stephen Bull, became the company's president. In his lifetime Jerome Case had made an invaluable contribution to the mechanizing of agriculture and a line of farm machinery – Case IH – still bears his name to this day.

The International Harvester Corporation was formed in 1902 through the merger of the McCormick and Deering companies. However, Cyrus McCormick's involvement with agriculture had begun in Rockbridge County, Virginia in 1831, when he demonstrated his grain reaper which was an improvement on ideas tried earlier by his father, Robert McCormick. Cyrus McCormick had patented his reaper by 1834 and sold one by 1840. It was a major step in the mechanization of the grain-harvesting process. The mechanical reaper obviated the need for endless hours of scything and trebled the output of even the best farm labourer with a scythe. The new machines meant that productivity could be increased massively.

Having proven the reaper in Virginia, Cyrus McCormick moved west because, like Jerome Case and John Deere, he was aware of the potentially massive agricultural market on the

■ LEFT *Cyrus Hall McCormick, whose involvement with agricultural machinery went back to 1831, when he demonstrated his improved grain reaper in Virginia.*

■ FAR LEFT *By the time the merger between McCormick's and Deering's companies was being worked out in 1902, the gasoline tractor was already a practical machine.*

■ ABOVE *The simple design of drawbar allowed the draft of numerous implements, especially ploughs and harvesting tools.*

■ BELOW *Pneumatic tyres and row crop machines were still to be developed at the time of the merger, but the company would survive against Henry Ford's price cutting.*

■ ABOVE *From early in its distinguished history the McCormick-Deering IH company relied on overseas sales and manufacture. These tractors and implements are awaiting sale in France.*

prairies. McCormick established a plant to manufacture reapers in Chicago, Illinois in 1847. Production was soon under way and McCormick's brothers, Leander and William, joined him in the blossoming business. The demand for reapers ensured that the company flourished and the brothers prospered.

William died in 1865 and in 1871 the company's plant was burned down. The firm struggled as a result of this catastrophe but, despite a financial loss, built a new factory on a larger site. In 1879 the company was incorporated as the McCormick Harvesting Machine Company. Cyrus was the second brother to die, in 1884. Six years later Nancy McCormick, his widow, and his son Cyrus Jr, bought the shares held by Leander McCormick. Cyrus Jr went on to head the McCormick Harvesting Machine Company successfully for several years.

■ RIGHT *Tractor design generally follows trends: having become more rounded in the post-war years, it again became more angular during the 1960s and 1970s.*

■ RIGHT *A classic F-Series Farmall tractor at a vintage tractor rally in the United States. It has the front wheels positioned close together in the standard tricycle row crop configuration.*

■ BELOW *A farmer seated on his International Harvester tractor against the blue sky of Nebraska.*

The company had a policy of buying patents that appeared to have potential, as well as making developments of its own, and so held its own against rival companies. The biggest rival faced by the McCormick concern was the Deering Harvester Company. As recently as 1870 William Deering, a successful businessman from Maine, had invested in the company which made the Marsh Harvester, a forerunner of the corn binder, patented by the brothers Charles and William Marsh in Illinois in 1858. The company prospered and by 1880 William Deering had become the owner of what was now known as the Deering Harvester

■ BELOW *The names McCormick, Deering, International Harvester and Farmall all appear on this tractor. IH owned McCormick-Deering, and Farmall was the name of the series of tractors.*

Company. As the years went by the two companies became embroiled in a sales war. Deering tried to sell his company to McCormick in 1897 but no agreement could be reached. Five years later a merger plan was worked out that combined the assets of both McCormick and Deering as well as some smaller companies. The new company was to be known as International Harvester and was massive by the standards of the day, being estimated to be worth approximately $120 million.

The new corporation set out to expand and did so considerably by exporting to much of the British Empire and beyond. A new factory was constructed in Hamilton, Ontario and other companies were purchased, including the Osborne Company, Weber Wagon Company, Aultman-Miller and the Keystone Company. This increased both the size of the operation and the number of product lines offered. As early as 1905 the company made inroads into Europe, building a plant in Norrkopping, Sweden and followed this with plants in Germany and Russia. Not for nothing had it prefixed its name with "International".

■ ABOVE *The Farmall Model M was one of three new models that made its debut in 1939 having been comprehensively styled by the noted industrial designer Raymond Loewy.*

■ BELOW *Tractor cabs were an innovation that were slow in coming despite Minneapolis-Moline's experimentation. Modern tractor cabs are now soundproofed and dustproofed.*

DANIEL BEST

Daniel Best was born in Ohio on 28 March 1838, the ninth child of 16 from his father's two marriages. As a youngster he lived for a time in Missouri, where his father ran a sawmill, before the family moved to Vincennes, Iowa to farm 400 acres. An older brother had already made the move to the West and encouraged Daniel to do the same. In 1859 he did so, working as a guard on a wagon train, and for the next ten years he earned a living in a variety of ways, mostly connected with the mining and timber industries.

During a spell working with his brothers, who produced corn in California, he designed and built a transportable machine for cleaning grain. The brothers operated the machine during the 1870 harvest season, and were able to clean up to 60 tons of grain per day. Best patented his machine in 1871 and entered a partnership with L. D. Brown; in the same year "Brown and Best's unrivalled seed separator" won first prize at the California State Fair. Best went on to patent a seed-coating machine and then a clothes-washing machine. He continued to dabble in the corn separator market, especially when Oregon mandated that grain be cleaned before sale or transport. He went into partnership with Nathaniel Slate in Albany, Oregon and they opened a branch of their business in Oakland, California, choosing the location because it was a shipping port for grain and wheat as well as being a broker's market. Best then moved with his family to Washington to pursue more mining and timber interests.

■ ABOVE *Daniel Best's patents left him in a position to charge a licence fee to other crawler manufacturers.*

■ BELOW *The Best 60 crawler was among the first machines to take crawler technology into the fields.*

The demand for Best's inventions continued to grow and he manufactured a variety of machines aimed at increasing productivity as well as mechanizing farming. Because of the growth in his business Best felt obliged to acquire larger premises. He sold some of his other interests in Washington and Oregon and bought the San Leandro Plow Company from Jacob Price. Renaming the concern the Daniel Best Agricultural Works, he moved production to San Leandro from both Albany and Oakland. At this time he also patented a combined header and thresher and a fan blast governor that allowed the machine to work at a constant speed regardless of variations in the speed at which it moved across the field. This innovation was acknowledged as a major step

■ RIGHT *Following the merger of Holt and Best, the new company's tractors became known as caterpillars. This is a 1929 model 30.*

towards quality control in grain harvesting and cleaning, as well as combining the two functions into a single machine. Over the next few years Best's company sold 150 of the machines to farmers in the states of Oregon, California and Washington.

■ BELOW *The 1939 caterpillar R2 is powered by a 25–31hp gasoline engine.*

The difference between Californian farms and those of the Midwest was their size. Most Californian wheat farms were much bigger and harvesting was a major labour-intensive task: some farms required the services of 150 horses. Best was of the opinion that the technology existed to mechanize the harvesting in order to save both man- and horsepower. That technology was steam power, which was already extant in two forms for agricultural use: the horse-drawn steam engine as a source of power and the self-propelled steam traction engine.

Best bought the rights to manufacture the Remington "Rough and Ready", a patented steam traction engine proven in both agricultural and logging applications. He went a step further than the blacksmith Remington had done, and contrived to make it both tow his combine harvester and power its auxiliary engine. He was successful and patented the machinery in 1889.

CHARLES HENRY HOLT

Charles Henry Holt was born in Loudon, New Hampshire. He went to school in Boston, where he subsequently studied accountancy. After periods working in his family's business, and then in the accounts department of a New York shipping company, he embarked on a ship in 1865 and sailed to San Francisco. He gained employment teaching and book-keeping some distance north of the city. Within two years he had amassed $700 and returned to San Francisco with ambition.

His family was in the timber business back in Concord, New Hampshire. They specialized in the supply of hardwoods used in the construction of wheels and wagons, so Charles Holt established himself, as C. H. Holt & Co, by buying timber from his father and selling it to Californian wagon and boat builders. There was considerable demand for this service because of the scale of developments then taking place in California. One of his brothers, Frank, also moved out to California and established a branch of the business to produce wheels and their respective components. This was not entirely successful as the wheels made in the wetter atmosphere of the east were not suitable for the much drier western summers

■ ABOVE *The Caterpillar D2 diesel was manufactured between 1938 and 1947 with only minor upgrades to the design.*

■ ABOVE *The Caterpillar diesel 40 is powered by a 55hp 3-cylinder diesel engine. It is seen here in highway yellow, the trademark colour adopted by the company to replace the previously used grey.*

■ LEFT *A 1935 Caterpillar 28. It produced 37hp at the belt pulley when tested at Nebraska.*

■ RIGHT *A Caterpillar 2 ton. On the early models such as this the Caterpillar brand name is arranged to resemble a caterpillar insect.*

and frequently failed. To try to overcome this problem, wood was shipped to California and seasoned before being made into wheels, but this, too, was not wholly successful and the brothers looked for a place where the climate was more suited to their particular needs. They settled on Stockton, 150km/90 miles inland from San Francisco and formed the Stockton Wheel company. After around 60 years of successful manufacture of steam engines, and some of the first viable crawlers, the Holt and Best companies merged to form the Caterpillar Tractor Company in 1925.

In 1931 the first Diesel Sixty Tractor rolled off the new assembly line in East Peoria, Illinois, with a new efficient source of power for track-type tractors. By 1940 the Caterpillar product line included motor graders, blade graders, elevating graders, terracers and electrical generator sets.

■ BELOW *A Caterpillar tractor exported to England to assist with the war effort.*

Henry Ford (1863–1947)

Henry Ford was born on his father's farm near Dearborn, Michigan in 1863. He grew up with the drudgery of farm work and horse-drawn implements and it was this experience that fuelled his interest in things mechanical. By 1893 Ford was an engineer and an employee of the Edison Illuminating Company in Detroit, Michigan. In his spare time he experimented with internal combustion engines and their potential for vehicles. Henry Ford completed his first four-wheeled vehicle, a twin-cylinder, four-stroke engined, gasoline-fuelled quadricycle, on 4 June 1896. It had two forward gears and was capable of 16kph/10mph in low and 32kph/20mph in high. The ex-farmer and skilled mechanic went on to build another car while still in Thomas Edison's employ – this was the "autobuggy", a tiller-steered two-cylinder car with planetary gear transmission and chain drive.

In 1899 he left the Edison Illuminating Company and founded the Detroit Auto Company, that was initially heavily involved in car racing. It metamorphosed into the Henry Ford Company, which Ford later left after a disagreement about the direction that the company should take: he wanted to build

■ ABOVE *Henry Ford sitting in one of his experimental automobiles constructed while he was still in the employ of the Edison Illuminating Company.*

■ LEFT *The Fordson E27N was a tractor manufactured at a Ford plant in Dagenham, England. It was a development of the World War II era when Fordson had contributed to Britain's war effort.*

■ LEFT *It is hard to overestimate Henry Ford's contribution to the development of the transport industry. As well as tractors he also progressed the methods of mass production and the success of the automobile.*

low-cost, affordable machines while his colleagues wanted to build luxury motorcars. After his departure, the company was re-formed as the Cadillac Company.

In 1902, Ford built an experimental people's car and in June 1903 he and 12 other men raised capital of $100,000 and set up the Ford Motor Company. Ford's Model A was staked as the equivalent of $25,000 and in the next few months 1708 of them were sold at $850 each. In 1905 the Society of Automobile (later Automotive) Engineers was formed and Henry Ford was elected as one of the vice-presidents. This was at a time when the proponents of steam and electric cars were falling by the wayside and the internal combustion engine was becoming dominant. In the 1906–7 sales year Ford became the world's largest car maker with the manufacture of 8423 four-cylinder 15hp Model N cars, retailing at $550 each. Ford owned 51 per cent of the company's stock and the company made a profit of $1 million. Henry Ford's reputation was assured.

In the same year Ford turned his attention to the possibility of making tractors and assembled a prototype with a view to building the world's first mass-produced agricultural tractor. It was based around the engine and transmission from a 1903 Model B car. Experimentation continued until 1915, when Henry Ford announced that his first tractor would be a light two-plough tractor that would sell for $200. His aim was to do for farmers with an affordable tractor what his affordable

■ RIGHT *These tractors are harvesting in the Rusitu Valley, Zimbabwe. Ford tractors were later given a distinctive blue livery which made them recognizable all over the world.*

■ ABOVE *Mass production of tractors by companies including Ford has led to the mechanization of farming in most countries around the world, regardless of the crop type.*

cars had done for motoring in general.

While development of the tractors was under way Henry Ford did not neglect car production or his workforce. In January 1914 he guaranteed that wages of not less than $5 per day would be paid to non-salaried employees and that there would be a profit-sharing scheme. In August he announced to the motoring public that if the company sold more than 300,000 Model T Fords in the next twelve months he would rebate up to $60 on the price paid. As a result, production soared to three times that of his competitors. The company had a dividend of $12.2 million in the next year and the employees divided up a $10 million bonus. In 1915, as he had promised, he refunded $50 to the purchasers of Model T Fords, having exceeded the 300,000 figure. The company made its millionth car in this year, with the Model T retailing at $440. The Model T was by this time so ubiquitous that a number of companies, such as the Pulford Company of Quincy, Illinois, offered axle conversions to enable the car to be used as a tractor to pull ploughs and harrows. Another similar conversion was offered by Eros.

In 1917 Ford was preparing to assemble his new tractors in Britain, but the pressures of the war meant that production had to be transferred to the United States instead. Within four months the Fordson Model F was being produced. The design appeared unconventional in an era of large tractors and three-wheeled machines. It was powered by an in-line, four-cylinder, gasoline engine and used the magneto ignition system of the Model T Ford car. However, the reputation of Ford's automobiles ensured that the new tractor would be taken seriously. Sales achieved a total in excess of 34,000 in 1918 and increased exponentially.

Ford produced tractors that were reliable and incorporated refinements gradually as technology advanced. As early as 1918 the Fordson had a high tension magneto, a water pump and an electric starter. Ford continued to make the Fordson Model F during the 1920s and sold the model in numbers commensurate with the recession. This period saw Fordson engaged in a sales war with the International Harvester Corporation. Cutting prices was one tactic and moving production was another. Production of tractors by Fordson in the United States ended in 1928 but it continued elsewhere, including Ireland and England.

The next step was to introduce even more innovative but affordable tractor technology.

■ RIGHT *A Ford tractor with the distinctive blue oval logo at work on a coffee plantation in Zambia. The driver is wearing protective clothing.*

■ BELOW *A Ford tractor being used in conjunction with the development of arable crop cultivation in Luanshya, Zambia.*

Henry Ford made a deal with Harry Ferguson, which was sealed with only a handshake. Ferguson had invented the three-point hitch and Ford agreed to put it on his new Ford 9N tractor. This innovative technology endeared Ford's tractors, and in particular the Model 9N, to his farming customers. This was one of Ford's last major achievements in agricultural technology. He died on 7 April 1947 and his grandson, Henry Ford II, assumed charge of the company. It is impossible to quantify the impact Henry Ford had, not just on the tractor industry with the 1.5 million tractors made by his company in his lifetime, but on industry as a whole with his pioneering of mass production and assembly line techniques.

ADOLPHE KÉGRESSE

Half-track crawler technology was conceived as a way of keeping vehicles mobile away from surfaced roads, where more conventional wheeled vehicles soon became bogged down. Its history extends as far back as the early decades of the 20th century. In the United States and Europe manufacturers sought to produce useful half-tracks, mainly for agricultural work. Holt, Nash and Delahaye were three such companies but their machines tended to be slow and cumbersome.

The breakthrough was achieved in France during the early 1920s as a result of the efforts of Adolphe Kégresse. Kégresse, a Frenchman, worked for the Russian royal family as technical manager of the imperial garages. Around 1910, the Tsar wanted to follow a winter hunt in one of his motorcars and would not accept Kégresse's argument that the idea was impractical. Kégresse drove one of the cars into the snow, embedded it in a snowdrift and produced photographs of the stranded car for the Tsar. To overcome the problem, Kégresse began to work on a system of continuous rubber tracks running on light bogies that would give a car mobility in snow. His system was a success and he converted the Packard and Rolls Royce cars belonging to Tsar Nicholas II to improve their performance in the snow. Subsequently, Austin armoured cars were also converted.

■ ABOVE ***One of the Citroën Kégresse machines built specially for the successful 1922-3 crossing of the Sahara desert.***

■ BELOW ***Adolphe Kégresse developed his half-track system in the Russian snow for Tsar Nicholas II.***

Following the Russian Revolution of 1917, Kégresse fled home to France via Finland. He left behind him about a dozen almost-completed converted cars, which were seized by the Bolsheviks and employed in military actions against the Polish. The Polish army captured one and despatched it to Paris, where it was examined by the French army.

In Paris, the industrialists André Citroën and M. Hinstin became interested in Kégresse's system. In 1921 the first "Autochenille" was manufactured based around a Citroën 10 CV Model B2 car. The Kégresse-Hinstin bogies pivoted on the driven rear axle to which they were fitted in place of wheels. An important difference between Kégresse crawler tracks and those used on tanks at the time was that the former were made from rubber and canvas. The advantage of this was lightness of weight and considerable flexibility, which ensured that the tracks followed every contour of the ground. The tracks were fitted with rubber teeth on the inside to engage with the pulleys. Experimentation had proved that steel teeth were prone to collecting snow, which was packed into the joints by movement until the tracks stretched beyond breaking point. The snow did not adhere to the rubber teeth.

Tests of the new vehicle were carried out in the snow of the French Alps and the innovative development was greeted with acclaim. Adolphe Kégresse went to work for André Citroën, who was fascinated by the potential of this development. The Swiss post office was one of Citroën's customers for the Autochenille, and its vehicles were equipped with skis at the front.

Citroën was of the opinion that if the machines were effective in snow they would work equally well in sand and loose stones. In the winter of 1921–2 trials took place in the deserts of North Africa and a few improvement were made as a result of this testing. The developed half-tracks earned a formidable reputation and widespread publicity when the first motor vehicle crossing of the Sahara Desert was carried out by a team driving five Kégresse machines. They were equipped with additional radiators and used aluminium in their construction to minimize weight. Power came from 1452cc/88.5cu in engines with a bore and stroke of 68 x 100mm/2.68 x 3.94in driving through a three-speed transmission. The back axle was a two-speed unit, thereby increasing the range of the three-speed transmission, and enabling the machines to deal with varied terrain. The Autochenilles

■ RIGHT *Adolphe Kégresse demonstrating the cross-country prowess of one of his converted Citroën machines with a general-purpose trailer.*

■ LEFT *As well as in the sand the Citroën half-track system excelled in snow, as here in the Alps.*

were capable of a maximum speed of 45kph/28mph. The 3,600km/2,250 mile trip took place between December 1922 and January 1923 and was led by Georges Marie Haardt, Citroën's managing director, and Louis Audouin Dubreuil, a man with considerable experience of the Sahara. Nine other men, including five Citroën mechanics, and a dog, Flossie, accompanied the vehicles. With relatively few problems the team made the crossing to Timbuktu. Haardt and Dubreuil together also led a Central Africa Expedition, the Croisiäre Noire, from Algeria to the Cape between November 1924 and July 1925.

The British experimented with the Kégresse system and installed bogies on Crossley lorry chassis, of both 1270kg/25cwt and 1524kg/30cwt capability. In Italy, Alfa Romeo built an experimental Kégresse crawler tractor that could be driven in either direction as it was equipped with two steering wheels and two driver's seats. The Kégresse system of endless rubber band tracks was a success from the start and soon there was demand for a heavier duty version of the system. Adolphe Kégresse redesigned the components, refining his idea considerably, and produced the new version with a completely new style of bogie. It differed from the original in that the driven axle was now at the front of the track and was fitted with sprockets rather than relying on friction. Citroën, Panhard, Somua and Unic all used the new design on vehicles throughout the 1930s. Somua built the MCL and MCG half-track tractors with four-cylinder petrol engines that produced 60bhp at 2000rpm. The company also produced the S-35 cavalry tank and the AMR Gedron-Somua armoured car. Unic built

■ ABOVE *The advantages of Kégresse's rubber tracks were immediately apparent in heavy soil conditions such as those experienced here.*

the Model P107 artillery tractor. In Poland, Polski-Fiat built their Model 621L with Kégresse bogies while in Britain Burford-Kégresse produced the MA 3 ton machine and in Belgium FN manufactured Kégresse-equipped machines. Most of these were used primarily as gun tractors. A third Kégresse-borne expedition in 1931 took French crews in seven half-tracks from Beirut to French Indochina (now Vietnam) between April 1931 and March 1932. A Kégresse P17 half-track was shipped from France to the United States for testing and evaluation in May 1931. Cunningham, Son and Company of Rochester, New York built their version, the T1, and in 1933 the Rock Island Arsenal built 30 of an upgraded model, the T1E1. This in turn led to the International Harvester half-track by the end of the 1930s. Although he was not as directly involved with agriculture as some of the other innovators, Adolphe Kégresse made a substantial contribution to the development of crawler track technology around the world. It is noteworthy that the most modern agricultural crawler tractors use rubber tracks like those pioneered by Kégresse.

■ RIGHT *A Kégresse converted machine being used to power a binder during an English harvest in the 1920s.*

HARRY FERGUSON (1884–1960)

Harry Ferguson was the son of an Irish farmer. He was still a young man when he showed a flair for mechanics and engineering. During his early twenties, he worked for his brother as a mechanic and a race pilot. Later, he designed and built several aeroplanes which he piloted. He became the Belfast agent for Overtime tractors (Waterloo Boy models renamed for the British market) and this first experience with tractors, together with a spell working for the Irish Board of Agriculture, started him thinking of better ways of attaching implements. After researching agriculture and, in particular, tractors and ploughs, he devised a two-bottom plough to be directly attached to a Model T Ford car. It was raised and lowered by a lever and, unlike other similar conversions available at the time, was simple to operate and did not

■ ABOVE *An enamelled lapel badge made to promote the Ferguson System used on Ferguson tractors in the aftermath of Harry Ferguson's split with Henry Ford.*

■ LEFT *Harry Ferguson, the Irish engineer who developed the acclaimed three-point hitch, which changed the face of farming and led to the manufacture of an eponymous range of tractors.*

■ BELOW *A Massey-Ferguson tractor in use in the village of Baaseli in the Rajasthan State of India.*

require wheels or a drawbar. Ferguson later developed a plough suitable for use with the Fordson Model F tractor. His first system was devised from a series of springs and levers. In 1925, with Eber and George Sherman in the United States, he founded Ferguson-Sherman Inc which produced a plough with the "Duplex" hitch system compatible with Fordson line tractors. He made his first Ferguson hydraulic system for his prototype tractor, for which the British David Brown Company had made the differential gear and transmission. In 1933, in partnership with David Brown, Harry Ferguson founded the Ferguson-Brown Company. The result was 1,250 Ferguson-Brown Model A tractors. All of these were equipped with the Ferguson hydraulic system. After this, Ferguson and Brown went separate ways as they had different ideas about the direction the development of tractors should take.

In 1938, Harry Ferguson met Henry Ford and as a result of their so-called "handshake agreement" Ford was able to produce Ferguson System tractors. Both parties brought different assets to the agreement: Henry Ford's reputation and manufacturing capacity were involved as well as an important part of his financial resources. Harry Ferguson brought the patents for the innovative ploughing system which offered Ford an advantage in his ongoing sales war with International Harvester.

Called the Ferguson System, the three-point hitch was put together using a combination of linkages, three different linkage points – two on the bottom and another one on the top – and hydraulics. Hooking up an implement to a tractor had previously been a complicated affair. Farmers used hoists, helpers, jacks and all kinds of imaginative ways to get heavy implements hooked up. With the Ferguson System they needed only to back up to the implement, hook it up, raise it on the linkage and drive off. The Ferguson System was used on Ford's 9N and

■ ABOVE *Following the split with the Ford company Harry Ferguson began manufacture of the TE20, seen here, ploughing, in England.*

■ RIGHT *The TE20 was similar in design to the Ford 9N but differed in that it had a four-speed transmission and an overhead valve engine.*

■ BELOW *In the UK mass production of the TE20 was carried out by the Standard Motor Company, and production frequently exceeded 500 tractors per week.*

■ LEFT *In Britain the TE20 became affectionately known as the "Grey Fergy". The number produced and reputation for reliability has ensured that many, including these two, have been preserved.*

2N Models. At the same time, through Harry Ferguson Inc, Ferguson continued to sell tractors, parts and equipment, including several machines produced by Ferguson-Sherman Inc. Towards the end of 1946, Henry Ford's grandson, Henry Ford II, advised Harry Ferguson that his agreement with Ford would be ending on 30 June 1947. Ford then introduced a new model, the Fordson 8N, that had similarities with the Ford-Ferguson 2N.

When the Ford Motor Company started to sell its new model, Harry Ferguson took two courses of action. First, he commenced litigation, pursuing the Ford Motor Company and its associates for millions of dollars. Second, he negotiated with the Standard Motors Company in Britain for it to produce his own tractor, the Model TE20 (TE was an acronym for "Tractor England"). This was similar to the Ford Models 9N and 2N. Nonetheless, it differed from the 9N in having a four-speed gearbox, an overhead valve engine, two foot-operated brake pedals on the left side and a one-piece bonnet (hood). Ferguson drove his first Model TO20 ("Tractor Overseas"), built in Detroit, in 1948.

The Models TO20 and TE20 were identical except for their electrical systems and transmission cases. The TO20 had a Delco electrical system and a cast-iron transmission case, whereas the TE20 had a Lucas electrical system and an aluminium transmission case.

The litigation with Ford dragged on for four years until in April 1952, Harry Ferguson settled out of court for $9.25 million. As by this time some of Ferguson's patents had expired, Ford had to make few changes to its designs in

■ LEFT *An unusual use to which the TE20 tractor was put was in support of the expedition to the South Pole led by Sir Edmund Hillary. The Ferguson tractors were fitted with special tracks and cabs, but were otherwise almost standard in specification.*

■ ABOVE *Harry Ferguson sold his company to Massey-Harris, of Canada, in 1953. The resultant company became known as Massey-Ferguson and later made machines such as this Model 180.*

order to continue building tractors with hydraulically controlled three-point hitches. The following year, Ferguson merged with Massey-Harris and Harry Ferguson turned his attention to developing a four-wheel drive system for high performance sports cars and racing cars. He died in 1960.

A particularly unusual task to which some of Ferguson's tractors were put was as vehicles for the Antarctic expedition led by Sir Edmund Hillary. The various accounts of the expedition contain numerous references to the tractors used during the course of the Commonwealth Trans-Antarctic Expedition. The tractors were used to tow sledges, unload ships and for reconnaissance in conjunction with tracked Sno-Cats and Studebaker Weasels. The Fergusons were, for at least part of the time, equipped with rubber crawler-type tracks around the (larger than standard) front and rear wheels, with an idler wheel positioned between the axles. The output of the four-cylinder engines of the Fergusons was only 28bhp, so on occasions the tractors were used linked together to increase their abilities. They were also fitted with makeshift cabs to keep the drivers warm in Antarctic conditions. The expedition members were glad of the Fergusons' abilities on numerous occasions and drove one to the South Pole itself. The tractors were commended for their simplicity, ease of maintenance and reliability, that helped them perform well in a situation never anticipated by their designer.

■ RIGHT *A Massey-Ferguson 6150 from the 1990s. Massey-Ferguson is now part of the AGCO Corporation, but the brand name still acknowledges the contribution to agriculture of the enigmatic Irishman.*

The Trend to Specialization

Much of the early experimentation in mechanizing agriculture focused on ploughing, and steam and gasoline-engined tractors were employed as an alternative to horses. It soon became apparent that a number of other implements could be pulled behind tractors or driven from their power take-offs, such as threshers, for example. After the invention of the three-point hitch, the versatility of the tractor could be exploited more fully. As a result tractors and implements became ever more specialized to suit specific farming applications. The development followed two distinct routes. One is the evolution of the specialized machine which is essentially a tractor that incorporates equipment designed to perform a specific task. Combine harvesters are examples of this. The second type of equipment is the range of increasingly specialized implements designed to be pulled behind and driven by a tractor, such as mowers, balers and seed drills.

Combine Harvesters

The combine harvester is an example of a tractor redesigned to do a single specialized job. The post-war years saw a plethora of such developments worldwide.

In its most general sense, harvesting is the picking or cutting and gathering of a crop. However, as crops are so many and various, the methods of harvesting also vary widely. Developments of the machine age have had to replace operations as diverse as the hand-cutting of wheat with a scythe and the hand-picking of fruit crops from trees. The machines referred to as "combine harvesters", or simply "combines", are so named because they combine two distinct operations in the harvesting of seed crops – namely, cutting and threshing. The combine harvester pulls the crop in with a reel over cutting blades, then compresses it and transports it to a thresher using an auger. In the thresher, the crop passes through a series of threshing rollers and sieves that separate the grain from the remainder. The grain is stored in a tank while the rest of the

■ LEFT *Prior to the development of engined harvesters, American combines were drawn by huge teams of horses such as this in Washington State.*

■ BELOW *The combine harvester became so known simply because it combined more than one harvesting operation.*

■ BOTTOM *Modern haymaking: a towed mower deposits mown hay into a trailer towed by another tractor.*

■ ABOVE *Harvesting machines, such as this John Deere 9976 designed for picking cotton, have been developed for harvesting specialized crops.*

■ FAR RIGHT TOP *The design of harvesters has progressed in recent years. This 1960s John Deere has little in the way of operator protection, while a comparable machine today would have an air conditioned cab.*

■ FAR RIGHT BOTTOM *This Claas grain combine cuts the crop and threshes it; the grain is then handled almost like a liquid as it is loaded into tractor-towed trailers that keep pace with the combine.*

plant material is discarded. Specialized combines are designed to harvest crops such as sugar cane, cotton and tobacco.

Hay, or green foliage, as it is referred to, is mowed by combine harvesters designed to cut the crop and produce tied bales. A relatively recent innovation has been the development of combines that produce large round bales

■ RIGHT *John Deere introduced the Forage Harvester in 1969 and by 1998 when this, the 480hp 6950 model was manufactured, the type had been considerably developed and refined.*

■ LEFT *The harvesting of fruits such as blackberries is also mechanized. Here such fruit is being harvested from the rows of bushes in Oregon, USA, in the shadow of the snow-covered Mount Hood.*

■ BELOW *An image of mechanized harvesting in Britain of the 1930s, where although towed implements are in evidence the process was still considerably more labour-intensive than it is now.*

■ BOTTOM *A comparable scene from the United States showing a John Deere row crop tractor towing a John Deere 12A reaper.*

instead of smaller rectangular ones. Forage harvesters are used in making silage: they cut the crop and, by means of a spout at the rear of the harvester, deliver it into a high-sided trailer which is towed by a tractor alongside the harvester. Noted combine harvester makers currently include Case-IH, Claas, John Deere, Massey-Ferguson and New Holland Inc.

■ HARVESTING IMPLEMENTS

The various tasks associated with harvesting are dealt with by a vast range of towed implements. These include straw choppers that pick up and chop the debris from wheat

■ ABOVE *A specialized Fendt F220 GT machine from 1962 designed to harvest cabbages. It is powered by a 1410cc/86cu in displacement two-cylinder engine and has a six forward speed transmission.*

■ RIGHT *A diesel Fordson Major haymaking in Earl Sterndale, Derbyshire, England with an English-made rotary mower.*

■ BELOW *Specialized machinery has been developed for the harvesting of root crops, such as this machine for lifting carrots.*

harvesting and distribute it so that it can be ploughed in. For applications where combine harvesters are not used, towed implements are designed to carry out the same functions. These include rotary and disc mowers, rotary tedders and rakes which allow cut green crops to be aerated and dried. Towed balers are variously designed to make circular bales of everything from dry straw to damp silage. Round balers have now largely superseded the square balers, but both work on similar principles, requiring drive from the tractor's power take-off to gather up the cut crop and compress it into manageable bales to be transported from the field. Baler manufacturers include Bamford, Claas, John Deere, Vicon and Welger.

■ ABOVE *A 1959 Fendt FL120 tractor powered by a 1400cc/85cu in two-cylinder engine, pictured in Germany with a hay rake*

■ BELOW *A 1998 John Deere 935 MoCo. MoCo is an acronym for mower conditioner. The 935 is intended for use with 90–150 PTO hp tractors.*

■ BELOW *A 1937 Fendt Dieselross F18 with a sidebar mower attachment. The noted Dieselross tractors were powered by a single cylinder 1000cc/60cu in engine.*

Once a crop has been harvested the land needs to be prepared for the next crop and many of the various machines used in preparing the land are of the pull-type – implements towed behind tractors. The process has to contend with widely varying ground conditions in different parts of the world. In many places with temperate climates, excessively wet soil is a problem. Not only can it be difficult for tractors to work without becoming bogged down, but excessive water impedes plant growth because no air can reach the roots in waterlogged soil. To contend with this, machines have been developed that can lay lengths of "land drain", perforated plastic piping, beneath the soil to drain the fields. A more basic method of draining fields is the excavation of ditches.

Ploughs are used to turn over the soil after harvest and the ploughed fields are then disced and harrowed to allow the seeds of next year's crop to be sown. The basic principle of the plough has remained almost unchanged since a single-furrow plough was towed behind horses or oxen. It still cuts the top layer of soil and turns it over. There have been enormous changes, however, in the materials from which the plough is made, the method of propulsion, the number of furrows that can be ploughed at one time and the methods of control of the plough. John Deere's self-scouring steel plough was rightly heralded as a major innovation and ploughing was one of the primary farming tasks to which early tractors were put.

The plough has to be pulled across the entire surface of the field and numerous ways of achieving this have been tried. One notable method was the use of pairs of steam "ploughing engines" that were employed for field cultivation. They worked by drawing a plough backwards and forwards between them using a winch system rather than towing it behind a single machine. This method endured in many areas until the 1930s but, once the

■ ABOVE *Steam ploughing taking place at Uppingham, England during the 19th century.*

■ BELOW *Over the course of a century ploughing has become more straightforward, as the machines designed for it have become more advanced.*

■ BELOW RIGHT *Once proven, the gasoline-engined tractor soon superseded the horse as the motive power for ploughing and harrowing operations.*

■ LEFT *By the 1960s tractors such as the Fendt Farmer 2 were a common sight on European farms.*

■ RIGHT *A 1998 John Deere row crop ripper, designed for various field applications including ripping and bedding. It requires a 25–45 PTO hp tractor depending on soil type.*

■ LEFT *The tractor has become a vital farm tool even in countries which are perceived as less developed, such as this machine seen in an Albanian field.*

■ RIGHT *This diminutive English crawler is hitched to a Cooper tiller.*

gasoline tractor was completely viable, plough development concentrated on using tractors for propulsion. Ferguson's three-point linkage made the attachment of implements, including ploughs, more straightforward. The three-point linkage has now been so refined that the depth of furrows can be automatically controlled. The advent of the reversible plough allowed a tractor driver to turn all the soil in the same direction despite driving the tractor in opposite ways, to and fro across the field.

Preparation of the field requires more than ploughing and an array of other specialized implements has been devised to do this, including cultivators, harrows and stone clearers. A disc harrow is used to prepare a ploughed field for seeding while a cultivator can be used for a variety of tasks including stubble removal, mulching, aerating and turning in manure and fertilizer. Rollers can be used to make an even seed bed. Stone clearers remove stones that are turned up during ploughing and other operations; if left lying on the surface they can inhibit crop growth and damage machinery.

■ BELOW *Ploughing, tilling and harrowing can be dusty operations which is one reason that air conditioned and dust proofed tractor cabs have become the norm within farming.*

Another group of specialized implements for attaching on to tractors includes those that are designed for the distribution of manure, slurry or chemical fertilizers. They range from the "muckspreader" to the broadcaster, which spreads seed via a spinning disc, and injectors which force material into the ground.

Sowing, Loading and Handling

The method of planting seeds depends on the type of crop being grown. Crops such as beet, lettuce, cabbage and artichokes need space to grow and therefore require planting at specific intervals. A precision seed drill is usually employed, set to plant single seeds at a specified distance apart. Seed drills for other crops can be many times wider than the tractor used for their draft. They cut numerous parallel grooves in the soil and run a supply of seed into each groove, then fill the grooves as they pass. It goes without saying that seed drills, though they still carry out the task for which Jethro Tull's machine was devised at the beginning of the 18th century, are now vastly more technically precise. The modern seed drill that enables a precise amount of seed to be sown has now generally supplanted the broadcaster type of seed distributor.

Once a crop is sown, weeds and pests have to be controlled. To do this farmers use sprayers, normally a tank mounted on the rear of the tractor, with booms to dispense the spray. Tractors adapted for this work have tall, row crop wheels that allow crop clearance and leave only narrow tracks to minimize soil compaction and crop damage. There are

numerous manufacturers of such specialized equipment around the world.

A variety of loaders have been developed, largely from the loader originally attached to the front of tractors. This purpose-built equipment includes handlers, loaders and rough terrain forklifts, all intended to speed up material and crop-handling operations for agricultural applications.

■ ABOVE *In recent years technology has been applied to the planting of seeds. John Deere developed the Max Emerge series of planters that plant several rows of seeds in one pass.*

■ LEFT *How quickly this technology has advanced is evidenced by this smaller 1958 Fendt F220 GT machine set up to do a similar job.*

■ OPPOSITE BOTTOM *A John Deere 1860 No-Till air drill is designed to open the soil, plant the seed and close the soil again in a single pass. Its tools adjust to soil types and depths with minimum work.*

■ LEFT *The John Deere 1560 No-Till drill is designed to speed up grain planting through tilling and seeding in one pass. It has a large capacity for grain and features low-maintenance till openers.*

■ RIGHT *Specialist high-clearance machines such as this self-propelled sprayer with a 24m/26ft boom are intended for use in fields of growing crops such as this oil seed rape.*

■ FAR RIGHT TOP *The sprayer booms are designed to fold in to the sides of the cab, as on this John Deere, to facilitate the sprayer's being driven on roads between fields. Note the high crop clearance.*

■ FAR RIGHT MIDDLE *This 1960 Fendt Farmer 2 FW 139 tractor is equipped with a hydraulic front loader suitable for loading hay and similar crops.*

■ FAR RIGHT BOTTOM *The JCB 520G is a loader that incorporates aspects of both the fork lift and front loader, and is suited for handling palletized products such as these rolls of turf.*

■ RIGHT *This specialized machine has sufficient clearance to pass over trees, which it sprays with a pesticide mist, as here in France.*

Specialist Tractors

While row crop tricycle tractors were among the first specialized tractors, increasing specialization led to the production of tractors designed for particular tasks including vineyard work, cotton picking and orchard use. Such tractors have been built by numerous manufacturers, either as purpose-built models or as variants of their other models. Specialist tractors are designed for a range of tasks and some are constructed to customers' specifications. One such contemporary manufacturer is Frazier, a small British company based outside York, that is typical of many companies that produce specialized farming machinery. The company's Agribuggy is assembled from a number of proprietary components, including axles, suspension and engines, and is intended as the basis for crop-spraying and fertilizer-spreading tasks. The machines are purpose-built and offered in both diesel and petrol forms. They are designed to be adaptable and are available

■ ABOVE *One of the first specialist tractors to be developed was the tricycle-type, intended for row crop work, such as this Oliver 60.*

■ LEFT *Tractors are often used for specialist tasks such as in orchards. This Massey-Ferguson 374S is being used to collect apples.*

■ BELOW *Crop sprayers have to be suited for use in fields of part-grown crops without causing unnecessary damage to the growing plants, hence high clearance.*

■ LEFT *Sprayers are designed to be driven between rows of crops in order to minimize damage to the plants, but also require the operator to wear a mask to avoid inhaling pesticides.*

in both low ground pressure and row crop variants. Early products available in Europe included crawlers and specialist machines from the likes of Citroën-Kégresse and Latil as well as smaller vineyard tractors.

In the United States, McCormick-Deering offered specialized orchard tractors, signified by an "O" prefix. In the early 1940s the company offered the OS-4 and O-4 models, variants of the W-4 models, for orchard work. The OS-4 had its exhaust and air filter mounted underneath in order to reduce its overall height while the O-4 was fitted with streamlined bodywork which allowed the branches of fruit trees to slide over the tractor without damage. The concept of the compact tractor is now well established so that they are recognized as a bona fide agricultural product. Similar to the Agribuggy are machines from Turner, Sanderson, Schulter, Vee Pee, Westrac Triolet, Matbro, Blank and Chaviot.

■ ABOVE LEFT *These specialized Frazier machines are fitted with flotation tyres to avoid soil compaction in wet conditions.*

■ TOP RIGHT *Roadless Traction enhanced the performance of many Fordson tractors, including this 1951 Fordson E1A Major, by converting them into half-tracks.*

■ ABOVE RIGHT *The lawn tractor originated as a development of a small size tractor.*

■ RIGHT *The French-manufactured Vee Pee has low ground pressure and is used for various agricultural roles.*

■ BELOW LEFT *Tobacco is another crop that requires specialized harvesting machinery such as this example seen working in Wilson, North Carolina.*

■ BELOW RIGHT *Elineau of France manufactured this machine for spraying pesticide mist on to the small trees of apple orchards. The machine has sufficient clearance to avoid damaging the trees.*

CRAWLER TRACTORS

Paralleling the developments of the steam-powered tractor were experiments with tracked machinery known as "crawlers". The first experiments involved wheeled steam engines that were converted to run with tracks. Benjamin Holt was a pioneer of this technology, and he tested his first converted steam tractor in November 1904 in Stockton, California. Holt gasoline-powered crawlers worked on the Los Angeles Aqueduct project in 1908. Holt viewed this as something of a development exercise and learned a lot about crawler tractor construction from it, simply because dust and heat took their toll on the machines. Downtime for repairs of all makes of crawler was considerable.

World Wars I and II helped speed the development of crawler machinery in several ways. During World War I the embryonic crawler technology was soon developed as the basis of the tank, now an almost universal weapon of war. American development and use of tanks lagged behind that of Europe, partially because the United States remained uninvolved in World War I until 1917. Prior to this date the US army was still steeped in the cavalry traditions of the fighting in the Old West; by the time America became involved in the European conflict, the European nations were using tanks on the Western Front. Orders went back to the United States for tanks but in the meantime US soldiers used British and French machines, namely the Mark VI and Renault FT17 respectively. These tanks were to be produced to take advantage of America's massive industrial capacity, but they had to compete for production-line space with trucks and artillery so there was some delay. It is perhaps difficult to understand this situation

■ ABOVE RIGHT *The 1904 prototype steam-powered crawler tractor made by Hornsby's of Grantham, England. The company later sold its patent to American Holt in 1912.*

■ RIGHT *Early crawlers such as this one made by the Bullock Tractor Co of Chicago were chain driven; steering was by a worm drive.*

■ RIGHT *Holt and Best were among the early pioneers of crawler technology. This early machine has a disc harrow and also belt-drive pulley.*

■ BELOW *Post-war International Harvester was among the makers of crawler tractors for agricultural use, as were Caterpillar, Fiat and Fowler.*

■ RIGHT *A diesel-engined Caterpillar crawler being used in conjunction with an elevator during haymaking in England during the late 1930s.*

■ MIDDLE RIGHT *An early 1930s Fordson Roadless crawler tractor, this was the narrow version intended for orchards and other confined areas.*

■ MIDDLE FAR RIGHT *Another version of the Fordson tractor which has been converted into a crawler.*

■ BOTTOM *The Bristol tractor was manufactured by a small English company that changed hands several times. In the late 1940s, while owned by Saunders, the Bristol 20 used Roadless tracks and a 16hp Austin car engine.*

■ RIGHT *Allis-Chalmers became involved in the manufacture of crawler tractors in 1928 when it acquired the Monarch Tractor Company. The Model 35 was a 1930s model.*

when the crawler track was already well established and there had been a couple of experiments in tank development. The experimental machines included the Studebaker Supply Tank and the Ford 3-ton tank. The French tank produced in the United States was designated the M1917 and was the only US tank to arrive in Europe before the Armistice.

Tractor and crawler technology progressed as a result of these military applications. The US army had become interested in crawlers and in half-tracks – vehicles with crawler tracks at the rear and a tyred axle at the front – and in May 1931 it acquired a Citroën-Kégresse P17 half-track for assessment. US products soon followed: James Cunningham and Son produced one in December 1932; in 1933 the Rock Island Arsenal produced an improved model; Cunningham built a converted Ford

■ LEFT *International Harvester started crawler production in 1928 when it offered the TracTracTor, which then became the T-20 in 1931.*

■ BELOW *Minneapolis-Moline made this Mopower crawler loader in 1960.*

truck later in 1933; General Motors became interested and the Linn Manufacturing Company of New York produced a half-track. In 1936 Marmon-Herrington also produced a half-track, converted Ford truck for the US Ordnance Department with a driven front axle.

■ ABOVE *A 1941 Allis-Chalmers WM crawler tractor. Allis-Chalmers had adopted the orange colour scheme of Persian Orange back in 1929 just as the Depression began.*

Towards the end of the decade a half-track designated the T7 made its appearance at the Rock Island Arsenal: it was the forerunner of the Models M2 and M3 to be produced subsequently by Autocar, Diamond T, International Harvester and White.

■ ABOVE *Cletrac was an acronym for the Cleveland Tractor Company which specialized in the production of crawlers including this 9-16 Model F of 1921.*

■ RIGHT *This 1950 Fowler-Marshall VF crawler was based on the long-running and popular English Field Marshall series of tractors.*

During the 1920s Robert Gilmour Le Tourneau, an American contractor who manufactured equipment for Holt, Best and later Caterpillar tractors, developed a new system of power control that began to widen the scope of the crawler. All the control systems featured winch and cable actuation until the development of hydraulically lifted and lowered blades. One of the first British machines to be so equipped was the Vickers Vigor, developed from the Vickers VR-series crawlers. Hydraulics was just one example of the advances in technology being applied to agricultural machinery. It was first used in the late 1930s in time for bulldozers and similar machines to make a lasting impression during World War II. During the war the bulldozer earned numerous accolades and led directly to the blade-equipped tank, a type of armoured fighting vehicle still in general use.

Throughout the war years the half-track evolved and although the designs were

■ ABOVE *Converting wheeled tractors to crawlers was employed for light 4x4 vehicles such as the Land Rover. This is the Cuthbertson devised by the Scottish firm of the same name.*

■ RIGHT *The rubber tracks used on the Claas Challenger show how the idea has been refined in four decades.*

■ ABOVE *Fowler's of Grantham, England also used the name Challenger on their crawlers in the 1950s. This 35 model predates the Challenger but is of a similar design overall.*

■ LEFT *The Track Marshall crawler is manufactured by Marshall of Gainsborough, England which specialized in crawlers from 1960 onwards, the last British maker to do so.*

■ LEFT *The Roadless RT20 crawler was powered by a Perkins P3 diesel engine. It was introduced in 1954 and intended for sales in South America.*

■ LEFT *The concept of converting wheeled machines to crawlers has endured until the present-day as this rubber tracked Toyota Landcruiser 4x4 illustrates.*

standardized there are certain differences between the models produced by the various manufacturers. As well as the crawler conversions to wheeled tractors made by companies such County, Roadless and Doe, there were even more specialized conversions to other machines. Trackson was a crawler track conversion offered for Fordson tractors in the late 1920s by Trackson of Milwaukee, Wisconsin. Later, Cuthbertson and Sons of Biggar, Scotland converted Land Rovers to crawler operation through the use of bogies on a subframe assembly and sprockets driven by the conventional axles. Recently a variation of this idea has been offered by Toyota on one of its luxury four-wheel-drive vehicles.

Current crawler tractor manufacturers, beside Caterpillar and Massey-Ferguson, include Claas, Track Marshall and Tractoroexport. The latter is based in the former USSR and makes the T-70 Crawler.

■ ABOVE *The Cuthbertson conversion for Land Rovers relied on toothed sprockets bolted to the driven hubs which interlock with the rubber and steel tracks.*

■ RIGHT *A surviving Cuthbertson-converted Land Rover from the early 1960s. Ground clearance was increased and ground pressure decreased.*

Military Tractors

During World War I Holt supplied crawlers to the allies while the English company Hornsby experimented with crawler tracks for tanks. The vast scale of World War II necessitated massive industrial production of all types and saw numerous tractors made that were designed for specific military purposes. The tractor types varied and included wheeled, half-track and full-track types.

In America an unusual military tractor was made by Allis-Chalmers. It was the M7 (T26E4) over-snow machine, a half-track tractor that used the entire 63bhp engine and transmission assembly from a Willys Jeep. Full-track tractors were made for the US army by International Harvester, Cletrac, Allis-Chalmers and the Iron Fireman Manufacturing Company. The International models included the TD9, TD18 and M5. The TD models were conventional full-track tractors powered by four-cylinder diesel engines, while the M5 was a high-speed tractor powered by a Continental six-cylinder engine that produced 207bhp. Cletrac manufactured the MG1 and MG2 models that were fitted with a six-cylinder Hercules engine that produced 137bhp. The Allis-Chalmers tractors were massive – the M4 weighed 18 tons and the M6 38 tons. Both were intended for use as artillery tractors and were powered by six-cylinder Waukesha engines.

In Britain a David Brown tractor became noted for its use by the Royal Air Force as an airfield tractor. The model was powered by an in-line four-cylinder engine of 2523cc/154cu in displacement that produced 37bhp at 2200rpm. It had a four-speed transmission and a conventional appearance.

The RAF also used a number of Roadless-converted Fordson tractors fitted with a

■ TOP *The Allis-Chalmers Model U was in production throughout the war years and among those exported to the UK to assist in the war effort.*

■ BELOW LEFT *The Minneapolis-Moline ZTX US military tractor of 1943 featured five gears that gave it a top speed of over 25kph/15mph.*

■ ABOVE RIGHT *During World War II tractors were used for a variety of non-agricultural tasks including work on airfields towing aeroplanes.*

■ ABOVE LEFT *As steam traction became viable the British army was quick to use Fowler engines as artillery tractors during the Boer War.*

■ RIGHT *British Royal Engineers in the years prior to World War II landing Royal Navy equipment from a landing barge with the assistance of a Fordson tractor.*

Hesford winch for aircraft-handling duties. The Germans, Japanese and Italians made use of tractors manufactured by Latil, Somua, Hanomag, Isuzu and Pavesi. French companies Latil and Somua were captured by Germany.

There are numerous current specialist military tractors: one such specially built to meet British Ministry of Defence specifications is made by JCB. This towing and shunting tractor is designed to be manoeuvrable and offers tremendous traction and torque. It is ideal for moving aircraft and trailers and has a high specification cab.

■ LEFT *The Studebaker Weasel was a light crawler machine designed by Studebaker's engineers during World War II that exerted minimal ground pressure. It was among the first of such specialist machines.*

■ LEFT *Minneapolis-Moline produced the Model NTX as an experimental military machine. It was four-wheel-drive and used standard military wheels and tyres.*

■ LEFT *A restored example of the David Brown VIG airfield tractor manufactured for the Royal Air Force and extensively used on British airfields during the conflict.*

Bulldozers first came to the military's attention after their use by the allies in removing beach defences, and even occupied pillboxes, in both Europe and the Pacific during World War II. Later, tanks would be equipped with bulldozer blades to assist in clearing obstacles. The Caterpillar D7 saw service in all theatres of operation during World War II and General Eisenhower credited it as being one of the machines that won the war.

As for the other US auto makers, World War II interrupted civilian vehicle manufacture, and production was turned to helping win the war. One of Studebaker's products at this time was the M29C Weasel, an amphibious cargo carrier that was a light, fully-tracked military vehicle, powered by a 65bhp six-cylinder engine, with three forward gears and a two-speed driven rear axle. It was fitted with 50cm/20in wide endless tracks and exerted a low ground pressure. This machine, designed by Studebaker's own engineers, can be regarded as one of the pioneers of the light crawler-tracked vehicle. Such machines have since become popular for specialist applications ranging from vineyard work to use on small agricultural sites where a conventional tractor or crawler would be too large.

4 x 4 Tractors

The 1920s saw much experimentation with four-wheel-drive tractors as an alternative to crawler machines. Wizard, Topp-Stewart, Nelson and Fitch were amongst those who manufactured machines in the United States. After World War II, companies such as Roadless Traction and County Tractors offered four-wheel-drive conversions to many tractors, often using war surplus GMC truck-driven front axles. Selene was an Italian company offering 4 x 4 conversions. As the benefits of four-wheel drive came to be seen by the larger manufacturers, including the likes of Ford, John Deere and Case, they began offering their own four-wheel-drive models. This squeezed some of the small companies offering conversions. Nowadays the 4 x 4 tractor is simply seen as another conventional tractor model and four-wheel drive is often offered as an extra-cost option on machines that are also available in a two-wheel-drive configuration.

■ BELOW *A County Fourdrive converted Fordson tractor being used in the Solomon Islands.*

■ LEFT *On state-of-the-art tractors such as this AGCO machine-four-wheel drive is considered as just another conventional but useful feature in enhancing the tractor's performance.*

■ BOTTOM *A mid-1980s U1700L38 model of the Mercedes Unimog.*

■ LEFT *A Massey-Ferguson tractor preparing a field for cultivation. Tractors have increased in size in recent years.*

■ BELOW LEFT *The four-wheel-drive version of Massey-Ferguson's streamlined Perkins engined 4235 Model tractor.*

■ BELOW RIGHT *Four-wheel-drive tractors such as this tend to have larger diameter front tyres than the two-wheel-drive variants.*

■ ABOVE RIGHT *Some four-wheel-drive tractors such as this Fiatagri machine have different sizes of tyres at the front and rear.*

■ RIGHT *Modern tractors feature comprehensive dashboards which allow operators to monitor engine and transmission functions.*

COMPACT TRACTORS

The concept of the compact tractor can be said to have its origin in southern Europe where it was used for vineyard work. In the years immediately after World War II, NSU sold a number of its light artillery tractor, the Kettenkrad, for agricultural use, and developments also took place in the Far East. The use of compact tractors spread quickly. In England the British Motor Corporation (BMC) offered a "mini" tractor and the major tractor makers added compact tractors to their ranges.

By the mid-1980s the Japanese firm Hinomoto was making the C174 compact, which is fitted with a 1004cc/61.2cu in three-cylinder diesel engine. It produces 20hp and has nine forward gears and three reverse. The C174 is equipped with a rear-mounted power take-off and a hydraulic linkage.

Shibaura makes compact tractors for Ford and Mitsubishi makes the MT372D model as well as Cub Cadet and Case compact tractors. Iseki is another Japanese manufacturer that

■ ABOVE *The British Motor Corporation Mini tractor was aimed at the same market as the Ferguson TE20. The tractor was announced in 1965 but was shortlived and production had ceased by 1970.*

■ ABOVE *The BMC Mini was based around a 950cc/58cu in diesel version of a car engine of the time. It proved to be underpowered and was later uprated to 1500cc/90cu in.*

■ LEFT *The 1998 John Deere 5210 tractor is only 239.5cm/94.3in tall to the top of the rollbar and has an 205cm/80.7in wheelbase. Power is from a 2900cc/175cu in three-cylinder engine.*

■ LEFT *The compact tractor is in use worldwide as this laden example in Bhutan shows.*

makes compact tractors for White, Bolens and Massey-Ferguson in addition to a range of larger conventional machines. In the compact category are tractors such as the TX 2140 and 2160 Models. They are powered by three-cylinder water-cooled engines, 776cc/47.35cu in and 849cc/52cu in respectively, in both two- and four-wheel-drive forms, and are suited for use with a wide range of farming implements.

Kubota is a Japanese company that was founded in the last decade of the 19th century. It began manufacturing tractors in the 1960s and claimed to be the fifth largest producer during the mid-80s. One of its products then was the compact B7100DP, a three-cylinder-powered tractor that displaced 762cc/46.5cu in and produces 16hp. It also featured four-wheel drive, independent rear brakes and a three-speed PTO.

Other compact tractor manufacturers around the world include Grillo that produces the Model 31 in Italy, Holder that makes the Cultitrac A40, and Howard that produces the Model 200 in Australia. A compact crawler, the V228, is made by Blank in Germany.

■ RIGHT *The International Harvester Cub Cadet was a diminutive tractor aimed at garden and grounds use rather than full-scale agriculture.*

■ FAR RIGHT *The BMC Mini tractor bore some resemblance to the Ferguson TE20 but struggled to compete in sales terms even with secondhand examples of the "Grey Fergy".*

The Sport of Tractor Pulling

In the early years of the 20th century, when agriculture in the United States was booming, huge numbers of boulders had to be removed with the help of horses from massive acreages before they could be cultivated. Folklore has it that one farmer told another that he could remove a larger boulder than the other, and so almost inevitably a competition started. At the time of the outbreak of World War II, the mechanization of agriculture was well under way and by then tractors were being used for clearing boulders. Such boulder-pulling was seen as a challenge and informal competitions were introduced. The tractor that was needed on the farm all week was used for "tractor pulling" on Sundays. Over the years the tractors became bigger and the competition became ever more serious. Eventually the boulders also became a little too large to handle so the "dead-weight sled" was introduced. This was a sled with weights on it, connected to the tractor by means of a chain. It was all or nothing: either the tractor took off with the sled or it lost grip and spun its driven wheels, digging itself into the track. To gain more grip, the tractors were soon loaded with anything that was heavy.

■ ABOVE *Smoky Joe is a Ford 8600, based tractor puller seen here competing in an event in Warwickshire, England.*

■ ABOVE *A Fiat 1000 tractor in the same event. Tractors compete in different classes depending on engine type and modifications.*

■ LEFT *One class is for modified tractors that have to retain a relatively standard appearance and bodywork. This German Deutz machine has been prepared for such a class.*

■ RIGHT *Kevin Brian's Volvo BM T800 tractor puller. Notice that the overall profile of the machine has been altered in order to accommodate the various modifications.*

■ BELOW *A Case IH tractor puller. To increase the all-important traction, much larger than standard rear tyres are fitted where class regulations permit.*

Later on came the idea of making the sled heavier during the pull. A number of volunteers stood next to the track and stepped on the sled as it went past: this was, unsurprisingly, called a "step-on sled". The greater the distance covered, the higher the position. If a tractor made it to the end of the track this was called a "full pull" and the driver qualified for the finals of the day's events. Over years of pulling, the tractors continued to grow. It became harder to recruit volunteers to step on the sled because it was going faster and faster and, naturally, safety became an issue. To solve the problem, the "weight-transfer machine" was developed. This is a sled which has wheels at the rear end. At the start of the pull the weights are placed above the wheels. As the tractor starts to pull, the weights travel forward to the sled-plate by means of a chain. The friction increases and at some point the tractor loses traction. This principle is still in use today. The best pull is made when the tractor has a quick start. At the start of the track the sled is easy to pull, so a lot of speed can be developed. As the friction increases, the speed of the sled and tractor means that the whole unit keeps powering on and goes a few metres further.

The distance covered is now measured with infra-red equipment, and the results of a pull,

■ ABOVE *In the least restricted classes tractors are especially built with multiple engines coupled together for a massive power output.*

so calibrated, show that sometimes tractors come as little as 1cm/½in short of a full pull, or stop at exactly the same point. At tractor-pulling events, it is not only power that counts. Almost as important is the balance of the tractor. The sport of tractor pulling could be described as the world's most powerful motor sport, albeit not the fastest.

The tractors compete in a complex array of classes. Within the modified class come specially designed tractors, that compete in different weight classes. All types of component parts are allowed as long as the overall weight and size are within the rules. The numbers and types of engines are similarly limited by the rules. There are now also strict safety rules to protect the tractor, driver and spectators from danger. Usually, the specially constructed chassis in this class is fitted with the rear axle of a truck or excavator shovel. The internal components are replaced with stronger gears. The tyre size is limited to a diameter of 77.5–81cm/30.5–32in by the rules. The original tractor-tyre profile is always decreased by reducing the pressure in order to generate sufficient wheel-spin to prevent the tractor digging itself in while giving enough traction to move the sled forwards.

In the largest-capacity classes aircraft engines are often used today, as are gas-turbines. In the United States V8 racing-engines are very popular and in Europe tractors are fitted with up to nine engines, depending on the type and weight class.

The Super Standard or Super Stock classes feature heavily tuned standard agricultural tractors, weighing 4.5 tons. The basis of the tractor is a normal agricultural model but not much of the machine is left – everything that is normally needed for field operation is removed. The block, the clutch housing, the gearbox housing and the rear-axle have to be original although the insides of these components can be modified. To increase the engine's power, a maximum of four turbos can be fitted, as long as it all fits under the original tractor hood. The great amount of air that flows into the intake means that a lot of diesel can be injected into the cylinders. When the air is compressed by the turbos a great deal of heat is produced and

■ BELOW *This German Q8 sponsored machine gets its power from no less than three V12 Allison aero engines.*

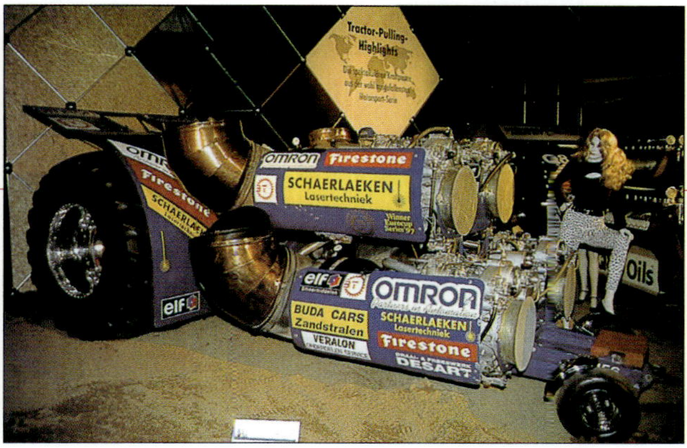

■ ABOVE LEFT *When too much is never enough: this German tractor pulling special has been constructed with four jet aircraft engines.*

■ ABOVE RIGHT *It provides spectacular tractor pulling action, but unlike some of the smaller power and weight classes, bears little resemblance to anything that can be seen in a field.*

to prevent the turbos from melting, a spray of water is injected into the intakes; this water leaves the exhaust as water vapour. To make sure this massive power reaches the wide rear tyres, numerous parts of the transmission are replaced by stronger versions, while all the unnecessary gears are removed.

Alky-burners which use methanol can be fitted: methanol burns for longer than diesel, so more power is generated and the engine suffers less stress. Numerous modifications are needed but up to 2500bhp is achievable.

The Garden Puller is the ideal start-up class. Drivers may compete from the age of eight and since this class requires little more than a former lawnmower or garden tractor it is available to those with limited funds.

Mini-pullers are small modifieds, whose weight must include both the weight of the driver and its fuel. This class uses its own special, small sled and the tractors are custom-designed and built. They use mainly V8 engines and helicopter turbines. The power produced can be up to 3000bhp, though the average is about 1700bhp. Due to the enormous power-to-weight ratio, these machines are very hard to handle. The rear axles are mostly custom-engineered and the gearbox is little more than a single speed with a reverse gear.

■ RIGHT *The same can be said for some of the machines that rely on internal combustion engines too, and the team's name reflects the cost of this sport.*

29 00252

A–Z of Tractors

The section that follows lists the major tractor manufacturers and their most important machines, stretching back to the beginning of the 20th century. It also illustrates how, throughout its history, the tractor manufacturing industry has been characterized by numerous mergers and amalgamations. Where once there were hundreds of minor manufacturers producing small numbers of farm machines, there is now just a handful of multinational corporations making thousands of tractors. Also apparent is how quickly innovations in tractor manufacture spread. For example, Henry Ford offered the new and innovative Fordson in 1917; within a few years his style of tractor had become the norm and the basic configuration of the Fordson is still followed by manufacturers today. Computers and global positioning systems are the latest technologies to be applied to the farm tractor, and undeniably have a place in today's modern agriculture.

■ OPPOSITE *Technology supersedes tradition in Tian Shan Province, China.*

■ LEFT *A gleaming 1951 David Brown Cropmaster.*

AGCO ALLIS

During the mid-1980s the well-known Allis-Chalmers tractor brand became Deutz-Allis under the ownership of Klockner-Humboldt-Deutz, based in the German city of Cologne. In 1990 the Deutz-Allis division was sold to the Allis-Gleaner Company (AGCO), which later reintroduced the brand as AGCO Allis tractors. These machines are produced as one of its numerous brands of AGCO farming equipment. The relatively recently established range of AGCO Allis tractors incorporates several different series, including those that are designated as 5600, 6670, 8700 and 9700 models.

The 5600 Series models are mid-sized machines and range from the 45hp 5650 to the 63hp 5670. They are powered by direct injection air-cooled diesel engines. The 5600 models are designed to be capable of tight turns and to drive a wide variety of equipment from the power take-off (PTO). The given horsepower figures are measured at the PTO. The AGCO Allis 6670 tractor is a row crop tractor that produces 63 PTOhp; it is powered by a four-cylinder direct injection air-cooled diesel engine. Reactive hydrostatic power steering is designed to end drift and what is termed the "economical PTO" setting is designed to save fuel by reducing engine speed by 25 per cent on jobs that do not require full PTO power.

The 8745 and 8765 Models are large capacity AGCO Allis tractors designed for large-scale farming. The 8765 is available with a choice of all-wheel drive or two-wheel drive and produces

■ RIGHT ***The Model 9690 is a two-wheel-drive AGCO Allis tractor manufactured in 1996. Seen here with twin rear wheels, it is one of the company's largest tractors.***

■ LEFT ***The 6690 is a four-wheel-drive AGCO Allis tractor. This is a 1994 example that uses different diameter front and rear wheels.***

■ ABOVE ***The AGCO Allis 6690 model is one of the company's 6600 Series and is powered by an air-cooled diesel engine.***

■ LEFT *Note the modern stylized curved hood on this four-wheel-drive 1995 AGCO Allis 9435 model.*

85hp at the PTO while the 8745 produces 70 PTOhp. Both come with 12-speed synchronized shuttle transmissions which are designed to offer sufficient power in all gears. These tractors have an AGCO Allis 400 Series turbocharged diesel engine providing the power under the bodywork, which is of a modern "low-profile" appearance. The larger tractors in the 8700 Series are the 8775 and 8785 Models, powered by a fuel-efficient AGCO Allis 600 Series liquid-cooled diesel. These tractors produce 95hp and 110hp at the PTO respectively. They are manufactured with a choice of all-wheel drive and two-wheel-drive transmissions. The transmission has four forward speeds and an optional creeper gear. The tractors are also equipped with a 540/1000 "economy PTO", a durable wet multi-disc clutch and electronically controlled three-point hitch. The 125 PTOhp 9735 and 145 PTOhp 9745 Models are tractors that have been designed with styling and performance in mind. Both are available in an all-wheel-drive version or as a standard model with either four- or 18-speed transmissions.

The two turbocharged 9600 Series models are fitted with a liquid-cooled engine of up to 8700cc/530cu in displacement. The 175 PTOhp 9675 and the 195 PTOhp 9695 tractors feature Powershift electronic transmission and a cab-forward design.

New advanced computer technology has recently been employed in the manufacture of the AGCO Allis range. The proprietary system known as DataTouch is designed to be a compact, easy-to-read, touch-screen display, from which all the functions of the in-cab systems can be controlled. The system has been designed so that there are no cables in the operator's line of sight. The system is based on simple touch-screen technology that is considered by the manufacturer to be easy to use despite the complexity of the operations and data it controls.

■ BOTTOM *A four-wheel-drive AGCO Allis 9815 model from 1996, seen in the field with a disc harrow.*

Allis-Chalmers

■ BELOW *From 1929 onwards Allis-Chalmers tractors were painted in a bright shade of orange. It was known as Persian Orange and was an attempt to attract new customers.*

This tractor maker has roots that stretch back to Milwaukee's Reliance Works Flour Milling Company that was founded in 1847. The company was reorganized in 1912 with Brigadier General Otto H. Falk as president. It remained based in Milwaukee, Wisconsin and, although it had no experience of steam traction, built its first gasoline tractor, the tricycle-type Model 10–18, in 1914. This had a two-cylinder opposed engine that revved to 720rpm and, as its designation indicates, produced 10 drawbar hp and 18 belt hp. It was started on gasoline but once the engine warmed up it ran on cheaper kerosene. The single wheel was at the front while the driver sat over the rear axle.

Unlike some of its competitors, Allis-Chalmers did not have an established dealer network around the United States so sales did not achieve their full potential. Between 1914 and 1921 the company manufactured and sold approximately, 2,700 10–18s. Some of these were sold through mail order catalogues, and during World War I some export sales were achieved. The French imported American tractors and sold them under their own brand names – the Allis-Chalmers 10–18, for instance, was marketed in France as the Globe tractor.

■ BELOW *The Allis-Chalmers Model B tractor was exported from the United States to Britain under the Lend-Lease policies of the war.*

The conventional Model 18–30 tractor, introduced in 1919, was powered by a vertical in-line four-cylinder engine. In the early days sales were limited, partially as a result of competition from the cheap Fordson, and only slightly more than 1,000 had been assembled by 1922, but over the course of the next seven years the total reached 16,000.

Allis-Chalmers acquired a few other companies when the end of the post-war boom led to numerous closures and mergers within the tractor industry. Among these acquisitions was the

■ RIGHT *The Allis-Chalmers Model U had a lengthy production run that extended between its introduction in 1929 and end of production in 1953.*

■ BELOW *On top of the orange paint, the A-C logo left no doubt as to which make the operator was driving.*

Monarch Tractor Company of Springfield, Illinois, that made crawler tractors. The company had started tractor production in 1917 and had reorganized twice by the time of the merger, when production of a range of six different-sized crawlers was under way. The smallest of these was the Lightfoot 6–10 and the largest the Monarch 75, which weighed 11.5 tons. Allis-Chalmers continued the production of crawlers in Springfield. Another of its acquisitions was the Advance-Rumely Thresher Company, that was taken over in 1931.

In 1929 as many as 32 companies making farm equipment merged to form the United Tractor and Equipment Corporation, which had its headquarters in Chicago, Illinois. Amongst the 32 was Allis-Chalmers, which was contracted to build a new tractor powered by a Continental engine and known as the United. The tractor was launched at an agricultural show in Wichita in the spring of 1929. The corporation did not stay in business long. Allis-Chalmers was fortunate enough to survive the collapse and continued to build the United tractor, albeit redesignated the Model U. The Model U and E tractors became the basis of the Allis-Chalmers range. Allis-Chalmers also introduced a distinctive colour scheme to attract new customers and differentiate its tractors from those of other makers. The colour chosen was called Persian Orange. It was a simple ploy but one that no doubt worked, as other manufacturers soon followed suit with brightly coloured paintwork and stylized bonnets, radiator grilles and mudguards.

The Model U later became famous as the first tractor available with low-pressure pneumatic rubber tyres. In 1932 Model U tractors fitted with aircraft-type tyres inflated to 15psi were successfully tested on a dairy farm in Waukesha, Wisconsin. Despite their proven ability, pneumatic tyres were greeted with scepticism by those who thought that such tyres would not be adequate for farming use. Allis-Chalmers indulged in a series of speed events involving pneumatic-tyred tractors to promote this latest breakthrough in tractor technology. They went as far as hiring professional racing drivers to demonstrate their pneumatic-tyred machines at agricultural shows and state fairs. In the late 1930s, Allis-Chalmers introduced its Model A and B

ALLIS-CHALMERS MODEL U	
Year	1933
Engine	Four cylinder
Power	34hp on kerosene
Transmission	Four speed (pneumatic tyres)
Weight	n/k

■ BELOW *The Allis-Chalmers Model U played an important part in the development of pneumatic tyres for tractors as the company used a number of them to demonstrate Firestone tyres.*

■ LEFT *A 1942 version of the long-running Allis-Chalmers Model U which pioneered the use of pneumatic tyres. Steel rims reappeared during World War II as a result of rubber shortages.*

tractors. The four-speed Model A replaced the Model E and was made between 1936 and 1942, while production of the Model B ran between 1937 and 1957. The Model B was powered by a four-cylinder 15.7bhp engine and more than 127,000 were made over the course of the lengthy production run. In 1936 the Model U was upgraded by the fitment of the company's own UM engine. The Model WC was introduced in 1934 as the first tractor designed for pneumatic tyres, although steel rims remained available as an option. In 1938 Allis-Chalmers offered the downsized Model B tractor on pneumatic tyres, a successful sales ploy. The tractor sold particularly well and was widely marketed. It was manufactured in Great Britain after World War II for sale in both the home and export markets. In another move to increase sales in the same year, the company increased the number of its tractor models with styled hoods and radiator grille shells.

Many established American tractor manufacturers quickly added new models to their ranges in the immediate post-war years. Allis-Chalmers introduced its Models G and WD. The Model WD-45 was fitted with a gasoline engine. In 1955 a diesel variant was offered and this marked something of a landmark for Allis-Chalmers as it was the first wheeled diesel tractor the company had launched, though it had been making diesel-engined crawlers since taking over Monarch in the late 1920s. The diesel engine selected for the WD-45 was an in-line six-cylinder of 3770cc/230cu in displacement. An LPG engine option was also made available for the WD-45 and it was the first model Allis-Chalmers offered with power steering. The WD-45 was a great success overall and more than 83,000 were eventually made.

■ BELOW *The three-point linkage, as seen on this WD-45, revolutionized the attachment of farm implements to tractors.*

■ BOTTOM *The Allis-Chalmers WD-45 was one of the first all-new post-World War II tractors.*

Allis-Chalmers produced the Model B tractor at a plant in Southampton, England, from 1948, although by then it was already considered an old-fashioned tractor. The British plant was moved to Essendine in Lincolnshire soon afterwards and the D270 went into production. This was in some ways an updated Model B, featuring high ground clearance – which made it suitable for use with mid-mounted implements – and a choice of three engines, all from later Model B tractors. These included petrol and paraffin versions of the in-line, four-cylinder, overhead-valve unit and a Perkins P3 diesel. The petrol and

■ LEFT *A restored Allis-Chalmers WD-45 with adjustable rear wheel tread.*

■ BELOW *The Model C was made between 1940 and 1948 and featured a tricycle-type wheel arrangement for row crop use.*

paraffin engines produced 27hp and 22hp at 1650rpm respectively. The D272 was a further upgraded version offered from 1959 and the ED40 was another new model introduced in 1960. Disappointing sales of these models, amongst other factors, caused Allis-Chalmers to stop making tractors in Britain in 1968.

In 1955, the company bought the Gleaner Harvester Corporation and introduced its D Series in the latter part of that decade. This was a comprehensive range of tractors that included numerous D-prefixed models including the D10, D12, D14, D15, D17, D19 and D21 machines. There were up to 50 variations in the series once the various fuel options of gasoline, diesel and LPG were considered. The D17 was powered by a 4293cc/262cu in engine that produced 46 drawbar and 51 belt hp in the Nebraska Tractor Tests. There were 62,540 Model D17s made during the tractor's ten-year production run.

In 1960 the company changed the livery used on its products, selecting an even brighter hue, named Persian Orange Number 2, which was contrasted with cream wheels and radiator grilles. The most important models to benefit from this change were the D10 and D12, tractors which had superseded the Models B and CA. Their production run lasted ten years but fewer than 10,000 were made.

The last Allis-Chalmers tractors were produced during the mid-1980s because in 1985 the company, hit by the recession, was taken over by a West German company. Klockner-Humboldt-Deutz acquired it and renamed the tractor division Deutz-Allis. It was shortlived: in 1990 the company was acquired by an American holding firm, known as Allis-Gleaner Company (AGCO), which soon renamed the tractor producer AGCO Allis.

One of the final Allis-Chalmers tractors was the Model 4W-305 of 1985. It had a twin turbo engine that produced power in the region of 305hp and a transmission that included 20 forward gears and four reverse. Production of tractors at West Allis, Wisconsin, ceased in December 1985.

OTHER MAKES

(ACME, Advance-Rumely, American Harvester, Avance, Belarus, Bolinder Munktell, Braud, Breda, Brockway, Bull)

■ ACME

ACME was one of a lengthy list of short-lived tractor manufacturers founded during the boom years that followed the end of World War I. The ACME tractor was advertised as being available in both wheeled and half-track form. It is hard to say with complete certainty but it is likely that many small companies which advertised tractors, such as this one, never made more than a handful of machines after their initial prototype. This was one reason why the Nebraska Tractor Tests, started in 1920, were to become such a useful consumer aid for farmers.

■ LEFT
A 40-60 Advance-Rumely tractor of 1929. Noted for the manufacture of large tractors, the company was acquired by Allis-Chalmers in 1931.

■ ADVANCE-RUMELY

Meinrad Rumely was a German emigrant who set up a blacksmith's shop in La Porte, Indiana during the 1850s. His smithy was gradually expanded into a factory that built farm machines and steam engines for agricultural use. In 1908 John Secor joined the company to develop an oil-fuelled engine, and Rumely, which had primarily been a thresher manufacturer, made its first OilPull tractor in 1909 after Secor had perfected a carburettor for kerosene or paraffin fuel. A later result of this development work was the Model B 25–45 tractor that in turn was superseded by the Model E of 1911. The Model E was a 30–60 tractor, the designation indicating that it produced 30hp at the drawbar and 60hp at the belt. These figures were substantiated when the Model E was tested in the 1911 Winnipeg Agricultural Motor Competition. In 1920 the same tractor was the subject of Nebraska Tractor Test Number 8, when the drawbar figure was measured at almost 50hp and the belt at more than 75hp. The engine capable of producing this horsepower was a low-revving, horizontal twin-cylinder with a bore and stroke of 25 × 30cm/10 × 12in. The measured fuel consumption of this engine was high at almost 50 litres/11 gallons of kerosene per hour. Notable features of the engine design included the special carburettor with water injection and air cooling induced by creating a draught through the rectangular tower on the front of the tractor. The company was renamed the Advance-Rumely Thresher Company in 1915 during the production run of the Model E 30–60 OilPull, which remained in production until 1923 when it was superseded by the similarly designed 20–40 Model G. By 1931, Advance-Rumely had produced more than 56,500 OilPulls in 14 configurations.

Advance-Rumely, noted for making large tractors, entered the small tractor market in 1916 when it first advertised its All Purpose 8–16 model. The operation of the machine was described as being "just like handling a horse gang". The machine had only three wheels – a single steering rear wheel and two front wheels, one driven and the other free-wheeling. It was powered by a four-cylinder engine that ran on kerosene. The tractor was intended for drawbar towing of implements and for the belt driving of machines such as threshers and balers.

While Advance-Rumely continued to refine its own OilPull line of tractors, it acquired Aultman Taylor in 1924 but was itself sold to Allis-Chalmers in 1931. In that year it marketed the Model 6A tractor, a modern-looking machine for its time. The 6A was powered by a six-cylinder Waukesha engine and fitted with a

■ BELOW LEFT
Early tractors such as this Advance-Rumely took many of their design features from the steam traction engines that had preceded them.

■ **RIGHT** *This large tractor was rated at 22-65hp at the drawbar and belt respectively and was made by the Advance-Rumely Thresher Company during 1919.*

■ **BELOW RIGHT** *Advance-Rumely was founded by Meinrad Rumely, a German emigrant blacksmith who opened a smithy in La Porte, Indiana in the mid-19th century.*

six-speed gearbox. Allis-Chalmers, however, sold the 6A only until existing stocks had been used up, and less than 1,000 were made in total.

■ AMERICAN HARVESTER

American Harvester diesel tractors are made under contract in the People's Republic of China and imported into the United States by a company called Farm Systems International. There are numerous tractor manufacturers in China but Farm Systems International claim to contract only with those manufacturers who are capable of matching or exceeding specified standards of quality and workmanship. The engines used in American Harvester machines incorporate features such as removable cylinder sleeves and forged pistons, aimed at ensuring the longevity of the tractors.

The Model 504 is one of a range of Compact American Harvester tractors that are engineered to last between 6,000 and 11,000 hours between overhauls and are also designed to be sufficiently powerful though small and fuel-efficient. The 504 is fitted with a low-pollution diesel engine coupled to an eight-speed transmission with four-wheel-drive capability. Options include a two-wheel-drive transmission with an adjustable width, row crop front end. The 504 has a full-size, mechanical

■ **BELOW** *This Advance-Rumely Model H tractor was rated at 16-30hp in 1920, but was superseded by lighter models from 1924.*

power take-off as standard and a full-size, three-point hydraulic hitch. A range of models is available, with engines that produce from 18 to 50hp. All have a 12 volt electrical system with emergency hand crank starting, glow plugs and compression release for cold weather. There is a built-in auxiliary hand-pump to purge fuel lines.

The American Harvester Model 250 is of smaller overall dimensions and is primarily intended for use with implements such as

OTHER MAKES

■ RIGHT *Belarus tractors are made in the Republic of Belarus, a member of the Commonwealth of Independent States previously known as Belorussia, in the former USSR, and are widely exported.*

■ BELOW *Belarus offers six series of tractors from 31 to 180bhp in almost thirty configurations. All the machines are of a simple design to ensure reliability.*

rotary cultivators, rotary disc ploughs, rotary harrows and reaping machines as well as ordinary ploughs and harrows. To enable it to do this it has a system of "live hydraulics" and large diameter tyres to aid traction in fields. It can also be used as the power for irrigation and drainage equipment, threshing machines and rice mills or to drive trailers.

The Model 250 is 268.7cm/105.8in long and 124cm/48.8in wide. The height to steering wheel is 143.3cm/56.4in while the wheel base is 152cm/60in. The turning circle varies depending on whether brakes are fitted to the front axle. With brakes fitted the turning circle is 2.5m/8.25ft while without them it is 2.8m/9.24ft. The Model 250 is powered by a vertical, water cooled, four stroke, three-cylinder diesel. Its displacement is 1432cc/87.4cu in achieved through a bore and stroke of 8.6x9.7cm/3.4x3.8in. The Compression Ratio is 22:1 and the engine produces 25hp @ 2500rpm. The engine is cooled by a pressurized system. The transmission has eight forward and two reverse gears and is assembled with a dry, single plate clutch. The gearbox is fitted with a differential lock to assist traction in wet or heavy soil. The drum brake is of the internal expanding shoe type while steering is of a traditional peg and

■ RIGHT *The Belarus 862 D is designed for high speed field work and has a 90hp engine and a four-wheel-drive system that only engages drive to the front axle when the rear wheels slip up to 6 per cent.*

worm design. The Model 250 has 6.0x15 and 8.3x24 tyres, front and rear respectively and its hydraulic linkage has a maximum lift capacity of 1878kg/4140lbs.

■ AVANCE

Avance was a Swedish tractor manufacturer active in the second decade of the 20th century when tractor innovations were accruing rapidly. Avance offered a tractor of an improved design, the first semi-diesel-engined machine. All oil products had to be imported into Sweden and were expensive, so a machine that could run on as cheap a fuel as possible – including waste oil – offered clear advantages. The engineers at Avance had considered the starting procedure of diesels in some detail and developed the semi-diesel, which ignited the fuel by its injection on to a red hot bulb in the cylinder head. The Avance machine offered this new technology in a machine that was in other ways dated, relying on both a chassis and tank cooling of the engine. By the end of the decade Avance were offering two-cylinder, hot-bulb, semi-diesel tractors of two capacities, 18–22 and 20–30hp. They utilized compressed air starters with glow plugs and batteries as additional options.

■ **ABOVE RIGHT** ***The Belarus 862 D is fitted with independent and ground speed PTO and category II live hydraulics with draught and position control.***

■ **RIGHT** ***The 862 D is powered by a 4075cc/248cu in, in-line four-cylinder engine which drives through a transmission with 18 forward and two reverse gears.***

■ BELARUS

Belarus Tractors are made in the Minsk Tractor Factory in the Republic of Belarus, a member of the Commonwealth of Independent States (CIS). The company's products have been exported widely and it offers numerous tractors in a variety of configurations.

The Belarus Model 862 D of 1986 was powered by an engine that displaced 4075cc/248cu in and produced 90hp. It featured an automatic, four-wheel-drive transmission that incorporated 18 forward and two reverse gears. Hydrostatic steering was fitted as standard.

The current Belarus range of four-wheel-drive tractors includes the 1221, which produces 130hp, the 115hp 1025, the 105hp 952 and the 862, which produces 90hp. The two-wheel-drive line of Belarus tractors ranges from the 105hp 950 machine to the 90hp 900 Model.

OTHER MAKES

■ **BOLINDER-MUNKTELL**
The Swedish tractor-maker Bolinder-Munktell was formed by the amalgamation of two Swedish companies. In 1932 the tractor manufacturer Munktell combined with its engine-maker, Bolinder, to form Bolinder-Munktell, which continued the production of the 15–22 and 20–30 tractors. Munktell is credited with having built the first tractor to be manufactured in Sweden, the BM 30–40 of 1913. It was powered by a two-cylinder Bolinder engine. The company also experimented with wood-burning tractors, because fuel was a major consideration in countries where oil had to be imported. In 1921 and 1922 the company offered a two-stroke, two-cylinder, hot-bulb engine that produced 15-22hp and, as a result, was designated the Model 22. Its engine was actually derived from a marine engine and used compressed air to start after the hot bulbs had been heated with an integral blowlamp. By 1930 the company was also offering a larger model, the 20–30, and both variants took part in the Oxfordshire World Tractor Trials of

■ ABOVE *Bolinder-Munktell later combined with Volvo to form Volvo BM but prior to this the company's two-stroke diesel engines proved popular.*

■ BELOW *Bolinder-Munktell was a merger of the Swedish tractor maker Munktell and engine maker Bolinder. This three-cylinder diesel was one of the company's products.*

1930. Another Swedish manufacturer was Bofors, the arms manufacturer, that entered the tractor market alongside Avance and Munktell with its 40–46hp two-cylinder tractor first built in 1932.

Bolinder-Munktell offered a 31hp twin-cylinder engined tractor in 1939 and in the aftermath of World War II offered the Model 10 tractor, a 23hp machine powered by a hot-bulb engine. It was not until the 1950s that the company abandoned the hot-bulb engine, when it introduced the BM35 and BM55 models with direct injection diesel engines. These tractors also featured five-speed transmissions and an optional cab. Bolinder-Munktell later merged with Volvo.

■ BRAUD

In 1870 Braud was founded in St Mars La Jaille, in France, to manufacture threshing machines. Over a century later, in 1975, Braud produced its first grape harvester and went on to specialize in this field. In 1984 Fiatagri acquired 75 per cent of Braud. Then in 1988 all of Fiat-Allis and Fiatagri's activities were merged to form a new company, FiatGeotech, the Fiat group's farm and earthmoving machinery sector. Within this restructuring, Hesston and Braud joined forces in a new company, Hesston-Braud, based in Coex, France. It later became part of New Holland Geotech.

■ BREDA

Breda was active in tractor production in Italy during the 1920s, and unlike many of its competitors, produced gasoline-engined tractors. These were powered by four-cylinder engines of 26 and 40hp. During the 1930s the range of models offered was expanded to include both a conventional four-cylinder gasoline/kerosene-engined tractor and an unusual two-stroke, two-cylinder, Junkers diesel-engined machine. After World War II the company offered multi-cylinder-engined crawler tractors.

■ BROCKWAY

During the years immediately after World War II, there was an influx of new tractor manufacturers into the industry. Brockway had made bridging equipment for the US Army during the war and was one of several American companies new to tractor manufacture. Others included Custom, Earthmaster, Farmaster, Friday, General, Harris and Laughlin.

■ BULL

The Minneapolis Steel and Machinery Company was primarily a structural steel-maker, producing thousands of tons per year in the late 1800s and early 1900s. The company also manufactured the Corliss steam engine, that served as a power unit for many flour mills in the Dakotas. In 1908, Minneapolis Steel and Machinery produced tractors under the Twin City brand name.

By the outbreak of World War I, the company was one of the larger tractor producers in the world, and had diversified into manufacturing tractors for other companies. One of these was the Bull tractor for the Bull Tractor Co: the company was contracted to build 4,600 machines, using engines supplied by Bull.

The acceptance that small tractors were practical for all kinds of farming tasks quickly changed the emphasis of the tractor-manufacturing industry and threatened some of the old-established companies and their larger machines.

The Bull tractor was a small machine based around a triangular steel frame. It had only one driven wheel, thereby eliminating the need for a differential. A single wheel at the front steered the machine and the other two simply free-wheeled. An opposed twin engine produced up to 12hp and the transmission was as basic as the remainder of the machine, with a single forward and single reverse gear.

At first the little Bull tractor sold well, but after an initial success, the limitations of its usefulness, and some inherent faults in the machine's design and construction became apparent. Sales quickly declined and as a result, little was heard of the company after 1915.

■ ABOVE *This 1950 Bolinder-Munktell BM10 tractor produced 20hp from its two-cylinder, two-stroke hot-bulb engine.*

CASE

■ BELOW *The new Case RC of 1935 was painted light grey in order to distinguish it from the CC models. The RC began production as a four-cylinder, engine-powered, tricycle row crop tractor.*

Case built its first viable gasoline-powered tractor in 1911 and by 1913 had developed a practical and small-sized tractor powered by a gasoline engine, although the company's history began long before this. J. I. Case and Company was formed in 1863, in Racine, Wisconsin, to build steam tractors. It became the J. I. Case Threshing Company in 1880, and its first experimental gasoline tractor appeared in 1892, but was not a success. In 1911 the massive Case 30–60 won first place in the Winnipeg Tractor Trials. It weighed almost 13 tons but clearly found a market, as it was

CASE RC ROW CROP 1935	
Engine	Waukesha in-line four cylinder
Power	18-20hp
Transmission	Three forward speeds, hand clutch
Weight	1180kg/2600lbs

■ BELOW *The Case L model of 1929 ended Case's production of Crossmotor models because the L used an in-line four-cylinder overhead valve engine for propulsion.*

■ RIGHT *The Case CC was a row crop version of the Model C with a distinctive steering arm, nicknamed the "chicken perch" and "fence cutter".*

■ BELOW LEFT *The Case RC of 1939 added the rounded sunburst cast grille and Flambeau Red paintwork.*

■ BELOW RIGHT *Production of Case RC models was moved to Rock Island, Illinois in 1937 after Case had purchased the Rock Island Plow Company.*

made until 1916. A smaller version, the 12–25, was made from 1913 onwards but it was the company's 20–40 model that garnered more awards at the Winnipeg Trials in 1913. All three of these Case tractors were powered by flat twin engines (horizontally opposed twin cylinders) of varying displacements and used other components taken from the Case range of steam engines.

It was generally accepted that the future lay in smaller tractors that had more in common with automobiles than steam engines. Case experimented with small-sized machines and developed the three-wheeled 10–20 Crossmotor tractor. This was powered by a vertical in-line four-cylinder engine mounted transversely across the frame. It had a single driven wheel and an idler wheel on the rear axle. The driven wheel was aligned with the front steering wheel and the machine was capable of pulling a two-tine plough. Between 1915 and 1922 approximately 5,000 10–20s were produced. Case introduced the four-wheeled Model 9–18 in 1916 to compete with the popular Fordson. It was the 9–18 tractor that, in many ways, established Case as a major manufacturer and more than 6,000 of the two versions, 9–18A and 9–18B, had been made by 1919. The 9–18 was a lightweight tractor designed to weigh around the same as a team of horses and capable of pulling a plough or driving a

■ LEFT *When pneumatic tyres were still considered innovative, tractor makers offered customers a choice of steel wheels, or pneumatic tyres as used by this Model L.*

Case had not abandoned production of larger tractors altogether and offered the 22–40 between 1919 and 1924 and the 40–72 between 1920 and 1923. Only 42 tractors of the latter design were made. Each weighed 11 tons and when tested in Nebraska in 1923 produced a record 91 belt hp, but used fuel in huge quantities.

A new president, Leon R. Clausen (1878–1965), was appointed to head the thresher. In 1917 the 10–18 was launched. It was similar to the 9–18 but featured a cast radiator tank and an engine capable of higher rpm. During the 10–18's three-year production run around 9,000 tractors were made. The 15–27 was a tractor designed for a three-tine plough and was the first Case tractor to have a power take-off fitted. Its capabilities matched the requirements of the market to the extent that more than 17,500 were sold between its introduction in 1919 and 1924 when it was superseded by the Model 18–32.

■ LEFT *Later the Case colour scheme was a combination of Flambeau Red and Desert Sand.*

■ BELOW LEFT *The row crop tractors' front wheels minimized crop damage.*

■ BELOW *The refined row crop Case DC included upgrades such as the streamlined cast radiator grille.*

■ RIGHT *The distinctive Case name and logo was always displayed.*

■ FAR RIGHT *What made the Case DEX different from other Case tractors from the early 1940s was that the DEX used the enclosed chain final drive system instead of gears.*

■ BELOW *A 1942 Case DEX model photographed in Yorkshire, England.*

J. I. Case Threshing Machine Company in 1924. Clausen had been born in Fox Lake, Wisconsin and in 1897 had graduated from the University of Wisconsin with a degree in electrical engineering. He had experience of the tractor industry as a former employee of John Deere. He also had an antipathy towards trade unionism and some disdain for customer demands, believing that product design should be solely the province of the engineering department. He started the company working on a redesigned range of tractors.

■ CASE MODEL L

In 1929 the Case Model L went into production based around a unit frame construction. It was notable because, for the first time in 15 years, the engine was not mounted transversely but longitudinally. The angular Model L was a great success and was to remain in production until 1939 when it was replaced by the Model LA, a restyled and updated version of the L. The restyling gave the tractor a more rounded appearance typical of the time, but much of the engineering was similar to that of the Model L. The engine was a 6.6 litre, overhead valve, in-line, four-cylinder unit. Drive to the rear axle was by a pair of chains and sprockets as in the Model L. The gearbox was a conventional four-speed unit with a single reverse gear. A lever-operated overcentre-type clutch allowed selection of the required gear. The tractor stayed in production until 1955.

The Case Model C also went into production in 1929 and it, along with

CASE 385 TRACTOR

Year	1988
Engine	Three cylinder, 2536cc/155cu in
Power	45hp (33.6 kW)
Transmission	Eight forward, four reverse
Weight	(2WD model) 2430kg/5356lbs

■ RIGHT *The Case LA debuted in 1939 although under its streamlined hood and Flambeau red paint it was essentially the earlier Model L tractor, albeit more powerful.*

the Model L, was one of the tractors that helped to establish the Case brand in Great Britain. It was tested in the 1930 World Tractor Trials in Oxfordshire where, in the class for machines fuelled by paraffin, it achieved the best economy figures. The model C recorded a maximum output of 29.8hp on the belt and 21.9hp on the drawbar, figures that were almost identical to those achieved in Nebraska the previous year. The results of the tests were widely advertised by Case, which later offered the Models CC, CI, CO, CV and CD (row crop, industrial, orchard, vineyard and crawler versions respectively). Under

■ BELOW *This is a 1943 version of the Case LA tractor, which had revised wheels over the initial model. The LA was designed to pull up to five ploughs.*

■ ABOVE *The plate that identifies the tractor as Case model number 11161 LA also bears the "Old Abe" mascot and is positioned next to the oil pressure gauge.*

■ LEFT *Despite the distinctive green and yellow colour scheme that suggests John Deere, the French company SFV was acquired by Case during the 1960s.*

CASE MX100C	
Year	1998
Engine	4 litre four-cylinder turbo
Power	75 kW at 2200rpm
Transmission	16 forward, 12 reverse
Weight	4750kg/10,470lbs

Clausen, progress and innovation were cautious and conservative which, in some instances allowed competitors to benefit at Case's expense. One area in which Clausen wanted to advance the company was to offer a full line of implements to complement the tractor range. To this end, Case bought out Emerson-Brantingham in 1928 and the Rock Island Plow Company in 1937. Following these acquisitions, and that of the Showers Brothers furniture factory in Burlington, Iowa, Case moved towards production of combine harvesters. A new line of tractors appeared in 1939, the Models D and DC, which were to be followed by the Models S and V and an upgraded Model L, the LA.

The Model D was a four-wheeled tractor and was designed to pull a three-tine plough. It had a belt pulley, PTO and Case's motor lift system for the implements. The DC was a row crop tricycle with adjustable wheel spacing

■ ABOVE RIGHT *Société Française Vierzon (SFV) incorporated the blue, white and red of the French tricolour in its company logo, seen here on the right-hand side of the 302 model.*

■ RIGHT *The two-stroke semi-diesel SFV tractors featured distinctively shaped exhausts, and a transverse, leaf-sprung beam front axle.*

RIGHT ***Case pioneered the loader backhoe to be sold as a single unit in the late 1950s and had considerable success with the resultant versatile machine. This is a 1990s version, the Case 580 SK.***

and what the manufacturers termed "quick-dodge" steering for close cultivation in uneven rows. The D Series tractors were the first Case machines to be painted in a bright hue – Flambeau Red – a colour that was to become standard for the next decade.

■ THE 1940S

As it did for most American industry, World War II changed things for Case. Between 1940 and 1945 three Case plants had made in excess of 1.3 million 155mm howitzer shells. Case also made specialized military tractors such as the Model LA1. Alongside these projects, Case made parts for army trucks, amphibious tracked vehicles and military aircraft. This war production did not adversely affect Case's tractor sales to farmers at a time when agricultural production was as crucial as armament production; in fact it ended the effects of the Depression on the company. Labour relations were not all that they might have been and in 1945 Case employees from the Racine plant went on strike for 440 days, the longest strike in the company's history. This had a disastrous effect on Case's dealers and customer base and has been credited by many historians as one of the reasons for John Deere's growth and consolidation of its position within the tractor market.

In the aftermath of both the war and the strikes, Case looked towards expansion. The company bought plants in Bettendorf, Iowa and Stockton, California, as well as the Kilby Steel Company of Anniston, Alabama. With these additional facilities Case sought to produce a wider range of farm machinery, including combine harvesters, rakes, ploughs and manure spreaders. The Alabama plant was to be used for the production of new machines, including tobacco harvesters for the south-east of the United States. In the wake of this expansion came a slump in profits for the years 1950–53, largely because many innovations that were being adopted by rival manufacturers – including the three-point hitch – were not offered on Case

ABOVE ***The SFV 201 was one of the models made by SFV prior to the company's acquisition by Case.***

LEFT ***Prior to the acquisition, SFV specialized in the production of two-stroke, semi-diesel engined tractors of an unusual design that proved popular in Europe.***

machines. An example of this failure to compete can be seen in Case's baling machines; in 1941 the company dominated the hay baler market because its baler had been the first to pick up the hay as it was towed along. Just before the outbreak of war New Holland introduced a baler that used twine instead of wire for baling and, more importantly, did not require two extra men to tie bales as the Case machine did. Case failed to make any improvements to its balers and sales slumped to the extent that in 1953 Case achieved only 5 per cent of sales.

■ LEFT *A Case tractor towing a Massey-Ferguson baler during haymaking on a hill farm in Yorkshire, England.*

■ JOHN T. BROWN

The company was in the doldrums and the situation was exacerbated when Clausen relinquished the presidency in 1948 and was succeeded by Theodore Johnson. Johnson resigned in 1953 to be replaced by John T. Brown. This change, along with impetus from the company's underwriter and a more dynamic board of directors, began to turn the company's fortunes around. New engineering practices and an acceptance of diesel engines, as well as new lines of implements including one-way disc ploughs, cotton strippers, disc harrows, Lister press drills and front loaders, all took the company forward. Most important among these advances was the 500 Series of tractors. This new line was soon followed by the 400 and the 300 Series.

These ranges of tractors were effectively the first completely redesigned Case models to appear since

■ BELOW *A four-wheel-drive tractor from the Case XL Series towing a disc harrow in a field in Normandy, France.*

■ RIGHT *The 1056XL is the largest model in the Case IH 56 Series. It is powered by a six-cylinder engine that produces 98hp and features a four-wheel-drive transmission.*

the 1930s. The 500 models of 1953 were powered by an in-line, six-cylinder, diesel engine that developed sufficient horsepower to pull five plough bottoms. The 500 also featured power steering, a push-button starter and live hydraulics, making them easy to operate. The 400 Series was unveiled in 1955 and incorporated all Case's new technology. Power came from an in-line four-cylinder engine with a choice of diesel, gasoline or LPG fuel, capable of pulling four ploughs. Final drive was now by means of gears and the transmission had eight forward speeds. A hydraulic vane steering system was fitted, as were a three-point hitch and suspension seat for the driver. The 400 Series models were the first made by the company to be advertised on television. Both the 400 and 500 Series models were made at the Racine, Wisconsin plant, and a third new model line was made at Rock Island and went on sale in 1956.

■ THE 300 SERIES

The 300 Series offered customers considerable choice: diesel or gasoline engine, and transmission with four, eight or twelve speeds. The other new feature of the 300 Series was its streamlined styling, which soon became the norm across Case's entire range. The next development in styling came in 1957 and was inspired by the automobile industry: the radiator grille was squared off and inclined forwards at the top, giving a slightly concave appearance. This styling continued through the Case-O-Matics and the 30 Series tractors, introduced in 1960, and even to the massive 1200 Traction King first produced in 1964.

CASE 1255XL 1990

Engine	Six cylinder turbo 5867cc/358cu in
Power	25hp/92KW
Transmission	20 x 9 syncromesh
Weight	6225kg/13,720lbs

■ ACQUISITIONS

In France, SFV – Société Française Vierzon – had entered the tractor market in 1935 with a machine not unlike the Lanz Bulldog. Despite World War II the company endured until 1960, when it was acquired by Case. In 1957 Case merged with the American Tractor Corporation, based in Churubusco, Indiana. This corporation manufactured "Terratrac" crawler tractors and Case continued production of such machines in Indiana until 1961 when it moved the production to Burlington, Iowa. One of the results of this merger was the

■ BELOW *The Case IH 1255XL, seen here harvesting, has a two speed PTO that produces 121.1hp @ 540rpm and 1000 rpm. The hydraulic system has a maximum pressure of 175kg/sq cm (2488lb/sq in).*

■ RIGHT *Tractors such as the Case IH 4230 have a forward tilting hood and swing out service panel to enable convenience of maintenance.*

■ BOTTOM *The Case 5150 is one of many tractors equipped with front weights which are positioned to improve traction as well as reducing turning radius.*

■ BELOW *Modern tractors such as this Case XL Plus model are fitted with transmissions that have up to 16 forward speeds as well as, in this case, a driven front axle.*

development of the loader/backhoe. Case's 320 loader/backhoe was the first such machine to be built and marketed as a single unit.

■ CHANGING TIMES

Case took over the British tractor-maker, David Brown Ltd, in 1972. This acquisition was seen as more than a purchase because the British company had a large distribution network in Great Britain, outlets in Europe, and even some in the United States. From then on David Brown tractors would be painted in David Brown White and Case Red. The ownership of Case itself had changed in the late 1960s. The Kern County Land Company was a majority shareholder in Case and in 1967 this company was acquired by Tenneco Inc from Texas. In 1974 new agricultural products from Case included the 2670 Traction King tractor, the 6000 Series of mouldboard ploughs and the F21 Series of wheeled tandem-disc harrows. A year later the 1410 and 1412 tractors appeared. There were further new tractors the following year, when the 1570 Agri-King and 2870 Traction King 300hp four-wheel-drive machines were announced. As it was America's bicentennial year Case also offered a limited-edition version of the Model 1570, known as the Spirit of 76. The 70 and 90 Series tractors were new for 1978 and were followed by another new line in 1983, the 94 Series.

In 1985 Tenneco Inc completed its purchase of International Harvester, after that company had been adversely affected by the recession in farming in the early 1980s. In a restructuring of Tenneco, Case IH became Tenneco's largest division. The Case IH range for 1986 included the Model 685L, with a four-cylinder engine that developed 69hp, an eight forward speed and two reverse 4x4 transmission and hydrostatic steering. A larger model in the same range was the Model 1594, with an in-line six-cylinder engine that produced 96hp and drove through a four-range, semi-automatic, Hydra-Shift transmission.

A decade after the restructuring Tenneco formed the Case Corporation and sold its agricultural products as Case IH machines. The current Case IH range includes Magnum and Maxxum tractors. The 8900 Magnum Series Tractors are powered by an 8300cc/506cu in displacement engine and assembled with an 18-speed Powershift

■ BELOW *The MX Series cabs are quiet with a 72dB(A) limit. The temperature is controlled and the air in the cab filtered.*

■ LEFT *The 1998 Case MX120 has sixteen forward gears, four wheel drive and hydrostatic steering.*

transmission. There are four models in the MX Series of Maxxum tractors, with outputs ranging from 85 to 115 PTO hp. They are suited to a variety of tasks including tillage, planting and loader work. They are also designed to adapt to speciality row crop, hay, forage and utility applications. The MX100 offers 85 PTO hp, while the MX135 produces 115 PTO hp. The Maxxum Series is fitted with a modern design of six-cylinder 5883cc/359cu in displacement turbocharged diesel engine. The Maxxum tractor transmission is a 16-speed fully synchronized unit and is standard on all models except on the MX 135, which has a Powershift transmission. Standard creeper and super creeper transmissions are available on all models. A compact series of three Maxxum tractors is also offered: Models MX80C, 90C and 100C. Alongside these are the CS 110-150 and CX50 to CX100 Models. A specialized agricultural machine manufactured by Case IH at its East Moline plant is the 2555 Cotton Express, a state-of-the-art cotton picker. Cotton picking is a specialized business and the machines designed for it have become increasingly technical. The 2555 is capable of holding up to 3855kg/8500lb of cotton and has a 32.5cu m/1150cu ft vertical lift basket. The design of components, such as straight-through front and rear outlets, are intended to enhance crop flow, reduce chokes, improve drum component life and decrease wear on moistener pads and pad holders. The 2555 is powered by a 260hp turbocharged diesel engine and offers on-road transport speeds of around 29kph/18mph as well as sufficient power for harvesting. A more conventional, but no less technologically advanced, combine harvester currently made by Case IH is the Axial-Flow 2100 Series.

■ LEFT *This 1998 Case MX tractor is equipped with a Miller PL-3 front loader, a versatile tractor attachment.*

■ OPPOSITE *Despite its apparent complexity the three-point linkage and hydraulic system on the rear of this Case IH tractor is similar to the one devised by Harry Ferguson.*

■ LEFT *The front loader, such as the unit attached to this Case tractor, is suited to a variety of farming tasks including the handling and loading of crops.*

■ WORLD PRODUCTION

Towards the end of the millennium, the Case Corporation is multinational. In North America it has numerous production facilities, each dedicated to specific products. In Burlington, Iowa, loaders, backhoes, forklifts, crawlers, dozers and hydraulic cylinders are produced. In East Moline, Illinois, the company manufactures combine harvesters, cotton pickers, grain and corn heads while in Fargo, North Dakota, the Case plant produces tractors, wheeled loaders and Concord air drills.

In the same state a plant in Valley City is dedicated to electronics. In Hamilton, Ontario, tillage, crop production and material handling equipment are made. In Racine, Wisconsin, Case produces its lines of Magnum and Maxxum tractors as well as transmissions and foundry products. Skid steer and trenching machines are made in Wichita, Kansas and directional drills are fabricated in Hugo, Minnesota. The company has numerous plants around Europe: St Valentin, Austria, is where Steyr tractors are made, while excavators, loaders and backhoes are produced in Crépy-en-Valois, France.

Another French plant at Croix produces agricultural and construction equipment cabs, while others at St Dizier and Tracy-le-Mont produce transmissions and hydraulic cylinders respectively. In Britain, tractors, gears and shafts are made in Doncaster, mini-excavators and skid steer machines in Manchester and sprayers are made in Lincoln. Forage harvesters, combines and square balers are produced in Neustadt, Germany. In South America, a plant in Sorocaba, Brazil, makes wheeled loaders, backhoes and excavators.

Case also has a factory in Australia in Bundaberg, Queensland, that produces Austoft sugar cane harvesters, transporters and planters. The corporation participates in a number of joint ventures, including those with Hay & Forage Industries of Hesston, Kansas, that produces hay and forage equipment, and the Consolidated Diesel Company of Rocky Mount, North Carolina, that makes engines.

Further afield, Case works with the Liuzhou Case Liugong Construction Equipment Company Ltd of Liuzhou, China, to make loaders and backhoes. Case has a similar arrangement with Brastoft Maquinas e Sistemas Agroindustrias SA in Piracicaba, Brazil, to produce sugar cane harvesters, and with UzCaseMash in Tashkent, Uzbekistan where cotton pickers are made. Case's East Moline, Illinois plant produces combine harvesters, cotton pickers, grain heads and corn heads, while its Fargo, North Dakota facility builds tractors and wheeled loaders as well as making Concord air drills. Case's 1997 revenue amounted to approximately $6 billion and the corporation has about 18,000 employees and 4,900 dealers and distributors.

CATERPILLAR

■ BELOW *The Caterpillar Sixty was one of the models of crawler manufactured in the Peoria, Illinois plant from 1925 onwards. It was a post-merger version of the Best 60hp model crawler.*

During the late 19th century Benjamin Holt and Daniel Best experimented with various forms of steam tractors for use in farming. They did so independently, running separate companies, but both were pioneers with track-type tractors and gasoline-powered tractor engines. Paralleling the developments of the steam excavator were experiments with tracked machines referred to as "crawlers". Crawler technology would later diverge into separate and distinct strands of activity, although the technology employed remained essentially the same. One of these strands of activity is, of course, the crawler's agricultural application.

The initial experiments involved wheeled steam tractors which were converted to run with tracks to overcome the problem of wheels sinking into soft ground. The first test of such a machine took place in November 1904 in Stockton, California, where a Holt steam tractor had been converted to run on tracks. This was accomplished by the removal of the rear wheels and their replacement with tracks made from a series of 7.5 × 10cm/3 × 4in wooden blocks 60cm/2ft long, bolted to a linked steel chain which ran around smaller wheels, a driven sprocket and idler on each side. Originally the machine was steered by a single tiller wheel, although this system was later dropped in favour of the idea of disengaging drive to one track by means of a clutch which slewed the machine around. From here it was but a short step to gasoline-powered crawlers, one of which was constructed by Holt in 1906. By 1908, 28 Holt gasoline-powered crawlers were engaged in work on the Los Angeles Aqueduct project in the Tehachapi mountains – something Holt saw as a proving-ground for his machines. By 1915, Holt "Caterpillar" track-type tractors were being used by the Allies in World War I.

In the years after World War I, the Best Company continued the work with crawler-tracked machinery. In 1921 it introduced a new machine, the Best 30 Tracklayer. This crawler was fitted with a light-duty bulldozer blade, was powered by an internal combustion engine and had an enclosed cab. At this time there was a considerable amount of litigation involving patents and types of tracklayers, and two companies were frequently named in the litigation: Best and Holt. Holt held a patent for track-layers which put him in a position to charge a licence fee to other manufacturers of the time, including Monarch, Bates and Cletrac. During World War I, much of Holt's production went to the US Army, while Best supplied farmers. After the war the two companies competed in all markets and neither had a significant advantage over the other. Eventually in 1925, the Holt and Best companies effectively merged to form the Caterpillar Tractor Company. Holt had in fact bought out Daniel Best in 1908 but later had to compete with Best's son, C. L. "Leo" Best.

In late 1925 the new Caterpillar Company published prices for its product line: the Model 60 sold for $6,050, the Model 30 for $3,665 and the two ton for $1,975. The consolidation of the two brands into one company proved its value in the next few years: the prices of the big tracklayers were cut, business increased and sales more than doubled.

The Caterpillar Twenty was a mid-sized crawler tractor put into production by the company in Peoria, Illinois late in 1927; production continued until 1933. It was powered by an in-line four-cylinder engine that made 25hp at 1250rpm. According to its makers it could pull 2174kg/4793lb at the

■ RIGHT *A Caterpillar crawler being used for orchard work. The operator is wearing protective clothes to protect himself from the effects of pesticides.*

■ BELOW *A 1950s Caterpillar D4 with dozer blade; the "D" prefix indicates a diesel engine.*

drawbar in first gear, but in the respected Nebraska Tractor Tests it recorded a maximum pull of 2753kg/6071lb. The transmission was a three-speed with a reverse, and steering was achieved through multi-plate disc clutches and contracting band brakes. With a width of only 1.5m/5ft and length of 2.7m/9ft the tractor was compact and helped to establish Caterpillar as a known brand on smaller farms and in export markets. In 1929 the company announced the Caterpillar 15, which increased its range of crawlers to five models of varying capabilities.

In 1931 the first Diesel Sixty-Five Tractor rolled off the new assembly line in East Peoria, Illinois, with a new, efficient source of power for track-type tractors. This year also saw the shift to the now familiar yellow livery of Caterpillar products; all Caterpillar machinery left the factory painted Highway Yellow, which was seen both as a way of brightening up the machines in an attempt to lift the gloom of the Depression, and as a safety measure since machines increasingly being used in road construction had to be visible to motorists. Highway Yellow caught on slowly at first but eventually became the standard colour for all construction equipment. New diesel-engined crawlers went into production in 1935. Their model designations began with RD – Rudolph Diesel's initials – and finished with a number that related to the crawler's size and engine power, so that RD8, RD7 and RD6 machines were soon followed by the RD4 of 1936. (Other accounts of where RD comes from have suggested that the R stands for Roosevelt and the D for Diesel.)

The RD8 was capable of 95 drawbar hp, while the RD7 achieved 70 drawbar

CATERPILLAR RD7

Year	1937
Engine	Four cylinder diesel
Power	61hp at 850rpm
Transmission	Three speed
Weight	9535kg/21,020lbs

■ LEFT *Crawler tractors such as this Caterpillar offer greater traction over wheeled models, especially in heavy or wet soils.*

■ BELOW *The Caterpillar 65 is the smallest model in the Challenger series. It weighs 32,875lbs.*

hp and the RD6 45 drawbar hp. By this time the US Forest Service was using machines such as the Cletrac Forty with an angled blade on the front, so Caterpillar built one fitted with a LaPlante-Choate Trailblazer blade. Ralph Choate specialized in building blades to be fastened to the front of other people's crawlers: his first one was used on road construction work between Cedar Rapids and Dubuque, Iowa.

In 1938, Caterpillar started production of its smallest crawler tractor, the D2. It was designed for agricultural use and was capable of pulling three- or four-tine ploughs or a disc harrow. The Nebraska tests rated it as having 19.4 drawbar hp and 27.9 belt hp. A variation of the D2 was the gasoline- or paraffin-powered R2, which offered similar power output.

By 1940 the Caterpillar product line included motor graders, blade graders, elevating graders, terracers and electrical generating sets and by 1942 Caterpillar track-type tractors, motor graders, generator sets and a special engine for the M4 tank were being used by the United States in its war effort. The agricultural applications of the larger Caterpillar diesel crawlers such as the D7 and D8 Models tended to be reserved for huge farms, where multiple implements could be used. The widespread use of Caterpillar products during World War II led the company to shift the emphasis of its operations towards construction in the post-war years. In 1950 the Caterpillar Tractor Co. Ltd was established in Great Britain, the first of many overseas operations created to help manage foreign exchange shortages, tariffs and import controls and to improve service to customers around the world. In 1953 the company created a separate sales and marketing division just for engine customers. Since then, the Engine Division has become important in the diesel engine market and accounts for one quarter of the company's total sales albeit not wholly in agricultural applications.

In 1963 Caterpillar and Mitsubishi Heavy Industries Ltd formed one of the first joint ventures in Japan to involve partial US ownership. Caterpillar-Mitsubishi Ltd started production in 1965 and was subsequently renamed Shin Caterpillar Mitsubishi Ltd, becoming the second largest maker of construction and mining equipment in Japan. Caterpillar Financial Services Corporation was formed in 1981 to offer equipment financing options to customers worldwide. During the early 1980s the worldwide recession took its

■ RIGHT *The Caterpillar Challenger tractors have found wide acceptance for farming around the globe. This one is seen working in Zambia, Africa.*

toll on Caterpillar, costing the company the equivalent of US $1 million a day and forcing it to reduce employment dramatically. During the later years of that decade the product line continued to be diversified, and this led the company back towards agricultural products. In 1987 the rubber-tracked crawler machines named Challengers appeared in fields, offering a viable alternative to wheeled tractors.

The Caterpillar range for 1996 included a model known as the Challenger 75C. Its engine displaces 10 litres/629cu in and produces a maximum power of 325hp. The operating weight is in excess of 16 tons. It is fitted with rubber crawler tracks known as Mobil-trac. The company continued to expand, acquiring the UK-based Perkins Engines in 1997. With the addition of Germany's MaK Motoren the previous year, Caterpillar became the world leader in diesel engine manufacturing. In the same year the company also diversified into the compact machine business, to offer a range of versatile small construction machines.

Considerable innovative technology is employed in the assembly of agricultural crawlers. The undercarriage is designed to transfer maximum engine power to the drawbar. Because there is less slip with tracks than wheels the crawler will do more work with less horsepower and requires less fuel to do so. Traction under heavy loads is a variable; a wheeled tractor typically experiences slip levels of up to 15 per cent while under the same heavy drawbar loads, a Challenger tractor with Mobil-trac technology experiences up to 4 per cent slip. The long, narrow footprint of the rubber crawler tracks allows the operator to get into the field in difficult conditions by lowering ground pressure and increasing flotation. By distributing the gross weight over more axles, Caterpillar's crawlers and combines achieve reduced soil compaction.

■ RIGHT *The Challenger crawler models use what the makers term Mobil-trac, a type of rubber track technology that offers advantages in traction and flotation over wheeled types.*

OTHER MAKES

(Claas, Claeys, Cletrac)

■ **CLAAS**

The Germany company Claas started to develop combine harvesters for European conditions in 1930 and continues to manufacture such machines, including those for specialized tasks such as sugar cane harvesting. The company claims that more than 80 crops are threshable with Claas combine harvesters ranging from cereals to maize, rice, beans, sunflowers, grass and clover seed. Claas machines range from the 212hp Model 35 to the 410hp Model 95E.

The company started the development of its range of sugar cane harvesters in the 1970s. It currently offers the CC3000 and the Ventor, that are designed for harvesting burnt or green cane. Early in the history of mechanical harvesting of sugar cane Claas recognized the need to develop machines suitable for harvesting green cane.

The current Claas range of balers for hay, silage and straw is wide and includes large square balers known as Quadrant models, Rollant round balers, Variant variable chamber balers and conventional Markant square balers. Self-propelled foragers harvest grass or lucerne to be used for drying, wilted grass silage and silage maize. The Claas Jaguar range is one of the large forager ranges suited to harvesting methods such as whole crop silage. Alongside the self-propelled models, Claas makes pull-type and mounted foragers. Claas also manufactures green harvest machines and its Saulgau plant is located in the heart of Europe's largest green harvest region.

■ ABOVE *The Claas Dominator 106, seen here receiving some maintenance during harvesting, is one of a range of harvesters from Claas that also includes the Jaguar 880 and the Mega 218 models.*

■ OPPOSITE *The Claas grain harvesters are equipped with a high capacity auger, that empties the full grain tank into a farm trailer that is towed alongside the harvester while harvesting continues.*

■ LEFT *The Claas Challenger 55 is a rubber-tracked crawler, aimed at agricultural users, and identical in all but detail to the similarly named Caterpillar model.*

■ **CLAEYS**

In 1910, Werkhuizen Leon Claeys, which had been founded in 1906, built its factory in Zedelgem, Belgium, to manufacture harvesting machinery. In 1952 Claeys launched the first European self-propelled combine harvester, and in 1964 Sperry New Holland purchased a major interest in Claeys, by now one of the largest combine manufacturers in Europe. By 1986 the Ford Motor Company had acquired Sperry New Holland and merged it with Ford Tractor Operations.

■ **CLETRAC**

Rollin H. White was one of a trio of brothers who established the White name in the US automotive industry. In 1911 he designed a self-propelled disc cultivator which, although it never went beyond the experimental stage, established his interest in agricultural machines. He then worked on ideas for a crawler tractor with a differential system that allowed the machine to be steered with a steering wheel rather than the more usual system of levers. The company was based in Cleveland, Ohio and was known as the Cleveland Motor Plow Company. The name was changed in 1917 to the Cleveland Tractor Company and then changed again in 1918 to Cletrac.

The Model R was the first commercial tractor to offer the newly developed controlled differential, that slowed the drive to one track and increased it to the other. It was effective and became standard on Cletrac tractors, later finding wide acceptance in crawler technology. Other tractors from Cletrac were the models H and W. The Model F appeared in 1920 and was made until 1922 as a low-cost crawler tractor available in high clearance row crop format. It was powered by a four-cylinder side-valve engine that produced 16hp at 1600rpm at the drawbar. Its tracks were driven by sprockets mounted high on the sides of the machine, which gave the tracks a distinctive triangular appearance. The Model F retailed for $845 in 1920.

Cletrac introduced its first wheeled tractor in 1939, the general GG. A crawler version of this model was also available and was referred to as the HG. Both were powered by a Hercules IXA engine which was an in-line four-cylinder that produced 19hp at 1700rpm at the belt, later increased to 22hp. The company also made a tricycle row crop tractor, although production of this model was taken over by B. F. Avery in 1941; it was subsequently sold as the Avery Model A. Cletrac was sold to the Oliver Corporation in 1944, which in turn was sold to the White Motor Corporation in 1960.

DAVID BROWN

David Brown manufactured Ferguson tractors in the mid-1930s as a result of Harry Ferguson approaching the company then known as David Brown Gear Cutters of Huddersfield, England, with a view to the manufacture of a tractor transmission. Brown was noted for the manufacture of gears and Harry Ferguson wanted to produce a tractor with an American Hercules engine and an innovative hydraulic lift. This machine came to be built by Brown at a plant in Meltham, near Huddersfield, after the prototype had been tested. Known as the Ferguson Model, it was at first fitted with a Coventry Climax engine and subsequently with an engine of Brown's own design. Production ceased in 1939 because Brown wanted to increase its power and Ferguson to reduce the costs.

■ DAVID BROWN VAK-1

Harry Ferguson travelled to the United States to see Henry Ford while David Brown exhibited a new model of a tractor built to his own design. The new machine was the VAK-1 and featured an

■ BELOW *The successful Cropmaster tractors were superseded by the 25 and 30 models, available in gasoline or diesel.*

■ BELOW *The Cropmaster was introduced in 1947 as the replacement for the successful VAK-1 and VAK-1a models.*

■ BELOW *A restored David Brown tractor on display within a few miles of the original David Brown factory in Meltham, England.*

■ ABOVE *A farmer driving a restored David Brown Cropmaster: the raised windshield was intended to divert cold winds away from the driver's hands.*

■ RIGHT *Farmers with a David Brown Cropmaster during a break in the ploughing competitions at the noted Great Dorset Steam Fair held annually in England.*

■ LEFT *The David Brown company was initially a gear manufacturer, but went on to make tractors with Harry Ferguson.*

DAVID BROWN VAK-1	
Year	1939
Engine	2.5 litre four cylinder
Power	35bhp @ 2000rpm
Transmission	Four forward gears
Weight	1625kg/3585lbs

hydraulic lift. After World War II the Yorkshire-based company reintroduced the VAK-1 in a slightly improved version, the VAK-1a, until it launched the Cropmaster of 1947. This became a popular machine, especially the diesel form which was introduced in 1949.

David Brown unveiled the Model 2D at the 1955 Smithfield Agricultural Show. This was a small tractor designed for small-scale farming and row crop work. Only about 2,000 were made during a six-year production run which

■ LEFT *Ben Addy's restored David Brown 880. The 880 was one of the restyled models of a design that was introduced with the 900 model of 1956. The 880 superseded the 950 in 1962.*

■ RIGHT *The driver's eye view from the seat of the later version of the David Brown 880 tractor.*

■ BELOW *The 880 designation endured and is found on this later David Brown tractor. The bar behind the driver's seat is to protect the driver if there was a roll-over when working on hillsides.*

accounted for a significant percentage of the market which the model was aimed at. Unconventionally, the air-cooled two-cylinder diesel engine was positioned behind the driver and the implements were operated from a mid-mounted tool carrier, operated by a compressed air system. The air was contained within the tractor's tubular frame.

■ DAVID BROWN 950

The styling of David Brown tractors remained closely based on the rounded VAK series until 1956, when the new 900 tractor was unveiled. The 900 offered the customer a choice of four

DAVID BROWN 950 TRACTOR	
Year	1958
Engine	four cylinder diesel or petrol option
Power	42.5hp
Transmission	Four forward speeds
Weight	n/k

■ RIGHT *A David Brown tractor fitted with a cab and a David Brown manufactured, hydraulically operated front loading shovel.*

■ BELOW RIGHT *A David Brown 995. David Brown was later acquired by Case.*

■ BELOW *A David Brown with a rotary hay rake during harvest in West Yorkshire, England. While David Browns were exported worldwide, this one never went more than ten miles from the factory where it was made.*

engines, but its production run lasted only until 1958 when the 950 was announced. This tractor was available in both diesel and gasoline forms, both rated at 42.5hp. The specification of the 950 was upgraded during the four-year production run, with improvements such as an automatic depth-control device being added to the hydraulics and a dual speed power take-off being introduced. A smaller model, the 850, was also available from 1960 onwards as a 35hp diesel. It stayed in production until it was replaced by the three-cylinder diesel 770 in 1965. During this period approximately 2000 Oliver tractors were also produced by David Brown in its Meltham factory for the Oliver Corporation. The David Brown company was taken over by Case in 1972.

OTHER MAKES

(Deutz, Eagle, Emerson-Brantingham)

■ DEUTZ

The company that became known as Deutz was among the pioneers of the internal combustion engine. Nikolaus August Otto, in conjunction with Eugen Langen, manufactured a four-stroke engine which the duo exhibited in Paris at the World Exhibition of 1867. The pair formed a company, Gasmotoren Fabrik Deutz AG, and employed the likes of Gottlieb Daimler and Wilhelm Maybach.

The company introduced its first tractor and motor plough, considered to be of advanced design, in 1907. In 1926 Deutz unveiled the MTZ 222 diesel tractor and the diesel tractor technology race was under way.

In Germany the diesel engine changed the face of tractor manufacture, and at the beginning of the 1930s, Deutz produced its Stahlschlepper ("Iron Tractor") models including the F1M 414, F2M 317 and F3M 315, with single-, twin- and three-cylinder diesel engines respectively. The smaller engines were started by an electrical mechanism while the larger one started with compressed air. When running, the largest displacement model produced 50hp. By this time Deutz was selling its engines to other tractor makers, including Fahr, with which it later merged. Ritscher was another company that used Deutz diesels in the construction of what was the only tricycle-type tractor built in Germany.

After World War II, Deutz became Klockner-Humboldt-Deutz AG, acquired Fahr and offered air-cooled diesel tractors such as the Models 514 and 612. The company was among the first European manufacturers to export its tractors to the United States. It also built tractors in South America and acquired a share of Steiger. In 1985 Deutz purchased Allis-Chalmers and formed Deutz-Allis, which later became part of the AGCO Corporation.

■ ABOVE *The lack of a radiator in the post-war Deutz meant the round front panel gave a distinctive appearance.*

■ LEFT *A four-wheel-drive Deutz-Fahr: Deutz acquired Fahr after World War II.*

■ BELOW LEFT *In the post-war years European tractors were considerably less advanced and less complex than those from the United States.*

■ BELOW RIGHT *This Deutz is equipped with PTO and drawbar.*

■ ABOVE LEFT *A diesel-engined Deutz 7206 tractor. This is a two-wheel-drive model so does not have open centre front tyres, but ribbed ones to assist steering.*

■ ABOVE RIGHT *This Deutz-Fahr DX 6.31 is four-wheel drive and so has open centre tyres that enhance traction at the front axle.*

■ BELOW *This Deutz-Fahr Agcotion shows the latest in tractor cab styling. The front ballast weights enhance traction at the front axle of the four-wheel-drive model.*

■ EAGLE

The Eagle Manufacturing Company was based in Appleton, Wisconsin and started tractor manufacture in 1906 with a horizontally opposed twin-cylinder engine powered machine. By 1911 it was producing a four-cylinder 56hp machine and by 1916 had a range of four-cylinder tractors in production that took it through the 1920s. In 1930 it changed course and moved from flat twins to vertical in-line six-cylinder machines. One of these was the 6A Eagle, designed for three- to four-plough use and powered by a Waukesha six-cylinder engine that produced 22 belt hp and 37 drawbar hp. Model 6B was a row crop machine and 6C a utility tractor. The Eagle stayed in production in its various forms until World War II when production ceased, not to be resumed.

■ EMERSON-BRANTINGHAM

Emerson-Brantingham was one of the pioneers of American agricultural machinery manufacturing, with roots that stretched back to John H. Manny's reaper of 1852. The company had purchased the Gas Traction Company of Minneapolis in 1912 and became heavily involved in the manufacture of gasoline-engined tractors. Its range included the Big 4 Model 30, a 30 drawbar hp 10 ton machine that was subsequently enlarged into the Big 4 Model 45. This was rated at 45 belt hp and 90 drawbar hp and was even heavier. The Model 20 of 1913 was a much smaller machine and this was followed by the Model AA 12-20 of 1918 that, in turn, was refined into the Model K of 1925.

The huge company, which was based in Rockford, Illinois, was facing financial difficulties in 1928 when it was bought by Case. This acquisition gave Case a boost as it acquired valuable sales territory in the heart of America's corn belt through a well-established dealer network, in addition to a proven line of farm implements.

Case later dropped the Emerson-Brantingham line of tractors but retained many of its implements.

One of the simplest tractors available in Germany during the 1930s was the Fendt Dieselross, or "diesel horse". It was little more than a stationary engine equipped with a basic transmission system and wheels. During World War II Fendt was among the German tractor manufacturers that developed gas generator-powered tractors that would burn almost any combustible material in response to the fuel shortages of the war. In the post-war years Fendt reintroduced its Dieselross tractors in different capacities. A 25hp version was powered by an MWM twin-cylinder engine, while a 16hp model used a Deutz engine. Fendt was acquired by the AGCO corporation in 1997.

■ ABOVE RIGHT ***A 1928 Fendt machine designed for mowing grass. It is powered by a single cylinder engine fuelled with benzine, and was assembled by Johann Georg Fendt and his son Hermann.***

■ RIGHT ***A 1992 four-wheel-drive Fendt Farmer 312 tractor ploughing an English field in heavy conditions.***

■ BELOW ***A 1932 Fendt Dieselross with a sidebar mower. This tractor was powered by a 1000cc/60cu in displacement single cylinder Deutz diesel engine.***

FENDT FARMER 312

Year	1998
Engine	In-line six cylinder turbo diesel
Power	110 PTO hp, 125 BS hp
Transmission	21 forward, 21 reverse
Weight	2363kg/5210lbs

■ ABOVE *A four-wheel-drive Fendt Farmer Turbomatik, working with rollers, during the field cultivation process.*

■ LEFT *The Dieselross name was used by Fendt on several of its tractors. This 1952 model had a diminutive MWM single cylinder diesel engine of 850cc/52cu in displacement, and six forward gears.*

■ ABOVE *A 1950s Fendt Farmer 2D diesel tractor with a two axled drawbar trailer, loaded up with logs.*

■ BELOW *Fendt used the Farmer designation on several models of its tractors through the decades. This is a Farmer 45 model which contrasts with the Turbomatik at the top of the page.*

FERGUSON

The Ferguson tractor evolved from an arrangement made with David Brown and later a partnership between Harry Ferguson and Henry Ford. Originally, Harry Ferguson, who came from Belfast, had installed his innovative three-point hitching system on David Brown tractors. He subsequently made a deal with Henry Ford, through their famous "handshake agreement", although Ford and Ferguson later went their separate ways. This split led to a certain amount of litigation when Ferguson opened his own Detroit factory. The lawsuit which followed suggested that Ford's use of the Ferguson System on its 8N tractors was considered a violation of Harry's patent. The upshot was that Ferguson won

■ ABOVE *The Ferguson-Brown tractor was manufactured in the latter part of the 1930s, through the collaboration of Harry Ferguson and David Brown. Only 1350 tractors were made.*

■ LEFT *A Ferguson TE20 at work in an English field with a Massey-Harris baler. The TE20 went into production in 1946 and became a familiar sight on British farms.*

FERGUSON-BROWN TYPE A	
Year	1936
Engine	Coventry Climax E Series four cylinder
Power	18 – 20hp
Transmission	Three forward, one reverse
Weight	n/k

■ ABOVE *Ferguson tractors, converted to full track configuration for the Commonwealth Expedition to the South Pole in the Antarctic, unloading stores.*

■ BELOW LEFT *Over 300,000 TE20s were manufactured in the production run of the TE20, which paralleled production of the TO20 in the United States.*

■ BELOW *The TE20 was marketed under a slogan that read, "It's what the implement does that sells the tractor". This is a 1949 model.*

■ BELOW *TE20 Fergusons were initially available with a gasoline engine but later diesel and TVO - Tractor Vaporising Oil - versions were made available. This is a 1955 TVO model.*

■ OPPOSITE *A Ferguson TE20 ploughing the fields with a two-bottom Ferguson plough, connected to the tractor by means of Ferguson's revolutionary three-point linkage.*

FORD FERGUSON 9N

Year	1939
Engine	1965cc/120cu in displacement four cylinder
Power	16.31 drawbar and 23.56 belt hp
Transmission	Three speed
Weight	n/k

■ LEFT *A 1951 TED20. At this time production of the TE models was often in excess of 500 per week.*

■ RIGHT *The TE20 inspired great affection and was renowned for its reliability and capacity for hard work.*

damages for patent infringement and loss of business from Ford.

Now on his own, Harry Ferguson set about making his own line of tractors, the TE and TO models. TE was an acronym for Tractor England while TO stood for Tractor Overseas. Both models were not dissimilar to the Fordson 9N but the Ferguson model featured a more powerful engine and a fourth gear ratio. Harry Ferguson came to an arrangement with Sir John Black of the Standard Motor Company in Britain to produce a new tractor in his factory in Coventry. Production started in 1946, using an imported Continental engine. Standard's own engine was substituted when it became available in 1947, with a diesel option being offered in 1951. The first Ferguson was the TE20, referred to as the TO20 in the United States. Over 500,000 TE20s were built in Britain from 1946–56, while some 60,000 TO20s were built in the United States during 1948–51. This tractor – the TE20 – was nicknamed the "Grey Fergy", a reference both to its designer and to its drab paintwork. It became enormously popular, to the extent of

■ BOTTOM ***This Ferguson TE20 has the original-type, closed centre pattern, agricultural rear tyres fitted. Attached to the three-point linkage is a device for carrying, in this case milk churns.***

being ubiquitous on British farms. In August 1951, Harry released the TO30 Series, and the TO35, painted beige and metallic green, came out in 1954. Ferguson sold his company to Massey-Harris in 1953.

■ FERGUSON RESEARCH

Harry Ferguson then established Harry Ferguson Research Ltd and experimented with numerous engineering innovations including a four-wheel-drive system for high performance sports cars. A modified version of this later made it into production in the Jensen FF Interceptor.

Ferguson sold his company to the Canadian agricultural company Massey-Harris in 1953. This was a complex deal that saw Ferguson receive $16 million worth of Massey-Harris shares and the company become Massey-Harris-Ferguson for a period. In 1957 Ferguson resigned from involvement with Massey-Harris-Ferguson and sold his share in the company. In 1958 he was working on the possibility of another tractor development in Britain, but partially as a result of the economic trends of the

■ ABOVE *On the Ferguson TE20 the operator sat astride the gearbox, with feet placed on the footpegs to either side of it.*

■ BELOW *This Ferguson 35, intended to be a successor to the TE20, has a front loader and is towing a muck spreader.*

■ RIGHT *Ferguson's revised line of tractors, designed to supersede the TE20s, featured a much more curved hood than earlier models.*

■ BELOW LEFT *A Ferguson TE20 tractor awaiting restoration in an English barn. It has been painted a non-standard red at some time.*

■ BELOW RIGHT *Harry Ferguson's trademark was his surname in italic script on the top of the grille surround.*

FERGUSON TE20	
Year	1946
Engine	In-line four cylinder
Power	28hp
Transmission	Four speed
Weight	1 ton 2 cwt/1.12 tonnes

time it came to nothing. Despite this, the Ferguson tractor and the three-point linkage are two of the landmarks in the development of the tractor. The linkage in particular, albeit in a refined form, is the norm throughout the world and still in use on almost every working tractor.

Harry Ferguson then established a consulting engineering company based in Coventry in the West Midlands. This company experimented with numerous engineering innovations including a four-wheel-drive system for high performance Grand Prix cars. The project initially known as the Ferguson Project 99 was eventually developed into a working car and driven by Stirling Moss in 1961.

FIAT

■ LEFT *The Fiat 70-90 is one of four tractors in Fiat's Medium 90 Series that ranges from the 55-90 to the 80-90. The first number in the designation refers to the tractor's power output.*

■ BELOW *Fiat Geotech acquired Ford New Holland Inc and merged into one company – New Holland Inc – during 1993.*

Several of the European nations involved in World War I began to see the value of tractors in increasing farm productivity. In Italy the motor industry undertook experiments with tractors of its own design, and by 1918 the Fiat company had produced a successful tractor known as the 702, while the Pavesi concern introduced an innovative tractor with four-wheel drive and articulated steering.

In 1919 the first mass-produced Fiat tractor, the 702, came off the assembly line. Fiat soon became the major producer of agricultural tractors in Italy and added a crawler to its range in 1932. This was the first tractor that can be considered an earthmoving machine: the 700C was a tractor equipped with a front blade to shift earth and welded devices to load trucks. It was powered by a 30hp four-cylinder engine. Later, but before the outbreak of World War II, Fiat produced the 708C and Model 40.

After the war, in 1950, Fiat launched the Fiat 55, a crawler tractor powered by a 6500cc/396cu in, four-cylinder diesel engine that produced 55hp at 1400rpm. The transmission incorporated a central pair of bevel gears with final drive by means of spur gears. The crawler tractor had five forward speeds and one reverse. The customer could specify whether they wanted lever or steering-wheel steering. The 6 volt electrical system functioned without a battery and was reliant on a 90 watt dynamo.

In 1962 Fiat created a joint venture with the Turkish company Koa Holding in Ankara, that was known as Türk Traktor. By 1966 Fiat had created its own Tractor and Earthmoving Machinery

FIAT 70-90

Year	1986
Engine	3613cc/220cu in
Power	70hp
Transmission	n/k
Weight	n/k

■ BELOW LEFT *Like the 90 Series, the 94 models from Fiat are a range of tractors with increasing power outputs. This four-wheel-drive 88-94 model is rated at 88hp.*

■ LEFT *A Fiat combine harvester at work during the harvest. Under the Fiatagri group Fiat produced Laverda combines and Hesston forage harvesters.*

Division. This was developed until 1970 when Fiat Macchine e Movimento Terra SpA was founded and carried on the company's activities in the earthmoving sector in its new plant in Lecce, Italy. Shortly afterwards, the new company took over Simit, then the leading Italian manufacturer of hydraulic excavators. In 1974 Fiat Macchine e Movimento Terra entered into a joint venture with the American tractor manufacturer Allis-Chalmers to form Fiat-Allis. In Italy Fiat Trattori SpA was also founded and in 1975 Fiat Trattori became a shareholder of Laverda. In 1977 Fiat Trattori acquired Hesston, as a way of gaining entry into the North American market, and later took over Agrifull, which specialized in the production of small and medium-sized tractors. In 1983 Fiat Trattori entered another joint venture when it combined with the Pakistan Tractor Corporation to pursue a joint venture in Karachi, Pakistan which became known as Al Ghazi Tractors Ltd.

In 1984 Fiat Trattori became Fiatagri, Fiat Group's holding company for the agricultural machinery sector. Things changed again in 1988 when all of Fiat-Allis and Fiatagri's activities were merged to form a new farm and earthmoving machinery company, FiatGeotech. FiatGeotech acquired Benati in 1991, which was later merged with Fiat-Hitachi. Fiat also acquired Ford New Holland Inc and merged it with FiatGeotech. The new company was named N. H. Geotech, but became New Holland Inc in 1993.

■ RIGHT *A Fiat F100 tractor at work. The four-wheel-drive tractor is towing a trailer laden with circular bales previously harvested.*

FORD

In 1907 the Ford Motor Company built the prototype of what it hoped was to become the world's first mass-produced agricultural tractor. The machine was based around components – including the transmission – from one of Ford's earliest cars. As Henry Ford had grown up on his father's farm, he was aware of the labour-intensive nature of farm work and was keen to develop mechanized ways of doing things. As a result, Ford built his first tractor in 1915, and by 1916 he had a number of working prototypes being evaluated. His aim was to sell to farmers a two-plough tractor for as little as $200, and to do for farmers and farming what the Model T Ford had done for motoring.

With a number of staff, Ford designed what would later become the Fordson Model F. Its secret was its stressed cast-iron frame construction. This frame contained all the moving parts in dustproof and oiltight units, which eliminated many of the weaknesses of early tractors. It had four wheels and was compact. This gave it an unusual appearance at a time when both three-wheeled and massive tractors were the norm.

■ **FORDSON MODEL F**
The Fordson Model F, Ford's first mass-produced tractor, went into production in 1917. Power came from an in-line four-cylinder gasoline engine that produced 20hp at 1000rpm. A three-speed transmission was fitted with a multiplate clutch that ran in oil and the final drive was by means of a worm gear. The ignition utilized a flywheel-mounted dynamo to supply high tension current to the coil that was positioned on the engine block. The tractor retailed at $750: this was more expensive than Henry Ford had predicted, but the reputation earned by his Model T car ensured that the new tractors sold in large numbers.

Ford's prototypes, seen in action at a tractor trial in Great Britain, were considered a practical proposition and the British government requested that they be put into production immediately to assist with winning the war. Ford was preparing to do exactly that when, in the early summer of 1917, German bombers attacked London in daylight. The Government viewed this new development in the war as a serious one and decided to turn all available

■ LEFT *The Fordson F and N models were the most important tractors in the history of mechanized farming and brought benefits of tractors to a massive number of farmers.*

■ RIGHT *A group of farmers with a Roadless Traction converted E27N Fordson Major tractor.*

FORDSON TRACTOR	
Year	1917
Engine	In-line four cylinder gasoline
Power	20hp
Transmission	Three speed
Weight	1225kg/2700lbs

■ OPPOSITE TOP *A restored example of a 1937 Fordson Model N. Fordson built them in Dagenham, England from 1933.*

■ ABOVE LEFT *The Fordson E27N Major was Ford's first new post-war tractor, and production started in March 1945 at Ford's Dagenham plant in England.*

■ ABOVE *The Fordson Major looked bigger and better than the Fordson Model N. A redesigned clutch, and a spiral bevel and differential drive featured in the new model.*

■ ABOVE *The E27N Major proved popular, and production soared to a peak of 50,000 made in 1948. Many were exported and production continued until 1951.*

■ LEFT *The Fordson Model N assisted Britain's war effort by helping the country grow a much higher percentage of its food requirements than previously.*

■ LEFT *The 1939 Ford Ferguson 9N was innovative because of its hydraulically controlled integral implement hitch. Rubber tyres, electric starter and a PTO were standard.*

■ ABOVE *Harry Ferguson's surname appeared on the Ford 9N as he devised the three-point implement hitch, linked to a hydraulic system.*

■ ABOVE *The Ford 9N sold well. As early as the end of 1940 more than 35,000 had been built and Ferguson's system led other manufacturers to reconsider the hitching of implements.*

■ BELOW *The English Fordson Super Major of the early 1960s, built on the success of the "new" Fordson Major that replaced the E27N Major in 1952.*

industrial production over to the manufacture of fighter aeroplanes in order to combat the German bombers. Ford was asked if he could manufacture his tractors in the United States instead. He agreed and only four months later Fordson F Models were being produced.

While this was only a temporary set-back, the delay and shift in production caused Ford another problem. His plans for his new tractor became public knowledge before the tractors themselves were actually in production, and another company tried to pre-empt his success. In Minneapolis the Ford Tractor Company was set up, using the surname of one of their engineers. The rival tractor produced from this shortlived company was not a great success, but it deprived Henry Ford of the right to use his own name on his tractors. He resorted to the next best thing: Henry

■ BELOW *The Fordson Dexta was a Perkins, three-cylinder, diesel-engined tractor introduced in 1958 to give Fordson dealers a small, low-priced tractor to sell.*

Ford and Son, shortened to Fordson.

The Model F immediately proved popular and US sales increased exponentially from the 35,000 achieved in 1918. By 1922, Fordsons were accounting for approximately 70 per cent of all US tractor sales. By this time the post-war boom in tractor sales had ended. Ford survived by cutting the price of his tractors but his major competitors, notably International Harvester, did the same and the competition became fierce. By 1928 IH had regained the lead in sales and had achieved 47 per cent of the market total.

■ CHANGING FACTORIES

In 1919 production of the Fordson tractor had begun in Cork, Ireland. This was the first tractor to be manufactured simultaneously in the United States and Europe. Production of Fordson tractors in the United States ended in 1928 in the face of major competition from IH and in 1929 all Ford's tractor manufacturing was transferred to Ireland. In 1933 production of Fordson tractors was moved again, this time to Dagenham in England. From Ford's Dagenham factory, Fordsons were

■ LEFT *The Ford 8N was introduced in 1948 after the collapse of the agreement made by Henry Ford and Harry Ferguson.*

■ LEFT *The blue and orange Fordsons were a familiar sight in British fields during the 1950s and 1960s as this one in Hampshire indicates.*

■ BELOW *Ford celebrated its golden anniversary in 1953 and redesigned its tractors for the occasion. By 1955 the three plough 600 Series was on sale, with a redesigned grille, and red and grey colour scheme.*

■ RIGHT *The Ford Workmaster series of tractors went on sale in 1959 with a choice of gasoline, diesel or liquid petroleum gas engines. This is a 1960 601 model.*

exported around the world, including back to the USA. Ford produced the All Around row crop tractor in Britain specifically for the USA in 1936. The Fordson was the first foreign tractor tested in Nebraska at the noted Nebraska Tractor Tests, to which it was submitted in both 1937 and 1938. Another Fordson plant was based in the USSR where production was halted in 1932 when the factory switched to making a Soviet copy of the Universal Farmall. Production of Fordson tractors was later restarted in the USA during the 1940s.

The next important innovation – one of the most important in the history of the tractor – was the introduction of the three-point system in the late 1930s. It was to be introduced on Ford's 9N model, having been designed by Harry Ferguson, and is still used on farm tractors today. This ingenious system, combined with a variety of compatible three-point implements, made the tractor a viable replacement for the horse and horse-drawn implements. Ferguson demonstrated the system to Ford in Michigan in autumn 1938 and through the famous "handshake agreement", by which each man's word was considered sufficient to seal the business partnership, production began. At that time the three-point hitch was known as the Ferguson System and was produced in cooperation with the Ferguson-Sherman Company until 1946.

The Model 9N was first demonstrated in Dearborn, Michigan, on 29 June 1939. This new agricultural concept revolutionized farming. The basic design principles and features incorporated into the 9N are still evident in many of the tractors currently being manufactured. The Ford 9N, the first of the N Series

■ LEFT *This row crop 961 diesel tractor from 1959 is one of the first Ford tractors to have an American-made diesel engine.*

■ BELOW LEFT *A 601 Ford Workmaster, made in 1961, the same year as Ford introduced its largest tractor until then – the five plough 66hp Model 6000.*

■ BELOW *The Ford Workmaster models were offered with a choice of engine types. The Model 501 Offset Workmaster increased the versatility of the Ford range.*

■ BELOW *In Britain, Ford tractors, such as this 1962 Ford 5000 diesel, were painted in shades of blue rather than the red and grey favoured in the United States.*

tractors, went on sale complete with the first three-point hitch in 1939. It was developed as a versatile all-purpose tractor for the small farm and was exceedingly popular. The 9N was powered by an in-line four-cylinder 1966cc/120cu in displacement gasoline engine. Many of the engine's internal components, including the pistons, were compatible with parts used in Ford's V8 automobile of the time.

The 9N went through subtle changes during each year of its three-year production run. For example, in 1939 the grille had almost horizontal bars and the steering box, grille, battery box, hood, instrument panel and transmission cover were made of cast aluminium. It also had clip-on radiator and fuel caps, which were changed in 1940 to a hinged

■ BELOW LEFT *The gasoline engine used in the Ford Powermaster models between 1958 and 1961 was this 2820cc/172cu in displacement in-line four-cylinder unit.*

■ BELOW RIGHT *The 861 Powermaster, in its gasoline-engined form.*

FORD 6610 TRACTOR

Year	1983
Engine	In-line four cylinder diesel
Power	86hp (64 kW)
Transmission	Eight forward, four reverse
Weight	n/k

■ LEFT ***A Ford 5000 tractor being used with a specialized implement for the unusual, but highly colourful, task of harvesting tulips.***

type. In 1941 the grille was changed to steel with vertical bars, and many other changes were also made. By the end of 1941 Ford had made so many changes, and had so many more ideas for changes, that the designation of the tractor was changed to the Ford 2N. There were over 99,000 9Ns produced from 1939 to 1942 and almost 200,000 2Ns produced between 1942 and 1947. The 9N's selling price in 1939 was $585, including rubber tyres, an electrical system with a starter, generator and battery, and a power take-off. Headlights and a rear tail-light were optional extras.

The Ford 2N had a relatively short production run. New features

■ LEFT ***A Ford TW20, with a large disc harrow, in a Colorado farmyard. The TW20 is one of the high-powered TW range made in American plants.***

■ BELOW LEFT ***A Ford 7640 four-wheel-drive tractor. Following the Fiat takeover the Ford name was phased out in favour of New Holland.***

incorporated in its design included an enlarged cooling fan contained within a shroud, a pressurized radiator and, eventually, sealed-beam headlights. Other changes were made here and there as a result of the constraints imposed by the war. For a while, only steel wheels were available because of the rubber shortage caused by Japanese conquests in Asia, and a magneto ignition system was used rather than a battery. When the war ended things reverted to what had been available before. Ford had made 140,000 Model N tractors in England during the war years.

■ LEFT *During the 1980s Ford manufactured its 10 series of tractors at Basildon in Essex, England, one of its eight plants. The 10 series consisted of 11 tractors ranging from 44 to 115hp.*

The Ford 2N eventually evolved into the Ford 8N, a model that officially started its production run in 1947 and was to last until 1952. 1947 was also the year that the much-vaunted handshake agreement on the three-point hitch came to an end. Ford and Ferguson failed to reach an agreement when they tried to renegotiate their deal in the immediate post-war years. Ford declared he would continue using the hitch, but would no longer give Harry Ferguson any money for doing so, nor would he continue to call it the "Ferguson System". As few official business documents existed this resulted in a lawsuit which eventually awarded Harry Ferguson approximately $10 million.

By the time the lengthy lawsuit was finally settled, however, some of Ferguson's patents had expired, enabling Ford to continue production of a hydraulic three-point hitch with only minimal changes. Ferguson then started producing the TE20 and TO20 tractors, in Britain and America respectively, that were similar in appearance to the 8N and effectively competed with it.

A completely new line of implements was introduced by Ford. Some of the noticeable differences between the 3N and 2N tractors were the change in wheelnuts from six to eight in the rear wheels, a scripted Ford logo on the fenders and sides of the bonnet and finally, the absence of the Ferguson System logo which was no longer displayed under the Ford oval even though the tractor still used Ferguson's three-point hitch.

Ford's first new post-war tractor made in Dagenham was the Fordson E27N. It was rushed into production at the

■ ABOVE RIGHT *A 1972 diesel-engined Ford 7000 tractor, finished in the distinctive colour scheme that had become standard.*

■ LEFT *A four-wheel-drive Ford 5095 tractor. This model has been additionally protected by the installation of tubular steel bars that extend over the cab for protection during forestry work.*

■ LEFT *The Ford 4110 is one of Ford's English-manufactured, standardized range of 10 Series tractors. A mid-range tractor, its power output is in the region of 50hp.*

request of the British Ministry of Agriculture. The basis of the machine was an upgraded Fordson N engine with a three forward, one reverse gearbox, a conventional clutch and rear axle drive. The Fordson E27N started rolling off the Dagenham production line in March 1945. Ford had made numerous improvements to this tractor over its earlier model. The new tractor featured a spiral bevel and conventional differential instead of a worm drive and a single-plate wet clutch was incorporated. The E27N was powered by an in-line four-cylinder side-valve engine that produced 30hp at 1450rpm. It came in four versions, each with different specifications for brakes, tyres and gear ratios. A variant using a Perkins engine was offered in 1948, and in that year over 50,000 E27Ns were made. Production continued until 1951, with various upgrades and options being made available. These included electrics, hydraulics and a diesel-engined version.

Ford's 50th Anniversary was in 1953 and in that year it introduced the Model NAA Jubilee. This was Ford's first overhead-valve engined tractor; it had a displacement of 2195cc/134cu in and produced 31hp. In 1958 Ford introduced the 600 and 800 Series

■ RIGHT *A Ford tractor, with a seed drill, planting peas. The tractor has dual wheels, front and rear, to reduce soil compaction.*

■ OPPOSITE BOTTOM *A four-wheel-drive Ford tractor, with a towed crop spraying unit, at work in Wiltshire, England. The tractor is equipped with weights at the front to improve traction.*

■ BELOW *County tractors, such as this hard-worked forestry tractor, used Ford components in their construction, and equal-sized front and rear wheels.*

tractors, powered by American-made diesel engines, although gasoline and LPG versions were also offered. These were followed by ranges of tractors known as Powermaster and Workmaster. The Model 8000 was the first Ford tractor to have a 100hp engine, displacing 6571cc/401cu in, while the smaller displacement Model 6000 produced 66hp.

■ CONSOLIDATION

By the 1960s Ford was producing tractors in Brazil, Britain and India as well as in the United States. In 1964 Ford Tractor Operations was moved to Basildon in England. In 1986 the Ford Motor Company acquired New Holland from the Sperry Corporation and merged it with Ford Tractor Operations, naming the new company Ford New Holland.

In Basildon, Ford was producing tractors such as the Model 4610, with an engine of 3300cc/201cu in displacement producing 64hp. This was one of 11 tractors in the 10 Series, ranging from the Model 2910 (2900cc/177cu in, 44hp) to the Model 8210 (6600cc/403cu in, 115hp). Another of the tractors from the 10 Series was the 4400cc/269cu in displacement, 103hp Model 7610. Basildon is one of Ford's eight manufacturing plants around the world, and the Company exported to 75 countries.

In 1991 Fiat acquired Ford New Holland Inc and merged it with FiatGeotech, renaming the company N. H. Geotech. Later Versatile Farm Equipment Company became part of Ford New Holland Americas, N. H. Geotech's North American division.

N. H. Geotech changed its name to New Holland Inc in 1993. The Ford name can be used by New Holland Inc only until 2001, by agreement with Fiat.

■ LEFT *The limited slip differential in the front axle of a four-wheel-drive Ford 6810 tractor engages automatically in difficult conditions when it senses wheel spin.*

OTHER MAKES

(Frazier, Gleaner, Hanomag, Hart-Parr, Hesston, HSCS, Hurlimann)

■ FRAZIER

Frazier is a small specialist company based outside York in England and is typical of many companies which produce specialized farming machines. The IID Agribuggy is assembled from a number of proprietary components including axles, suspension and engines, and is intended as the basis for tasks such as crop-spraying and fertilizer spreading. The machines are purpose-built and offered in both diesel and petrol forms. The diesel variant is powered by a four-cylinder Ford engine of 1608cc/98cu in displacement. The Agribuggy is designed to be adaptable, and is available in both low ground pressure and row crop variants.

■ LEFT *A pair of Frazier IID Agribuggies. The Agribuggy is designed as a low ground pressure machine for specialist tasks.*

■ LEFT *An Agribuggy with low ground pressure tyres designed to minimize soil compaction.*

■ GLEANER

Gleaner has been a manufacturer of combine harvesters for more than 75 years. The company currently offers a range of four rotary combine models as well as the C-62 conventional combine, all of which are powered by Cummins liquid-cooled engines. Gleaner combine harvesters are built on a one-piece, welded mainframe and feature a centre-mounted "Comfortech" cab. Rotary combines are designated as the R Series, while the C62 is a conventional combine harvester.

The R42 Gleaner Class 4 combine has a 6200 litre/170 bushel grain tank and a 450 litre/100 gallon fuel tank, with a 185hp Cummins engine. The R52 Gleaner Class 5 combine has a standard 8200 litre/225 bushel or optional 8900 litre/245 bushel grain tank. Its polyurethane fuel tank has a capacity of 450 litres/100 gallons. A 225hp Cummins engine is fitted.

The R62 Gleaner Class 6 combine offers a 260hp in-line six-cylinder engine, and has as standard an 8200 litre/225 bushel bin or as an option a 10,900 litre/300 bushel grain tank. The R62 offers accelerator rolls, chaff spreader, two distribution augers and a 680 litre/150 gallon fuel tank. The R72 Gleaner is the only Class 7 combine currently built in North America. It features a 12,000 litre/330 bushel grain tank and a 300hp in-line six-cylinder engine. The R72 includes two distribution augers, accelerator rolls, a chaff spreader and a 680 litre/150 gallon fuel tank.

The C-62 conventional combine harvester is, according to its manufacturers, built to exceed others in its class. The C-62 has a 10,900 litre/300 bushel grain bin and a high-capacity, turret unloading system that delivers grain into trucks and carts at a rate of 80 litres/2.2 bushels per second. The C62 is constructed around an all-welded frame using heavy-duty final drives and is designed with even weight distribution and the strength needed for large loads. Under it all is fitted a 260hp Cummins diesel engine.

Gleaner is part of the AGCO Corporation – indeed AGCO is a acronym for the Allis-Gleaner Corporation.

■ BOTTOM LEFT *Gleaner is now part of the AGCO corporation. This is a 1991 model.*

■ LEFT *As can be seen from this 1967 Gleaner CR combine, provision for the operator has progressed considerably in only thirty years. Air conditioned, dust-proofed cabs are now standard.*

■ **HANOMAG**

The German company Hanomag of Hanover was offering a massive six-furrow motor plough at the outbreak of World War I. It was, like other German machines of the time, intended for the plains of Germany. In the years after the war it offered a larger version with an eight-furrow plough and an 80hp four-cylinder gasoline engine. By the 1930s Hanomag was thriving, partially as a result of exports of both its crawler and wheeled machines. In 1930 it offered the R38 and R50 wheeled models and the K50 crawler. All were diesel-powered and featured a power take-off.

Hanomag contributed to the German war effort and its factories suffered extensive damage. The company resumed production of tractors in the late 1940s and offered the four-cylinder diesel R25, finished in red.

A Hanomag twin-cylinder diesel engine was later incorporated in the European versions of the Massey-Harris Pony, built in France. Hanomag continued to offer its R-range of tractors, including the small R12 and R24 Models alongside larger R45 and R55 Models, through the 1960s.

A change of ownership of the company in 1971 resulted in the cessation of all tractor manufacture.

■ LEFT *Hanomag had success with export sales of both wheeled and crawler tractors during the 1930s.*

■ ABOVE *A four-wheel-drive Hanomag 35D hydraulic loader, working on corn silage in England.*

OTHER MAKES

■ HART-PARR

Charles Hart and Charles Parr were engineering students together at the University of Wisconsin and graduated in 1896. They formed a company in Madison, Wisconsin to build stationary engines. These were unusual in that they used oil rather than water for cooling, which was an asset in areas that suffered harsh winters. As oil freezes at a considerably lower temperature than water, damage to engines caused by freezing coolant could thereby be avoided. Hart and Parr moved to Charles City, Iowa in 1901 and made their first tractor in 1902. The Model 18–30 followed it in 1903. This had a distinctive rectangular cooling tower which then became a distinguishing feature of all Hart-Parr tractors for the next 15 years. The cooling system circulated the oil around vertical tubes within the tower and air flow through it was maintained by directing the exhaust gases into the tower. The engine was rated at 30hp and was of a two-cylinder horizontal design with a large displacement that operated at around 300rpm. The 17–30 was a further development, and this was followed by numerous others, including the 12–27 Oil King.

Hart-Parr redesigned its machinery for the boom after World War I. The 12–25 was one of the new models and featured a horizontal twin-cylinder engine. Later these tractors were offered with an engine-driven power take-off, but the full import of this advance was not realized until later. Oliver acquired Hart-Parr in 1929.

■ LEFT *Hart-Parr became the Oliver Farm Equipment Corporation of Chicago in a merger of 1929.*

■ BELOW LEFT *Early Hart-Parr tractors were characterized by the rectangular cooling tower.*

■ HESSTON

In 1947 the Hesston company was founded in Kansas, United States. It became a respected manufacturer of hay and forage machinery, recognized for its innovative products and with industrial and marketing offshoots in Europe. In 1977 Fiat Trattori took over Hesston in order to gain entry into the North American agricultural machinery market. In 1988 all of Fiat-Allis and Fiatagri's activities were merged to form a new company, FiatGeotech, Fiat's group farm and earthmoving machinery sector. As part of this restructuring Hesston and Braud joined forces in a new company, Hesston-Braud, based in Coex, France.

■ HSCS

Hofherr, Schrantz, Clayton and Shuttleworth was formed in Hungary after Clayton and Shuttleworth's withdrawal from the steam traction engine market in that country. Initially the company's headquarters was in Kispest but it later moved to Budapest. The company started making gasoline engines in 1919, leading to the production of its first tractor in 1923. This used a single-cylinder gasoline engine for its motive power and was assembled around a steel frame. Production versions of the HSCS tractor used single semi-diesel engines, a configuration that was popular in much of Europe but not in the UK nor the United States. The perceived advantages of the semi-diesel engine are that it is mechanically simple and will run on almost any type of fuel, including waste oil. The HSCS engine was rated at 14hp and was intended for ploughing and as a source of stationary power.

The company persevered with semi-diesels throughout the production of numerous wheeled and crawler tractors. An HSCS tractor competed in the 1930 World Tractor Trials held in Britain.

In 1951, under the auspices of the communist regime, the company name was changed to Red Star Tractor. From 1960 onwards the products were sold under the

DUTRA brand name – an amalgamation of the words "Dumper" and "Tractor", representing the company's product range. Tractors were exported to other eastern bloc countries and beyond. Later the company produced RABA-Steiger tractors under licence from Steiger.

■ **HURLIMANN**

Hurlimann tractors reflect the farming conditions peculiar to Switzerland, a small mountainous country. It has little room suited to the production of arable crops and Hans Hurlimann started in business to build tractors suited to the country. His first machine used a single cylinder gasoline engine, and was fitted with a power bar grass mower.

The first tractors were considered to be old fashioned but development work and upgrades through the 1930s led to a new model introduced in 1939. This was fitted with a direct injection, four-cylinder diesel engine and led to Hurlimann exporting tractors, and selling them to the Swiss military as gun tractors. These tractors proved popular, and another new model – the D-100 – was introduced in 1945.

The D-100 was equipped with a PTO, two speed belt pulley and a differential lock. It also featured both hand and foot throttles and a five speed transmission. The tractor produced 45hp at 1600rpm, and had a low centre of gravity achieved by the use of 56cm/22in diameter rear wheels. Hurlimann continued exporting tractors and later became part of the Italian Same company.

■ TOP RIGHT *A Hungarian-manufactured HSCS tractor from the 1940s. HSCS stood for Hofherr Schrantz Clayton and Shuttleworth.*

■ RIGHT *A Hurlimann S200 tractor manufactured during the 1970s. Hurlimann was one of several Swiss tractor makers at the time.*

■ RIGHT *Hurlimann's D-100 was acknowledged as a well-engineered tractor retaining a low centre of gravity through the fitment of smaller than normal diameter rear wheels.*

■ ABOVE *Hurlimann used a diesel engine in its 1930s tractors, supplied to the Swiss Army as gun tractors.*

INTERNATIONAL HARVESTER

■ BELOW *The Farmall series became popular during the 1930s, when pneumatic tyres were still only available as an extra-cost option. The range included the F-12, F-20 and F-30 models.*

The International Harvester Corporation was formed in 1902 through the merger of two small tractor makers, McCormick and Deering.

The history of International Harvester really began in 1831, when Cyrus McCormick invented a reaper which quickly became known as the "Cornbinder". The fledgling IH at first marketed two ranges of tractors, the Mogul and Titan models. The former was sold by McCormick dealers and the latter by Deering dealers. The first IH tractors appeared in 1906 when the Type A gasoline tractor was marketed with a choice of 12, 15 and 20hp engines. The Type B soon followed and lasted until 1916. IH was noted for its production of the giant 45hp Mogul tractor during the second decade of the 20th century. It followed this in 1919 with the Titan, a 22hp machine. International Harvester also produced light trucks alongside its tractors.

During World War I many American tractors were exported to Great Britain and International Harvester Corporation marketed the models from its range that were considered most suited to British conditions. These were the Titan 10–20 and the Mogul 8–16.

■ TITAN 10–20

The International Harvester Titan 10–20 was built in the Milwaukee, Wisconsin factory and was the smallest and most popular model in the Titan range. Mogul tractors were built in parallel in the Chicago, Illinois factory. Production of the 10–20 started in 1914 and lasted for

■ RIGHT *The F-12 tractor had a four-cylinder engine that operated at 1400rpm.*

■ LEFT *The Farmall F-12 was introduced in 1932. It was a row crop tractor, rated as a one to two plough tractor. One benefit was its infinitely adjustable rear hubs.*

FARMALL F-20

Year	1932
Engine	Four cylinder
Power	16.12 drawbar and 24.13 belt hp
Transmission	Four speed
Weight	n/k

■ RIGHT *The Farmall M was introduced in 1939 as a row crop tractor styled by Raymond Loewy. It was to become one of the classic American tractors of all time.*

■ BELOW LEFT *The switch from grey to red paint was made in 1936 but rubber tyres were available prior to this as this tricycle row crop model suggests.*

■ BELOW MIDDLE *Pneumatic tyres were offered for both the front and rear of the Farmall row crop models as seen on this tractor at a South Dakota vintage rally.*

■ BELOW RIGHT *Dwayne Mathies on the Farmall row crop tractor bought new by his family for their South Dakota, USA farm. Four generations of Mathies have now sat astride it.*

a decade because the simplicity of the design ensured a reputation for reliability. The 10–20 was powered by a paraffin-fuelled, twin-cylinder engine of large displacement that achieved 20hp at only 575rpm. The engine was cooled by water contained in a cylindrical 180 litre/40 gallon tank positioned over the front wheels. The Titan 10–10 was assembled on a steel girder frame. It was chain driven and had a two-speed transmission. More than 78,000 were made and it was one of several models of tractor that were to carry the company into the 1920s. Others produced in that decade included the 8–16, the 15–30 and the Farmall Regular.

■ IH 8–16 TRACTOR

The International Harvester 8–16 was produced in the United States during World War I and proved popular. It had a distinctive appearance, with a sloping hood over the engine and radiator. Production commenced in 1917 and lasted until 1922. The design, although inspired by the IH truck line, was old-fashioned at the time of its introduction as it was based on a separate frame and featured chain and sprocket final drive. However, the availability of a power take-off as an optional extra gave the 8–16 an advantage over its competitors as the tractor could be used to drive other machinery. While IH could not claim to have invented the PTO (it had been used on a British Scott tractor in 1904) it was the first company to have commercial success with the innovation. IH made it a standard fitting on its

■ LEFT *The Farmall F-14 replaced the F-12 in 1938. It was a slight upgrade of the earlier model with an engine that operated at 1650rpm and made 14.84 drawbar and 17.44 belt hp at Nebraska.*

■ RIGHT *It was industrial designer Raymond Loewy who gave the Farmall tractors the horizontal barred grille and rounded radiator grille shell during the 1930s.*

■ BELOW *Diesel engines were another innovation introduced to the Farmall range during the 1930s.*

McCormick-Deering 15-30 tractor introduced in 1921.

As the initial post-war wave of prosperity subsided in the early 1920s. Ford cut its prices to keep sales up and, faced with this competition, IH offered a plough at no extra cost with each tractor it sold. This had the effect of shifting all IH stock, allowing the company to introduce the 15–30 and 10–20 models in 1921 and 1923 respectively. These machines were to give Ford competition in a way that that company had not experienced before. The new IH models were constructed in a similar way to the Fordson, around a stressed cast frame, but incorporated a few details that gave them the edge on the Fordson. These included a magneto ignition, a redesigned clutch and a built-in PTO, setting a new standard for tractors.

■ MCCORMICK-DEERING

The International Harvester 10–20 of 1923 was said to offer "sturdy reliability" and power, and it went on to become an outstanding success in the United States where it was generally known as the McCormick-Deering 10–20. It remained in production until 1942, by which time 216,000 machines had been sold. The styling of the 10–20 owed a lot to the larger 15–30: both models were powered by an in-line four-cylinder petrol and paraffin engine with overhead valves that were designed for long usage with replaceable cylinder liners. A crawler version of the 10-20 was unveiled in 1928 and was the first crawler produced by International Harvester; known as the TracTracTor, it was to become the T-20 in 1931.

In 1924 the company progressed further with the introduction of the Farmall, the first proper row crop tractor. It could be used for ploughing but could also turn its capabilities to cultivation. It

■ ABOVE *The Farmall M was offered on pneumatic tyres as standard at the time of its introduction, although steel wheels were a lower cost option. An electric starter and lights were also optional extras.*

■ LEFT *A mix of famous brands as a red Farmall row crop ploughs using a two-furrow plough in the familiar yellow and green colour scheme that shows it was made by John Deere.*

was suitable for use along rows of cotton, corn and other crops. It was refined and redesigned for the 1930s, when the Farmall Regular became one of a range of three models as the F-20, with the F-12 and F-30. These machines were similar but had different capacities.

In 1929 the 15–30 had become the 22–36 and was subsequently replaced by the W-30 in 1934. The 10–20 had a long production run, being made until 1939. IH dropped its hitherto traditional grey paint scheme during the 1930s and replaced it with red. The effect of this was twofold: first, it allowed the tractors to be more visible to other motorists as they became more widely used on public roads; secondly they were more noticeable to potential buyers. In the USSR at Kharkov and Stalingrad the International Harvester 15-30 went into production as the SKhTZ 15-30 and engines based on

■ ABOVE LEFT *Later International Harvesters were fitted with additional equipment such as the front loader on this Farmall model.*

■ ABOVE RIGHT *A restored example of the Farmall Super FC-D tractor. It retains the adjustable rear wheel spacing and the streamlined Raymond Loewy design.*

■ BELOW *This Farmall M is the tricycle row crop type and is fitted with a hydraulic front loader.*

Caterpillar units were produced at Chelabinsk in the Ural Region.

The first IH wheeled, diesel-powered tractor appeared in 1934, designated the WD-40. It was powered by a four-cylinder engine and the numerical suffix referred to its power, in the region of 44bhp. The engine was slightly unorthodox in that it was started on petrol and once warm switched to diesel through the closure of a valve.

■ THE W-MODELS

The International Harvester W6 was announced in 1940 as part of a range of new tractors. The range also included the W4 and W9 models and all were powered by an in-line four-cylinder engine that produced 36.6hp when running on gasoline and slightly less on paraffin. A diesel version was designated the WD6.

■ LEFT *The Farmall A was also new in 1939, it was a small machine with adjustable tread front wheels and an engine and transmission offset to the left of the tractor.*

■ RIGHT *Clearly visible on this standard tractor is the steering arrangement to the front axle and the infinitely adjustable rear track by means of the splined hubs.*

■ RIGHT *The International 584 tractor, seen with a muck spreader on an English winter's day.*

■ BELOW *The International 955 was a four-wheel-drive model, made before Tenneco Inc merged Case and International Harvester.*

In the late 1930s the industrial designer Raymond Loewy redesigned IH's trademark before moving on to deal with the appearance of the company's range of tractors. It was he who gave them their rounded radiator grille with horizontal slots. The new styling initially appeared on the crawler tractors but soon after the Farmall M models were restyled in the same way.

During World War II IH manufactured a range of machinery for the war effort, including half-track vehicles for the allied armies. The company produced more than 13,000 International M-5 half-tracks at its Springfield plant. It also made a number of "essential use" pick-ups for civilians who required transport in order to assist the war effort.

■ RIGHT *International Harvesters from different decades. International Harvester suffered during the United States farm crisis of the early 1980s.*

■ BELOW *Hay bales being loaded by hand on to a farm trailer on a Yorkshire Dales farm in England.*

■ OVERSEAS OPERATION

The W6 was improved in the first years of the 1950s, when the model was redesignated as the Super W6 and Super M, from International Harvester and Farmall respectively. The bore was increased slightly to give the tractors an extra 10hp. The more established American tractor manufacturers quickly added new models to their ranges in the immediate post-war years and IH was no exception. The company replaced the Model A with the Super A, which gained a hydraulic rear-lift attachment as hydraulics began to be more widely used.

In the post-war years IH was one of the three large American tractor manufacturers to establish factories in Britain. It opened a factory in Doncaster,

■ RIGHT *International Harvester still manufacture harvesting machinery including combine harvesters such as these.*

■ FAR RIGHT TOP *The Farmall Cub was the smallest tractor in the range, built throughout the years between 1949 and 1979.*

■ FAR RIGHT MIDDLE *A 1965 International Cub.*

■ BOTTOM RIGHT *A restored example of a Farmall Model C. This model replaced the earlier Model B when introduced with the Farmall Cub in 1947.*

South Yorkshire, while Allis-Chalmers opted for Hampshire and Massey-Harris for Manchester, although it moved to Kilmarnock, Scotland in 1949. IH was the only company to have noteworthy commercial success, assembling the Farmall M for the British market.

■ DIESEL TECHNOLOGY

In 1959 the American tractor manufacturers adopted industry standards for the increasingly popular three-point hitches to make farm implements more versatile by increasing their interchangeability between makes. To meet this standard, IH offered new tractors for 1960 – the 404 and 504 models – that offered the first American-designed, draught-sensing three-point hitch. The 504 also came with power steering while both models featured dry air cleaners and a means of cooling the hydraulic fluid. The 1960s saw increasing refinements made to the diesel engine as turbochargers and intercoolers were developed. IH embraced the new technology and developed better transmissions and four-wheel-drive systems as farming became more mechanized. By the 1970s the Farmall 966 was a 100hp machine with 16 forward and two reverse gears and a 6784cc/414cu in displacement engine.

The economic crisis of the early 1980s was to have far-reaching consequences within the American agricultural industry. International Harvester was a casualty of the recession. In the 1980 financial year the company's losses exceeded $3,980 million and the following year they were similarly high. In 1982 the situation worsened as losses totalled more than $1.6 billion. Despite this catastrophe the losses were reduced to $485 million for 1983, but IH could not survive. In 1984 Tenneco Inc, which already controlled Case, bought IH's agricultural products division and formed Case IH.

JCB

■ BELOW *A JCB 1115 Fastrac, spreading granular fertilizer from an Amazone N1209 spreader. The 1115 produces 115hp and can haul as much as a 24 tonne gross train weight.*

The British plant manufacturer JCB currently produces a comprehensive range of machines including the famous "digger", with a front loader and backhoe. JCB also produces wheeled and tracked excavators. It is the company's range of crawler tractors, the Fastracs, that are wholly designed for agricultural applications.

■ JCB FASTRAC

The JCB Fastrac is a modern high speed tractor. The Fastrac features a unique all-round suspension system and a spacious ROPS (rollover protective structure) and FOPS (falling objects protective structure) cab with air-conditioning and passenger seat as standard. It has four equal-sized wheels. The Fastrac has a three-point implement mounting position and the optional JCB Quadtronic four-wheel steering system is available on the 2115, 2125 and 2135 Fastrac models. This automatically switches between two-wheel and four-wheel steering for quicker headland turns. Power comes from turbo diesel engines that produce 115–170hp. The diesel Perkins 1000 Series high torque engine is quiet and fuel-efficient. All models are turbocharged: the 2135 has a waste guard turbo while the 2150 has a waste guard and intercooler. This is coupled to a three-speed Powershift transmission and an electronic transmission controller which has been designed to ensure smooth changes under load. The suspension and chassis use equally advanced technology, including a three-link front suspension that allows the tyres to tuck in against the chassis for a tight turning circle.

JCB FASTRAC 2150	
Year	1998
Engine	Perkins 1000 Series turbo diesel
Power	133 PTO hp, 150hp
Transmission	54 forward, 18 reverse
Weight	6365kg/14,032lbs

■ LEFT *The JCB Fastrac is designed to be versatile. It operates both at the slow speeds required in fields, and at up to 72kph (45mph) on roads. Many of the machine's functions are controlled by computer.*

■ RIGHT *The JCB Fastrac, introduced in 1991, features self-levelling suspension and a turbo diesel engine. Different models in the range had different outputs ranging from 115 to 170hp.*

Self-levelling on the rear suspension compensates for the additional weight of implements and self-levelling from side to side assists boom stability which is useful when working on hillsides. Optional adjustable wheel-slip control, working in conjunction with a radar sensor that measures true ground speed, helps reduce tyre wear and soil smearing. Air over hydraulic disc brakes are fitted on all four wheels and the external disc brakes allow cooling.

■ **TRANSMISSION**

Inside the cab, the JCB electrical monitoring system (EMS) provides a performance assessment of the numerous machine functions on the dashboard. It includes the engine rpm, PTO rpm, selected Powershift ratio and a full range of warning indicators, such as one indicating whether the front or rear PTO is selected.

The axle drive shafts have double seals on the bearing cups to retain more grease for longer life. Improved axle drive shafts and cross serrated drive shaft location is designed to ensure durability and longer component life. The heavy-duty front axles feature a solid bearing spacer between the pinion bearing for improved durability. Soft engage differential-lock, fitted as standard to the rear axle, can be selected when wheels are spinning. It engages smoothly to protect the drive train and then automatically disengages when four-wheel steering is operated or when the "differential-lock cut-out" is selected.

■ BELOW *A JCB Fastrac 150, working with a Claas Quadrant 1200 square baler. Unusually for a tractor, the Fastrac cab has room to accommodate a passenger, and a seat has been fitted for them.*

OTHER MAKES

(HST, Iseki, Ivel, Jeep)

■ H.S.T. DEVELOPMENTS

H.S.T. Developments was formed as Taylor Engineering Developments Ltd in 1972 and change its name in 1989. The company pioneered what it refers to as the Trantor, an acronym for Transport Tractor. The Trantor is designed to offer off-tarmac farm use as a normal tractor but to offer greater versatility on the road where a high percentage of farm products need to be transported. The Trantor has been designed, through a sprung drawbar, to tow a ten tonne load on road and have a top speed of 55mph. In the field the Trantor has the capability to pull an eight tonne load. The Trantor 904 has a 90hp diesel engine which drives through a ten forward speed transmission (with two reverse gears). It has a two speed PTO that can be operated at 540 and 1000rpm, an independent PTO clutch and a Category Two three-point linkage. Power steering, a differential lock and fully suspended pick-up hitch are all fitted. The 904 has air brakes on all four wheels – 71cm/28in diameter rear and 41cm/16in front – and an air operated hand brake. There are a variety of cab options, power ranges and transmissions on offer. The initial models were unveiled in the late 1970s at British agricultural shows and a revised version, the fully suspended Trantor Mk II, was made in limited numbers. Production is now underway in the UK and plans are being developed to market and manufacture Trantor tractors in third world countries. In these countries within Asia and South America the requirements for a tractor are less specialized and sophisticated than in North America and western Europe.

■ ISEKI

Iseki is a Japanese manufacturer of both compact and larger conventional tractors. In the former category are tractors such as the TX 2140 and 2160. They are powered by three-cylinder water-cooled engines of

■ ABOVE *Engineer's sketches of the Trantor range prepared in the 1980s after the production of a prototype.* LEFT *The Trantor tractor was designed to offer versatility and is shown here with a canvas tilt over the rear load area.* MIDDLE *The Trantor tractor features a three-point rear linkage for implement applications.*

■ LEFT *A 1982 Trantor Mark II tractor in a Welsh farmyard.*

■ RIGHT *The CJ5 Jeep such as this 1973 model was one of the last jeeps intended for agricultural use. The company then moved to sport utility production.*

■ BELOW RIGHT *The CJ2A Jeep, introduced in 1945, was a civilian version of the wartime Jeep, and was aimed at farmers and ranchers.*

776cc/47.3cu in and 849cc/51.8cu in respectively in both two- and four-wheel-drive forms and are suited for use with a range of implements. One of Iseki's larger machines is the Model T6500 which is powered by a 3595cc/219cu in four-cylinder water-cooled diesel engine. The transmission offers twenty forward and five reverse gears. It has equal-sized wheels all round, which makes it suitable for use with crops where high clearance is required.

■ IVEL AGRICULTURAL MOTOR

In England in 1902 Dan Albone patented something he termed the "agricultural motor": it was of a tricycle tractor design and went into production in 1903 in a Biggleswade, Bedfordshire factory. Albone called it the Ivel after a river near his home and the production Ivel tractor developed 20bhp at 850rpm. The Ivel weighed 1650kg/3638lbs and was a viable machine.

Albone died in 1906 and little further work was done on his patented machine: in fact the company gradually declined without his impetus and went into receivership in 1920. The legacy Albone left to agriculture, however, is a rich one. He demonstrated that agricultural motors were to be the farming power source of the future and paved the way for the acceptance of the new machines.

■ JEEP

As World War II drew to a close it was apparent that the four-wheel-drive Jeep would be invaluable to farmers, so Willys-Overland began to manufacture civilian Jeeps designated as CJ models. The first was the CJ2A. Initially the Jeep CJs were marketed for agricultural purposes, equipped with power take-offs and agricultural drawbars. They were promoted for a variety of farming tasks, such as towing ploughs and disc rotavators. The second of the CJs was the CJ3A. This Jeep went into production in 1948 and was built until 1953. In 1953 the CJ3B was introduced and would stay in production until the 1960s: a total of 155,494 were constructed. Gradually Jeeps became more refined and were sold as transportation rather than as farming vehicles. Currently Jeep is a

JOHN DEERE

■ BELOW *Soon after its introduction, the John Deere GP tractor was offered in a variety of configurations. These included the tricycle row crop, and its derivatives the Models A and B.*

The history of the massive John Deere company starts in 1837. In that year John Deere, a 33-year-old pioneer blacksmith from Vermont, designed and made a "self-polishing" steel plough in his small blacksmith's shop in Grand Detour, Illinois. He made it from the steel of a broken saw blade and found that the plough was capable of slicing through the thick, sticky prairie soil efficiently without becoming stuck or forcing itself out of the ground. As it cut the furrow it became polished and this ensured that the soil would not stick. It was a major breakthrough in farming technology and became the first commercially successful steel plough in America. The plough was fundamental in opening the American Midwest to agriculture and ensuring high levels of crop production.

■ EXPANSION

With a succession of partners, John Deere made an increasing number of ploughs each year. The supply of broken saw blades was of course limited, so at first Deere had steel shipped from England. In 1846 the first plough steel ever rolled in the United States was made to order for John Deere in Pittsburgh. In 1848 Deere moved his

■ RIGHT *The John Deere GP model: the designation GP stood for General Purpose. It was introduced in 1928 and was designed as a three-row cultivating tractor.*

■ BELOW *A restored John Deere GP Model A, with a two-furrow plough. The Model A was introduced in 1934 and most were like this tricycle row crop version.*

JOHN DEERE MODEL A

Year	1934
Engine	Two cylinder, 5047cc/308cu in
Power	18.72 drawbar hp, 24.71 belt hp
Transmission	Two speed
Weight	1840kg/4059lbs

operation to Moline, Illinois, to make use of the Mississippi River to power his factory's machinery and for distribution of his products. By 1852 Deere, Tate and Gould were making approximately 4000 ploughs per year. This partnership did not last long – in fact Tate later became a competitor – and by 1856 John Deere's son Charles was working at the company. In 1868 it was incorporated as Deere & Company.

Charles Deere went on to expand the company established by his father. He was reputed to be an outstanding businessman, and established marketing centres, called branch houses, to serve his network of independent retail dealers. During the 1880s John Deere was able to offer financing to retail customers for its agricultural products. By the time of Charles Deere's death in 1907, the company was making a wide

■ ABOVE *Steel lugged wheels gave traction while in the field, but meant the tractor was not permitted to run on roads.*

■ LEFT *The advent of the pneumatic agricultural tyre can be considered a major step on the road to the modern complex tractor.*

■ RIGHT *For all the technological advances that have been made within tractor technology, some things have changed remarkably little. In John Deere's case the brand name and colour scheme of the tractors have remained constant.*

■ LEFT *The John Deere Model B was introduced in 1935. It was smaller than the Model A and rated at 11.84 drawbar and 16.01 belt hp in the Nebraska Tests.*

■ BELOW LEFT *Industrial designer, Henry Dreyfuss, redesigned the Model A and B tractors to give them aesthetically pleasing lines, and to keep up with the competition.*

■ BELOW RIGHT *The Model A and B GP tractors both featured infinitely adjustable rear wheel tread.*

■ BOTTOM *In excess of 322,200 John Deere Model B tractors were made between 1935 and 1952.*

range of steel ploughs, cultivators, corn and cotton planters, and other farming implements.

■ ACQUISITION

In 1911, under Deere & Company's third president, William Butterworth, six farm equipment companies were acquired and incorporated into the Deere organization, going a long way to establishing the company as a manufacturer of a complete range of farm equipment. In 1918, the company purchased the Waterloo Gasoline Engine Company in Waterloo, Iowa, and this put it in the tractor business. Tractors, of course, went on to become one of the most important parts of the John Deere business and meant that the modern era of the John Deere Company had begun.

■ RIGHT *A Dreyfuss-styled, John Deere tricycle row crop tractor, with a two row planter. The success of the design ensured a long production run for this tractor.*

■ RIGHT *New for 1937 was the John Deere Model G, capable of pulling a three furrow plough. The Model G produced 20.7 drawbar and 31.44 belt hp.*

■ RIGHT *A 1935 John Deere Model A, with the more utilitarian pre-Dreyfuss styling. Numerous variants of the Model A were produced, including orchard models.*

At the time of the acquisition, the Waterloo Gasoline Traction Engine Company was making its Model N tractor and under John Deere's supervision this model was kept in production until 1924. It was the subject of the first ever Nebraska Tractor Test in 1920. The Model N was rated as a 12–25 model when the tests confirmed outputs of 12.1 drawbar and 25.51 belt hp.

■ JOHN DEERE MODEL D

During the 1920s the company introduced its two-cylinder Model D tractor. Many other tractor-makers were offering four-cylinder machines at the time but Deere's engineers, aware that the post-war boom in tractor sales was over, considered the economics of both manufacture and maintenance and designed the two-cylinder engine. History showed that their decision was correct as the Model D was a particularly successful machine. It was Deere's interpretation of the cast frame tractor, powered by a two-cylinder

■ LEFT *The provision of a belt drive pulley on tractors was originally as important as the fitment of a drawbar, as it enabled the farmer to drive a variety of equipment.*

kerosene/paraffin engine and fitted with a two forward and one reverse speed gearbox. From this basic machine a production run of sequentially upgraded tractors continued until 1953, by which time more than 160,000 had been made. The scale of upgrades can be gauged from the fact that the 1924 model achieved a rating of 22–30hp when tested in Nebraska while the 1953 model achieved 38–42hp in the same tests. The distinctive exhaust note made by these two-cylinder machines earned them the nickname of "Johnny Poppers".

JOHN DEERE 4010 TRACTOR

Year	1959
Engine	In-line six cylinder
Power	73.65 drawbar hp
Transmission	Eight speed
Weight	3175kg/7000lbs

■ JOHN DEERE GP

John Deere brought out a row crop tractor in 1928 known as the GP. In the same year, Charles Deere Wiman, a great-grandson of John Deere, took over direction of the company. During the period when modern agriculture was developing, his strong emphasis on engineering and product development resulted in rapid growth. The GP designation indicated General Purpose. It was designed as a three-row row crop machine and was the first John Deere tractor with a power lift for raising attached implements. Sufficient crop clearance was achieved by having a curved front axle and step-down gearing to the rear wheels. Unfortunately it did not prove as successful as had been hoped, so John Deere's engineers went back to the drawing board and produced the GPWT. The WT part of the designation indicated Wide Tread and the machine was of a tricycle configuration. In subsequent years a number of variants of this model were produced, including models for orchard use and potato farming – the GPO and GP-P models.

■ FAR RIGHT *The power take-off (PTO) shaft and linkage for hitching up implements are clearly visible on the rear of this restored row crop John Deere.*

■ RIGHT *A restored example of a 1931 John Deere GP. The engine flywheel is clearly visible on this side, and the belt pulley is on the other.*

■ BELOW *The row crop tricycle tractor was one of the first specialist designs of tractor to be developed, and it found appreciative customers in a short space of time.*

Through the Great Depression, and despite financial losses in the early 1930s, Deere elected to carry debtor farmers as long as was necessary. The result was a loyalty among the primary customer base that extends across three generations to the present day. Despite the setbacks of the Depression, the company achieved $100 million in gross sales for the first time in its history in 1937, the year of its centennial celebration.

■ **JOHN DEERE MODEL A**

The Model A was a John Deere machine produced between 1934 and 1952. It was a tricycle row crop tractor that incorporated numerous innovations. The

■ ABOVE *Although John Deere came late to the tractor manufacturing business, after its acquisition of Waterloo Boy, the company wasted no time in catching up and developing new models.*

■ BELOW *The size and scale of prairie farming in the United States led to the development of larger tractors with much more powerful engines.*

wheel track was adjustable through the use of splined hubs and the transmission was contained in a single-piece casting. The first Model A was rated at 18 drawbar and 24 belt hp but this output was subsequently increased. By the time production of the Model A was halted in 1952 over 328,000 had been made. Another tractor to have a long and successful production run was John Deere's Model B, manufactured between 1935 and 1952. It was smaller than the A and rated at 11 drawbar and 16 belt hp. It was later produced in numerous forms including the model BO and the crawler-track equipped version of the 1940s. The MC model made later was purpose-built as a crawler tractor.

■ ECONOMIC RECOVERY

By 1937 the American economy was well on the way to recovery and in 1938 the company unveiled a range of tractors

■ ABOVE ***A row crop 630. The 30 Series was the last range of two-cylinder John Deere-engined tractors.***

■ LEFT ***The new diesel-powered Model R was Deere's most powerful tractor when introduced in 1949.***

■ LEFT ***The two tone 20 Series made its debut in 1956, and featured a yellow stripe on the sides of the hood and radiator shell. The engines of tractors such as the 620 had redesigned cylinder heads to increase their power.***

■ RIGHT *A John Deere tractor in preservation. It is easy to understand the high regard in which these iron beasts of burden are held after years of reliable service.*

■ BELOW *The Model G Series was in production between 1942 and 1953.*

■ BOTTOM *A restored John Deere tractor at a summer vintage machinery rally in South Dakota, United States.*

that had been redesigned by the industrial designer, Henry Dreyfuss. The company's management was conscious that the John Deere line had changed little between 1923 and 1937, while many of its competitors were moving towards stylized tractors and taking their design cues from the automobile makers of the time. The Models A and B were the first restyled tractors, although mechanically the Model B was similar to the one originally introduced in 1935. They were followed by the similarly styled D and H Models in 1939 and the Model G in 1942. The Model H was a lightweight two-row tricycle tractor and in excess of 60,000 were made. The Model G was a three-plough tractor rated at 20–31hp. It was the most powerful tractor in John Deere's line-up at the time. By the time of its manufacture pneumatic tyres were supplied as the standard fitment, although the rubber shortages caused by World War II caused the maker to return to steel wheels.

■ POST-WAR YEARS

John Deere's factories produced a wide range of war-related products, ranging from tank transmissions to mobile laundry units. Throughout this period John Deere nonetheless maintained its emphasis on product design, and developed a strong position for the post-war market through the efforts of Messrs Wiman and its wartime president, Burton Peek. Before Wiman's death in 1955, the company was firmly established as one of the nation's 100 largest manufacturing businesses. Through the first post-war decade, from 1946 to 1954, many new products and innovations were introduced, including the company's first self-propelled

■ BELOW *John Deere unveiled its new generation of power tractors in 1959. From then on, the size and power output of agricultural tractors continued to increase.*

■ BELOW *The 5010 tractor was a large diesel-powered machine, more than capable of pulling a forage harvester and drawbar trailer, as seen here.*

combine harvester, cotton picker and combine corn head. The latter was one of John Deere's most successful harvesting innovations. The company also made electric starting and lights standard on its post-war tractors.

■ LEFT *During the 1960s John Deere developed products that were aimed at specialist markets, such as this ride-on lawn mower.*

■ BELOW *A John Deere No 45. The operator is in the open, exposed to all the dust and noise of harvesting.*

■ OPPOSITE BELOW *A John Deere Model 55-H sidehill combine in Wenatchee, Washington, USA during 1954.*

■ **JOHN DEERE MODEL M**

All the more established American tractor manufacturers quickly added new models to their ranges in the immediate post-war years. John Deere was no exception and replaced the Models H, LA and L with the Model M in 1947. This was followed by two derivatives, the Models MC and MT, a crawler and tricycle, in 1949. The Model M was made between 1947 and 1952 while the MT was made between 1949 and 1952. Production of both models totalled more than 70,000. The MC was John Deere's first designed and constructed crawler machine and in the Nebraska Tractor Tests it achieved a rating of 18–22hp. A variety of track widths was made available to customers and more than 6,000 tractors had been made by 1952. The MC and the industrial variant of the Model M, the MI, went on to become the basis of John Deere's Industrial Equipment Division.

John Deere's first diesel tractor was produced in 1949 and designated the Model R before the company switched to

■ LEFT ***The modern combine harvester contrasts with the earlier machine, not least because of the increased level of comfort afforded to the operator, which inevitably has a positive effect on productivity.***

a numerical designation for its tractors. The Model R was the replacement for the Model D and was based on engineering and design that had been started during the war years. It was a powerful machine that gave 45.7 drawbar and 51 brake hp in the Nebraska Tests. The large displacement diesel that powered the Model R was started by means of an electric start, two-cylinder gasoline engine. More than 21,000 Model Rs were built between its introduction in 1949 and 1954 when production ceased.

■ JOHN DEERE 20 SERIES

John Deere switched to a system of numerical designations for its tractors in 1952 and the machines that followed were the 20 Series of the mid-1950s, the 30 Series introduced in 1958 and the 40, 50, 60, 70 and 80 Series that followed in sequence through the 1950s and 60s. The 50 and 60 Series, for example, replaced the Models B and A respectively in 1952 while the 80 Series replaced the Model R.

In 1956 the John Deere 20 Series tractors were announced as a range of six different machines designated sequentially from 320 to 820. Of these, the 820 was the largest and was the only diesel model. Despite this it had a horizontal twin-cylinder engine – John Deere's established configuration. The 820, in many ways an upgraded Model R tractor, produced 64.3hp at 1125rpm, meaning that it was the most powerful machine John Deere had built up until that time. The engine displaced 7726 cc/471.5cu in through a bore and stroke of 15.5 × 20cm/6.125 × 8in. Starting was by means of a small-capacity V4 gasoline engine. The 820 was fitted with a hydraulic lift as standard although

■ RIGHT *This John Deere tractor has been fitted with a hydraulically operated bale and silage grapple, one of six different units that can be fitted on John Deere's hydraulic front loader.*

PTO was an optional extra. The 820 weighed in excess of 4 tons and was, according to its manufacturer, capable of pulling six 35cm/14in furrows. This tractor had a short production run that ended in 1958, but it was one of the first in the trend towards ever larger and more powerful tractors.

■ WORLDWIDE MARKETING

In the mid-1950s manufacturing and marketing operations had been expanded into both Mexico and Germany, marking the beginning of the company's growth into a major multinational corporation. In 1958 Deere's Industrial Equipment Division was officially established, suggesting future diversification. In fact, Deere had

■ LEFT *John Deere's first four-wheel-drive tractor was added to the company's range in 1959. This is a later 2130 model.*

■ BELOW *The John Deere Pro-Series offers up to 24 row spacing configurations.*

■ RIGHT *The 1956 John Deere 20 series comprised of six tractors ranging from the 320 to the 820.*

■ BELOW *The 20 range featured a two-tone colour scheme, a revised layout of the controls, and a sprung seat to make operation of the tractor easier for the driver.*

been doing business in industrial markets since the 1920s, providing machines for road maintenance, light earthmoving and forestry work. In the same year the John Deere Credit Company was established and currently John Deere Credit is one of the 25 largest finance companies in the United States of America.

■ MULTI CYLINDERS

The 30 Series tractors of 1958 were the last two-cylinder machines to be made by John Deere. The company introduced its first four-wheel-drive tractor – the 8010 – in 1959 and then for 1960 it launched a completely new line of multi-cylinder engines capable of meeting the growing demands for more

JOHN DEERE 9976 PRO-SERIES COTTON PICKER

Year	1997
Engine	Six-cylinder 8144cc/497cu in turbocharged diesel
Power	300hp (224kW)
Transmission	Three speed
Weight	17,975kg/39,630 lbs six row

■ BELOW *Contemporary John Deere loaders have a lift height of up to 3.5m (11ft 5in) and a reach of up to 109.2cm (43in).*

powerful tractors. These new John Deere tractors were unveiled in Dallas, Texas in August 1959.

There were four models, 1010, 2010, 3010 and 4010, and they were completely new. The smaller models were powered by in-line four-cylinder engines and the larger ones by an in-line six-cylinder engine.

■ JOHN DEERE 4010

The six-cylinder 4010 and four-cylinder 3010 were offered as diesels, although both gasoline and LPG versions were available. The tractors were designed to have higher operating speeds and a

better power-to-weight ratio to increase productivity. The 4010 produced more than 70 drawbar hp while the smaller 3010 achieved more than 50hp. Power steering, power brakes and power implement raising were up-to-the-minute features and an eight-speed transmission enhanced the versatility of the machines. The smaller models in the range, the 1010 and 2010, had features such as adjustable track to make them suitable for row crop work. The tractors were immediately greeted with acclaim and sales were very successful. The new range accounted for a significant increase in John Deere's market share over a five-year period. In 1959 John Deere had 23 per cent of the US tractor market and by 1964 the figure had increased to 34 per cent. This pushed Deere into the position of market leader.

In 1963, in a move to a related, if smaller, type of machinery, Deere

■ TOP *The John Deere 7520 was developed by John Deere during the 1960s and relied on the economies of scale offered in large acreage farming.*

■ ABOVE *A two-wheel-drive John Deere 3040 tractor in an English farmyard. It features a curved windscreen for enhanced visibility for the operator.*

■ LEFT *A 1990s John Deere, equipped with an hydraulic front loader and the standard rear three-point linkage to maximize versatility.*

■ LEFT *A four-wheel-drive John Deere 7520 fitted with dual tyres.*

■ LEFT *A hard worked John Deere tractor, fitted with a Farmhand bale and silage grapple.*

■ BELOW *A John Deere 4055 tractor towing a forage harvester, which is blowing hay into the trailer it is also pulling.*

entered the lawn and grounds care business. During the second half of the 1960s the company's industrial equipment line was expanded to include motor graders, four-wheel-drive loaders, log skidders, backhoe loaders, forklifts and excavators. New models of elevating scrapers, utility crawler dozers and loaders were all introduced. In 1969 John Deere entered the insurance business with the formation of the John Deere Insurance Group, which also offers credit-related insurance products for John Deere dealers.

■ THE 1970S

From 1970 onwards there were broad expansions throughout the equipment divisions of John Deere, with major advancements in all product lines, worldwide market development, and a programme of capital investment to enlarge and improve facilities. More than $1.5 billion was invested in this programme between 1975 and 1981.

At this time the 40 Series tractors were becoming more popular as by now they were being assembled with V6 turbocharged diesel engines that produced in excess of 100bhp. This figure was exceeded by the end of the next decade, when John Deere's 4955 Model tractor produced 200bhp. The 7800 has dual rear wheels at each side and a 7636cc/466cu in engine that produces 170bhp and drives through a 20 speed transmission. In 1978 sales had reached $4 billion, which represented a quadrupling of sales over the previous ten years. Expansion of the credit business continued in 1984 with the acquisition of Farm Plan, that

■ RIGHT *One of the important design considerations with four-wheel-drive tractors, such as this John Deere, is the turning radius. This figure is the official SAE standard for measuring tractor turning, so making comparisons between models.*

offered credit for agricultural purchases, including, for the first time, non-John Deere products.

■ THE 40 SERIES

The 1986 John Deere Model 2040 was powered by an engine of 3900cc/238cu in displacement using diesel fuel and producing power in the region of 70hp. It was one of the 40 series of three tractors: the 1640, 2040 and 2140 models. Also made in the same year was the John Deere Model 4450 of 7600cc/464cu in displacement that produced 160hp and featured a 15-speed transmission with a part-time 4×4 facility. Diversification continued in 1987 when John Deere entered the golf and turf equipment market and again in 1988 when the company diversified into recreational vehicle and marine markets. In the same year a worldwide Parts Division was established to increase sales of spare parts to owners of both John Deere and other makes of equipment. In 1989, John Deere Maximizer combine harvesters were introduced. In 1991 the worldwide Lawn and Grounds Care Division was established as a separate division within the company, in order to distinguish the specialist products from those of the agricultural equipment business.

■ LEFT *In the early 1960s John Deere diversified into the lawn and grounds care business.*

■ BELOW *The 1998 John Deere 7810 model is powered by a turbocharged diesel engine.*

■ THE 8000 SERIES

The 1990s were auspicious. 1992 saw the introduction of an entirely new line of 66 to 145hp tractors, the 6000 and 7000 Series, designed from the ground up as a complete range of products to meet the varying demands of worldwide markets and to facilitate on-going product updates quickly and at minimum cost. In 1993, the company's 75th year in the tractor business, the

tractor line spanned a range from 40 to 400hp. Under a distribution agreement reached in 1993 with Zetor, a tractor manufacturer in the Czech Republic, Deere became the distributor of a lower-priced line of 40 to 85hp tractors in emerging markets, starting with selected areas of South America and Asia.

The 8000 Series tractors set new standards for power, performance, manoeuvrability, visibility, control and comfort in 1994. The 8400 was the world's first 225hp row crop tractor. In

■ ABOVE *A Cotton Picker picking the cotton off the plants with the spindle units and transferring the balls into the basket.*

■ BELOW LEFT *John Deere tractors feature a curved tempered glass area.*

■ BELOW *Late 1990s John Deere tractors are equipped with what the manufacturers describe as the ComfortGard cab. It is ergonomically designed so that controls are conveniently positioned.*

■ LEFT *Dual tyres as fitted on this 8850 model have to be weighted, balanced and correctly inflated to increase productivity, reduce soil compaction and optimize minimum fuel consumption.*

■ BELOW *A two-wheel-drive 65hp (49.2kW) John Deere 6110 model, fitted with the ComfortGard cab. Also available with an open operator station.*

the same year Deere acquired Homelite, a manufacturer of hand-held and walk-behind power products for both the home-owner and commercial markets. Then in 1995 the company introduced a new line of mid-priced lawn tractors and walk-behind mowers branded as "Sabre by John Deere" for distribution through John Deere dealers and national retailers. In that year it also announced the "GreenStar Combine Yield-Mapping System" as the first in a series of precision-farming systems that was designed to help measure crop yield in different parts of a field.

■ STOCKS AND SHARES

The company made significant financial moves in 1995 when stock was split three-for-one from 17 November, 1995. The previous stock split had been a two-for-one split in 1976. In this year the company's consolidated net sales and revenues exceeded $10 billion. Financial moves continued in 1996 when the Board authorized a $500 million share repurchase. For the year

■ ABOVE *The 8400 tractor is the largest model in the John Deere 8000 Series.*

■ RIGHT *The John Deere Advantage Series of tractors. From the left they are the 7405, 6605 and 6405 models producing 105, 95 and 85hp respectively.*

■ BELOW *The John Deere 1860 No-Till Air Drill's no-till opener features no-tool adjustments and minimum maintenance.*

■ LEFT *The John Deere 9610 row crop combine harvester is one of the company's Ten Series of combines and is powered by a six-cylinder, turbocharged diesel engine of 496cu in (8.1 litres) displacement.*

■ BELOW LEFT *Combine harvesters such as this make harvesting a one-person operation.*

Deere's consolidated net sales and revenues were a record $11.2 billion. In the same year the Lawn and Grounds Care Division name was changed to Commercial and Consumer Equipment Division. 1995 was successful for tractor and harvester manufacture too with both the largest introduction of new agricultural products in the company's history and the largest single John Deere agricultural sale ever. This was an order worth $187 million for combine harvesters to be supplied to the Ukraine. Although John Deere is an American tractor manufacturer, the company has production plants in other countries including Argentina, Australia, Germany, Mexico, South Africa and Spain.

■ DEERE'S LEGACY

The importance of John Deere's contribution to agriculture (and America's development) is indicated by the degree of veneration attached to the site of his original smithy in Grand Detour, Illinois. In 1962, an archaeological team from the University of Illinois unearthed the exact location of the blacksmith's shop where John Deere developed his first successful steel plough in 1837. The location has been preserved in an exhibit hall which shows how the dig was performed and contains artefacts found on the site. The centre contains numerous exhibits, including a reconstruction of John Deere's blacksmith shop enhanced with the sounds of horses' hooves on the treadmill, hammers on the anvil and

■ TOP *The John Deere 9300 is a 360hp tractor with four-whee- drive capability and a range of three optional transmissions.*

■ ABOVE *The 9300 is one model in John Deere's 9000 Series that offers power outputs that range from 260- to 425hp. They are designed to maximize visibility.*

■ RIGHT *The 9400 can be fitted with dual (seen here) or triple tyre combinations that offer optimum traction and minimum soil compaction.*

JOHN DEERE 9400 TRACTOR	
Year	1997
Engine	In-line six-cylinder turbo diesel
Power	425hp (316kW)
Transmission	12 speed (24 speed optional)
Weight	33,770lbs (13,295kg)

conversations between workers. It was in a place such as this that John Deere developed the self-polishing steel plough that opened the prairie to agriculture. His home has been preserved to provide a glimpse of pioneer life. Deere built it when he arrived in Grand Detour in 1836 and later added extensions to accommodate his growing family. The rooms are furnished as they would have been then, and show how pioneers cooked, cleaned, bathed and spent their leisure hours. The home of Deere's neighbour, furnished with many period items, has also been preserved and provides a different perspective of early prairie life, as well as serving as a visitor centre.

OTHER MAKES

(Kirov, Komatsu, Kubota)

■ KIROV

Kirov was based in the former USSR and among its products of the mid-1980s were the K-701 giant tractors. These were 12-ton machines powered by a liquid cooled V12 four-stroke diesel that produced 300hp and had a liquid vibration dampener on the front end of the crankshaft. The engine oil pump is electrically driven and switched on prior to firing up the engine in order to build the lubrication system up to operating pressure. The gearbox is driven through a semi-rigid coupling and a reduction unit which can be disconnected to facilitate engine starting in cold weather. The planetary gearbox is mechanically controlled and features hydraulically controlled friction clutches. The frame of the K-701 is articulated to aid traction and manoeuvrability, and to increase fuel economy the rear axle drive can be disconnected when not required.

■ KOMATSU

Komatsu is a long-established Japanese crawler manufacturer with a factory in the Ishikawa Prefecture of Japan. Like Caterpillar, much of Komatsu production has been directed to the manufacture of bulldozers. Production of the company's D50 series started in 1947 when the D50A1 was manufactured. It was a conventionally designed machine and was powered by the company's own 60hp 4D120 diesel engine. By June 1970 Komatsu had made 50,000 D50 machines. The current Komatsu range encompasses 23 crawlers including the world's largest, the Komatsu D575A-2 Super.

■ KUBOTA

Kubota is a Japanese company that was founded in the last decade of the 19th century. It began manufacturing tractors during the 1960s and claimed to be the fifth largest producer in the mid-1980s. One of its products was the compact B7100DP, a three-cylinder powered tractor that displaces 762cc/46.5cu in and produces 16hp. It also featured four-wheel-drive, independent rear brakes and a three speed PTO. The company offers a range of grounds maintenance equipment, mowers and implements, a series of ride-on mowers and a range of compact tractors. In the current range of ride-on mowers are models including the 656cc/40cu in G1700 and 719cc (43.9cu in) G1900-S machines with four-wheel steering. The company also offers the T1560 and TG1860 models of 423 and 719cc (25.8 and 43.9cu in) displacement respectively. All are diminutive machines of the ride-on mower type. One of the current four-wheel-drive compact tractors is the 7100HST which is powered by a 16hp three-cylinder diesel engine. The largest Kubota compact tractor is the Grandel L-series of L3300, L3600 and L4200 models. Of these, the latter is the largest with an engine displacement of 2197cc (134cu in) that produces 45.3hp and is intended for service applications. Kubota also supply engines for use in other company's agricultural machines: the Swiss manufactured Bucher Tractomobil TM 800 of the mid-1980s was powered by a 24hp Kubota engine for example.

■ BELOW *Kubota manufacture a range of compact tractors and a line of implements. This four-wheel-drive has both a back hoe and a front loader shovel.*

■ ABOVE *A Kubota B8200 compact tractor, it has a diesel engine and four wheel drive capability.*

■ BELOW *Kubota manufacture a range of mowers, including those based around their compact tractors (left) and ride-on tyres (right).*

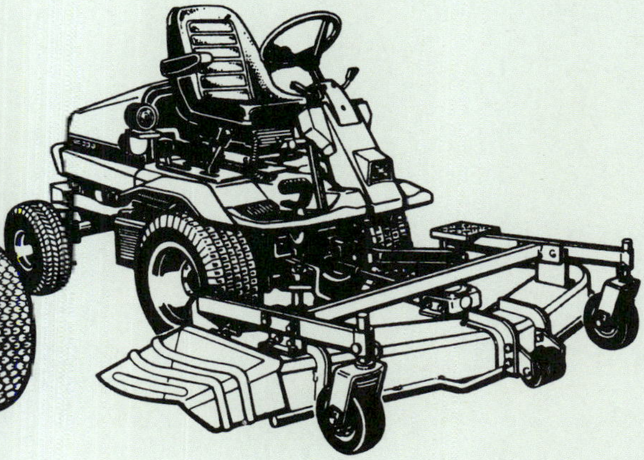

LANDINI

The illustrious Landini company – the oldest established tractor manufacturer in Italy – was founded by Giovanni Landini, a blacksmith who set up his own business in Fabbrico in Italy's Po Valley. As early as 1884, Giovanni Landini began a mechanical engineering concern in that small Emilian town. His business was successful and gradually he progressed from simple blacksmithing to fabricating machinery for local farms. He produced winemaking machinery, then steam engines, internal combustion engines and crushing equipment. In 1911 Landini built a portable steam engine and from here he progressed to semi-diesel-engined machines. The way forward to a modern and mechanized agricultural industry in Italy was clear and Landini started work on his own design of tractor. His death in 1925 prevented his completion of the first prototype Landini tractor.

■ LEFT *The Velite of the 1930s was one of the Landini company's first successful tractors. It was powered by a 7222cc/440cu in single-cylinder semi-diesel engine.*

Giovanni Landini's sons took over the business and saw the completion of the tractor project. In 1925 the three sons built the first authentic Italian tractor, a 30hp machine. It was a success and was the forerunner of the viable range of Landini 40 and 50hp models which appeared in the mid-1930s and were to become renowned under the names of Velite, Buffalo and Super. The first production tractors were powered by a

■ ABOVE LEFT *In the post World War II years Landini manufactured the L25 tractor. It was powered by a 4300cc/262cu in semi-diesel engine, producing 25hp.*

■ LEFT *This is a 1954 model Landini L25. The semi-diesel engine was capable of running on remarkably poor grade fuels including vegetable oil, creosote and used engine oil.*

■ RIGHT *The 130 Legend incorporates state-of-the-art engine and transmission management techniques.*

■ BELOW *A 1996 Landini 9880 model with a 3870cc/236cu in displacement engine which produces 88hp.*

40hp semi-diesel engine which was a two-stroke single-cylinder unit. The company continued to produce semi-diesel-engined tractors until 1957, since this type of engine was popular in many European countries, including Germany. For a period Landini and other Italian makers, such as Deganello and Orsi, produced Lanz machines under licence.

In the early 1930s the Landini brothers designed a more powerful tractor which they named the Super Landini: in 1934 it was the most powerful tractor on the Italian market. It produced 50hp at 650 rpm through an engine displacement of 1220cc/74.4cu in. The tractor was driven through a three-speed transmission with a single reverse gear and it stayed in production until the outbreak of World War II.

Following the war the Fabbrico factory both redesigned its range of tractors and expanded the company's output. In the post-war years the L25 was announced, a 4300cc/262.3cu in displacement semi-diesel engined tractor that produced 25hp. It was made in a new Landini factory in Como, Italy. Production of the 55L model, the most powerful tractor to be equipped with the single-cylinder "Testa Calda" (hot-bulb) engine, started in 1955.

Another key aspect of this redesign was the replacement of the "Testa Calda" engine used until then, with English manufactured multi-cylinder Perkins diesel power units. It marked Landini's first step towards becoming an international concern. This was later consolidated further through the agreement signed with Massey-Ferguson in 1960, by which Landini became part of the Massey-Ferguson company. As the trend towards full diesel engines continued, Landini entered an agreement with the British company Perkins in 1957 to produce its diesels in Italy under licence. This agreement between Landini and Perkins Engines of Peterborough has endured, as they are still used and are now fitted across the entire Landini range.

In 1959 the C35 model was the first Landini crawler tractor to be manufactured and the precursor of another tradition – crawler machines – that continues to the present time. The renowned 6500, 7500 and 8500 Series models were introduced in 1973 with a redesigned transmission. With the launch of the 500 Series of two- and four-wheel-drive machines in the same year, Landini advanced its wheeled tractors by applying engineering that was to remain standard for years to come. Once the four-wheel-drive models were proven, work began on the design

■ LEFT *The current Landini tractor range encompasses 50 different models that range in power from 43 to 123 PTO hp. This is the Advantage 65F model.*

■ BELOW *Landini has constructed a number of compact tractors, and collaborates with Iseki of Japan.*

of high-powered machines, aimed at producing power in excess of 100hp using in-line, six-cylinder Perkins engines. The range was widened to give tractors with power outputs from 45 up to 145hp. In 1977 production of this new series of tractors commenced.

The 1980s saw the company diversifying its products as well as specializing. Having identified the requirements of the growing wine and fruit production sector, Landini started production of the Series Vineyard, Orchard, Standard and Wide models, the V, F and L machines. Landini soon had a 25 per cent share of the worldwide market and was established as a leading manufacturer of these products. In 1986 Landini launched a new Vineyard tractor range which allowed the Fabbrico factory to become the sole supplier of orchard and vineyard versions of both crawler and wheeled tractors branded as Massey-Fergusons. In 1988 the company launched a redesigned series of tractors, the 60, 70, 80 Series. It achieved a sales record that year for the Fabbrico factory, retailing more than 13,000 tractors.

In 1989 Massey-Ferguson sold 66 per cent of its Landini shares to the Eurobelge/Unione Manifatture holding company. This company later sold the controlling interest in its affairs to the Cameli Gerolimich Group. The move took Landini SpA into Unione Manifatture and into the 1990s at the forefront of the tractor industry, both in Italy and worldwide. Landini redesigned its tractors and offered a new range with the launch of the Trekker, Blizzard and Advantage Series. The result was that for the first time, sales of Landini tractors exceeded 3000 units in the company's export markets.

In February 1994 Valerio and Pierangelo Morra, as representatives of the Argo SpA family holding company, became president and vice-president of Landini SpA respectively. They and Massey-Ferguson contributed to a substantial recapitalization of Landini and in March 1994 Iseki joined Landini SpA. In December of the same year, Landini SpA announced a net profit of 7 billion lire and an increase in tractor sales of more than 30 per cent over the previous year. Change continued into the following year when in January 1995 Landini acquired Valpadana SpA, a prestigious trademark in the Italian agricultural machinery sector. During the following month the company made an agreement for the distribution of Landini products in North America through the established AGCO sales network, and renewed the agreement for

SUPER LANDINI	
Year	1934
Engine	1219cc/74.4cu in
Power	50hp at 650rpm
Transmission	Three speed, one reverse
Weight	n/k

the sole supply of specialized wheeled and crawler tractors to AGCO. Overseas markets were not ignored and in March 1995 Landini Sud America was opened in Valencia, Venezuela. This company was aimed at promoting the Landini brand in Latin America, a market that was considered to have potential for sales of tractors. In 1995 Landini sales, including those of imported Massey-Ferguson tractors and the Valpadana tractors manufactured in the San Martino plant, reached a total of 14,057 units, of which 9415 machines were sold under the Landini name.

In 1996, in order to meet the growing demand for the Legend Series of tractors, a significant investment was made when assembly line Number 2 in the Fabbrico factory was dismantled and replaced with a new assembly line, designed to double the factory's production capacity. In San Martino a new factory was opened in 1996, entirely dedicated to machining operations, gear manufacture and prototype component assembly. The presidents of both the Landini and Iseki companies were at the opening of the new plant, signalling agreement between the two companies on long-term technological co-operation between Landini and Iseki.

The current Landini range includes 50 different models, with power outputs ranging from 43–123 PTO hp. Landini tractors are distributed in North America by AGCO and the current range includes the following models: Advantage, V, F and GT Series, HC Series, Trekker Series, 60 Series, 80 Series, Blizzard, Legend and Globus Series.

■ ABOVE ***This compact Landini is working with a round baler on a hill meadow.***

■ LEFT ***Traditionally narrow tractors have been used in vineyards, and this Landini Discovery, with a specialist loader, is suitable for between rows.***

■ BELOW ***The Landini Discovery 85 compact tractor has many additional features of larger tractors.***

OTHER MAKES

(Lamborghini, Land Rover, Lanz, Laverda, Leyland)

■ LEFT AND BELOW *By the time the Lamborghini 950 Premium tractor was manufactured, the car-and tractor-making portions of Lamborghini's business had been sold to separate companies.*

■ BOTTOM LEFT *This four-wheel-drive 874-90 Lamborghini tractor is powered by a turbocharged diesel engine.*

■ LAMBORGHINI

This company is perhaps better known for the production of sports cars than of tractors. Ferruccio Lamborghini was born in Renazzo di Cento, near Ferrara, on 28 April, 1916. His enthusiasm for machinery led him to study mechanical engineering in Bologna, after which he served during World War II as a mechanic in the Italian army's Central Vehicle Division in Rhodes. On his return to Italy at the end of the war, Lamborghini began to purchase surplus military vehicles which he then converted into agricultural machines. Three years after the end of the war, the Lamborghini tractor factory was designing and building its own tractors.

It is hard to say what made Lamborghini turn his attention from agricultural machinery to luxury sports cars. He may have been motivated by the success of his neighbour, Enzo Ferrari. Folklore suggests that the idea came to him after a discussion with Enzo Ferrari, when Lamborghini complained about the noisy gearbox in his Ferrari. Ferrari's reply was allegedly that Lamborghini should stick to tractors and let Ferrari build sports cars.

Ferruccio Lamborghini extended his interests into various fields of engineering, including heating and air conditioning systems and even helicopter design. While the cars, which were added to the Lamborghini line in 1963, were extremely successful and are still in production, the attempts to manufacture helicopters were hindered due to complex bureaucratic controls imposed by the government, and as a result, the idea was abandoned.

The Lamborghini 5C was a crawler tractor unveiled at the Paris Agricultural Show in 1962. The tractor was unusual in that, as well as crawler tracks, it had three rubber-tyred wheels that allowed use on the road as the wheels lifted the tracks clear of the road surface. The tracks were driven from the rear sprockets and it was to these sprockets that the wheels were attached for

driving on the road. The small front wheel was effectively an idler and steering was achieved by moving the same levers that slewed the tractor around when using tracks. The 5C was powered by a three-cylinder diesel engine that produced 39hp.

When it became clear to Ferruccio Lamborghini that his son Antonio had little interest in the automobile business, he began to contemplate retirement. In 1973 Lamborghini sold all his companies and retired to his vineyard in Umbria, dedicating the last twenty years of his life to the production of fine wines. It was here, at the age of 77, that Lamborghini died on 20 February 1993.

In 1972 the car and tractor portions of Lamborghini's business had been split. The tractor production operations were taken over by Same which has continued to develop the Lamborghini range and increased the volume of production.

■ LAND ROVER

In the years after World War II Rover, which had a reputation for building quality motor cars, was in a difficult position because of the shortage of steel. Rover engineers Maurice Wilks and his brother Spencer considered building a small utility vehicle with an aluminium body and four-wheel drive. The intention was that the machine, specifically intended for agricultural use, would merely be a stopgap until sufficient steel was available for the company to return to building luxury cars.

The Wilks brothers delegated much of the design work of the utility machine. The first prototype Land Rovers had a tractor-like centre steering wheel to enable them to be sold in either left- or right-hand drive markets. Because a conventional chassis would have required expensive tooling, the engineer Olaf Poppe devised a jig on which four strips of flat steel could be welded together to form a box-section chassis.

The first Land Rover, with a 2m/80in wheelbase, was shown to the public at the 1948 Amsterdam Motor Show. Orders flowed in, especially when early Land Rovers were displayed at agricultural shows around Britain, and the company began to look seriously at export markets. The vehicles were demonstrated ploughing and driving mowers. Power take-offs and winches were optional extras and between 1948 and 1954 numerous details were refined and improved. To make the vehicle more capable it was redesigned for 1954: the wheelbase was increased by 15cm/6in and the rear overhang increased by 7.5cm/3in. This enabled the rear load area to be increased. A long wheelbase variant, at 2.7m/107in, was also made available as a pick-up and these models had the 1997cc/121.8cu in engine which had been available in the later 2m/80in models. Changes were again made to the Land Rover for 1956 when both models were stretched another 5cm/2in to give wheelbases of 2.24m/88in and 2.77m/109in. The diesel engine was introduced in June 1957 and by 1958 Rover had produced in excess of 200,000 Land Rovers. In April 1958 the company introduced the so-called Series II Land Rover. The Series II featured a redesigned body that was 4cm/1½in wider than its predecessors, together with other minor improvements including more modern door hinges and bonnet (hood) latches.

While Land Rover products are still made and widely exported, the emphasis of the range is now on sport utility vehicles, with the exception of the Defender 90 and

■ ABOVE ***The prototype Land Rover with its centre steering position, operating a Massey-Harris elevator during the construction of a haystack, in 1947.***

■ BELOW ***A Series II Land Rover, adapted to tow an especially designed swan-neck articulated trailer, seen here loaded with a Perkins diesel-powered tractor.***

■ LEFT ***The most modern version of the Land Rover is the Defender 90, still widely used by farmers, although the company's more luxurious models are considered as sport utility vehicles (SUVs).***

OTHER MAKES

110 Models, which are refined versions of the original Land Rovers and are still popular for agricultural applications. Numerous specialized agricultural conversions have been made to Land Rover vehicles during the course of their production to suit them to specific tasks, such as carrying and operating implements, in the manner of the Mercedes Unimog.

■ LANZ

In Germany, Lanz produced Bulldog tractors including the Model T crawler and the L, N and P wheeled models offering 15, 23 and 45bhp respectively. The machines were imported into Britain and were popular because of their ability to run on low-grade fuel, including used engine and gearbox oil thinned with paraffin. In 1924 Ford upped the ante when the Fordson F tractor went on sale in Germany, meaning that German manufacturers had to compete. The differing types of fuel employed by Ford and the German manufacturers illustrated a divergence of ideas about tractors. The German companies, such as Stock and Hanomag, compared the Fordson's fuel consumption unfavourably with that of their own machines, which were moving towards diesel fuel. Lanz introduced the Feldank tractor, that was capable of running on poor fuel through its use of a semi-diesel engine.

The initial Bulldogs were crude. The HL model, for example, had no reverse gear: the engine was stalled and run backwards to enable the machine to be reversed.

■ ABOVE *Lanz built farm machinery from 1859 and its Bulldog tractor was regarded as a simple, reliable machine. Prior to World War II Lanz was one of the two major German tractor makers.*

■ LEFT *Lanz Bulldog production was resumed after World War II, despite the company's factory being razed to the ground by Allied bombing. The post-war political situation in Germany affected Lanz's sales adversely.*

Power came from a single horizontal-cylinder two-stroke semi-diesel engine that produced 12hp. The HL was gradually improved, becoming the HR2 in 1926. Lanz was later acquired by John Deere.

■ LAVERDA

Laverda was founded in 1873 in Breganze, Italy, and by the beginning of this century had become the leading Italian manufacturer of threshing machines. The company is also noted for its production of motorcycles. In 1975 Fiat Trattori became a shareholder in Laverda, then in 1984 Fiat Trattori became Fiatagri, the Fiat group's holding company for the agricultural machinery sector.

■ LEYLAND

In Great Britain, Morris Motors eventually became part of the British Leyland conglomerate. This company was concerned by poor sales of Nuffield tractors, so renamed the brand as British Leyland. Along with this renaming, a new two-tone blue colour scheme was adopted for the tractors.

British Leyland built tractors such as the 270 and 344 models. However, the tractor maker did not have sufficient funds to develop its products and it was gradually overtaken in sales by other tractor makers. Leyland tractors was sold in 1981 and joined with Marshall as a part of the Nickerson organization.

■ ABOVE *A late-1970s British Leyland 344 tractor, in the two-tone blue colour scheme favoured by BL after it had acquired Nuffield as part of the merger with Morris Motors.*

■ RIGHT *The British Leyland badge on the front of this 344 tractor could also be seen on a variety of cars during the 1970s.*

■ BELOW LEFT *Lanz Bulldogs were manufactured in Mannheim, Germany, but when John Deere had acquired the company production of the long-running model was halted.*

■ BELOW *This decaying British Leyland tractor retains its factory-fitted safety cab.*

MASSEY-FERGUSON

In 1953 Harry Ferguson merged his company with the Massey-Harris company. As the deal was being finalized, there arose the question of which exchange rate was to be used. Harry suggested settling the matter with the toss of a coin. He lost the toss, and about a million dollars, but appeared not to care, no doubt realizing that his patents and equipment were in capable hands.

Once Harry Ferguson had sold his tractor company to Massey-Harris the face of tractor manufacturing was profoundly altered. Before the merger the Massey-Harris company had been competing with both Ford and Ferguson. For a while the newly formed Massey-Harris-Ferguson company produced two

■ LEFT *A 1970s Massey-Ferguson 135 photographed in Cappadocia, Turkey.*

MASSEY FERGUSON MF 362 4WD	
Year	1998
Engine	Perkins four cylinder diesel
Power	60 PTO hp, 62bhp
Transmission	Eight forward, two reverse
Weight	2666kg/5877lbs

■ ABOVE LEFT *Massey-Harris was noted for the manufacture of self-propelled combine harvesters, and neglected tractor development to a degree. To catch up they merged with Ferguson in 1953.*

■ LEFT *The 1970s styling of the Massey-Ferguson range was much more angular than that which went before, as evidenced by the line of hood and grille on this MF135 model.*

■ RIGHT *A little modified, probably repainted more than once, but still working more than 30 years after it was made.*

■ LEFT *The two-wheel-drive MF 399 has 41cm/16in diameter front wheels, and 97cm/38in diameter rear ones. It is powered by a six-cylinder Perkins diesel, and has a 12 speed transmission.*

■ BELOW LEFT TOP *The four-wheel-drive version of the Massey-Ferguson MF 362. This tractor is powered by a naturally aspirated, four-cylinder Perkins A4.236 engine.*

■ BELOW LEFT BOTTOM *A dilapidated MF 20 during a break from haymaking.*

■ BELOW RIGHT *A four-cylinder, Perkins diesel-engined Massey-Ferguson 375, donated by the World Business Council to farmers in Tanzania, East Africa.*

separate lines of tractors, continuing with both the Massey-Harris and the Ferguson makes, as both tractors had loyal followers amongst dealers and customers. The MH 50 and Ferguson 40 had different bodywork but were mechanically identical as both models were based on the Ferguson 35. In November 1957 the now Massey-Ferguson Company produced its first "Red and Grey" tractor, the Model MF 35 powered by Perkins engines.

The company was Canadian-based and produced tractors all around the

MASSEY FERGUSON MF 32 CONVENTIONAL COMBINE

Year	1998
Engine	Valmet 620DSL
Power	129kW (175 DIN hp)
Transmission	Hydrostatic
Weight	10,299kg/22,706lbs

■ ABOVE *Combine harvesters are required to cut the standing crop, then lift it on to the conveyor which takes it to the rasps, which then remove the grain from the straw.*

■ RIGHT *This Massey-Ferguson combine from the 1960s carried out the same task, but the styling of combines and provision of operator comfort were still ahead in the future.*

■ LEFT *This Massey-Ferguson 530 S combine harvester features an open operator station, something that is becoming rarer as cab technology continually progresses.*

■ BELOW *This MF 31 combine was the largest one in the Massey-Ferguson range in 1986 and was powered by a 153hp, turbocharged Perkins engine.*

■ ABOVE *Combines, like tractors, need to maintain traction in fields, but rely on hydrostatic transmissions connected to their large capacity diesel engines.*

■ RIGHT *For harvesting on fields with slopes of up to 11 degrees, Massey-Ferguson has devised the Auto Level system, designed to keep an even spread across the machine's grain-separating components.*

■ ABOVE LEFT *A Massey-Ferguson 3070 tractor, with a Cambridge roller, preparing the land for the next year's crop.*

■ ABOVE RIGHT *A four-wheel-drive Massey-Ferguson tractor, equipped with a hydraulic front loader. This is a versatile and perennially popular farmyard tool.*

■ LEFT *Two generations of Massey-Ferguson tractors at work. The older model is being used to load round hay bales on to the trailer, pulled behind the newer four-wheel-drive model.*

■ BELOW *The Massey-Ferguson 2775 tractor of the 1980s features a V8 Perkins engine of 10,488cc/640cu in displacement.*

■ RIGHT *The four-wheel-drive MF 6180, of 1998, is powered by a Perkins 1006-6T engine, a six-cylinder turbo diesel unit that drives through a gearbox offering 16 forward and reverse gears.*

world. The all-new MF 35 was followed by a range of tractors including the MF 50, MF 65 and MF 85. In 1976 Massey-Ferguson introduced new tractors, the 1505 and 1805 Models, both powered by the 174hp Caterpillar V8 diesel engine.

In the mid-1980s the 3000 Series of Massey-Ferguson machines was made available with a turbo-diesel, 190hp, six-cylinder engine. A smaller Massey-Ferguson tractor was the MF 398, powered by a 3867cc/236cu in diesel engine and featuring a 4x4 transmission. Two Massey-Ferguson tractors from 1986 were the Models 2685 and MF 699. The former had a 5800cc/353.8cu in Perkins turbo-diesel engine that produced 142 hp and was one of the 2005 Series of three tractors: 2645, 2685 and 2725. Each had a four-wheel-drive transmission that incorporated 16 forward and 12 reverse gears. The MF 699 was the most powerful in the MF 600 Series of four tractors, MF 675, 690, 698T and 699. It was powered by a 100hp engine.

Massey-Ferguson itself became part of AGCO in 1994. According to the manufacturer, "For 33 straight years more people have purchased MF tractors than

■ LEFT *A 1993 MF 3095 Autotronic. This is one of the 3000 series of tractors that was among the first Massey-Ferguson tractors to make extensive use of electronics.*

■ BELOW *The Massey-Ferguson MF 3690 Autotronic was another of the 3000 series of tractors of 1993.*

■ ABOVE *The MF 185 is an American-made rectangular baler, designed to be towed behind a tractor. It is capable of producing bales of up to 320kg (700lbs). It rides on wide flotation tyres.*

MASSEY-FERGUSON MF 4245 4WD TRACTOR

Year	1998
Engine	Perkins 1004-4T
Power	75.8 PTO hp, 88bhp
Transmission	Eight forward, eight reverse
Weight	4330kg/9548lbs

■ LEFT *The MF 844 loader is one of the 800 series loaders, designed to be used in conjunction with 60–90hp tractors. It can lift 1700kg/3748lbs to a maximum height of 3.75m/12.3ft.*

■ LEFT *A four-wheel-drive Massey Harris 4245 tractor, haymaking with an MF 146 variable chamber round baler.*

■ OPPOSITE *A 1998 six-cylinder 114hp MF 4270 tractor working in conjunction with a Massey-Ferguson Forage Harvester during haymaking.*

■ RIGHT *The MF 40 conventional combine has a section where grain is stored after the threshing and separating processes. A Valmet 612DSJL engine supplies the power.*

■ BELOW *The MF 8120, seen here in four-wheel-drive form, has a six cylinder turbo diesel engine driving it through a 32 speed transmission.*

any other brand." Massey-Ferguson's current range is comprehensive and includes tractors offering 130–180 PTO hp, 86–110 PTO hp, 55–95 PTO hp, 34–67 PTO hp, 37–53 PTO hp and 16–40 engine hp, as well as conventional combine harvesters, rotary combine harvesters and loaders.

The 130–180 PTO hp tractors in the 8100 Series are designed as high-performance tractors, while the 4200 Series 55–95 PTO hp tractors are available as a selection of models of varying configurations with different options and attachments. The 200 Series of 34–67 PTO hp tractors features Perkins diesel engines. Another small range of tractors from Massey-Ferguson is the 1200 16–40 PTO hp Series. Massey-Ferguson manufactures Class 5 and 6 combine harvesters, including the 8680 conventional and 8780 rotary combines.

■ BELOW *The MF 6130 is a 1998 model tractor with a 16 forward and reverse speed transmission. Power comes from a four-cylinder turbo diesel engine.*

MASSEY-HARRIS

■ BELOW *One of the earliest four-wheel-drive tractors was the Massey-Harris General Purpose of 1930. A 226cu in displacement engine powered it.*

■ BOTTOM *The Massey-Harris 101 was introduced in 1938 as a streamlined row crop tractor. It is powered by a high compression, gasoline-fuelled Chrysler six-cylinder engine.*

Massey-Harris was formed in 1891 in Toronto, Canada from the merger of two companies who manufactured farm implements. Daniel Massey had been making implements since 1847 while A. Harris, Son & Company were competitors for the same market. The Model 25 was a popular tractor through the 1930s and 40s. Another Massey-Harris tractor of this era was the 101 of 1935. This machine was driven by a 24hp Chrysler in-line six-cylinder engine. A third was the Twin Power Challenger powered by an I-head four-cylinder engine that produced approximately 36hp. The company chose a red and straw-yellow colour scheme for its tractors in the mid-1930s.

After World War II, Massey-Harris introduced the Model 44 based around the same engine as the pre-war

■ RIGHT *A Massey-Harris combine in Britain during the 1950s.*

■ BELOW RIGHT *The Challenger was rated as a 26-36hp tractor, power came from an in-line, four-cylinder, gasoline engine.*

MASSEY-HARRIS MODEL 101	
Year	1939
Engine	Chrysler L-head T57-503 gasoline
Power	23.94 drawbar hp
Transmission	Three speed
Weight	2597kg/5725lbs

■ BOTTOM *The Massey-Harris Challenger of 1936 was the last from the company to have the Wallis tractor-style boiler plate unit frame. The rear wheels were adjustable to cater for different row widths.*

Challenger and using a five-speed transmission. The company brought out a new range in 1947 which still included the Model 44, to which were added the Models 11, 20, 30 and 55. The Model 30 featured a five-speed transmission and more than 32,000 were made before 1953 when the company merged with Ferguson.

The tractor built in the largest numbers by Massey-Harris prior to the merger was the Massey-Harris Pony. This was a small tractor and proved more popular in overseas markets than in the United States and Canada, where it was considered too small for many farming applications. It was produced in the Canadian Woodstock plant from 1947 and at the Marquette factory in France from 1951. A decade later the production total exceeded 121,000. The

■ LEFT *The Massey-Harris Pony was produced in Massey-Harris's French and Canadian plants and production eventually totalled in excess of 121,000.*

first version of the Pony was powered by a four-cylinder Continental engine driving a three-speed transmission with one reverse gear. Its top speed was 11kph/7mph and it produced 11hp. The Pony was basic in its initial form, but was refined over its production run. Canadian production was halted in 1954, but in 1957 the 820 Pony was offered from the French factory with a five-speed gearbox and a German Hanomag diesel engine. It was further refined for 1959, when it was redesignated the 821 Pony. Around 90,000 of the Pony tractors manufactured were built in the French factory and this was Massey-Harris's first real European success. The post-war Model 44 had been a success for the Massey-Harris company in the United States, where 90,000 were made in

■ LEFT *Many European manufactured Massey-Harris 820 Ponys were fitted with diesel engines made by Hanomag.*

■ BELOW LEFT *A distinctive feature of the 820 Pony was its rounded radiator grille.*

Racine, Wisconsin. It featured the rounded pre-war styling but was mechanically new. The customer had a choice of four-cylinder engines that used either petrol, paraffin or diesel fuel. A hydraulic lift system for implements was introduced in 1950. The company chose the Model 44 as its tractor to enter the British market and started by manufacturing them in Manchester in 1948, although operations were later moved north to Kilmarnock, Scotland. This was largely an assembly process because the components were imported from Racine. The models offered included row crop, high clearance and Roadless-converted

MASSEY-HARRIS MODEL 44	
Year	1949
Engine	Four cylinder I-head
Power	27.75 drawbar hp
Transmission	Three speed
Weight	2307kg/5085lbs

■ ABOVE *Massey-Harris started production of the 744 PD tractor in Manchester in 1948. Production was later moved to Scotland and the tractor redesignated as the 744D.*

■ BELOW *The Massey-Harris 33 was made between 1952 and 1955. It was an upgraded version of the two plough 30 that had been introduced in 1947.*

half-track versions. Around 17,000 were made in total and in later years approximately 11,000 of a Perkins-engined variant – the 745 – were made before production was halted in 1957. In that year, after the merger with Ferguson, the company was renamed Massey-Ferguson and another new line of tractors was introduced.

The following three examples of results from Nebraska Tractor Tests give an illustration of how the Massey-Harris tractor range progressed in the post-war decades. Nebraska Test Number 306 was on the Massey-Harris Model 101 S made by the Massey-Harris Co, Racine, Wisconsin, and tested between 22 and 26 May 1939. The tractor's equipment consisted of 10–36 rear tyres, 5.00–15 front tyres, a six-cylinder L-head Chrysler T57–503 engine, run at 1500 and 1800rpm, 3.125in bore × 4.375in stroke, and an Auto-Lite electrical system. The tractor's weight was 1726kg/3805lb on steel wheels and 2597kg/5725lb on rubber tyres.

The Test H Data obtained with rubber tyres was as follows: gear: 3, speed: 7.27kph/4.52mph, load: 901.3kg/1987lb, rated load: 23.94 drawbar hp, fuel economy: 9.85hp hours per gallon. The Test H Data on steel wheels was as follows: gear: 2, speed: 5.92kph/3.68mph, load: 844kg/1862lb, rated load: 18.29 drawbar hp, fuel economy: 7.46hp hours per gallon. The fuel economy at 1800rpm maximum with a load of 36.15 belt hp was 10.89 hp

hours per gallon. Fuel economy at 1500rpm with a rated load of 31.5 belt hp yielded 11.86hp hours per gallon.

Nebraska Test Number 427 was carried out on the Massey-Harris 44K Standard made by the Massey-Harris Co, Racine, Wisconsin, and tested between 29 September and 14 October 1949. The tractor's equipment included a four-cylinder I-head engine, 1350rpm, 3.875in bore × 5.5 in stroke, a 6 volt Auto-Lite electrical system, a Zenith 62AJ10 carburettor. The tractor's weight was 2306kg/5085lb and the Test H Data obtained was as follows: gear: 3, speed: 4.29mph, load: 1182kg/2608lb, slippage: 4.4 per cent, rated load: 27.7 drawbar hp, fuel economy: 10.42hp

■ ABOVE *Despite the familiar colours of this tractor on a French beach it is not a John Deere, but a repainted Massey-Harris Pony from the French Marquette factory.*

■ LEFT *The Massey-Harris 745 was a Perkins diesel-powered tractor intended as an improved version of the 744. Approximately 11,000 were made between 1954 and 1958 in the Kilmarnock, Scotland plant.*

■ BELOW *A hard-worked example of a French built, Massey-Harris Pony, more than forty years after it was made. The mudguards and seat are not the originals.*

■ BELOW *A gasoline-engined version of the European-manufactured Massey-Harris Pony. The engine is an in-line four-cylinder unit.*

hours per gallon. 506kg/1116lb of ballast was added to each rear wheel for tests F, G, and H. Test G resulted in a low-gear maximum pull of 2128kg/ 4692lb. Fuel economy at Test C maximum load of 35.66 belt hp was 11.3hp hours per gallon. Test D rated load of 33.64 belt hp yielded 11.19hp hours per gallon. Tractor fuel was used for the 45.5 hours of engine running time.

Nebraska Test Number 603 was carried out seven years later on a Massey-Harris 333 made by Massey-Harris-Ferguson Inc, Racine, Wisconsin, and was tested between 25 October and 3 November 1956. The tractor's equipment included a four-cylinder I-head engine, 1500rpm, 3.688in bore × 4.875in stroke, 12–38 rear tyres, 6.50–16 front tyres with a tractor weight of 2685kg/5920lb. The Test H Data recorded was: gear: 3, high range, speed: 7.94kph/4.93mph, load: 1026kg/ 2262lb, slippage: 3.76 per cent, rated load: 29.71 drawbar hp, fuel economy: 10.69hp hours per gallon. 466kg/1028lb of ballast was added to each rear wheel for tests F, G and H. Test G resulted in a low-gear maximum pull of 2452kg/ 5407lb at 2.1kph/1.31mph with a slippage of 12.08 per cent. Fuel economy at Test C maximum load of 39.84 belt hp was 12.37hp hours per gallon.

■ BELOW *One reason that production of the Massey-Harris Pony was continued in Europe, after being halted in Canada, was that the size of the tractor proved more suitable to the smaller scale farms of Europe than those of North America.*

MERCEDES-BENZ

Benz started building tractors in 1919 when it offered the 40 and 80hp gasoline-engined "Land Traktors", but the Benz-Sendling S7 of 1923 was the first diesel-engined tractor manufactured by Benz. It featured power from a 30hp two-cylinder, vertical engine. The machine itself was a three-wheeled tractor with a single driven rear wheel, although outriggers were supplied to ensure stability during use. A four-wheeled machine, the BK, quickly superseded the S7.

■ BENZ AND DAIMLER

In 1926 Benz and Daimler merged, adopting the name Mercedes-Benz. During the 1930s the company

■ ABOVE *The MB-trac 1500 Mercedes Benz tractor is fully reversible which means it can be used as a dual directional tractor by rotating the controls, instruments and seat through 180 degrees in the cab.*

MERCEDES-BENZ U1200 UNIMOG	
Year	1998
Engine	OM 366 A in-line six cylinder 5958cc/ 363cu in
Power	125hp
Transmission	Eight forward, eight reverse
Weight	8500kg/18,739lbs

■ LEFT *The dual directional nature of the MB-trac 1500 means it can be used to push or pull implements where appropriate. A 150hp turbo diesel engine of 5675cc/346cu in displacement provides ample power.*

■ RIGHT *Mercedes-Benz Unimogs are supplied in numerous configurations, and have been manufactured for several decades, offering four-wheel drive.*

produced the OE model that was powered by a horizontally arranged single-cylinder, four-stroke diesel engine that produced 20hp. One of these machines competed in the 1930 World Tractor Trials held in England. Prior to World War II tractor production in Germany was relatively small in scale and even in the coming conflict the German army was to rely heavily on horse-drawn vehicles, in stark contrast to the mechanized armies of the Allies.

In the post-war years two of the first popular and successful tractors were of a four-wheel-drive configuration. One was the MAN 325, that remained in production for two decades until the company shelved tractor production in favour of trucks. The second was the Boehringer Unimog which was later sold to Mercedes-Benz. Mercedes-Benz has continued to produce this machine, still known as the Unimog, for several decades in a variety of configurations including models designed for agricultural use as implement carriers.

■ ABOVE *A short wheel base platform variant U900 Unimog from the mid-1980s. The Unimog is designed to accept a variety of specialist implements.*

■ MERCEDES UNIMOG

The Unimog has evolved into the Unimog System of vehicle and implements, based on a wide range of vehicles and an almost unlimited number of implement attachment options. Several ranges are offered, from compact to heavy-duty models and each has at least three standard implement attachment points and a hydraulic system that ensures implement operation. The Unimog has been designed so that its wheels distribute pressure evenly on the ground in order to minimize soil compaction. It is of all-wheel-drive configuration to ensure optimum traction.

Another advanced Mercedes-Benz tractor was the MB-trac 1500, introduced in 1986. This tractor featured a turbo-diesel engine of 5675cc/346cu in displacement that produced power in the region of 150hp. The MB-trac was designed as a dual-direction tractor.

■ RIGHT *To enhance ground clearance, the Unimog, such as this 1990s U1200 model, are based on portal axles.*

OTHER MAKES

■ MINSK

The Minsk Tractor Works sells its tractors through agricultural machine distributors in 35 countries around the world. Current production includes models such as the MTZ-320, MTZ-682, MTZ-1221 and MTZ-920.

MINNEAPOLIS-MOLINE

■ BELOW *The Minneapolis-Moline Universal Model J was a row crop tractor with infinite rear wheel adjustment, capable on rubber tyres of 12.2mph (19.5kph).*

In the hectic 1920s, many new tractor-making companies were formed while others merged to form new corporations. In 1929 three extant companies, Minneapolis Steel and Machinery, the Minneapolis Threshing Machine Company and the Moline Implement Company, all merged and Minneapolis-Moline Power Implement Company was the result. Amongst these companies' assets were Twin City Tractors and Minneapolis Tractors, and in the wake of the merger came the rationalization of their products and factories. The Twin City tractor range was chosen as the one to spearhead the Minneapolis-Moline push into the market, with production continuing in the Minneapolis factory. Initially the machines were marketed as Twin City tractors with the Minneapolis-Moline name added, but as the range evolved, the Twin City brand name was reduced in prominence and Minneapolis-Moline became the brand name. The constituent companies are detailed here.

■ BELOW *The Minneapolis-Moline Model R was a two-plough tricycle, row crop tractor, manufactured between 1939 and 1941.*

■ MOLINE UNIVERSAL

In 1915 the Moline Plow Company had purchased the Universal Tractor Company of Columbus, Ohio. The product line was moved to Moline, Illinois and a new building was constructed for the production of the Moline Universal Tractor. This was a two-wheel unit designed for use with the farmer's horse-drawn implements as well as with newly developed Moline tractor-drawn implements. The Universal was commonly referred to as the first row crop tractor. It was equipped with electric lights and a starter, components that were considered advanced for the time.

After World War I, a number of automobile manufacturers wanted to produce tractors and the Moline Plow Company was courted by manufacturer John N. Willys. Willys purchased Moline from the owners, the Stephens

■ LEFT *The Minneapolis-Moline Model U was available in both row crop tricycle and standard tread forms. The UDLX was available with a cab, but was only made in small numbers.*

MINNEAPOLIS-MOLINE UNIVERSAL MODEL J	
Year	1935
Engine	F-head four cylinder
Power	16hp
Transmission	Five speed
Weight	2222kg/4900lbs

family, and subsequently his automobile company began producing the Universal tractor. Willys had as his partners in the tractor trade George N. Peek, a well-known farm equipment executive, and General Hugh Johnson. Willys continued to produce the Moline Universal tractor into the 1920s. In this decade the tractor boom subsided; Willys withdrew from the Moline Flow Company and sold out to his partners. General Johnson became president and R. W. Lea

■ BELOW *The Model U was tested in the Nebraska tractor tests in 1938 and produced 30.86 drawbar and 38.12 belt horsepower at 1275rpm.*

■ LEFT *The Minneapolis-Moline Model V was a compact tractor. This example was produced in 1944.*

■ BELOW *The Minneapolis-Moline Model Z was introduced in 1937 as a row crop tractor, painted in the new Prairie Gold colour.*

became vice-president of the Moline Plow Company. When they retired their associates took over and operated the business as the Moline Implement Company, which it remained until joining the Minneapolis-Moline organization in 1929.

■ TYPES A AND B

The Minneapolis Threshing Machine Company began producing steam traction engines in 1889 just west of Minneapolis, where the town of Hopkins was founded, and flourished solely because of the company. In 1893, a Victory threshing machine and steam engine built by the company won several medals at the World Exposition in Chicago. By 1911 the Minneapolis Threshing Machine Company was building tractors under the Minneapolis name and went on to build many large tractors before the Minneapolis-Moline merger, but these tractors were better suited to sod-breaking than for row crop applications. After building a couple of row-type tractors the company marketed its Minneapolis 17-30 Type A and Type B. These were cross-motor row crop tractors and remained in production even after the merger. During the 1920s, even before the Minneapolis-Moline organization, the company's products were advertised as being part of "The Great Minneapolis Line".

In the late 1800s and early 1900s the Minneapolis Steel and Machinery Company was primarily a structural steel producer, turning out thousands of tons per year. The company also produced the Corliss steam engine, that served as a power unit for many flour mills in the Dakotas. In 1910 Minneapolis Steel and Machinery produced a tractor under the Twin City name, the Twin City 40. At the outbreak of World War I, the company was one of the larger tractor producers. It also manufactured a number of tractors under contract, such as the Bull tractor for the Bull Tractor Co. Through the 1920s, Twin City tractors were promoted with slogans such as "Team Of Steel" and "Built To Do The Work". After 1929, this line was still produced in the

■ LEFT *Minneapolis-Moline came about from the merger in 1929 of three companies involved in the production of farm machinery.*

■ RIGHT *The UTS, like others in the Minneapolis-Moline range, was equipped with red-painted wheels.*

MINNEAPOLIS-MOLINE MODEL U	
Year	1938
Engine	In-line four cylinder
Power	30.86 drawbar and 38.12 belt hp
Transmission	Five speed
Weight	n/k

■ RIGHT *Although the M-M logo stands for Minneapolis-Moline, the tractor manufacturers lost no time in using it to suggest that M-M made Modern Machinery.*

■ BELOW *The Minneapolis-Moline UTS was a wartime model in the U-series of tractors. The similar UTU was a tricycle row crop tractor.*

old Minneapolis Steel and Machinery Lake Street Plant under the Minneapolis-Moline Twin City tractor banner.

In the new Minneapolis-Moline Power Implement Company, two of the major historic agricultural machine-producing cities were represented. After the merger, the Minneapolis-Moline Power Implement Company Officers for 1929 were as follows: J. L. Record (MSM) Chairman of the Board; W. C. Macfarlane (MSM) President and Administrative Officer; George L. Gillette (MSM) Vice-President of Sales; Harold B. Dineen (Moline) Vice-President of Production and Design; N. A. Wiff (MSM) Vice-President; W. C. Rich (MSM) Secretary; W. S. Peddle (MSM) Treasurer. In reality most of the top officers of the three companies were content to retire instead of becoming involved in Minneapolis-Moline Power Implement, preferring that the younger generation take over.

After experiments with the luxury UDLX tractor with an enclosed cab,

■ ABOVE *This 1947 Minneapolis-Moline GTA tractor of 1947 was designed to run on liquid petroleum gas (LPG).*

■ LEFT *Minneapolis-Moline tractors were restyled in the immediate post-war years. This is a restyled, row crop tricycle Model Z from 1949.*

■ LEFT *One of the last new tractors to be added to the M-M range before the outbreak of World War II was the GT, a standard tread tractor that was tested at Nebraska in 1939.*

MINNEAPOLIS-MOLINE M-5	
Year	1960
Engine	5506cc/336cu in Diesel
Power	58.15hp at 1500rpm
Transmission	Six speed
Weight	n/k

Minneapolis-Moline launched the GT as a five-plough tractor in 1939. In the Nebraska Tractor Tests its measured power output was 55hp at the belt, despite being rated at only 49hp by its manufacturer. Powered by a gasoline-fuelled in-line four-cylinder engine, it developed its maximum power at 1075rpm. Later, in the aftermath of World War II, increased power versions, the G and GB Models, were offered.

The White Motor Company purchased Minneapolis-Moline in 1963. AGCO purchased White Tractors in 1991, and in doing so acquired the rights to the Minneapolis-Moline name.

■ ABOVE LEFT *By the time this 1969 M670 tractor had been made, Minneapolis-Moline had been owned by White for six years. The company was later acquired by AGCO.*

■ RIGHT *The fact that this 1970 Minneapolis-Moline G1050 tractor, of 504cu in displacement, is designed to run on LPG gas, is made clear by the provision of a tank in front of the radiator.*

NEW HOLLAND

The New Holland Machine Company was founded in 1895 in Pennsylvania and specialized in the manufacture of agricultural equipment. It endured until 1940 when New Holland changed owners and, following a company reorganization, began production of one of the first successful automatic pick-up hay balers. In 1947 the Sperry Corporation acquired the New Holland Machine Company and formed Sperry New Holland. In 1964 Sperry New Holland purchased a major interest in Claeys, which was by this time one of the largest combine manufacturers in Europe. Sperry New Holland launched the haybine mower-conditioner, Model 460. This was capable of accomplishing what had previously required two or three machines to do and was perceived as a significant innovation in hay-harvesting technology.

FORD NEW HOLLAND 8830	
Year	1998
Engine	6571cc/401cu in, diesel
Power	170hp
Transmission	18 forward, nine reverse
Weight	6804kg/15,000lbs

■ BELOW ***New Holland is a noted manufacturer of an automatic pickup hay baler. The company expanded its operations by buying a major interest in Claeys, an established European company.***

■ MERGER

In 1986 the Ford Motor Company acquired Sperry New Holland and merged it with Ford Tractor Operations, naming the new company Ford New Holland. In 1991 Fiat acquired Ford

■ RIGHT *During the 1970s companies such as Case, Claas and New Holland began to dominate the increasingly international European market.*

New Holland Inc, merged it with FiatGeotech and named the new company N. H. Geotech. In 1993 this company was renamed New Holland. At its second worldwide convention held in Orlando, Florida, New Holland launched 24 tractor models in three different ranges alongside the Fiat-Hitachi Compact Line.

The articulated tractors in the Versatile 82 Series are high-powered machines designed for the biggest of fields and the heaviest applications. The range includes the Models 9282, 9482, 9682 and 9882, all of which are powered by six-cylinder engines of varying horsepower with twelve-speed transmissions in both two- and four-wheel-drive configurations. The Series 70 tractors have power outputs that range between 170 and 240hp. They incorporate New Holland's own "PowerShift" transmission which offers single lever control of the 18 forward

■ ABOVE *A New Holland 8070 combine harvester loading a trailer with the grain which has been threshed and separated in the combine.*

■ RIGHT *A New Holland combine in Wiltshire, England during the harvest. The few weeks of the harvest are crucial to the economics of the farming year, and the cost effectiveness of combine harvesters.*

and nine reverse gears. They are manufactured in Winnipeg, Canada and marketed worldwide. The tractors are available with or without cab, or with ROPS (Rollover Protection Structure). The third range of New Holland tractors is the 90 Series, whose models have a range of transmissions. The 100–90 and 110–90 Models are manufactured in Jesi, Italy while the 140–90, 160–90 and 180–90 Models are manufactured in Curitiba, Brazil.

In 1997 New Holland completed its purchase of Ford Motor Credit Company's partnership interests in the two joint ventures that provide financing for New Holland's products in the United States. New Holland also signed an agreement with Manitou, for the design and production of a New Holland range of telescopic handlers. In India in 1998, New Holland completed the construction of a new plant for the manufacture of tractors in the 35–75hp range and commenced production. The company also signed an agreement with Flexi-Coil, a Canadian manufacturer of air seeding systems and tillage equipment. In Turkey, New Holland made a new agreement with its partner, KoÁ Group, increasing its share in the joint venture Türk Traktor to 37.5 per cent. New Holland Finance expanded its activities from the UK to other European markets, starting with Italy.

NEW HOLLAND NH 6635

Year	1996
Engine	Turbo diesel
Power	85hp (63 kW)
Transmission	Optional with creeper
Weight	n/k

■ TOP *The 40 Series of New Holland tractors such as this model 7840 of 1996 can be considered state of the art, with its ergonomically designed cabs and modern four-wheel-drive systems.*

■ LEFT *A 1996 New Holland 7740 tractor from the 40 Series, with a New Holland 640 round baler in tow. The baler is capable of producing circular bales of up to 1.5m/5ft diameter.*

■ LEFT *A 1996 Ford New Holland four-wheel-drive 7840 Model tractor. Note the ballast weights at the front.*

■ ABOVE *A Ford New Holland 8340, one of the last to bear the Ford name.*

■ BELOW *New Holland still produces a range of towed harvesting implements including small rectangular balers, large square balers, and circular balers such as this Model 640.*

NUFFIELD

■ BELOW *The Nuffield Universal was introduced to British farmers at the 1948 Smithfield, London show.*

William Morris made his reputation as the force behind Morris cars, which became one of the British motor industry's most renowned names. As early as 1926 he had become interested in the tractor market and produced a small crawler tractor based on the track mechanism of a light tank. This project was later abandoned, but not forgotten, and work was progressing on another machine as the world moved towards the end of the war in the mid-1940s. A dozen prototypes were being tested in Lincolnshire by 1946 and, boosted by the success of these machines, plans for full-scale production at the Wolseley car factory were made. So Nuffield entered the tractor market with the Universal, which it unveiled at the 1948 Smithfield Agricultural Show.

The Universal was offered in two versions: the M4 was a four-wheeled

tractor and the M3 was a tricycle type for row crop work. The engine was derived from the wartime Morris Commercial engine, a four-cylinder side valve, and its tractor application was started on petrol and run on paraffin. It produced 42hp at 2000rpm. Later a diesel variant was offered, initially with a Perkins P4 unit, then later with a 3.4 litre British Motor Corporation (BMC) diesel following the Austin and Morris merger. In 1957 came the Universal 3, a three-cylinder diesel-engined tractor. The Universal 4/60 was announced in 1961. This was a 60hp tractor and the increased power had been achieved by boring out the existing 3.4 litre engine to 3.8 litres.

Production was eventually moved to the Bathgate plant in Scotland via the Morris Motors plant at Cowley in Oxfordshire. The Nuffield tractors were

■ ABOVE LEFT *Sir William Morris was the man behind Nuffield tractors, allegedly after being asked to build tractors in the UK to compete with the numerous imported models available in Britain after World War II.*

■ LEFT *This is a restored version of the 1955 M4, powered by a version of the Morris Commercial truck engine that had been proven in numerous Morris vehicles during the war years.*

■ RIGHT *A diesel version of the Nuffield M4. The engine was initially sourced from Perkins, then a 3.4 litre displacement British Motor Corporation diesel was used.*

■ BELOW *The 1949 M4 had a three-point linkage, drawbar and rear PTO drive.*

■ BELOW *The early Nuffield M4 was regarded as a viable British alternative to imported American models. It had a five-speed transmission and a truck engine, and was noted for speed.*

given a facelift in 1964 and became the 10–60 and 10–42 models. The tractors were redesigned for 1967, but before they could find widespread acceptance, Nuffield was involved in the merger that created the British Leyland Motor Corporation, making Nuffield tractors into Leylands. In 1981 Leyland was sold to the Nickerson organization.

NUFFIELD M4	
Year	1948
Engine	Morris Commercial ETA
Power	42hp at 2000rpm
Transmission	Five speed
Weight	n/k

OLIVER

Many of the major tractor manufacturing corporations were formed from the merger of numerous small companies, and Oliver is an example of this. In 1929, Hart-Parr, Nichols and Shepard and the American Seeding Machine Company all merged with the Oliver Chilled Plow Company to form the Oliver Farm Equipment Sales Company. The company then began to design a completely new line of tractors. Oliver itself dated back to 1855 and bore the name of its Scottish-born founder, James Oliver, who had developed a chilled steel plough. He had patented a process that gave the steel used in his ploughs a hard surface and tough consistency.

Once the Oliver Farm Equipment Sales Company was formed, the original Oliver company's prototype row crop models Models A and B could go into production. Oliver was the first company to use laterally adjustable rear wheels to suit the differing row spacings of different crops, but other manufacturers soon followed. These tractors were powered by a 18–27 four-cylinder engine that was also fitted to the company's line of conventional tractors, the Oliver Hart-Parr standard models. These were available in Standard, Western, Ricefield and Orchard versions and built until 1937. With a choice of four- or six-cylinder engines, these models became the Oliver 90 during the late 1930s. This was a three-speed 49hp machine.

■ ABOVE AND RIGHT ***The Oliver Row Crop 60 made its debut in 1940 as a compact version of the already extant Row Crop 70.***

OLIVER 60 ROW CROP	
Year	1940
Engine	1894cc/115cu in
Power	n/k
Transmission	Four speed
Weight	907kg/2000lbs

■ BELOW ***An Oliver Model 70 from 1937, by which time Oliver had dropped the Hart-Parr name.***

■ ROW CROP 70 HC

The company achieved unexpected success with the Oliver Hart-Parr Row Crop 70 HC, which was introduced to the farming public in October 1935. This streamlined machine was fitted with a high compression, gasoline-fuelled, six-cylinder engine and was noted as being quiet and smooth running. By February 1936 Oliver had

■ ABOVE LEFT *The Oliver 80 was another new model for 1940 although it did not have the streamlined styling of the 60 and 70 models.*

■ ABOVE RIGHT *The 80 was available with a gasoline engine, seen here, or one suited to running on kerosene distillate.*

sold in excess of 5000 examples, which was 3000 more than anticipated. An electric starter and lights were options.

In 1937 the Hart-Parr suffix was dropped from the company name so that the Model 70 Row Crop models carried only the Oliver name on their streamlined hoods. In the Nebraska Test the high-octane-fuelled, six-cylinder Row Crop 70 produced 22.64 drawbar hp and 28.37 belt hp. The Models 80 and 90 followed in 1938. The 80 had the angular look of earlier models while the 90 was run on kerosene. Oliver made both 90 and 99 Models between 1938 and 1952. After this date both were referred to as Model 99s. In 1940 the company introduced a smaller tractor, the 60, in a row crop configuration and in 1944 it acquired Cletrac.

■ FLEETLINE MODELS

In 1948 Oliver unveiled a line of tractors to mark its 100th year in business. They were known as Fleetline Models 66, 77 and 88 and identified by a new grille and sheetmetal. Each was fitted with a power take-off and the range of engines offered something for every customer. Engine displacements ranged from the 2113cc/129cu in diesel to 3784cc/231cu in diesel installed in the 99 Model. Other diesel options in the new range included the 77 and 88 Models; otherwise the tractors used four-cylinder gasoline and paraffin engines. PTO equipment was standard but hydraulic lifts were not.

These models were followed by the Super Series of 44, 55, 66, 77, 88 and 99 Models. The Super 44 was the smallest model in the range, powered by a four-cylinder Continental L-head engine that was offset to permit the operator better visibility for field use. The Super 55 was a compact utility tractor which on gasoline produced 29.6 drawbar hp and 34.39 belt hp. Production of the Oliver 55 continued after Oliver was taken over by White. The Super 99 of 1954 was available with a three-cylinder, two-stroke, supercharged, General Motors diesel engine with a displacement of 3770cc/230cu in or an Oliver diesel. It was equipped with a three-point hitch and a cab was an extra-cost option.

In 1960 White Motor Corporation bought Oliver and later Cockshutt and Minneapolis-Moline. All eventually merged as White Farm Equipment.

■ LEFT *The Oliver 1955 model featured an angular cab, and was built during the 1970s, more than a decade after Oliver had been acquired by White. Both companies later became part of AGCO.*

RENAULT

■ BELOW *A Renault 145.54. This is one of a modern range of different capacity tractors, of a similar design, powered by turbocharged diesel engines.*

In the early days of European tractor production France lagged behind the main European countries; tractor production was confined to the Renault Car Company although some Austin tractors were assembled in France. In the years immediately after World War I Renault (along with Peugeot and Citroën) announced the production of a crawler tractor. Renault's crawler was based on its experience of tank manufacture during the war. The tractor was subsequently designated the GP. It used a four-cylinder 30hp gasoline engine and a three-speed transmission with a single reverse gear; steering was by means of a tiller. An upgraded version, the H1, went on sale in 1920. Renault then developed the HO, a wheeled version of the H1. These models were powered by a four-cylinder engine that produced 20hp at 1600rpm and featured epicyclic reduction gears in the rear wheels. All these tractor models were based around a steel girder frame and the engine was enclosed within a stylish curved bonnet (hood) that bore a close resemblance to Renault's trucks and cars of the time. The PE tractor was introduced in 1922 and was considerably redesigned from the earlier models. Renault introduced the VY tractor in 1933, powered by a 30hp in-line, four-cylinder diesel engine. It had a front-positioned radiator and the engine was enclosed. This model was painted yellow and grey and became the first diesel tractor to be produced in significant numbers in

■ BELOW *The four-wheel-drive Renault Ceres 610RX, along with the smaller 85hp 95X, is part of a current range with a similar streamlined design.*

RENAULT 106.54 TRACTOR	
Year	1996
Engine	Six cylinder turbo diesel
Power	100hp, 75kW
Transmission	12 forward, 12 reverse
Weight	n/k

■ RIGHT *Renault produces general tractors, such as this one seen ploughing in England, and specialist machines for orchard use.*

■ BELOW LEFT *A Renault tractor equipped with a French-manufactured hydraulic front loader.*

■ BELOW RIGHT *The Renault 106.54 is a four-wheel-drive 100hp tractor. The dual tyres and four-wheel drive help traction in heavy clay soils.*

France. Renault was also the major force in the World War II French tractor industry and had built in excess of 8500 tractors by 1948. Many of these were of the 303E model, although Renault followed this with the 3042 in 1948.

More recent tractors from Renault have included the Model 61 RS, a low-profile machine designed for operation in confined areas and powered by a three-cylinder diesel engine that makes 60hp and gives a maximum of 57hp at the PTO. The 80 TYX is a four-cylinder, water-cooled, diesel-powered tractor capable of producing 78hp. The Model 61 RS is available as either a two- or four-wheel-drive model with twelve forward and reverse gears. The Model 106.14 is a larger tractor with a six-cylinder diesel engine of 5656cc/345cu in displacement. It develops 96bhp and is available in both two- and four-wheel-drive configurations.

Roadless Traction Ltd

In the UK, Roadless Traction Ltd of Hounslow designed numerous half-track bogie conversions for vehicles as diverse as a Foden steam lorry and a Morris Commercial. It later devised tracked conversions for various makes of tractor, including the Fordson E27N and forestry tractor conversions for Land Rover.

■ PHILIP JOHNSON

The company name Roadless Traction Ltd was registered on 4 March 1919 by Lieutenant Colonel Henry Johnson. Johnson was born in 1877 and attended the King Edward VII School in Birmingham before studying engineering at the Durham College of Science. After Durham he gained work experience in the heavy industries of South Wales before the outbreak of the Boer War in 1899. Johnson volunteered for the army, but was not selected because of defective eyesight, and found his way to South Africa by working his passage on a cattle boat. Once in Cape Town he was able to get seconded to a steam road transport company of the Royal Engineers as a result of his experience with steam engines. The unit was responsible for towing howitzers and field guns as well as ammunition, mostly behind Fowler steam engines. It was here in South Africa that Johnson was able to study the use of mechanized transport in off-road situations. Johnson returned to England in 1906 and took up employment with the Leeds-based firm of Fowler and Compan. This required him to assist in the export of steam engines and involved a period of living in India. There Johnson is reputed to have delivered many Fowler engines under their own steam to the remotest parts of the sub-continent.

Johnson returned from India in 1915 to take up a wartime post with the Ministry of Munitions. He spent much of those war years working on tank development and went out to France to the Front once the tanks were being used in combat. His tank development work, including that with rubber tracks and a spring and cable suspension system, continued after World War I.

Johnson's military duties ended in 1918 and during the 1920s he started converting Foden and Sentinel team lorries to half-tracks by substituting the driven rear wheels with tracks and bogies. It is estimated that the company invested £50,000 in the development of its products in the seven years following 1921. The company moved into Gunnersbury House, a former nunnery, in Hounslow, Middlesex in 1923. Johnson bought the house, leasing part to the company and living in the remainder.

Motor lorries of varying sizes were also converted to half-track in this period, including those from Peugeot,

■ RIGHT *A 1941 Fordson N Roadless, equipped with a front-mounted, chain drive, Hesford winch.*

■ OPPOSITE BOTTOM *A Fordson Roadless half-track, in service with the Royal Air Force during World War II, towing a refuelling trailer. A group of WAAFs are refuelling a Hawker Hurricane.*

■ BELOW *A Fordson E27N converted to a half-track through the installation of Roadless DG4 tracks.*

Vulcan, Austin, Guy, Daimler, FWD and Morris Commercial. These were sold to customers in places as diverse as Scotland, Sudan and Peru. One of the company's first major commercially successful orders was for a batch of lorries for the Anglo-Persian Oil Company for use in connection with oil exploration in Iran. Roadless supplied converted Morris Commercial lorries to fulfil this order.

FORDSON N ROADLESS TRACTOR	
Year	1944
Engine	In-line four cylinder gasoline
Power	20hp
Transmission	Three speed
Weight	1225kg/2700lbs plus track bogies

■ CRAWLER TRACTORS

Following on from this growing success, the company turned its attention to tractors and potential agricultural applications for its technology. One of the first machines to be converted was the Peterbro tractor, manufactured by the Peter Brotherhood Ltd of Peterborough, Cambridgeshire.

This tractor used a four-cylinder gasoline-paraffin engine of Ricardo design that produced 30hp. Few of these tractors were made and even fewer – possibly only one – converted to half-track configuration using the Roadless components. Roadless also cooperated with another Peterborough-based firm, Barford and Perkins Ltd, to produce a half-track tractor. This was based on that company's THD road roller and powered by a rear-mounted, vertical, two-cylinder McLaren-Benz engine driving through a three-speed forward and reverse transmission. It utilized Roadless tracks and had a drawbar pull rated at 6858kg/17,419lb, but as it weighed 11 tons it was of limited use off-road and the project was abandoned.

The development of rubber-jointed tracks eventually enabled Roadless to

■ ABOVE *This 1950 Roadless Model E is powered by a TVO engine. It is thought that a total of only 25 machines were ever made.*

produce viable agricultural machines. Its system, known as "E tracks", was easily adapted to many tractors and required little maintenance, so endearing it to farmers. The company converted AEC-manufactured Rushton tractors to full-tracks using E3 rubber-jointed tracks that were skid-steered, Ferodo-lined and differential-braked. Rushton Tractors was formed as a subsidiary of AEC in 1929 to manufacture Rushton and Roadless Rushton tractors. There were two variants of the Roadless Rushton with different lengths of track: the standard version had two rollers on each side while the other had three. These tractors were amongst those successfully demonstrated at the 1930 World Agricultural Tractor Trials held at Wallingford, Oxfordshire. The tractor was a success and sold in both the UK and export markets, although Rushton went out of business after an Algerian customer defaulted on payment for 100 tractors shipped there for use in vineyards.

The Fordson tractor was gaining in popularity and in 1929 the first Roadless conversion on a Fordson tractor was carried out on a Fordson Model N. It was successfully demonstrated on Margate Beach early in 1930, when it hauled 3 tons of seaweed off the beach. Roadless-converted Fordsons soon became popular and were offered in two track lengths. Fordson tractor production was moved from Ireland to Dagenham in 1931 and Fordson approved the conversion for use with its machines. The association between Ford and Roadless Traction would endure from then until the 1980s.

ROADLESS FULL-TRACK MODEL E

Year	1950
Engine	Fordson TVO or diesel option
Power	40hp
Transmission	Three speed
Weight	n/k

Another major tractor maker to take advantage of Roadless crawler technology was Case of Racine, Wisconsin. A number of Case tractors, including the Models C, L and LH, were converted and, unlike the other conversions, the Case tractors retained their steering wheels. Roadless built experimental machines for McLaren, Lanz, Bolinder-Munktell, Mavag and Allis-Chalmers, although many never progressed beyond prototypes. Forestry and lifeboat hauling were two tasks that were ideally suited to the Roadless converted machines.

The war years saw Roadless building a variety of machines for the British Air Ministry to use as aircraft tugs. Despite being almost blitzed out of its factory, the company's production was entirely devoted to war requirements, whether it was experimental work or track conversions to imported American tractors from manufacturers such as Case, Massey-Harris and Oliver.

In the immediate post-war years

■ BOTTOM LEFT *The full-track Roadless Fordson used the company's E3 rubber jointed tracks, but even after considerable development, production of the machines was very limited.*

■ BOTTOM RIGHT *Roadless put the Model E into production in 1950 when this TVO variant was manufactured.*

Roadless converted a large number of the popular Fordson E27N tractors, that were sold through advertisements in many Ford publications. The conversion received an accolade when it was awarded a silver medal at the 1948 Royal Show in York. Subsequently several versions of the E27N were built and exported widely.

Through the 1950s the company diversified, turning its attention to full-track and four-wheel-drive tractors. This and its connections with the forestry industry would ultimately lead to the Roadless-converted Land Rover. In the same way as the company's half-tracks were built by converting wheeled tractors, so too were the full-track models. The Fordson Model E was converted and later the Fordson Diesel Major was converted as the Roadless J17. At the same time the company also developed a row crop tricycle conversion for the Fordson E27N Major for sale in the United States and this stayed in production until 1964.

The first Roadless 4×4 Tractor appeared in 1956, overseen by Philip Johnson who was now running the company. He travelled widely to see his company's products in use. While in Italy to visit Landini he met Dr Segre-Amar who had founded the Selene company, based near Turin. Selene converted Fordson tractors to 4×4 configuration using a transfer box and war surplus GMC 6×6 truck front axles. A working relationship between the two men developed that ultimately led to the Roadless company producing the 4×4 Fordsons in Britain. This tractor was a great success and subsequently Roadless converted the Power Major of 1958 and the later Super Major in large numbers, together with a small batch of Fordson Dextas. International Harvester also marketed a Roadless converted 4×4 tractor known as the B-450, that was constructed in International's Doncaster factory in England. It stayed in production until 1970.

■ ROADLESS ROVERS

Around the end of the 1950s the Hounslow company focused its attention on the light 4×4 Land Rover which had now been in production for a decade. The Forestry Commission was experiencing some difficulty with its use of conventional Land Rovers, which were prone to getting stuck on rutted forest tracks and were hampered by fallen trees in cross-country use. The Machinery Research Officer for the Forestry Commission, Colonel Shaw, suggested that tractor-type 25 × 70cm/10 × 28in wheels should be fitted to the Land Rover. A prototype was built and evaluated in the Alice Holt Forest in Hampshire, England. The verdict was that the machine had potential but required further development in order to be viable. A 2.77m/109in wheelbase Land Rover was despatched to the Hounslow premises of Roadless for a redesigned and properly engineered conversion to be effected.

Roadless used a combination of components to make the machine functional: it retained the original gear- and transfer boxes and coupled them to a pair of Studebaker axles with GKN-Kirkstall planetary hub reductions and the same 25 × 70cm/10 × 28in wheels that had been used before. The front axle had a track 35cm/14in wider than the rear in order to facilitate sufficient steering lock to retain the vehicle's manoeuvrability. The turning circle was approximately 12m/40ft. In order to

■ **RIGHT** *To convert the Rover Company's Land Rover to the Roadless specification, with 28in diameter wheels, it was necessary to alter the front wings (fenders).*

■ **BOTTOM LEFT** *The Roadless conversion to the British Land Rover was approved by the Rover Company from 1961 onwards. This steel rear body was an extra option.*

accommodate the large wheels and tyres the normal Land Rover front wings (fenders) were removed and replaced with huge flat wings while the rear ones were fabricated in the manner of tractor rear wheel arches. With the change in gear ratios and wheel diameter the complete machine was capable of approximately 48kph/30mph.

This machine was despatched to the Forestry Commission's test site at the Alice Holt Forest. Roadless prepared a second prototype that was sent to the Special Projects Department of the Rover Co Ltd. It was thoroughly tested – reportedly at the Motor Industry Research Association (MIRA) cross-country course at Lindley. Roadless made some further modifications to the Land Rover, including strengthening the chassis and altering the axle clearances, and after a couple of years of tests Rover approved the conversion. This approval meant that the converted Land Rover could be marketed as the Roadless 109 from 1961. In December of the same year the 2286cc/139cu in gasoline engine model retailed at £1558 and the diesel variant at £1658. A special pick-up body was listed as an extra at £172. The Roadless was capable of returning 35kpg/10mpg and had a 68 litre/15 gallon tank. Tests showed that the machine understeered when cornering at 24kph/15mph, the steering was heavy at low speeds and that the machine was capable of wading in up to 75cm/2½ft of water. This latter fact was one of the features that Roadless Traction Ltd mentioned in its advertisements, also pointing out that the wide track ensured stability on side slopes – a useful asset for forestry work. The Land Rover project was something of a side-show for Roadless, as by the mid-1960s the major portion of its business was the production of four-wheel-drive tractors. Approximately 3000 Roadless four-wheel-drive Fordson tractors had been manufactured when production of the Fordson Super Major ended in 1964.

■ ROADLESS 4X4s

Over the next decade things would change considerably for the company. The first major change was brought about by the death of Lieutenant Colonel Philip Johnson on 8 November 1965 at the age of 88. Johnson had been active in Roadless right into his last years and had only relinquished the managing director's post in 1962. His death meant that a reshuffle took place. Four-wheel-drive tractor production continued, with Roadless conversions being supplied for Ford's new range of 2000, 3000, 4000 and 5000 tractors. The 5000 was the most powerful, a 65hp unit with a choice of eight- or ten-speed transmissions and in Roadless converted form known as the Ploughmaster 65, still using a GMC front axle. This was followed by the Ploughmaster 95.

These tractors, like their predecessors, had smaller front wheels than rear ones but the technology employed in the Land Rover had taught lessons, because in the mid-1960s the company had drawn up plans for four-wheel-drive tractor conversions that had equal-sized wheels all round, like the Roadless 109. The Roadless 115 was one of the first tractors of this design to be produced.

Successful demonstrations of Roadless' products at the Long Sutton Tractor Trials in Lincolnshire meant that through the 1970s the company was not

short of work. Increasingly stringent legislation affected Roadless' tractors, and from the end of the 1970s the company was required to fit its machines with "Quiet Cabs".

In 1979 the company relocated from its original premises in Hounslow to Sawbridgeworth in Hertfordshire, England. Sales of Roadless 4×4 tractors had started to slacken simply because of increasing competition from other 4×4 tractor makers, including cheaper machines from Same, Belarus and Zetor from Eastern Europe, as well as machines from the other international major tractor makers.

Roadless then diversified into the manufacture of log-handling machinery and forestry tractors, but with hindsight it appears that Roadless had had its day. A combination of circumstances and the recession of the early 1980s forced the companies that made up Roadless into voluntary liquidation.

ROADLESS 109 LAND ROVER	
Year	1961
Engine	In-line four cylinder diesel
Power	67bhp (50kW) @ 4000rpm
Transmission	Eight forward, two reverse
Weight	3052kg/6728lbs

■ **TOP AND LEFT** ***The Roadless Traction conversion was made to the 109in wheelbase Land Rover models. This is a diesel-powered Series II version, and the conversion was aimed at forestry work. The conversion involved swapping both the front and rear axles for Studebaker ones that increased ground clearance and track.***

OTHER MAKES

(Same, Somua, Steyr)

■ SAME

Same is an Italian company that was founded in 1942 and currently owns the Lamborghini brand. One of the company's earliest tractors was the 4R20M of 1950 which was powered by a 2hp, twin-cylinder, gasoline and kerosene engine. Same production included the Condor 55 and Models 90 and 100 of the mid-1980s. The Condor 55 is a conventional tractor powered by a 2827cc/172.4cu in 1003P, direct-injection, air-cooled diesel with three cylinders that produces 55hp. The 90 and 100 Models are from a range where the numerical designation approximates to the number of horsepower that they produce. Each has 12 forward and three reverse gears and can achieve 30kph/19mph. Both have two-speed power take-off and hydrostatic steering.

■ LEFT *Same was founded by Francesco Cassani in 1942. This is a Same Antares 100 from 1990.*

■ ABOVE *Same now builds machines such as the 130 Antares and is noted for 4x4 tractors.*

■ BELOW *The Same Silver 90 of 1995 is a four-wheel-drive tractor from a range of similar tractors with different outputs.*

■ BELOW *The Same Silver 90 has a turbo diesel engine that produces in the region of 90hp.*

■ RIGHT *Somua was one of the numerous French manufacturers that produced agricultural tractors in the inter-war decades. This one is working at Courtelin, France.*

■ SOMUA

Somua was a French manufacturer of agricultural machinery in the inter-war years and among its products was a machine with a rear, power-driven rotary cultivator. Other French makes of similar machines included Amiot and Dubois. The former was a machine with an integral plough while the latter was a reversible motor plough.

■ LEFT *An earlier Somua tractor in use on the Normandy coast of France for transporting fishing boats from the water across the long, sloping beach.*

■ STEYR

The Austrian manufacturer Steyr entered the tractor market in 1928 when it announced an 80hp machine of which only a few were made. After World War II Steyr returned to tractor manufacture with the Model 180, a two-cylinder diesel, in 1948 and the smaller Model 80 in 1949. These were followed during the 1950s by the models 185 and 280, three- and four-cylinder diesel tractors respectively. The company was based in St Valentin, Austria and through the 1980s and 1990s offered a range of row crop and utility tractors ranging from 42 to 145hp.

In 1996 the Case Corporation acquired 75 per cent of the shares in Steyr Landmaschinentechnik GmbH (SLT) from Steyr-Daimler-Puch AG.

■ LEFT *Austrian Steyr resumed tractor manufacture after World War II, and has manufactured tractors ever since. This is a modern, four-wheel-drive example of the company's products.*

STEIGER

The first Steiger tractor was built in North Dakota in the late 1950s. Named after the brothers who designed it, this tractor is reputed to have gone on to achieve more than 10,000 hours of field time and is now on display in the museum at Bonanzaville in West Fargo, North Dakota. The first Steiger manufacturing plant was a dairy barn on the Steiger brothers' farm near Thief River Falls in Minnesota. By the late 1960s, the company had been incorporated and moved into larger facilities in Fargo. Several moves and several years later, Steiger tractor manufacturing arrived at its current Fargo location. The distinctive lime-green Steiger tractors were constructed around engines that produced up to 525hp. The tractors were named after animals including Puma, Bearcat, Cougar, Panther, Lion and Tiger, and each name denoted a specific horsepower class.

In 1986, Steiger was acquired by Case IH. To consolidate the merger, both companies' four-wheel-drive tractor lines were unified in both colour and name. The name Steiger was associated with high-power tractors and in a survey of farmers in four-wheel-drive tractor markets, this name was cited as the most popular and well-known four-wheel-drive tractor brand. As a result the name was later revived for the Case IH 9300 Series tractors which were then claimed to be the industry's leading line of four-wheel-drive machines. For a period a Hungarian tractor-making company produced RABA-Steiger tractors under licence from the Steiger company.

The current range, the 9300 Series of massive four-wheel-drive tractors from Case IH, consists of a range of ten

■ LEFT *Steiger tractors were finished in a distinctive shade of lime green, and named after animals. This Cougar II is one such tractor.*

■ ABOVE *Steiger built large tractors for other manufacturers including this, the Allis Chalmers 440 of 1973, which was followed by the 4W-305 of 1986.*

■ ABOVE *This 1992 Steiger Case IH 9280 is fitted with triple tyres and has been specifically designed for the needs of the large acreage farmer.*

■ LEFT *Case IH acquired Steiger in 1986. Following the merger both companies' tractors bore the red and grey of Case IH. This 9280 model dates from 1992.*

STEIGER 9310 4WD TRACTOR	
Year	1996
Engine	Case 6TA, six cylinder
Power	207 PTO hp, 240 bhp
Transmission	12 forward, three reverse
Weight	9537kg/21,026lbs

Steiger machines. The models range from 240 to 425hp, with two row crop special models and the Quadtrac tractor which features four independent crawler tracks. The current 9300 Series tractors are designed and manufactured in Fargo, North Dakota.

Four-wheel-drive tractors have the perceived advantage of superior flotation compared to two-wheel-drive tractors. Weight and pull are evenly distributed with less slippage, less rolling resistance and more drawbar pull. The 9300 Steiger tractors offer fuel efficiency through the use of the Case 8.3 L, Cummins N14 and Cummins M11 engines. These have been engineered to provide the optimum balance of torque rise, power curve and fuel economy. The 9300 Series models range from the 240hp 9330 to the 425hp 9390. The optional transmissions are as follows: a 12-speed SynchroShift standard, a 24-speed hi-low SynchroShift and a 12-speed full Powershift, although not all these transmissions are available on all models. This series of tractors is comprehensively equipped in terms of hitches, hydraulics and power take-offs. Lift capacities range from 6662–8884kg/14,689–19,586lb, depending on the model.

■ ABOVE ***The diesel-powered Steiger ST-310 Panther has a Cummins engine, as does the larger Tiger ST-470.***

■ BELOW ***The Steiger Panther ST-310 has a 855cu in displacement, six-cylinder, diesel engine, which produces 310bhp.***

OTHER MAKES

(Tung Fung Hung, Twin City, Universal, Ursus, Valmet, Versatile, Volvo, Waterloo Boy)

■ TUNG FUNG HUNG

Tractor production has always had a place in Chinese agriculture despite the availability of a huge pool of labour. Tung Fung Hung is one of several Chinese manufacturers. During the 1950s the company built a tractor known as the Iron Buffalo and a crawler in state factories. It also built a version of the MTZ tractor from the Minsk Tractor Works. A number of Chinese factories produce tractors for export, and these machines are marketed under a variety of other names, such as American Harvester.

■ ABOVE *Both conventional tractors and crawlers have been widely built in China.*

■ TOP *In China agriculture is not as reliant on technology as in other parts of the world, although compact tractors such as this machine in Nanking are widely used.*

■ ABOVE *Small farm machines, such as this in the Hunan Province of China, rely on small engines with tractor-type tyres.*

■ ABOVE *A machine in the Yixing Province of China used for a plethora of tasks.*

■ RIGHT *Over the years the Universal name has been used by a variety of tractor makers both as a brand and a model designation. This is a UTB Universal 530.*

■ TWIN CITY

Twin City was the brand name used by the Minneapolis Steel and Machinery Company which produced tractors for a time. In 1910 it introduced the Twin City 40. Its steam engine influences were obvious: it had an exposed engine in place of the boiler, a cylindrical radiator and a long roof canopy. The Twin City 40 was powered by an in-line four-cylinder engine and its larger cousin the 60–90 by an in-line six-cylinder of massive displacement. The 90 suffix indicated 90hp at 500rpm. The machine also had 2.1m/7ft diameter rear wheels and a single speed transmission which made it capable of 3kph/2mph. In 1929 Minneapolis Steel and Machinery became part of Minneapolis-Moline.

■ UNIVERSAL

In 1915 the Moline Plow Company purchased the Universal Tractor Company of Columbus, Ohio. The product line was moved to Moline, Illinois and a new building was built for the production of the Moline Universal Tractor. The Moline Universal Tractor was a two-wheel unit design for use with the farmer's horse-drawn implements as well as newly developed Moline tractor-drawn implements. It was commonly referred to as the first row crop tractor, and was equipped with electric lights and a starter, which was very advanced for its time.

■ ABOVE *The UTB Universal 600 is a diesel-engined tractor made in Brasov, Romania, where production started in 1946. Like other Eastern Bloc tractor makers UTB considered exports important.*

■ LEFT *The UTB logo indicates that the 600 model, seen here at a European vintage machinery rally, was made by Universal Tractors of Brasov.*

OTHER MAKES

■ ABOVE *Ursus tractor manufacture started in Poland, with a design based on that of the Lanz Bulldog, and then a standardized Eastern Bloc tractor. This much later 106-14 is working in Ireland.*

■ LEFT *An Ursus tractor, photographed in the Kielce province of Poland. Exports of Ursus tractors were made to the United States as well as much of Europe.*

■ OPPOSITE TOP *The Valmet 8450 is a modern, four-wheel-drive tractor, powered by a 140hp turbocharged diesel engine.*

■ OPPOSITE *Canadian company Versatile offered massive articulated tractors from 1966 onwards. The 895 is a 310hp 14,010cc/855cu in displacement machine that articulates behind the cab.*

■ **UNIVERSAL**

Another company to use the Universal brand name was a Romanian company based in Brasov. They began production in 1946 and exported widely. A mid-1980s product was the Model 1010 which is powered by a 100hp 5393cc/329cu in six-cylinder diesel engine. In the United States the Romanian Universal tractors are marketed under the Long brand name.

■ **URSUS**

Ursus was a state-owned Polish tractor maker whose tractors were very similar to those from other State-owned companies elsewhere in the Eastern Bloc including 1950s models from the East German (DDR) ZT concern and Czechoslovakian Zetor. Tractors were also produced in Bulgaria under the Bolgar name.

■ **VALMET**

Valmet is a Finnish tractor maker which was amalgamated with Volvo BM from Sweden in 1972. The company has specialized in forestry tractors such as the Jehu 1122. This machine is a wheeled tractor although provision has been made to install tracks over the tyres to improve traction in deep snow. Volvo BM Valmet also made the 2105, a 163hp six-cylinder, turbo diesel tractor as part of a range.

■ **VERSATILE**

In 1947 the Hydraulic Engineering Company was formed in Toronto, Canada and began production of small-size agricultural implements under the Versatile name. In 1954 the Hydraulic Engineering Company launched its first large machine,

OTHER MAKES

an innovative self-propelled swather. The Hydraulic Engineering Company was incorporated in 1963 as a public company, adopting the name Versatile Manufacturing Ltd. Then in 1966 Versatile, operating out of Winnipeg, Canada, became involved in the manufacture of huge four-wheel-drive tractors that produced power in excess of 200hp. Versatile Manufacturing Ltd changed ownership in 1976 and changed names in 1977, becoming the Versatile Farm Equipment Company, a division of Versatile Corporation. In 1991 the Versatile Farm Equipment Company became part of Ford New Holland Americas, N. H. Geotech's United States division.

■ LEFT ***Versatile is a Canadian tractor maker who from the early 1970s specialized in the production of large four-wheel-drive tractors such as the 895.***

■ BELOW ***In 1991 Versatile became part of Ford New Holland which led to machines such as the articulated four-wheel-drive 946 model being produced in Ford's blue colours.***

■ VOLVO

The Sweden based Volvo group is a massive motor manufacturer and a long-established tractor maker. During the 1920s it produced tractors alongside Munktells who it later acquired.

Volvo tractors have a history of diesel engine fitment: during the 1950s the T30 model used a Perkins L4 engine, for example. Another Scandinavian merger occurred in 1972 when Volvo began to cooperate with Finnish Valmet in the manufacture of tractors, offering the Nordic range specifically designed for Scandinavian countries. During the 1980s Volvo manufactured the 805 model in two forms: the 805 was a two-wheel-drive tractor, while the 805-4 was a four-wheel-drive variant. Both were powered by a 95hp four-cylinder turbocharged diesel engine. A larger tractor from the same era was the 2105 model. Volvo was among the first to design and fit safety cabs to its tractors. Its machines have been exported widely around Europe and to the United States.

■ ABOVE *A Volvo BM Valmet 405 tractor. Its maker's name carries the heritage of Volvo, Bolinder, Munktell and Valmet.*

■ **WATERLOO BOY**

John Froelich built a machine powered by a Van Duzen single-cylinder engine in Iowa that many consider as the first practical tractor. The engine of the machine was mounted on the Robinson chassis from a steam engine and Froelich devised a transmission system. He was experienced in the agricultural business and had worked as a threshing contractor, so was aware of the requirements of mechanized harvesting.

Froelich bought a large Case thresher and transported it together with a wagon for the crew to live in, by rail to Langford, South Dakota. It is reported that hundreds turned out to see the machines at work, as over a seven-week period his crew threshed wheat full time. His machinery suffered no breakdowns and as a result many were convinced of the benefits of mechanization. As a result Froelich gained backing from a group of Iowa businessmen and they formed the Waterloo Gasoline Traction Engine Company. In 1893 the company built four more tractors, of which only two were fully workable, and others in 1896 and 1897. The company dropped the word "Traction" from its name in 1895 and concentrated on the manufacture of stationary engines. John Froelich's interest was primarily in tractors so he left the company at this time.

The company took a renewed interest in tractors in 1911 and by 1914 had produced the forerunner of what became the Model R. It was powered by a horizontal two-cylinder engine and soon superseded by the Model N. This went on sale in 1916 and over its eight-year production run, around 20,000 were made. The Waterloo Boy Model N was sold in Britain as the Overtime by the Overtime Farm Tractor Company, based in London. The Model N had a massive chassis frame on which was mounted the fuel tank, radiator, twin-cylinder engine and driver's seat. The engine, which was started with petrol and then run on paraffin, produced 25hp. The use of roller bearings throughout the machine was considered innovative at the time of its manufacture.

This early tractor had differing but equally important influences on two other tractor companies. The Belfast agent for Overtime Tractors was Harry Ferguson: this was his first experience with tractors and started him thinking of better ways of attaching implements. It was also the Waterloo Boy that brought John Deere into the tractor business. In 1918 Deere and Company bought the Waterloo Gasoline Engine Company for $1 million and initially kept the Model N in production as a John Deere tractor.

■ ABOVE *The Waterloo Boy Model N kerosene tractor, the machine that brought John Deere into tractor manufacture.*

WHITE FARM EQUIPMENT

The White Motor Corporation of Cleveland, Ohio became established in the tractor manufacturing industry during the early 1960s when the corporation bought up a number of relatively small tractor-producing companies. These companies were, in the main, established concerns with a long history of involvement in the tractor industry, often going back to its earliest days. In 1960 White bought Oliver but continued to produce the successful and popular Oliver 55 Models throughout the decade. Oliver had been in business since 1929 when it, too, had come about as a result of combining several small companies.

■ LEFT *Cockshutt was a long-established tractor maker and was acquired by the White Motor Corporation in 1962, after White had acquired Oliver and before it acquired Minneapolis-Moline.*

White purchased the Cockshutt Farm Equipment Company in 1962. This company's history stretched back to 1839. In more recent times Cockshutt manufactured tractors such as the Models 20 and 40. The 20 was introduced in 1952 and used a Continental L-head 2294cc/140cu in, four-cylinder engine and a four-speed transmission. The Model 40 was a six-cylinder, six-speed tractor. Following these acquisitions, White acquired Minneapolis-Moline a year later. The brand names of all three companies were retained by White until as late as 1969, when the entire company was restructured as White Farm Equipment. During the 1970s White produced a tractor named the Plainsman. This was an eight-wheeler powered by an 8260cc/504cu in displacement engine that produced 169hp. Subsequently, White was itself acquired. A company based in Dallas, Texas, the TIC Investment Corporation, bought White Farm Equipment in 1981 and continued its business under the acronym WFE. The Allied Products Corporation of Chicago bought parts of WFE including the Charles City, Iowa tractor plant and stock. In 1987 Allied combined White with the New Idea Farm Equipment Company, forming a new division known as White-New Idea. In 1993 the AGCO Corporation of Waycross, Georgia purchased the White-New Idea range of implements, and has retained the White name for its brand of tractors. The current White tractor models range from 45 to 215hp, and include proprietary systems, such as Synchro-Reverser, Powershift and Quadrashift

■ ABOVE *The White 2-60 Field Boss was marketed as a White tractor during the latter part of the 1970s.*

■ LEFT *The 4-150 Field Boss was one of the large tractors made by White Farm Equipment.*

■ LEFT *This Model 60 White tractor was made in 1989 when the company was under the control of the Allied Products Corporation of Chicago.*

transmissions. They are powered by Cummins direct-injected diesels. The range includes the following models: 6045 and 6065 Mid-Size, 6090 Hi-Clearance, six Fieldmaster and three Powershift models.

■ WHITE 6045

The 45 PTO hp 6045 Mid-Size has a 50 degree turning angle and there is a choice of two-wheel-drive or a model with a driven front axle. The Synchro-Reverser transmission has twelve gears in forward and reverse. The 6065 Mid-Size develops 63hp at the PTO and has a 12 speed Synchro-Reverser transmission and a four-cylinder engine. Both two- and four-wheel-drive models are available. The 6090 Hi-Clearance tractor is an 80 PTO hp tractor with generous ground clearance. It gives 69cm/27.2in of crop clearance and 59cm/23.2in of ground clearance under the front and rear axles as well as 55cm/21.7in of ground clearance under the drawbar. The 6090 in this form has a synchromesh transmission with 20 forward and 20 reverse gears as standard. The 6175 and 6195 Powershift Series ranges from 124–200 PTO hp and offers an electronically controlled full power-shift transmission. It has 18 forward and nine reverse gears. The White 6215 Powershift has 215 PTO hp and a Powershift transmission with 18 forward and nine reverse gears. It is powered by a Cummins 6-cylinder, 8300cc/506cu in displacement, turbo-charged, aftercooled engine.

WHITE 8410 4WD TRACTOR

Year	1998
Engine	Cummins B5.9 six cylinder
Power	145 PTO hp
Transmission	32 forward, 32 reverse
Weight	7303kg/16,110lbs

■ BELOW *The White A4T Plainsman of 1971 was a large articulated tractor with a 8260cc/504cu in displacement engine.*

OTHER MAKES

■ WIKOV

In the mid-1920s, in a Czecho-slovakia recently independent from the Austro-Hungarian Empire, the two-cylinder Wikov 22 was made by Wichterie and Kovarik of Prostejov. Other noted Czechoslovakian motor manufacturers who offered tractors were Praga and Skoda, whose constituent companies had previously offered motor ploughs.

Praga offered the AT25, KT32 and U50 models while Skoda offered a four-cylinder powered, three-speed tractor designated the 30HT. It could be run on either kerosene or a mixture of alcohol and gasoline which was known as "Dynalkol".

ZETOR

The Zetor tractor company was established in 1946 in Brno, Czech Republic, and became one of the largest European tractor manufacturers. More than half a million Zetor tractors have been produced and have been sold in over 100 countries around the world. Zetor tractors are marketed and currently sold worldwide through two major distribution channels. The first of these is the companies of the Motokov Group, with offices around the world, while the second is the John Deere dealer network. This was made possible through long-term marketing agreements reached between the Motokov Group, John Deere and Zetor. Zetor tractors have been sold in the United States since 1982 and in 1984 American Jawa Ltd took over the distribution. Zetor tractors are distributed in America through two major service and distribution centres, one in Harrisburg, Pennsylvania and the other in La Porte, Texas. In 1993, under a distribution agreement reached with John Deere, Zetor was able to distribute a lower-priced line of 40–85hp tractors in what are considered to be emerging markets, starting with selected areas of Latin America and Asia.

Zetor designs and manufactures most of its own tractor components, including the engines that are designed to be fuel-efficient. Throughout its history Zetor has endeavoured to pioneer various innovations. It had one of the first hitch hydraulic systems, known as Zetormatic, which it introduced in 1960. Later, Zetor was the among the first tractor

■ ABOVE *A Zetor tractor exported to England and fitted with the Zetormatic hitch system, a hydraulic system for hitching implements such as this hay rake.*

■ LEFT *Zetor has always seen exports as an important part of its business. This 1970s model is in France but the company has exported to more than 100 countries worldwide.*

■ ABOVE *The Zetor 25 was a 25hp tractor with a two-cylinder diesel engine, introduced in 1945, and one of the earliest Zetor tractors to be exported from the Czech Republic.*

■ BOTTOM *The 1966 Zetor 3011 Diesel tractor was wholly conventional. The steering arm runs alongside the engine to the front axle.*

■ BELOW *For a time Zetor tractors, Polish Ursus tractors and ZT tractors from East Germany were almost identical, as the result of Soviet control.*

■ BELOW *This Zetor 3011 diesel tractor was manufactured in Zetor's Brno, Czechoslovakia plant and exported to Britain, although others went to Ireland and as far as New Zealand in the 1950s.*

companies to manufacture fully integrated safety cabs with insulated, rubber-mounted suspension. The Zetor 8045 Crystal Model of 1986 had an engine of 4562cc/278cu in displacement and used diesel fuel. It produced power in the region of 85hp. It is a 4×4 tractor with 8 forward gears and two reverse. In 1997 the Zetor product line included ten different tractors. These ranged from the 46hp Models 3320 and 3340 to the 90hp Models 9640 and 10540. While Zetor is a Czechoslovakian company, versions of its tractors are assembled in numerous countries around the world including Argentina, Burma, India, Iraq, Uruguay and Zaire.

ZETOR 8045 CRYSTAL	
Year	1986
Engine	4562cc/278cu in in-line four cylinder diesel
Power	85hp
Transmission	Eight forward, two reverse gears
Weight	n/k

Farming Implements

The versatility of tractors is enhanced through the use of specialist implements designed for specific farming tasks, both for preparing the land and harvesting the crop. The implements are generally one of two types: those that are attached to the tractor and those that are towed behind it.

In some farming areas the soil can be too wet for the propagation of crops so machines that drain fields are used as well as machines capable of working in wet and heavy soils without becoming bogged down. Draining the fields can sometimes be achieved through the use of a mole plough which cuts narrow drainage channels into the surface of a field, allowing a network of such channels to carry away excess water. More recently machines have been developed that lay lengths of perforated plastic pipe that drains fields.

Maintenance of hedges is quickly achieved through the use of hedge trimmers while the quality of fields is upgraded through the application of

■ LEFT *Tractors such as this Farmall Row Crop model are designed for use in the cultivation of crops, and pass through fields with minimum damage to a growing crop.*

■ ABOVE *Four-wheel-drive tractors such as this Massey Ferguson offer sufficient traction to enable them to pull implements such as rippers and sub-soilers as here.*

■ LEFT *Modern tractors are often equipped with implements to the front and rear to maximize productivity by combining several sowing tasks into a single-pass operation.*

■ RIGHT *A four-wheel-drive John Deere tractor with a seed drill being towed by the tractor and pwered by its PTO. The drill delivers metered amounts of seed and fertilizer.*

■ BELOW RIGHT *Ploughing remains one of the timeless farming tasks for which tractors are essential.*

various chemical fertilizers in both powder and liquid form, and implements exist for the distribution of these fertilizers as well as the more traditional use of manure.

While ploughs are now more massive and complex than they have ever been, the concept of ploughing remains unchanged. The purpose of ploughing is to break up the top layer of soil in order to allow the roots of growing plants to penetrate the soil. Ploughs are designed to slice into the top layer and, through the curve of the mouldboard, invert it. John Deere's contribution to ploughing with the development of the self-scouring steel plough suitable for heavy

■ ABOVE *The hydraulic front loader is a versatile farming implement, especially when it can be fitted with a variety of tools as on this John Deere.*

■ RIGHT *A John Deere ploughing. The plough is attached to the tractor's three-point hitch and is adjustable to take into account soil conditions.*

■ ABOVE *John Deere is a manufacturer of a full line of tractors and implements incluidng tandem disc harrows such as this 235 model.*

■ BELOW *John Deere's air seeding system is a complex, efficient system of planting that makes sowing a one-pass operation, opening, seeding and closing as it goes.*

prairie soils cannot be overestimated. Ploughs are manufactured around the world by specialists such as Ransomes in the UK, Kverneland in Norway, both Niemeyer and Krone in Germany as well as the major full-line manufacturers such as John Deere, Massey-Ferguson and constituent parts of the AGCO Corporation. Cultivators are a vital part of preparing the land after ploughing and these are made by a similar range of companies. Rotary power harrows, soil packers, sub-tillers, tine cultivators and rollers are all specialized implements for dealing with a variety of field conditions.

Seeding is just as mechanized a process as ploughing and massive seed drills made by the likes of John Deere illustrate how far mechanization has come since Jethro Tull devised his seed drill. Despite this the machines still carry out the same task, namely that of depositing the seeds below the surface of the soil where they will germinate. Once the seeds are planted by means of

■ RIGHT *A John Deere planter behind a John Deere tractor. To enable such large implements to be transported to fields they are designed to fold up behind the tractor.*

a broadcaster or the increasingly popular seed drill, the farmer is likely to spray fertilizer and pesticides. The implements (and tractors) for this must pass through and over the crop with minimal damage, which has led to numerous high-clearance machines being devised and, of course, the row crop tractor. Drills and planters are made by the full-line manufacturers and specialists such as Smallford, Reekie and Hestair in the UK, and the likes of Vaderstad, Kuhn and Westmac in

■ LEFT *A John Deere rotary disk mower, designed for cutting grass and hay.*

■ BELOW *Planting is increasingly scientific, with tools controlling the depth at which the seed is planted and adding precise amounts of fertilizer.*

■ LEFT *The hay rake such as this, seen in England behind a Fergy TE2,0 was used to turn the mown grass to allow it to dry before being baled.*

■ BELOW *This vintage haymaking equipment indicates how the harvest is more precisely managed now.*

■ BOTTOM *A twin axle trailer, behind an International Harvester tractor, being used to carry away grain.*

Europe. Sprayers are produced by a considerable number of companies including Hardi, Vicon, ETS Matrot and Moteska.

Once the growing cycle is completed another array of specialist harvesting machinery is used. Apart from combine harvesters for grain and balers for hay there are specific harvesters for crops that include peas, beans, beet, cotton, sugar cane, root vegetables and tobacco. Geography and climate mean that some of these machines are specific to certain parts of the world. Massey-Ferguson, Claas, Deutz-Fahr, New Holland and John Deere are among the noted manufacturers of combines worldwide. In addition to self-propelled harvesting

machines there are a considerable variety designed to be towed behind tractors. One of the largest groups of these are mowers and rotary rakes, both of which are used for haymaking. In recent years balers have been developed considerably and towed balers are now capable of producing much larger hay bales than previously. Some of the new generation of balers produce large circular bales which pose their own problems of handling and storage, and specific loaders have been devised for this. Forage harvesters are also available in both self-propelled and towed implement forms for the harvesting of grass and for silage making.

The scientific approach to farming has led to the development of specialized loading and handling machinery including the rough-terrain fork lift and the loader. The hydraulic front loader was one of the first machines of this type, although the capabilities of even these have been increased in recent years. John Deere currently manufactures a range of tools for hydraulic loaders that include various sizes of bucket, a bale hugger, a pallet fork, a round bale fork and a bale and silage grapple.

■ ABOVE LEFT *The shift to round bales led to the development of a spike tool for handling the bales, to be fitted to hydraulic loaders.*

■ ABOVE RIGHT *This photograph from the late 1960s shows square bales being taken by trailer from the fields where they have been harvested to storage in a barn.*

■ RIGHT *A small Fendt Dieselross tractor equipped with a sidebar mower.*

■ RIGHT *Self-propelled aquatic harvesters are particularly specialized implements, designed for marine plants and weed beds.*

HEAVY TOWING SALVAGE
WIDE
LOAD
Transpecs
Transpecs

JAYS

ESSO
ESSO
5024 SY 75

BULWARK
63
EAM 375

BMC
PRO 620
09 PL 639

BRITISH ROAD SERVICES
290 HOA

MAGIRUS DEUTZ
UGS 742R

Balutrans AG
WHITE

TRUCKS

READY
16
UQ3101

ALLIED PICKFORDS
The Careful Movers
MITSUBISHI
TURBO

GTI
159
FREIGHTLINER
159
18641PR
MKZ 775

THE WORLD OF TRUCKS

In one sense the world of trucks has changed enormously, as new technology and improvements in the infrastructure have enabled heavier, faster trucks to be developed. In another sense the basic function of a truck is the same as it ever was – to transport a load from one place to another as economically and as safely as possible. Trucking companies undertake to deliver the goods on time, regardless of the weather and the distance involved. For most of the time it is the driver who takes responsibility for the safe arrival of the load. While some truck drivers are engaged on regular hauls with one type of load, others, known as "roamers" or "trampers" in the UK, travel from one location to another and can be away for a week or more, hauling a variety of loads ranging from soap powder or coffee beans to steel or breakfast cereal. In this modern age, truckers can be likened to the resourceful pioneers of old.

■ OPPOSITE *The timeless lines of this Freightliner cabover typify the United States trucking scene.*

■ LEFT *A dual-steer bonneted Pacific concrete mixer operating in British Columbia. It is powered by a Cummins L10 diesel engine.*

History of the Truck

Seen against thousands of years of history, the truck is a relatively new invention – it has existed for little over a century. During that period it has developed from a crude powered cart into a highly efficient marvel of modern technology. No one invented the truck *per se*; it emerged from a succession of early experiments by inventors in pursuit of a means of propulsion. When steam power became a reality in the 18th century it was only a matter of time before the high pressure rotative engine was developed. Alternative energy sources such as gas, oil and electricity gradually appeared, paving the way for a practical, self-propelled vehicle. The earliest vehicles were passenger carriers, but practical designs for steam wagons were emerging in the last decade of the 19th century. The first gasoline-engined truck appeared in 1896, and that's where the story begins.

What is a Truck?

■ ABOVE *Smooth aerodynamic lines characterize the modern-day urban delivery truck such as this Leyland DAF 60 series.*

■ RIGHT *Four-wheeled box vans are much the same throughout Europe. This late 1970s FBW milk truck is typical of Switzerland.*

A truck can be described as a self-propelled load carrier but, within that general definition, there are so many variations that it is virtually impossible to single out a "standard" truck. Each country has its own system of transport legislation, which distinguishes trucks from other types of vehicle. In the UK and Europe, for instance, any goods vehicle over 3500kg/3.1 tons gross vehicle weight qualifies as a truck. Large goods vehicles (LGVs) are those over 7500kg/6.7 tons gross vehicle weight. In the United States trucks are divided into classes, heavy-duty trucks coming within Class 8.

The nearest thing to a standard truck is a general-purpose "flat" or box van used to transport a wide variety of goods. In this day and age such vehicles have diminished in numbers as more and more trucks are tailored to specific types of loads. Purpose-built self-loading equipment has become commonplace on trucks, especially in the construction industry. Temperature-controlled truck bodies are indispensable for the transport of fresh foods such as meat, fish, fresh produce, fruit and dairy products. Bulk tankers come in a variety of forms for liquids, powders and gases. These are often tailored to specific commodities, which can range from liquid chocolate and liquid tar to granulated sugar or cement powder.

■ BELOW *North America is noted for its spectacular trucks like this Peterbilt conventional doubles outfit delivering bulk cement.*

Because of the vast number of different tasks performed by trucks, they are often custom built for specific types of operation. In specifying a truck, account has to be taken of axle loadings and the loaded truck's centre of gravity. Often auxiliary drives are installed for special equipment such as hydraulic pumps and compressors. At the same time a close eye has to be kept on unladen weight to ensure that the truck can take the net payload specified by the customer.

In the past 30 years or so the word "truck" has become almost universal, but this wasn't always so. "Truck" is an American term. In the UK the term was "lorry" or "wagon" and these terms are still popular among old established hauliers. In French it translates to "camion", in Spanish "camión", in German "lastwagen",

■ LEFT *The UK scene is dominated by articulated outfits grossing 38 to 41 tons. This Scottish Scania 4 series hauls a tri-axle curtainsider.*

■ ABOVE *In the 1980s Swiss trucks like this Volvo CH230 garbage vehicle, were restricted to a maximum width of 2.3m/7.5ft.*

in Swedish "lastbil" and in Dutch "bedrijfswagen". Even so, the word "truck" figures in most vocabularies today. Though a truck is designed to carry loads, there are numerous variations which have fixed equipment but still come under the general heading of "trucks". These include recovery trucks, fire trucks, mobile cranes, cement pumps, drilling rigs, hydraulic platforms, ballast tractors and mobile exhibition trucks.

Despite efforts, especially within Europe, to harmonize weight legislation, there are wide variations between countries. Similarly, in the United States, transport law varies from state to state. Most other countries also set their own weight and length limits. The main factors on which truck legislation is based are axle weights, gross vehicle weight and overall length. Often individual axle weight limits are set low, while high gross vehicle weights are allowed by adding more axles. Road wear from heavy trucks is generally calculated on a combination of axle weights and outer axle spread – theoretically, the longer the outer axle spread and the higher the number of axles, the less road damage. With such a diverse range of national and state legislation, trucking companies have to conform to the lowest weights they are likely to encounter when their journeys take them across international or state borders.

■ RIGHT *Like the United States, New Zealand has some impressive long-haul trucks. This Seddon Atkinson Strato cabover grosses 44 tonnes on eight axles.*

EARLY ORIGINS

■ LEFT *In the 17th century the means of transporting goods was by teams of pack horses.*

■ ABOVE *Cugnot's steam artillery tractor of 1770 was acknowledged as the world's first self-propelled road vehicle.*

■ BELOW *Trevithick's steam carriage of 1803 looked decidedly top heavy. Even so, it completed a number of successful journeys within London.*

From earliest times man has sought ways to transport heavy objects from one point to another. Ancient civilizations devised ways of moving large rocks to build monuments. It was discovered that wooden logs could be used as rollers to ease their task. The wheel was a logical development of the roller. Earliest evidence of the wheel dates from 3500 BC in the Sumerian civilization of Mesopotamia. By 2000 BC there were crude ox-drawn carts. The ox and horse served man's transport needs until the last two centuries, when the horseless carriage turned from a fantasy into a reality. The modern truck has evolved over the past hundred years, although indirectly it owes its existence to many bizarre experiments, which can be traced back more than 400 years.

As early as 1472 an Italian inventor came up with a carriage propelled by windmills. In the late 17th century, a Frenchman thought he had found the answer in rewindable clock springs. Steam power emerged as a practical means of propulsion during the 18th century, although the earliest record of steam power appeared in the writings of Hero of Alexandria in 116 BC with his description of the Ball of Aeolus – a rudimentary reaction turbine. In 1629 an Italian, Giovanni Branca, invented an impulse turbine.

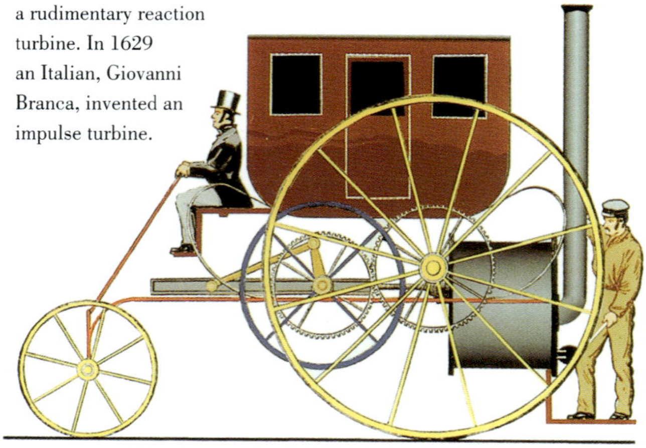

Sir Isaac Newton (1642–1727) is said to have designed a steam carriage in which steam was released through a jet pipe, providing forward thrust. It is doubtful if any of these ideas met with success, but the quest for self-propulsion continued. The 17th century saw experimental carriages from Englishmen Ramsay and Wildgoose.

Experiments with heat engines had taken place in various European countries during the 16th and 17th centuries. In 1663 the Marquis of Worcester patented a simple atmospheric engine which was used to raise well water at Vauxhall in London. In 1673 Dutchman Christian Huyghens is on record as exploding gunpowder inside a cylinder to operate a piston, but he was unable to control the violence of the explosion or to achieve any kind of regular cycle. In 1698 the earliest steam engine using a piston was being patented in England by Thomas Savery. Referred to as the Savery "Fire" engine, it worked not just by steam but by atmospheric pressure combined with a vacuum created by condensing the steam in the cylinder.

■ ABOVE *Britain's first commercial vehicle was this Thornycroft 1-ton steam van of 1896.*

By 1712 Thomas Newcomen, a Dartmouth blacksmith, had developed an improved engine based on Savery's design, and for the next 50 years or so his "atmospheric" engine was the most efficient means of powering machinery. In 1765 James Watt patented an atmospheric engine with a condenser, achieving greater efficiency and considerable fuel savings. Watt also filed a patent for a steam carriage in 1769, but it was not built. High pressure rotative steam engines for road vehicles were still to be developed.

In the same year that Watt was granted his steam carriage patent, Captain Nicolas Joseph Cugnot of the French Artillery completed the world's first steam-powered road vehicle. Cugnot was commissioned to build a second vehicle, his world famous Artillery Tractor, which was completed in 1770. Though crude and cumbersome, the vehicle was capable of hauling up to 5 tons at 5kph/3mph and had a range of about 1.5km/1 mile before running out of steam. Cugnot's design was inherently unstable, having a heavy boiler overhanging its single front wheel which was 1.3m/4.25ft in diameter and only steered through 15 degrees. Its instability was its undoing since it overturned while negotiating a corner, demolishing a wall. Cugnot was jailed for what was the first-ever motoring offence, and no further development took place.

About 15 years later William Murdock, a pupil of James Watt, designed a high-pressure engine and produced a working model, but Watt discouraged further development, dismissing high-pressure steam as impractical and dangerous. At the same time, steam development was beginning to take place in America with Welsh-born Oliver Evans of Philadelphia being granted a licence to operate steamers, although there are no records of any being built. However, Evans did build a 20-ton steam dredger which he mounted on a wheeled chassis in 1804 to travel under its own power the 2.5km/1.5 miles from his works to the Schuylkill River.

An important step forward was made in 1798 when Richard Trevithick built his first high-pressure steam carriage. He patented his design in 1802 and the following year produced a second carriage, which was to complete a number of trips carrying passengers from Leather Lane to Paddington in London.

Over the first four decades of the 19th century, new ideas were rife. There were numerous practical designs for steam road carriages, but they were all for passengers rather than goods.

For the next 50 years road vehicle development in the UK was stifled by draconian legislation

■ BELOW *This 1901 5-ton steam lorry won the Mann Patent Steam Cart & Wagon Co. a silver medal in the Liverpool Trials.*

laying the foundations of an anti-road culture which has survived to the present day. Other countries, mainly Europe and America, moved ahead with new ideas.

Britain's attitude was summed up by the Locomotives on Highways Act of 1861, passed in 1865. Under it, all mechanically propelled road vehicles needed three attendants, one of whom had to walk 55m/60yd in front carrying a red flag. A speed limit of 3kph/2mph was imposed in towns, while 6.5kph/4mph was permitted on rural highways. The requirement for the red flag was dropped in 1878.

France, Germany, Italy and the United States continued to develop new, more efficient means of propulsion as well as inventing new systems for steering, suspension and drive transmission. In France during the late 19th century, Amédée Bollée, Georges Bouton and Leon Serpollet made important advances in high-pressure steam engines. In 1873 Bollée completed his advanced 12-seater carriage "L'Obéissant" which was one of the first with Ackerman steering. Another breakthrough was Serpollet's liquid-fuelled flash boiler announced in 1890.

In spite of legislation, there were brave attempts at building steam wagons in the UK during the 1870s. What must be the earliest British self-propelled load carrier was a massive vehicle built in 1870 by John Yule of Rutherglen. The 7.9m/26ft long by 4.9m/16ft wide wagon with driving wheels 2m/6.5ft in diameter was used to transport boilers to Glasgow docks, a distance of 3.2km/2 miles. In 1875 another one-off steam wagon weighing 4 tons was built by Brown & May of Devizes.

Progress was also being made on internal combustion engines. Jean-Joseph Etienne Lenoir built the first practical gas engine, albeit a rather inefficient affair relying on a single-stroke in which the charge in the cylinder was not compressed before ignition. The idea of compressing gas prior to firing had been thought of as early as 1838 by William

■ ABOVE *In 1896 this Daimler Phoenix 1½-tonner with 4hp engine was the world's first gasoline-engined truck.*

■ BELOW LEFT *George Selden filed a patent for his road engine in 1879 and other manufacturers had to pay him royalties until 1911.*

■ BELOW RIGHT *All four-stroke engines operate on the Otto cycle. The third "ignition" stroke in the diesel cycle is the "combustion" stroke following fuel injection.*

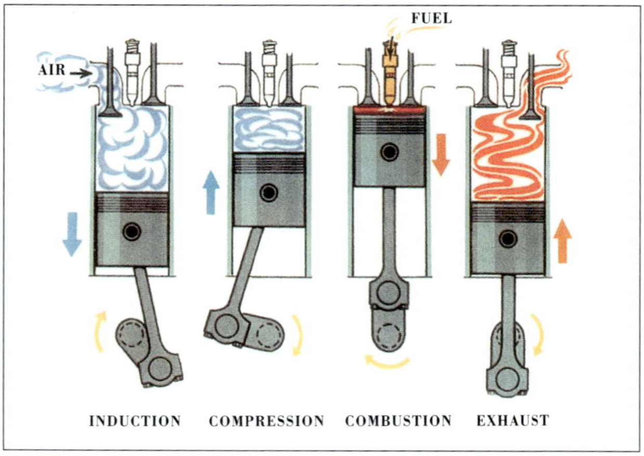

Barnett, but 20 years elapsed before it was put to practical use. Early experiments with a four-stroke cycle (induction, compression, ignition, exhaust) were conducted by Alphonse Beau de Rochas in 1862 and patented by Dr Nikolas August Otto in 1876. All subsequent four-stroke engines have been based on the Otto cycle. The alternative two-stroke principle was patented by Sir Dugald Clerk in 1881.

There was rapid progress in engine design during the latter half of the 19th century. The discovery of oil in the late 1850s was an important step forward. By the early 1870s gasoline had become available and one of the earliest gasoline-engined vehicles was built by Siegfried Markus of Mecklenburg, Austria, in 1873. Significant development was also taking place in America during the 1870s, where George Brayton of Boston designed the first practical liquid-fuel engine. This was introduced into the UK in 1878 where further development was carried out by Priestman Bros. of Hull, who devised a method of blowing vaporized fuel into the cylinders, igniting it with a spark plug.

In 1879 George Baldwin Selden filed an idea for a "road engine" with the United States Patents Office. The patent was not approved until 1895. Following this, every manufacturer of gasoline-engined vehicles had to pay royalties to the holder of the Selden patent up until 1911. Ransom Eli Olds of Lancing, Michigan was helping to pioneer the United States motor industry in 1886 when, at the age of nineteen, he built his first steam car.

Britain was reawakening in the 1890s, thanks to a small number of entrepreneurs who recognized the importance of the motor

industry. One was Sir David Salomons, who took the initiative to organize the first-ever horseless carriage exhibition. This was staged at Tunbridge Wells in 1895. Ironically, all five exhibits were European. Shortly after the exhibition, he organized the Self Propelled Traffic Association in collaboration with Frederick Richard Simms, who was a director of Daimler Motoren Gesellschaft. The association's objective was to persuade the British government to repeal the Locomotives on Highways Act, a goal finally achieved in 1896. The new Locomotives Act of that year lifted most of the restrictions but speed limits were still low, any truck over 2 tons being restricted to 8kph/5mph.

In Europe development of the gasoline engine had progressed dramatically during the late 1880s, the two leading figures being Germany's Gottlieb Daimler and Karl Benz. It was Daimler who introduced the first production gasoline-engined truck in 1896. The same year John Isaac Thornycroft built Britain's first practical self-propelled load carrier, the Thornycroft 1-ton Steam Van. The modern truck began to evolve from that point on.

THEY HELPED MAKE HISTORY ***(left to right, then down page)***

- ***Gottlieb Wilhelm Daimler (1834–1900) introduced the world's first truck.***
- ***Dr Rudolph Diesel (1858–1913) invented the diesel engine.***
- ***Edwin Richard Foden (1870–1950) developed Foden steamers and founded ERF.***
- ***Lawrence Gardner (1840–90) founded Gardner Engines.***
- ***Marius Berliet 1866–1949) founded Automobiles M. Berliet.***
- ***William Crapo Durant (1861–1947) founded General Motors Corporation.***
- ***Ransom Eli Olds (1867–1950) founded Oldsmobile and Reo Trucks.***
- ***John Michael Mack (1864–1924), with his brothers, founded Mack Trucks.***

The Truck Evolves

In the space of 100 years trucks have evolved from crude self-propelled carts into highly advanced machines which the early pioneers would not have thought possible. Innovative engineering, legislation, competitive rivalry and customer demands all push technology on to new frontiers. Often refinements are forced by legislative changes concerning safety, pollution and road damage.

Quite apart from meeting legislative changes, trucks undergo periodic development to keep ahead of their competitors. Driver comfort and safety are important factors. At one time the driver sat on a hard wooden seat without even a windshield, let alone a cab roof to protect him. By World War I he had the luxury of a canvas hood, and by the 1920s semi-enclosed cabs brought a greater degree of comfort. Of course, the need for improved cabs was not just a comfort issue – as speeds and weights increased, safety considerations became more relevant.

■ ABOVE *In the earliest trucks the driver had precious little protection from the elements. This Vabis dates from 1909.*

■ RIGHT *By the 1930s fully enclosed cabs provided a degree of driver comfort, as on this Thornycroft Jupiter.*

■ BELOW *Enclosed cabs came in 1930, but styling had progressed little by 1946 when this Maudslay Mogul was built.*

Recent developments have been related to environmental issues, safety and efficiency. During the past decade exhaust emission laws have put increasing demands on engineers to develop eco-friendly diesels. Alongside these, there have been major advances in "intelligent" automatic transmission systems that leave the driver free to concentrate on the road conditions. These also aid fuel economy and component life by selecting the optimum gear ratio at all times. Another important advance has been the increased use of recyclable materials.

Perhaps the most exciting recent development is DaimlerChrysler's Promote Chauffeur. Conceived as a novel solution to traffic congestion, the system raises the possibility of truck convoys invisibly coupled by "electronic drawbars". A lead truck is driven conventionally, followed by another truck which automatically mimics the steering, acceleration and braking of the first truck, while maintaining a gap of 6 to 15m/20 to 49ft according to speed. Successful demonstrations of this have already taken place on the Lake Constance Freeway in June 1999.

■ ABOVE LEFT *Current sleeper cabs such as the new Mack Vision are a real home-from-home for today's truckers.*

■ LEFT *Mercedes-Benz electronic drawbar function in Promote Chauffeur couples two trucks electronically into a single unit, optimizing performance.*

■ ABOVE *The shape of trucks to come? The Mercedes-Benz Ext 92 concept truck was unveiled for the first time in 1992.*

MILESTONES FROM A CENTURY OF TRUCK EVOLUTION

1890s

1896 First gasoline-engined truck, from Daimler Motoren Gesellschaft.
1896 Thornycroft Steam Van introduced.
1898 Alexander Winton builds first gasoline-engined van in the United States.

1900s

1901 First mechanical road sweeper by John Collins, Connecticut.
1903 Dennis introduces worm-drive axle.
1909 Knox fifth wheel patented.
1909 First air suspension tried on commercial vehicles.

1910s

1912 All-wheel drive truck developed by FWD.
1917 Goodyear promotes pneumatic tyres on heavy trucks.
1919 Clessie Cummins begins diesel production.
1919 Dunlop and Goodyear pneumatic truck tyres introduced.

1920s

1920 Electric lighting taking over from paraffin and acetylene.
1922 Pagefield introduces first demountable swap body system.
1924 First rigid six-wheelers announced.
1924 MAN announce world's first direct-injection diesel engine.
1926 Hendrickson introduces walking beam suspension.
1926 Pneumatic tyres taking over from solids.
1928 First diesel-engined truck in UK (Mercedes-Benz).
1928 Hydraulic brakes available on trucks.
1928 Diesel engines under development in UK by Gardner, Leyland and AEC.
1929 Air brakes for trucks (invented by George Westinghouse for railway use, 1868).
1929 First British-built diesel truck, the Kerr Stuart.
1929 Enclosed cabs on most trucks.

1930s

1930 Rear-view mirror compulsory fitment in UK.
1930 First rigid eight-wheeled steamer from Sentinel.
1931 Cummins diesel demonstrated in an Indiana truck.
1933 Kenworth first to offer Cummins diesel as standard.
1933 Kenworth offers sleeper cab.
1933 UK legislation leads to decline of steam trucks.
1934 First diesel and gasoline rigid eight-wheelers by AEC.
1936 Cabover trucks gain popularity in United States.
1937 Sterling introduces tilt cab.
1938 Kenworth launches torsion bar suspension.

1940s

1941 Producer gas trucks overcome fuel shortages.
1948 Cab improvements, more emphasis on styling.

1950s

1950 Kenworth experiments with gas turbine, later followed by Ford and GMC.
1952 Reo and International Harvester introduce LPG-powered trucks.
1954 Volvo introduces turbocharged diesel engines.
1955 Glass fibre used in cab construction by Bristol.
1955 Firestone introduces tubeless truck tyres.
1956 Single-piece curved windscreens appearing.
1958 Dunlop Pneuride heavy-duty air suspension available .

1960s

1960 Synchromesh gearboxes on some heavy trucks.
1960 Rockwell taper leaf springs.
1962 First UK truck with tilt cab, the Foden S24.
1965 Fail-safe spring brakes in United States.
1966 First UK truck with spring brakes from ERF.
1968 Leyland builds gas turbine trucks.

1970s

1973 Opec oil crisis leads to more economical engines.
1974 Chevrolet Titan gas turbine on operational trials.
1977 Roof air deflectors gaining popularity to improve fuel economy.

1980s

1982 Length limits for tractors relaxed in United States. Long-nose conventionals gain popularity.
1985 Aerodynamic styling appearing on trucks in United States, influenced by Europe.
1986 Anti-lock braking systems for trucks.
1987 Detroit Diesel 60 Series first with electronic fuel management.

1990s

1998 Volvo introduces driver's safety airbag.
1998 All-round electronic control disc brakes from Mercedes and Scania.
1999 Mercedes "driverless" trucks under development.

THE DIESEL ENGINE

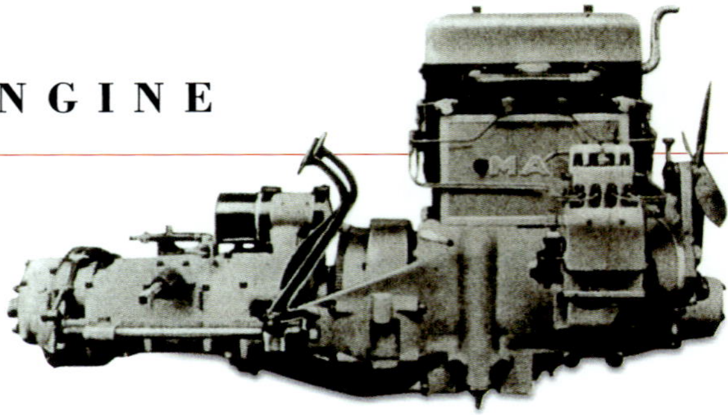

■ ABOVE *MAN's direct-injection 4-cylinder diesel engine of 1924 was the forerunner of the modern truck engine.*

The high-speed, automotive oil engine has been with us since the mid 1920s and, for the past half century, has been the staple power unit of heavy trucks all over the world. For most of that time it has gone under the name "diesel", although it has been argued that an automotive engine based strictly on Dr Rudolph Diesel's theory has never been built. Dr Diesel was born in Paris of German parents in 1858 and, after studying at the Universities of Augsburg and Munich, he developed his theory of an "economical thermal motor" which he patented in 1892.

■ LEFT *The unusual opposed-piston 3-cylinder Rootes TS3 two-stroke diesel introduced on Commer trucks in 1954.*

The essence of his idea was that when air is highly compressed it reaches a temperature hot enough to spontaneously ignite fuel brought into contact with it. His original design was fuelled by coal dust instead of oil, but a much modified engine developed at MAN of Augsburg in 1897 used fuel oil. Prior to Diesel's successful engine a number of other engineers had experimented with "crude oil" engines, which would run on high flash-point oil as opposed to gasoline.

Among them were George Brayton of Boston in 1874, Priestman Bros. of Hull in 1885 and Ackroyd Stuart, who took out patents for oil engines between 1886 and 1890. These included a compression-ignition engine with jerk pump injection, but with a lower compression ratio than Dr Diesel's. This required pre-heating when starting from cold. It was in December 1924 at the Berlin Exhibition that the first practical direct-injection engine appeared. This was the MAN 5 litre/305cu in 4-cylinder unit, which is regarded as the forerunner of the modern diesel. It developed 45bhp and was governed to a maximum of 1050rpm.

By the early 1930s new diesels were being developed by many leading truck manufacturers and specialist engine builders. Though the Cummins Engine Co. was by then well established, heavy-duty gasoline engines were to remain popular in the United States through to the 1960s. The economy benefits of the diesel became increasingly important with the oil crisis of the early '70s. Cummins, Caterpillar and Detroit Diesel are all major proprietary manufacturers in the United States,

■ BELOW *The Gardner 6LXB 180 was renowned for durability. Most British heavies used it, including Atkinson, Bristol, ERF, Foden, Guy and Scammell.*

■ ABOVE *The 400bhp Detroit Diesel 8V-92TA Silver Series two-stroke thrived on high-speed long-haul operations.*

while in the UK and Europe the most significant makers have included MAN, Mercedes-Benz, Deutz, Saurer, Volvo-Penta, Gardner, Perkins, Meadows and Rolls Royce.

Some manufacturers favoured the two-stroke diesel, which can develop a high power output from a smaller cubic capacity and is therefore lighter and more compact than four-stroke engines of equivalent power ratings. Noted two-stroke diesels were those of Detroit Diesel, Krupp, Foden and Rootes, the latter being of an unusual 3-cylinder opposed-piston type. Common drawbacks of two-stroke diesels are their tendency to generate high temperatures and to lack torque in the lower speed range. Four-stroke engines present less cooling problems and have a flatter torque curve, giving greater "lugging" power at low speed.

■ ABOVE *The new Cummins 11 litre/ 671cu in M series 6-cylinder diesel features CELECT Plus electronic engine management.*

As demands for bigger, more powerful engines grew, some manufacturers, notably Detroit Diesel, Cummins, Mercedes-Benz, Deutz, Tatra, Perkins and Scania, turned to V engines with between 4 and 12 cylinders. These have the advantage of more compact dimensions than in-line units. Gardner, on the other hand, favoured the traditional in-line approach with their 150bhp 8LW, designed during World War II, and later their 8LXB 240 which was a highly successful design of the 1970s era. In recent years tough new emission laws have brought big advances in diesel engine technology with increasing use of electronic engine management, controlling fuel injection and timing with great precision. Not only has this reduced pollution to

■ BELOW *Announced in 1987, the new Detroit Diesel 60 series 6-cylinder four-stroke was the first to feature electronic fuel injection.*

negligible levels, but it has paid dividends in massive fuel economy improvements of up to 25 per cent. Progress towards even leaner, cleaner and more efficient engines continues, and new generations of eco-friendly diesels will doubtless remain the preferred truck power units.

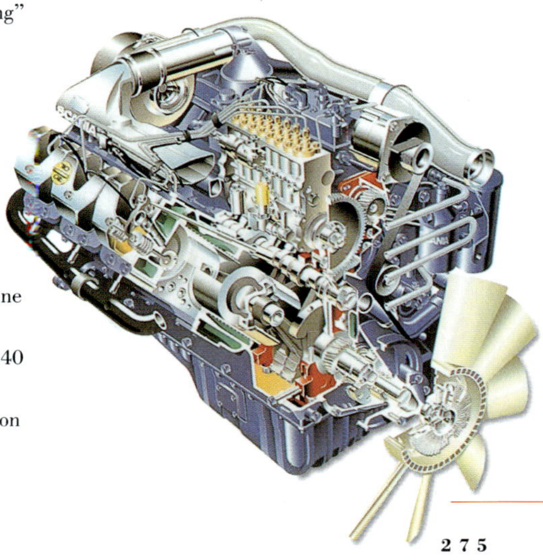

■ RIGHT *The current Scania 14 litre/ 854cu in turbocharged and intercooled V8 has power ratings between 460 and 530bhp.*

TRUCK ANATOMY

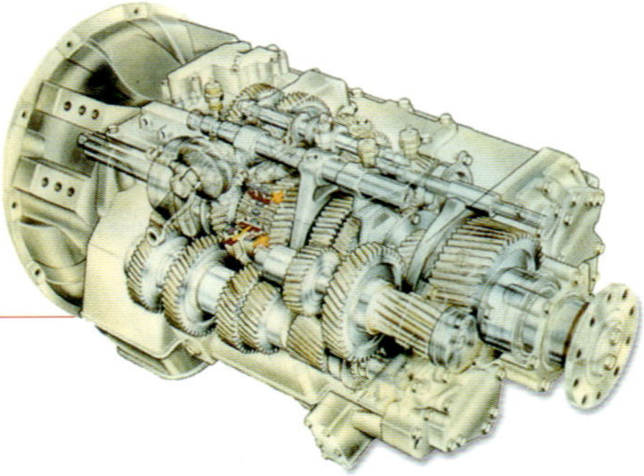

■ ABOVE *A modern-day heavy truck synchromesh twin countershaft gearbox – the Eaton RTS 17316 16-speed range-change plus splitter.*

■ BELOW *A typical Meritor single-reduction hypoid heavy-duty rear axle as used by many leading truck manufacturers.*

While huge advances in technology and component design have taken place, the fundamental anatomy of a truck has not changed for more than half a century. Most modern trucks still consist of a ladder-type chassis frame on to which the engine, transmission, suspension, axles, steering, braking system, electrics and cab are attached. Most chassis frames are constructed from high-tensile steel and can be of riveted, bolted or, in some cases, welded construction. Where weight is critical, frames are sometimes built from aluminium.

At one time most trucks had semi-elliptic multi-leaf springs front and rear, but big advances have been made in suspension over the past 30 years or so. Parabolic tapered leaf springs for improved ride and greater reliability became available in the 1960s. Most premium-quality trucks now feature air suspension. Hydraulic dampers are standard fitment for safe handling and even ride. Front axles, up to 8 tonnes capacity, are usually of I-section, forged from nickel steel for greater strength. Recirculating ball steering with integral hydraulic power assistance provides almost effortless control for the driver. Power steering pressure is delivered by an engine-driven pump.

The engine is the heart of the truck, and virtually all modern heavy trucks have turbocharged and intercooled in-line-six V8 or V10 direct-injection diesels. Typically these have net power outputs of between 300 and 600bhp. Most modern diesels are quiet-running with low exhaust emissions, achieved by sophisticated electronic fuel injection and timing control. Electric starting is most common, but some heavy diesels have compressed air starters.

Power is transmitted to the road through a clutch, gearbox and differential drive. To cope with high torque loadings most modern clutches are of the twin-plate type with air-assisted hydraulic actuation giving light pedal effort. Gearboxes can be constant mesh with sliding dog engagement or synchromesh and can have eight, nine, ten, thirteen or sixteen ratios. Most have a mainshaft and twin countershafts. As an alternative to manual gearboxes, semi and fully-automatic "intelligent" transmissions are available, relieving the driver of the responsibility of gear shifting.

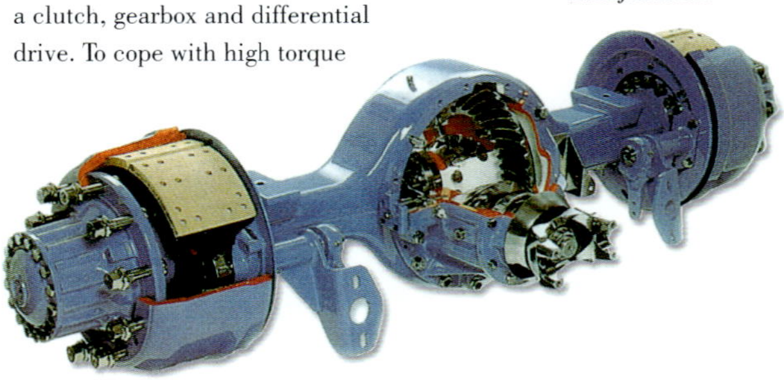

Rear axles of between 10 and 13 tonnes capacity are generally of spiral bevel or hypoid gear type with single or double-reduction. Some axles have the secondary reduction gearing in the wheel hubs, reducing drive-shaft stress and enabling a smaller

■ LEFT *Since the 1960s most heavy trucks have featured tilt cabs. This is a 1981 Bedford TM4400 with Cummins E370 diesel.*

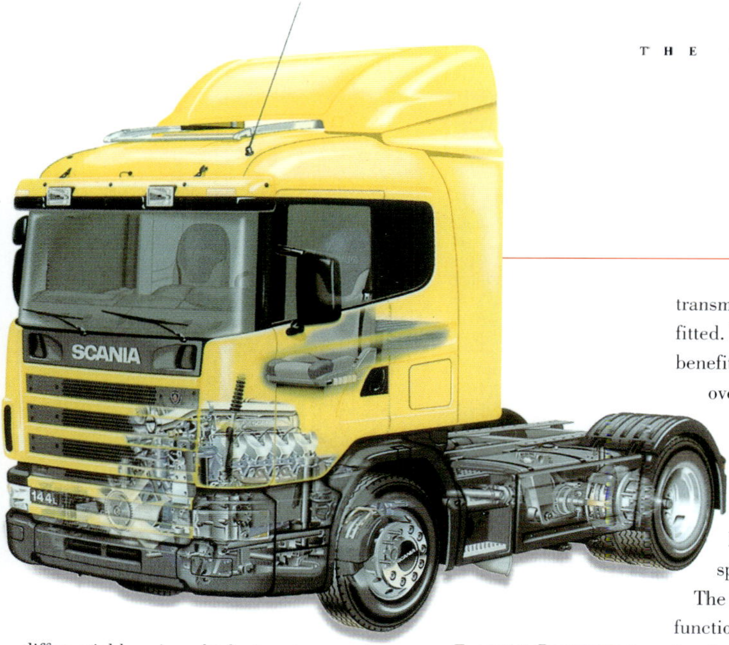

differential housing which gives improved ground clearance. The drive from the gearbox to the rear axle is transmitted by a propeller shaft with universal joints.

Braking is of paramount importance and modern systems are highly sophisticated. While internal expanding drum brakes are still the most common, increasing numbers of manufacturers are fitting disc brakes. Some fit front discs and rear drums, while some of the latest trucks have electronically controlled disc brakes front and rear. In nearly all cases brakes are actuated by compressed air through a complex system of valves. All trucks must have an independent secondary system by law.

Spring brake actuators keep the brakes applied on a stationary vehicle and they cannot be released until air pressure has been built up. Compressed air is supplied to chassis-mounted air tanks from an engine-driven compressor. Air systems have alcohol antifreeze equipment and are self-draining to expel moisture. To save wear and tear on the service brakes, many heavy trucks have engine brakes which utilize engine compression to retard the vehicle. In mountainous territories other auxiliary brakes such as electric

■ ABOVE *Representing state-of-the-art present-day trucks is the Scania 144L with a 50-tonne gcw, 14 litre/854cu in V8 diesel and disc brakes.*

■ BELOW *This sleeper cab on a 1999 Mercedes-Benz Actros is typical of current European sleeper cabs.*

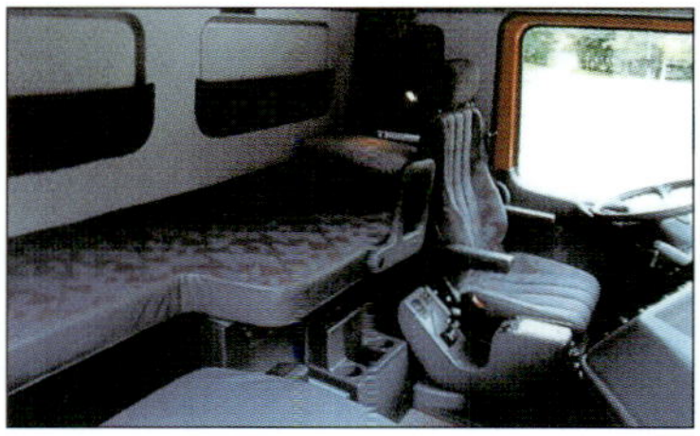

transmission retarders are frequently fitted. Wheels and tyres have also benefited from technological advances over the years. Tubeless radials on single-piece wheel centres are standard on most modern trucks, and wheel centres are often of forged aluminium for lightness and smart appearance. For accurate concentricity, wheels are spigot-mounted.

The truck's electrical system serves vital functions, not only for starting and lighting, but for the many electronic devices that keep a modern truck operational. Most systems incorporate two high-capacity 12-volt batteries to give 24 volts. These are kept charged by an engine-driven alternator incorporating current voltage control.

The one feature that gives the truck its identity and means most to the driver is the cab. Over the past 20–30 years cabs have improved enormously inside and out. Modern styling not only adds prestige, but reduces wind drag to improve fuel economy. Interior appointments on long-haul cabs are now up to the best passenger-car standards, featuring velour or soft leather upholstery, carpeting, tinted glass, electric windows and many other refinements. Comprehensive instrumentation on wrap-around dash panels have become the norm, while interior noise has been reduced to car levels so that the modern trucker can listen to music or receive calls on his cab phone. Nearly all long-haul cabs now have well-appointed sleepers.

ROLE OF THE TRUCK

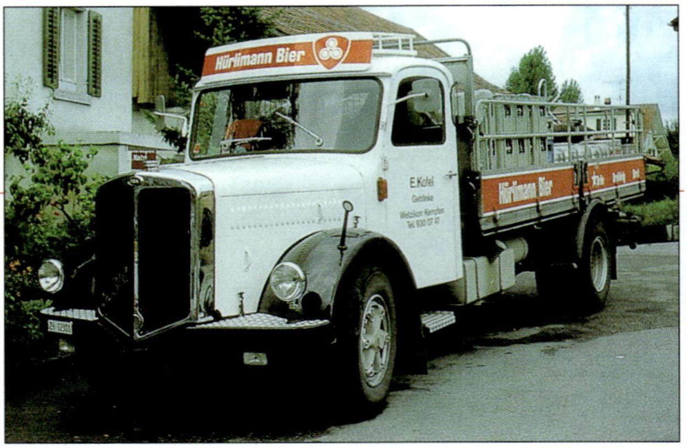

The average citizen spares little thought for trucks, save perhaps to complain at their presence on the highway. In doing so he is probably unaware that those very trucks might be delivering the goods that he expects to find at the supermarket the next day. Just about everything we own, from the bread we eat to the shoes on our feet, has to travel by truck. Likewise, the raw materials that go into manufacturing these products are also delivered by trucks. It is no exaggeration to say that modern society would quickly grind to a halt without an efficient, around-the-clock road-haulage industry.

Commodities that we take for granted have to be transported from factory to wholesaler and on to retailers. Beer, gasoline, milk, fresh vegetables, clothing, children's toys, newspapers, TV sets, soft drinks, sports gear and even motor cars all rely on trucks for delivery. Further back down the line, other

■ OPPOSITE TOP *Brewers rely extensively on their truck fleets to keep bars and clubs supplied with beer. This is a Swiss FBW.*

■ OPPOSITE MIDDLE *Food distribution is dependent on trucks. This famous New Zealand brand runs long-distance ERF B-trains.*

■ OPPOSITE BOTTOM *Keeping filling stations supplied is down to the large tanker fleets run by major oil companies.*

■ RIGHT *Car dealers are kept supplied by transporters carrying up to 10 cars at a time.*

trucks carry the grain, steel, plastic, fertilizer, cotton, chemicals, timber and countless other materials that go into the manufacture of such products. We rely equally heavily on other types of trucks too – those that collect our garbage, sweep our streets, clear the snow in winter, fight fires all year round and tow away broken-down vehicles.

A fundamental difference between road and rail is that road transport can survive without rail but rail freight is entirely dependent on road transport to provide collection and delivery at rail terminals. For complete flexibility and rapid turnaround, especially important when handling perishable cargoes, road transport is the only option. As long as we continue to expect the goods demanded by modern society, trucks will be needed to deliver them.

■ ABOVE LEFT *Supermarkets could not keep going without the thousands of trucks that deliver to them on a regular basis.*

■ ABOVE RIGHT *Hauling fresh milk over long distances requires large tankers.*

■ BELOW *Our daily bread supplies rely entirely on an efficient supply of flour from the millers. This is an Iveco EuroTech bulk flour tanker.*

Peterbilt
87803
Peterbilt
Peterbilt

Truck Types

As the trucking industry developed, so did the need for various types of bodywork. The open truck was fine for most goods, and in inclement weather a tarpaulin could be used to cover the load. The box van or "tilt" van offered extra load security and complete weather protection. While liquids were originally carried in cans or churns on an open truck, bulk tankers were much more efficient. Loose loads such as coal, sand and gravel involved a lot of hard work with shovels until the dump body appeared. Eventually the variety of bodywork was almost endless. Box vans were adapted into insulated vans for meat and perishable goods. Later still, refrigeration equipment was available. Tankers were developed for powders and gases as well as a vast range of liquids. Over the years bodywork has carried on being adapted to suit customer requirements.

GENERAL-PURPOSE TRUCKS

■ ABOVE *The open "flat deck" or "platform" truck is the basic general-purpose vehicle. This is a Mack MC working in New Zealand.*

Any truck not adapted for a particular product is a general-purpose truck. The most basic type is the flat-platform truck, usually fitted with a front loading board to prevent the load from moving forward under braking. In the UK they are known as "flats" or "platform trucks" while in Australia and New Zealand they are called "flat decks" or "trays". In the United States the popular term is "flatbed".

They have the advantage of lightness and ease of loading from the side, rear or above, but once loaded the cargo has to be restrained by ropes, chains or webbing straps, and loads needing weather protection have to be sheeted over. Sheeting and roping a large load demands special skill, and usually it is the driver's responsibility to ensure that the cargo is secure and does not pose a risk to other road users. Securing different types of products requires different techniques according to how stable they are and whether or not they can be damaged by the lashings themselves.

A sided body offers some load security. In most cases the sides are hinged so that they can be lowered to facilitate loading and

■ LEFT *For heavy international transport throughout Europe, TIR tilts, such as this Swiss-registered White Road Commander, are the ideal option.*

■ BELOW *For all-round loading access, the platform truck is unrivalled, as clearly seen in this photograph of a Canadian Freightliner.*

■ CENTRE LEFT *Stake sides, as seen on this GMC, are popular as general-purpose trucks in many countries, including the United States.*

■ CENTRE RIGHT *The dropside truck has the advantage of greater load restraint. This early 1970s AEC is pictured at a large steel stockholder.*

■ BOTTOM RIGHT *For weather protection certain loads must be securely sheeted, as with this 21-ton load of bagged cement on a Leyland Constructor.*

unloading. One type of sided truck popular in many countries is the stake side which features fixed high sides made up of spaced-out horizontal boards. Such bodywork is well suited for agricultural use and for the carriage of loose, bulky items such as tyres.

A type of general-purpose bodywork common in Europe is the tilt, which is basically a dropside body with a tarpaulin cover supported by a strong framework. One advantage is that it can be sealed by Customs for cross-border international traffic while still offering the flexibility of an open platform truck for loading and unloading. It does, however, take considerable time and effort to strip down and reassemble.

Curtainsiders & Box Vans

By far the most common bodywork to come on the scene over the past 30 years is the curtainsider. This is, in effect, a van body with open sides and slide-back plastic curtains. These provide access for loading by forklift trucks. Once the body is loaded, the curtains are drawn along the full length and tensioned up – usually by special straps and buckles. As an extension to the curtainsider principle, there are now versions with sliding roofs for overhead loading. Another type, mainly for steel haulage, has a full-length sliding canopy that can concertina to either end of the load platform for overhead loading.

■ ABOVE *Maximum-capacity reefers such as this MAN five-axled artic from Aberdeen, haul meat to London's Smithfield market.*

The other type of body seen in most countries is the box van. This usually has double doors or a roller shutter at the rear and often has a side door or shutter near the front end. It has the benefit of greater load security but the drawback of inferior loading access. Such bodies are sometimes fitted with sliding tracks or roller conveyors in the floor to facilitate the loading and unloading of goods in bins or on pallets. A relatively recent development has been the double-deck van body featuring an intermediate load platform. Van bodies are frequently fitted with hydraulic or electric tail lifts.

Another important version of the box-van body is the temperature-controlled van which

■ LEFT *Temperature-controlled box vans are essential in dairy-products distribution. This cab-forward Peterbilt 320 operates in Canada.*

■ RIGHT *Curtainsiders provide full-length access for loading by forklift truck while offering load security for high-value cargo.*

■ BELOW RIGHT *Curtainsiders originated in the UK as Boalloy Tautliners. This International is New Zealand-based.*

■ BOTTOM *Box vans are popular in the United States, where this seven-axled International A-train is based.*

has insulated panelling and a built-in temperature control unit, usually used to chill the interior for the transport of fresh produce, meat, poultry and fish. These are frequently referred to as "fridge" bodies or "reefers" and generally have a refrigeration plant powered by its own small diesel engine which can be heard running even when the vehicle is stationary or unattended. All the bodywork described here can come in an almost endless variety of sizes, from compact units for 1 tonne or less to long semi-trailers for payloads of up to 30 tonnes.

TANKERS

Tankers come in two basic types – those for bulk liquids and those for bulk powders. The latter only became common during the 1950s, and during the past 40 years or so have become more and more sophisticated in design. The first bulk liquid tankers date from the early 1920s. Some early tankers for fuel oil were built in rectangular form, but as manufacturing techniques improved cylindrical and elliptical barrels became the norm. Because different commodities have different specific gravities, tanks tend to be tailored to particular products. Also, loading and unloading methods have to suit the behaviour of the product. For instance, some products foam profusely when poured while others can only be pumped when kept within a certain temperature range.

Some tanks consist of one single compartment while others can have up to five or six separate compartments for different grades or types of product. Most tanks for foodstuffs are manufactured from stainless steel for hygiene. Others may be glass-lined. Most are insulated and, where a higher than ambient temperature must be maintained, as with liquid chocolate, they can be fitted with

■ OPPOSITE TOP *An Iveco EuroTech articulated bulk powder tanker seen unloading near the Port of Rotterdam.*

■ OPPOSITE MIDDLE *Some tanks are housed in ISO frames which can be stacked with standard containers and loaded on to skeletal trailers.*

■ RIGHT *Highly polished modern tankers are among the best-looking trucks on the highway. This New Zealand Kenworth is a good example.*

heating jackets. Depending on the product, tanks can be top filled or, where the product foams through agitation, they can be filled from below. The load may be discharged by gravity or pumped out, and tanks are usually lightly pressurized to assist discharge. When hazardous chemicals are carried, strict safety codes are applied and drivers undergo special training.

There are also flexible, portable rubber tanks which lie flat when empty so that other goods can be carried.

A whole range of powders are now transported in bulk tanks and these too require highly sophisticated unloading equipment. Commodities most commonly carried include cement, flour, gypsum, limestone, china clay, salt, pulverized coal, plastic granules, farm feeds and silica sand. Sometimes vehicles are equipped with a number of identical smaller tanks instead of one large one.

■ ABOVE *Not all powder tankers tip. This ERF with Metalair-Feldbinder cement bulker is non-tipping and has pneumatic discharge.*

■ RIGHT *This Spanish Dodge foodstuffs tanker is passing through the dock area of Almeria.*

■ OPPOSITE BOTTOM *A large fuel distributor in Portland, Oregon, runs this impressive eight-axled A-train hauled by a Freightliner conventional.*

■ RIGHT *Doubles outfits are not legal in the UK. This smart chemical tanker is typical of a maximum-weight British artic, plated at 38 to 41 tonnes.*

DUMP TRUCKS

Dump trucks or "tippers" are mainly employed for the transport of construction materials such as earth, stone aggregates, sand and rock. However, dump trucks come in a wide variety of types, from four-wheelers for 2 or 3 tons payload to massive, heavy-duty articulated and drawbar outfits grossing 50 to 60 tons or more. Most dump trucks are equipped with hydraulic rams to raise the body. These can be front-mounted or underbody-mounted, the latter being the only option for three-way dump trucks, which can be tipped to either side as well as to the rear. Most hydraulic pumps are driven from a gearbox power take-off. As well as "open" dump trucks there are covered versions commonly used for grain and bulk feed. Even most open dump trucks carrying sand and aggregates are sheeted over nowadays, since stricter regulations regarding safety and pollution have come into force in many countries.

Dump-truck bodies, like those on tankers, generally tend to be purpose-built to cater for

■ TOP *The Peterbilt transfer dump is designed to tip its own load and then the trailer's load which is transferred into the truck body.*

■ ABOVE *Three-way dump trucks are common in Europe, especially in Germany, Italy and Switzerland. This is a Fiat with Romanazzi bodywork.*

■ LEFT *Seen at a quarry in the Spanish town of Carboneras is this 36-tonne Pegaso 2431K 8×4. It has forward-mounted underbody gear.*

■ ABOVE LEFT *Grossing 35 tonnes, this Mercedes-Benz 3538 end dump truck is seen working on a major road-building project near Iraklion Airport in Crete.*

■ ABOVE RIGHT *The MAN 35-332 8×8 dump truck has great performance on rough terrain. Here it is seen at work on a large drainage scheme at Magdeburg.*

certain types of loads. Those for heavy, dense materials like earth, clay and sand have lower sides and therefore less cubic capacity than those used on lighter materials such as coke, coal and grain. The latter are generally referred to as "high-sided bulk dump trucks" in the UK. Materials used in the construction of dump-truck bodies also vary. While light alloys are suited to lightweight, bulky goods, materials such as rock and granite ballast require harder wearing steel. Massive earthmovers, which operate off-highway, are designed to tip, but they are generally known as "quarry dumpers" as opposed to "tippers". Many bulk tankers are also equipped with tipping gear to aid discharge of the load.

■ RIGHT *With a design weight of 44 tonnes, this six-axled Foden outfit is limited to 41 tonnes in the UK. It has Harsh triple-ram gear.*

Furniture-Removal Vans

The furniture-removal van, referred to as a "moving van" in some countries, is basically a large-capacity box van adapted for easy loading and unloading of furniture. In the UK it usually has a Luton head, which is an extension over the driver's cab. This takes its name from a type of high-volume van developed to carry hats, Luton once being the centre of the UK hat trade. Removal vans also have a dropped rear floor section behind the rear axle to save effort when loading and unloading. The rear door is usually in the form of a full-width tail board which is lowered to form a convenient ramp. Sometimes mechanical tail lifts are fitted instead.

■ ABOVE *Pickfords, the oldest removal company in the world, ran this solid-tyred Leyland drawbar outfit in the 1920s.*

Removal vans are operated by professional crews, specially trained in handling awkward and often valuable pieces of furniture, as well as being sensitive to customers' concerns about cherished possessions. Furniture moving can be strenuous work and very often access to properties is difficult in a large van. The cabs of many removal vans have extra seating to accommodate crew members. Journeys can vary from a few hundred metres/yards to

■ LEFT *A medium-weight Mitsubishi articulated removal van operated by the New Zealand division of Allied Pickfords.*

■ OPPOSITE BOTTOM *Longer distances covered in the United States demand larger removal vehicles like this Kenworth K100 of United Van Lines.*

■ ABOVE LEFT *This old-style bonneted Büssing with integral van body is typical of the furniture trucks once popular in Europe.*

■ ABOVE RIGHT *Volvo FL6 with Luton-type van body represents the current scene in the UK. This one is engaged in office removal.*

■ RIGHT *Lighter vans such as this GMC are useful for small consignments.*

hundreds of kilometres/miles. In the case of international removals, the furniture is sometimes transferred at the depot into an ISO container and a local crew takes over at the final destination.

As well as being used on household removals, furniture vans are used to deliver new furniture to shops and retail superstores. Similar vehicles are engaged in home deliveries of new furniture, and the skills needed for such deliveries are similar to those of the professional removal crews.

56

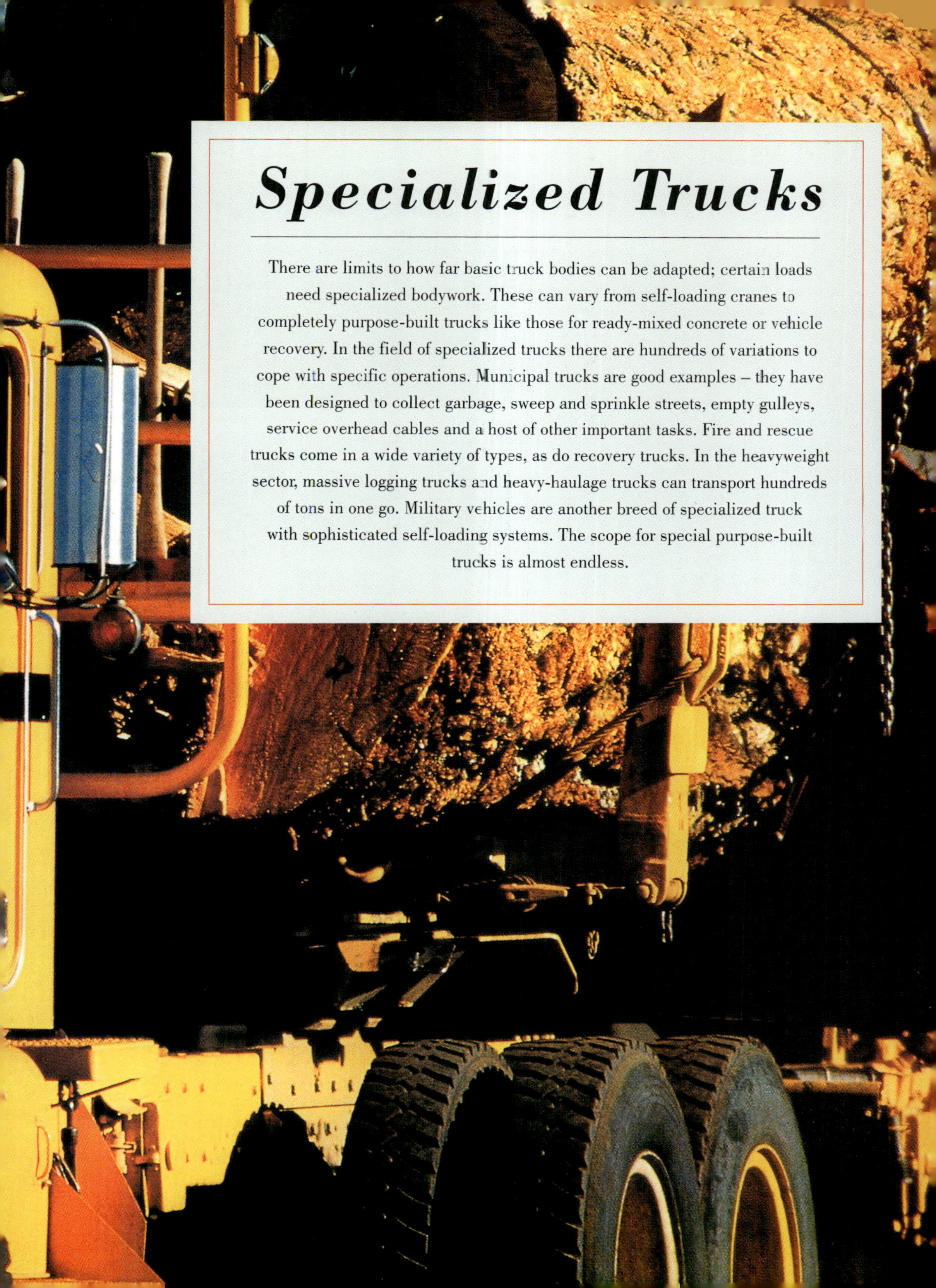

Specialized Trucks

There are limits to how far basic truck bodies can be adapted; certain loads need specialized bodywork. These can vary from self-loading cranes to completely purpose-built trucks like those for ready-mixed concrete or vehicle recovery. In the field of specialized trucks there are hundreds of variations to cope with specific operations. Municipal trucks are good examples – they have been designed to collect garbage, sweep and sprinkle streets, empty gulleys, service overhead cables and a host of other important tasks. Fire and rescue trucks come in a wide variety of types, as do recovery trucks. In the heavyweight sector, massive logging trucks and heavy-haulage trucks can transport hundreds of tons in one go. Military vehicles are another breed of specialized truck with sophisticated self-loading systems. The scope for special purpose-built trucks is almost endless.

CONCRETE MIXERS

Concrete mixers or "readymix" trucks have become an increasingly common sight over the years as the use of concrete has grown in the construction industry. Early designs by Jaeger & Co. and T. L. Smith Co. in the United States were built under licence in the UK by Ransomes & Rapier of Ipswich and Stothert & Pitt of Bath. Today a large proportion of concrete mixers are 6×4s with drums of 6 to 7cu m/7.8 to 9.1cu yd capacity, but often a customer might require larger or smaller quantities. To operate economically, concrete suppliers often run a variety of trucks with two, three, four or five axles to cater for various load capacities. A typical 8×4 truck can deliver 8 to 9cu m/10.5 to 11.8cu yd and some larger multi-axle mixers have drums of between 12 and 15cu m/15.7 and 19.6cu yd capacity.

Most concrete mixers have a separate engine to rotate the drum at various speeds. Some

■ TOP *1993 MAN 32-292 four-axled mixer truck with 9cu m/11.8cu yd drum in the Hasselhorst district of Berlin.*

■ ABOVE *This Terberg F2850 10×4 12cu m/15.7cu yd machine is one of a large fleet based near Rotterdam in The Netherlands.*

■ LEFT *In New Zealand the International ACCO is a popular basis for transit mixers. This is a 1997 ACCO-G with a lowered version of the Iveco Group cab.*

■ **RIGHT** ***A construction site near Burnaby, Canada, is the setting for this Freightliner 40-ton dual-steer cabover of Kask Brothers.***

■ **BELOW LEFT** ***A Foden 3000 series 8×4 concrete mixer.***

■ **BELOW RIGHT** ***A nicely liveried DAF 85 series 8×4 of the John Fyfe Group.***

■ **BOTTOM LEFT** ***Spanish Dodge 6×4 mixer grosses over 30 tonnes and carries around 7cu m/9.2cu yd.***

■ **BOTTOM RIGHT** ***Canada is one of the best places to see giant mixers such as this dual-steer Mack in Vancouver.***

have a P.T.O. or hydraulic drive. The trucks are loaded at batching plants, which today have computerized controls to ensure correctly measured quantities of ballast, cement and water. Drum rotation is reversed during discharge. The trucks have special chutes that distribute the concrete on site. With the abrasive nature of the materials used, drums can suffer rapid wear. Regular cleaning is necessary to maintain efficient operation. Drivers take special care when cornering, owing to the vehicle's high centre of gravity.

SELF-LOADING TRUCKS

■ ABOVE *A 1994 Iveco Ford Eurotrakker with Atlas 100.1 self-loading grab with a Kingshoffer 50 litre/3050cu in bucket.*

Self-loading trucks come in a very wide variety of shapes and sizes, from the basic 2/3-tonne four-wheeler with truck-mounted hydraulic crane to 50-tonne multi-axle rigids and heavy-haulage tractors. Such vehicles are most widely used in the construction industry, where heavy loads often need to be handled on remote sites. Self-loading cranes are a virtual necessity on trucks delivering bricks, building blocks and similar materials. Another common type of self-loading vehicle is the skip truck or "bin lifter", which has a hydraulically operated gantry for delivery and collection of garbage bins. An extension of this idea is the roll-on-and-off garbage container which is hooked to a hydraulic arm and dragged up on to the truck. Many dump trucks engaged on road repairs have their own truck-mounted loading shovels.

One self-loading truck popular in the UK during the 1960s and '70s was the Brimec, which could slide its loading platform rearwards and then tip to form a ramp on to which vehicles or plant machinery could be driven or winched. Similar vehicles are currently in wide use for car recovery. A Japanese system that appeared in the '60s involved raising the whole front end of the truck on big hydraulic rams until the rear of the body platform descended to ground level.

In recent years many trucks engaged on container traffic have been fitted with their own hydraulic swing lift equipment capable of lifting heavy ISO containers from alongside the truck. Yet another device that has become popular recently is the portable forklift truck, which can be carried on the rear of the trailer or truck, to be demounted at the delivery point.

■ LEFT *This 1995 Foden 4380 can lift up to 60 tonnes in one go with its Bonfiglioli P.67000TL self-loading crane.*

■ OPPOSITE BOTTOM *1995 ERF EC Olympic 6×2 for machinery transport has a rear-mounted Cormach 30000SE crane with a 30-ton capacity.*

■ LEFT *Side-lifter equipment, popular in New Zealand, can lift ISO containers weighing around 30 tonnes.*

■ RIGHT *Mitsubishi truck's novel system using hydraulic jacks that raise the whole front up until the body forms a ramp.*

■ LEFT *Brick and block deliveries are made easier by truck-mounted cranes, such as this Hiab mounted on a 1988 Seddon Atkinson 3-11.*

■ RIGHT *A common form of self-loader is the skip truck or "bin lifter". This one is mounted on a 1987 DAF 2100.*

GARBAGE TRUCKS

Garbage trucks were once little more than covered dump trucks with hatches through which dustbins or trash cans could be emptied. Over the past three or four decades they have become more and more sophisticated, beginning with the introduction of hydraulic compression equipment. In recent years increasing volumes of domestic refuse and garbage have led to bigger and bigger garbage trucks. Three and four-axled trucks at up to 32 tonnes gvw are now commonplace in most parts of Europe and the United States.

At one time garbage trucks were built on low-loading chassis with small wheels to make it easier for crews to manually empty the bins. Crew cabs have become standard in the UK, while in the United States crews generally ride on a platform at the rear of the truck. While many garbage trucks were once built on standard off-the-peg chassis, most are now on specially designed chassis providing low-entry crew cabs with large glazed areas. Automatic transmissions are the norm, making the driver's job much easier. At the same time many authorities have standardized wheeled bins of increased capacity, which can be pushed into place on mechanical hoists to relieve the crews of lifting. This not only improves hygiene, but speeds up operations for greater efficiency.

■ ABOVE *A GMC 6×4 garbage truck of the early 1980s engaged on household garbage collection.*

■ LEFT *Garbage trucks have become larger in recent years. This 1996 Seddon Atkinson Pacer 325 grosses 32 tonnes.*

■ ABOVE *This White GMC garbage truck in Canada has a tight turning circle for accessing service roads in housing estates.*

■ BELOW *The latest Mercedes-Benz has large glazed areas and a walk-in cab. Special "wheelie" bins ease the operator's workload.*

Fire Trucks

There is always an air of excitement when the sirens sound and traffic pulls to one side to give the speeding fire truck right of way as it hurries to an emergency. Fire trucks have captured the imagination of children and adults alike. The design and complexity of fire engines have advanced dramatically since open appliances with warning bells roared through the streets with the brass-helmeted crew clinging bravely on to their handrails. Wooden escape ladders were superseded by alloy and, later still, by hydraulic platforms.

Gasoline engines remained popular for many years after most trucks had turned to diesel, as gasoline engines offer faster acceleration. In recent years, though, most UK and European appliances have favoured diesel power. Manual transmissions have also given way to automatic.

In the United States articulated fire appliances have been popular for many years, classic examples being from American LaFrance and Seagrave. Another noted manufacturer is Hahn. In Europe, Magirus is recognized as one of the pioneers of fire-appliance design, while Merryweather, Dennis, HCB Angus and Carmichael led the industry in the UK. Today, many UK brigades have turned to European makers.

■ ABOVE LEFT *A heavy-duty Mack CF pump escape operating in Auckland, New Zealand.*

■ ABOVE *Hydraulic hoists, as shown on this Dodge, have replaced the traditional turntable ladder.*

■ BELOW *Articulated fire trucks are seen mainly in the United States. This Seagrave dates from 1960.*

Recovery Trucks

Since the humble manually operated equipment of the 1920s, recovery trucks have evolved into highly sophisticated machines capable of removing a broken-down truck weighing anything up to 50 tonnes. Recovery specialists take pride in their trucks, which require considerable expertise to operate. Technology made great advances during World War II, and during the 1950s ex-army vehicles were to be seen in civilian guise at most garages. Much of the recovery equipment in common use originated from the United States, including the Holmes Twin Boom principle which first appeared in the '30s. Large transport fleets often purchased their own recovery trucks to be self-sufficient.

While most recovery vehicles once used a crane jib to lift the stricken vehicle, a revolutionary new underlift design appeared,

■ ABOVE *Dutch recovery trucks like this four-axled Scania 144G have enormous reserves of power and strength. It is powered by a 530bhp, 14 litre/ 854cu in V8 diesel engine.*

■ LEFT *This British-registered Magnum 6×4 is kept ready for heavy truck recovery on the M1 motorway and in mainland Europe.*

■ LEFT *Veteran International Harvester 6×4 heavy tractor forms the basis of this well-equipped New Zealand recovery truck.*

■ OPPOSITE *When a truck comes to grief, the heavy lifting gear is brought in. Air bags are being used to right this rolled artic on a British motorway.*

■ RIGHT *This ex-British Army Foden 6×6 features Swedish Ekalift AK6500 EA12 top hamper recovery gear with an 11-ton lift capacity.*

■ ABOVE *This ERF EC10 has 50/30 T3DWX Century underlift gear with a 15-ton extending top boom.*

originating from Sweden. It featured a powerful hydraulic boom which could be extended under the truck to support the front axle. This system is far superior to the high mounted jib, and in recent years it has become state-of-the-art It is not unusual now to see purpose-built four-axle recovery vehicles with engines up to 500bhp and 12-tonnes underlift capability. At the other end of the scale there is still a call for lightweight self-loading recovery trucks for private cars, popular with motoring organizations and small garages.

Logging Trucks

Logging trucks are among the largest and most powerful of vehicles. Some of the best examples are found in Canada, New Zealand and Scandinavia. There are two classes of logging truck – those which can operate on the public highway and those which are restricted to internal journeys on private forestry roads. The on-highway trucks must conform to length and weight limits, while no such restrictions apply on private roads.

Certain manufacturers specialize in extra-heavy-duty logging trucks, among them the Pacific Truck & Trailer Co. and the Hayes Manufacturing Co., both of Vancouver. Autocar, Kenworth, Mack and Western Star are also renowned for their rugged tractors tailored to the logging industry. In Sweden, both Scania and Volvo produce high-powered, bonneted logging trucks, as does Sisu in Finland.

Some of the heaviest outfits feature a torque converter, engine brake, water-cooled service brakes and electric transmission retarder. Special trailers with bolsters are used to carry logs, and the larger outfits regularly haul three or more trailers, each carrying around 50 tons. Depending on the type of logs, the timber is either taken direct to pulp mills for paper making, to sawmills to be cut into standard sizes, or to the docks for export.

■ ABOVE *A 38-tonne MAN six-axled artic loaded with pulpwood from the Welsh forests heads over the Plynlimon Pass en route to a paper mill.*

■ BELOW *Typical of Canada's on-highway logging trucks is this Kenworth W900 seen at work in British Columbia.*

■ ABOVE *Grossing 150 tons, this nine-axled Mack outfit is restricted to the private forestry roads in the Kaingaroa forests on New Zealand's North Island.*

■ RIGHT *This early 1980s 24m/79ft seven-axled drawbar outfit can gross 52 tonnes under Swedish regulations.*

■ BELOW *A Bedford TM2600 6×4 prepares to load logs at a forestry site in the Scottish border region during the late 1970s.*

■ BELOW *Murupara, New Zealand, is the setting for this view of two on-highway logging trucks. In the lead is a 6×4 Pacific.*

HEAVY-HAULAGE TRUCKS

They're big, they're powerful, they're spectacular – heavy-haulage outfits are, by far and away, the most impressive of trucks. Gross train weights for such outfits can be anything from 500 to 1000 tonnes and sometimes as many as three or four tractors are coupled together to provide the tractive effort. Such colossal tractors can individually weigh up to 40 tonnes and are powered by turbocharged and aftercooled diesels producing over 600hp. They tend to be custom-built to individual operator's specifications by such companies as Faun and Titan in Germany, MOL in Belgium and Nicolas in France. Another specialist manufacturer is MAN-ÖAF of Vienna.

Among the traditional makers once famous for such super haulers were Scammell in England, Pacific in Canada, Kenworth in the United States, Willème in France and Trabosa in Spain. Depending on the type of load, special girder-frame trailers supported on front and rear bogies, each with up to 12 rows of wheels may be used. Alternatively, multiples of modular bogies might be used, linked together.

Often the movement of such massive loads is planned months in advance and involves specialist teams, including structural engineers to test the strength of bridges and to advise on any obstructions such as overhead cables. Normal traffic is usually stopped to keep the route clear and such loads are escorted by police outriders. So spectacular are some of the larger heavy-haulage outfits that enthusiasts will travel great distances to see them.

■ ABOVE *Hookers, the well-known New Zealand heavy-haulage specialists, are the owners of this British-built Scammell Contractor photographed on North Island in 1993.*

■ BELOW *Grossing around 530 tonnes, this outfit is carrying a GEC steam turbine with two German-built Fauns providing the traction.*

■ TOP *This transformer is being hauled by a 240-ton Scammell Contractor, typical of the British scene up until the 1980s.*

■ ABOVE LEFT *Waiting on the outskirts of Vienna is this Austrian MAN-ÖAF 48.792 8×8 with jeep dolly and Goldhofer trailer.*

■ ABOVE RIGHT *This impressive Mack-hauled outfit is seen loading up at Oslo Docks in Norway during the early 1980s.*

MILITARY TRUCKS

Mobility is crucial to military operations and, ever since the birth of the truck, the armed forces of the world have capitalized on the rapid movement of troops, supplies and equipment being made possible by motorized transport. Military and civilian vehicle development has progressed steadily since World War I and in many instances civilian trucks have benefited from the spin-off of advances in military designs. Military-vehicle production soared during World War II with the United States being the largest producer. Between 1939 and 1945 it supplied well over three million military vehicles for the Allied Forces.

Broadly speaking, military vehicles are divided into three classes – low, medium and high-mobility. Low-mobility 4×2, 6×4 and 8×4 types are usually based on standard civilian types. Medium-mobility 4×4, 6×6 and 8×8s are specially designed for on-off highway use with a good rough terrain capability, while high-mobility vehicles are designed for tactical support in combat areas and are often tracked types. Interchangeability of components is an

■ ABOVE *This Foden 8×6 medium-mobility DROPS vehicle features Demountable Rack Offloading and Pick-up Systems.*

■ LEFT *For over 20 years the Bedford MK 4-ton 4×4 was the workhorse of the British Army as well as many foreign armies.*

■ BELOW *1992 Oshkosh M1074 10×10 five-axled PLS (Palletized Loading System) truck, powered by a Detroit Diesel 8V-92TA.*

important consideration within each class to facilitate rapid repairs and maintenance. As a rule, military vehicles have lower weight ratings than their civilian counterparts – for instance, a 10-ton civilian truck would be rated at about 6 to 7 tons in military form. Often one basic chassis can be put to a number of roles, such as a general-service cargo truck, fuel and water tanker, troop carrier, field ambulance, radio truck or workshop.

There are hundreds of military vehicle types, from the humble Jeep up to the massive tank transporter, each with an important role to play. In recent years sophisticated designs for mechanical loading and unloading have been developed, like DROPS (Demountable Rack Offloading and Pick-up Systems) equipment which was adopted by the British Army in the late 1980s. This is mounted on Foden and Leyland/Scammell 8×6 chassis.

■ ABOVE LEFT *The legendary Diamond T 980 earned its battle honours during World War II hauling 45-ton tank transporters.*

■ ABOVE RIGHT *An Oshkosh M983 HEMTT tractor with a Detroit Diesel 8V-92TA two-stroke engine hauling a launch platform for patriot missiles.*

■ BELOW LEFT *A British Army DROPS truck based on the Scammell 8×6, showing self-loading equipment.*

■ BELOW RIGHT *The last tank transporters supplied by Scammell to the British Army were Commanders with Rolls Royce CV12 TCE turbocharged V12 diesels.*

The United States Army has a similar system called the PLS (Palletized Loading System) based on an Oshkosh M1074 10×10 and M1076 three-axled trailer with a combined load capacity of 33 tons. The PLS has a degree of commonality with the 10-ton HEMTT (Heavy Expanded Mobility Tactical Truck) which is in wide use in a number of roles, including cargo truck with self-loading crane, fuel tanker, fifth-wheel tractor for Multiple Launch Rocket System and recovery truck. The Czech Republic manufacturer Tatra has a broadly similar range of logistic support trucks based on their latest T816 8×8.

In the UK, Alvis Unipower is now a leading manufacturer of heavy-duty, all-wheel drive military trucks, including the massive MH8875 8×8 75-tonne tank transporter which is matched to a six-axled Nicolas trailer and can operate over dirt roads at speeds up to 80kph/50mph.

Mobile Cranes

Though not designed to carry a load, mobile cranes qualify for mention as heavy-duty road vehicles. Indeed, many early examples were mounted on truck chassis. Over the years they have become more highly specialized and virtually all current mobile cranes are purpose-built, Germany being the leading manufacturing country. Among the most impressive examples of mobile cranes are the eight-axled Mannesmann Demag-Gottwald TC3600, with a 650-tonne lifting capability, and the AC1600 18×8, nine-axled telescopic crane for a 500-tonne lift.

Liebherr also offer some massive examples, like the 800-tonne capacity 16×8 LTM1800.

Other German specialists are Faun with six-axled models up to 120 tonnes and Krupp with their KMK8400 16×8 for 400 tonnes and their colossal KMK11000 for 1000 tonnes. The latter travels in two sections on a total of 19 axles, the combined weight of the crane and the ancillary vehicle for the telescopic jib being 210 tonnes.

Of course, not every situation calls for such massive equipment, and there are numerous

■ LEFT *This 1987 Krupp 220 GMT eight-axled machine is capable of lifting 220 tonnes. It weighs 96 tonnes and has a 99m/325ft reach.*

■ BELOW *This eleven-axled monster, a Demag HC920, is one of the largest cranes operated by Hewden Stewart in the UK.*

■ ABOVE *A 1989 16×8 eight-axled Krupp KMK8400 operated by Grayston White & Sparrow, with a 400-tonne lifting capacity.*

smaller mobile cranes with lifting capacities ranging from 10 tonnes to 100 tonnes. One notable Spanish manufacturer is Luna Cranes of Huesca, which manufactures an eight-axled giant, the GT-300, for lifting up to 300 tonnes. Luna also build lighter cranes for between 20 and 75 tonnes. Historically, Fodens Ltd and Coles Cranes were significant builders of mobile cranes in the UK. Fodens were in the mobile-crane business as far back as the 1930s in conjunction with Smiths of Rodley, Leeds. A tie-up with Demag in Germany during the 1960s saw Foden mobile cranes powered by air-cooled Deutz diesel engines.

■ RIGHT *This 1980 Gottwald AMK200-103 weighs over 100 tonnes and lifts 200 tonnes up to 96m/315ft. The cab is adapted from MAN.*

■ RIGHT *This impressive machine is a 1981 Gottwald AK68-1 with a maximum lifting capacity of 850 tonnes. Fully extended, it has a reach of 178m/584ft and weighs 110 tonnes.*

National Differences in Truck Design

Despite the globalization of the modern truck industry, there are still wide variations in trucks of different nations. In much the same way as living creatures adapt to their surroundings, trucks evolve to suit the conditions in various parts of the world. What is right for hot, equatorial regions simply would not suit the freezing conditions of the arctic. Likewise, what suits the long, deserted highways of parts of Australia and America would not be right for the Alpine passes of Switzerland and Italy. Coupled with the climatic and geographical differences, there are wide variations in local legislation, itself being influenced by local conditions. Then there is the influence of local culture, which is reflected in the way trucks are styled and liveried. Such diversity adds great interest for the foreign visitor who cares to observe the transport scene.

EUROPE

Despite some progress towards harmonization, the trucking scene in Europe still reflects the different priorities of individual nations. The growth of international traffic has gone some way to shaping a pan-European truck that can operate profitably without infringing local laws. The nearest thing to this is a 40-tonne gcw six-axled artic.

While the diversity of European trucks has diminished through federalization under European Community rule, full harmonization is still a long way off. Countries with high weight limits, such as The Netherlands, Sweden, Italy and Spain, are reluctant to agree to a lower weight limit, and Sweden in particular would not want to accept a shorter length limit. Such a move would render existing trucks and trailers illegal.

In Britain, traffic law favours forward-control or "cabover" trucks. Until the 1960s most British heavy trucks were rigids, the largest long-distance trucks being eight-wheelers with drawbar trailers grossing up to 32 tons. Artics gained popularity from 1964 when the law was changed to allow them to run at 32 tons instead of 24 tons. By European standards, British trucks tended to be under-powered, but the advent of new motorways from 1959 led to more powerful machines. This period also saw the beginning of roll-on/roll-off ferries between Britain and Europe.

Germany is the dominant force in European truck manufacture, while Sweden is also a major player. Germany's weight and length laws are similar to those in the UK, but Sweden

■ ABOVE *Belgium uses vehicles of Swedish, German and Dutch origin. This Scania was seen in Antwerp.*

■ RIGHT *The French stay loyal to home-produced trucks. This Renault Premium belongs to one of France's largest hauliers.*

■ BELOW LEFT *Trucks from the old Eastern Bloc are a common sight in Western Europe, like this Polish Magnum.*

■ BELOW RIGHT *For a long time the Italian scene was dominated by eight-axled drawbar outfits like this OM.*

■ RIGHT *The Netherlands is the place to see magnificent multi-axle outfits like this Scania drawbar rig in Rotterdam.*

■ BELOW RIGHT *Long-haul trucks in the UK are predominantly six-axled 41-ton artics like this ERF EC10.*

permits the use of drawbar combinations up to 24m/79ft, weighing 52 tonnes. The Netherlands has a thriving trucking industry and houses Europe's largest port at Rotterdam. The Dutch scene is dominated by heavy six, seven and eight-axled outfits grossing up to 60 tonnes.

Switzerland has lower weight limits, especially away from its borders, and since the 1970s has favoured the use of high-powered, rigid four-axled trucks. Until recently, many Swiss trucks were restricted to 2.3m/7.5ft width. France has had high axle and gross weight limits for many years, and this is reflected in the absence of French multi-axle outfits.

Spain also has high axle weights but there the preference, until recent years, has been for four-axled rigids on long-distance traffic. These are usually high-powered 8×2 vehicles with self-tracking fourth axles, grossing up to 36 tonnes. They were a development of the twin-steer six-wheeler which was originally adopted for its safety benefits on mountain roads.

Italian heavy trucks have something in common with those in Spain in that many are twin-steer six-wheelers with fourth axle conversions. However, most such Italian eight-wheelers operate with four-axled drawbar trailers grossing 44 tonnes. Traditionally, most Italian trucks featured right-hand drive for added safety when negotiating narrow mountain roads. The current trend in Europe is towards greater standardization in legislation, with the ultimate aim of a unified federal system. It will be some time before that aim is achieved and, as things stand, common weights and dimensions are confined to trucks operating on international traffic.

■ BELOW LEFT *Liberal length limits allow Swedish trucks to run at 24m/79ft.*

■ BELOW RIGHT *German companies support their own truck industry. Drawbar outfits are very popular, such as this MAN.*

United States & Canada

■ ABOVE *Canadian and United States trucks have much in common. Freightliner cabovers, such as this Canadian example, are a common sight in both countries.*

With the stepping up of the Interstate highway network during the 1950s and '60s road transport overtook rail freight in America. In the late '30s the railways dominated freight movement but over 35 years that has been reversed. Road improvements enabled larger and more efficient trucks to be introduced. Many states allowed "doubles" outfits with two 12.2m/40ft trailers on a total of nine axles. These could gross over 60 tons and had high-power engines to maintain the 32kph/20mph minimum speed limit. Gasoline engines remained popular in America long after most countries had switched to diesel. The fuel crisis of the early '70s led to the decline of big, thirsty gasoline engines. A 16.8m/55ft length limit applied in many states while axle weights and bridge formulas, which stipulate minimum legal outer axle spreads, vary from state to state. In some cases truck and trailer combinations have very long drawbars to achieve the required outer axle spread. Michigan is noted for its liberal weight laws where rigs with 11 axles can gross over 74 tons. These have earned the nickname "centipedes".

While the majority of big Class 8 trucks are typical five-axled eighteen-wheelers, there are other types popular in certain states. One of these is the dromedary outfit, which consists of an artic with a very long tractor with its own van body. Such tractors can have three or four axles. Trucks engaged on long hauls must conform to the regulations in each state they enter or cross. Such are the variations in laws that the truck industry is geared to custom building. Unlike those in the UK and Europe, American manufacturers do not list standard specifications, but offer a wide choice of available options. This is generally referred to as a "modular build" approach.

East Coast rigs are generally workmanlike outfits, Mack and Volvo being popular makes, while the West Coast is dominated by glamorous long-nosed conventionals from Kenworth, Peterbilt and Western Star. The vast distances and extreme climatic variations encountered

■ BELOW LEFT *A classic eighteen-wheeler conventional photographed on Interstate 5 near the United States-Canadian border.*

■ BELOW RIGHT *Visitors to Michigan will be confronted by these spectacular centipede outfits grossing up to 74 tons. This photograph shows a Brockway.*

■ RIGHT *Kenworth W900 Studio Sleeper conventional is the archetypal West Coast tractor, an icon of the United States trucking scene.*

■ BELOW RIGHT *The stretch-reach drawbar rigs, common in Washington State, are designed to meet local bridging formulas.*

by long-haul truckers in the States put extra demands on both driver and truck. To cope with this, most long-haul rigs have well-appointed sleepers that are like motor homes compared to the cramped sleeper cabs seen in Europe.

The American trucker has long been regarded as the modern-day cowboy – a resourceful free spirit upholding the legends of the great pioneers. This glamorous association, particularly true on the West Coast, has reached far beyond the shores of the United States – many truck drivers in the UK and Europe emulate the "steel cowboy" image with customized trucks and stetsons. The influence is particularly strong in The Netherlands, where truckers take enormous pride in their rigs. Australia and New Zealand have also developed their own trucking culture along American lines.

Canada's trucking industry parallels that of the United States to some extent, in that operators are faced with similar legislative differences between one province and another. Over the years trucking has overtaken rail freight. Trucks benefit from greater flexibility especially in accessing remote regions. Operators running to the Northwest Territories face extremely cold conditions and the climate varies greatly over such a huge country. High-powered doubles outfits are a common sight in most parts of Canada, some provinces allowing gross weights of up to 70 tons. Canadian doubles are usually of the B train type, consisting of two semis linked by a fifth wheel, while in the United States A trains, basically artics hitched to drawbar trailers, are more common

In the past two decades there has been a marked increase in the use of dual-steer straight trucks hauling drawbar trailers, especially in British Columbia and the northwest of the United States. Canada is also noted for its four and five-axled concrete mixers. Most impressive of all are the massive logging trucks, particularly evident in British Columbia.

■ BELOW *Dromedary outfits, such as this Peterbilt 362E, consist of a load-carrying tractor hitched to a normal semi-trailer.*

Other Countries

■ ABOVE *This proud Moroccan driver is posing with his locally built Volvo N88. Note the large air filter on the far side.*

■ RIGHT *A Russian MAZ with TIR tilt trailer engaged on long-distance haulage in Eastern Europe.*

Road transport has become a vital part of the economy in most countries of the world. Eastern Europe had a truck-manufacturing industry from the beginning of the 20th century while the Russian Federation, formerly the USSR, entered the scene in the mid 1920s. Russia has some of the coldest regions on earth, and their trucks must be geared to cope with temperatures that few European makes could withstand. The emphasis is on ruggedness rather than driver comfort. As a consequence, most sales are within Russia and its neighbouring Eastern European countries.

Japan was also a relative latecomer to the truck industry, but by the '70s it had become a major player. Among Japan's most important export markets are Australia and New Zealand. Japanese trucks are now seen as state-of-the-art machines that can hold their own against any European and American competition.

■ RIGHT *Zimbabwe is the only place one is likely to see rarities like this Panda 6×4 tractor.*

■ BELOW *Recently, Israel has seen a growth in multi-axle 60-tonners like this DAF 95 cement bulker with 8×4 tractor.*

Africa has a very varied transport industry. Within such a vast continent the conditions and priorities can be completely different according to the territory. In Morocco, Algeria and the Sahara regions many of the trucks are locally assembled Volvos featuring large heavy-duty air filters suited to the arid conditions. Bonneted trucks, including the Renault C range, are a common sight. In Central Africa road conditions demand particularly rugged trucks with "no frills", easy-to-repair specifications. Southern Africa has the most sophisticated transport system within the continent and, while there is little indigenous manufacturing, trucks are tailored to local needs by assembly plants set up by a number of European, American and Japanese companies. Heavy-duty long-haul trucks often consist of

30.4m/100ft long 55-tonne gross doubles outfits known locally as "interlinks".

Trucks in the Middle East are a mixture of European and American types, and legislation on weight and length tends to vary from country to country. Heavy trucks are generally of very rugged build and some regions now permit multi-axle outfits of 60 tons gross. These are particularly prevalent in Israel. Doubles outfits are allowed on certain roads in Saudi Arabia. Trucks have to be specifically equipped to work in high temperatures and dusty conditions, so heavy-duty cooling systems and air filters are called for. Mercedes trucks have a strong presence in the region, with a well-established assembly plant located in Iran. Turkey has its own manufacturing industry building trucks under the BMC and Chrysler marques.

Pakistan and Afghanistan are noted for their highly colourful trucks, with elaborate bodywork featuring intricate decoration. Indian trucks are also individualistic in style. Most are locally built by Tata, which began as licence-built Mercedes, and Ashok Leyland which are now a mixture of old Leyland and Iveco-Ford Cargo designs. They are built along simple, rugged lines for ease of repair. This approach is prevalent in other parts of the world such as Southeast Asia, Indonesia and parts of Latin America. Cuba has a particularly interesting trucking scene, with many ageing trucks of American, Russian and Japanese origin, some of which date from the 1960s.

The most advanced trucking nations in the Southern Hemisphere are Australia and New Zealand where a wider variety of makes can be seen than almost anywhere else in the world. New Zealand heavies run at 44 tons, either in truck and drawbar trailer form or as doubles outfits, often on eight axles. They are noted for their smart liveries and impressive appearance. When it comes to impressive trucks though, there is nothing to compete with the spectacular Road Trains in Australia. These massive outfits, usually hauled by powerful American tractors, can consist of up to four trailers hauling payloads in excess of 100 tons. Many run on eighty or more tyres and have engines of between 600 and 750bhp. Most Road Trains are to be seen in the Northern Territory along the Stuart Highway which links Alice Springs to Darwin some 1500km/932 miles to the north. Such outfits are restricted to certain routes and are excluded from built-up areas.

■ ABOVE LEFT *India has its own breed of truck, represented by this ruggedly built Ashok-Leyland tanker*

■ ABOVE RIGHT *Basic, easy-to-repair trucks like these old Bedford TJs abound in Nigeria and Central Africa.*

■ BELOW *The largest on-highway trucks are found in Australia. This is a typical road train hauled by a Mack Super-Liner with 400bhp V8 engine.*

27
27
5922 TJ

A–Z of Trucks

The truck-building industry has been established for over a century. During that time many hundreds of manufacturers have come and gone: some have prospered to become world leaders while some have fallen by the wayside. Throughout history the industry has seen countless takeovers and mergers, and in recent years the trend has been towards globalization, with the bulk of manufacture in the hands of a few multi-national companies. This A–Z does not set out to include every single make, many of which are so obscure as to be of little relevance. Instead it lists all the leading truck manufacturers, focusing on famous makes, while taking a brief look at some lesser-known makes and short-lived specialist types, included for their historic interest. Takeovers and mergers are continually in progress, and in the future it is doubtless that more makes will be consigned to history.

■ OPPOSITE *A Western Star dual-steer four-axled concrete mixer loads up at a batching plant near Whistler in British Columbia.*

■ LEFT *A 1949 Gardner-engined Scammell Rigid 8 22-ton box van, once a common sight on Britain's trunk routes.*

SOUTHALL, LONDON, ENGLAND

AEC

■ BELOW *AEC's first volume-produced truck was this gasoline-engined solid-tyred Y type of 1916.*

The earliest truck from AEC was the 3 to 4-ton Y-type of 1916. The Associated Equipment Company was formed in Walthamstow, East London, in 1912 to build buses for the London General Omnibus Company. The factory was the former works of the Vanguard Omnibus Company which was merged into the LGOC in 1908. It was one of the first factories to use a moving assembly line. An estimated 10,000 Y-types were produced for the War Department and a civilian version went into production after World War I. Early AECs were powered by gasoline engines from Daimler or Tylor but from about 1920 the company built its own engines.

Development continued throughout the 1920s, the range consisting of the 201 and 204 (for 2½ tons), the 418 and 428 (4 tons), the 506, -07 and -08 (5/6 tons) and the 701, which was an experimental articulated vehicle. From 1928, pneumatics were becoming an option.

AEC joined forces with Daimler in 1926 but that association, under which the vehicles were sold as ADC, was to last only two years.

In 1926–27 AEC's truck sales were beginning to improve and a major investment was made in a new factory at Southall in London. Following the appointment of a new design engineer, John Rackham, the model line-up was transformed. From 1930 onwards, the trucks were given model names. The Mercury and Monarch for 3½ to 4-ton payloads were powered by a 4-cylinder engine, while the Majestic 6-tonner and Mammoth 7 to 8-tonner took a 6-cylinder unit. A new 6-cylinder diesel engine was also introduced.

New improved models were added to the AEC range during the 1930s, including the Matador 4×2 four-wheeler, the Mammoth Major 12-ton payload six-wheeler, and its larger counterpart, the 15-ton Mammoth Major 8. This was the first production rigid eight-wheeler. Its successors included the Mk.II (1935), Mk.III (1948), Mk.V (1958) and the Ergomatic (1964).

■ ABOVE *Large numbers of Matador 4×4s were supplied to the armed forces. Many went on to serve in civilian timber haulage.*

■ LEFT *AEC was the first to offer a rigid eight-wheeled diesel truck. This 1936 Mammoth Major Mk.II grossed 22 tons.*

■ LEFT *The Mandator Mk.V was AEC's last model type before the Leyland takeover. This one has an Oswald Tillotson cab.*

In 1948 AEC began a program of expansion, taking over the Maudslay Motor Co. and Crossley Motors, forming a new holding company, Associated Commercial Vehicles (ACV). Maudslay vehicles were phased out during 1950, replaced by AECs. The AEC range was expanded with the introduction of the lighter Mercury model in 1953, powered by the AV410 6-cylinder diesel. This was later developed into the AV470. Developments of the Mercury included the twin-steer Mustang of 1956 and the six-wheel Marshal introduced in 1960.

Heavy-duty Mk.IIIs were the Mandator (4×2), Mammoth Major 6 (6×2/6×4) and Mammoth Major 8 (8×2/8×4). There was a tractor-unit version of the Mandator. Bonneted versions of most models were offered, mainly for export. Until the mid 1950s AEC Mk.IIIs still featured exposed radiators but they were modernized from about 1956 with a concealed radiator and a wide "dummy" grille.

In 1958 the Mk.III range was replaced by the Mk.V (there was no Mk.IV except on bus models) which was a completely new design. The Mk.V had a very stylish cab built mainly by Park Royal Vehicles. AEC built only chassis with front panels so that customers could specify their own choice of cab.

During the 1950s AEC went from strength to strength, developing export business throughout the world. Plants were established in South Africa, Spain, Portugal, Belgium and South America, while AEC engines were supplied to Willème in France, Vanaja in Finland, OMT in Italy and Verheul in The Netherlands. In the late '50s AEC embarked on the production of dump trucks at the old Maudslay factory. AEC's empire continued to grow with the takeover of the old established Thornycroft company in 1961.

In 1962 AEC's expansion was brought to an end when the company was taken over by its rival, Leyland Motors Ltd. One by one, AEC's overseas interests were dissolved and, since Leyland Group products were competing with one another, some rationalization of model types was inevitable.

Very soon a new range was launched featuring a common style of Leyland Group cab, the Ergomatic. While it lacked the tasteful lines of the AEC's handsome Mk.V, it had the benefit of being a tilt cab, thus providing improved servicing access. The Mercury was also updated to take the Ergomatic cab and the AV470 was replaced by the more powerful 8.2 litre/500cu in AV505. The main power unit for the leading heavy models, the Mandator tractor and the maximum-weight Mammoth Major eight-wheeler, became the AV691 of 11.3 litres/689cu in capacity. The largest tractor units were the Mammoth Major Six and the twin-steer Mammoth Minor. For these and later Ergomatic models, the higher powered AV760 became a popular fitment.

An unsuccessful project to develop a new, high-powered V8 diesel engine to suit the heavy trucks of the 1970s tarnished AEC's image. A number of the engines went into production but they proved unreliable in service. The problem was blamed on lack of funding by Leyland. In reality Leyland itself was being starved of investment since it was led, under pressure from the UK government, into an ill-planned merger with British Motor Holdings in 1968. BMH car plants were subsequently being propped up by the truck business which, in turn, suffered big losses. AEC was one victim of this unhappy episode and, by the mid '70s, the writing was on the wall for the Southall company. The factory closed down in 1979.

■ LEFT *After 1964, most AECs featured the Leyland Group Ergomatic cab, as seen on this 1975 Marshal six-wheeler.*

GLASGOW, SCOTLAND

ALBION

Founded in 1899, the Albion Motor Car Company produced its first commercial vehicle – a half-ton van – in 1902. Its founders, Norman O. Fulton and T. Blackwood Murray, were formerly employed by the Glasgow based Mo-Car Syndicate which later became the Arrol Johnston Company, who themselves built trucks between 1904 and 1913. Albion's early vehicles were lightweight machines but in 1910 they launched their A10 truck for 3 to 4-ton payloads. This had a 4-cylinder gasoline engine and chain drive. The A10 met War Office requirements and a total of 6000 were built for service in World War I.

During the 1920s Albion's truck range expanded to include forward-control models, and shaft drive took over from chain drive. The distinctive rising-sun trademark appeared on their

■ RIGHT *One of Albion's most famous trucks was this chain-drive A10 3-tonner produced between 1910 and 1926.*

■ LEFT *The LK51 forward-control 4-tonner was a short-lived model built between 1931 and 1933. It had a 4-cylinder gasoline engine.*

■ BELOW *Albion entered the heavy-weight market with the CX range in 1938. This is a 1948 diesel-engined CX7N tanker.*

■ RIGHT *One of Albion's most successful post-war trucks was the Chieftain FT37. This dropside truck dates from 1958.*

radiators around 1928. Albion referred to their forward-control trucks as "overtypes", a term normally associated with steam lorries.

With the introduction of pneumatic tyres in the late 1920s, Albions began to take on a more modern appearance although their cab designs were still very basic. The heaviest truck model of the period was a 5-tonner, built along very rugged lines. During the early '30s a 6-ton payload four-wheeler and an 8-ton payload six-wheeler became available and some models were offered with diesel power using Gardner and Dorman engines. Albion developed their own diesels by the end of 1933. 1935 saw the introduction of one of Albion's most successful four-wheelers – the KL127.

That same year, the company took over Halley Motors Ltd of Yoker, Glasgow, who were building a similar product range. The Halley factory provided Albion with the additional capacity they needed to expand their range. In 1936 a short-lived maximum-capacity eight-wheeler – the T561 – was introduced, but few were built. Very soon a completely new heavy-duty truck range – the CX – appeared. This embodied two, three and four-axled trucks with payload ratings from 7 to 15 tons.

Albion were important suppliers of military trucks during World War II, their range including 3-ton 4×4s, 10-ton 6×4s and heavy-duty tank transporters. The immediate post-war range was the CX, more or less carried over from before the war, plus a choice of four-wheelers which were now given type names – the Clansman (5-tonner), Chieftain (5/6-tonner) and Clydesdale (7/8-tonner). An updated range of heavy trucks, designated the HD range, was launched in 1951, but almost immediately afterwards Leyland Motors announced the takeover of Albion.

Most of Albion's heavy trucks were then phased out as they competed with Leyland's own products, and the much reduced Albion offering consisted of medium-weight four and six-wheelers. Leyland's influence began to show in the late 1950s when an all-new pressed-steel cab – the LAD – became standard.

The same pattern of cab appeared on Leylands. Albion briefly returned to the eight-wheeler market in 1958 with their Leyland-powered Caledonian, which was outwardly similar to Leyland's Octopus.

Following the formation of the British Leyland Motor Corporation in 1968, under which BMC trucks became part of the Leyland group, a new factory built by BMC at Bathgate was to become BLMC's medium truck plant. By 1972 production of Albions at their Scotstoun plant had been phased out, along with the Albion name. However, a Leyland range called the Blue Line continued to be built at Bathgate until 1981. These embodied Albion components and retained the Chieftain, Clydesdale and Reiver names.

■ ABOVE LEFT *The underfloor-engined Claymore of the mid 1950s was popular as a furniture van and as a brewery distribution truck.*

■ LEFT *The Reiver and Super Reiver were Albion's heaviest models during the 1960s. This example features the LAD Vista-Vue cab.*

MILAN, ITALY

ALFA ROMEO

■ RIGHT *A 1959 Alfa Romeo Mille 14-tonne gvw truck powered by a 6-cylinder diesel engine.*

The Alfa Romeo name is more usually associated with fast cars than with trucks. However, the company, whose origins go back to 1906, was a significant truck producer between 1930 and 1967. After launching a light truck at the 1930 Milan Show, Alfa (derived from Societa Anonima Lombarda Fabbrica Automobili) Romeo went on to build heavier trucks based on Büssing designs. These were generally of normal-control layout but the heaviest, including a three-axled model for 10-tonne payloads, had forward-control cabs. From 1945 onwards the range was predominantly forward-control. They were noted for their ample power output, their 900 model for 8-tonne payloads having a 9.5 litre/579cu in diesel developing 130bhp. In 1948 an unsuccessful design for independent front suspension using torsion bars was made. A stylish new model, the Mille, was introduced in 1957 for use as a 14-tonne gross four-wheeler, 32-tonne articulated outfit or 36-tonne drawbar combination. A 10-tonne six-wheeler with steering rear axle was also available. The Mille and its 900 fore-runner were also built under licence by the Brazilian company FNM of Rio de Janeiro.

LITTLETON, COLORADO, USA

AMERICAN COLEMAN

From the beginning, Coleman Motors Corporation specialized in all-wheel drive trucks. Coleman, later known as American Coleman, began production in 1925. The first trucks were 4×4 and 6×6 types. They found favour with the highway authorities, the army, fire departments and airports. Off-highway trucks for the logging and oil industry also appeared. Crane carriers were supplied to the army during World War II, production of bonneted trucks restarting from 1945. The factory closed temporarily from 1949 to 1951 as the result of a strike. In 1968 American Coleman built a most unusual truck consisting of a four-wheel steer tractor which could be coupled to a semi-trailer to form a rigid, the tractor axles effectively acting as a dual-steer front bogie. They dubbed it the "Space Star" and it was powered by an 8V-71N Detroit Diesel. It never proceeded beyond prototype stage. The company continues to build 4×4 specialized trucks for airport, highway maintenance, dockyard shunting and fire-fighting, as well as carrying out four-wheel drive conversions to other vehicles.

MOSCOW, RUSSIA

AMO

AMO (Automobilnoe Moskowvoskoe Obshchestvo) began production in November 1924, exactly seven years after the end of the Great October Revolution, and marked the start of Russia's own motor-vehicle industry. The first truck, the AMO-F15, was based on a Fiat 1½-tonner. Predicting a massive demand for trucks in the USSR, the Moscow factory was extended in 1931 and another model, the AMO-2 for 2½-ton payload, entered production. This was replaced by an improved version, the AMO-3, in 1932. The factory was renamed Zavod Imieni Stalina in 1933 and the products were accordingly relaunched as ZIS. ZIS trucks were to continue in production until 1956 when the factory was once again renamed as the Zavod Imieni Likhacheva (ZIL).

■ ABOVE *The 1924 AMO F15 was basically a Fiat 1½-tonner built under licence. It was the first Russian truck, and forerunner of the ZIS.*

EAST KILBRIDE, SCOTLAND

ARGYLE

Argyle trucks were produced in small numbers between 1970 and 1973. The company was formed by Argyle Diesel Electronics Ltd but competition from larger manufacturers rendered the enterprise non-viable. Only one type of any significance was built, the Christina 16-ton gross four-wheeler powered by a Perkins 6.354 diesel engine with an Eaton Yale & Towne 5-speed gearbox and Eaton 2-speed rear axle. The cab was a standard off-the-peg pressed-steel unit from Motor Panels of Coventry and resembled those used on Seddon and Guy trucks. There were plans for a tractor unit and a rigid six-wheeler but the company ceased trading before they entered production. However, Argyle did produce one Cummins-engined heavy tractor called the Trilby for the British Steel Corporation. This one-off was designed to haul a 120-ton load.

■ ABOVE ***The Argyle Christina was a short-lived make. It was assembled from proprietary components, including a Perkins 6.354 diesel, Eaton 2-speed axle and Motor Panels cab.***

NEWCASTLE-UPON-TYNE, ENGLAND

ARMSTRONG SAURER

■ BELOW ***Early 1930s Armstrong Saurer trucks were built in the UK but based on Swiss engineering.***

During the 1920s a number of imported Saurer trucks had entered the UK and, in 1930, the Saurer company was seeking to set up a British manufacturing base. It was the Newcastle engineering company of Sir W. G. Armstrong-Whitworth that acquired the manufacturing rights and production commenced in 1931. The trucks were called Armstrong Saurers but were primarily of Saurer design. While bonneted trucks were typical of the Swiss market, British operators demanded forward-control or "cabover" types, so these were added specially for the UK.

The range included the Defiant four-wheeler with 4-cylinder diesel and the 6-cylinder Dauntless four-wheeler. A six-wheeler went under the name Dominant. Gasoline engines were offered initially but were soon dropped. Saurer was renowned for its well-engineered diesel engines. Armstrong Saurer launched their Samson eight-wheeler in 1934. This was a very advanced machine with overdrive gearbox and eight-wheel air brakes. Despite encouraging sales during the mid '30s, production ended in 1937.

■ LEFT ***The 22-ton gross Samson was a British development and was one of the first rigid eight-wheelers on the market in 1934.***

PRESTON, ENGLAND

ATKINSON

In 1907 Edward Atkinson and his brother Harry, together with a partner George Hunt, set up an engineering business, Atkinson & Co. at Frenchwood Avenue, Preston. The company soon moved to bigger premises at Kendal Street, undertaking motor and steam wagon repairs. It took on a repair agency for Alley & MacLellan, the founders of the famous Sentinel Steam Waggon, built at that time in Polmadie, Glasgow. By 1916 Edward Atkinson had decided to build a wagon of his own design, having relinquished the Alley & MacLellan agency when Sentinel moved to Shrewsbury in 1915.

While Atkinson produced a successful steam wagon, the post-war slump of the 1920s saw the company in financial difficulties. A brief but unsuccessful merger with Walker Bros. of Wigan, under which the products were called Atkinson-Walker wagons, ended in 1930. With no prospect of recovery, the company fell into the hands of the receivers who eventually sold it to St Helens-based speculators J. Jenkins, H. Johnson and J. Lytheer in 1931. At first the rescued company carried on with steam wagon repairs as well as carrying out third-axle conversions, but some experimental trucks were built in 1931 – one being a bonneted four-wheeler with Dorman diesel engine. Following the death of Edward Atkinson in 1932, a London businessman, W. G. Allen of Nightingale's Garage, bought the business and it was renamed Atkinson Lorries (1933) Ltd.

Soon it was decided to build diesel-engined trucks to compete with the likes of Foden and ERF. In 1935 Atkinson moved to bigger premises in Marsh Lane, Preston. Early Atkinsons featured Gardner diesels, Kirkstall axles and vacuum hydraulic brakes. In the six years up to the beginning of World War II only 50 trucks were built but they included four, six and eight-wheelers as well as twin steer six-wheelers. Atkinson was one of the few UK manufacturers to be allowed to continue civilian truck production during World War II, under

■ TOP *An early Atkinson L1266. This 1937 six-wheeler was powered by a Gardner 6LW.*

■ ABOVE LEFT *Atkinson briefly used a Krupp steel cab. This rare example operated in the UK.*

■ LEFT *Atkinsons changed little during their first 20 years. This 1951 L1586 was basically a 1930s design.*

■ RIGHT *Atkinson retained the traditional exposed radiator to the last. This is a 1972 Defender with Mk.2 fibreglass cab.*

■ LEFT *One of Atkinson's largest trucks was the mighty Rolls Royce-powered Omega of the late 1950s.*

the direction of the government. Shortages of Gardner engines led to the use of AEC diesels during the war.

Post-war demand was such that Atkinson moved again, into a new factory at Winery Lane, Walton le Dale in 1947. It was, by then, one of the UK's leading truck builders and it soon built up a healthy export trade. Throughout the 1950s and '60s Atkinson went on to produce a huge variety of road-going and specialized trucks. Its mainstream products were forward-control load carriers and it diversified into heavy-duty dump trucks and special oil-field tractors such as the massive bonneted Omega of 1957, which was powered by a 333bhp supercharged Rolls Royce C6.SFL coupled to a Self Changing Gears 8-speed semi-automatic gearbox and capable of hauling 90 tons over desert terrain.

The haulage range consisted of four, six and eight-wheelers powered almost exclusively by Gardner diesels. From 1958 all models could be ordered with a new Mk.1 fibreglass cab with a panoramic two-piece wrap-around windscreen. During the late 1960s the company offered an increasing choice of tractor units, including twin-steer and rear-steer six-wheeled versions. Engine choice was widening to include Rolls Royce and Cummins diesels. From 1963–64 a weight saving specification was offered in the form of Weightmaster models with a trimmed-down specification and lower-powered engines for the lightest possible unladen weight.

As Atkinson's world markets expanded, assembly plants were established in Australia, South Africa and New Zealand where vehicles were tailored to local operators' requirements. In 1968 it tried to increase its share of the European market by fitting Krupp steel tilt cabs when Krupp of Essen in Germany phased out truck production. Atkinson Vehicles (Europe) was set up in Antwerp, Belgium, but the venture was short- lived.

In the late 1960s models were given type names and the taller Mk.2 fibreglass cab was introduced. The main tractor units were the 4×2 Borderer and 6×2 rear-steer Leader. The most popular rigid was the Defender eight-wheeler, although some six-wheeled Searchers and four-wheeled Raiders were also built.

The highly successful Atkinson company, renamed Atkinson Vehicles Ltd from 1954, was the subject of a takeover by Seddon Diesel Vehicles Ltd of Oldham in 1970 and Seddon-Atkinson Vehicles was born. The last Atkinson-badged trucks were built just five years later. Seddon-Atkinson's independence was short lived – the company was taken over by International Harvester of North America in 1974.

The last hint of Atkinson's identity is the presence of their "circle A" badge on current Seddon Atkinson trucks.

■ BELOW *The Viewline, seen here on a 6×4 heavy-haulage tractor, was offered between 1966 and 1972.*

LONGBRIDGE, ENGLAND

AUSTIN

■ LEFT *The Austin K2 box van of the late 1940s was nicknamed the "Birmingham Bedford".*

■ BELOW LEFT *One of the first volume-built UK trucks with a tilt cab was the 1964 Austin FJ.*

■ BOTTOM LEFT *The 1950 Loadstar was a modernized version of the earlier K4, dubbed the "K4 Series II".*

The Austin Motor Co. Ltd was established in 1908 but did not begin building trucks, other than light commercials, until 1913. Their first truck was a 2 to 3-tonner of unusual design, having a 29hp 4-cylinder gasoline engine mounted ahead of the radiator, a layout featured in Renaults and Macks of the era. Drive to the rear wheels was via a 4-speed gearbox and twin propshafts – one to each rear wheel. The semi-forward-control driving position and raked steering wheel meant that the steering column was fully exposed ahead of the dash panel.

Approximately 2000 of the early Austin trucks were built but the company left the truck market and did not return until 1939, when it launched a completely new range. That range was modelled to a degree on Bedford's, covering the 1½ to 4/5-ton payload bracket. They bore such similarities that they were often referred to as the Birmingham Bedford. Austin dubbed them the "K" models. Large numbers were built for military use during World War II.

After the war the K range continued with little change, but a stylish new model named the Loadstar entered the scene in 1950. Austin also began to offer a Perkins diesel-engine option. A significant event took place in 1951 with the formation of the British Motor Corporation by the merger of Austin and the Nuffield organization who produced Morris Commercial trucks. By the mid 1950s Austins and Morris Commercials were being commonized. A new range of forward-control models featured a bought-in steel cab manufactured by the Willenhall Motor Radiator Co. BMC's own diesel engines became available on the new models, the largest being a 5.1 litre/311cu in 6-cylinder unit for the 701 7-tonner launched in 1955. A 5.7 litre/347cu in version was introduced later.

Austin's (or by now BMC's) next design was the unusual "angle-planned" FG range which featured a new concept in cabs with entrance doors on the back corners. This was claimed to be a safety feature although it did allow the occupant to step out into the path of other traffic. By this time Austin and Morris trucks ("Commercial" had been dropped) were virtually identical under the BMC umbrella.

In 1961 a completely new BMC truck plant was opened at Bathgate in Scotland. A new model, the FJ, appeared in 1964 and was one of the first British trucks to feature a tilt cab. After the formation of the British Leyland Motor Corporation in 1968, created by the merger of British Motor Holdings and the Leyland Motor Corporation, Austins and their Morris counterparts were all badged as BMC, and from 1970 all carried the Leyland name and were marketed as the Redline range.

OGDEN, UTAH, USA

AUTOCAR

Louis S. Clarke, in partnership with his brother John, founded the Pittsburgh Motor Vehicle Co. in 1897 to build cars and light commercials. Fearing that the company name sounded too provincial, Clarke decided to change it to the Autocar Company in 1899. It was in 1908 that a small cabover truck, the XVIII ("18" in Roman numerals), was introduced. This rudimentary vehicle was very sturdily built and featured shaft drive. Just one year later a longer version, the XXI.U (21.U) appeared, the "U" signifying "under-cab" engine. That model remained in production until 1926. In 1919 it was joined by a larger, more powerful truck for 5-ton payloads, the Model 26.

In the late 1920s a new range of bonneted conventionals was launched, the largest being a six-wheeler with 6-cylinder gasoline engine. Payloads were up to 7½ tons. Throughout the 1930s Autocar built a wide range of medium and heavy trucks for loads of 3 to 12 tons, plus a heavy-duty 4×4, the DC10044. While most were bonneted there were cabovers too, such as the stylish UD model of 1937 which remained in production for over a decade. From 1938 certain Autocar types were also built by Kromhout in The Netherlands.

In 1953, following a downturn in the United States truck market, Autocar was taken over by White Trucks. Production was transferred to a new factory at Exton, Pennsylvania. From that point on Autocar concentrated on heavy-duty trucks tailored to customers' requirements and their name became synonymous with high-powered trucks for logging, mining and heavy haulage.

In 1974 Autocar production was transferred from Exton to a new plant in Ogden, Utah. New models with a stronger White influence appeared, such as the Construcktor 2 which featured a White Road Boss cab. In 1980 the White Motor Corporation went into receivership and Volvo of Sweden stepped in to purchase the company, which then became the Volvo White Truck Corporation. Autocar trucks continued to be marketed by the new organization and, as well as their heavy-duty machines, a new highway truck,

the AT64F, was launched. This was aimed at the owner operator.

A joint venture between Volvo and GMC trucks was announced in 1986, at a time when General Motors were pulling out of heavy truck production. The resulting organization was called Volvo White GMC. The Autocar name was still retained and in late 1987 a new model, the White GMC Autocar, aimed at the construction industry, was launched. This was offered in 4×2, 4×4, 6×4, 6×6 and 8×4 form. Since 1995 the White GMC name has been dropped and Autocar has become Volvo Autocar. Volvo Trucks North America, the company's official title since 1997, continues to offer five basic Autocar models, two 4×2s and three 6×4s, all of which are powered by Volvo diesels.

■ TOP *1994 Autocar five-axled mixer has all-Volvo running units.*

■ ABOVE LEFT *Concrete mixer based on Autocar 8×4 at work in Auckland, New Zealand*

■ LEFT *Rugged build and powerful performance made Autocars a popular choice in the construction industry.*

BRUSSELS, BELGIUM

AUTOMIESSE

■ LEFT ***A late 1950s Automiesse with licence-built Gardner diesel, seen in Antwerp, Belgium.***

■ BELOW LEFT ***Among the last Automiesse tractors was this sleeper-cabbed Büssing-engined machine operating in Brussels during the 1960s.***

Miesse SA was an old established heavy vehicle manufacturer which, prior to 1939, traded as Jules Miesse et Cie. The original company dated back to the turn of the century and built steam cars and trucks. Heavy trucks up to 5-tonnes payload with gasoline engines were introduced in the mid 1920s and car production ceased in 1926. Some of their heavy trucks were powered by their own 8-cylinder gasoline engine while others, in the early '30s, had Junkers two-stroke opposed piston diesels. From 1932 Miesse were given a licence to build British-designed Gardner diesels and these became standard fitment in most of their extensive truck range. One interesting vehicle introduced in 1939 was a rigid eight-wheeler with steering fourth axle and a payload capacity of 16 tons. One notable feature of this was a roof-mounted radiator. In 1939 the company was renamed Automiesse and the trucks were badged as such during the last few years of production.

After World War II Automiesse concentrated on heavy-duty trucks using Gardner engines, including the 8LW. To meet the higher power demands of their heavy 38-tonne tractors, Detroit Diesel and Büssing engines were specified. Production was dwindling in the late 1960s and the company closed in 1972.

OTHER MAKES

■ **ADC (ASSOCIATED DAIMLER COMPANY)**

SOUTHALL, LONDON, ENGLAND

Between 1926 and 1928 the Daimler Company, owned by BSA, and the Associated Equipment Company (AEC) formed a joint marketing agreement. Daimler had already been supplying engines to AEC for some years. The first ADCs were existing AEC designs but in 1928 a new lightweight ADC model, the 423/424, appeared. AEC-based goods vehicles such as the 418 3-tonner, the 507 5-tonner and the Ramillies 6-tonner, were all built as Associated Daimlers for a brief period but from 1928 ADC was disbanded, AEC and Daimler becoming separate companies again.

■ **ASHOK LEYLAND**

ENNORE, MADRAS, INDIA

Beginning in 1948 as Ashok Motors to assemble Austin cars, the company went on to assemble Leyland trucks in 1950. In 1954 Leyland Motors took a stake in Ashok and the company became Ashok Leyland. Products consisted of certain Leyland types, many of which continued in production long after they had become obsolete in the UK. Most Ashok Leylands had locally built cabs and bodies. In 1987 Leyland's holding was taken over by the Hinduza Group and Iveco Fiat SpA, and manufacture of the old-style Ford Cargo, also badged Ashok Leyland, began alongside the Leyland-based trucks which still remain in production.

■ LEFT ***This late 1920s ADC fuel tanker was based on an AEC design.***

■ ABOVE RIGHT ***The 1999 Ashok Leyland Comet 1611.***

■ RIGHT ***The latest Ashok Leyland Cargo 1614 dump truck.***

OTHER MAKES

■ ASTRA

PIACENZA, ITALY

Astra was founded by Mario Betuzzi in 1948. After a few years in business reconditioning war-surplus trucks, Astra turned to assembling heavy dump trucks in 1954. In the 1960s it began building its own dump trucks powered by engines from Detroit Diesel, Mercedes and Fiat. By the late '70s it had cornered 50 per cent of the Italian market for such vehicles. Since 1985 Astra has been part of the Iveco Group and still produces heavy construction vehicles on two, three and four axles.

■ AVAILABLE

CHICAGO, ILLINOIS, USA

Available trucks were in production for 47 years, the company having been founded in 1910. The first truck was a chain-drive machine powered by an underslung 2-cylinder gasoline engine for ¾ ton. Larger trucks for 2-ton payloads were added and within five years or so Available was offering a choice of four types, the heaviest of which took a 5-ton payload. A Continental 4-cylinder engine was used. In 1920 a bonneted 7-tonner was announced, powered by a 50hp Waukesha engine, but demand was insufficient to continue production for more than a short period.

Throughout the 1930s and '40s Available offered a range of 4×2s and 6×4s in "normal" and "forward" control with a choice of engines. Models ranged from 4-tonners up to maximum-weight tractor-trailer combinations. Most of Available's modest production, which totalled around 2500 trucks, were sold to local customers. In 1957 the company was taken over by the Crane Carrier Corporation of Tulsa, Oklahoma.

■ ABOVE RIGHT ***DAF engineering went into the development of the AVM heavy-duty trucks built in Zimbabwe.***

■ LEFT ***Part of the Iveco Group, Astra specialize in heavy-duty chassis for the construction industry.***

■ AVM

HARARE, ZIMBABWE

Since 1972 AVM heavy trucks, based on DAF designs but fitted with locally built cabs, have been assembled by Dahmer & Co. The company is 80 per cent owned by the British-based Lonrho Group. The vehicles, mainly 6×4s, are heavily built to withstand the demanding local operating conditions. Gross weights go up to 55 tonnes. DAF diesels and ZF gearboxes are used. The heaviest outfits have two trailers, built by Zambesi Coachworks in Harare.

■ ABOVE RIGHT ***AWD used the Bedford TM cab for its prototype heavy tank transporter.***

■ LEFT ***An Available 10-ton payload six-wheeler from 1947.***

■ RIGHT ***The AWD MTL33 was a Cummins-engined 8×6 with a driven trailer bogie.***

■ AWD

DUNSTABLE, ENGLAND

AWD trucks were built at the former Bedford GM plant following General Motors' decision to withdraw from the UK truck market in 1986. David J. B. Brown, the founder of Artix Ltd, an articulated dump-truck company subsequently sold to Caterpillar, took over the business in 1987 and continued to build selected Bedford models under the AWD name. The Bedford name was retained by GM for its van range. Numerous special all-wheel drive prototypes were built, aimed at the military and export markets. Existing Bedford trucks were used as the basis for David J. B. Brown's patent Multidrive articulated 8×6 and 10×6 machines. Limited sales resulted in the closure of AWD in 1992 when the business was sold once again to Marshall SPV of Cambridge, who were granted permission to reinstate the Bedford name.

BOREHAMWOOD, ENGLAND

BARON

■ LEFT *The Baron 7-tonner was a simple, ruggedly built export truck for local assembly in developing countries.*

In 1957 Peter Boulas anticipated a demand for a rugged, no-frills truck that would withstand the harsh operating conditions of third-world countries. Historically, British manufacturers had dominated such markets with the likes of the Bedford TJ which was basic, reliable and easy to repair. Boulas feared that foreign influence was threatening British industry and designed the Baron 6 and 7-tonners, officially announced in 1964, after carrying out a seven-year market survey in the developing countries of Africa and the Far East. They were powered by a Perkins 6.354 diesel with 4-speed gearbox and Eaton 2-speed axle. Prototypes were built featuring pressed-steel front cowls by Airflow Streamlines who supplied similar designs to Commer and Dodge. Barons were to be exported in CKD (Completely Knocked Down) form for assembly in the third world. Just two versions were released – the 6-ton Master BN6 and the 7-ton Senior BN7. Baron withdrew from the market in 1970 through lack of demand.

MADRID, SPAIN

BARREIROS

■ LEFT *A Barreiros 82/35 twin-steer rigid eight-wheeler of the late 1960s with self-steering rear lift axle.*

■ BELOW LEFT *Twin-steer six-wheelers like this Barreiros 26/26 had safety benefits on twisting mountain roads.*

The manufacture of Barreiros trucks began in 1958 but the company's founder, Eduardo Barreiros Rodriguez, had begun an engineering business at Orense in north-west Spain some 18 years earlier. He specialized in converting gasoline engines to diesel and in 1951 transferred his business to Madrid where he began manufacturing diesel engines and, later, complete trucks. The first Barreiros truck was a 6-tonner called the Victor. Further medium-weight models bearing the names Halcyon, Condor, Azor and Super Azor appeared during the 1960s.

From 1963 the Chrysler Corporation bought into the company and by 1967 owned a majority holding. The name was changed to Chrysler Espana SA but the Barreiros nameplate was still used on the trucks until 1978. From then on the range was marketed under the Dodge brand. During the 1960s and '70s the range broadened to include maximum-weight tractor units and six and eight-wheelers.

In 1978 the French group Peugeot-Citroën acquired Chrysler's European truck interests when the American giant ran into financial difficulties. Just three years later Renault Véhicules Industriels took control of the Dodge truck operations both in the UK and Spain and the last vehicles to have the distinctive Barreiros cab were badged as Renaults. Renault updated some models with their Premier cab.

TIPTON, ENGLAND

BEAN

■ LEFT *A 1928 Bean 30cwt truck powered by Bean's own 4-cylinder gasoline engine.*

While Bean was not a significant truck builder, it qualifies for brief mention. After setting up as A. Harper, Sons & Bean Ltd in 1923, the company produced a few light vans. It changed its name to Bean Cars Ltd in 1924 with plans to become a major volume producer with financial backing from the Sheffield steel-making company, Hadfields. Their products consisted of 1½ and 2½-ton payload trucks, the latter appearing in 1929 as the Empire model. A forward-control development of the Empire model for a 4-ton payload was announced in 1930 but, in the difficult trading conditions of the economic depression, the company was forced to close in 1931.

DALMUIR, SCOTLAND

BEARDMORE

Beardmore trucks might be seen as one of the lost causes of the UK industry. The name Beardmore became famous on taxicabs which were built in Paisley, Glasgow from 1919 to 1933. In 1933 production was transferred to Hendon in north London where taxi production continued until 1969. After the business left Paisley, William Beardmore Ltd – another branch of the Beardmore Engineering concern set up at nearby Dalmuir to build heavy trucks. They drew up plans for maximum-weight four, six and eight-wheelers for payloads of 8 tons, 13 tons and 15 tons respectively. A handful of four-wheeled 8-tonners were actually built but the company folded in 1937 before its final plans could be realized. William Beardmore Ltd had earlier been involved in the production of Beardmore-Multiwheeler road tractors.

■ ABOVE *A 1924 Beardmore 1½-ton truck with integral van body.*

■ BELOW *Beardmore-Multiwheeler tractors were based on the French Chenard-Walcker and were built at Beardmore's London factory. This is a 10-ton Cobra.*

LUTON & DUNSTABLE, ENGLAND

BEDFORD

■ LEFT ***Bedford's 6-cylinder WLG 2-tonner of 1931 became a market leader in the UK.***

■ LEFT ***The A type 5-tonner was built between 1953 and 1957 and had the option of a Perkins P6 diesel engine.***

The old established Vauxhall car company was taken over by General Motors in 1925. Around the same time GM had begun assembling Chevrolet trucks, first at Hendon in north London and then at Luton, in order to get a foothold in the UK market and, even more importantly, to gain access to the vast export markets of the British Commonwealth. Luton-built Chevrolet 30cwt U types with their powerful 6-cylinder gasoline engines sold well, and GM marketed them with a strong "British-built" message, choosing to brand the 1930 model as the Chevrolet Bedford. In 1931 a new 2-ton gasoline model, the W type, was launched as a "pure" Bedford and it featured many developments, including a heavy-duty rear axle with fully floating hubs and dual rear wheels. The new Bedford 2-tonners won a substantial share of the light truck market. An improved 30cwt model cloned from the last Chevrolet U type was introduced in 1932 as the Bedford WS. From that point the American identity disappeared completely and Bedfords were presented as a purely British product.

During the 1930s the range expanded to include the WT semi-forward-control model for 3-ton payloads, although the company openly described it as the truck for a 50 per cent overload, making it in effect a 4½-tonner. Plans for a completely new range – the K (1½ tons), M (2 to 3 tons) and O (4 to 5 tons) – were afoot in the late '30s but the launch coincided with the start of World War II. Full production was delayed until 1946. Meanwhile Bedford became a major supplier of military trucks and tanks. Around 250,000 were built for the war effort, including a hastily designed 4×4 called the QL.

In the post-war years the K, M and O models went into full production and they were joined in 1950 by the S type 7-tonner, called the Big Bedford. All were hugely successful and gave Bedford a big share of the home market as well as healthy worldwide export sales. From 1953 the K, M and O models were replaced by the A models which were mechanically similar but had a stylish new cab with strong American influence in its styling. Perkins diesel engines became a factory-fitted option to the standard gasoline engine.

Bedford's wartime experience with building 4×4s was put to use in developing their new 3-ton military R type, which was launched in 1952 and became the standard 3-ton truck for the Ministry of Defence. It also sold well in civilian form and to overseas military

■ BELOW LEFT ***The OSS was a joint development between Bedford and Scammell Lorries and used Scammell's automatic coupling.***

■ LEFT *Announced in 1950, the S type 7-tonner had a 110bhp 6-cylinder gasoline engine with an optional Perkins R6 diesel from 1953 and, later, a Leyland O.350.*

customers. By 1954 Bedford production had outgrown Luton and was transferred to a new factory in Dunstable. The next significant launch was the legendary TJ model which won Bedford massive export business in the developing countries of the third world. The TJ continued to be built, often for local assembly abroad, right through to the 1990s.

In 1960 Bedford announced a new forward-control range, the TK, which replaced the S type. Heavier versions appeared during the 1960s and in 1966 the company entered the heavy-duty scene with the completely new KM featuring a 7.63 litre/466cu in diesel engine of their own design. Nineteen seventy-two saw another bold move when a 32-ton tractor powered by General Motors' own two-stroke 6V-71 Detroit Diesel was announced. Just two years later a complete range of heavy-duty trucks, the tilt-cab TM range, appeared. This did not enjoy the same success as earlier Bedfords and this, combined with the economic recession of the late 1970s, saw Bedford's business decline.

From 1980 General Motors' car and truck divisions were separated and Bedford became the UK Division of the GM Overseas Commercial Vehicle Corporation. Into a declining market Bedford launched a tilt-cab medium truck, the TL, but it was an underfunded development of the old TK and Bedford continued to lose orders to competition. Bids by GM to strengthen their UK truck manufacturing operations by the acquisition of the Leyland Group failed as a result of UK government intervention and, partially as a result of this, the American giant decided to withdraw from the UK truck business in 1986. The Bedford plant was sold to David J. B. Brown who resumed production of selected models under the AWD name. AWD only survived for five years and the remains of the once giant Bedford operation were sold to Marshall Special Purpose Vehicles of Cambridge. A handful of Bedfords have been built in the 1990s.

■ BELOW *The TK range was in production from 1960 to 1984.*

■ BOTTOM *The TM heavy-duty tilt-cab range appeared in 1974. This EVV3 32-tonner had a Detroit Diesel 6V-71.*

FRONT ROYAL, VIRGINIA, USA

BERING

■ LEFT *Bering's cabover HD80ST tractor is based on the Korean Hyundai and has a Cummins or Caterpillar diesel.*

Bering is a completely new United States truck manufacturer, established in 1997. The Bering Truck Corporation and its subsidiary, Bering Distribution LLC, manufactures, imports and distributes Class 3 to 8 trucks. The product range comprises 13 models using Cummins and Caterpillar engines combined with chassis designs sourced from the Korean company, Hyundai. The range is divided into Light-Duty (LD), Medium-Duty (MD) and Heavy-Duty (HD) groups. The lightest HD model, the two-axled HD33M, grosses 33,000lbs/15 tonnes, putting it in Class 7, while six other HD models, the HD60ST, HD80ST and HD80TT tractor units and the HD67MX, HD65DP and HD83DP rigids, fall within Class 8. The Class 8 rigids are specified for concrete-mixer and dump-truck duties, the HD83DP being a cab-forward 8×4 for 38 tons gvw. Tractor units, including the maximum-weight 6×4s, are of cabover layout.

LYON, FRANCE

BERLIET

■ LEFT *Berliet's chain-drive 3-tonne CAT forward-control truck of 1913.*

■ BELOW LEFT *The revolutionary Stradair 5-tonner of 1967 featured air suspension.*

■ BOTTOM LEFT *The mid 1950s TLM was noted for its extravagant styling. This 35-tonne artic has those classic lines.*

The history of the company that was to become one of France's largest and most famous truck manufacturers dates back to the very beginning of motoring history. As long ago as 1894 Marius Berliet began experimenting with his own design of gasoline engine which he installed in a primitive car. In 1902, with financial backing from a rich Lyon merchant called Giraud, he produced a dual-purpose twin-cylindered vehicle with chain drive which could be transformed from a car into a truck by exchanging bodywork in a matter of minutes. This led to the introduction in 1906 of Berliet's first true commercial chassis, a chain-drive 2-tonne cab-over-engine machine powered by a 4-cylinder gasoline engine. Within a couple of years Berliet were offering models with 1½ to 4 tonnes payload capacity.

By the onset of World War I Berliet had added a forward-control 6-tonner to the range and a normal-control chain-drive 4/5-tonner designated the CBA. This was a particularly successful machine and 25,000 were built for the armed services. In the depressed market following the war, when sales were stifled by a glut of war-surplus trucks, matters were made even worse by the French government imposing a tax on profits gained during the war. Berliet ran into financial difficulties, going into receivership in 1921. By taking on reconditioning work and disposing of some assets, the company was able to survive to introduce a new and successful range of light commercials in 1924. Within two or three years Berliet was adding new models including heavier trucks up to 7½ tonnes payload. By now most models of 4 tonnes and below had pneumatic tyres and virtually all were of normal-control layout.

Experimental diesel engines were being tried in 1930 and by 1931 they

■ RIGHT ***This 26-tonne GBH12 6×4 dump truck featured a 250bhp 6-cylinder diesel.***

■ BELOW RIGHT ***This mid 1970s 880KB box van had a 5.8 litre/360cu in 4-cylinder diesel and a payload of 8 tonnes.***

were offered in what was an updated CBA chain-drive. The early engines were not as reliable as hoped but by 1933 an improved version was available and was offered in the new shaft-drive GD2. The CBA model was discontinued after 22 years in production. By the late 1930s diesel power was available in models from 3 tonnes and upwards, the heavy models being bonneted six-wheelers for 12 to 15-tonnes payload.

A few years after World War II Berliet's range took on a completely new look. The plain, sober styling of the late 1930s, appealing though it was, gave way to the sensational new GLR model with its protruding bonnet (hood) and curvaceous lines. Berliet built up an extensive export business in overseas countries. Trucks were exported as far afield as China. Berliet also began trying out some specialized heavy trucks including their biggest – the 1957 TOO 6×6 for oil exploration in the Sahara.

In 1967 Berliet was absorbed into Citroën. The first product of that joint operation was the highly unusual Stradair truck which embodied many innovative features. It had variable height air suspension, front-wheel drive options and a distinctive protruding bonnet (hood) with offset radiator which gave it a very striking appearance.

While bonneted heavy vehicles continued to be popular in France, Berliet also offered forward-control models which, from 1959, featured a stylish new cab dubbed the "Relaxe" cab. During the 1960s Berliet's range was quite complex with up to 120 different types on offer. They also had many overseas production facilities throughout the world, including Eastern Europe, China, North Africa, South America, Spain and Portugal. In spite of this, the French government felt that Berliet was vulnerable to foreign takeover and sought to merge the company with Saviem, which had been formed in 1955 by the merger of Renault, Latil and Somua. Eventually the merger did take place, in 1974 and, through Saviem, Renault took control of the Berliet empire.

In the meantime Berliet had come out with new models, the most notable being their TR260 with its Premier cab which was to become a familiar sight in many parts of the world. Another development in the 1970s was the Club of Four cab. This was a joint development by Saviem, Volvo, DAF and Magirus-Deutz. The cab, most familiar on Volvo's F7 and Renault's GR and GF ranges, was for a while fitted to Berliet-badged trucks.

However the Berliet name was shortly to disappear after Saviem was reorganized into RVI (Renault Véhicules Industriels) in 1978. Indeed, by 1980 Berliet's history had drawn to a close.

■ BOTTOM ***The Berliet GAK drawbar outfit features the Relaxe cab which was very advanced when introduced in 1959.***

LONGBRIDGE, ENGLAND, & BATHGATE, SCOTLAND

BMC

■ LEFT *The 701 7-tonner made its debut in 1955 and was the first truck to carry the BMC badge.*

After the Austin Motor Company and Morris Commercial Cars Ltd were merged into the British Motor Corporation, formed in 1951, Austin and Morris trucks were progressively commonized and a new 7-ton payload model, the 701 was launched in 1955 as a BMC 7-tonner. The vehicle was powered by a BMC 5.1 litre/311cu in diesel engine.

Later the trucks reverted to being Austin or Morris but in 1968, after the formation of the British Leyland Motor Corporation, the trucks, by then produced at a new plant in Bathgate, Scotland, were badged BMC for a period of just two years. They were then integrated into the Leyland product range as Redline models and were all badged as Leyland.

■ ABOVE *A BMC Mastiff artic powered by a Perkins V8 diesel engine.*

■ BELOW *The BMC FG medium truck featured the "angle plan" safety cab.*

■ BOTTOM *A 1970 BMC Laird six-wheel, low-loading brewery truck.*

■ BELOW *The BMC VA was specially designed for parcel deliveries.*

IZMIR, TURKEY

BMC

In 1964 the British Motor Corporation licensed a new Turkish assembly plant, BMC Sanayi ve Ticaret A.S., at Izmir to build BMC trucks. Production began in 1966. Some were built with the familiar UK pattern cab while others featured locally built cabs. BMC Turkey also assembled Land Rovers and agricultural tractors.

Trucks built at Izmir were powered by Leyland engines built under licence at the plant. In 1983 BMC signed a licence agreement with the Swedish Volvo Truck Corporation and two years later with the Cummins Engine Co. Following the link-up with Volvo, BMC launched their Fatih series of trucks powered by turbo-charged diesels. There are four models from 17 to 27-tons gross weight. The cab fitted is a development of the old Leyland Redline G cab. More recently, in 1994, BMC launched their Professional range, covering the same gross weights but featuring a completely new cab designed by the renowned stylist Pininfarina. These are powered by the Cummins B-series 6 litre/366cu in diesel. The same truck is marketed in the UK through MAN's subsidiary ERF as the EP6.

■ ABOVE RIGHT *The 1999 BMC Fatih garbage truck used a modified version of the old Leyland G cab.*

■ RIGHT *Ultra-modern styling by Pininfarina is a feature of the latest BMC Professional range.*

BRISTOL, ENGLAND

BRISTOL

■ LEFT *The Bristol HG6L was developed as an eight-wheeler for use by the British Road Services organization.*

■ BELOW *When British Road Services demanded articulated vehicles, Bristol introduced the HA6G with Gardner diesel.*

Production of Bristol trucks was twice interrupted by long spells of inactivity. The origins of the manufacturer can be traced back to 1874 and the formation of the Bristol Tramways Company which, in turn, became the Bristol Tramways & Carriage Company in 1887. This should not be confused with the Bristol Wagon & Carriage Works Ltd, which built steam wagons between 1904 and 1908.

Bristol was mainly concerned with the manufacture of gasoline-engined buses, but some were fitted with truck bodies during the period 1908 to 1914. After a small number of trucks were built for the War Department in 1915, production was suspended until 1919 but a few trucks were built during the 1920s.

The company was purchased by the Thomas Tilling Group in 1931 after which production was turned over fully to buses for Tilling's own operations. The Tilling Group was nationalized by the British government in 1948 so Bristol was then under state control. With the formation of British Road Services (BRS) as part of the new nationalized transport system, the controlling body, the British Transport Commission, decided to utilize the Bristol manufacturing plant to design and build a standardized maximum-weight goods vehicle. The trucks were built in two forms. The first was a 22-ton (later 24-ton) gvw rigid eight-wheeler (HG6L), the second a 24-ton gcw articulated tractor-trailer combination (HA6G, HA6L and HA6LL).

Leyland's O.600 diesel was standard for the HG6L while the HA6G, HA6L and HA6LL were built with a Gardner 6LX or a Leyland O.600 or O.680. The first models, HG6Ls, appeared in 1952 and Bristol truck production continued until 1964 when new UK weight legislation rendered them obsolete. A plan to build a 30-ton gcw Bristol tractor unit, the HD, was shelved. From then on BRS, by then partly denationalized, only bought off-the-shelf trucks. Bristol themselves continued to build buses, with Leyland taking a substantial shareholding in the company during the late 1960s.

CORTLAND, NEW YORK, USA

BROCKWAY

■ LEFT *This multi-axle Brockway 761 series based in Michigan features a Mack R series cab.*

The Brockway Motor Truck Co. built its first truck in 1912 but the company's origins as the Brockway Carriage Co. dated back to the 1870s. The 1912 machine was an open-cabbed, chain-driven buggy-style vehicle with large-diameter cart wheels and was powered by a 3-cylinder two-stroke engine with air cooling. Four-cylinder Continental engines became standard fitment on subsequent trucks and Brockway was a significant supplier of military vehicles during World War I.

After the war they introduced models for 1½ and 3-ton payloads, with a more conventional layout and worm drive. A 5-tonner was added in 1921. Brockway soon grew to become one of the largest truck manufacturers in the United States. Four-cylinder Wisconsin engines were fitted in the late '20s and from 1928 that company's 6-cylinder engines were also used. The same year Brockway took over the Indiana Truck Corporation but in 1932, during the difficult trading conditions of the depression, they re-sold Indiana to the White Motor Corporation.

In 1934 Brockway launched what was one of the largest trucks on the market – the V1200, capable of hauling loads of 27 tons and powered by a massive American La France V12 gasoline engine delivering 240bhp. Sales were limited as axle weight restrictions in many States discouraged such machines. It was withdrawn from the range in 1937. During the late '30s the Brockway range listed 16 different models from 1½-ton trucks up to artics for 10-ton payloads, powered by Continental 6-cylinder gasoline engines.

From 1942 Brockway were engaged in defence work but the post-World War II era saw the introduction of the impressive 260 bonneted highway tractors for gross combination weights up to 32 tons. These were powered by 6-cylinder Continental gasoline engines and had Fuller gearboxes and Timken rear axles. This range was still Brockway's core product when the company was taken over by Mack Trucks. Under Mack ownership Brockway were to remain autonomous, although their first venture into forward-control tractors saw them adopting the Mack F Series cab. The first range announced under Mack ownership was the all-new Huskie, which featured a three dimensional Huskie emblem on the bonnet, echoing the famous bulldog motif of its parent.

From 1963 diesel engines from Cummins, Caterpillar and Detroit Diesel became alternatives to the standard Continental gasoline units, which were phased out completely in the late '60s. In 1968 Brockway dubbed their 5-speed gearbox and 2-speed axle package "Huskidrive". An 8-speed gearbox and 2-speed axle were also offered. One of Brockway's last models was the low profile, cab-forward Huskiteer in two and three-axled rigid form. In April 1977 Mack decided to close the plant down.

■ BELOW *A Brockway N527TL artic with Cummins NHC250 from the mid 1970s.*

BRUSSELS, BELGIUM

BROSSEL

■ BELOW *A late 1950s Brossel 32-tonne gcw tractor engaged on brewery transport in Belgium.*

Ets Brossel Frères (later Brossel Frères Borg et Pipe SA) built medium-weight bonneted trucks. In the post-war years the company produced derivatives of the FN 4×4 and the Ardennes artillery tractor. In the 1960s Brossel was absorbed into the Leyland Motor Corporation and some Leyland models were marketed in Belgium and France as Brossel before the company was wound up in the mid '60s. The last new range launched in January 1961 was called the Europ. This featured an adaptation of Leyland's fibreglass Vista-Vue cab and Power Plus diesel engine similar to the Leyland Beaver.

CHARLOTTE, NORTH CAROLINA, USA

BROWN

■ BELOW *Initially, all Brown tractor units were built for exclusive use by Horton Motor Lines.*

Brown was one of a number of low-volume manufacturers set up as an offshoot of a transport operator. In this case it was J. L. Brown, chief engineer of Horton Motor Lines, who designed and gave his name to the marque. Horton's had been operating a mixed fleet of Mack, Autocar, White and Corbitt tractor units, and J. L. Brown aimed to combine the best features of existing trucks into his own design. The first, designated the 21-R, appeared in 1939, powered by a Continental gasoline engine. Production continued until 1953 – an improved model, the 513, appearing in 1946. Cummins diesels were available from 1949. In all, approximately 1000 Browns were built.

BRASOV, ROMANIA

BUCEGI

■ LEFT *The 1962 Bucegi 5-tonne truck was based on Russian technology and powered by a V8 gasoline engine.*

Bucegi trucks for 3 to 5-tonne payloads were built at the AB (Autocamioane Brasov) works from 1962 to replace the original SR 101 models. Based on a Russian ZIL design, they were also marketed as the Carpati. Power unit was a V8 gasoline engine. Bucegis wore an SR badge on their bonnets (hoods) which stood for "Steagul Rosu" ("Red Star"), the works where they were built. Production ended during the 1970s when Autocamioane Brasov switched to building trucks based on MAN designs. Since 1990 the company has traded as Roman SA and currently markets a wide range of trucks under the DAC brand. (see "DAC", "Roman" and "SR").

BRAUNSCHWEIG, GERMANY

BÜSSING

■ BELOW *The driver of this 1903 Büssing 3-tonne truck had no protection from the elements.*

The motor-truck industry was still in its infancy when Heinrich Büssing set up his company at Braunschweig in 1903. That was the year he built his first truck – a 2-tonne payload machine powered by a 2-cylinder gasoline engine and featuring worm drive. That successful design was later built under licence by other companies in Germany, Austria, Hungary and by Straker Squire in England. Before World War I Büssing had already progressed to building heavy-duty trucks for loads of between 5 and 11 tonnes, powered by 6-cylinder engines. In 1923 Büssing introduced what was the first rigid three-axled truck and bus chassis in Germany and, during the '20s, cornered the market for such machines.

A number of other manufacturers were taken over by Büssing in the late 1920s. The first acquisition was Mannesmann-Mulag Motoren und Lastwagen AG of Aachen. Then the Elbing plant of Automobilfabrik Komnick AG was bought, followed a year or so later by Nacionale Automobil AG (NAG). After the last takeover Büssings was called Büssing-Nag until 1950. Büssing began building trucks with diesel engines around 1930 and pioneered the horizontal underfloor diesel in 1936.

During World War II Büssing once again supplied military vehicles,

■ RIGHT *A 1953 Büssing 12000 with 200bhp underfloor diesel engine. The truck grosses 24 tonnes or 32 tonnes with trailer.*

including 6×4 armoured cars and an 8×8 with all-wheel steering. After the war, civilian production resumed with a 5-tonne and later a 7-tonne truck chassis. In 1950 the company name became Büssing Nutskraftwagen GmbH and production was concentrated on underfloor-engined trucks which were to become the firm's speciality. Most tractor units and all normal-control trucks had vertical engines, but in the mid 1960s there was a version of their Commodore maximum-weight tractor unit, the 16–210, which had a horizontal diesel mounted under the cab ahead of the front axle, the gearbox being mounted halfway along the truck's chassis.

Büssing took over the Borgward plant at Osterholz-Scharmbeck in 1962 and built their military 4×4 4-tonner under the Büssing name until 1968. The factory was then sold to Faun-Werke GmbH. In 1969 links were formed with another major German truck manufacturer, MAN, and two years later the MAN takeover of Büssing was announced. The unique underfloor-engined truck range continued in production under the MAN-Büssing name through to the late 1980s.

■ LEFT *A Büssing BS22L with U12DA 280bhp underfloor engine for 38 tonnes gtw.*

■ BELOW *A 15-tonne gross Büssing with 7.5 litre/457cu in underfloor diesel engine engaged on furniture transport in Switzerland.*

■ ABOVE *The imposing Büssing 8000 bonneted tractor was a true classic of the early 1960s.*

OTHER MAKES

■ BELAZ

ZHODINO, BELORUSSIA

In November 1958, in the former road-building machinery works of Dormash at Zhodino, a heavy-duty 25-tonne tipping truck was assembled from components made at MAZ (Minsk Auto Zavod). That vehicle was designated a MAZ-525. The following year production began of 25-tonne dump trucks under the BELAZ (Belorussian Auto Zavod) name. In 1961 the first experimental 27-tonne BELAZ-540 dump truck was produced, followed in 1963 by the BELAZ-548 for 40-tonne payloads.

Full-scale production of the 540 27-tonner began in September 1965 and the 25-tonne version was discontinued. The 540 was a half-cab with 375bhp diesel engine. There was also a 540-A with 360bhp V-12 diesel and 3-speed hydro-mechanical transmission. In 1975 two 75-tonne and one 120-tonne BELAZ dump trucks were made. Two years later prototypes of a 110-tonne dump truck, the BELAZ-7519, were built and the 75-tonne dumper went into production.

■ ABOVE ***The Russian Belaz 256D of the early 1970s was powered by a V8 diesel engine and grossed 26 tonnes.***

Throughout the 1980s and '90s the product range has expanded with the introduction of airport tow tractors capable of hauling aircraft weighing up to 200 tonnes. An experimental 180-tonne dump truck, the 7521, was built in 1979. An even bigger machine, aimed at the mining industry, was a 280-tonne dump truck put into operation in 1990 at a Russian open-cast mine. The current BELAZ range covers dump trucks for 32, 42, 55, 80 and 120 tonnes. Since 1996 BELAZ has built the 75131 dump truck for 130-tonne loads.

■ BELSIZE

MANCHESTER, ENGLAND

Belsize Motors Ltd was not in the truck market for very long and is better remembered for its fire engines. The company existed from 1901 to 1925 but did not begin truck building until 1911 when a shaft-drive 3-tonner was introduced. This was also used as a basis for charabanc bodywork. A 1½-ton truck appeared in 1914. Production tailed off after World War I and Belsize concentrated on vans and taxis.

■ ABOVE ***The 1911 Belsize 3-tonner had a 4-cylinder gasoline engine and shaft drive.***

■ BERNA

OLTEN, SWITZERLAND

Berna was an old established manufacturer that built its first truck, the K model, in 1905. It featured chain drive and a 2-cylinder gasoline engine located under the driver. At that time the company was called J. Wyss Schweicherische Automobilfabrik Berna. Not many of these early trucks were built. The same is true for a larger version which was also tried for a short period. The first successful heavy truck was a remarkably advanced machine launched in 1906. The G1 was a 5-tonner with a 6.3 litre/384cu in 4-cylinder gasoline engine, 4-speed gearbox and shaft drive to a double-reduction rear axle.

■ ABOVE ***Berna trucks were virtually identical to Saurer. This Swiss outfit is a 4VF with drawbar trailer.***

In 1906 the company was renamed Motorwerke Berna AG. In spite of their high standard of engineering, Berna trucks failed to sell in sufficient quantities to be viable and the company was faced with financial crisis within the first three years of its existence. Berna was rescued from closure in 1908 by a British firm, Hudson Consolidated, and was renamed once again as Berna Commercial Motors Ltd. A new range of goods vehicles for payloads of 1½ to 6 tonnes was introduced. After five years in British hands it returned to Swiss ownership as Motorwagenfabrik Berna AG. From 1914 to 1918 Bernas were also built under licence in the UK by Henry Watson & Sons Ltd of Newcastle-upon-Tyne.

In 1915 Berna launched the highly successful C2 with 4-cylinder gasoline engine. It was supplied in large numbers to the Swiss, British and French armies and was renowned for its ruggedness. Many thousands were built up until 1928, adapted to civilian operations. A new heavy truck, the G type, appeared after World War I and, to meet demand from Germany, Austria and other areas, licensed assembly plants were set up in Vienna and Budapest. By the late 1930s Berna sales were rivalling those of Switzerland's leading truck manufacturer, Saurer. In 1928 Berna began building Deutz diesel engines under licence.

The following year Adolph Saurer AG took a controlling interest in Berna and, although the Olten products continued to be marketed as Berna, an increasing Saurer influence was evident in their design. Saurer diesel engines ousted the licence-built Deutz units. The distinctive bonneted U range, based on the C type Saurer, appeared in 1936. During World War II a large number of Berna trucks were built for the Swiss army. They were virtually identical to the corresponding Saurer models.

After the war Berna added forward-control versions to the U range with a traditional but nevertheless pleasing

OTHER MAKES

appearance. For the remainder of Berna's existence their products were largely identical to those of Saurer. In the 1960s some Italian OM trucks were badged as Bernas following a marketing tie-up between Saurer and the Fiat group. Saurer themselves vanished in the early 1980s – after merging with FBW to form Nutzfahrzenggesellschaft Arbon & Wetzikon (NAW), the joint operation was absorbed into Daimler-Benz in 1982.

■ BERNARD

ARCUCIL, FRANCE

Camions Bernard was neither the oldest nor the largest of French truck manufacturers but in their 43-year history they did produce some very impressive road-going trucks. The company began as SA des Bennes Basculantes E. Bernard, who built hydraulic tipping gear. In 1923 Bernard produced a complete vehicle for a 2-tonne payload. Pneumatic tyres came as standard and the power unit was a side-valve, 4-cylinder gasoline engine of

■ ABOVE ***The Bernard TD15035 was powered by a licence-built Gardner 6-cylinder diesel.***

2.6 litres/158cu in. Three years later they introduced a high-speed, low-frame coach chassis powered by an American-built 6-cylinder engine.

The company name became Camions Bernard in 1929 and began building its own 3.6 and 5.2 litre/219 and 317cu in engines. A new range of bonneted heavy trucks was launched, developed from the earlier coach chassis. In 1932 an 8-cylinder 6½-tonner with 5-speed gearbox was launched. This had automatic chassis lubrication as standard. Shortly afterwards Bernard turned to diesel power, having acquired a manufacturing licence from the British company Gardner. Four and 6-cylinder engines were built plus a 3-cylinder unit for lighter models. In 1935 a 15-tonne bonneted heavy six-wheeler with the 6-cylinder diesel and a remote mounted gearbox was launched.

Pre-war designs were continued after 1945, but production was concentrated entirely on trucks. New models in the early '50s featured full air brakes, 12.1 litre/738cu in diesels, disc transmission handbrakes and power steering. During the late '50s Bernard introduced higher-powered engines up to 200bhp and 10-speed transmissions. The early '60s range included 4×2 trucks and tractor units and long-wheelbase six-wheel rigids. The bonneted Bernard was perceived as old fashioned and sales declined. In 1963 Bernard launched forward-control versions of their trucks with a futuristic cab designed by Philippe Carbonneaux. Though modern it lacked the solid elegance of the old Bernard. In any case it came too late – in 1963 Mack Trucks took over the company and renamed it Automobiles Bernard. The trucks began to appear with Mack engines and transmissions. The alliance did not last and in 1966 Bernard closed down.

■ BORGWARD

BREMEN, GERMANY

Borgward were not a major player in the truck market. In their early existence from 1924 to 1938 they built light vehicles. In 1928 they took over Hansa Lloyd and used the brand names Goliath and Hansa Lloyd. From 1938 the company was re-established as Carl F. W. Borgward Automobile und Motorenwerke and trucks from 1½ to 5 tonnes were introduced. All were available with diesel engines. Military vehicles, including half tracks, were built during World War II and after the war Borgward reintroduced a civilian 3-tonner. In 1949 the company became Carl F. W. Borgward GmbH. A 4-tonner, including a tractor-unit version, was listed. Improved models appeared in 1954 and forward-control versions in 1958. Financial problems forced the closure of the company in 1962.

■ ABOVE ***A late 1950s Borgward B544 powered by a 6-cylinder, 5 litre/305cu in diesel engine.***

■ BRUCE-SN

EDINBURGH, SCOTLAND

Unorthodox designs of truck sometimes emerge aimed at a specific type of operator. Brewery fleets have come up with various designs of ultra-low loading trucks for distribution work. The Bruce-SN was one example. Built in 1984 to Scottish & Newcastle Brewery's design, it was of front-wheel drive layout, the load carrying section being virtually a large box. The truck took its name from the late Alan Bruce, S & N's transport manager, who masterminded the design. Using a modified Bedford TL cab, the Bruce-SN was powered by a Cummins B-series diesel mounted with flywheel and gearbox facing forward, a transfer box taking the power to a Kirkstall steer-drive front axle. The truck featured single rear wheels. A similar experimental design was based on the Leyland Freighter. Neither type was to enter quantity production.

■ ABOVE ***This experimental front-wheel drive Bruce SN was developed specifically for brewery distribution.***

DETROIT, MICHIGAN, USA

CHEVROLET

■ LEFT ***Chevrolet's production concentrated on light commercials during the 1920s and '30s.***

■ BELOW LEFT ***A Chevrolet 2-ton payload truck of the early 1930s.***

Chevrolet's early history is more concerned with cars, the first commercials – lightweight ½-tonners – appearing in 1918. The company was founded in 1911 by Louis Joseph Chevrolet, a Swiss racing driver, and William Crapo Durant, who had just lost control of the GM empire he had started in 1908. Through a number of shrewd business moves Durant regained control of GM, which absorbed Chevrolet in 1918. GM was already well established in the truck market. Chevrolet trucks, as distinct from car-based commercials, first appeared in 1926 and in 1929 the company introduced its famous "cast iron wonder" 6-cylinder of 3.2 litre/ 194cu in. The engine gained an enviable reputation for durability and smooth power.

From 1925 Chevrolet had begun fitting fully enclosed cabs as opposed to just offering chassis cowls. In 1930 they purchased the body works of the Martin-Parry Corporation of Indianapolis which enabled them to offer complete trucks with a variety of bodywork. Production was still largely concentrated on light trucks and pickups and Chevrolet boasted impressive truck sales volumes which had exceeded half a million by 1930.

Late 1930s models included the 1½-ton R model with its spoked wheels and splash-lubricated 4-cylinder engine. This was marketed in the UK. An important development was the LQ of 1929 which took the new 3.2 litre/ 194cu in overhead valve six. It was this that formed the basis for the British Bedford launched in 1931. At that time GM's heavy trucks were all badged as GMC and it wasn't until the late '30s that Chevrolet began to produce heavier models up to 2-tons payload, and true heavy-duty trucks were not to appear in the Chevrolet line-up until 1960.

The 60 and 70 series bonneted range came in 1961 and these marked a move into heavier trucks and artics. The forward-control T series tilt-cab range set Chevrolet firmly on the truck scene and from then on they progressed to maximum-weight line-haul trucks generally similar to their GMC stable mates. Detroit Diesel two-stroke engines and Fuller Roadranger transmissions were typical of the drivelines but during the 1960s big V6 and V8 gasoline engines were still available.

In the late 1960s Chevrolet developed a futuristic gas-turbine truck which was attractively styled and dubbed the "Titan 3". It boasted automatic

■ BOTTOM LEFT ***By the late 1930s Chevrolet had adopted a more stylish cab for their 2-tonner, designated the VD.***

■ BOTTOM RIGHT ***The 1964 M80 tandem with dump body had a choice of V8 gasoline or V6 diesel engine.***

■ BELOW LEFT *The 1970s Titan 90 was Chevrolet's heaviest cabover and offered a choice of Detroit Diesel or Cummins engine.*

■ BELOW RIGHT *This 1963 TM 80000 features a 180cm/72in BBC tilt cab.*

■ RIGHT *The Chevrolet Bison, with a choice of 6V-92TT Detroit Diesel or Cummins 14 litre/854cu in diesel engine, was introduced in 1976.*

transmission, power-operated tilt cab, electric windows, retractable headlights and built-in stereo radio and radio telephone. The truck did not go into production since it was basically a concept vehicle but it made quite an impact when it was exhibited at the New York World's Fair.

In 1970 the Titan name was reintroduced on a new cabover range for up to 34 tons gcw. Cummins diesels up to 320bhp were available. In 1976 the Chevrolet Bison conventionals, similar to GMC's General, were launched. One year later came the 90 Series Bruin for heavy-duty line-haul work. This too came with a choice of Detroit or Cummins diesels, and gasoline engines had by then been discontinued. Chevrolet continued to offer a full range of light and medium-weight trucks. Production of heavy-duty trucks was discontinued from 1980 and the company reverted to producing lightweight models.

PARIS, FRANCE

CITROËN

■ LEFT *The medium-weight bonneted Citroëns of the 1960s era featured car-like styling.*

While Citroën's production was mainly concentrated on light vehicles from 1919 until the early 1930s, bonneted trucks in the 2 to 4-tonne payload class appeared in 1934. Frontal styling was clearly based on Citroën cars. A new truck range with modern styling appeared in 1954 as the 23 or 55 models for gvws of 3.5 to 9.3 tonnes. The lighter models had a 4-cylinder Perkins diesel option. A heavier 60 model was added for 9.8 tonnes gvw but, in tractor-unit form, could gross 13.75 tonnes or 17.4 tonnes with drawbar trailer. Semi-forward-control versions also appeared. The heavier models had a choice of Citroën 6-cylinder diesel or gasoline engines. Citroën's heavy trucks were phased out after the company acquired Automobiles M. Berliet in 1967. Some trucks were marketed as Citroën-Berliet until Citroën was merged into Automobiles Peugeot in 1974.

LUTON & DUNSTABLE, ENGLAND

COMMER

■ ABOVE *The updated Superpoise of the late 1940s had styling reminiscent of the Humber car.*

■ LEFT *The Commercar 3-ton truck of 1920.*

The Commer name came on to the market in 1926, but the history of the company began some 20 years earlier. A prototype truck was built in 1903, its design being centred around a revolutionary design of pre-selective gearbox invented by a talented engineer called Linley. The new enterprise was set up by Julian Halford who saw great possibilities for the new gearbox which eliminated sliding gears and thus the dreadful crashing sounds that drivers made with conventional gearboxes. The Commercial Car Company had been formed in 1905 at Lavender Hill in south London. The premises were unsuitable for large-scale truck production so, almost immediately, a site for a new factory was selected at Biscot Road, Luton, some 56km/35 miles away. The first Luton-built vehicles were completed in 1906.

While the initial prototype had been a 4-ton chain-drive forward-control machine of rudimentary design, the production trucks were bonneted types of similar load rating. In the ensuing five years the range expanded to include 1½, 2 and even a 7-ton model and Commercial Cars began exporting trucks to the United States, Canada, Australia, New Zealand and as far as Siberia. Their leading product was the chain-drive RC type although shaft-drive models were also tried. Some 3000 military trucks were supplied to the War Office during World War I.

■ BELOW *The Q type Commer Superpoise was announced in 1939 and production carried on after World War II.*

Tough post-war trading conditions saw Commercial Cars struggling to survive and in 1926 the Coventry-based car manufacturer Humber took over the company and the name was changed to Commer Cars. Just two years later both were absorbed into Rootes Ltd – a car distribution company set up by William and Reginald Rootes some years earlier. Under new ownership Commer designs were modernized and vehicles were built along more mass-produced lines. The Invader 2-tonner appeared, powered by a Humber Super Snipe engine. This

■ LEFT *The 1951 Commer QX featured a forward-entry cab and underfloor 6-cylinder gasoline engine.*

was followed by the G6 6/7-tonner with set-back front axle and a 100hp 6-cylinder gasoline engine. A 1½-tonner, the Raider, was also added to the range.

In 1935 the LN models entered the scene and with them came the first appearance of a radiator design which was later to grace the first Q model, Superpoise, launched in 1939. Karrier had joined the Rootes empire in 1934 and in subsequent years some commonization began to take place between Commer and Karrier models. In the post-war era a modernization program began with a restyled Superpoise introduced in 1948 with frontal styling borrowed from the Humber car. A completely new forward-control model, the QX, had many advanced features, including a forward-entry cab and an underfloor 6-cylinder gasoline engine. In 1954 Commer introduced their revolutionary Rootes TS3 (Tilling Stevens, 3 cylinder) two-stroke, opposed-piston diesel. Maidstone-based Tilling Stevens, who developed the engine, had joined the Rootes Group in 1949.

By 1953 Commer had outgrown the Biscot Road plant and moved to a new factory in Dunstable some 8km/5 miles west of Luton. Normal-control models were given a restyled cab which was also used on certain Dodge trucks.

■ ABOVE *The last model to carry the Commer name was the 1974 Commando.*

■ BELOW *This 1960 six-wheeler was powered by the unusual Rootes 3-cylinder opposed-piston TS3 engine.*

Commer introduced a factory-approved 10-ton six-wheeler with Unipower third axle. In 1962 a completely new forward-control cab was introduced on the C (TS3-engined) and V (Perkins-engined) ranges. Two years later, with the raising of UK weight limits, Commer launched their 16-ton gvw Maxiload. At about the same time, Dodge's parent company Chrysler bought a 46 per cent share in Rootes and by 1967 had gained full control of the group.

A process of integration between the Dodge, Commer and Karrier ranges began, all production being centred on Dunstable. Ultimately, the Commando range was launched in 1974 at which time the TS3 engine was phased out. By 1976 the Commer name had followed suit and all products were marketed as Dodge. Chrysler UK sold out to PSA Peugeot-Citroën in 1978. Later still, in 1981, Renault Véhicules Industriels took control of the company and the Commando models which had initially been Commer and featured new black plastic grilles became Renaults.

HENDERSON, NORTH CAROLINA, USA

CORBITT

■ LEFT *The 1948 Corbitt tractor was characterized by its exceptionally high driving position.*

One of America's pioneer automobile manufacturers, Corbitt was formed in 1899 and began truck manufacture in 1913. The early trucks were bonneted chain-drive 1-tonners with 4-cylinder Continental gasoline engines. By the '20s, as the Corbitt Motor Truck Co. (founded in 1916), they were one of America's largest truck producers with a range for 1 to 5-ton payloads. Heavier models up to 15 tons gvw were added during the 1930s. Medium-weight trucks of the '30s utilized the radiator grille and front-end sheet metal from the contemporary Auburn car. Military and civilian trucks were produced during World War II, including heavy-duty 6×4 tractor units. The post-war years saw an impressive range of bonneted and cabover heavy tractors. Volume truck production came to an end in 1952 when the founder, Richard Corbitt, retired. In 1957 there was an attempt to revive the Corbitt business with a build-to-order approach but this was short-lived.

MANCHESTER, ENGLAND

CROSSLEY

■ LEFT *A 25/30hp Crossley ambulance, a type supplied in large numbers to the allied forces in World War I.*

Although Crossley's origins date back to the 19th century when Sir William Crossley acquired world rights (excluding Germany) from Nicolas August Otto to develop his newly invented four-stroke gas engine of 1869, the company did not enter the truck market until 1932. Prior to that it specialized in engine manufacture and, from 1912, in military vehicles. In 1932 a range of forward-control diesel trucks for payloads of 3 to 7 tons was introduced. Three years later came their Atlas forward-control model, including a double-drive six-wheeler for 12 tons. Their brief presence in the civilian market was brought to an end at the outbreak of war in 1939. During World War II a 4×4 forward-control 3-ton truck, the Q type, was supplied in large numbers to the RAF. No further trucks were built and the company was absorbed, along with the Maudslay Motor Company, into Associated Commercial Vehicles in 1948. ACV marketed certain AEC vehicles under the Crossley name in some export markets through to the late 1950s.

BUDAPEST, HUNGARY

CSEPEL

■ LEFT *Csepel's forward-control range of the 1970s featured a French-designed Chausson cab.*

The Csepel Engineering Works near Budapest began truck production in 1950 with a bonneted 3-tonner based on a design from Steyr Daimler Puch of Austria. Much of Csepel's production was for export. The company developed all-wheel drive trucks of 4×4, 6×6 and 8×8 configuration. At first Csepel built their own diesel engines but went on to buy in engines from Rába for their heavier trucks. In the late 1970s the company became Csepel Autogyar. The trucks were exported to Asia and Africa under the Mogurt name. Some medium-weight Csepels featured the Chausson forward-control cab as fitted to Star trucks in Poland. The company still markets a full range of medium-weight trucks and buses.

OTHER MAKES

■ CALEDON

GLASGOW, SCOTLAND

The company that built Caledon trucks was originally Scotland's Commer (Commercial Cars) agent called Scottish Commercial Cars. In 1914 supplies of Commers dwindled as the War Department commandeered the company's production. In 1915 Scottish Commercial Cars marketed a bonneted chain-drive four-wheeler with a Dorman 4-cylinder gasoline engine which they named Caledon. The vehicle was fitted with a French-designed Dux gearbox built under licence.

Some heavier vehicles were built using Buda and Hercules engines. A Buda powered their largest truck, a 10-ton payload six-wheeler in 1924 which had a 6m/20ft long body. This was believed to be the first rigid six-wheel truck in the UK. Declining sales during the depression led Caledon into financial difficulties and the company was sold to Richard Garrett & Sons Ltd of Leiston, Suffolk. A couple of Garrett-Caledons were built but further production was abandoned.

■ LEFT *Caledon trucks built in Glasgow were originally inspired by World War I Commers.*

■ BELOW *Chenard-Walcker tractors had a unique coupling system to pull trailers.*

■ CANADA

MONTREAL, CANADA

Between 1956 and 1958 the Canadian Car Co. Ltd, a member of A.V. Roe, Canada, and the Hawker Siddeley Group developed a heavy-duty tractor unit in both 4×2 and 6×4 form, in co-operation with Leyland Motors (Canada) Ltd. The trucks, for gcw ratings of 58,000lbs/26 tonnes up to 99,800lbs/45 tonnes, were powered by Leyland 0.680 6-cylinder diesel engines and had a choice of Spicer and Fuller transmissions. Eaton axles were used. Canadas were of bonneted layout using an International Harvester steel cab. The leading model was designated the 680WT. Canadas were manufactured at CCC's Diesel and Engineering Division of Can-Car at Longueuil near Montreal. Can-Car, Canada's leading producer of railway carriages, also built semi-trailers at their Fort William plant.

■ CHENARD-WALCKER

SEINE, FRANCE

Based at Gennevilliers, Seine in France, Chenard-Walcker was set up in 1905 but only built light vehicles until turning to heavy-duty road tractors in 1919. These were bonneted short-wheelbase "tugs" for hauling independent trailers and featured the company's own unique design of trailer coupling. Load capacity of the early machine was around 5 tonnes but there was a later version for 10 tonnes. The tractors were marketed by subsidiary S.A. des Trains Chenard-Walcker-FAR. Licensed production by Minerva of Antwerp began in 1920 and, from 1930, they were also built under licence by Beardmore Multiwheeler in the UK. Those built in Antwerp were badged as Minerva. Heavy tractors for train weights of up to 25 tonnes were also offered. Some production of ordinary load-carrying 5 to 6-tonne trucks took place from the mid 1930s. The company was acquired by S.A. des Automobiles Peugeot in 1951.

■ CHINGKANGSHAN

NANJING, CHINA

The Chingkangshan bonneted 2½-tonne truck was first built in 1968 and is typical of Chinese vehicles that were produced in large numbers in several different factories. Chingkangshan trucks are built at the Chingkang Mountains Motor Vehicle factory in Kiansi province and are based on a Russian GAZ design, similar to the T'iao Jin and Yuejin 2½-tonne trucks from Nanjing which are built in large numbers for both military and civilian use.

■ LEFT *The Canada truck of the late 1950s was powered by a Leyland diesel.*

EINDHOVEN, THE NETHERLANDS

DAF

Production of DAF trucks began in 1950 when the first forward-control 5-tonner was launched, powered by a Hercules 6-cylinder side-valve gasoline engine. A Perkins P6 diesel was optional. Prior to that, as DAF Aanhangenwagenfabrik NV, it had built trailers. The origins of the company date back to 1928 when its founder Hubertus van Doorne and his brother Wim began in general engineering. During the German occupation of The Netherlands experimental military vehicles were built. In the post-war period the brothers shrewdly foresaw a boom in demand for civilian trucks and, with support from the Dutch government, a new truck plant was built at Eindhoven in 1949. So successful were the early DAFs that the factory was enlarged just a few years later to six times its original size.

From 1953 DAF began using Leyland engines and from 1956 began building them under licence. The model range expanded rapidly as did export sales. By 1958 they commanded a third of the Dutch domestic truck market. Soon DAF undertook its own development of Leyland's O.350, O.375, O.600 and O.680 diesels and was experimenting with turbocharged versions. Normal-control trucks were added to the range.

An important new model, the 2600, was launched in 1962 and this was to put DAF among the world leaders. It included maximum-weight rigids and artics for gross combination weights up to 40 tonnes, and featured a modern well-appointed cab for long-haul operations. DAF underwent further rapid expansion and a new cab and axle plant was opened at Ophasselt in Belgium.

In 1970 a new tilt-cab range was announced with increased power and gross weight ratings. DAF lost its independence in 1972 when the International Harvester Group bought a third of the company's shares. Some International components began to be introduced and for a brief period DAF offered a version of the American company's Paystar bonneted truck using DAF running units. DAF ran into further

■ LEFT ***DAF 30-ton rigid eight-wheelers became popular on the UK scene in the 1970s.***

■ BELOW ***The 16DD bonneted range was powered by a licence-built Leyland O.350 engine.***

■ ABOVE ***The T1800 was DAF's first volume-produced heavy articulated truck.***

■ BELOW ***DAF's flagship of the 1990s was the superbly appointed 95 series.***

■ **RIGHT** ***The 2600 range became DAF's most important seller of the 1960s.***

■ **BELOW** ***This DAF 2000 articulated bulk powder tanker dates from 1959.***

difficulties in 1975 following heavy investment in new facilities. Van Doorne's shareholding was reduced to 61 per cent in 1975 when the Dutch State Mines came to the rescue and purchased 25 per cent of DAF's shares.

Rigid eight-wheelers for 30 tons, the 2205s, became available in the UK from 1975. Models were added to the lighter end of the range in 1978 when DAF became involved with the Club of Four tilt-cab project. At the same time heavier-duty models up to 100 tonnes gtw were added, based on the 2800.

After International bought shares in DAF it took over Seddon Atkinson in the UK and bought a stake in the Spanish ENASA group which built Pegaso trucks. From 1978 International was forced, for economic reasons, to sell its European interests but the link between DAF, Seddon Atkinson and ENASA resulted in a joint Cabtec project which developed a new heavy truck cab used on all three makes. It went on DAF's new 95 series.

In 1987 when the British manufacturer Leyland ran into insolvency problems, DAF agreed a merger and subsequently the trucks were badged as Leyland DAF in the UK and DAF elsewhere. DAF were then to concentrate on heavy vehicles while Leyland produced light and medium trucks, these being marketed as DAFs in The Netherlands. All was not well, however, and by 1993 Leyland DAF collapsed when DAF became bankrupt and had to be rescued by the Dutch and Belgian governments. The Leyland plant became Leyland Trucks Ltd but the Leyland DAF dealer network continued to market both makes.

The last significant DAF launch was that of the 75 and 85 series that appeared in 1993, but various improvements have taken place in recent years including the introduction of their flagship long-haul tractor, the 95XF in May 1997. Since November 1996 DAF has been a wholly owned subsidiary of Paccar Inc., who also own Foden Trucks. Since taking over DAF, Paccar has also, in June 1998, acquired the Leyland truck business. During 1998 assembly of certain DAF trucks was introduced at the UK Foden plant. From January 2000 the Leyland name has been dropped from Leyland DAF.

GUILDFORD, ENGLAND

DENNIS

Dennis Brothers Ltd was formed in 1904 but John Dennis had began a cycle manufacturing business in 1895 and was joined by his brother Raymond in 1898. By 1901 they had begun producing cars, followed by their first commercial vehicle in 1903. A notable feature was its worm-drive rear axle, the first in Britain. As early as 1907 Dennis was offering a 5-ton payload truck with worm drive. From 1913 all production was to be concentrated on commercial vehicles, which included trucks, buses and fire appliances. The latter were to become synonymous with Dennis throughout its history. Engines were supplied by White & Poppe of Coventry, a company which Dennis took over in 1918 to become their engine plant until the early 1930s.

During World War I 7000 subsidy trucks were supplied to the War Department. Immediately after the war Dennis introduced a new 2½-tonner and in 1926 a truck range covering payloads of 4, 5 and 6 tons. These were powered by 5.7 litre/347cu in 4-cylinder gasoline engines. By then Dennis were building a very wide range of trucks, buses and municipal vehicles and had already achieved extensive export sales in many parts of the world. In 1933 the distinctive Ace 2½-tonner appeared, while a whole new truck range, including the Max 7½-tonner and the twin-steer Max Major for a 10½-ton load, was introduced in 1937. By now the heavier trucks had Dennis' own 4-cylinder diesel engine.

After World War II Dennis chose Pax (Latin for "peace") as the name for its popular 5-ton truck. New truck models were coming thick and fast in the late 1940s. These included the 1946 Horla 12-ton payload artic tractor, the 1946 Centaur four-wheeler and the Jubilant heavy-duty six-wheeler, which also appeared in 1946, powered by a 7.6 litre/463cu in 6-cylinder diesel. A very small number of rigid eight-wheeled Jubilants, no more than three, were also built in the early 1960s. As the 1950s drew on, Dennis concentrated more on buses and municipal vehicles but one interesting goods vehicle worthy of mention was the underfloor-engined Stork 3-tonner in 1952.

In 1957 the 14-ton gvw Hefty replaced the Max and by then Perkins engines were in wide use, as well as the occasional Gardner. In that same year the Centaur was replaced by the Condor. This and a lighter model, the Heron, had a modern style of forward-control cab.

■ ABOVE *The 1933 A model dropside truck took a payload of 2¼ tons.*

■ LEFT *The Dennis Horla tractor unit was based on the Pax and had a Dennis gasoline or Perkins P6 diesel engine.*

■ LEFT *1937 saw the launch of the Dennis Max for payloads of 7 to 8 tons.*

■ RIGHT *The Pax in both normal and forward-control was Dennis's best seller.*

■ BELOW LEFT *The 1974 Dominant had a fibreglass cab and Perkins 6.354 diesel.*

■ BELOW RIGHT *Dennis' last bid for a share of the market was with the Delta.*

One short-lived machine was the Paravan, a specially designed delivery van of 1958. It had an unusual angled up-and-over door on the left front corner and a Perkins P4 engine located behind the driver.

Dennis' position in the truck market was declining but in 1964 they made a bold effort to re-establish themselves with a Cummins V8-engined 32-ton tractor unit, the Maxim, plus a special low-loading Pax six-wheeler aimed at the brewery industry. By the late '60s Dennis' fortunes were at a low ebb, its once thriving truck and bus business having diminished, and it was relying almost entirely on municipal and fire vehicles, but the volume was insufficient. In 1972 the company was taken over by the Hestair Group, who also owned Yorkshire Vehicles and Eagle Engineering, both of whom specialized in municipal bodywork. A brief re-entry into the truck market came in the mid '70s with the Delta 16-tonner but home sales were few, the bulk of production being exported to the Middle East. With much of their business now given over to buses and municipal vehicles, Dennis were virtually out of the truck business, but they had one last assault on the 16-ton four-wheeler market in 1978 with a modernized Delta featuring a very square cab designed by the Ogle Design Group. This had the turbocharged Perkins T6.354 or a Gardner 6LXB but domestic sales amounted to a paltry 20 trucks per year. In 1983 Dennis pulled out of trucks completely. The company was taken over by Trinity Holdings in 1989 and became part of the Mayflower Group in 1998.

NORWICH, ENGLAND

DENNIS-MANN EGERTON

The Dennis-Mann Egerton was a semi-experimental one-off truck jointly designed by bodybuilder Mann Egerton of Norwich and the British Aluminium Co. of Greenford. It explored the benefits of super-lightweight-aluminium integral construction. With a gvw of 12 tons, the truck could carry an 8½-ton payload. It featured an attractively designed cab built on an aluminium frame and skinned with embossed aluminium sheeting that did not require painting. A Dennis 5.5 litre/335cu in, 92bhp horizontal 6-cylinder diesel engine was used, similar to that fitted in the Dennis Pelican bus. The drive was taken to an Eaton 2-speed axle through a Dennis 5-speed gearbox. Other running units were those used in the Dennis Centaur truck. The truck was used on the British Aluminium Co.'s own transport fleet for about eight years and was later scrapped. A similar experimental Mann Egerton truck, rated at 14 tons gvw, was built in 1956 using Albion components.

■ ABOVE *The all-aluminium integral Dennis-Mann Egerton was one of the lightest trucks of its era.*

RATHCOOLE, REPUBLIC OF IRELAND

DENNISON

■ LEFT *The Dennison eight-wheeler used Rolls Royce diesel power.*

In 1977 Dennison Trailers of Rathcoole, Dublin, entered the truck manufacturing business with a small range of maximum-weight 4×2 tractors and 6×4 and 8×4 rigids. Its founder George Dennison had built up a successful semi-trailer business. That was sold to Crane Fruehauf and truck manufacture took over. The trucks had a choice of Rolls Royce or Gardner engines and a Motor Panels cab similar to that used on Fodens. Fuller gearboxes and Eaton rear axles were used. In 1979 Dennison began fitting Finnish Sisu cabs. Most of its sales were in Ireland but some 8×4 rigids and 4×2 tractors were sold in the UK. Stiff competition and low volumes forced Dennison to withdraw from the market in 1981. Dennison reverted to trailer manufacture.

CHICAGO, ILLINOIS, USA

DIAMOND T

■ LEFT *Diamond T trucks sold well, and some were built in semi-forward-control layout.*

■ BELOW LEFT *An early 1970s Diamond Reo C11464 6×4 conventional.*

C. A. Tilt began building cars in 1905 and when one of his customers requested a truck he obliged. That was in 1911 and the truck was a 1½-tonner with chain drive. Tilt's emblem of the Diamond T Motor Car Co. was his initial "T" set within a diamond which symbolized quality. The company built only trucks from 1911 onwards and as early as 1915 had built up a national reputation for its products which ranged from 2 to 5-ton payload. Diamond T Model B Liberty trucks were built in large numbers during World War I and development took place throughout the 1920s and '30s. In 1928 the trucks boasted 6-cylinder engines, spiral-bevel rear axles and all-wheel braking. By then heavier six-wheeled trucks were being offered for 12-ton payloads. In the mid '30s the trucks were given stylish new cabs and by 1937 the first cabover models were appearing. During World War II Diamond T built their legendary 6×6 trucks and 6×4 12-ton tank tractors which were widely used as heavy-haulage tractors after the war.

A new range was launched in 1947 and by 1951 lighter trucks had been dropped. From then on production was concentrated on heavy-duty trucks, both normal and forward-control. Also in 1951 a new design of forward-control tilt cab appeared. This was also used on certain Hendrickson and International trucks. Diamond T was taken over by the White Motor Co. in 1958 and the word "Car" in the company title was changed to "Truck". In 1961 production was transferred to the company's Reo factory, also in White ownership from 1957. From 1967 Diamond T and Reo products were merged and the trucks were renamed Diamond Reo, a sub-division of the White Motor Corp.

A range of heavy-duty conventionals and cabovers were built under the new name up until 1971 when White sold the division to Francis L. Coppaert of Birmingham, Alabama. Under new ownership and independent once again, Diamond Reo Trucks Inc., as it was now

■ RIGHT ***This Diamond T 6×4 five-axled fuel tanker dates from the mid 1960s.***

called, developed some successful new models. These were the Royale cabovers with a choice of straight six, V8 or V12 engines, and the Apollo conventionals with a choice of Caterpillar, Cummins or Detroit Diesel power units. Their bonneted, heavy 6×4 tractor, the Raider, appeared in 1974. While sales were healthy in the early 1970s, Diamond Reo fell into financial problems in 1975 and the receivers were called in. The company was then purchased by one of the Diamond Reo parts distributors, Osterlund Inc. of Hansbury, Pennsylvania. From that point on one basic model, the bonneted Giant, was available in 4×2, 4×4, 6×4 and 6×6 form mainly for the construction industry.

CUIDAD SAHAGUN & MONTEREY, MEXICO

DINA

■ LEFT ***The DINA 761 6×4 tractor was powered by Cummins NTC-335 diesel and grossed 35 tons.***

DINA Trucks was founded in 1953, taking its name from Diesel Nacional SA. The government-owned company began by building trucks based on bonneted Diamond T designs but later DINAs became based on 4×2 and 6×4 International Harvesters. In 1975 a new factory was opened at Monterey, mainly for smaller pickup trucks. In 1985 DINA came under the control of General Motors. Recently Grupo DINA launched its HTQ (High Technology and Quality) truck range which conforms to North American and European legislation.

DETROIT, MICHIGAN, & DELAWARE, OHIO, USA

DIVCO

■ LEFT ***The Divco was the ultimate in purpose-built door-to-door delivery trucks.***

Although Divco specialized in door-to-door delivery vans they were such a memorable part of the American scene that no truck history would be complete without them. The distinctively styled vans were the invention of George Bacon, chief engineer of the Detroit Electric Vehicle Co. In 1922 he designed an electric delivery truck that could be driven from any one of four positions – front, rear and either running board. When it was discovered that electric traction was not as successful as gasoline power, Bacon set up the Detroit Industrial Vehicle Co. (Divco) to build a similar vehicle but with a Le Roi gasoline engine. The vans entered production in 1926. Numerous improved versions appeared up until the mid 1930s but the depression saw Divco being taken over by Continental Motors and renamed Continental-Divco Corp. In 1937 Continental Motors acquired the Twin Coach Co. of Kent, Ohio, and the vans were renamed Divco-Twin. It was at this stage that the famous snub-nosed pressed-steel van bodies appeared, a design that remained virtually unchanged until production finally ceased in 1986.

During its history Divco underwent many name changes. After Divco-Twin Truck Co. it became the Divco Corporation; the Divco Truck Division of Divco Wayne; and finally, in 1972, the Divco Truck Co., Correct Mfg. Co. The largest truck to bear the Divco name was a forward-control 6-ton refrigerated box van with separate cab and 5.4m/18ft long box-van body. The company's chassis cabs were also used for garbage trucks and a variety of other purposes.

KEW & DUNSTABLE, ENGLAND

DODGE

Dodge Bros. (Britain) Ltd was set up in Fulham, London, in 1922 as a subsidiary of its American parent. At first it was marketing American vehicles including light commercials up to 30cwt payload. In 1928 it moved to new premises at Park Royal, west London, by which time a wider range of trucks was being imported. Three years later Chrysler bought the Dodge operations. Chrysler had already absorbed the Maxwell Car Co., which had a UK distribution centre set up in 1914 at Kew in Surrey. Under Chrysler ownership the two operations were merged and Kew became the new home of Dodge Bros. (Britain) Ltd.

By 1932 a British Dodge 2-tonner was in production, powered by the American Dodge side-valve gasoline engine. Heavier models for 3, 4 and 5-ton payloads were added to the range in the '30s while the first all-British Dodge, with a Perkins diesel option, appeared in 1938. Some exports were already taking place to Australia and New Zealand where the trucks were badged Fargo. Wartime production was very limited as the factory switched to building aircraft, but from 1945 full production was resumed, the models being similar to the pre-war range. The largest truck was the 6-ton Major of semi-forward-control layout.

■ TOP *A 1955 Dodge 7-ton dump truck with Perkins R6 diesel engine. It was nicknamed the "Parrot-Nose" Dodge.*

■ ABOVE *The wartime Dodge Major 6-ton dump truck was powered by a Dodge gasoline engine with optional Perkins diesel.*

■ BELOW *The Dodge 300 series had the forward-control Motor Panels LAD cab and a Perkins or Leyland diesel engine.*

The first new post-war range appeared in 1949 – the stylish 100 series with a modern Briggs steel cab which shared the same basic shell as the Thames ET6 and the Leyland Comet. It was sometimes referred to as the "Parrot-Nose" Dodge owing to its beak-like bonnet (hood). A 7-ton version with a Perkins R6 engine was added in 1953. In later years the 100 series formed the basis for the Premier truck range in India.

A completely new forward-control range, the 300 series was announced in 1957, taking Dodge into a heavier weight category. A 14-ton gvw model was available powered by an AEC AV470 diesel. Other power units for the 300 range included Perkins and Leyland. The range featured a Motor Panels steel cab dubbed the "LAD" (Leyland-Albion-Dodge), modified versions being used by both Leyland and Albion.

Meanwhile, in 1958 the bonneted range, now called the 200 series, received a more modern cab of streamlined appearance with a wider grille. An almost identical cab was introduced on Commer's Superpoise at the same time. In 1963 the 200 was

■ LEFT *The Spanish-built Dodge 38-tonne tractor was marketed in the UK as the R38 throughout the 1970s.*

revamped once again as the 400 series taking an American design of cab. Very few of these were actually sold in the UK, the model being aimed at the export market. An important new range entered the scene in 1964, the tilt cab 500 series. These marked the introduction of a Chrysler V8 diesel which was, in fact, a Cummins VALE built under licence. The heaviest model was now a 28-ton gcw tractor unit. The Chrysler V8 proved unpopular and Dodge later offered the Perkins V8-410 in response to demand. The successful 500 series enjoyed a 13-year production run.

Chrysler, Dodge's parent company, had owned a stake in the Rootes Group, owners of both Commer and Karrier, since 1964 and gained full control of the company by 1967. Dodge production was moved from Kew to the Commer-Karrier factory in Dunstable. The process of integrating Dodge, Commer and Karrier was completed by 1973 and from 1976 the Dodge name was applied to former Commer models, including the tilt-cab Commando that was launched in 1974.

In the early 1970s there was a strong demand for heavy tractor units but the 500 series had been developed to its limit at 28 tons. To cater for 32 tons and over, Dodge took the unusual decision to import the Spanish-built Dodge (formerly Barreiros) 38-tonne tractor and market it in the UK as the Dodge R38. Barreiros in Madrid had been bought out by Chrysler in 1967 and was renamed Chrysler Espana when the Barreiros name was replaced by Dodge. Dodge UK also imported the Barreiros-Dodge rigid eight-wheeler. Sales of the Spanish-built Dodges took off quite well but demand soon fell away and the model was dropped in 1982.

Chrysler were to suffer financial losses in their European operations in the late 1970s and decided to sell out to the French Peugeot-Citroën Group in 1978. Chrysler UK's business was renamed Talbot Motor Co. with the Dunstable truck operations being Karrier Motors. A few years later Peugeot sold Karrier Motors to Renault Véhicules Industriels and eventually the Dodge name was phased out.

■ LEFT *The tilt-cab 500 series, launched in 1964 and powered by a Chrysler Cummins V8 diesel.*

■ BELOW *A 28-ton gvw eight-wheeled version of the 500 series was marketed during the early 1970s.*

DETROIT, MICHIGAN, USA

DODGE

■ LEFT *The 1966 Dodge D800 conventional had a 6.7 litre/408cu in V8 gasoline engine.*

■ LEFT *The 1967 L700 223cm/88in wheelbase tilt-cab tractor was designed for urban distribution.*

■ BELOW LEFT *1953 marked the introduction of the Dodge 4-ton payload Job Rated truck.*

John F. Dodge and his brother Horace formed a company in 1910 to manufacture automotive components and four years later began building cars. The cars formed the basis for light commercials. Following the death of the two Dodge brothers in 1920, their widows sold the company to a New York banking firm and the vice president and general manager, Frederick J. Haynes, linked up with Graham Brothers of Evansville, Indiana, who had supplied cabs and bodies for Dodge trucks, while their own Graham truck range used Dodge engines and drivelines. In 1927 Dodge Brothers absorbed Graham Brothers and the following year the bank sold the company to Chrysler. The heaviest truck at that time was a 2½-tonner and the products were called Dodge Brothers. A 4-tonner powered by a 6-cylinder gasoline engine was introduced in 1931. A heavier truck for up to 7½ tons with a straight-eight gasoline engine was available briefly from 1933–35, but Dodge's production was centred mainly on light to medium trucks. In 1936 the name was shortened from Dodge Brothers to Dodge. The heaviest truck model until the early 1950s was a 3-tonner. In 1951 a 4 to 5-tonner was introduced, but Dodge did not really enter the heavy truck market until 1960, their first tilt-cab L-line heavies appearing in 1964. Dodge's presence in the heavy truck market was relatively brief. After offering a range of maximum-weight tractor units with power ratings up to 335bhp from Cummins and Detroit Diesels, the company decided to pull out of heavy trucks in 1975 and concentrated once more on light commercials.

■ BELOW LEFT *The Dodge CNT900.*

■ BELOW RIGHT *The LN1000 had a choice of 121cm/48in, 185cm/73in or 200cm/79in BBC tilt cab.*

ADELAIDE, AUSTRALIA

DODGE

■ LEFT *The Australian-built Dodge Series 7 was available with gasoline or diesel engine.*

Dodge became established in Australia in 1939 but did not enter the truck market until 1958, when they introduced their own range of normal and forward-control trucks. They were a peculiar blend of American and British products, the normal-control models having a distinctly American looking cab while the forward-control versions featured the UK LAD cab. They were designated the 10 series and powered by V8 gasoline engines. In 1962, the Series 7 had a new cab with a strong American influence. This was to become the top seller with V8 gasoline engine and Rockwell 2-speed rear axle. Until then the trucks had also been marketed as Fargo and De-Soto.

A new truck plant was opened at Adelaide in 1974 and in 1975 more new Australian Dodge trucks were announced, including a version of the UK-designed Commando. In mid 1975 the range was further extended by marketing imported Mitsubishi Fuso heavy trucks which were badged Dodge. At the lighter end, the Mitsubishi Canter was also offered. Soon after Chrysler's withdrawal from the European truck business in 1978, Dodge of Australia were also to pull out of the market.

BOMBAY, INDIA

DODGE

Premier Automobiles Ltd (PAL) was established in 1944 and entered into an agreement with the Chrysler Group. The company went on to build a range of Dodge-based trucks in the 1 to 8-ton payload range. While some had locally built cabs, others featured the British Kew Dodge cab and some had American-style cabs. The trucks had a high local content and used licence-built Perkins engines or locally built gasoline engines. Some trucks were sold under the Fargo name. Both the Dodge and Fargo names were replaced by their own brand, Premier from 1972. (See "Premier".)

KADIKOY, TURKEY

DODGE

Chrysler Sanayi AS began building Dodge trucks in 1964 based on American types but with locally built cabs. Heavier models were sold in chassis-only form. The trucks were also marketed under the De-Soto and Fargo names. Production of light, medium and heavy trucks continues today.

CHELTENHAM, ENGLAND

DOUGLAS

■ LEFT *The Douglas transporter had a high AEC content, including their 9.6 litre/588cu in diesel engine.*

Douglas specialize in heavy tractors beginning in 1947 with the four-wheel drive Transporter. This might be described as a development of the wartime AEC Matador 4×4 medium artillery tractor produced from 1939 to 1945. Although many ex-Army Matadors later entered service with timber hauliers, there was also a role for the Douglas Transporter in such work since it had the benefit of the more powerful AEC 9.6 litre/588cu in diesel rated at 125bhp. The Douglas also featured the more modern AEC Mk.III pattern cab. Other Douglas tractors included the Tugmaster forward-control for industrial and airport use. This was mainly powered by a Perkins diesel. A special elevating fifth-wheel Tugmaster RO-RO tractor for use at ferry terminals appeared in 1955.

Today Douglas, as part of the Dennis Group Plc, continues to be a major supplier of heavy-duty terminal tractors. The current Tugmaster range includes the NS8-220, for a fifth-wheel loading up to 35 tonnes, the NS8-210 for 25 to 30 tonnes and the HM-50 for 16.5 tonnes. The standard power unit is the 5.9 litre/360cu in Cummins B-series diesel, but Volvo diesel engines are optional on the NS8.

OTHER MAKES

■ DAC
BRASOV, ROMANIA

DAC trucks were introduced in 1973, built at the Intreprinderea de Autocamione Brasov (Brasov Truck Manufacturing Works). Prior to that it was the S.R. (Steagul Rosu) Works, whose history dates back to 1921 when it was the ROMLOC Factory, which produced locomotives and rail wagons. The first DACs were based on the Bucegi which was powered by a V8 gasoline engine. As DACs they had a licence-built Saviem 6-cylinder diesel. DACs are also built as heavy dump trucks based on Russian designs. In 1990 the company was privatized under the name of ROMAN S.A. Currently ROMAN trucks are badged DAC. The range includes two, three and four-axled trucks from 7 to 40 tonnes gvw and tractor units from 16 to 40 tonnes gcw, plus military and specialized trucks. Engines include Deutz, Navistar, Caterpillar and Renault diesels according to model. (See also "Bucegi", "Roman" and "SR".)

■ DAEWOO
CHOLLABUK-DO, KOREA

Daewoo are relative newcomers to the heavy truck market, having begun production at their Kunshan plant in 1994. Annual production has already reached 2000 units and total output has exceeded 9000. The trucks are modern, well-equipped four and six-wheelers in rigid and tractor-unit form. Daewoo claims to be the first Korean manufacturer to have developed its own in-house trucks as opposesd to licence-built designs. The company has adopted an aggressive marketing strategy and are establishing assembly plants in the Czech Republic, Poland, Vietnam and the Philippines.

■ LEFT *Current DAC tractor units have a wide choice of power units including Deutz, Navistar, Caterpillar and Renault diesels.*

■ DAIMLER
STUTTGART & BERLIN-MARIENFELDE, GERMANY

The name Daimler is linked to the origins of the motor vehicle. Having produced the world's first motor car in 1886, Gottlieb Wilhelm Daimler announced the world's first motor truck in 1896. That was based on the Riemenwagen car and was equipped with a rear-mounted V-twin gasoline engine, which drove the rear wheels through a system of belts and gears to ring gears on the wheels. Similar designs were built for loads of 1½ to 5 tonnes. Another model in 1897 had shaft drive and the engine was mounted underneath the driver at the front. By 1900 the final drive gearing was semi-enclosed to keep out dirt and to aid lubrication. By then a 4-cylinder engine had been introduced.

In 1901 Daimler Motoren-Gesellschaft took over a company previously set up by Daimler at Marienfelde called Motorfahrzeug und Motorenfabrik Berlin AG, and production of Daimler trucks was transferred there until 1914. Early experiments with diesel power were taking place during World War I and in 1923 a diesel-engined truck was exhibited at the Berlin exhibition. From 1924 Daimler began collaborating with Benz Werke and in 1926 the two companies merged to form Daimler-Benz, their products being sold as Mercedes-Benz from then on.

■ ABOVE *Daimler's 1896 Phoenix was the world's first motor truck.*

■ LEFT *Korean manufacturer Daewoo offer a comprehensive truck range.*

■ DART
WATERLOO, IOWA, & KANSAS CITY, MISSOURI, USA

Since 1958 the Dart Truck Co. has been part of Paccar Inc. of Bellevue, Washington, but its history dates back to 1903. The very first Dart was a ½-ton "high-wheeler" with underfloor engine and double chain drive. Between 1903 and 1907 Dart was based at Anderson, Indiana, as the Dart Manufacturing Co. but then the company opened a new factory at Waterloo, Iowa, where it was based until 1924. Early truck designs had 4-cylinder gasoline engines with chain drive but shaft drive was adopted in 1912. Bonneted 2 and 3-tonners were built up until the 1920s. For a brief period in 1924–25 it changed hands and became the Hawkeye-Dart Truck Co. In 1925 the name became Dart Truck Co. again and a factory was set

OTHER MAKES

■ ABOVE *This bonneted De Dion Bouton with gasogene equipment dates from the late 1920s.*

up in Kansas City. During the 1930s a new range of 1½ to 8-ton trucks appeared while heavy models for 10-ton payloads, plus an articulated version, were added in the late '30s.

At this stage Dart began building heavy off-highway trucks for the mining industry, a type in which it was to specialize later. Post-war models continued to include conventional medium and heavy tractor units but from the early 1950s Dart concentrated on heavy dump trucks. After the Paccar takeover they became KW-Dart until 1970, from which time the "KW" was dropped. Current products include heavy dump trucks for up to a 150-ton payload, powered by Caterpillar, Detroit Diesel and Cummins engines.

■ DE DION BOUTON

SEINE, FRANCE

The company frequently referred to as De Dion began in 1884 as De Dion Bouton & Trepardoux. In their early years they built steam vehicles, including what is said to be the world's earliest articulated vehicle in 1894. Count Albert De Dion and Georges Bouton severed their relationship with Bouton's brother-in-law Trepardoux over Bouton's growing interest in gasoline engines. Gasoline-engined trucks appeared in 1906, the heaviest of which was a 5-tonner. In 1910 the distinctive circular radiator made its appearance. After World War I De Dion Bouton went through difficulties that lasted well into the 1930s. In 1930 a 5-ton truck was launched while a larger 6½-tonner, the LY, followed in 1936. Truck sales failed to reach sufficient numbers, and in the post-war era up to their closure in 1950, De Dion were not significant players in the truck business.

■ DE-SOTO

DETROIT, MICHIGAN, USA, & ISTANBUL, TURKEY

Initially the De-Soto truck was the result of "badge engineering" on the part of the Chrysler Corporation who chose to use the De-Soto name on Dodge and Fargo trucks in certain export territories up until about 1960. For some years British Dodges were marketed as De-Soto in Australia and New Zealand.

In the 1960s Chrysler Sanayi AS of Kocaeli, Turkey, introduced their range of D series bonneted trucks which were marketed as Dodge and De-Soto and built at Kadikoy, Istanbul. Some of these were powered by Perkins diesels. Current Turkish trucks are still badged Chrysler, Fargo and De-Soto.

■ DELAHAYE

TOURS & PARIS, FRANCE

The very old established company of Emile Delahaye dated from 1898 and some early light trucks were built along similar lines to Daimler using rear-mounted 2-cylinder engines with belt drive. By 1904 chain drive had been introduced and a wide truck range was available by 1906. In the 1920s Delahaye were building ¾-tonne and 2-tonne bonneted trucks with 4-cylinder engines, shaft drive and pneumatic tyres, although heavier trucks retained solid tyres with chain drive.

Delahaye advanced into true heavy-duty trucks with diesel-engined 7-tonners in 1931. These had 6-speed gearboxes and 10 litre/610cu in 6-cylinder direct-injection engines built under licence from Fiat. By 1939 their 149 model had air brakes and a Gardner diesel engine. After World War II the company's main truck model was the modern, forward-control 163 type but sales were never to match those of the pre-war era. In 1954 Delahaye joined forces with Hotchkiss becoming Société Hotchkiss-Delahaye, but within two years the Delahaye truck operations came to an end.

■ DONGFENG

SHIYAN, HUBEI PROVINCE, CHINA

Since about 1977 DongFeng (translated this means "East Wind") trucks have been built at Shiyan No.2 Automobile Factory (or Second Automobile Works) which was established in the early '70s. This has now been renamed DongFeng Motor Corp. The EQ1406 was a gasoline-engined bonneted 5-tonne payload truck, while a heavier version, the EQ144, was built in 6×2 form. An end dump truck based on the EQ140 was designated the DD347. Similar models were made at the same factory carrying Renault badges and engines, following technological co-operation with the European manufacturer.

■ ABOVE *Dodge trucks are badged De-Soto in certain countries. This example operated in Belgium during the 1960s.*

■ ABOVE *A military-specification chain-drive Delahaye 3-tonne truck built in 1913.*

■ ABOVE *The Chinese Dongfeng DD347 dump truck has a 5.4 litre/330cu in 6-cylinder gasoline engine and a 4½-ton payload.*

SANDBACH, ENGLAND

ERF

■ LEFT *ERF's first truck was this CI4 6/7-tonner with Gardner 4LW engine, built in 1933.*

Edwin Richard Foden was the youngest son of Edwin Foden who founded the famous Foden steam-wagon company whose history dated back to 1856. By the early 1930s Fodens were struggling to sell steamers and ER, as he was called, was firmly convinced that the company should build diesels instead. His brother, William, had retired in 1924 and emigrated to Australia. A disagreement over policy led ER to resign and he and his son, Dennis, set up their own company called E R Foden just a short distance from Fodens' factory.

Production began in 1933 with a modern 6/7-ton payload forward-control four-wheeler powered by a Gardner 4LW engine. All the running units were bought in and, unlike Fodens, E R Foden were assemblers. The trucks sold well and very soon the E R Foden badge was altered to ERF. During the six years up to the outbreak of World War II the range expanded to include three and four-axled rigids and two-axled tractor units. They were also the first company to build a twin-steer six-wheeler. ERF was one of the few UK truck manufacturers to be allowed to continue production during the war and some wartime models were fitted with AEC engines when Gardners were in short supply. After the war, in 1948, a completely new range was introduced under the general designation of the V range, masterminded by chief engineer Ernest Sherratt who himself was an ex-Foden man. ERF went from strength to strength, developing an extensive export business.

■ BELOW LEFT *Introduced in 1948, this 22-ton eight-wheeler was part of ERF's V range with Jennings coachbuilt cab.*

Domestic vehicles had Jennings coachbuilt cabs, Jennings being an old established coachbuilder with whom ERF shared their premises at Sandbach. Later, in 1963, ERF absorbed the company as their in-house cab builder. For export, a steel cab was introduced in 1951, produced by the Willenhall Motor Radiator Co. This was also available on the home market but after a couple of years a completely new and strikingly modern cab with panoramic windscreen and oval radiator grille was introduced as the KV cab. A semi-forward-control version, nicknamed the "Sabrina", was added in 1958. The first appearance of the KV in November 1953 added to

■ LEFT *The KV models, first introduced in 1954, were noted for their ultra-modern styling and panoramic vision.*

■ RIGHT *The 34-ton gcw A series tractor units of 1972 had a choice of Cummins 6-cylinder or Gardner 8-cylinder diesels.*

ERF's prestige and the new models featured many improvements, especially in the braking system. ERF also became involved in building specialized export models for heavy-duty operation and options of Cummins and Rolls Royce diesels were offered during the late '50s. South Africa was a particularly strong export market for ERF.

The next major launch was the LV-cabbed range of 1962. It was with this range that ERF became the first UK manufacturer to offer fail-safe spring brakes. With an increasing demand for articulated vehicles in the UK, ERF began offering a complete matched artic during the '60s. Export demand continued to be healthy and an assembly plant was set up in South Africa in 1965 to build vehicles tailored to local requirements.

In the early 1970s Ernest Sherratt retired as director of engineering and his replacement, an ex-Chrysler man, brought in the A series which was based on a new design philosophy more akin to mass production ideas, especially in the design of frame and suspension. Engines included the Cummins NH220 and Gardner 8LXB 240. The A series formed the basis for a 38-ton European tractor with a steel Motor Panels tilt cab which ERF aimed specifically at the European market. Soon after, ERF's first true tilt-cab range, the B series, was announced. This featured the SP (Steel/Plastic) cab produced by a revolutionary new moulding technique.

Continuous improvements have been introduced to the ERF range since the mid 1970s resulting in the C series and later the E series, all using developments of the SP cab structure. The last major launch was in 1993 with the EC range which soon became a leading seller in the UK. A top-of-the-range heavy tractor unit for long-haul operations appeared as the Olympic.

In 1996 ERF, Britain's last independent truck builder, was bought out by Western Star of Canada. Since the takeover, certain ERF-based models are now marketed as Western Star, like the Commander range that has sold well in Australia and New Zealand. The mechanical content of the Commander series is predominantly American-sourced. ERF also markets the Turkish-built BMC Professional as the ERF EP and assembles Isuzu trucks.

In August 1999 it was announced that ERF production was to be transferred from Sandbach to nearby Middlewich, and in February 2000 Western Star sold the company to MAN in Germany.

■ ABOVE *The B series of 1974 featured a composite steel and plastic tilt cab as on this 1976 eight-wheeler.*

■ RIGHT *ERF's latest EC range was launched in 1993 and is still in production.*

CLEVELAND, OHIO, USA

EUCLID

Euclid have always specialized in heavy off-road dump trucks, beginning with the 11-ton payload Trak Truck in 1934. The company was called the Euclid Crane & Hoist Company when it was founded in 1931. It was renamed the Euclid Road Machinery Co. in 1936 and a larger dump truck for 15-ton payloads was introduced. These early machines were the first purpose-built site dump trucks with scow-end bodies. Euclid added a range of specialized plant and vehicles including graders, loaders and crawler tractors. The load capacity of its dump trucks steadily increased. In 1953 the company was taken over by General Motors and remained under their control until 1968 when they were forced to sell it off under the Anti-Trust (Monopolies Commission) Regulations. By that time GM had set up Euclid (Great Britain) Ltd at Newhouse in Scotland where a wide range of Euclids were assembled. GM sold their Cleveland operations to the White Motor Corporation and the UK products were marketed under the Terex name. There were Euclid dump trucks for payloads from 22 to 170 tons. Daimler-Benz AG purchased the business in 1977 and in 1984 it passed to Clark Michigan. One year later Euclid was taken over by Volvo Construction Equipment but it was sold again in 1992 to Hitachi. The company now trades as Euclid Hitachi.

■ LEFT *Euclid heavy dump trucks are powered by Detroit Diesel or Cummins engines.*

■ LEFT *This articulated dump truck of the 1960s era is the nearest thing to a conventional truck in the Euclid range.*

OTHER MAKES

■ **EBRO**

BARCELONA, SPAIN

Ebro truck production began at Motor Iberica SA in 1956 with licence-built Ford Thames models. Just as the UK trucks took the name of a major English river, the Thames, so the Spanish-built Fords were called Ebro. Initially Ebros were similar to the Thames ET6 bonneted trucks while there was a semi-forward-control model loosely resembling the Thames Trader but having a locally designed cab. The D-series tilt-cab models formed the basis for a new range in 1968 for payloads up to 7 tonnes. Heavier models were added in 1976 as the P series for up to 27 tonnes gvw. In 1980 Motor Iberica was taken over by the Nissan Motor Co. who have recently announced their new Atleon medium trucks.

■ LEFT *In the late 1970s Ebro moved up the weight scale with their P range, using Perkins diesels.*

■ BELOW LEFT *In the 1960s semi-forward-control Ebros bore a vague resemblance to Thames Traders.*

OAKLAND, CALIFORNIA, USA

FAGEOL

Fageol Motors Co. was founded in 1916. An initial plan to build cars and tractors was dropped to concentrate on truck production. Bonneted trucks from $2\frac{1}{2}$ to 6 tons payload capacity were offered. These had 4-cylinder Waukesha gasoline engines and solid tyres. During the 1920s the heaviest model was discontinued and a new range was introduced for $1\frac{1}{2}$ to 5 tons as well as coaches. In 1925 coach manufacture, centred on another plant at Kent, Ohio, was absorbed into the American Car & Foundry Co., while truck production continued at Oakland. Trucks continued to undergo improvements, with the introduction of pneumatic tyres and electric lighting and starting. Heavier models for up to 10 tons with trailer appeared in 1930. Fageol ran into financial problems at this point and were reorganized as the Fageol Truck & Coach Company in 1932. Some impressive heavy-duty 6×4 tractor units were introduced during the 1930s but Fageol's trading position did not improve and the company was sold to Sterling in 1938. Sterling retained Fageol's distribution network but sold the manufacturing facilities on to T. A. Peterman who introduced the Peterbilt.

PRIBOJ, YUGOSLAVIA

FAP

■ RIGHT ***The Yugoslavian-built FAP is based on a Mercedes design. This photograph shows the similarities of the two makes.***

Fabrika Automobila Priboj na Limu built medium-weight Austrian Saurer trucks under licence from 1951. Originally these were of normal-control layout but forward-control models were added to the range. Power units included Perkins and Leyland as well as locally built Famos diesels. From 1972 FAP's licence agreement with Saurer was replaced by an agreement with Daimler-Benz AG and subsequent vehicles, which include heavy-duty FAP-Famos 6×6 and 8×8 trucks, have featured Mercedes cabs.

GENNEVILLIERS, FRANCE

FAR

■ RIGHT ***This FAR Pony Mécanique of the French Railways SNCF was derived from Scammell's Mechanical Horse.***

Tracteurs FAR began in 1919 by building Chenard-Walcker-designed road tractors. From 1937 they built the Scammell Mechanical Horse under licence as the Pony Mécanique. These continued in production until 1970.

KADIKOY, TURKEY

FARGO

■ RIGHT ***The Fargo name badge is still used on trucks built at Chrysler's factory in Turkey.***

The Fargo name badge was used to market Dodge trucks in certain territories from 1931. It is still used in Turkey.

NÜREMBERG, GERMANY

FAUN

■ LEFT *This early 1960s Faun F66/47K was powered by an air-cooled Deutz diesel and grossed around 16 tons.*

Faun's history begins in 1918 with the merger of Fahrzeugfabrik Ansbach and Nürnberg Feuerloschgerate Automobillastwagen und Fahrzeugfabrik Karl Schmidt. The combined company was called Fahrzeugfabriken Ansbach und Nürnberg until the name was shortened to Faun-Werke AG in 1920, the trucks carrying the name Faun. Much of the production during the 1920s consisted of municipal vehicles, but a new range of trucks from 2 to 6-tonne payload appeared in the early '30s. There was also a heavy-duty 9-tonner powered by a Deutz diesel engine. 1934 marked the introduction of a six-wheeler and four years later a forward-control twin-steer four-axled rigid was introduced for a 15-tonne payload.

After World War II Faun offered a comprehensive range of trucks, both normal and forward-control. The normal-control models presented a very impressive appearance and covered the heaviest weight categories for articulated and drawbar operation. From 1969 Faun ceased production of normal on-highway trucks to concentrate on special vehicles, including crane chassis, airport crash tenders and heavy-haulage tractors which are still in production. Many feature 8×8 drive and high-powered diesels of between 700 and 800bhp. For a brief period during the mid 1970s a joint marketing agreement was established with Fodens Ltd in the UK to market dump trucks as Foden-Faun.

■ LEFT *This 1978 Faun HZ40.45/45 has a Daimler-Benz OM404 V12 diesel and was built for the Czech government.*

■ BELOW *A 1988 Faun 8×8 300-ton heavy-haulage tractor powered by a 19 litre/1158cu in 456bhp diesel with Allison automatic transmission.*

WETZIKON, SWITZERLAND

FBW

■ LEFT *A forward-control 16-ton gross FBW four-wheeler with single-axle "pup" trailer.*

The founder of Franz Brozincevic et Cie Motorwagenfabrik Wetzikon AG was a Croatian engineer, Franz Brozincevic, who in 1909 designed a chain-drive truck for the Swiss Post Office powered by his own design of gasoline engine. Called the Franz, the truck was further developed into a range of shaft-drive machines for up to 5 tonnes payload. In 1914 the Franz operations were absorbed into Motorwagenfabrik Berna AG, Franz Brozincevic becoming Berna's general manager. After differences with Berna's management he resigned and established his own company, FBW, at the former premises of Schweizer Motorwagenfabrik. In 1922 FBW built their first 4-cylinder gasoline engine and introduced a double-reduction rear axle. Two years later a licence was granted to Henschel & Sohn to build FBW vehicles in Kassel, Germany.

During the 1920s FBW introduced a very advanced design for 5-tonne payloads. They were powerful trucks featuring small turning circles, pneumatic tyres and four-wheel braking, suiting them to mountain roads. FBW gained an excellent reputation for engineering. By the late '20s they had built their first heavy-duty chain-drive six-wheeler. FBW engines were fitted with a patented exhaust brake.

The first FBW diesel engine was announced in 1934, an 8.5 litre/518cu in 6-cylinder unit producing 100bhp. Wartime production concentrated on military vehicles for the Swiss army. The post-war years brought increased demand for heavy trucks in the construction industry. From the late 1940s a range of trucks was available, including forward-control models for 7-tonne payloads. A powerful new 11 litre/671cu in 6-cylinder horizontal engine with 145bhp was introduced in 1949. The range of trucks expanded during the '50s and '60s extending up to maximum legal weight. In 1968 lighter models were added to gain wider market coverage.

The 1970s saw impressive new models with turbocharged diesels in both vertical and horizontal forms. A very handsome tilt cab appeared on the forward-control models. In the late '70s there were 18 basic models in the FBW heavy-duty range. The 70N 4×2 and 80N 6×4 were bonneted types also marketed as the all-wheel drive 70X and 80X. Seven forward-control tilt-cab models included a 17-tonne gvw 4×2 (50V type), 21-tonne 6×2 (75V), 26-tonne 6×4 (80V) and, perhaps FBW's most impressive machine, the 28-tonne 85V 8×4 which appeared following increases in the Swiss weight limits during the '70s. In addition there were seven underfloor-engined models designated the U range in 4×2, 6×2 and 6×4 form. These were especially suited to municipal operations as well as general haulage. The lightest was the 13-tonne gvw 40U while the heaviest was the 6×4 80U at 26 tonnes gvw. To cover the lighter end of the range FBW marketed the Mitsubishi Canter 2-tonner and the heavier Fuso 6½-tonner as MMC-FBW.

In a declining market Switzerland's two truck makers, Saurer and FBW, joined forces in 1982 to form NAW (Nutzfahrzeuggesellschaft Arbon & Wetzikon) and were absorbed into Daimler-Benz.

■ LEFT *FBW built a wide variety of heavy-duty trucks, including bonneted tractors.*

■ RIGHT *Many FBWs were powered by the maker's own 5 and 6-cylinder underfloor diesel engines.*

TURIN, ITALY

FIAT

■ LEFT ***Fiat's 18BL was typical of their products from the World War I era.***

Though Fiat's origins as a car manufacturer date from 1899, the company did not build trucks until 1903. Beginning as F.I.A.T. (Fabbrica Italiana d'Automobili, Torino) the company became Fiat SpA from 1918. The original 4-tonne payload truck was a well thought-out design with cab-over-engine layout and a 4m/13ft load deck. It was powered by a 6.4 litre/390cu in 4-cylinder engine rated at 24hp. A shaft took the drive to a mid-mounted gearbox from which the drive to the rear wheels was by chains. A larger machine for a 5-tonne payload, powered by a 7.4 litre/451cu in 40hp engine came in 1906. The following year a normal-control layout was adopted.

In 1911 Fiat supplied motor trucks to the Italian forces engaged in the Italo-Turkish conflict in Libya. These were based on the Tipo 15 Bis and a more powerful version, the 15 Ter. They were believed to be the first motor vehicles used in war. Just before World War I the larger 18 series truck had entered production and this became one of the company's most important models during that era. There was also a larger 20B model and a type 30 heavy-duty tractor capable of towing up to 100 tonnes. Huge numbers of trucks were supplied to the Allied Forces during 1914–18.

In 1925 a new range of 2 to 2½-tonne trucks had pneumatic tyres. Light trucks based on these were built under licence by AMO in Moscow as well as by Mitsubishi in Japan, effectively founding those countries' truck industries. The same year, Fiat took over SPA Commercial Vehicles. Fiat concentrated on lighter trucks in the late '20s while heavier bonneted models up to 5 tonnes were built by SPA. In 1929 the Consortium Fiat Veicoli Industriale was formed, concentrating the marketing and production of Fiat, SPA and (from 1931) Ceirano vehicles at Fiat.

The first diesel engine appeared in 1930 and was installed in an 8-tonne Ceirano chassis. In 1931 the diesel-engined normal-control Fiat 632 4-tonner and 634N 6-tonner were introduced. The engines were 5.5 litre/335cu in 4-cylinder and 8.4 litre/512cu in 6-cylinder units. In 1938 Fiat acquired the share capital of OM (Officine Meccaniche) of Brescia but OM was allowed relative autonomy until finally absorbed into Fiat in 1970. Attractive, streamlined forward-control trucks for payloads of 3½ to 6½ tonnes were announced in 1939. These were the 625, 665 and 666 for gross train

■ ABOVE ***This Fiat 690N2 with Viberti fourth-axle conversion seen in Naples represents a typical Italian outfit of the 1970s era.***

■ LEFT ***A Fiat 6×2 with self-steering rear axle and a large-capacity integral van body.***

■ RIGHT *The 1939 Fiat 626N was powered by a 5.7 litre/348cu in diesel and could tow a 6-tonne trailer.*

■ BELOW RIGHT *This amusement-contractor's truck, a 626N, was still in service after more than 35 years.*

weights of 12 tonnes. The 666 was the heaviest, powered by a 9.4 litre/573cu in 6-cylinder diesel. They featured an easily removable engine which could be withdrawn from the front. A six-wheeler Fiat-SPA version, derived from the 666, in single and double-drive form, was developed as the A10,000 during World War II but finally went into production in 1945. It was designed for a 10-tonne payload.

Forward-control layout was now standard on Fiat heavies, as was right-hand drive which was considered safer when negotiating narrow mountain roads. In 1949 an improved range was launched, developed from the pre-war models. A completely new truck cab was introduced in 1952 and was to last right through to the late 1960s, gracing such models as the 642N and 643N four-wheelers, the 682T tractors, the 690N twin-steer six-wheelers, the 690T twin-steer tractor, the 693N six-wheeler and 683N and 683T rigids and tractors. Fiat France came into existence in 1966 with the acquisition of Unic and Turin-based Lancia Veicoli Speciali SpA was taken over in 1969.

A new generation of models appeared in 1970. Typical of these was the 4×2 619N rigid and 619T tractor unit, the 697N and T six-wheelers and the twin-steer 691N and T of 1971. Many of these twin-steer trucks were converted to 8×2 form by the addition of a fourth axle. All the new models were fitted with a new-style cab with wide grille and bumper-mounted headlights. Tilt-cab versions began appearing in the mid 1970s. In 1974 Fiat Veicoli Industriali SpA signed a joint agreement with the German manufacturing group Klockner Humboldt Deutz AG to form the Industrial Vehicle Corporation IVECO, which came into being on January 1st 1975. The Fiat name continued to appear on trucks until 1982 when the Iveco brand name was adopted for the group products.

■ BELOW *A maximum-weight five-axled articulated outfit used on international haulage by the large Polish company, Pekaes of Warsaw.*

SANDBACH, ENGLAND

FODEN

■ LEFT *The 1937 Foden DG4/7½ was powered by a Gardner 4LW diesel engine. DGs were built between 1936 and 1948.*

■ BELOW LEFT *Foden reluctantly gave up steamer production in 1934. This Speed Six was the last type built.*

The origins of the old established Foden company can be traced back to 1856 and the founding of an engineering business called Hancock & Foden which built agricultural machinery and steam engines. Its co-founder Edwin Foden went on to build steam traction engines and, in 1901, a successful steam lorry. Edwin's two sons William and Edwin Richard joined the company, and steam wagon production continued throughout the 1920s with such famous machines as the C type 5/6-tonner. By the late '20s steam wagon sales were losing out to internal combustion-engined trucks but Fodens Ltd (the company's title from 1902) still persevered with steamers. Edwin, the founder, had died in 1911 and his eldest son William had emigrated to Australia in 1924 leaving only Edwin Richard (ER) on the Board. ER foresaw the inevitable demise of steam and advocated a switch to diesel power, but he failed to convince other members of the Board. As a result ER left in 1932 and set up his own company, ERF, in partnership with his son Dennis.

ER's early experiments with diesels, beginning with a Gardner-engined 6-tonner in 1931, eventually formed the basis, albeit after he had departed, of a new range of Foden diesels that were phased in during 1934. Meanwhile steam-wagon production was discontinued, the last steamers being the highly advanced Speed Six and Speed Twelve under-types. The early '30s were difficult times for Fodens and the company came close to collapse. William Foden was persuaded to return to the company in 1935 and his presence raised the morale and fortunes of the firm. A new range of diesel trucks, the DG was launched in 1936, setting Fodens on a successful course to recovery. The Gardner-powered DGs were offered in 4×2, 6×2, twin-steer 6×2, 6×4, 8×2 and 8×4 form, plus tractor units for articulated use. Military versions of the 4×2 and 6×4 DGs were developed during World War II and DG production was resumed after the war.

Fodens' first new post-war model was the FG of 1948, featuring the stylish S.18 cab. Another development that had been underway during the 1940s was a two-stroke diesel engine. This was fitted in an eight-wheeled vehicle announced in 1948. The 4.09 litre/249cu in 6-cylinder two-stroke developed 126bhp at 2000rpm and

■ BOTTOM LEFT *This 1967 S21 represents Foden's leading type in the 1960s era.*

■ BOTTOM RIGHT *A 1971 S39 artic with 150 Gardner and 12-speed box.*

■ RIGHT *A 1979 30-ton gvw Foden eight-wheeled bulk cement tanker featuring the S83 cab.*

weighed only 500kg/1100lbs. A 4-cylinder version of 2.7 litre/164cu in capacity appeared in the FE.4/8 cab-ahead-of-engine four-wheeler in 1952. This truck, with its ultra-modern styling, was only built for three years. Meanwhile Fodens had entered the heavy-duty dump truck market, a field in which they were to become leading manufacturers.

Fodens' on-highway range continued to be updated throughout the 1950s and '60s. Twelve-speed range-change gearboxes became common fitment, especially on trucks with two-stroke engines. Gardner engines remained optional on all models. Fodens frequently introduced new cab designs, fibreglass becoming widely used from 1958 when their distinctive S.21 cab appeared. In 1962 came their S.24 cab, the first production tilt cab in the UK. Fodens was particularly successful in the field of rigid eight-wheelers. New UK weight limits introduced in 1964 led to a decline in eight-wheeler demand and most manufacturers were obliged to switch to building tractor units. One interesting machine offered by Fodens was the Twin-load – a dromedary-style load-carrying eight-wheeled tractor unit coupled to a single-axle semi. Unfortunately UK length limits made it impractical and only a handful of twin-loads were built.

Fodens Ltd was enjoying a substantial share of the truck market both at home and abroad during the 1960s but their fortunes took a down turn in the '70s. A substantial order for military vehicles helped them regain a footing in the mid '70s but more financial difficulties returned at the end of the decade. Meanwhile they had launched a heavy-duty range aimed at the European market but a combination of heavy investment and insufficient sales led the company into receivership in 1979.

Fodens Ltd was taken over by the Paccar Company in 1980 and renamed the Sandbach Engineering Company. Truck production restarted in a small way in 1981 with a much reduced workforce and a simplified range. Paccar, who also owned Peterbilt and Kenworth in the United States, introduced sweeping changes and a new breed of Foden emerged, benefiting from Paccar technology and production techniques. Most of the specialized vehicles were dropped and in-house component manufacture was discontinued. Production was concentrated on a rationalized range. Eight-wheelers, Fodens' traditional speciality, continued to be offered and a strong presence was maintained in that market.

The name Foden was reinstated into the company title, which became Foden Trucks in 1983. Military vehicles continued to form an important part of Foden's production. The civilian range was divided into the medium-weight 2000 series, the heavyweight 3000 series and the 4000 heavyweights. A wide variety of power units, including Caterpillar which in 1984 Paccar were the first to offer in the UK, and a wide choice of drive-lines and rear suspensions became available.

In 1996 Foden launched a top-of-the-range tractor unit in the form of their 4000 XL series featuring a high roof cab for long-haul operations. In 1998 a redesigned 3000 range was launched, marking a move away from fibreglass cabs. The new model, named the Alpha 3000, features a steel cab similar to that used on the DAF 85 series, DAF having become part of Paccar in 1996. There are plans to replace the 4000 series cab with the DAF 95 cab. In September 1999 it was announced that Foden's Sandbach factory is to close and production will be transferred to the Leyland plant near Preston.

■ RIGHT *In 1998 Foden Trucks introduced their new Alpha range with a steel cab similar to the DAF 85 series.*

DAGENHAM, ENGLAND

FORD & FORD THAMES

■ BELOW *The Thames Trader was built from 1957–65. This is the Mk.II introduced in 1962.*

Ford's UK truck manufacturing operation went under the name Fordson from 1933–39, Fordson Thames from 1939–57 and Ford Thames from 1957–65. Prior to 1929, assembly of American Ford TT light trucks had taken place at the Trafford Park plant in Manchester which opened in 1911. In 1931 production was transferred to a new factory on the banks of the River Thames at Dagenham. The Thames name was adopted to give the trucks a distinct British identity. Fordson and Fordson Thames models are dealt with in their own sections.

The first significant Ford Thames model was the semi-forward-control Trader of 1957. It took Ford into a higher weight category, the heaviest model being a 7-tonner. This was also available as a tractor unit for 13.4 tons. There were six basic models for 1½, 2, 3, 4, 5 and 7-ton payloads. Those up to 3 tons had a choice of 4-cylinder gasoline or 4-cylinder diesel engine. Above that weight, 6-cylinder diesel and gasoline engines were also offered, while 6-cylinder engines were standard on the 7-tonners. An improved Trader Mk.II was introduced in 1962 for payloads up to 7½ tons and included a 17-ton gross tractor unit. At the same time a normal-control Trader featuring the German-style Koln cab became available. After the Thames name was dropped in 1965 this truck became the Ford K series.

■ LEFT *Ford's tilt-cab D series was launched in 1965 and became a market leader.*

■ BELOW LEFT *In 1975 Ford entered the heavy-duty market with their Transcontinental H series, built in Amsterdam.*

The dropping of the Thames name coincided with the introduction of the all-new tilt-cab D series in 1965. Henceforth UK-built trucks were marketed simply as Ford. The new D series was a highly successful range. Initially it covered the payload range from 2 to 8 tons while the heaviest D800 artic grossed 19 tons. A 16-ton gvw

■ LEFT *Ford built on the success of the D series with an even better range – the Cargo, launched in 1981.*

model, the D1000, was added in 1967. This was powered by a Cummins Vale V8 diesel. An artic version grossed 28 tons. The medium-weight D series took slant-six diesels developed from Ford's earlier 6D engines while the lighter models took a slant-four. For the first couple of years Ford also offered 4 and 6-cylinder Canadian-built gasoline engines mainly for the export market.

In addition to their 4×2 models Ford offered 6×2 and 6×4 versions for gross weights of 16 to 24 tons. A luxury Custom cab option was available on light and medium models while it was made standard on the heavy-duty models. Within a year of the launch of the D1000, Ford began offering their own V8 (actually the Perkins V8.510 built under licence) as an alternative to the Cummins Vale. Having achieved a leading position in the medium-truck market, Ford set their sights on entering the maximum-weight sector and designed a completely new range of heavies for up to 44 tons gcw, powered by Cummins 14 litre/854cu in diesels. However, though designed in the UK, the trucks were produced at Ford's Amsterdam plant in both left and right-hand drive. Dubbed the "Transcontinental", the big Ford featured an adaptation of Berliet's Premier cab. Assembly of the Transcontinental was transferred to the Sandbach Engineering Co. in 1981 when Paccar had spare capacity, but production finished altogether in 1982.

Ford's next major launch was that of the Ford Cargo range in 1981. This proved to be a market leader, putting Ford ahead of its traditional rival, Bedford. The new Cargo featured modern, up-to-the-minute styling and a high degree of driver comfort. With the demise of the Transcontinental, Ford introduced a range of heavyweight Cargo tractor units ranging from 28 to 38 tonnes gcw. The 38-tonners were powered by the Cummins L10 while those at 28 and 32 tonnes had Perkins, Cummins or air-cooled Deutz diesels.

In 1986 Ford sold its UK truck operations to the Italian Iveco group and subsequent vehicles have been badged Iveco Ford. After making heavy losses, the Langley plant closed in October 1997, bringing UK Ford truck production to an end.

■ LEFT *The Transcontinental featured an adaptation of Berliet's Premier cab and Cummins 14 litre/854cu in diesel engine.*

■ BELOW *After production of the Transcontinental ended in 1982, Ford introduced heavier Cargo tractor units.*

DEARBORN, MICHIGAN, & LOUISVILLE, KENTUCKY, USA

FORD

■ LEFT *Ford's legendary TT 1-tonner of the 1917–27 period was built at Trafford Park in the UK as well as in Dearborn.*

■ LEFT *The W series cabovers of 1970 were face-lifted with a new grille in 1975.*

While Ford built light commercials from their early days, they were generally car-derived. The TT launched in 1917 was a lengthened, heavier-duty version of the old Tin Lizzie for payloads of 1 ton. A succession of light trucks in the 1 to 2-ton payload class was built in the 1920s and '30s. In 1927 the famous Model T and TT – of which some 15 million were produced – ended. The more modern AA 1½-ton truck appeared in 1928. At first the AA had worm drive but in 1929 a spiral-bevel axle was made standard, as were offset steel disc wheels with dual rears on the heaviest model. The AA formed the prototype for the first Russian-built GAZ trucks (Gorkovoka Automobilova Zavod) in 1931.

The AA was joined by the BB in 1932, the first Ford commercial to feature the legendary V8 gasoline engine. Facelifted cabs offered in 1933/34 had raked radiator grilles resembling Ford cars. Semi-forward-control versions appeared later in the 1930s. Many thousands of military vehicles and armoured cars were produced for the war effort. It wasn't until the late '30s that Ford began to move up the weight range with their truck models. Restyled F6, F7 and F8 models for up to 3-ton payloads came in 1948, with a 6×4 version of the heaviest F8 model. Overhead-valve engines were introduced in 1952, replacing the old side-valve units which were phased out in 1954.

It was at this time that heavy-duty Fords began to appear for gross weights up to 24 tons. In 1957 the old fixed-cab forward-control models were replaced by the all-new tilt-cab C range and some diesel options became available. By 1960 big Ford commercials were in full production, the tandem drive T.950 Super Duty being the largest of these. The Super Duty V8 gasoline engine produced 270bhp. Other features included full air brakes, Fuller Roadranger transmission and power steering. The largest tilt-cab model, the C.800, was designed in articulated form and had the 205bhp HD V8. Fully automatic transmission was also available.

In 1962 the H series heavy-duty cabovers became available featuring a raised version of the C series tilt cab. This was Ford's first true line-haul

■ BELOW LEFT *A seven-axled drawbar outfit in New Zealand being hauled by an LTL-9000 6×4 conventional.*

■ LEFT *An L-9000 six-axled refrigerated outfit operated by Southern Transport of Invercargill on New Zealand's South Island.*

truck. The H-1000 took Ford's Super Duty 8.5 litre/534cu in V8 gasoline engine developing 266bhp while the HD-1000 featured the Cummins in-line-six NH.220 at 220bhp. Drive-line choice included Fuller or Spicer gearbox, Eaton or Timken rear axles and Hendrickson rear suspension. In 1964 Caterpillar and Cummins V6 and V8 diesels were also offered.

In 1965 production of heavy trucks was transferred to a new plant at Louisville, Kentucky. The normal-control T range continued until 1972 but the new L line Louisville range was launched to replace it in 1970. A new heavy-duty tilt-cab model, the W series, also made its debut in 1970. This was a completely new heavy tractor with a 132cm/52in BBC cab of very square appearance. An 208cm/82in BBC sleeper version was also offered. By then there was a choice of four different Cummins diesels covering 13 power ratings, two Detroit diesels covering five power ratings and Caterpillar diesels at 250 or 270bhp.

The Louisville or L line became one of Ford's best-known truck ranges and survived through to the 1990s. The W series was facelifted in 1975 with a grille resembling that of the Louisville. The old C series was also to survive into the early 1980s. In the late '70s the W series was replaced by the impressive new aluminium-cabbed CL-9000. A bonneted derivative of this model, the LTL-9000 for maximum-weight line-haul operation, was launched in 1981. While Ford's dominance of the light and medium market continued, it was losing sales in the highly competitive Class 8 heavy-duty sector. The superbly equipped Aeromax 120 conventional of 1991 was aimed to challenge the best that Kenworth and Freightliner could offer, but Ford's disappointing Class 8 sales led them to sell their heavy truck operations to the Freightliner Corporation in 1997. The products were subsequently renamed Sterling. Freightliner is a subsidiary of the DaimlerChrysler Corporation.

■ ABOVE *A 1960 C.750 milk tanker powered by a 302-HD V8 gasoline engine with the option of 5-speed synchromesh or Transmatic auto.*

■ RIGHT *Ford's F-700 medium-weight conventional grosses 12.5 tons and uses a V8 gasoline engine.*

■ BELOW *An L-9000 concrete mixer based in Vancouver, British Columbia.*

BARCELONA, SPAIN

FORD

Between 1920 and 1954 a range of Ford light trucks, based on American and British models, was built at Ford Motor Iberica, production being curtailed during the Civil War years from 1936–40. In 1956 a new range developed from British designs was launched under the Ebro name. The name was taken from the Ebro River, just as Thames was adopted for Ford's UK trucks.

COLOGNE, GERMANY

FORD

■ ABOVE ***German Ford FK4500 4½-tonners were powered by V6 two-stroke diesel engines of 120bhp.***

German-built Ford trucks appeared in 1935 with the BB 2-tonner. In 1936 a 3-tonner with the 3.6 litre/219cu in V8 gasoline engine was introduced. After World War II production of the 3-tonner continued and in the late 1940s it became known as the Ford Rhine. A 4-cylinder version was also available called the Ford Ruhr. From 1951 German Ford trucks were designated the FK series (standing for Ford-Köln). In 1956 a restyled range for payloads of 1.5 to 4.8 tonnes was announced, powered by V4 and V6 two-stroke diesel engines. The cab was also used on the normal-control Thames Trader and the later K series built in the UK. Truck production at Cologne ceased in 1971, the last models being based on the UK D series.

DAGENHAM, ENGLAND

FORDSON & FORDSON THAMES

The Fordson name appeared on British-built Ford trucks in 1933, the first new model to appear with it being the forward-control BBE 2-tonner. This was launched in December 1934. Unlike its Ford BB predecessor, the BBE featured longitudinal front semi-elliptic springs instead of the traditional Ford transverse arrangement. The power unit was Ford's 3.6 litre/219cu in V8 gasoline engine producing 85bhp. As well as the basic 4×2 model there were 6×2 and 6×4 factory-approved conversions called the Surrey and Sussex respectively. These were converted by County Commercial Cars Ltd and took a payload of up to 6 tons. A normal-control V8-engined 2-tonner with a similar choice of drive configurations was the Model 51 of 1935. This had cab styling along the lines of the Ford Y type car. Another interesting model that was in production from 1935–37 was the Tug light artic for 3-ton payloads.

■ ABOVE ***The Fordson Thames ET (English Truck) models of 1949 had a Briggs cab.***

■ LEFT ***The BBE model launched in 1933 was the first truck to carry the Fordson nameplate.***

■ RIGHT *The Fordson Thames 7V with V8 gasoline engine appeared in 1939 and production carried on until 1949.*

■ BELOW RIGHT *A Fordson Model 51 3-ton dump truck with 85bhp V8 gasoline engine and torque tube drive.*

It featured a three-wheeled tractor based on the Y type 8hp car. There was also a 4-ton version taking the 10hp engine of the C model passenger car. All the heavier Fordson trucks of 1936 had V8 engines. The forward-control range was enlarged in 1938 with a new 4/5-ton forward-control model. It was in 1939 that the name Thames was first introduced and the trucks were then marketed as Fordson Thames, although they were generally referred to as Thames.

During World War II Ford built large numbers of light and medium military vehicles powered by V8 gasoline engines. These included 1½-ton 4×2s, 1½ and 3-ton 4×4s and 3-ton 6×4s. Normal civilian production resumed in 1945 with forward-control 7V trucks in the 2 to 5-ton payload sector. The design was now almost eight years old. There were 10 different models, including a tractor version, based on the short-wheelbase dump-truck chassis, for articulated use with an 8-ton payload. Unlike its nearest rival, Bedford, which offered only bonneted trucks at that time, Ford only had forward-control models and the 7V cab was cramped compared with most normal-control cabs. This led Ford to revert to normal control for its new range of Fordson Thames trucks – the ET6 and ET7 of 1949. The ET6 took the V8 gasoline while the ET7 had a Perkins P6 diesel

for greater economy. The new models covered a similar payload range to the 7Vs and still included the Surrey and Sussex 6×2 and 6×4 conversions by County. The new cab was supplied by Briggs Motor Bodies, and a similar design was used by Dodge on its bonneted Kew models and on Leyland's Comet. In 1953, conscious of the fuel economy aspect of V8 gasoline engines, Ford introduced its 3.6 litre/219cu in Cost Cutter 4-cylinder gasoline with overhead valves. This formed the basis for Ford's first diesel, the 3.61 litre/220cu in 4D in 1954. With the Thames Trader forward-control range of 1957, the Fordson Thames name changed to Ford Thames.

DETROIT, MICHIGAN, USA

FREEMAN

Freeman trucks were of an unusual four-wheel drive design in which the front wheels were driven via a "live" axle positioned above a fixed axle, a system of bevel gearing eliminating the need for a differential. The trucks were in production from 1928–34 and there were three weight ratings. Power came from Buda 6-cylinder gasoline engines rated at 65, 75 and 100bhp. The heaviest model was capable of hauling two drawbar trailers, enabling a total payload of 20 tons to be carried. Initially trading as Freeman Motor Co., it later became the Freeman Quadrive Corporation.

■ ABOVE *The early 1930s Freeman 4×4 truck could haul two drawbar trailers and was powered by a Buda 6-cylinder gasoline engine.*

PORTLAND, OREGON, USA

FREIGHTLINER

■ BELOW *The Freightliner 6×4 conventional grosses up to 40 tons and features an aluminium cab to reduce tare weight.*

Freightliner is an example of an enterprising haulier building a truck to meet his own exacting standards and later successfully launching it on to the market. Leland James, president of Consolidated Freightways Inc. of Spokane, Washington, wanted something better than the existing truck manufacturers could offer in the late 1930s. In 1939 he set up a subsidiary under the name Freightways Manufacturing Corp. at Salt Lake City, Utah, to build a truck to suit CF's own needs. The aim was to build the lightest possible tractor unit through the use of light alloys. The product of Freightways' endeavours was the CF-100 diesel-engined cabover built in 1940. The Freightliner nameplate appeared in 1942.

CF were the only users of the early tractors, which were produced up to 1942 when war-time restrictions on materials forced a temporary shutdown. After the war, production was resumed at Consolidated Freightways' maintenance workshops in Portland, Oregon, and a new company, the Freightliner Corporation, was formed. The trucks were highly successful and by careful design and extensive use of aluminium, they could carry 1 ton more than most other trucks of similar size. In 1948 it was decided to market the Freightliner, and one of the first private carriers to purchase one was the Hyster Company. That truck, an 800 model, eventually clocked a total of four million miles and on retirement it was restored and presented to the Smithsonian Museum of History and Technology.

A sleeper cab was offered from 1949 and in 1951 Freightliner joined the White Motor Company of Cleveland, Ohio, in a joint marketing agreement whereby White became responsible for sales, service and distribution of Freightliners. The trucks were then badged White Freightliner. Many

■ BELOW LEFT *This dual-steer four-axled rigid can gross 60 tons with a trailer.*

■ BELOW RIGHT *An aluminium-cabbed 6×4 cabover with Cummins 14 litre/854cu in diesel.*

■ LEFT *An A train doubles outfit hauled by a Freightliner FLB-COE. Available power units include a 410bhp Cummins Celect diesel engine.*

■ RIGHT *Business Class Freightliners include the FL80 in various axle configuration.*

■ BELOW RIGHT *Freightliner's original cabover range was launched in 1942.*

■ BOTTOM RIGHT *An FLC 6×4 conventional A-train bulk tanker.*

refinements were introduced in the 1950s, with a newly designed cab appearing in 1953. That basic design continued with relatively little change for about three decades. A tilt version appeared in 1958 which could tilt to 90 degrees for complete maintenance access. The all-aluminium cab was designed as a strong riveted structure and featured a V-shaped windscreen with flat glass.

In 1974 Freightliner began offering a long-nosed conventional with a high degree of interchangeable parts with their cabovers. Once again these were among the lightest conventionals around. Freightliners use mainly Cummins diesels. By the late '70s the company had become one of America's major heavy-duty truck producers and had opened plants in Fremont, Chino, Indianapolis, and a Canadian plant in Vancouver. White trucks were forced to pull out of the joint marketing arrangement in 1977, and from that point on the trucks reverted to Freightliner. Daimler-Benz (now DaimlerChrysler) had established a North American presence as long ago as 1964 and in 1981 it took over the Freightliner Corporation. As part of the world's largest producer of heavy trucks, Freightliner went from strength to strength and since 1991 has made significant in-roads into export markets. In 1992 Freightliner became the United States' number one Class 8 truck producer.

In 1995 the company entered the lighter Class 4, 5, 6 and 7 truck markets with the formation of their Custom Chassis Corporation. Freightliner also purchased American La France, the world's oldest manufacturer of fire appliances.

Some European influence has become evident in the cabover tractors with set-back front axles and a greater degree of aerodynamic styling, following a trend in United States cab design over the past two decades or so. The Century Class truck was unveiled in 1995, incorporating many technological advancements. In 1997 Freightliner took over Ford's heavy-duty truck operations and shortly after introduced the new Sterling name badge for Ford products.

OTHER MAKES

■ LEFT *A 1½-ton payload Federal E6 type dating from 1931.*

■ LEFT *This 6×4 Federal 2902 Styliner with dump body was built in 1954 and worked all its life in Australia.*

■ FEDERAL

DETROIT, MICHIGAN, & MINNEAPOLIS, MINNESOTA, USA

After originally being set up as the Bailey Motor Truck Co. in 1910, the company name was changed that same year to the Federal Motor Truck Co. The first Federal was a bonneted chain-drive 1-tonner with a 4-cylinder Continental gasoline engine. Shaft drive was introduced in 1916, by which time a range of trucks from 1½ to 3 tons was available. A 5-ton model appeared in 1917 followed by a 7-tonner in 1918. The lighter models had pneumatic tyres from 1921. By the mid '20s Federal was one of America's major truck producers. As early as 1929 a sleeper cab was being offered on the larger tractor units and pneumatic tyres and front-wheel brakes had become the norm. Bold cab styling was adopted in the late '30s and cabover trucks were added to the range from 1937. By 1939 Federal had produced over 100,000 trucks.

During World War II Federal built heavy-duty 6×6 wreckers with 180bhp Hercules gasoline engines plus a 20-ton 6×4 tractor powered by a Cummins two-stroke diesel of 130bhp. The distinctive Styliner range appeared in 1951, powered by Federal's own 145bhp Power Chief gasoline engine. In 1952 the company became the Federal Fawick Corporation but was taken over by Napco Industries in 1955, production being relocated at Minneapolis. For the last few years the company built specialized heavy vehicles in ever-diminishing numbers, and production ceased altogether in 1959.

■ FLEXTRUC

ONTARIO, CANADA

Specialized 8×6 and 10×6 construction vehicles in articulating four-axle form are the main product of this company which took over the manufacturing rights of the Rubber Railway Company in 1979. The trucks are steered hydraulically by having a pivoted chassis. They have gross weights of 40 tons plus.

■ FOWLER

LEEDS, ENGLAND

Most of Fowler's products are outside the scope of this book since the company was mainly concerned with steam traction engines. Founded in 1880 as John Fowler & Co., they began building under-type steam lorries in 1924 using a vertical V-twin compound engine of 3hp. These never achieved the same success as vehicles from Sentinel or Foden. In 1931, when it was becoming clear that steam was losing out to the internal combustion engine, Fowler bid for a share of the diesel truck market by introducing their semi-forward-control Marathon 6 to 7-tonner. This had a 12.2 litre/745cu in direct-injection Fowler diesel developing 90bhp at 1400rpm. A three-axled version was also offered, plus a short-wheelbase dump-truck chassis called the Crusader. The trucks were heavy and expensive so sales were very limited. Gardner engines were tried in 1934 with little more success and Fowler production ceased in 1935.

■ LEFT *Fowler were famous steam-engine builders who tried to market this Marathon 7-ton diesel truck in 1931.*

OTHER MAKES

■ LEFT *Dutch manufacturer FTF used a British Motor Panels cab on its 6×4 tractor unit.*

■ BELOW *The UK-built British Quad of 1918 was based on the FWD.*

■ **FTF**

WIJCHEN, THE NETHERLANDS

Floor's was once a transport company which, during the early 1950s, began building its own trailers. It turned to importing and assembling Mack trucks in 1952 and, following Mack Truck's decision to set up its own assembly plant in 1964, Floor's Handel en Industrie BV began building its own trucks under the FTF name from 1966. The trucks incorporated many Mack components, but later models used Detroit Diesel engines, Fuller gearboxes or Allison automatics and a British-designed Motor Panels cab. In recent years production has been centred on 6×2, 6×4, 6×6, 8×4, 8×8 and 10×4 types, all in the heavy-duty category.

■ **FWD**

CLINTONVILLE, WISCONSIN, USA

Inventor Otto Zachaw came up with a patent constant-velocity joint in 1910 that led to the production of a steer-drive axle and in 1912, in partnership with his brother-in-law William Besserdich, founded the FWD (Four-Wheel Drive) Auto Company. A primitive 2-ton truck had been built as early as 1910 but it was during World War I that FWD trucks for 3 and 5-ton payloads began volume production. William Besserdich left to set up Oshkosh in 1917. FWD went on to build a wide range of trucks in conventional and cabover form. During World War II cabover versions of their SU bonneted truck were built for the armed forces – the familiar SU-COE models.

The 1950s saw a huge range of trucks for both on and off-highway use, including sleeper-cab 6×4 tractors for line-haul work. Specialized multi-wheel drive trucks like the Tractioneer appeared in the '50s and '60s, plus the unusual Teracruzer for desert use. From 1960 the company became the FWD Corporation, and in 1963 took over the Seagrave Corporation which specialized in fire-fighting equipment. Production of specialized trucks and fire appliances has continued into the 1990s.

■ **FWD**

SLOUGH, ENGLAND

Considerable numbers of American FWD trucks were shipped to the UK during World War I, many finding their way into civilian ownership after the war. A British version, the British Quad was built under licence from 1918, using a Dorman engine. In 1927 FWD Motors launched a 6×6 powered by a 6-cylinder Dorman. Later, in 1929, FWD entered an agreement with AEC of Southall under which the trucks were fitted with AEC engines instead of Dormans. By then the British-built FWDs were so far removed from the original American-sourced trucks that the FWD name was dropped, and from 1931 the trucks were renamed Hardy.

■ BELOW *A late 1960s FWD LB46-2641 Tractioneer with air load transfer.*

BIRMINGHAM, ENGLAND

GARNER

■ LEFT *A 2-ton Garner truck of the early 1930s.*

From 1915 Henry Garner of Moseley, Birmingham, assembled American Gramm-Bernstein trucks to meet wartime demand for civilian trucks in the UK. In 1925 Garner began building its own design of truck, a 2-tonner with Dorman engine. Production moved to a new factory at Tylesley in 1926 and in 1931 a new range of forward-control trucks up to 6-ton payload was introduced. For a brief period from 1934–36 Garner was taken over by steam-wagon builders Sentinel of Shrewsbury and the trucks were marketed as Sentinel-Garner. However, it was re-sold in 1936 to a consortium of ex-Dodge employees who set up a factory at Willesden in west London. A modernized truck range for 2 to 5-ton payloads was offered from 1937 up to World War II. After the war the company concentrated on building commercial bodywork.

LEISTON, ENGLAND

GARRETT

■ LEFT *A 6-ton Garrett undertype steam wagon of the early 1920s.*

One of the oldest names in the industry, Garrett's history dates back to 1856. They specialized in agricultural machinery and steam traction engines until 1904, when an experimental steam lorry was built. Garrett entered the steam-wagon market in earnest from 1909, first with overtypes and then, from 1927, with the more practical undertype layout. Garrett acquired the Scottish Caledon truck company in 1926 but a planned Garrett-Caledon gasoline truck did not enter full production, although two or three prototypes were completed. In 1928 a couple of oil-engined trucks were built, basically steamers fitted with McLaren diesel engines – these are reputed to be the first-ever UK diesel trucks. Just before the company folded in 1932, a 6-ton forward-control four-wheeler with a choice of Meadows gasoline engine or Blackstone diesel was announced, but there is no record of it entering production. From 1932–60 Garrett turned their attention to engineering.

GORKY, RUSSIA

GAZ

■ LEFT *The GAZ 53A 4-ton truck of 1969 had a V8 gasoline engine, but this example has a Perkins P6 engine fitted.*

GAZ (Gorkovoka Automobilova Zavod) began in 1931 by assembling Ford AA trucks under licence. Products were based on American Fords until after World War II and were lightweight models with both civilian and military specifications. Post-war models consisted of the GAZ-51 general cargo truck for 5 tonnes, the 1½-tonne GAZ-63 4×4 and a dump truck designated the GAZ-93. A 2-ton payload 4×4, the GAZ-66 was a cabover design powered by a 4.2 litre/256cu in V8 engine. Some GAZ production was transferred to the UAZ (Ulyanovsk) factory from 1957, where they were further developed and badged UAZ.

SEATTLE, WASHINGTON, USA

GERSIX

Gersix was the forerunner of today's Kenworth. The company was formed in 1917, having briefly been set up as Gerlinger in 1916. Louis and Edgar Gerlinger completed their first truck in 1917. This was powered by a 6-cylinder Continental gasoline engine leading to the choice of Ger-six as the make. The truck was a well-engineered, worm-drive bonneted machine. Until 1922 Gersix remained a low-volume producer, then two of the major shareholders, H. W. Kent and E. K. Worthington, reorganized the company, renaming it the Kenworth Motor Truck Co.

HIGH WYCOMBE, ENGLAND

GILFORD

■ LEFT *The early 1930s Gilford truck was partly inspired by Gilford's bus chassis.*

Gilford is probably remembered more for its buses than its trucks. The company began as E. B. Horne & Co. in north London in 1925 and became the Gilford Motor Co. Ltd in 1926. At first it imported Garford trucks from America but, because of import restrictions, it began building its own light commercials for 1½ to 2½-ton payloads powered by 4-cylinder Buda engines. During the 1930s it built trucks generally based on bus chassis. One model, the 1680T, was noted for its instantly recognizable Westinghouse Gruss air springs mounted on the front dumb irons. A normal-control version, the 168SD, was also available with goods bodywork. From 1927–33 Gilfords were built at High Wycombe, but production moved back to London in 1934. Poor sales forced the company into liquidation in 1935. For a brief period the factory was taken over by HSG (High Speed Gas) to build HSG-Gilford producer gas-powered trucks, but very few were built and HSG relocated to the Sentinel Waggon Works, Shrewsbury, in 1938, closing shortly afterwards.

EDERVEEN, THE NETHERLANDS

GINAF

In the 1950s Gebr Van Ginkel NV reconditioned old United States army trucks, converting them for civilian use, but in 1967 it began building its own 6×6 trucks – often based on Diamond T chassis. The company became Ginaf Automobielbedrijven BV from 1967 and went on to specialize in heavy-duty 4×4, 6×4, 6×6, 8×4, 8×6, 8×8, 10×4 and 10×8 trucks, aimed chiefly at the construction industry. Some early models had cabs by Van Dijk Coach-builders but DAF cabs became standard, the latest models having the Cabtec unit of the DAF 95 or the 85 series cab. DAF engines and axles are also used.

■ ABOVE *Ginaf's speciality is extra-heavy-duty construction vehicles based on DAF engineering.*

PONTIAC, MICHIGAN, USA

GMC

■ BELOW *A 1915 GMC SC type 1½-ton chain-drive truck with 4-cylinder gasoline engine.*

GMC trucks first appeared in 1912 following the earlier takeover of two pioneer truck manufacturers – Rapid and Reliance. Rapid trucks were the brainchild of brothers Max and Morris Grabowski, who built a rudimentary single-cylinder truck capable of 16kph/10mph back in 1900. The Rapid Motor Vehicle Co. of Detroit was officially incorporated in 1904 and in 1905 production was moved to Pontiac, Michigan. Max Grabowski fell out with his partners and left the company in 1907, setting up the Grabowski Power Wagon Co. but that enterprise was short-lived, going bankrupt in 1912. Shortly after taking over the Rapid Motor Vehicle Co., GM purchased the Reliance Motor Truck Co. of Owosso, Michigan, which had been formed in 1902. A new company, the General Motors Truck Co., was established following the acquisition of Reliance, to market both Rapid and Reliance trucks. In 1911 the two companies were merged and all production centred on Pontiac, the GMC nameplate being adopted the following year. Rapid trucks were generally of bonneted layout with 4-cylinder engines and chain drive to take payloads of up to 2 tons. Reliance trucks, on the other hand, were heavier-duty cabovers for 3½ to 5 tons payload, also primarily chain-drive. GMC trucks switched to shaft drive with worm axles in 1915.

■ ABOVE *This veteran 1906 Reliance 2-tonner was the forerunner of the GMC truck.*

■ ABOVE *The 1936 GMC T74 5-ton cabover had a 5.4 litre/330cu in gasoline "six".*

■ BELOW *The L5000 with 183cm/72in BBC tilt cab had a 182bhp V6 gasoline engine.*

After World War I production concentrated on the bonneted K series, covering payloads from 1 ton to 5 tons plus an artic version, the K101, which could take 15 tons. The heavier models had solid tyres. A Canadian production plant got underway in 1922. From 1925–29 GMC built the massive Big Brute K102.

During the late 1920s the K models were replaced with the more modern T-line trucks with pneumatic tyres and fully enclosed cabs. By 1931 GMC were offering four-wheelers, six-wheelers and artics for payloads of up to 15 tons. The company even built a range of semi-trailers. In 1933 engine improvements were introduced, the heavy trucks having new 10 litre/610cu in and 11.7 litre/713cu in gasoline engines with 7-bearing crankshafts. The same year saw the introduction of a full forward-control range. Sleeper cabs were now available too and all cabs were of very functional design. New streamlined cabs began appearing in 1935 on the T range. Medium trucks now had hydrovac servo brakes while the heaviest models had full air systems. Diesel power became available on some models in 1939, the engines being 3 or 4-cylinder two-stroke Detroit Diesels built by GM.

GMC's wartime production was an astonishing 560,000 military CCW 2½-ton 6×4 trucks plus 20,000 DUKW amphibious vehicles, making it the largest producer of the war period. From 1939 the company became the

GMC Truck & Coach Division of the General Motors Corporation. In the post-war era a comprehensive range from pickups to maximum-weight 6×4 tractors was offered. Memorable classics like the DW-970 conventional and the DF-860 cabover were available in the late 1950s, powered by the 6-71SE Detroit Diesel two-stroke rated at 210bhp. Noteworthy models of that same era were the 800/860 4×2 and W860 6×4 tractors with GM's own all-round air suspension, where compressed air was stored in a tubular front axle and in the rectangular section rear-radius arms.

The slab-fronted DFR 8000 cabover and DLR 8000 cab-forward models appeared in 1958 with aluminium 122cm/48in BBC tilt cab and air suspension. These originally had unusual I-section chassis rails. In 1963 they opted for conventional channel sidemembers and steel leaf suspension. While Detroit two-stroke diesels were common fitment, GM also offered their Torq-Flow four-stroke V8 diesels from 1964. Some medium-duty trucks were fitted with independent front suspension in the early '60s, but this was abandoned in 1963.

During the 1970s GM began commonizing more on the design of GMC and Chevrolet trucks. The Astro 95 cabover, launched in 1969, was the main line-haul tractor powered by the 71 series Detroit Diesel or with a Cummins option. The Chevrolet Titan was virtually identical. New additions to the range in the '70s were the Brigadier and General conventionals, the latter being the top-of-the-range Class 8 tractor. GM also offered Astro glider kits consisting of a new cab and chassis with front axle, aimed at owners who wanted to update an old truck, of any make, or to rebuild an accident-damaged truck. From 1980 the Astro 95 took on a new look with a full-width grille, but very little more came from GMC in the way of new heavy truck models after that. It entered a joint venture with Volvo of Sweden towards the end of 1986 resulting in the Volvo GM Heavy Truck Corporation, which eventually became Volvo Trucks North America.

■ ABOVE LEFT ***A late 1950s bonneted GMC 620 tandem-axle truck.***

■ ABOVE RIGHT ***This semi-forward-control articulated car transporter dates from the early 1950s.***

■ RIGHT ***The 1979 GMC Brigadier tandem-axle tractor had a choice of Straight Six, V6 and V8 Detroit Diesel two-strokes or Cummins 14 litre/854cu in, with power ratings up to 350bhp.***

WOLVERHAMPTON, ENGLAND

GUY

■ LEFT *The 1920 Guy 2½-ton truck had shaft drive and solid tyres. It was powered by a 4-cylinder gasoline engine.*

The founder of Guy Motors, Sidney Slater Guy, was one of the pioneers of the UK truck industry. In 1913 he resigned from his position of works manager at the Sunbeam Motor Car Company and in 1914 formed Guy Motors at Fallings Park, Wolverhampton. The first truck was built that same year – a 1½-tonner which featured an overdrive 4-speed gearbox. In its early history Guy Motors was a significant producer of buses as well as trucks. In 1922 a heavy-duty articulated six-wheeler was introduced, plus a 3-ton electric truck. A number of military trucks were developed in the 1920s, including half tracks. Lighter trucks had pneumatic tyres from 1923. Already Guy were developing export sales in many parts of the world. Some heavy trucks were built in the early '30s, including the Warrior four-wheeler and Goliath six-wheeler powered by Gardner diesels.

■ LEFT *The 1954 Guy Otter 6-ton payload dump truck had a choice of Gardner 4-cylinder or Perkins 6-cylinder diesel.*

■ BELOW LEFT *In 1958 Guy Motors launched their Invincible Mk.II and Warrior range featuring bold styling and wrap-around windscreen.*

From 1933 the earliest examples of the famous Wolf 2-tonner, Vixen 3 to 4-tonner and Otter 6-tonner were appearing in both bonneted and forward-control form. There was also a low-loading six-wheel version of the Vixen called the Fox. Guy's famous Indian's head began appearing on the radiator caps in 1934. During World War II Guy designed and built the military 4×4 Quad Ant and a 4×4 rear-engined armoured car. During the war some civilian austerity models were offered, including the Vixant which was basically the Vixen with angular front-end sheet metal.

After the war the Wolf, Vixen and Otter resumed full production and in 1952 a new bought-in cab from Motor Panels began to appear. This was also fitted to the Otter tractor unit, specially developed in conjunction with British

■ RIGHT *A 1960 Otter 6-ton platform truck powered by a Gardner 4LK diesel engine.*

■ RIGHT *Guy's first heavy eight-wheeler was the 1954 Invincible, based on an AEC chassis.*

Road Services, the nationalized UK transport organization.

In 1954 Guy extended up the weight range with new maximum-weight trucks of 4×2, 6×2, 6×4, 8×2 and 8×4 configurations. These were at first called Goliath, but were almost immediately relaunched as the Invincible range since the old Guy name "Goliath" had been claimed by a German van manufacturer. The Invincibles were based on AEC chassis engineering but were powered by Gardner or Meadows diesels. The heaviest Invincible grossed 24 tons gvw or 32 tons with trailer. The following year Guy launched the 14-ton gross Warrior with a stylish Motor Panels cab plus a more powerful version named the Formidable built mainly in tractor-unit form.

In 1958 Guy invested heavily in developing a completely new heavy-duty range, the Invincible Mk.II. This had a completely new chassis of very heavy proportions and a wide choice of engines from Gardner, Meadows, Leyland, AEC, Cummins and Rolls Royce. Perhaps its most memorable feature was its new ultra-modern cab with wrap-around windscreen and distinctive trans-Atlantic styling. A lightweight version, the Warrior, powered by an AEC AV470 engine, appeared the following year, developed from a prototype built by Guy's main dealer, TGB Motors, in 1958. However, Guy's finances were under some strain and the company was taken over by the Jaguar Car Company in 1961.

Jaguar breathed new life into Guy, which then traded as Guy Motors (Europe) Ltd. The range remained unchanged for three years or so until a new model, the Big J (signifying "Jaguar") was announced in 1964. This was a comprehensive range of four, six and eight-wheelers powered by a choice of engine but with the Cummins V6-170 and V6-200 as the leading fitment. The Big J featured a steel Motor Panels cab.

In 1964 the Jaguar company merged with the troubled British Motor Corporation to form British Motor Holdings. This in turn merged with the Leyland Motor Corporation in 1968 to form the equally troubled and top-heavy British Leyland Motor Corporation. Under Leyland ownership Guy was a small cog in the LMC machine and during the mid 1970s Guy was gradually phased out, disappearing completely by 1979.

■ BELOW RIGHT *Guy's last truck model was the Big J4T launched after the company had been taken over by Jaguar Cars.*

OTHER MAKES

■ GENOTO

ISTANBUL, TURKEY

The General Motors-owned Genoto company, General Otomotiv Sanayi ve Ticaret A.S. of Istanbul, assembled Bedford TK trucks during the 1970s and '80s. The main model was the MSLR based on the KHL 13.5-tonne gvw chassis but with the addition of a 5-tonne capacity trailing third axle, bringing the gvw to 18.5 tonnes. Chassis engineering, including frame, suspension, brakes and steering, were all Bedford but Genotos were powered by a 130bhp 6-cylinder Mercedes-Benz OM352 diesel engine.

■ GOTFREDSON

WALKERVILLE, CANADA, & DETROIT, MICHIGAN, USA

Originally named the G & J (from the original company name of Gotfredson & Joyce Corporation) the Gotfredson was assembled from well-known proprietary units including Buda engines, Timken axles and Fuller transmissions. Production began in 1920 at Walkerville, Ontario, while an American plant in Detroit, Michigan, started production in 1923. The range included normal-control trucks for up to 7 tons payload. Gotfredson trucks sold well in Canada and many were exported to the UK. They were well-built trucks with handsome cast-aluminium radiators. From 1923 the company was called the Gotfredson Truck Corporation Ltd. Canadian production ceased in 1932 and the company was sold to the Ford Motor Company. The Detroit plant had run into financial problems in 1929 and had been rescued, reformed and slimmed down as the Robert Gotfredson Truck Co. As such it survived through to 1948. Products included heavy-duty trucks for up to 50 tons gtw powered mainly by Cummins diesels, Gotfredson having a Cummins sales and service franchise. Production figures were small, the trucks being custom-built.

■ GRÄF & STIFT

VIENNA, AUSTRIA

The Wiener Automobilfabrik vom Gräf & Stift was founded in 1895 and built its first truck, a 45hp 2½-tonner in 1909. It went on to build heavier machines for 3 and 5-tonne payloads, many being supplied to the Austrian Army. From 1926 production was concentrated on a 2½-tonne truck with pneumatic tyres. During the 1930s trucks up to 4½ tonnes payload were produced and the first diesel engines were offered.

After World War II the company became Gräf & Stift Automobilfabrik AG and

■ ABOVE *The 1970 Genoto was based on British Bedford engineering, but powered by a 6-cylinder Mercedes-Benz diesel engine.*

■ LEFT *The 1923 Gotfredson took its power from a Buda gasoline engine and featured pneumatic tyres and semi-enclosed cab.*

OTHER MAKES

■ RIGHT
A 1958 Graf & Stift LF-200/50 19-tonne gvw truck with sleeper cab.

■ BELOW RIGHT
GV flourished in the 1920s when heavy-duty electrics were in vogue.

production was concentrated on the 120 6-tonner powered by a 6-cylinder diesel of 125bhp. Forward-control models with a very attractive cab design appeared in 1957. These included maximum-weight trucks and tractor units powered by 6-cylinder Mercedes-Benz diesels, plus a twin-steer six-wheeler with a 200bhp two-stroke diesel. In 1970 the company merged with ÖAF, also of Vienna, becoming Österreichische Automobilfabrik Gräf & Stift AG, but henceforth all trucks were badged ÖAF.

■ GRUBE

WERDAU, GERMANY

Grube trucks were built from 1952–67 by VEB IFA Kraft Fahrzeugwerke, Ernst Grube, but were also marketed under the IFA badge (Industrieverband Fahrzeugbau Association) from the former East Germany. Prior to 1952 the factory had built steam tractors for road haulage. These went under the Lowa name and were introduced in 1949. Grube's distinctive bonneted H6 truck was at various times also marketed as the Horch H6 and the Sachsenring S4000, all these manufacturers being part of the IFA combine.

■ GV

LONG ISLAND, NEW YORK, USA, & BIRMINGHAM, ENGLAND

The General Vehicle Co. produced a wide range of battery electric trucks between 1906 and 1920. Payloads ranged from 1 to 5 tons. Production of GV trucks also took place in Birmingham, England, from 1916 and that operation continued until 1935. After 1921 lighter models were discontinued but heavy-duty models became popular with municipal users, breweries and railway companies. The largest machine was the articulated Giant for 10-ton payloads. GV in America briefly entered the gasoline-engined market from 1913–18, building German Mercedes 6-tonners under licence. They were first known as American Daimler but were renamed GV Mercedes.

GLASGOW, SCOTLAND

HALLEY

■ LEFT *This Scottish-built Halley chain-drive 2½-ton truck was exported to a customer in Sydney, Australia.*

Established as Halley Industrial Motors Ltd in 1906, the company was formerly called the Glasgow Motor Lorry Co. Ltd, which was formed in 1901. Between then and 1906 it built steam wagons, the early ones being called Glasgow wagons. During the period up to World War I, Halley gasoline-engined trucks from 1½ to 6 tons appeared, the heaviest of which had Tylor engines. During the war Halley built some 400 3-ton subsidy lorries. By then Halley were building their own engines, including a 6-cylinder unit. In the post-war years the firm concentrated on a solid-tyred 3½-tonner but sales were poor in the depressed market. Nevertheless the range was expanded to include forward-control models.

After running into financial difficulties in 1926 they were rescued by the North British Locomotive Company. They re-formed towards the end of 1927 as Halley Motors Ltd. Much of Halley's sales around that period were of buses, municipal vehicles and fire engines. A rigid six-wheeler, the B53 model for 8-ton payload, was announced in 1929 and in the early '30s a range of trucks from 4 to 13 tons payload was offered. Diesel power was growing in popularity at that time and Halley offered a Perkins Leopard in their 4-tonner of 1934. However, Halley's fortunes did not improve and the company went into liquidation in 1935, their factory being purchased by Albion Motors Ltd.

DARTFORD, ENGLAND

HALLFORD

■ LEFT *A Hallford chain-drive truck of the Bristol Tramways & Carriage Co.*

The very old established J & E Hall Dartford Ironworks originated in 1785 and the company's Hallford lorries appeared in 1907. The first 3-ton chain-drive was based on a Saurer design. By 1911 Hallford were producing their own engines and the truck range included models from 1½ to 5 tons. World War I production concentrated on 3-ton subsidy trucks powered by Dorman engines. After the war Hallford reverted to building their pre-war range, which still featured chain drive. From 1923 they offered a rigid six-wheeler for 10 tons payload, but in 1925 they withdrew from the market.

HANOVER, GERMANY

HANOMAG

■ LEFT *A 1970 Hanomag-Henschel F-190 19-tonne gross four-wheeler with tilt body.*

Hanomag began building gasoline-engined trucks in 1925 but had built a number of steam lorries some 15 to 20 years earlier. Those early steamers dating from 1905–08 were Stoltz designs built under licence. Hanomag's first gasoline-engined truck was a ¾-tonne forward-control model. In 1933 an innovative design appeared in the form of an underfloor-engined forward-control 4-tonner with a horizontal 4-cylinder diesel. Hanomag went on to build heavier tractors for artic and drawbar use up to 15 and 20-tonne payloads, the heavier one having a 5-cylinder diesel. Hanomag's post-war range mainly consisted of light trucks up to 2½ tonnes payload. In 1967 a new range appeared, extending up to 5 tonnes payload. In the meantime, Hanomag had taken over the Tempo company which specialized in front-wheel drive vans. In 1968 Hanomag merged with heavy truck maker Henschel of Kassel to form Hanomag-Henschel. Only two years later Hanomag-Henschel was taken over by Daimler-Benz (now DaimlerChrysler). Production of Hanomag-Henschel was phased out in 1973.

SLOUGH, ENGLAND

HARDY

The Hardy name replaced FWD in 1931 after the British FWD company signed an agreement with AEC Ltd to use AEC engines in their all-wheel drive trucks which previously used Dorman engines. AEC-engined Hardys also featured radiators and cabs closely resembling those of contemporary AECs. In the mid 1930s Hardy was absorbed completely into AEC and production was transferred to Southall in London. Hardy-AEC designs included the 8×8 roadtrain tractors exported to Australia during the mid '30s. The Hardy pedigree was also to be seen in AEC's famous Matador 4×4 medium artillery tractor of World War II. The Hardy name was not used after 1935.

WOLVERHAMPTON, ENGLAND

HAULAMATIC

■ LEFT *The 1980 Haulamatic dump truck featured a Perkins V8 diesel engine and Allison automatic transmission.*

From 1969 a new design of two and three-axled dump truck was introduced as the Haulamatic. Haulamatic had earlier marketed a Commer-based dump truck with beefed-up chassis and suspension. Power units included GM and Perkins V8 diesels, and models featured Allison transmissions. Haulamatic became part of Clarke Chapman in 1982 and since 1989 it has been owned by the NEI (Northern Engineering Industries) Group.

VANCOUVER, CANADA

HAYES

■ LEFT *Hayes specialized in massive heavy-duty logging tractors powered by a wide variety of engines.*

From 1934 trucks built by the Hayes Manufacturing Co. Ltd of Vancouver were referred to simply as Hayes but, prior to that, from their inception in 1928, they were called Hayes-Anderson. The company offered a wide range of trucks from 1½ tons upwards but came to specialize in logging trucks for the local lumber industry. Power units included Continental, Hercules and Leyland. They also built special low-loading dockside trucks.

In the late 1930s Hayes became Leyland distributors, supplementing their own range with Leylands. They also began using more Leyland components including axles and gearboxes. In the post-war years a range of on-highway trucks appeared and these continued to be updated and marketed throughout the 1950s and '60s. Engine choice now included Detroit Diesel, Cummins, Rolls Royce and Caterpillar. Three members of Hayes' management left in 1947 to form the Pacific Truck & Trailer Co. which was also to specialize in logging trucks. Meanwhile Hayes went on to build larger and more powerful logging trucks themselves throughout the 1960s and early '70s. The most impressive of these was the HDX1000, capable of hauling five trailers grossing up to 150 tons. The power unit for the HDX was a 430bhp Detroit Diesel V12. Mack Trucks took a two-thirds stake in Hayes from 1969 but in 1974 the company was sold to Paccar. Production ceased in 1975.

LYONS, ILLINOIS, USA

HENDRICKSON

■ RIGHT *1980 Hendrickson H3-38 6×4 tractor with Detroit Diesel.*

Swedish-born Magnus Hendrickson emigrated to the United States in 1887, settling in Chicago. A brilliant engineer, he built his first truck in 1900 and became chief engineer at the Lauth-Juergens truck company. Among his early innovations was a tilt cab, around 1911. Hendrickson left Lauth in 1913 and set up his own truck company, his first product being a chain-drive cabover. By 1920 he was offering three models from 2½ to 5 tons with shaft drive. A lighter 1½-ton model of 1922 had pneumatic tyres. From the outset Hendrickson built trucks for specialized operations, setting the pattern for their whole history. A significant development was the unique rocking-beam tandem-axle suspension unit that appeared on their first six-wheeler of 1926.

From 1933 Hendrickson formed close ties with the International Harvester Co. of Chicago, who gained exclusive rights to use the Hendrickson rear bogie. This arrangement lasted until 1948 when Hendrickson bogies were made available to other manufacturers. Meanwhile, some Hendrickson trucks featured International Harvester cabs. During the 1950s Hendrickson turned more and more to custom-built trucks and crane chassis, and a vast array of models was on offer, including aircraft refueller chassis, super-heavyweight trucks for 200 tons and more, fire appliances, dockspotters, as well as a range of on-highway trucks and tractor units. Production of these was centred on their Mobile Equipment division at Lyons, Illinois. In 1977 Hendrickson was acquired by the Boler Company and, while truck production did continue into the 1980s, the main products were suspension units and truck equipment of which Hendrickson continues to be one of the world's leading suppliers.

KASSEL, GERMANY

HENSCHEL

■ LEFT *A 1963 Henschel HS12KV powered by 132bhp 6-cylinder diesel.*

Prior to 1925 Henschel & Sohn GmbH built railway locomotives, but it was granted a licence in 1924 to build FBW trucks. The early FBW-based Henschel was a chain-drive 5-tonner but within a year a shaft-drive machine was available. In 1928 the company, now Henschel & Sohn AG, began building its own diesel engines and by 1930 the truck range included models from 2½ to 10 tonnes, the largest being a three-axled rigid. An articulated model was also available for payloads of up to 16 tonnes. Henschel then concentrated on a program of steam truck development based on the advanced Doble principle. Up to 18 heavy-duty steamers of modern appearance were built up until 1936. That year marked the appearance of a 300bhp 12-cylinder opposed-piston diesel engine. A range of military trucks was produced, but civilian production was resumed in the late 1950s. Bonneted trucks predominated but during the '50s a range of forward-control models became available, including some with underfloor engines. The company became Henschel-Werke GmbH in 1957, and in 1961 it formed a joint arrangement with Saviem under which Henschel was marketed in France as Saviem-Henschel. This arrangement only survived two years and was followed by an equally short-lived tie-up with the British Rootes Group, manufacturers of Commer trucks, to market their products as Commer-Henschel in Europe. That arrangement ceased in 1967 when Henschel was taken over by Rheinstahl, who already owned Hanomag and its subsidiary Vical & Sohn Tempo-Werke which built Tempo vans. Rheinstahl-Henschel AG was formed into Hanomag-Henschel Fahrzeugwerke GmbH in 1968 and the trucks carried Hanomag-Henschel name badges. Shortly after that, in 1970, the whole organization was absorbed into Daimler-Benz (now DaimlerChrysler). The last trucks to bear the Henschel badge were built in 1969.

HEANOR, ENGLAND

HHT

Although HHT trucks were not available on the open market, they are worthy of mention as an example of a specialized product developed to suit a transport company's own needs. Heanor Haulage of Heanor, Derbyshire, specialize in the movement of heavy, abnormal loads. Having operated heavy tractors from Scammell, they used a Scammell Contractor frame as a basis for their own heavier and more powerful machine, which featured a four-axled 1+3 arrangement. The first HHT had a 388bhp Detroit Diesel 8V-92 two-stroke diesel, Lipe-Rollway clutch and 15-speed Fuller Roadranger transmission. Three Leyland 11-ton axles formed the rear bogie, one being a lift axle for unladen running. A Volvo F89 cab was used. Approximately five tractors were built in all, most of which were three-axle types.

■ ABOVE *A three-axled HHT ballast tractor of 1978 built by Heanor Haulage.*

■ LEFT *Heanor's first HHT was this Detroit Diesel-powered four-axled machine built in 1975.*

CALCUTTA, INDIA

HINDUSTAN

Hindustan Motors Ltd was founded by the C.K. Birla Group in 1942 at Okha in the erstwhile state of Baroda, and was reregistered in 1950 with its head office in Calcutta. At first the company built a variety of British and American vehicles under licence but, from 1968, used the Hindustan nameplate on its trucks, which were based on the Bedford TJ. The normal-control J6, with detailed engineering changes to increase the gvw from 10.7 tons to 12 tons, used a cab based on the standard Bedford TJ, while a forward-control J6 featured a locally designed cab. Both were powered by Indian-built developments of the Bedford 5.4 litre/330cu in diesel and Bedford 4-speed gearbox. In 1982 the forward-control J6 was relaunched as the T.480 Mascot with 5-speed ENV gearbox as standard and larger fuel tank. By the early 1990s truck production had dwindled to nothing and Hindustan now build only cars and pickup trucks.

■ ABOVE *Hindustan's forward-control 7-tonner of the late 1970s was based on the British Bedford's normal-control TJ, but uprated to 12 tons gvw.*

TOKYO, JAPAN

HINO

Hino's roots can be traced back to 1910 and the establishment of the Tokyo Gas Industry. This became the Tokyo Gas & Electric Industry Ltd in 1913 and from 1917 the subsidiary Motor Vehicle Division began building T.G.E. trucks. The first truck was the A type of 1918 followed by the B type 1½-tonner of 1921. Truck production continued through to the formation of Hino Heavy Industries in 1942 after which the Hino name badge was used. In 1946 the division was renamed the Hino Industry Co. Ltd and the first 15-tonne heavy articulated truck was introduced. The company was again renamed in 1948 as Hino Diesel Industry Co. Ltd to manufacture heavy-duty diesel trucks, and the range expanded to include dump trucks and 6×6 construction vehicles. Japan's first twin-steer

■ LEFT *A Hino TE dump truck for 6.5 tons payload powered by DS70 140bhp 6-cylinder diesel engine.*

■ LEFT *A 1966 Hino tilt-cab KC series for payloads up to 7½ tons. The KC was launched in 1961.*

■ BELOW *Hino's TC362E twin-steer 6×2 of the early 1970s had a gvw of 22 tons and carried around 15 tons payload.*

■ LEFT *A 1979 KL645 9.5-ton gvw four-wheeler with 165bhp 6-cylinder diesel operating in Norway.*

six-wheeler was launched by Hino in 1958. In 1959 the company became Hino Motors Ltd. At that time the leading truck types were the bonneted TA, TH and HD models. The TA and TH specifications were virtually identical at 12 tonnes gvw, the TA being a shorter-wheelbase version of the TH for dump-truck bodywork. The HD was shorter still for articulated use at gcws up to 22 tonnes. Visually their cabs echoed the American International KB8 styling. A six-wheel version, the KE100 for 13 tonnes gcw, was also available.

The 1960s saw a comprehensive truck range of both normal and forward-control layout, the latter having tilt cabs. Hino came under the control of the Toyota Motor Co. in 1966 and from then on it concentrated on medium and heavy-duty diesel trucks, the heaviest of which was their ZM 6×4 logging truck. In 1972 a new forward-control tractor unit, the HE model for 40 tonnes, was introduced. Hino assembly plants were established in numerous countries throughout the world, including one in Dublin, Ireland, where Harris Ltd built Hino's first 30½-tonne 8×4 model aimed at the Irish and UK market. This was a forward-control ZM type. Australia and New Zealand became particularly important markets for Hino. During the 1980s and '90s Hino's principal medium and heavy trucks have been the F series, the lightest being the 10-tonne gvw FC and the heaviest being the FS three-axled and FY four-axled rigids.

For a period during the 1980s Hino was second only to Daimler-Benz as the world's largest truck producer, but it has since been overtaken by expanding organizations like Paccar, Navistar and Volvo. In 1992 Hino introduced their advanced Super Dolphin PROFIA truck with motor-operated tilt cab. The newest versions of this in three and four-axled rigid form have restyled, air-conditioned sleeper cabs and a host of luxury and safety features such as a glazed roof, electronic navigation aids, cruise control, collision-avoidance system, pre-tensioned seat belts and safety airbags. Other safety features include anti-lock braking and hydrodynamic retarder.

■ LEFT *In the late 1970s this UK-registered HE335E grossed 32 tons and was powered by Hino's ED100 diesel engine of 235bhp.*

■ BELOW *New Zealand is an important market for Hino. This is a 1997 380bhp FY1K drawbar outfit grossing 44 tons.*

BARCELONA, SPAIN

HISPANO-SUIZA

■ LEFT *Exceptionally modern styling characterized the 66 7-tonner launched in 1944 by Hispano-Suiza.*

Hispano-Suiza's origins can be traced to 1898 and an unsuccessful project on the part of Emilio de la Cuadra to build a gasoline-electric truck, a project for which he enlisted the help of Carlos Vellino, a Swiss battery manufacturer. Vellino sent for his compatriot Marc Birkigt to help. Unfortunately Cuadra ran into financial difficulties and his enterprise was renamed J. Castro (one of the creditors) Fabrica Hispano Suiza d'Autómoviles, signifying the joint Spanish and Swiss enterprise in which Birkigt became a partner.

Up to 1908 Hispano-Suiza built cars, but a truck was then introduced. This was a 12/15hp 1-tonner. A chain-drive truck for 3 tonnes payload appeared in 1911 and larger trucks were built in military form. An even larger truck for 4 tonnes payload and powered by a 6.8 litre/415cu in 4-cylinder engine at 53hp appeared in 1915. Between 1916 and 1923 national pride saw truck production move to a new factory in Guadalajara and the products were called La Hispano. Hispano-Guadalajara ran into financial problems and was taken over by Hispano-Suiza, Barcelona, but the plant was closed down completely in 1931. During the Spanish Civil War truck production was very limited, and Hispano-Suiza's first important new model was the 66 announced in 1944. This beautifully styled 7-tonner had unique lines that were later to be inherited by Pegaso trucks. The 66G had a 110bhp side-valve 6-cylinder gasoline engine while the 66D had a 128bhp 6-cylinder diesel.

Just two years after the 66 appeared, the Spanish INI (Institute Nacional d'Industries) purchased Hispano-Suiza's truck operations as part of a nationalization plan and the Empresa Nacional de Autocamiones SA (ENASA) was formed to build trucks under the Pegaso name.

ZWICKAU, GERMANY

HORCH

■ LEFT *The Horch H3 was also marketed as the Grube, the Sachsenring, and later the IFA.*

Formed in 1912, Horch built trucks from 1913 mainly for military use. After World War I, as A. Horch & Co. Motorenwagenwerke AG at Zwickau, it continued to build trucks of between 1½ and 3 tonnes payload up to 1925. Production then turned to specialized vehicles and military trucks. From 1945 the name Sachsenring was applied to the products, which subsequently came under the IFA (Industrieverband Fahrzeugbau Association).

SEINE, FRANCE

HOTCHKISS

■ LEFT *The 1966 Hotchkiss Type 80 featured a tilt cab and a choice of 4-cylinder gasoline or diesel engine.*

The Hotchkiss Company was formed in 1914 but only cars were built until 1936 when a bonneted 2-tonne truck was introduced. It had a 4-cylinder, 2.3 litre/140cu in ohv gasoline engine. After World War II the truck evolved into the PL20 model which featured hydraulic brakes. Hotchkiss were not significant producers of trucks, their products being limited to the medium-weight class. In 1954 they merged with Automobiles Delahaye and in 1961 a short-lived arrangement began under which Hotchkiss marketed Leyland Albion and Scammell trucks in France. The PL range continued in production until 1967, with heavier trucks up to 4 tonnes payload being added from the early '60s. Hotchkiss' last completely new truck was the forward-control tilt-cab model launched in 1965 for payloads of 3.7 to 5.7 tonnes and with a choice of gasoline or diesel engines. Jeeps were also built under licence from Willys. Hotchkiss' truck production was merged into Citroën around 1970.

LONDON, ENGLAND

HSG

■ RIGHT *There were plans to build a wide range of gas-powered HSG trucks in 1938, but full production never got underway.*

HSG, which stands for "High Speed Gas" was formed in 1936 to develop producer gas plant for road vehicles. As Gilford-HSG, based at the former Gilford Park Royal factory in west London, the company produced a couple of experimental bonneted 4 to 5-tonners, the first of which had a side-valve Coventry Climax 4-cylinder engine under the cab floor. Plans were drawn up for a full range of trucks, but production never got underway except for some semi-experimental military vehicles. In 1938 the business was acquired by the Sentinel Waggon Works of Shrewsbury. Two Sentinel-HSG prototype 5-tonners with horizontal, 4-cylinder underfloor engines were built, but the type never went into full production.

SHINTUNG, CHINA

HUANGHE

The Tsingtao Motor Vehicle Plant in Shintung Province, China, built an 8-ton payload diesel truck designated the JN-150 from 1964. Prototypes had been built in 1959. The power unit was a Chinese built, 160bhp 6-cylinder engine with a 5-speed gearbox. Since 1982 Huanghe trucks have been built at Jinan Factory.

SEOUL, KOREA

HYUNDAI

The Hyundai Motor Company was established in December 1967 and entered the truck market in 1978, drawing largely on British technology. Early Hyundai trucks were powered by Perkins diesel engines, the heaviest being for 7 tonnes. During the 1980s and '90s Hyundai have developed an ever-widening range using Japanese technology. A comprehensive range is offered, from 4×2 medium models to heavy-duty 6×4 tractor units and 6×4 and 8×4 rigids. Hyundai trucks form the basis of the Bering truck range recently launched in the United States.

HIGHLAND, ILLINOIS, USA

HUG

The Hug Company produced trucks, bodywork and trailers between 1922 and 1942, their products gaining a reputation for ruggedness and job fitness. This is not surprising since they understood the business from the customer's angle. Hug were a classic example of haulier turned manufacturer. The firm's founder G. J. Hug couldn't find a truck that would meet his needs on tough road-building work so he built his own prototype in 1921 – a solidly built 1-ton dump truck with a 34hp Buda gasoline engine and pneumatic tyres. During the 1920s and '30s Hug geared up to produce a wide range of trucks, many of which were fitted with dump-truck bodies. Heavy-duty bonneted 6×2 and 6×4 versions for payloads of up to 20 tons appeared in the '30s. The company also built cabover tractor units for maximum-weight line-haul operation. Typical were the 43LD and 43T powered by Cummins or Caterpillar 6-cylinder diesel or Buda gasoline engines. Fuller transmissions and Clark axles were used. At the lighter end of the range Hug offered models for payloads of 1½ to 2½ tons in both bonneted and cabover form. The company closed in June 1942.

■ LEFT *The D & R Transportation Co. of Lansing, Michigan, operated this seven-axled Hug 43LD A-train tanker with Cummins HA6 diesel in 1935.*

SALT LAKE CITY, UTAH, USA

IBEX

■ LEFT *The 1970 Ibex all-wheel drive tractor was powered by a Caterpillar 1676 8-cylinder diesel developing 340bhp.*

The Ibex Motor Truck Corporation specialized in heavy-duty, high-powered on/off-road trucks for construction, exploration and oilfield duty. They were mainly bonneted 4×4, 6×4 and 6×6 models powered by Cummins, Detroit Diesel and Caterpillar engines. Some cabover versions also appeared as well as specialized "dockspotter" tractors, and production began in 1963. In the 1980s production was concentrated on specialist airport service vehicles and terminal tractors.

ZWICKAU, WERDAU, & LUDWIGSFELDE, GERMANY

IFA

■ LEFT *The IFA W50 cabover 5-tonner was the workhorse of Eastern Europe for three decades.*

An association of manufacturers was formed in 1948 in East Germany to manage and co-ordinate state-owned truck production. The plants included Horch and Sachsenring at Zwickau and Ernst Grube of Werdau where production of the H3, H6 and Sachsenring S4000 took place. From 1965 VEB IFA (Industrieverband Farzeugbau Assn.) Automobilwerke Ludwigsfelde began production of the long-running W50 forward-control truck which was built mainly in four-wheeler and articulated form, many thousands of which are still to be seen in the old Eastern Bloc regions. The other model was the L60. In 1990 IFA Ludwigsfelde was taken over by Daimler-Benz (now DaimlerChrysler) and shortly afterwards production was switched to Mercedes light trucks and vans.

MARION, INDIANA, USA

INDIANA

■ LEFT *This model 95 box van for 2-ton payload dates from 1933.*

Indiana trucks were produced from 1911 through to the late 1930s. The bulk of production was in the light to medium-weight range. For the first nine years Indianas were built by Harwood-Barley Manufacturing Co., but in 1920 that became the Indiana Truck Corporation. Indiana used mainly proprietary engines and components. Engines in the earliest models were Rutenber gasoline units. Heavier models were added in the mid '30s. Five and 7-tonners were available using Waukesha and Hercules engines respectively. In 1928 the company was taken over by Brockway, but during the depression Brockway were forced to sell Indiana to the White Motor Co. From joining White in 1932 Indiana's production was moved to Cleveland, Ohio. Indiana claimed to be the earliest American manufacturer to offer a diesel truck, having co-operated with Cummins in 1931 to stage demonstration runs. The following year a 5-tonner with a 6-cylinder Cummins was offered. During the '30s production concentrated on the 2 to 7½-ton class, although a few heavier models were offered. Between 1936 and the company's demise in 1939, assembly of Indianas was undertaken in the UK by Indiana Sales of Wolverhampton.

MELBOURNE, AUSTRALIA

INTERNATIONAL HARVESTER

■ BELOW *The Australian-born ACCO range survives in the current ACCO-G series 2350 with choice of Cummins or International diesel power.*

Although International Harvester had a presence in Australia from 1912, production of Australian-designed trucks did not commence until the late 1950s. The first design was the military 4×4 2½-tonner for the Australian Army. The civilian AACO (Australian A-line Cabover) was developed from this in 1961. The squat, angular cab could not disguise its military origins but it proved a practical truck that would soon be seen all over Australia and New Zealand. Early models had a choice of International V.392 V8 gasoline engine or Perkins 6.354 diesel. Production was centred on Dandenong Works, Victoria. A large proving ground was built at Anglesea. A modernized tilt-cab range – the ACCO-A (Australian C-line Cabover) – was introduced in 1971. Normal-control trucks from 5 to 11.8 tonnes gvw and 24 tonnes gcw were also available, the cab on these being shared with Dodge. Twin-steer four-axled versions of the ACCO-A appeared in 1975 for a gcw up to 30 tonnes.

During the 1970s and '80s International's Australian operations underwent several changes of ownership. Following the formation of Seddon Atkinson in the UK in 1970, the Atkinson Australia subsidiary was sold off, becoming part of International Harvester Australia in 1973. Seddon Atkinson itself was absorbed into International Harvester's European operations in 1974, only to be sold to the Spanish group ENASA in 1983. ENASA had been part of International Harvester since 1978. By this time the ACCO-B range was in production with additional heavier-duty models up to 50 tonnes gcw.

International Trucks Australia Ltd (ITAL) became a separate operation from the parent company, International Harvester, when the latter curtailed its expansion plans and was re-formed as Navistar. ITAL built both Atkinson and International trucks for the Australian market, including Atkinsons fitted with the ACCO (or T-line) cab during the 1980s. In 1990 Iveco (Industrial Vehicle Corporation, formed in 1975), acquired ENASA, including its Seddon Atkinson subsidiary, followed in 1992 by ITAL. From the late '80s Iveco's influence had already shown itself in the E-series forward-control heavy-duty tractors that were based upon the Iveco TurboStar.

Under Iveco ownership the range in Australia became a mixture of Iveco and International lines, the long-running ACCO cab surviving on the T-line. The ACCO was revamped in 1996 as the ACCO-G, using a low version of the Iveco EuroTech cab. From 1995 ITAL began marketing Iveco's EuroTech forward-control range specified for the Australian market, and in 1996 an Australian-designed conventional was launched as the 500E44 PowerStar using the EuroTech cab shell adapted to normal control with a unique, locally designed sloping bonnet (hood). Alongside this, the American-designed Transtar conventional is also available.

■ LEFT *An Australian-built 44-tonne New Zealand B-train with an International Transtar 4670 6×4 bonneted tractor powered by a Caterpillar diesel.*

CHICAGO, ILLINOIS, USA

INTERNATIONAL HARVESTER

International Harvester's history dates from 1902, but the company's roots can be traced back to 1831 when Cyrus Hall McCormack invented the first mechanical reaper. By the turn of the century there were two large manufacturers of harvesters – McCormack and Deering – both in Chicago. In 1902 they merged with three other smaller manufacturers to form the International Harvester Co. Cyrus H. McCormack, the son of the original inventor, was president of the new organization. In 1907 IHC decided to expand into the production of light trucks aimed especially at farmers, and so was born their distinctive high-wheel Auto Buggy. Over the next few years more conventional trucks, including a 2-tonner, appeared and the International name badge was adopted in 1914.

By 1921 a range up to 5 tons payload capacity was available and a new production plant at Springfield, Ohio, was commissioned. A fully enclosed cab was introduced for trucks in 1927. The first diesel-engined models came in 1933. The C line heavy truck in rigid and articulated form featured new styling with a sloping, V-shaped aluminium radiator grille. There were 18 models in the range, including a 7-tonner. Six-wheelers for 10-ton payloads also appeared in the mid 1930s, featuring Hendrickson rear bogies. The D series replaced the C series in 1937, and further refinements were made to the styling. Cabover models were added to the range and a sleeper cab appeared in 1938.

In 1940 International's famous K line was introduced, and by then the company was one of America's largest truck producers. Wartime production included many thousands of military trucks, such as the semi-forward-control H-542, production of these also taking place at Marmon Herrington and Kenworth. The K re-entered production in 1946 as the KB, a truck to become a familiar sight in the UK and many other parts of the world. It formed the basis for the Russian ZIS and China's Jiefang trucks, which were virtually straight copies. The new

■ TOP *International Harvester's early high-wheel Auto Buggy.*

■ ABOVE *In 1921 International's Speed range included this 1-ton truck with shaft drive and pneumatic tyres.*

■ BELOW *XL series cabovers, such as this Eagle 6×4 loaded with steel, could have Detroit Diesel or Cummins power up to 475bhp.*

■ RIGHT *A New Zealand specification heavy-duty bonneted 6×4 in the same class as the Fleetstar.*

■ BELOW *The KB8 conventional range was a great classic of the early post-World War II years.*

R series conventionals in the early 1950s featured a stylish all-steel cab built by the Chicago Manufacturing Co. and referred to by International as their Comfo-vision cab. It had a single-piece curved windscreen, sleeper option and distinctive grille with three horizontal bars on the lower portion. A lower version with high mounted headlights and a trapezoid grille went on the S series. The Fleetstar replaced the R series in the mid 1960s, this having a wide bonnet (hood) and grille. A version of this cab design became familiar on UK roads for a short period after International set up a manufacturing plant to build the medium-weight Loadstar models.

One attractively styled cab was the COF cabover. This tilt cab was originally a Diamond T design and had a long production run. A raised version of the same basic shell appeared on the heavy-duty VCO series. From the mid 1960s International used the "Star" suffix in most of their model types. The Loadstar was the medium and heavy range; the Fleetstar was the heavy-duty conventional range; the Paystar was the bonneted construction range; the Transtar, launched in 1971, was a maximum-weight line-haul range in bonneted and cabover form, while the Cargostar medium cabovers were developed from the COF range.

By the 1970s International was one of the largest truck manufacturers, with assembly plants and distributors throughout the world. In 1972 International were keen to expand into Europe, the UK assembly operations having petered out through lack of sales. The company entered talks with DAF of Eindhoven and acquired a 33 per cent holding in 1972. In 1974 International strengthened their European presence further by acquiring the newly formed Seddon Atkinson operations in Oldham, England. DAF had already undertaken a joint cab-development program with the Spanish group ENASA and in 1981 International bought a 35 per cent stake in that group too. However, after the series of European acquisitions, the International Harvester Group itself ran into difficulties and in 1984 was forced to pull out. In 1986 it was re-formed as the Navistar International Transport Co., which has marketed International trucks since the late '80s and throughout the '90s. Current products range from the 8100 city trucks, the 9200 tractor units – the workhorses for regional bulk haulage in the 280 to 470bhp class – the sleek 9400 line-haul tractors with power ratings up to 550bhp, and the top-of-the-range 9950 and 9900 Eagle IX premium conventionals with power ratings from 430 to 600bhp. The Eagle version is the fully specced tractor and International's flagship for the new millennium. Most current models feature aluminium cabs for lightweight, aerodynamic styling and a choice of engines from Caterpillar, Cummins and Detroit Diesel.

■ LEFT *The Transtar cabover offered a choice of Cummins, Detroit Diesel and Caterpillar engines up to 450bhp.*

TOKYO, JAPAN

ISUZU

Isuzu's predecessor, the Tokyo Ishikawajima Shipbuilding & Engineering Co. Ltd, began building British-designed Wolseley A9 trucks under licence from 1922. These were built mainly for military use. The agreement with Wolseley terminated in 1927. Typical of the company's products in the early 1930s was the bonneted 2-tonne Sumida truck. In 1934 a research program into diesel engine production was put in place, and 1936 saw the development of a 5.3 litre/323cu in air-cooled diesel. The TX40 2-ton truck, with modernized cab strongly influenced by contemporary American styling, was in production in 1936. A new factory for heavy trucks was completed at Kawasaki in 1938, the Tokyo Jidosha Kogyo (Tokyo Automotive Industry) Co. Ltd having been formed in 1937, combining the motor divisions of the Ishikawajima Shipbuilding & Engineering Co. and the Tokyo Gas & Electric Co. The latter produced Japan's first truck in 1917 and also formed the basis for Hino Heavy Industries which went on to become a separate truck-building concern, being renamed Hino Motors Ltd in 1959 and which eventually merged with Toyota in 1966.

Diesel trucks were in full production by 1941. The company became Isuzu Motors Ltd in 1949 and the main truck model during the 1950s was the TX550 bonneted 6-tonner powered by a 6.1 litre/372cu in, 125bhp 6-cylinder diesel driving through a 5-speed overdrive gearbox. A military 6×6 development, the TW540, was also offered as well as a 5-tonne 4×2 with military pattern bonnet (hood) and wings powered by a choice of 5.6 litre/341cu in, 145bhp 6-cylinder gasoline or the 6.1 litre/372cu in diesel. In 1959 Isuzu's heaviest truck was the TD150 bonneted four-wheeler for 9-tonne payload. This was powered by a 10.18 litre/621cu in 6-cylinder diesel developing 180bhp and had air-assisted brakes.

During the 1960s, heavier and more powerful models were introduced. Typical of these was the bonneted 8-tonne gvw TD with a completely new pressed-steel cab with single-piece curved windscreen and four headlights. The power unit was the 10.18 litre/621cu in diesel uprated to 200bhp. The same engine powered a forward-control TD-E 8-tonner as well as 10-tonne payload 6×2 versions – the TP (bonneted) and TD-E (cabover). At the lighter end of the weight scale Isuzu offered the Elf forward-control

■ ABOVE ***The 1963 TD50-D 8-tonne hydraulic end dump truck has a 10.18 litre/621cu in DH100 6-cylinder diesel.***

■ BELOW LEFT ***A 1968 Isuzu TD50 for 15-tonne gvw.***

■ BELOW RIGHT ***The 1981 TWD25 all-wheel drive truck has 14-tonne gvw and a 150bhp 6BD1 diesel engine.***

■ RIGHT *The 1993 EXR300 A-train milk tanker has Isuzu's 6RA1-TRC 12 litre/732cu in turbo-intercooled diesel engine with 295bhp.*

2-tonners which were built at the Fujisawa car plant and embodied some Rootes Group engineering.

General Motors acquired a 35 per cent holding in Isuzu in 1971 and in 1973 a new range, the Forward, was introduced. The SBR and JBR at 9 tonnes and 12 tonnes gvw respectively were at the lower end, while the SLR grossed 16 tonnes. The SBG was a twin-steer six-wheeler at 21 tonnes gvw and the SPZ a 6×4 for 24 tonnes. There were two 38-tonne gcw tractor units too – the VPR 4×2 and the VPZ 6×4. Models from 21 tonnes gvw upwards were powered by the Isuzu E120 direct injection 12 litre/732cu in diesel. It was selected models from this range that GM chose to market as Bedfords in Australia and New Zealand, GM Holden carrying out the assembly.

Alongside the Forward range, Isuzu continued to offer their medium-weight TXD45/55 4×2 and TWD55 6×4 bonneted models, which by the 1980s were looking very old-fashioned. Heavier bonneted models were also available as the TDJ (16 tonnes gvw) and TDH (17.5 tonnes gvw) 4×2 and the 24-tonne gvw TMH and TMQ six-wheelers. An all-wheel drive range with a military-style cab, unchanged since the 1950s, the TSD 4×4 and TWD 6×6 also soldiered on into the '80s.

For 1980 Isuzu launched a facelifted forward-control range with the new 10PB1 14 litre/854cu in V10 diesel producing 292bhp. The range featured a new larger radiator and a set-back front axle. Throughout the 1980s and '90s Isuzu have maintained a strong position in the truck market with healthy export sales. During the last decade of the 20th century the principal models were the EXR (4×2) and EXZ (6×4) tractor units and the C range. In its latest form this is being marketed as the Giga, featuring a premium-cab specification. During the '90s, assembly of medium-weight Isuzu trucks has taken place in the UK, first at Leyland Truck's, and later at Western Star's UK subsidiary, ERF.

■ RIGHT *Early 1980s SPH rigid eight-wheeler and four-axled drawbar trailer operates up to 44 tonnes gtw in New Zealand.*

EUROPE

IVECO (INCLUDING IVECO FORD)

In the early 1970's Fiat of Turin recognized the need to increase its share of the world truck market if it was to survive in the face of competition from the market leaders like Daimler-Benz and Volvo. While Fiat had a virtual monopoly of its home market, commanding nearly 80 per cent of truck sales, it needed to expand if it was to remain profitable. It had already absorbed most of the major Italian manufacturers over the years, including OM and Lancia, while it also owned Unic, giving it a foothold in the French market. Fiat found a partner in Germany's Magirus-Deutz, the truck manufacturing division of KHD (Klockner Humboldt Deutz) of Ulm. The old established company was also looking for a partnership that would ensure its future independence and strengthen its position in the market, but in Germany there were no suitable companies. After a worldwide survey, Magirus-Deutz and Fiat agreed to set up a joint company to co-operate on truck development and manufacture. The earliest meetings took place in 1973 and IVECO (Industrial Vehicle Corporation) came into being on January 1st 1975. Part of the agreement was that Magirus-Deutz would be allowed to continue building the air-cooled diesels for which it was renowned. Group production facilities were to be reviewed to make best use of factories by concentrating like with like. Turin was to build heavy trucks, Ulm medium trucks and heavy construction vehicles, including the air-cooled-

■ LEFT ***After the formation of Iveco in 1975 Fiat trucks began to display the new name badge on otherwise unaltered models.***

■ BELOW LEFT ***Some, like this five-axled articulated cement bulker photographed near Pompeii, simply had the "I" logo on the grille.***

■ ABOVE ***Iveco badges were added to UK Ford Cargos after 1986.***

■ LEFT ***The 1997 Super Cargo has a design gross weight of 26 tonnes and 266bhp turbo-intercooled low-emission diesel.***

■ **LEFT** ***Iveco became a make in its own right with the arrival of the TurboTech and TurboStar models of the 1980s.***

■ **BELOW RIGHT** ***This UK-registered Iveco Cargo also carries a Ford badge. Outside the UK the model was badged Iveco EuroCargo.***

engined bonneted trucks. Brescia's OM factory was to build medium-weight vehicles and Trappes in France medium to heavy.

To satisfy all parties it was decided to locate Iveco's headquarters in a neutral country – The Netherlands. However, Iveco was still faced with problems integrating the various companies and factories into one corporate organization. While UNIC, along with the likes of OM and Lancia, had gracefully given up their individual identity and accepted their place under the Fiat dominated Iveco umbrella, Magirus-Deutz were no pushover. They fought to retain their individuality, while pride in their 110-year-old company made them reluctant to be swallowed up by a foreign group. As a result, after five years of uneasy co-habitation with Fiat, KHD pulled out of Iveco. The Magirus name remained with Iveco but Deutz regained its independence as an engine manufacturer and continued to supply engines to Iveco.

During these five years bold attempts had been made to give the Iveco Group products a corporate identity, but this had never gone beyond the addition of an italic "I" logo to their radiator grilles. From an early stage, however, heavy trucks from Fiat, OM, UNIC and Magirus-Deutz had all been given the Fiat tilt cab. Magirus was the only one to insist on including its famous "cathedral spire" trademark as well as the "I" logo. By the mid 1980s the Iveco brand name had replaced individual makes, and major restructuring was taking place to establish Iveco as a manufacturer in its own right. The truck that signified the true breakthrough for Iveco was the TurboStar of 1984. The important features of this highly successful truck were its cab and engine. While the cab bore a resemblance to its Fiat cousins, it was extensively redesigned with a 1.7m/5.5ft internal height and

■ **RIGHT** ***Both Fiat eight-wheelers and their OM lookalikes were transformed into Ivecos after 1975.***

■ **BELOW RIGHT** ***Iveco's new EuroTech range of heavy-duty tractor units was launched in 1992. In the UK they carried a small Ford badge too.***

■ LEFT *The EuroStar with high datum cab and power options up to 520bhp is Iveco's flagship truck of the 1990s.*

a sophisticated suspension system. There were two engines available – the 8210 13.8 litre/842cu in straight six turbo with 330bhp, or the 8280 17.2 litre/1049cu in V8 with 420, making it one of the most powerful trucks of the era and eminently suitable for long-distance inter-continental haulage.

The next major landmark in Iveco's development came in 1986 with the merger of Iveco and Ford's UK truck division. The result was Iveco Ford Trucks Ltd, with Iveco and Ford holding equal shares of 48 per cent each, the remaining 4 per cent being held by a merchant bank. Following the link-up, Ford badges were added to Iveco trucks for the UK market. Four years later came another milestone when Iveco added Pegaso (ENASA) to its ranks. This included Seddon Atkinson of Oldham, England which had become part of ENASA in 1983 when International Harvester sold off its European truck interests. Iveco made another important acquisition in 1992 in the form of International Trucks Australia Ltd.

A major model-replacement program came to fruition between 1991 and 1993. An attractive new design of forward-control Steel/Plastic cab, the Multi Purpose or MP cab, was introduced in various widths and heights to cover all models from 6 to 44 tonnes gvw. At the lighter end came the 1991 Eurocargo (badged Cargo in the UK) with rigids from 6 to 15 tonnes gcw and tractors up to 34 tonnes gcw. Then came the Super Cargo 17-tonne, two-axled and 26-tonne three-axled rigids. Four-axled Eurotrakker rigids built at Iveco's Spanish plant appeared in 1993. A lighter-weight version, the Trakker, was also available and built at the Seddon Atkinson factory in the UK. The old TurboTech with Fiat-style cab was replaced by the new EuroTech in 1992, featuring the new MP cab. The TurboStar premium long-haul tractor was replaced in 1993 by the high-cabbed EuroStar. UK operations had to wait until 1995 for right-hand drive versions. From the outset it was evident that Iveco was the dominant partner in the Iveco Ford merger and in 1996 it acquired the 4 per cent neutral holding, making it the major shareholder with 52 per cent. One year later UK truck production was phased out and the Langley plant was closed. With its comprehensive model line-up, Iveco is now well and truly established as a manufacturer in its own right.

■ LEFT *Former Magirus-Deutz trucks with air-cooled diesels were also rebranded Iveco in the late 1970s.*

■ BELOW *Iveco's current heavy-duty eight-wheeler is the 8×4 EuroTrakker with a design gross weight of 34 tonnes.*

COLORADO SPRINGS, COLORADO, USA

JARRETT

James C. Jarrett Jnr of the J C Jarrett Motor and Finance Co. was in the business of selling trucks, but most of them were not up to the hilly conditions in the Colorado region. In 1921 he drew up a design for a more powerful truck with more suitable gearing. The specification included a Waukesha 6-cylinder gasoline engine, a 7-speed gearbox and a double-reduction rear axle. There were two load ratings of 2½ and 5 tons. The trucks were badged JCJ. No more than 300 were built during a 13-year production period, most going to local authorities.

KENOSHA, WISCONSIN, USA

JEFFERY QUAD

■ RIGHT *The versatile Jeffery Quad 4×4 was built in large numbers during World War I.*

The four-wheel drive, four-wheel steer Jeffery Quad for loads of 1½ to 2 tons was developed primarily for military use in 1913. Prior to this the Thomas B. Jeffery Corporation had built a number of lightweight delivery trucks which were discontinued to allow volume production of the Quad. Production was also farmed out to other manufacturers to try to meet demand. The Quad was a very versatile machine with its 13.7m/45ft turning circle. Power came from a 36hp 4-cylinder Buda gasoline engine. Production continued until 1919 but from 1917 onwards the Jeffery Company was taken over by Nash Motor Co. of Pacine, Wisconsin, and the trucks were called Nash Quad.

JELCZ, K.OLAWY, WARSAW, POLAND

JELCZ

■ LEFT *Some Jelcz trucks of the 1980s era still used diesel engines based on Leyland designs.*

Zaklady Samochodowe Jelcz SA formerly produced trucks under the Zubr name beginning in 1960, but from 1968 the Jelcz name badge was adopted. The Zubr A.80 8-tonne forward-control model featured a Wola diesel engine. The Jelcz 8-tonner appeared from 1968. From 1972 the range was updated using licence-built Wola-Leyland Power Plus diesels. The principal models were the 316 rigid six-wheeler and 317 tractor unit for 32 tonnes with the SW.680 diesel of 200bhp. A more powerful turbocharged version with 240bhp was also introduced. As well as using Leyland-based engines, Jelcz used Steyr V8 diesels with 320bhp output for higher powered 6×4 tractors. Steyr axles were also used on some models. As part of the Grupa Zasada, which also builds Star trucks and Mercedes vans, Jelcz currently offers an extensive range of some 27 different trucks from 16 to 42 tonnes, including 4×2, 6×2, 6×4, 8×4 and 4×4 types. Engines used include Mielec, Mercedes-Benz, Iveco, Steyr and Star.

WEST BROMWICH, ENGLAND

JENSEN

■ LEFT *Jensen's long lightweight chassis formed the ideal basis for large-volume furniture vans.*

Originally coachbuilders, the Jensen brothers decided to enter the truck business in 1938 with a lightweight integral design that could carry the maximum permitted payload but still be eligible to operate at 48kph/30mph. UK regulations passed in the 1930s restricted trucks over 2.5 tons unladen weight to 32kph/20mph. Jensen, by using a unique form of construction developed in conjunction with the Reynolds Tube Co., managed to build trucks to the maximum legal length of 8.4m/27.5ft with a load platform up to 7m/23ft and a payload capacity of 5 to 6 tons, while still not exceeding the 2.5-ton "tare" weight. A number of prototypes were built between 1939 and 1944 and production began in 1946. While the prototypes used Ford engines, production vehicles had Perkins P6 diesels and Moss 5-speed gearboxes. Later, an Austin 4-speed gearbox was used and a Moss rear axle was standard. When the UK length limit was increased to 9.1m/30ft in the mid 1950s, Jensen responded with their Freighter 6-ton models with a 7.7m/25.5ft body and an unladen weight of just 2-ton 19cwt as by this time the 32kph/20mph rule applied only to trucks over 3 tons. As well as the lightweight truck, Jensen produced a small articulated vehicle known as the Jen-Tug for urban deliveries. This was powered by a Ford gasoline engine, but later models had the 1.2 litre/73cu in 4-cylinder gasoline engine used in the Austin A40 car. Jensen's truck building activities ended in 1959.

■ BELOW *Jensen's chassis, cab and body were built as one integral structure to save weight.*

HEFEI, CHINA

JIANG-HUAI

During the period of Mao Tse-tung's Cultural Revolution of the late 1960s many provincial truck plants were established. The Jiang-Huai (or Chiang-Huai) HF.140 3-tonne forward-control entered production in 1969. It was powered by a 4.4 litre/268cu in, 120bhp 6-cylinder gasoline engine. Jiang-Huai also built a lighter model, the 2-tonne HF.130 and a heavy-duty 8-tonner designated the HF.150. Most are operated in Anhui province.

SHANGHAI, CHINA

JIAOTONG

The Shanghai Heavy Motor Vehicle Factory built trucks under the Jiaotong name, meaning "Communication". They are now called Datong. Gasoline and diesel engines of Shanghai manufacture are used and there are normal and forward-control models for 8 to 30 tonnes gcw. Truck production began in 1958. Applications include general cargo trucks, dump trucks, crane trucks, tractor units for semi-trailers and various municipal types such as fire appliances, street sprinklers and garbage trucks.

■ ABOVE *This mid 1980s Datong (formerly Jiaotong) SH161 heavy-duty six-wheeled truck grosses 28 tonnes and carries a 15-tonne payload.*

CHANGCHUN, CHINA

JIEFANG

Jiefang is one of China's leading makes of truck. Sometimes called the Jay Fong (an anglicized form of Jiefang), the make dates back to 1956 when the first CA-10 models were built, based on the Russian ZIL.164/ZIS.150 which was itself a copy of the American International K series. The CA-10 was built in huge numbers, many assembled in various plants throughout China. Other more modern Jiefang trucks from Dan Dong Automobile works in Lianoning Province have included the CA-141B cargo truck with single-piece curved windscreen and four headlights, and a dump-truck version of this designated the DD349. The No.1 Automobile Plant at Changchun, responsible for the production of Jiefang, also build off-road dump trucks.

■ ABOVE *The Jiefang CA102 dropside truck was powered by 95bhp gasoline engine and carried a 4-tonne payload.*

■ LEFT *The dump-truck version of the later Jiefang range carries a 4.5-tonne payload and has a gvw rating of 9.4 tonnes.*

BACKNANG, GERMANY

KAELBLE

■ LEFT *This 6×6 forward-control tractor was one of a wide range of Kaelble's custom-built heavy vehicles.*

Carl Kaelble Motoren- und Maschinenfabrik specialized in road tractors, crane carriers and, more recently, quarrying vehicles. The company history can be traced back to 1903, when it built its first high-speed gasoline engine. The first road tractor – the Suevia – appeared in 1925 and in 1933 a heavy six-wheel tractor was built for the German Railways. During the '30s larger tractors were produced with diesel engines up to 200bhp. After World War II Kaelble continued to build road tractors but entered the truck market too with a bonneted 7-tonne rigid with a 130bhp 6-cylinder diesel. From 1953 forward-control trucks for 6.5, 8 and 11 tonnes payload were introduced with in-line 6-cylinder diesels, plus a 13-tonner with a V8 diesel. During the late '50s Kaelble's K680 4×2 was a particularly impressive machine with its protruding bonnet (hood) and set-back front axle. This had the Kaelble GO130S indirect-injection 192bhp diesel and ZF AK6-75 gearbox. Payload ratings of 8.2, 10.2 and 11.4 tonnes were specified. Forward-control and tractor-unit versions were also available. Trucks were built through to the early 1970s when the company decided to concentrate entirely on specialized heavy vehicles, including a massive 500-tonne gtw 8×8 powered by a MAN V12 turbocharged diesel of 615bhp. During the late 1980s the company became CKG Kaelble-Gmeinder GmbH.

NABEREZHNYE CHELNY, RUSSIA

KAMAZ

In 1969 the Russians drew up plans for what was to be the world's largest truck plant at a site, determined by computer analysis, next to the Kama River east of Moscow. The plant, covering 103.6sq km/40 square miles and with a planned capacity of 150,000 trucks per annum, began production in February 1976. The models were all based on a new design of 6×4 heavy-duty tilt-cab truck powered by a 210bhp (later uprated to 220bhp), 10.85 litre/662cu in Kamaz 740 V8 naturally aspirated diesel engine. A turbocharged version, the 260bhp 7403, was also available. The rigid truck version for 22 tonnes gvw, or up to 36 tonnes with drawbar trailer, was designated the 53211 while the 54112 tractor unit grossed at 36 tonnes. Kamaz aimed to achieve export sales in many of the world's markets, including Western Europe, the UK, Australia and New Zealand. Their biggest markets have been the East European countries such as Hungary and Poland. Another important export country has been Cuba. While production at times exceeded the 100,000 per annum mark during the 1980s and early '90s, more recently the plant has been running at between 10 per cent and 20 per cent of its vast capacity. In 1998 a new 65115 15-tonne dump truck with modernized cab was announced. A 20-tonne model, the 6520 is being developed.

■ ABOVE *The Kamaz five-axled artic of the mid 1980s grosses 36 tonnes and is powered by a V8 diesel engine.*

HUDDERSFIELD & LUTON, ENGLAND

KARRIER

■ LEFT *The 1956 Karrier Bantam 2-ton low-loader was a popular vehicle for drinks distribution.*

■ BELOW *A 1949 Karrier CK3 3/4 ton chassis forms the basis for this telephone maintenance truck.*

Karrier Motors Ltd of Huddersfield was formed in 1920 but, prior to that, back as far as 1907 was called Clayton & Co. Those early Karriers were noted for their excellent hill-climbing and manoeuvrability. They were A-types powered by Tylor gasoline engines. Bonneted models, called B-types, appeared in 1911 and by 1913 Karrier were building War Office subsidy-type B4 trucks. After 1920 a K-type for 3 to 6 tons was added, developed from the subsidy truck. Forward control was readopted in 1922 and lighter 1½ and 2-ton models were added to the range. From their early years Karrier were to be significant suppliers of municipal vehicles, including the low-loading CYR 2½-ton garbage truck. At the heavy end of the range Karrier introduced an 8-ton six-wheeler, the KW6 and KWF6, the latter being of forward-control layout. The lightest truck was the 1½-ton ZA model, built in 1929–30 and powered by a Dorman gasoline engine. The Karrier Cob 3-tonner, a rival to Scammell's Mechanical Horse, was introduced in 1931. There was also a 4-ton version called the Cob Major. This was also built with truck and municipal bodywork in rigid form. A most unusual vehicle of the early '30s was the Road Railer, which was designed with an extra set of special wheels so that it could run on the road or on rails. In 1932 a 12-ton six-wheeler, the Colossus, was introduced.

By 1934 Karrier were in difficulties and called in the receivers. A buyer was found in Humber Ltd of Coventry, which was part of the Rootes Group. Rootes had taken over Commer Cars of Luton in 1928 and they decided to transfer Karrier production to the Commer factory. Truck production at Huddersfield was discontinued in 1935. The company was now called Karrier Motor Successors Ltd. After the takeover Karrier was to become more and more specialized in light to medium municipal vehicles, their leading models being the 2-ton Bantam, the 3-ton CK3 and the 6-ton CK6. From 1950 the Bantam was relaunched with a stylish new cab based on the Commer QX. This also went on a new model, the 3 to 4-ton Gamecock which replaced the CK in 1952. A completely new cab design was introduced in 1962, fitted to both Karrier and Commer models. By 1967 Rootes was under the control of Chrysler, and Dodge production was moved to the Commer Karrier plant. A process of integration began, resulting in a new range, the Commando, launched in 1974. Chrysler UK sold out to PSA Peugeot Citroën in 1978. For a brief period the name Talbot Motor Company was adopted but then, in 1981–82, Peugeot resurrected the Karrier Motors Ltd title, but that was short-lived, disappearing when Renault Véhicules Industriels took control in 1981.

KUTAISI, GEORGIA

KAZ

■ RIGHT *A late 1970s KAZ 608V four-axled artic with tilt sleeper cab.*

Production of trucks to ZIL design began at Kutaisi in 1956, the 600V model being based on the old ZIL.150 which was originally inspired by the International Harvester K model. KAZ went on to design their own tractor units with forward-control layout, including the 606 Kolhida and 608 Kolhida. In 1973 the KAZ 608V with tilt sleeper cab was introduced. In the mid 1980s production at the Kutaisi factory was concentrated on agricultural dump trucks.

SEATTLE, WASHINGTON, USA

KENWORTH

In 1923 Harry W. Kent and Edgar K. Worthington adopted the new name Kenworth for the former Gerlinger Motor Car Co., which Edgar Worthington had acquired in 1917. Between 1917 and 1922 Gerlinger had produced the ruggedly built Gersix truck and the early Kenworths were developed from this. The success of this venture was helped by the closure of two competitive companies in Seattle – the HRL Motor Co. and Vulcan.

Kenworth's early models were solid-tyred bonneted types for payloads of 1½ to 4 tons, powered by Buda 4-cylinder gasoline engines. Eighty trucks were sold during 1924 and sales reached approximately two per week the following year. By 1925 there were five types on offer, the heaviest being a 5-tonner. A 78bhp 6-cylinder gasoline engine was introduced in 1927 and two years later Kenworth opened an assembly plant in Vancouver, B.C., to develop sales in Canada. Already Kenworth was adopting a customizing approach. Though a "standard" range was available, almost any vehicle could be built to the customer's special requirements.

In 1933 Kenworth became the first American truck manufacturer to install diesel engines (in this case Cummins) as standard equipment, and the same year began offering a sleeper cab option. Kenworth had stuck exclusively to bonneted types, but in 1936 launched their first forward-control truck prompted by legislation in the Motor Carrier Act. During World War II Kenworth was a significant producer of military trucks, especially their famous M-1 6×6 wrecker. In the mid 1940s increased use of aluminium in chassis frames, cabs and running units resulted in important weight savings.

In 1944 Kenworth became a wholly owned subsidiary of Pacific Car & Foundry (PACCAR) of Seattle. Kenworth was relocated at the former Fisher Body plant and a production plant was also built later at Kansas City. Sugar plantations in Hawaii became large customers for Kenworth in the immediate post-war period. Export sales were accounting for 40 per cent of Kenworth's turnover by 1950. In the early 1950s the company introduced the massive 853 for Middle East oilfield duties. In 1958 the 953 powered by a Cummins NTC350 was introduced. A half-cab CBE (cab beside engine) tractor unit was introduced in 1954. This was said to provide improved vision for drivers using mountain roads, but not all drivers

■ TOP *The W900 represents the timeless classic eighteen-wheeler conventional and offers a range of sleeper options.*

■ ABOVE LEFT *A 1980 K100 6×4 cabover engaged on heavy haulage in the UK.*

■ LEFT *A T800 dump with pusher axle and four-axled pony trailer.*

■ LEFT ***A Canadian W900 with heavy-duty "low boy" trailer for transport of mechanical plant.***

liked it since it lacked interior space. In 1956 two icons of the company's history were launched, the W900 conventional and the K100 cabover. In the same year Kenworth produced an unusual underfloor-engined eight-wheel tractor unit for Pacific Intermountain Express. This formed part of a "dromedary" outfit. The Kansas City plant became operational in 1965 and the success of the new W900 and K100 saw record sales of heavy trucks, reaching 2037 in that year. In 1971 the PD series of cab-forward urban trucks, later marketed as the Hustler models, entered the market. At the other end of the weight scale Kenworth brought in their 6×4 Brute aimed at the construction industry.

A new plant at Chillicothe, Ohio was opened in 1974. Kenworths were also assembled in Australia where twin-steer four-axled rigids were developed. Kenworth also established a plant in Mexico building Kenmex trucks. Kenworth pioneered the high-roof long-haul tractor in 1976 with their top-of-the-range Aerodyne sleeper for both conventionals and cabovers. The archetypal American-style trucks underwent a new wave of styling changes in 1985 when the aerodynamic T600 claimed to reduce wind drag by 40 per cent. Cost conscious operators could benefit from fuel savings of up to 22 per cent from the sleeker lines of the new sloping bonnet (hood). Kenworth's new plant at Renton, Washington was opened on June 4th 1993, joining those in Seattle, Chillicothe, Vancouver, Mexicali and Bayswater, Australia. The same year Kenworth announced its Aerocab sleeper which could be described as a "home-from-home".

While European styling had been allowed to creep into the T600 and the lighter T300, the traditional United States style W900 with its slab-fronted radiator grille soldiers on, as does the long-established K range cabovers which have made only slight concessions to styling over the years. Meanwhile, the ultimate in aerodynamics can be found in Kenworth's latest T2000 range which boasts smooth flowing lines combined with an exceptionally spacious integral sleeper compartment. Kenworth's parent, Paccar, also owns Peterbilt, Foden, DAF and Leyland. Increasing international development has recently seen Americanized versions of Leyland-DAF's 55 Series with the Kenworth name badge, as the K37 urban delivery truck, and there are plans to produce similar versions of the 45 Series.

■ LEFT ***A T600 Chipliner powered by a Detroit Diesel 60 series at work in New Zealand.***

■ BELOW ***A 1998 K100G cabover four-axled tractor engaged on heavy haulage in New Zealand.***

STOKE-ON-TRENT, ENGLAND

KERR STUART

■ LEFT *Britain's first production diesel truck was this short-lived Kerr Stuart 6-tonner.*

Kerr Stuart was a short-lived truck project but is worthy of its place in history as the first production British diesel truck, introduced in 1929. Kerr Stuart built locomotive boilers but designed a 6-ton chain-drive semi-forward-control diesel truck in 1928 using proprietary components. Initially a 6-cylinder Helios diesel engine was tried, but the first production vehicle had a 60bhp 4-cylinder McLaren-Benz. This had a governed speed of 800rpm and required a single-cylinder air-cooled JAP gasoline engine to start it. Within a year of their formation Kerr Stuart went bankrupt, and only five production models are believed to have been sold.

NICOSIA, CYPRUS

KMC

Truck assembly began at KMC Motors in 1973 using British-sourced designs from Dennis powered by Perkins diesels. When supplies of Dennis parts diminished, KMC based their trucks on Dodge and Commer, including Spanish Dodges. Trucks ranged from 16 to 30 tonnes gvw. During the 1980s KMC sourced their designs and components from a wider number of manufacturers, MAN becoming a major supplier of cabs and engines. Detroit Diesel engines are also available in some models.

■ ABOVE *The Cypriot-produced KMC 26/38DT 6×4 dump truck was based on the Spanish Dodge. It was powered by the Chrysler BS36 11.95 litre/728cu in 6-cylinder diesel engine.*

SPRINGFIELD, MASSACHUSETTS, USA

KNOX/KNOX MARTIN

Knox Martin is universally regarded as the world's pioneer of the articulated truck. As the Knox Automotive Co. it produced a variety of light and medium trucks from its formation in 1901 through to 1908. The earliest of them was a three-wheeler van version based on the Knox car. It was in 1909 that Charles Henry Martin, a former Knox employee, rejoined the company and patented his Martin Rocking Fifth Wheel. This was a device for coupling semi-trailers to tractor units. The weight of the semi-trailer front end was taken by the tractor rear axle as opposed to the tractor chassis. The first Knox Martin tractors were three-wheelers with a steerable single front wheel capable of an almost 90-degree lock angle. This made the outfit extremely manoeuvrable. Later a four-wheel truck was introduced. It is worth noting that it was the Knox Martin principle that formed the basis of the highly successful Scammell articulated six-wheeler in the UK in 1922. Knox Martin themselves ceased trading in 1924.

TOKYO, JAPAN

KOMATSU

■ BELOW ***Komatsu are a major supplier of heavy dump trucks. This is their HD1200 of the late 1970s.***

Komatsu is a large Japanese manufacturer of dump trucks and other construction vehicles. Dump-truck production got underway from 1951 powered by licence-built Cummins diesel engines. Over the years Komatsu dump trucks have grown larger and more powerful. In the late 1970s the largest machine was the HD1200 with a 130-tonne payload, powered by a 37 litre/2220cu in, 1200bhp Cummins KTA-2300 V12 turbocharged, aftercooled diesel which drove an alternator providing current for the electric final-drive system. Each rear wheel had its own traction motor. Komatsu Mining Systems, formed in 1996 in a link-up with United States-based Modular Mining System Inc., is now Komatsu's global mining-equipment headquarters, and currently their range of eight dump trucks spans the 54 to 290 tonnes (59.5 to 320 US tons) payload range. The largest of these, machines employing diesel electric traction, is the 930E with a design gross vehicle weight of 480 tonnes (530 US tons) and a horse-power rating of 2500.

KREMENCHUG, UKRAINE

KRAZ

■ BELOW ***The 1999 KrAZ 5444 32-ton tractor is powered by 288bhp 14.86 litre/906cu in diesel.***

Production of YAZ trucks at the Yaroslavi works was transferred to a new factory at Kremenchug in 1959 and YAZ trucks were renamed KrAZ. The products were largely carried-over YAZ designs until 1966 when a new range of heavy trucks was launched. These were of 6×4 and 6×6 normal-control layout for use as dump trucks and as tractor units for articulated use. Their V8 diesels were built at the former YAZ plant which then became YAMZ. When marketed in Europe, KrAZ were badged as Belaz.

The current KrAZ range includes 37 bonneted 4×2, 6×4 and 6×6 heavy-duty tractors and truck chassis for gross weights from 17.3 to 75 tonnes, featuring a modern design of cab. The principal power unit is a 14.8 litre/903cu in V8 turbocharged diesel rated between 230 and 318bhp. The 4×2 tractor unit, type 5444, is for 32 tonnes gcw and has the 288bhp engine. The largest tractors, the 6×6 6443 models, are marketed with a 48-tonne Warz 9592 dump truck semi-trailer. Eurocargo medium-weight trucks are also assembled by KrAZ in a joint venture with Iveco.

AMSTERDAM, THE NETHERLANDS

KROMHOUT

Kromhout's history began in the mid 1920s when it built marine diesels, but in 1935 the company acquired a licence to build Gardner 4, 5 and 6-cylinder diesels which it used to power a range of Kromhout trucks. By the outbreak of World War II Kromhout Motoren Fabriek NV was offering a range of trucks and tractor units from 3 to 30 tonnes gcw. These were mainly of bonneted layout. Production was suspended during the war, but the range was reintroduced in 1945. In the late '40s Kromhout undertook assembly of Leyland vehicles for the Dutch market. Forward-control trucks for 10-tonne payloads appeared in 1953, and by 1955 normal and forward-control six-wheelers were added to the range. These featured Kirkstall overhead worm double-drive rear bogies. Kromhout developed higher powered diesels based on the 8.4 litre/512cu in Gardner up to 140bhp. Rolls Royce engines were also fitted as an option on the heavy six-wheelers.

Kromhout production ended in 1961 after the company merged with Verheul who, up until the merger, were mainly bus builders. Some Verheul trucks based on Kromhouts were fitted with the Kromhout-Gardner engine while others had Rolls Royce power units. Truck production at Verheul ended in 1965, by which time the company was AEC-owned.

■ ABOVE ***A Kromhout 4VS-AN long-wheelbase dropside truck dating from 1956.***

ESSEN, GERMANY

KRUPP

Production of Krupp trucks began in 1919 with a chain-drive 5-tonner, although some early steam wagons had been built at the company's Kiel ship building works between 1905 and 1908. Fried Krupp Motoren- und Kraftwagen-fabriken went on to build a mixture of types in the early 1920s, including a 10-tonne payload bonneted tractor unit, and then, in contrast, a three-wheeled road sweeper. By 1925 the range was shaft-driven and consisted of 1½, 2, 5 and 10-tonners. Krupp's first forward-control trucks appeared in 1930 in both 4×2 and 6×4 form. From 1932 Krupp built Junkers opposed-piston two-stroke diesel engines. During the '30s a whole range of trucks continued to be built, but by the latter part of World War II the Krupp organization faced collapse. It was renamed Sudwerke GmbH and rehoused in a plant at Kulmbach where, between 1944 and 1951, trucks were also built under the name Sudwerke.

■ ABOVE ***The 1963 Krupp 801 drawbar outfit for 34 tonnes gtw featured a 5.8 litre/355cu in 4-cylinder two-stroke diesel engine developing 192bhp.***

■ LEFT *A S960/12 articulated five-axled bulk cement truck powered by a Krupp-Cummins four-stroke V6 diesel engine.*

Production transferred back to Essen in 1951 and a new range was launched, including the famous 8-tonne Titan and 5.5-tonne Buffel. A completely new range of normal and forward-control models, including the 701, 801, 901, 1001 and 1051, of very handsome appearance, was announced in 1956. These were powered by Krupp two-stroke diesels which were water-cooled, uniflow scavenged designs with 3, 4, 5 or 7-cylinders with power outputs ranging from 132 to 310bhp. From 1963 Krupp began offering the licence-built Krupp-Cummins V6-200 four-stroke diesel and most heavy-duty forward-control models became available with a tilt cab. All-wheel drive bonneted models such as the 760 4×4 and 360 6×6 were also available, as was a range of half-cab quarry dump trucks in 4×2 (MK) and 4×4 (AMK) form for payloads of 18, 23 and 30 tonnes. The heavy-duty on-highway trucks went up to 43 tonnes design gross train weight. In 1967 Krupp introduced a new 4×4 on-highway tractor unit with a 265bhp V8 engine, but the following year production of all trucks ceased owing to a fall-off in demand.

In 1968 Daimler-Benz took over the distribution of Krupp trucks, including their existing stocks and real estate. A small residue of forward-control tilt cabs was purchased by Atkinson Vehicles (Europe) SA to produce their Atkinson-Krupp models, of which very few were built. Krupp itself switched to the production of heavy-duty mobile cranes.

■ BELOW *A 1964 SF960/12 with sleeper cab powered by four-stroke Krupp-Cummins V6 developing 220bhp.*

■ BOTTOM *The 1960 Mustang 801 with 186bhp Krupp 4-cylinder two-stroke grossed 14 tonnes.*

ALMA, MICHIGAN, USA

LaFrance

LaFrance is a name normally associated with American LaFrance fire appliances of Elmira, New York, but the company produced a 5-ton truck just before World War I. From 1914 onwards production was discontinued to concentrate on fire engines, but in 1923 a separate operation called the American LaFrance Truck Co. was formed in Bloomfield, New Jersey, offering a range of models from 2 to 7½ tons payload capacity. That enterprise was short-lived and in 1929 it was merged into the Republic Motor Truck Co. of Alma, Michigan, forming the LaFrance Republic Corp. Republic trucks went up to 6½ tons payload while heavier models of LaFrance design were added to expand up the weight range. The heaviest was a massive 20-ton gvw three-axled rigid called the Mogul, powered by an American LaFrance V12 gasoline engine of 240bhp. It attracted few sales and the whole business was taken over by the Sterling Motor Truck Co. in 1932, production being centred on Sterling's plant at West Allis, Wisconsin.

JURA, FRANCE

Labourier

■ LEFT *Labourier's 3-tonner of 1960 had an unusual fibreglass cab with forward-sloping windscreen.*

While Labourier's main products were timber trucks and agricultural tractors, they produced a 5/7-tonne low-loading truck in 1947. Labourier's largest tractor was a 10-tonne 4×4 for oilfield work powered by a Deutz air-cooled diesel. In 1960 the company produced its only normal type of load carrier in the form of the TL3 forward-control 3-tonner. This had a modern fibreglass cab and a 1.8 litre/110cu in Peugeot diesel engine. Labourier continued to build specialized tractors, dump trucks and snowploughs through to their closure in the 1970s.

LETCHWORTH, ENGLAND

Lacre

■ RIGHT *The 1913 Lacre O model had a 4-cylinder gasoline engine and chain drive. The payload was 2½ tons.*

The Lacre Motor Car Company's history began in January 1902 at Long Acre near Covent Garden in London, the name being an abbreviation of Long Acre. Until 1909 the products consisted of cars and light vans, the earliest being based on an Albion chassis. From 1909 a full range of trucks up to 9 tons payload capacity was available, one of the best-known models being the 2-ton O type with chain drive. Production moved to a new site at Letchworth Garden City in 1910. After World War I, during which they built military vehicles, Lacre switched to building road sweepers. For the first two years of the war all of Lacre's military production was sold to the Belgian Army, but trucks were also supplied to the British, Canadian and Indian forces. Road-sweeper production doubtless helped Lacre remain profitable during the post-war slump. Some ordinary load-carrying trucks were offered until the late 1920s, including the forward-control E type 2½-tonner noted for its easily removable engine which was mounted on a subframe. In 1928 Lacre was hit by financial problems and was wound up, the Letchworth factory being sold. A reconstituted company named Lacre Lorries Ltd was set up in Kings Cross, London, concentrating on road sweepers. In 1936 the company relocated again to Welwyn Garden City. During World War II the Ministry of Aircraft Production commandeered their factory so production of sweepers was suspended until 1947. From 1952 onwards Lacre only supplied sweeper bodywork on Bedford chassis.

TURIN, ITALY

Lancia

■ LEFT *The Lancia Esatau B of the early 1960s was powered by Lancia's own 6-cylinder diesel.*

Vincenzo Lancia and Claudio Fogolin formed Lancia in 1906. In 1912 the first trucks were built for the Italian army. The Iota and Diota of 1915 featured built-in electrics. The 2½-tonne Triota and Tetriota appeared in 1921. The Pentaiota of 1924 was Lancia's first true heavy truck, having a payload of 5.3 tonnes. In 1932 Lancia built their first diesel truck, the RO for 9.3 tonnes gvw powered by a vertical opposed-piston two-stroke engine built under licence from Junkers.

By 1938 Lancia had developed its own Type 102 5-cylinder diesel which was installed in the 3RO truck for 6½-tonne payload. More powerful 6-cylinder diesels were available in the Esatau of 1947, which was in production until 1963. Forward control appeared in 1955 with the 864A. These became the Esatau type B. During the 1960s Lancia's heavy trucks were the Esagamma and Esagamma E for 19 tonnes gvw, while heavier 6×2 and 6×4 versions were also available. Lancia joined Fiat in 1969.

SURESNES, FRANCE

Latil

■ LEFT *A Latil tractor purpose-built for shunting heavy trailers.*

Georges Latil was in vehicle building as early as 1898, having pioneered front-wheel drive in the Blum-Latil truck before establishing Cie des Automobiles Industriels Latil in 1914. The company specialized in all-wheel drive, all-wheel steer tractors. From the mid 1920s a range of trucks from 1½ to 10 tonnes was offered. In 1929 pneumatic-tyred trucks were introduced. Licensed production of Gardner engines began in the early 1930s. Latil tractors were licence built in the UK by Shelvoke & Drewry as Trauliers. After World War II Latil's comprehensive range was mainly diesel-powered. Until 1955 Latil remained independent, but it then became part of Saviem.

TOOWOOMBA, AUSTRALIA

Leader

■ RIGHT *The fibreglass-cabbed A6 three-axled rigid was part of Leader's Mid Ranger series.*

Leader trucks were the inspiration of a transport company that wanted a rugged truck tailored to Australian requirements. Cyril Anderson formed a transport firm in 1934. It grew into the nationally-based Western Transport. He also formed the Great Western Group. In 1972 it was decided to enter truck manufacture. The A series featured Caterpillar diesels, Fuller Transmissions and Rockwell axles. Detroit Diesel two-stroke V diesels were also available. Cabs were modelled on the Mack F series but built of fibreglass. There were two strains of Leaders – the Mid Ranger for short-haul work and the Overlander for long distance. These could be ordered with the Sundowner sleeper cab. A bonneted tractor, the Challenger, was also introduced. Leader were forced to pull out of truck manufacture in 1983.

LEYLAND, ENGLAND

LEYLAND

■ LEFT *A 1928 Leyland GH2 4-tonner powered by 4-cylinder gasoline engine. Pneumatic tyres were introduced in 1925.*

■ BELOW LEFT *The very first wagon to be built by the Lancashire Steam Motor Co. in 1896.*

The origins of the UK's most famous truck maker lie in the Lancashire Steam Motor Co. set up in 1896 at Leyland in Lancashire. The young man at the centre of the enterprise was James Sumner, the son of Elias Sumner, who was village blacksmith at Leyland. Between 1884 and 1896 James had experimented with numerous steam-propelled vehicles. The passing of the 1896 Act, which lifted certain restrictive legislation, encouraged James to set up the Lancashire Steam Motor Co., for which he received financial backing from the Spurrier family. With the help of just 20 employees, Sumner completed his first vehicle, a 1½-ton steam van with oil-fired boiler, cart wheels and tiller steering. As orders for the steamers came in, new premises were found, being the "North Works" of Leyland's factory in later years. No less than 72 steamers were built over the first six years, and larger machines for payloads of up 3, 4 and 5 tons were developed. By 1904 the company was experimenting with gasoline-engined trucks, and following the first rudimentary machine, nicknamed the "Pig", an improved model appeared in 1905, production reaching 16 chassis. In 1907 the Preston-based engineering company, Coulthards, was taken over and the business was renamed Leyland Motors Ltd.

■ ABOVE *Leyland's first gasoline-engined truck of 1904 was nicknamed the "Pig".*

■ BELOW *The Leyland Marathon introduced in 1973, developed by AEC.*

While steam-vehicle production continued until 1926, based at the company's Chorley works, Leyland's main focus was on the internal combustion engine. A bonneted 3-ton gasoline truck was approved under the War Office subsidy scheme in 1912. This became the famous RAF type. In its final form this had a 34hp 4-cylinder engine, cone clutch and 4-speed crash gearbox driving a double-reduction bevel rear axle. Over 5500 of these trucks were built, and they are regarded as one of Leyland's most famous machines. Notable classics of the 1920s were the Q-type 4-tonner, the SQ2 semi-forward-control 7-tonner of 1925 and the SWQ2 10-ton six-wheel derivative, which appeared in 1927. Leyland's early experiments with diesel power began in 1925 when a prototype engine of spark-ignition design was tried. By 1930 a direct-injection diesel was fitted into a six-wheeled Rhino for exhibition at the Olympia Show in London. By 1933 diesel engines were in full production.

From 1929–30 Leyland's famous Zoo range of trucks appeared with familiar names such as Beaver, Bison, Buffalo, Bull and Hippo, soon followed by the Rhino 6-tonner and the Cub 2-tonner in 1931. By now Leylands had taken on a more modern look, with fully enclosed cabs. UK legislation in 1933 led manufacturers to keep weight to a

■ RIGHT *Leyland's Hippo 12-tonner of 1937.*

■ RIGHT *Leyland's last important truck launch was that of the Roadtrain, which arrived on the scene in 1980.*

minimum to avoid the excessive road tax that was based on unladen weight. Another phenomenon of the period was the rigid eight-wheeler. Though Leyland was not the first to exploit the 22-ton four-axled rigid, it had one available within a year of its rivals AEC, ERF and Foden. It took the appropriate name Octopus. A by-product of the twin-steer eight-wheeler was the Chinese Six. Leyland offered one from 1937 called the Twin Steer Beaver, but later renamed it just Steer.

Leyland became an important producer of battle tanks during World War II and also built thousands of trucks for military and essential civilian users between 1939 and 1945. In the late '40s Leyland rivalled AEC as Britain's largest heavy-truck builder. From that point on both companies embarked on ambitious expansion plans. Leyland took over Albion Motors in 1951 and Scammell Lorries in 1955. By this time AEC had become ACV Group and had taken over Maudslay and Crossley.

The post-war products of the two companies were also broadly similar. As part of the post-war export drive, Leyland introduced its bonneted Comet in 1947. A forward-control version came in 1953 and AEC matched it with their Mercury. Both companies built normal and forward-control heavies of similar weights and power outputs. AEC established numerous joint projects with European manufacturers, as did Leyland. Leyland's range, which consisted of the Comet and Super Comet four-wheelers and the heavier-duty Beaver four-wheeler, Hippo six-wheeler and Octopus eight-wheeler, received a new cab in 1960. This was the heavily styled LAD steel cab which, compared to its predecessor, lacked interior space.

■ BELOW RIGHT *The mainstay of Leyland's early post-war range was this 22.O/1 rigid eight-wheeler powered by their O.600 diesel.*

■ RIGHT *Although badged Leyland, this Reiver was of Albion pedigree but was built at BLMC's Bathgate factory.*

In 1961 Leyland had bought out Standard Triumph and gained a facility to build a lighter truck, namely the Leyland 90. The same year ACV acquired Thornycroft. This was ACV's last expansion move as Leyland bought out the entire group in 1962. The resulting combine was called the Leyland Motor Corporation Ltd. It wasn't long before Leyland group products began to take on a family likeness. Their Ergomatic tilt cab of 1964 appeared on Leyland, AEC and Albion models. In the late '60s Leyland experimented with gas-turbine propulsion following the acquisition of the Rover Co. in 1966 which had extensive experience in this field. While a number of gas-turbine prototypes were built, the project was abandoned. Until the late '60s Leyland had remained reasonably successful and was easily the UK's largest producer and exporter of heavy trucks. Sadly, Leyland's fortunes were to take a down turn following an ill-planned merger with British Motor Holdings (BMH), which included BMC trucks and Guy Motors. BMC's range, built at Bathgate, was later marketed as Leyland Redline. The outcome of the merger, under which the company was now part of the British Leyland Motor Corporation (BLMC), was that BMH's ailing car operations starved the truck divisions of resources and investment.

The situation worsened until 1975 when the UK government was forced to nationalize the whole group and try to rescue what remained viable. Funds were put into a new range of trucks, desperately needed since Leyland had been unable to improve its range through lack of resources in the BLMC era. That new range was the T45, announced in 1980, which was highly successful. Unfortunately, by that time Leyland had lost most of its credibility and foreign competition had robbed most of its potential market, both at home and abroad. The BLMC years had all but ruined Leyland, which was once the jewel in the UK truck maker's crown. In spite of the excellent new T45 or Roadtrain range, Leyland suffered mounting losses and in 1987 the decision was reached by the UK government to sell off the company to DAF Trucks. Ironically, the relatively young Dutch company had originally built its reputation on Leyland technology during the 1950s. Henceforth Leylands were marketed as Leyland-DAF in the UK.

■ LEFT *During the 1990s Leyland Trucks Ltd. built the rugged Super Comet for export.*

THAME, ENGLAND

LEYLAND-DAF

■ RIGHT *Under Leyland-DAF the former Roadrunner was relaunched as the 45 series.*

The history of Leyland-DAF begins in 1987 with the sale of the UK's most prestigious truck manufacturer into foreign ownership, symbolizing the decline of Britain's once-thriving truck industry. Leyland's fortunes took a down turn after a series of expansion moves during the 1950s and '60s when it absorbed Albion (1951), Scammell (1955), ACV Group encompassing AEC, Maudslay and Thornycroft (1962), and finally the ailing car giant BMH, which included Austin and Morris trucks, as well as the Jaguar Group's Guy range, in 1968. It was the link-up with BMH to form the British Leyland Motor Corporation (BLMC) that eventually led to Leyland's problems. The car manufacturing divisions drained the group's resources until it faced collapse in the mid 1970s.

The British government stepped in and rescued the company in 1975 and British Leyland's truck and bus divisions were given greater autonomy, but the damage was done. All the truck plants except Leyland were either closed or sold off, including Southall, Wolverhampton, Scotstoun, Watford and Bathgate, and Leyland made a final bid to re-establish itself with the launch of the T45 series in 1980. In spite of the slimming measures and the launch of a first-class product, the company continued to suffer heavy losses. It changed its name to BL to disguise the British identity that was thought to convey a poor image. It was then relegated to being a member of the Rover Group. By 1986 the taxpayers could no longer be expected to prop up the state-owned truck maker and a buyer was sought. Bids were turned down from General Motors and Paccar, but in 1987 it was agreed that DAF would take a 60 per cent controlling share in Leyland and Freight Rover. Leyland was to be responsible for light and medium trucks while DAF concentrated on heavy trucks, and a new UK-based sales company would market the products as Leyland-DAF in the UK. In other markets the trucks were to be badged as DAF. Initially the new organization appeared to flourish, but then DAF ran into financial problems following heavy investment in a new range, the 65, 75 and 85 series. In February 1993 the company collapsed and was rescued by the Dutch and Belgian governments. However, the UK manufacturing plant at Leyland was not part of the deal and was the subject of a management buy-out, returning it to 100 per cent British ownership. The new company, Leyland Truck Manufacturing, formed an agreement to supply Leyland trucks to DAF to be marketed in the UK through Leyland-DAF Ltd, which is still owned by DAF. Leyland Trucks also builds certain DAF models and, for a period, undertook assembly of Isuzu trucks.

In 1996 it was announced that the American company Paccar, which owns Kenworth, Peterbilt and Foden, had taken over DAF. Just two years later in June 1998, Paccar acquired Leyland Truck Manufacturing too. Recently Kenworth and Peterbilt trucks for city deliveries in the States have begun using Leyland cabs and chassis. Plans were announced in September 1999 to transfer all Foden production to the Leyland plant. From the beginning of 2000, Leyland-DAF became DAF.

■ ABOVE LEFT *A heavy-duty 95 series 8×4 tractor engaged on UK heavy haulage.*

■ LEFT *The 85 series Leyland-DAF eight-wheeler is of DAF pedigree throughout.*

JABLONEC NA NISOU, CZECH REPUBLIC

LiAZ

■ LEFT *The latest LiAZ 300 series long-haul tractor is this 19/41 TBV with 300bhp diesel.*

Liberecké Automobilové Zavody took over production of Skoda 706 trucks in Prague in 1951 at the former Avia plant which had built Skodas since 1946. The Skoda 706RT and 706RTS forward-control models appeared in 1957 with the direct injection 11.78 litre/719cu in diesel. The LiAZ name was adopted from 1974 when the long-running 706 models were joined by the modernized 100.05 trucks and 100.45 38-tonne tractor units powered by a turbocharged version of the 11.94 litre/729cu in diesel which had powered the 706 models in 1968. In turbocharged form for the 100 series it was rated at 270 or 340bhp. From 1989 LiAZ trucks have been produced by the Truck International AS division of Skoda and the current range includes 4×2 trucks rated at 18 and 19 tonnes gvw or up to 40 tonnes gcw, 6×2 models up to 24.5 tonnes or 40 tonnes with drawbar trailer. Also available is a range of trucks and dump trucks with 4×2, 4×4, 6×4 and 8×4s spanning the 18 to 40 tonnes gross weight range. Some trucks still feature a facelifted version of the 100 series cab, while long-distance tractor units have a new design of sleeper cab.

USA

Liberty

■ RIGHT *Liberty trucks were built by a number of manufacturers and some were later converted for civilian use.*

Though Liberty was not officially a truck make in its own right, it was the name adopted for a standardized design of truck for the United States Army. In 1917 the United States Army drew up a specification for a standard Class B 3 to 5-ton heavy truck, to overcome the problems of having scores of different types needing huge stocks of non-interchangeable spare parts. Such was the demand for trucks in World War I that over 8000 Libertys were shipped to France during the latter part of the war. The Model B was built mainly by Selden of Rochester, New York, and Gramm Bernstein of Lima, Ohio, but they were also built by Garford, Pierce Arrow, Republic, Bethlehem, Diamond T, Brockway and Sterling. After the war a Belgian company based in Brussels began reconditioning the surplus United States Army Liberty trucks. Soc. Franco-Belgique de Camions Liberty went on to build modernized versions through to the start of World War II, the later ones having diesel engines. Liberty trucks were also rebuilt by Willème during that period before the company in Seine, France, went on to launch its own designs.

BRIDGEPORT, CONNECTICUT, USA

Locomobile

Locomobile existed for a very short period, its name being changed to Riker after just five years. The first Locomobile of 1912 was a cabover 5-tonner with chain drive. Other models for 3, 4 and 6 tons were added during 1915. Production ended in 1920.

■ RIGHT *A World War I Locomobile 3-ton truck with a 4-cylinder engine.*

ROUEN, FRANCE

LOHÉAC

The Lohéac story is an example of a transport contractor developing his own breed of truck to suit his specific needs. Beginning in the early 1950s Antoine Lohéac based his first tractor units on ex-United States Army H-542 Internationals introducing other makes of engine, mainly Berliet diesels. Over the years Lohéac introduced an increasing number of his own components, building the distinctive semi-forward cabs from fibreglass "in house". During the 1970s and '80s Lohéac used DAF and Scania engines and introduced a full forward-control tractor with Aramid fibre-reinforced cab. The Lohéac fleet is made up mainly of bulk liquid tankers. The company has also built its own semi-trailers.

■ ABOVE ***Lohéac built heavy trucks solely for their own use.***

■ LEFT ***Early Lohéac trucks were developed from the ex-army International H-542.***

COLNBROOK, ENGLAND

LOMOUNT

Lomount was a new name applied to Rotinoff heavy-duty tractors from 1960 to 1962. (See "Rotinoff".)

■ RIGHT ***One of two Rotinoff Viscount road-train tractors supplied for Australian livestock transport.***

LORRAINE, FRANCE

LORRAINE-DIETRICH

Formerly known as De Dietrich, whose history dated from 1896, Lorraine-Dietrich trucks first appeared in 1905. De Dietrich's earliest truck, a 3-tonner, took part in the 1897 Versailles Heavy Vehicle Trials achieving a top speed of 15kph/9mph. The early vehicles had complex transmissions combining belt drive and gearing, but a 2-tonne truck available in 1902 had chain drive. In 1907 the design rights were acquired from Turcat-Méry for a highly unusual three-axled truck with a central chain-driven axle and a lightweight steered axle fore and aft. By 1909 the truck range included bonneted models from ¾ tonne to 5 tonnes, the heaviest having a 5½ litre/335cu in gasoline engine. A cab-over-engine layout was adopted for a 3-tonner in 1911. Some shaft-drive 1-tonne trucks were built during the early part of World War I, but after that production ceased. A small number of trucks badged Lorraine were built under licence from Tatra in the 1930s, plus a few road-rail terminal tractors in the 1940s.

ALLENTOWN, PENNSYLVANIA, USA

MACK

■ LEFT *The 1999 Mack Vision tractor has a 460bhp E-Tech turbo diesel with V-MAC electronic vehicle management and control.*

■ BELOW LEFT *An early example of Mack's legendary AC Bulldog dating from 1917. Around 40,000 ACs were built between 1915 and 1938.*

The Mack Brothers Company was incorporated in New York in 1901 with John M. (Jack), Augustus F. (Gus) and William C. (Willie) Mack as directors.

From 1904 the brothers adopted the Manhattan name for their vehicles and in 1905 formed Mack Brothers Motor Car Co. in Lehigh County, Pennsylvania, with production facilities at Allentown. From 1910 it was decided to drop the Manhattan name and call the trucks Mack. The first trucks of 1905 were a bonneted 1½ to 2-tonner and forward-control models for 3, 4 and 5 tons payload – all powered by Mack's own design of gasoline engine.

To raise further capital the International Motor Company was formed in 1911 as a holding company for the Mack Brothers Motor Car Co. and the Saurer Motor Co. The latter built Swiss Saurer trucks under licence. A significant development was the introduction of the medium-weight AB of 1914 followed in 1915 by the legendary AC. It was the AC's rugged performance during World War I that impressed the British soldiers, so much so that they dubbed it the "Bulldog". The name stuck and from 1922 the famous bulldog motif was adopted as Mack's corporate symbol.

■ ABOVE *The A50T tractor was launched in 1950 in the lead-up to Mack's 50th anniversary.*

■ BELOW *An F series engaged on long-distance European international haulage.*

Over the years more famous models appeared, such as the BJ and BB of 1927. Then came the streamlined medium-duty Mack E models of 1936 with payload ratings up to 4 tons. Heavier E models followed, including the 6-ton shaft-drive EM, 6-ton chain-drive ER and EQ tractors for 10 to 12 tons.

During World War II Mack was a major supplier of trucks, including prime movers, personnel carriers, wreckers and tank transporters.

The 1950s saw important new models, including the B, H and G series. The bonneted B series of 1953 was one of Mack's best-known trucks. A total of 127,786 were built through to 1966, when it was replaced by the R series. The Thermodyne diesel was also introduced in 1953. A series of cab-forward medium-duty trucks began with the D series in 1955, followed by the N series which shared a design of Budd tilt cab with Ford. Then, in 1962, came the MB with Mack's own tilt cab. This was later developed into the MC in 1978. The H cabovers, nicknamed "Cherry Pickers" on account of their tall cabs, were specially designed to operate with 10.6m/35ft trailers within the 13.7m/45ft legal length limits. The G series of 1959 featured an all-aluminium cab and a choice of Mack or Cummins engine and was aimed at the West Coast users. Another significant development in the 1950s was the acquisition of the Brockway

■ **RIGHT** ***The Ultra-Liner range came on the scene in 1982 with power ratings up to 500bhp.***

■ **BELOW** ***A late 1950s H60 series cabover-engine tractor. Early H60s were nicknamed "Cherry Pickers".***

Motor Co. of Cortland, New York. This was allowed to continue with its own product line although Mack F series cabs appeared on certain models. Brockway was finally closed in 1977.

The famous F series appeared in 1962 and was sold in vast numbers throughout the world. For heavy-duty construction duties Mack introduced their rugged DM models. During the mid '60s assembly plants were set up in various countries, including an Australian plant in Queensland where specialized twin-steer four and five-axled rigids were built for roadtrain use. In 1963 Mack took over Camions Bernard in Arcueil, France, renaming it

Automobiles Bernard. The tie-up only lasted until 1966 when Bernard was closed down. Owing to a shortage of working capital, Mack merged with the Los Angeles-based Signal Oil & Gas Co. in 1967. The late '60s saw Mack introducing the Maxidyne constant-horsepower diesel, Maxitorque triple-countershaft transmission and, in 1971, Dynatard, Mack's own patented engine brake. A 66 per cent interest was acquired in Hayes Manufacturing, the Canadian heavy truck builder, in 1969.

The W series Cruise-Liner was announced in 1975 as Mack's premium long-haul cabover while the RW Super-Liner conventional followed in 1978. In 1979 Renault bought a 10 per cent share in Mack, increasing this to 20 per cent in 1982. That year also marked the launch of the new MH Ultra-Liner range with the Max-Glass composite cab made of fibreglass around a steel frame.

During the 1980s closer ties were forming with Renault, including an agreement to market the Renault Midliner city truck as the Mack Midliner in the United States. Mack's famous CH bonneted range was launched in 1988 and two years later it was announced that Mack had become a wholly owned subsidiary of Renault Véhicules Industriels. The new Vision, Mack's latest premium long-haul tractor, was launched in 1999.

BARKING, ENGLAND

MACK

■ **BELOW** ***The British-built Mack of 1956 featured a Bedford TA cab shell and front wings.***

From 1954–64 a British-based company, Mack Trucks (Great Britain) Ltd, produced a small number of vehicles to its own design. Initially the company reconditioned World War II American Macks but, after an unsuccessful plan to import new Macks from America, the company marketed a Perkins-engined 7-tonner. Similar vehicles appeared, including a Leyland-engined forward-control 7-tonner with Albion gearbox and a Bonallack cab. A normal-control version at 14 tons gvw was also marketed, featuring an adaptation of the Bedford TA cab. In all, it is understood that the company only built around 20 trucks, closing its doors in 1964.

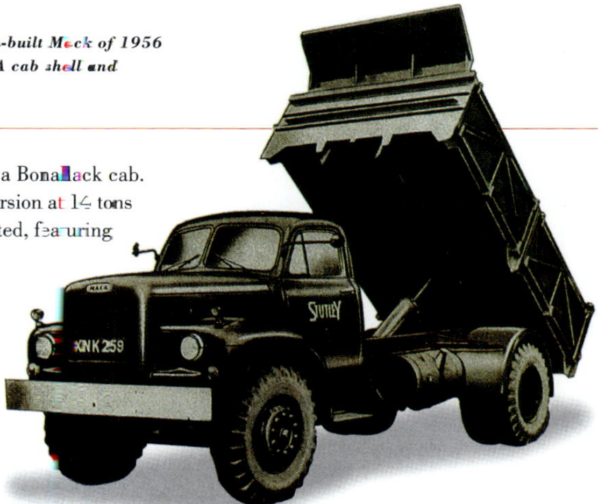

ULM, GERMANY

MAGIRUS-DEUTZ

■ LEFT *The 32-ton 200D16FS had a Deutz 12.6 litre/769cu in air-cooled V8 diesel engine.*

Prior to 1938, when Klockner Deutz Motoren absorbed Conrad Dietrich Magirus of Ulm, the latter was mainly concerned with the production of fire-fighting vehicles under the Magirus name. With its origins in 1903, Magirus first entered the truck market with a 3-tonner in 1916. This was followed by a 4-tonner in 1920. During the '20s many improvements were introduced, including pneumatic tyres and fully enclosed cabs, and the common power unit was a 4-cylinder 4.7 litre/287cu in gasoline engine. Six-cylinder engines appeared in the early '30s and in 1933 a range of military trucks featured a 7.5 litre/457cu in diesel. The 6.5-tonne M65 heavy-duty forward-control trucks of 1936 used a 150bhp horizontal 12-cylinder diesel with two opposing banks of 6-cylinders and a central crankshaft. The 10.63 litre/649cu in Z95D flat-twelve was mounted amidships behind the cab. This and the L265 bonneted 6½-tonner of 1939 were

■ ABOVE *In the mid 1930s the trucks were simply badged Magirus and prior to 1936 were all of bonneted layout.*

■ BELOW *Launched in 1951, the round-nosed Jupiter models had unique styling, as seen on this aircraft refueller.*

■ BELOW *A 1976 232D24K bonneted dump truck powered by FBL-413 V8 11.3 litre/689cu in air-cooled diesel.*

■ RIGHT *The 38-tonne gcw 340D22FS artic took its power from the Deutz air-cooled V12 340bhp diesel.*

■ BELOW RIGHT *This 209D14FS artic with day cab had a design weight of 35 tonnes gcw. The power unit is a 206bhp air-cooled V8 diesel.*

magnificent-looking machines and flagships of the Magirus range. The Magirus name badge, with its distinctive motif consisting of a letter "M" surmounted by the spire of Ulm cathedral, was still in use even though Klockner Deutz had acquired the company in 1938. Gradually the make was to become Magirus-Deutz, but the famous Magirus motif was retained. From as early as 1943 Deutz air-cooled diesels were beginning to oust the Magirus engines. The factory suffered extensive air-raid damage during World War II and was forced to close in 1945. Production resumed in a small way in 1946 with a mixture of products, including turntable ladders, tractors and a civilian half-track 2-tonner that was an important aid in post-war reconstruction.

A new 3-tonne payload truck was announced in 1946, outwardly resembling the pre-war designs that had the F4L 514 air-cooled diesel. They could actually handle 3.5 tonnes and were designated 53500 models. It was in April 1951 when Magirus-Deutz launched their sensational new Mercury and Jupiter ranges with their ultra-modern rounded bonnets (hoods) and ovoid grilles. The Mercury models for 5-tonne payloads had a 5.3 litre/323cu in, 85bhp 4-cylinder or 7.9 litre/482cu in, 125bhp 6-cylinder Deutz air-cooled engine. The heavier Jupiter for 8 tonnes payload had a 10.6 litre/647cu in producing 175bhp. In 1955 a number of heavy-duty 6×6 and 6×4 Uranus tractors were built mainly for military tank transporter duties. They were also used as a base for heavy armoured cars and as oilfield trucks. The planet names were dropped in favour of numeric designations from 1964. Forward-control trucks as well as bonneted versions became available from 1956 and an experimental tilt cab was tried in 1955. The fixed-cab 32-tonne 200D 16FS model was a particularly handsome machine. This carried the Deutz name badge plus the famous "M" and spire symbol. It was powered by the Deutz FBL714 12.6 litre/769cu in air-cooled V8 indirect-injection engine, but a 210bhp direct-injection version was also available.

During the 1960s a new design of forward-control cab in fixed or tilt form was introduced. This was of squarer appearance and had bumper-mounted oblong headlights but, in terms of styling, it was a retrograde step. That cab survived through to the late 1970s when it was replaced by the Fiat-Iveco cab and, in some dump-truck models, the cab was still fitted until the mid '80s. In 1971 Magirus-Deutz was one of four leading European manufacturers (the others were DAF, Volvo and Saviem) to form the Club of Four (officially called The Euro Truck Development Group) to develop a new range of medium trucks using a common steel tilt cab. In 1974 the company was reorganized as Magirus-Deutz AG and the following year was merged into the Fiat-led Iveco Group.

MUNICH, GERMANY

MAN

■ LEFT *The 10.212F has MAN's own cab. A Saviem cab appeared in the late 1960s.*

■ LEFT *A late 1950s 735L1 artic fuel tanker powered by 8.3 litre/506cu in 6-cylinder diesel.*

Although Maschinenfabrik Augsburg-Nürnberg AG began truck building in 1920, its history dates back further to 1915 when it built Saurer trucks under licence in a former Saurer plant in Lindau. From 1916 the company was entitled Kraftwagenwerke MAN-Saurer GmbH and the licence-built Saurers were produced until 1918. In 1897 MAN made history by pioneering the first diesel engine in close co-operation with Dr Rudolf Diesel. In 1923 MAN built the first automotive diesel engine featuring direct injection. The 4-cylinder four-stroke engine developed 40bhp at 900rpm. A MAN truck powered by the engine was exhibited at the 1924 Berlin Show, but it was about three years before diesels were offered in production models.

In 1926 MAN launched a chain-drive six-wheeler with a 150bhp 6-cylinder gasoline engine. This became available with a new 6-cylinder diesel of 100bhp in 1927. During the early 1930s an impressive new range of trucks offered a choice of gasoline or diesel. The largest model was the imposing S1H6 of 1932, a long-wheelbase bonneted six-wheeler for drawbar use, powered by a 16.6 litre/1013cu in 140bhp diesel. During the '30s a comprehensive diesel truck range for payloads of 3, 3.5, 4, 5, 6 and 8 tonnes was available.

In 1936 MAN acquired ÖAF (Österreichische Automobilfabrik). For a period ÖAF manufactured axles for MAN but, during World War II, ÖAF assembled 4×4 4-tonne military trucks for the Wehrmacht. ÖAF operated as an autonomous division during the 1950s and '60s developing its own range of trucks, often using Leyland, Cummins and Mercedes engines as well as MAN, but the company came under closer MAN control in the early '70s when it also absorbed Gräf & Stift. MAN's wartime production was severely disrupted by bomb damage, but some production was resumed with the 5-tonne payload MK model from 1945. This had a 110bhp 6-cylinder diesel. There were two interesting engine developments in 1951 – the first turbocharged diesel and the first V8 diesel. In 1955 truck production was transferred to a new factory in Munich. By 1960 the MAN range included 4×2 trucks and tractor units for load capacities of 5 to 20 tonnes, and in 1961 six-wheelers for payloads of 16 to 20 tonnes. A program of technical co-operation with Saviem of France began in 1968, under which Saviem began using MAN engines while MAN benefited from Saviem's new tilt cab

■ BELOW LEFT *A late 1970s 16.200 HAK bonneted four-wheel drive dump truck.*

■ LEFT *A 1992 F90 cabbed 35-332 8×8 dump truck with Meiller body, loading in Magdeburg.*

which replaced its own long-running all-steel forward-control cab. The latter had also been available as a tilt cab in the '60s.

At the same time MAN had acquired a financial interest in Büssing Automobilwerke AG and took over the company completely in 1971. This resulted in the demise of the famous Büssing range, which included a high proportion of underfloor-engined trucks. Such was the following for these among Büssing's former customers that MAN reintroduced them rebadged as MAN-Büssing. Demand was so great that the range survived through to the mid 1980s, the latter-day models featuring the Saviem-MAN pattern cab. During the early '70s MAN developed a rigid eight-wheeler aimed at the UK market and many European countries adopted the type. The Hungarian RÁBA company of Györ built MAN-based trucks under licence from 1970, renewing an association that had begun in the 1930s. From 1984 RÁBA began using DAF cabs but continued to use RÁBA-MAN engines. A similar agreement was formed with Autocamioane Brasov of Romania to build MAN trucks under the Roman name from 1971. These were also marketed as DAC.

During the 1980s MAN marketed their comprehensive F8 range from 16-tonne two-axled trucks up to 44-tonne tractor units, as well as special heavy-haulage tractors for gtw up to 105 tonnes. The F8 models were replaced in 1986 by the restyled F90, which featured a more modern MAN-designed cab. Further improvements came in 1994 with the launch of the 2000 range. When MAN needed a lighter range of trucks during the 1970s it entered a joint development program with Volkswagen. The result was the MT range using VW's LT cab. The MT continued in production for almost 10 years, after which it was relaunched as the MAN G90. Later still, after MAN took over Steyr Nutzfahrzeuge AG in 1991, the range was replaced by the L2000 models featuring a Steyr cab.

MAN Nutzfahrzeuge AG, as it is now known, also has truck-building facilities in Turkey (MAN-A.S.) and in India (Shakti-MAN) and has recently acquired a 51 per cent stake in the MAZ (Minsk Automobil Zavod) company of Minsk in Belarus. MAN's latest range of heavy-duty trucks is the F2000 Evolution launched early in 1999. In February 2000 MAN bought Western Star's British ERF subsidiary.

■ ABOVE *MAN's original diesel-powered truck of 1924.*

■ RIGHT *This 1999 26.414 6×2 tractor is part of MAN's new F2000 Evolution range with design gcw up to 50 tonnes.*

STOCKPORT, ENGLAND

MANCHESTER

■ LEFT *The 1929 Manchester $1\frac{1}{2}$-ton dump truck originates from the American Willys Overland.*

The Manchester was really an Anglo-American hybrid built between 1928 and 1933 by Willys Overland Crossley of Stockport near Manchester. The division of Crossley was set up in 1920 to assemble Willys Overland vehicles for the UK market and began using the Manchester name on the Willys Overland 25cwt truck in 1926.

The first British-designed Manchester was a 35cwt which was sometimes sold with a third-axle conversion. In 1930 a bonneted $2\frac{1}{2}$-ton truck appeared and a forward-control version was planned, but the company folded in 1933.

INDIANAPOLIS, INDIANA, USA

MARMON-HERRINGTON

Marmon-Herrington's origins date back to 1851, but trucks were not produced until 1931 when the Marmon Car Co. was joined by Col. Arthur W. S. Herrington, an engineer with experience in all-wheel drive. The company went on to build specialized all-wheel drive vehicles and, later, some massive trucks for the Iraq Pipeline Co. It also carried out all-wheel drive conversions on Ford light trucks. A variety of military trucks were built during World War II.

In 1963 Col. Herrington's share was acquired by a private conglomerate. Designs for a new truck were sold to its south-west distributor, who put it into production under the name of Marmon. In 1985 Marmon-Herrington became part of Fontaine Inc. at Louisville, where it makes driveline components.

■ ABOVE *Marmon-Herrington had this 6×4 cabover on the stocks when it pulled out of trucks in 1963.*

DENTON & DALLAS, TEXAS, USA

MARMON

■ LEFT *The Marmon 6×4 cabover is part of a range of hand-built premium trucks made in Denton, Texas.*

In 1963, after Marmon-Herrington ceased truck production, a new company, Marmon Motor Co. of Denton, Texas, was formed by one of its distributors to build trucks that Marmon-Herrington had been planning. Marmon are premium trucks aimed at the owner operator. In 1973 the company was purchased by the Interstate Corporation of Chattanooga. In the 1980s Marmon's P 6×4 range became their main product, while a lower-specced F (fleet) range was also available. Current Marmon trucks have taken on a more streamlined look in their D, L. R and S types, while the long-nosed P models retain the classic angular lines popular with long-haul owner operators.

COVENTRY & ALCESTER, ENGLAND

MAUDSLAY

■ LEFT *The 1927 forward-control Maudslay was heavily built and featured solid tyres.*

■ LEFT *A 1944 Maudslay Mogul II with AEC 7.7 litre/470cu in 6-cylinder diesel and 1500-gallon fuel oil tank.*

The name that graced the front of Maudslay lorries from 1903–59 is older than almost any other name in the industry. Henry Maudslay was born in 1771 and founded his own engineering company in 1798 off London's Oxford Street. In 1831 it became Maudslay Sons & Field who built steam engines for the British naval fleet. It also pioneered one of the world's first commercial vehicles, Sir Charles Dance's steam carriage. Maudslay Sons & Field Ltd closed in 1900 and in 1901 Reginald, a great grandson of Henry Maudslay, founded the Maudslay Motor Co. A lightweight commercial vehicle was introduced in 1903. Advanced features included overhead camshaft engines and shaft drive. In 1912 Maudslay introduced new 1½ and 3-tonners with 4-cylinder gasoline engines.

In 1923 a forward-control 7-tonner appeared. An even larger 8-tonner was announced in 1925. In 1929 it was joined by the L10 – a most impressive forward-control 10-ton six-wheeler.

During the 1930s truck sales all but dried up. The company was facing closure in 1935 when it was rescued by its major shareholder, Oliver Douglas Smith. A new truck range entered production at the end of 1939, consisting of the Maharajah six-wheeler, Mikado eight-wheeler and Mogul and Militant four-wheelers. Owing to the war, only a handful of six and eight-wheelers were built up until 1941, but four-wheelers were allowed to continue for essential civilian use. A wartime shortage of Gardner engines led to the use of AEC 7.7 litre/470cu in diesels in the Mogul while the Militant had the Gardner 4LW.

In 1946 a tractor unit named the Maharanee was introduced, and the following year a twin-steer six-wheeler, the Mustang. Production was transferred to a new plant at Great Alne, which was built as a shadow factory to escape Coventry's wartime blitz. Maudslay's last new models in 1948 were six and eight-wheelers. The six-wheeler was still called the Maharajah but the eight-wheeler became the Meritor. In May 1948 Maudslay was taken over by AEC, who discontinued the range and used the Maudslay plant to build AECs under the Maudslay badge. This continued through to late 1959 when the Maudslay name vanished. The Great Alne factory was sold in 1972 to the Rockwell Axle company.

■ BELOW *Built in January 1951, this Meritor with AEC 9.6 litre/588cu in diesel was one of the last Maudslays ever made.*

MINSK, BELARUS

MAZ

■ LEFT *MAZ 504A articulated tanker seen at work in Budapest in 1992.*

■ BELOW *MAZ 64221 6×4 cabover with sleeper cab coupled to a tandem-axle tilt.*

The Minsk Automobil Zavod (or Minsk Motor Works) was formed in 1947 to build a range of bonneted four and six-wheel trucks and four-wheel tractor units, a typical example being the MAZ-200 7-tonne payload cargo truck. This was of dated appearance and continued through to the mid 1960s when a forward-control range, generally known as the 500 series, entered production. This had an attractively styled steel cab of modern appearance and, in 4×2 form, had a payload rating of 8 tonnes. A 10-tonne payload six-wheeler version was also available. In the early 1970s the 500 models underwent extensive redevelopment and became the 9-tonne payload 500A. This had an 11.15 litre/680cu in 6-cylinder diesel developing 210bhp. Gross vehicle weight was 15.8 tonnes while the MAZ-504A tractor unit was rated for a gcw of 28 tonnes. The early '80s saw the launch of a modern heavy-duty model line-up more in tune with the advanced designs of Western Europe. Typical of new MAZ long-haul tractor units were the 5432 two-axled and 6422 three-axled cabovers powered by JaMZ V8 turbo diesels with power ratings of 280 to 320bhp. These were further developed into the 54321 and 64221 with increased output engines up to 360 and 425bhp.

During the 1990s MAZ began to form closer ties with MAN of Munich, switching to the use of MAN's in-line-six turbo inter-cooled diesels for their updated 54326 and 64226 models. Gross combination weights are up to 48 tonnes. In 1999 MAN acquired a controlling interest in MAZ which will probably lead to greater commonization in the products.

HAYES & SLOUGH, ENGLAND

McCurd

The McCurd Lorry Mfg. Co. Ltd was a relatively short-lived maker. Between 1912 and 1914 some bonneted worm-drive trucks for 2, 3 and 5 tons were built at Hayes by engineer W. A. McCurd. After World War I, production of these was continued until 1921 but then suspended. In 1925 the company was relocated to Slough in Buckinghamshire as McCurd Motors and a few newly designed 2½-tonners were built up to 1927 when the company ceased trading.

■ LEFT *This 1913 McCurd 5-ton box van was powered by a 4-cylinder gasoline engine with an RAC rating of 32.4hp. The type was only built for two years.*

STUTTGART, GERMANY

MERCEDES-BENZ

■ LEFT *The Gaggenau cabover truck of 1910, built at the Süddeutsche Automobilfabrik (SAF), was the forerunner of the Mercedes-Benz.*

As the 21st century dawns, Daimler-Chrysler (formerly Daimler-Benz AG) is the world's leading truck manufacturer. The Mercedes-Benz marque has existed since 1926, but the company's origins go back to the late 19th century and the earliest recorded motor truck. Daimler-Benz was formed by the merger of Benz & Cie, Rheinische Gasmotorenfabrik of Mannheim and Daimler Motoren-Gesellschaft of Stuttgart-Unterturkheim. Daimler pioneered the truck industry with its 1896 rear-engined 1½-tonner, while Benz & Cie completed its first truck, of similar size to Daimler's, in 1899. In 1899, the year before Gottlieb Daimler died, his partners formed a separate truck-building company called Motorfahrzeug und Motorenfabrik Berlin AG at Marienfelde. This was subsequently absorbed by Daimler in 1914. Benz & Cie formed a syndicate involving Süddeutsche Automobilfabrik (SAF) of Gaggenau. Benz concentrated on cars while SAF became responsible for truck production. In 1908 Benz took over Süddeutsche to form Benz-Werke, Gaggenau. After developing along separate lines with broadly similar products over the next decade or so, Daimler Motoren-Gesellschaft and Benz & Cie were to merge in 1926. Gaggenau was to become the truck plant while Berlin Marienfelde became a repair centre.

From 1931 model designations had the prefix "L" (for "Lastwagen"). During the war years over 64,000 commercial vehicles were produced by Daimler-Benz, almost exclusively for military use. In 1938 the German government introduced restrictions on the industry and Daimler-Benz was only allowed to produce 3, 4½ and 6-tonne two-axled trucks, while all other production was suppressed. For a brief period towards the end of the war the company also built a batch of 3-tonne Opel Blitz trucks. The factories had been extensively damaged by Allied bombing, bringing production to a virtual halt.

When production resumed in 1949 the range was limited to the bonneted L3250 3¼-tonners and the L3600 and L4500 for 3.6 and 4.5 tonnes payload. Medium and heavy truck production was allowed to resume in 1951 and soon the bonneted L models were joined by the first cab-over-engine trucks, designated the LP. The "P" stood for "Pullman", implying Pullman car comfort. Heavy trucks were built at Gaggenau plant which also built the versatile new Unimog 4×4, while medium trucks were produced at Mannheim. The first LP model was the LP315 7-tonner of 1955. This was joined in 1958 by the LP333 twin-steer six-wheeler which operated at 16 tonnes gvw or 32 tonnes gtw, the 32-tonne limit having been approved in that year by the German government. An LPS333 tractor ("S" meaning "Sattelschlepper") was also available for 32 tonnes gcw. The second steering axle on this was mid-mounted 1.6m/5.25ft ahead of the drive axle. All these models

■ LEFT *An NK56 six-wheeler with Balloon tyres and a payload of 10 tons.*

■ BELOW *The LPS1620 tractor was powered by the OM346 6-cylinder diesel engine.*

had a bulbous full-width cab with split windscreen. A more compact version of the cab with single-piece screen was featured on the LP321, LP322 and LP337 for payloads of 6 to 7 tonnes.

By this time Daimler-Benz AG had several factories in Germany and had set up assembly plants in 24 countries. Gaggenau, near Baden-Baden, was still the main heavy truck plant and Mercedes-Benz accounted for nearly 75 per cent of Germany's medium to heavy truck exports. An ultra-modern production plant came into operation in 1963 at Wörth, located between Mannheim and Gaggenau. At first only cabs were built, but by 1965 full-scale truck assembly was underway. By 1967 the new Wörth factory had taken over totally from Mannheim and Gaggenau. A completely redesigned forward-control cab of squarer appearance was launched at the 1963 Frankfurt Motor Show. This was taller, and the engine was mounted very low to minimize engine cover intrusion. Coincidental with this Mercedes-Benz announced its first direct-injection diesel engine, the 10.8 litre/659cu in OM346. This effectively replaced the OM326 which, like all previous types, was of pre-combustion design.

Another important development of the mid 1960s was the new LPS2020 three-axled "rear-steer" tractor unit designed to take advantage of the legal weight increase from 32 to 38 tonnes. In anticipation of the higher power requirements Daimler-Benz developed a new family of V diesels in V6, V8, V10 and V12 form with power outputs ranging from 192bhp to 400bhp. The first to appear was the 16 litre/976cu in V10, designated OM403, with an output of 320bhp. This went in a range of new tilt-cab models in 1969 featuring a tilt version of the old "square" type cab. These were LP/LPS 1632, 2032 and 2232 models and were recognizable by their deeper front wheel arches, split near the cab rear face.

In 1970 Daimler-Benz took over Hanomag-Henschel Fahrzeugwerke GmbH, whose truck plant was at Kassel. The company's Bremen van plant was also an important acquisition, enabling Daimler-Benz to fill a gap in its weight range. In addition to its main truck plant at Wörth, Daimler-Benz now had 18 factories, including its car plant and headquarters at Unterturkheim. Truck plants had been established in Brazil, Argentina, South Africa and Spain while others in Turkey, Iran and Indonesia were mainly concerned with buses. Technical and financial collaboration with the Indian Tata Engineering & Locomotive Co. had begun in 1954 to build Mercedes-Benz designs under licence. In 1964 the company had formed Mercedes-Benz of North America. In 1968 it took over the distribution, including existing stocks and real estate, of Krupp Trucks when production ended at Essen. In 1972 it formed an agreement with FAP-Famos of Yugoslavia to supply cabs. A United States truck assembly plant was built in 1980 at Hampton/Newport News. The following year Daimler-Benz acquired the Freightliner Corporation of the United States. A further acquisition came in 1982 with the purchase of NAW, the joint company formed by Saurer and FBW at Arbon and Wetzikon, Switzerland. There were more takeovers to come.

■ TOP LEFT *The stylish L6600 bonneted 6.6-tonne truck, produced from 1950–54, was powered by a 145bhp 6-cylinder diesel.*

■ TOP RIGHT *An early 1960s LP333 twin-steer six-wheeler operated at 32 tonnes gtw with drawbar trailer.*

■ LEFT *In the late 1960s this LPS1418 could operate at 32 tonnes gcw when coupled to a tri-axle trailer.*

■ RIGHT *This five-axled 38-tonne gcw dump truck features the attractive New Generation cab.*

■ RIGHT *Mercedes-Benz's most recent range is the medium-class Atego. This 1217 has the L sleeper cab.*

The most important truck launch of the 1970s was the New Generation range of 1973, so-called because of the "softer" styling of its new tilt cab. From that point on Mercedes-Benz trucks were predominantly forward-control, and bonneted types were gradually phased out after their production was moved to the old Henschel factory at Kassel. The first models to feature the New Generation cab were two and three-axled construction vehicles. By 1975 the cab had been introduced across the heavy truck range. In 1988 the cab was facelifted with a new black grille and relaunched as the SK. Detailed technical advances continued to be made during the 1970s and '80s, like the availability of ABS (anti-lock braking system). In 1983 new heavy-duty four-axled rigids were introduced, aimed mainly at the construction industry. The driver-friendly EPS (electro-pneumatic shift) gearbox was introduced in 1985, followed in 1991 by its environmentally friendly LEV (low-emission vehicle) range. In 1989 the Daimler-Benz AG group underwent restructuring and was renamed Mercedes-Benz AG. IFA at Ludwigsfelde in the former GDR was acquired by Mercedes-Benz in 1990.

On the heavy vehicle front, Mercedes-Benz's first all-new range for over 20 years – the Actros – was launched in September 1996. This embodies many technological advances and a completely new cab design, though still bearing a family resemblance to the SK. V diesels of various power ratings are available. There are 12 litre/732cu in V6 units with power ratings from 235 to 428bhp and 16 litre/976cu in V8s for 476, 530 and 571bhp. Medium-weight trucks have also received a new cab of similar basic design and have been relaunched as the Atego range.

In 1997 it was announced that the Daimler-Benz and Freightliner Corporation subsidiary had absorbed Ford's heavy truck operations, and in December 1998 Daimler-Benz announced its most recent merger – with the American Chrysler company of Auburn Hills to form DaimlerChrysler AG.

■ BOTTOM *This 1999 Actros 1857/LS is Mercedes-Benz's current top-of-the-range tractor unit with 500 series V8 Telligent diesel engine.*

TOKYO, JAPAN

MITSUBISHI

■ LEFT *A 1998 FV 6×4 tractor unit with side-lift container-handling equipment.*

■ BELOW LEFT *The 1934 TSS-28 2-tonner had a 4.8 litre/292cu in 6-cylinder gasoline engine.*

■ BOTTOM LEFT *Based on the FK model, this medium-weight artic is part of Allied Pickford's New Zealand fleet.*

Mitsubishi Shipbuilding & Engineering Co. Ltd built small numbers of light trucks of up to 2½ tonnes payload during the early 1920s, but large-scale commercial vehicle production did not begin until 1930. At first the company concentrated on buses, but trucks up to 3 tonnes payload also appeared in the mid 1930s when Mitsubishi developed its own diesel engines. Limited motor-vehicle production was centred at a factory in Kawasaki during World War II, but Mitsubishi were mainly preoccupied with military production. A range of heavy bonneted trucks was launched immediately after the war, these being diesel-powered 6 to 7-tonners bearing some resemblance to contemporary American designs.

In 1950, while under American occupation, the large Mitsubishi Group was dissolved and re-formed into separate companies. The two responsible for truck production became Mitsubishi Heavy Industries, Reorganized, Co. Ltd and Mitsubishi Nippon Heavy Industries Ltd. The former concentrated on the production of light vehicles, and later introduced the Jupiter 2 to 3-tonners.

Mitsubishi Nippon Heavy Industries was to build the heavier trucks under the Fuso name. A 7-tonner, the T3, developed from the 1946 design, appeared by 1956. This had the company's own DB31 8.55 litre/522cu in 6-cylinder diesel engine developing 155bhp. By 1961 this had been given a stylish new front-end treatment with a steeply sloping bonnet (hood) and full-width grille. It was now designated the T330 (long wheelbase) and T335 (medium wheelbase) and had the Mitsubishi DB31A 8.55 litre/522cu in diesel developing 165bhp. Options included power-assisted steering. Mitsubishi Fuso's other models for 1961 included T350 tractor units for 10-tonne payloads with a similar specification to the T330 but on a wheelbase of 3.45m/11.3ft. The W11D 6×6 dump truck and the W21 6×6 heavy-duty fifth-wheel tractor were based on World War II American designs. The W11D had the DB31W 8.55 litre/522cu in diesel with a 160bhp output, while the W21 had the 13.74 litre/838cu in DH21W producing 200bhp at 2000rpm. Both were fitted with air brakes. The W21, despite its heavy-duty specification was also designed for 24 tonnes gcw. The range also included a variety of forward-control two and three-axled mobile crane chassis with half-cabs such as the T380C, derived from the T330 truck, and the W13 and W25A 6×4s derived from the W11 and W22 trucks. A lighter half-cab 4×2 dump truck was also offered as the T52 for 6.5 to 7 tonnes. This had a downrated version of the 8.55 litre/522cu in DB31W producing 145bhp.

■ LEFT *This FS rigid eight-wheeler and drawbar trailer grosses 44 tons. It is powered by an 11.1 litre/677cu in 6-cylinder turbo diesel.*

■ BOTTOM *An FV Shogun 6×4 tractor coupled to tri-axle fridge trailer.*

In the early 1960s a range of tilt-cab forward-control trucks was launched. This included the T380 8-tonne four-wheeler and the T390 11.5-tonne six-wheeler plus two tractor units, the T386 and T386S for 27 tonnes and 32.6 tonnes gcw respectively.

In 1964, just 14 years after the break-up of Mitsubishi, the two separate divisions, Mitsubishi Heavy Industries, Reorganized, and Mitsubishi Nippon Heavy Industries, rejoined forces, becoming Mitsubishi Heavy Industries Ltd, Motor Vehicle Division. The lighter Jupiter range carried on, joined by the Canter for payloads of up to 6 tonnes. The bonneted Jupiters consisted of the T10DAH (4.8 tonnes gvw), the T22DBH (6 tonnes gvw), the T30B and T33B (6.8 tonnes gvw). The T30B was diesel-powered while the T33B had the 3 litre/183cu in gasoline engine. A forward-control Jupiter T40B (diesel) and T41B (gasoline) was also introduced for 6.4 tonnes gvw.

The Canter was now called the Fuso Canter, Fuso being the name given to the heavy trucks. The Fuso Canter was, however, only rated at 3.7 tonnes gvw. A heavier version at 7.4 tonnes gvw using a similar cab design was introduced as the Fuso T620. All heavy trucks were now simply badged as Fuso.

In the early 1970s the American Chrysler Corporation acquired a 15 per cent interest in Mitsubishi, and technical collaboration took place between the companies. By now the Mitsubishi range covered most weight categories. Restyled cabs appeared in 1972, and the heaviest 6×4s were rated at 30 tonnes gvw. V6 and V8 turbocharged diesels of 190 and 310bhp were developed. The lightest trucks were the Canter (4.2 to 5.4 tonnes gvw) while the FK series (9.15 tonnes gvw) and FM (11.8 to 14 tonnes gvw) catered for the medium 4×2 market. The heaviest 4×2 was the FP at 15.4 tonnes. FU 6×2 and FV 6×4 three-axled models were rated at 21.4 and 25.4 tonnes gvw respectively. Heavy-duty bonneted trucks, the NP, NV and W series were also available. Articulated versions of the FP and FV series were for gcws of between 34 and 51 tonnes. These took the turbocharged V8 diesel engines. The range was marketed by Chrysler in Australia as the Dodge Fuso, as was the lightweight Canter. The company was now called the Mitsubishi Motor Corporation. A black plastic grille gave the Fuso cab a new image in 1980, by which time the Mitsubishi name badge had replaced Fuso.

A brand new FP, FV and FS (8×4) range with new cab was launched in 1984. Power units included the 6D22-1A 11.15 litre/680cu in 6-cylinder with 225bhp, the LD22-1AT3 turbo version at 330bhp and the 16 litre/976cu in V8 in two ratings – 320bhp (naturally aspirated) and 400bhp in turbo form. Eaton Fuller transmissions were featured in these models. The top-of-the-range FV415 V8 truck was marketed as the Shogun. In 1998 another new generation of FP, FV and FS Shoguns with a new and stylish cab was launched. These feature higher power ratings and a completely new V8 naturally aspirated diesel of 19 litres/1158cu in capacity. The 8M22-OAT1 produces an impressive 550bhp.

BIRMINGHAM, ENGLAND

MORRIS

■ LEFT *A Morris FFK140 dump truck with 6-cylinder diesel engine.*

Following the merger of the Austin Motor Co. of Longbridge, Birmingham, and Morris Commercial Cars of Adderley Park, Birmingham, in 1951, a process of commonization began between the two companies' truck ranges, both of which consisted of mass-produced light and medium-weight vehicles in the 1½ to 5-ton bracket. A rationalized range of trucks that were virtually identical apart from the badges were announced in 1954. Although the Adderley Park company still traded as Morris Commercial Cars Ltd, the word "Commercial" was dropped from the badge in 1956. Thus, for the 12 years up to the formation of BLMC through the merger of British Motor Holdings (Morris Commercial's parent company) and British Leyland in 1968, the trucks were called Morris. After that they were all badged BMC. (See also "Austin" and "BMC".)

BIRMINGHAM, ENGLAND

MORRIS COMMERCIAL

William Morris, who later became Lord Nuffield, founded a cycle business back in 1893 and turned to motor-car production in 1912. In the early 1920s there were increasing numbers of low-cost American light trucks getting on to the UK market, and Morris saw an opportunity to compete in this sector with a mass-produced 1-tonner. A factory was purchased at Soho, Birmingham, in 1924 and the first

■ LEFT *This Morris Commercial T-Model has single rear wheels and semi-enclosed cab.*

■ BELOW LEFT *The semi-forward-control Equiload 5-tonner was first announced in 1938 and continued until 1948.*

Morris Commercial T type went into production using largely car-based running units. Commercial was added to the Morris name to distinguish the new trucks from the Cowley-built cars.

Very soon Morris Commercial began introducing heavier models like the D type six-wheeler for up to 2-ton payloads, introduced in 1927. This proved successful in both civilian and military roles. In 1930 Morris Commercial took over the old Wolseley Works at Adderley Park, Birmingham, and began to expand its truck range further. Following the appointment of a new chief engineer from AEC at

■ RIGHT *A 1946 LCS 1¼-ton Post Office truck with 240cu ft/6.8cu m integral box body.*

■ BELOW *A 1947 LC 1½-ton truck still at work in New Zealand in 1998.*

■ RIGHT *The FV forward-control 5-tonner announced in 1948 was available with a 6-cylinder diesel engine based on a Saurer design.*

■ BELOW RIGHT *The CV11/40 was a bonneted 3-tonner with 3.5 litre/213cu in side-valve gasoline engine.*

Southall, Morris Commercial began to develop heavy-duty models like the 4/5-ton Courier, and there were plans to produce four and six-wheelers for payloads of 8 to 12 tons but some of these never left the drawing board.

A 2½-tonner called the Leader or P type appeared in 1933 followed by the C type in 1934, which was built in normal and semi-forward-control form. A heavier version of the Leader for up to 4 tons payload was also available. By 1938 the stylish CV range entered production. This was marketed as the Equiload and covered payload ratings up to 5 tons, the heaviest model being marketed as the semi-forward-control CVF 13/5 with a 4.9m/16.4ft body. The power unit was Morris Commercial's 3.48 litre/212cu in 6-cylinder gasoline engine developing 85bhp. The Equiload range, in reduced form, continued after World War II and in 1948 a full forward-control 5-tonner was announced. This was the FV with a simple but attractively styled cab featuring rear-hinged "suicide" doors. For the FV, Morris Commercial offered their own 4.25 litre/259cu in 6-cylinder diesel engine, a Saurer design built under licence. The diesel models were designated FVO. An 80bhp 4-cylinder gasoline engine was also available.

In 1953 a 6-cylinder gasoline engine developing 100bhp was offered. The diesel engine was not as successful as hoped, but was still offered up to 1953. In 1954 the forward-control trucks took on a completely new appearance with a new steel cab bought in from the Willenhall Motor Radiator Co. By this time Morris Commercial had entered the BMC empire, formed with the Austin-Morris merger of 1951. From then on Austin and Morris Commercial trucks began to develop along common lines, and the Morris Commercial name was discontinued from 1956 when the trucks were simply badged Morris. (See "BMC" and "Morris".)

OTHER MAKES

■ MANN

HUNSLET, LEEDS, ENGLAND

Mann & Charlesworth Ltd built their first steam wagon in 1897, an "overtype". The following year an undertype was tried. From 1900 the company became the Mann's Patent Steam Cart & Wagon Co. Ltd. Mann's 5-ton overtype of 1909 sought to provide extra load deck by having a side-fired boiler. Just after World War I a new 6-tonner replaced the 5-ton wagon. In 1924 Mann announced their shaft-drive Express undertype. The company went into liquidation in 1928.

■ MINERVA

ANTWERP, BELGIUM

Minerva Motors SA built its first truck, a 2½-tonne payload cab-over-engine machine with overhead worm rear drive, in 1913. Power came from a 4-cylinder sleeve-valve gasoline engine. Production was suspended in World War I, but in 1923 a new model was introduced for 2 to 4-tonne payloads using the sleeve-valve engine. In 1925 Minerva absorbed SA Auto-Traction who were building Chenard-Walcker type tractors under licence. Production of these continued under the Minerva name. By 1927 a range of heavier trucks appeared with four-wheel braking and double-reduction rear axles. In 1932 they tried out sleeve-valve diesel engines, the largest being an 8.7 litre/531cu in 6-cylinder unit. In the last few years up to their closure in 1957 Minerva built very few trucks.

■ LEFT ***A mid 1950s Minerva 10-tonne artic with Perkins P6 diesel loaded with wool at Antwerp Docks.***

■ ABOVE ***This Moreland cabover with Cummins diesel features a sleeper cab.***

■ BELOW ***A Mol 8×8 500-tonne gtw tractor for Algeria's Electricity Company.***

■ MOL

HOOGLEDE, BELGIUM

Mol Cy. Nv. began by building specialized municipal chassis with low-line cabs and air-cooled Deutz diesels in 1966. The company used GKN Kirkstall axles and Allison Automatic transmissions. During the 1970s an increasing variety of types appeared, including massive 6×6 bonneted dump trucks and heavy-haulage tractors. Low-profile multi-axle crane chassis, half-cab dock spotters and even on-highway 38-tonne tractor units were built. The current range of products consists of specialized trucks and tractors. Typical of Mol's heavy tractors are two 8×8 TG300 models built for use by Algeria's Electricity Co. These have 600bhp Cummins diesels with Clarke Powershift transmissions and can haul up to 500 tonnes train weight.

■ MORELAND

BURBANK, CALIFORNIA, USA

The Moreland Motor Truck Co. was a significant manufacturer of heavy trucks during the 1911–41 period, employing some innovative engineering that influenced standards of truck design on the American West Coast. Moreland's earliest range included four models from 1½ to 5 tons in bonneted or cabover form. In 1924 a 6-tonner was in production and a rigid six-wheeler, the TX6, appeared to take advantage of more liberal weight limits that the company's founder, Watt Moreland, fought to bring in. This had

OTHER MAKES

a significant effect on the development of efficient long-haul trucking. Moreland also built bodywork and trailers. During the 1930s truck production was in decline and products became more and more custom-built. Production ceased in 1941.

■ MOWAG

KREUZLINGEN, SWITZERLAND

Formed in 1948 to take over the bodybuilding activities of Seitz und Ruf AG, Mowag (Mowag Motorenfabrik AG) began vehicle manufacture in 1951 with a 2-tonne 4×4 for military use. This was powered by a Chrysler 6-cylinder engine. Of more relevance to the truck world was the new range of forward-control heavy trucks launched in 1953. These were noted for their underfloor horizontal SLM (Swiss Locomotive & Machinery Works) diesel engines. Mowag built specialized trucks such as narrow-cabbed models for the carriage of long steel tubes. Other products included fire and armoured vehicles. One of Mowag's most interesting trucks was a forward-control 8×4, introduced in 1977, with an underfloor V8 two-stroke diesel. The 10.8 litre/659cu in Mowag M87K engine was turbocharged and intercooled, producing 500bhp at 2300rpm. An Allison 5-speed automatic transmission took the drive to Mowag double-reduction rear axles. The truck had a design gvw of 32 tonnes but was limited to 28 tonnes in Switzerland. Mowag continued to build specialized trucks and in 1999 it was announced that the company had been taken over by General Motors.

■ LEFT *A 1977 Mowag 32-tonne 8×4.*

■ BELOW LEFT *A 1920s Moreland truck.*

■ BOTTOM LEFT *An MTN 7-ton cabover.*

■ BOTTOM *A Multiwheeler Anaconda.*

■ MTN

CROYDON, ENGLAND

MTN was the name used by Motor Traction Ltd of Croydon for most export territories. It is derived from the surname of Frank Manton, who founded the company. Rutland was used in the UK, while MTN was used for Spain, Portugal, South America and other export markets. The MTN model range was extensive, covering payload ratings from 2 to 3 tons up to 17 tons and the trucks were hand-built using bought-in propietary engines and drivelines. (See also "Rutland".)

■ MULTIWHEELER

SOUTH HARROW, ENGLAND

Between 1933 and 1941 a small number of Multiwheeler tractors, descendants of Beardmore-Multiwheeler, were built by Multiwheeler (Commercial Vehicles) Ltd. They used AEC and Gardner diesels, but with the outbreak of war the company turned to building trailers for military use. Multiwheeler Anaconda tractors feature the unique type of trailer coupling designed by Chenard-Walcker, giving them exceptional manoeuvrability.

CHICAGO, ILLINOIS, USA

NAVISTAR

■ ABOVE *The Navistar International 9000 series conventional 6×4 is available with a wide choice of diesel power from Caterpillar, Cummins and Detroit Diesel.*

The Navistar International Transport Co. was formed in 1986 after International Harvester were forced to abandon their worldwide expansion in the early 1980s. During the '70s the International Harvester Co. bought into numerous overseas companies, including DAF, ENASA, Seddon Atkinson and Pacific but, after being beset by financial problems, these interests were sold off and the company was reorganized under the Navistar International name. It still produces a full range of heavy trucks under the International name badge. (See "International Harvester".)

ZARAGOZA, SPAIN

NAZAR

■ LEFT *This mid 1960s Nazar forward-control 8-tonner has bold Spanish styling typical of its era.*

A range of forward-control trucks for 1½ to 9-tonne payload was offered by Factoria Napoles SA of Zaragoza from 1957. The lighter models used Perkins diesels, while heavier models featured Henschel diesels. They had heavily styled cabs, typical of Spanish designs in the 1960s, and production continued until 1967 when the factory was taken over by Barreiros.

CHAMPS-SUR-YONNE, FRANCE

NICOLAS

■ LEFT *A Nicolas Tractomas TR88G8C 400-ton 8×8 tractor.*

Nicolas specialized in heavy trucks for indivisible loads, and in 1979 the company turned to building heavy-haulage tractors too. The Tractomas range was developed during the 1980s. Their TRB6602 was a typical 6×6 for train weights up to 200 tonnes. It was powered by Mercedes-Benz's 20.9 litre/ 1275cu in OM404A V12 diesel engine producing 480bhp, while the ZF transmission incorporated a torque converter. The cab was a modified version of Berliet's Premier cab. An even more impressive machine is the 8×8 Tractomas TR88G8C powered by an 800bhp Detroit Diesel two-stroke 16V-92N. Gross train weight was 400 tonnes. An earlier 350-tonne version used a Cummins KTA-600 in-line-six engine and a Willème cab. Tractors of similar appearance were produced by Willème and Mol NV. Nicolas is currently one of the world leaders in heavy transport equipment, manufacturing Automas self-propelled transporters and modular trailers with steering multi-pendular axles capable of transporting payloads from 40 up to 8000 tonnes.

KAWAGUCHI, JAPAN

NISSAN/ MINSEI

■ LEFT ***A Nissan UD TWA52T bonneted 6×4 tractor for 42 tonnes gcw powered by 14.3 litre/870cu in V8 diesel.***

■ FAR LEFT ***A 1959 Minsei T80 7-tonner with 4.9 litre/300cu in two-stroke diesel engine.***

What has, for the past 40 years or so, been marketed as the Nissan Diesel UD had its roots in the Nippon Diesel Engineering Co. Ltd founded in 1935. This became Minsei Diesel Industries in 1950. During the late 1930s Nippon were granted a licence to build Krupp-Junkers two-stroke opposed-piston diesel engines, which were used to power a 7-tonne truck that continued in production until after World War II. From 1950 trucks were built under the Minsei name and, after several years of research, Minsei introduced its own two-stroke diesel, the UD, which stands for Uniflow-scavenged Diesel. The engine was used to power the new T80 7-tonne truck which was similar in appearance to the Krupp.

Forward-control Nissan/Minsei trucks appeared in 1960, forming the basis for later CK tilt-cab 8-tonners. A heavy-duty 6×4 for 15 tonnes was also launched, powered by a turbocharged 7.4 litre/451cu in two-stroke diesel developing 230bhp. In 1962 Nissan/Minsei developed new four-stroke diesels. Two-stroke engines were still offered until about 1970. At that time Nissan/Minsei had a comprehensive line-up comprised of their PT81 bonneted 4×2 8-tonners, the PTC815D forward-control 4×2 dump truck for 9 tonnes gcw and the 6TCL81T forward-control tractor for 32 tonnes gcw. There were also 6×2s and 6×4s to take 15-tonne payloads. The largest truck was the 40 tonne gcw bonneted 6×6 heavy-haulage tractor.

During the 1970s Nissan began to build up export sales to Australia and New Zealand, where the trucks were marketed as Nissan-UD. Lighter trucks were also introduced, like the CMA for 9.5 tonnes gvw. Nissan-UD's main forward-control heavy truck of the 1980s was the CWA45 available in 6×4 and 8×4 form. In 1993 Nissan-UD launched its new Mikado model with a 350bhp version of the PF6TB 12.5 litre/763cu in diesel. The CW350 26-tonne 6×4 and CG350 30-tonne 8×4 are designed for up to 55 tonnes gtw.

■ ABOVE ***A Nissan Mikado CG380 eight-wheeler and trailer.***

DARLEY DALE, ENGLAND

NORDE

■ LEFT ***The 1964 Norde six-wheeler with Cummins V6 diesel and Bedford TK cab grossed 20 tons.***

With the advent of motorways in the UK in 1960, there was a demand for more powerful trucks. One haulage company set up its own manufacturing operation in 1961. Toft Brothers & Tomlinson formed Norde (short for North Derbyshire Engineering Co. Ltd) to build trucks of its own design. The first was a 24-ton outfit capable of 110kph/70mph over long distances. Power was from a 262bhp turbocharged Cummins, the drive being taken to an AEC axle through an SCG RV.30 semi-automatic transmission. Hendrickson-Norde suspension was used. Other models were introduced, including six-wheel rigids with Perkins 6.354 or Cummins V6.200 diesels and a Bedford TK cab. Sales were very limited and the company survived for one year, after which it concentrated on truck suspension systems.

VIENNA, AUSTRIA

ÖAF

■ LEFT ***A mid 1960s Tornado FS9-200L 32-tonne artic powered by Leyland O.680 diesel of 200bhp.***

ÖAF's origins go back to 1907 when Austro Fiat AG was set up to assemble Fiats. The association ended in 1925 and the company became Österreichische Automobilfabrik AG. The name AFN was used for a period. ÖAF began licence-building MAN diesels in 1934 and, in 1936, became a subsidiary of MAN. Production was suspended following the war and it wasn't until the early 1960s that ÖAF re-entered the heavy truck market. Their most important model was the Tornado. Engine choice included Leyland, Cummins, MAN or ÖAF's own diesel. The cab on forward-control versions was shared with Gräf & Stift, with whom ÖAF merged in 1970.

The last ÖAF announced before switching to MAN-based designs in the early 1970s was the 13-tonne gross Hurricane. ÖAF began to lose their individuality after 1970 and became almost identical to MAN. Since the late '70s ÖAF have specialized in the production of heavy-duty multi-axle trucks.

BRESCIA, ITALY

OM

■ LEFT ***An early 1960s OM Tigrotto 4-tonne truck powered by a 75bhp 4-cylinder diesel engine.***

S.A. Officine Meccaniche was formed at the turn of the 19th century. In 1928 it became OM Fabbrica Bresciana Automobili. It acquired a licence to build Saurer trucks, which were marketed with OM badges. In 1933 the OM Brescia factory came under the control of the Fiat Group. One of the first new trucks was the 1CRD 3-tonner with a 60bhp diesel, still built under Saurer licence. In 1936 came the new BUD bonneted 7½-tonner. OM's Titano model – the Titano 137 six-wheeler – first appeared in 1937. Wartime production was disrupted through bomb damage but production was to resume, after reconstruction, in 1946. Now the first forward-control trucks began to appear, such as the Taurus 3-tonner and Supertaurus 5-tonner. In 1950 an important new range, including the Leoncino 2½-tonner, updated versions of the Taurus and Supertaurus, plus the Orione and Super Orione 9-tonner powered by the 10.6 litre/647cu in V8 diesel engine, was introduced.

The 1950s and '60s saw new models added, like the Tigre 6.3-tonner (12 tonnes with trailer) and the re-emergence of the Titano model, this time as a completely new maximum-weight range that made its debut in 1961. It boasted a 260bhp, 10.3 litre/629cu in in-line-six DG-L diesel and was claimed to be the most powerful truck in Europe at that time. It was offered in 4×2, 6×4 and 8×4 rigid form plus 4×2 and 6×4 tractor units. The 8×4 was rated for 22 tonnes gvw or 44 tonnes gtw and was OM's heaviest and most powerful truck.

In 1968 OM was fully incorporated into Gruppo Veicoli Industriali Fiat, which also included Unic of France. From that point on OM ceased to exist as an independent company, but the OM badge appeared on Fiat-based trucks through to the formation of the Iveco Group in 1975.

■ LEFT ***Grossing 14 tonnes, this 1970 OM 150/L carries a 9-tonne payload. It has a 176bhp 6-cylinder diesel engine.***

TORTONA, ITALY

OMT

■ LEFT *The 1963 OMT MF4 with AEC AV690 diesel was one of Italy's first rigid eight-wheelers.*

Officine Meccaniche Tortonisi specialized in trailer manufacture but in 1963 introduced a heavy truck. To benefit from the maximum possible gross weight under Italy's legislation, it developed a twin-steer 8×2 truck using a Fiat cab and some Fiat running units. For its power it used an AEC AV690 6-cylinder diesel, but some were also built with Fiat diesels. The truck could gross 22 tonnes and carry a net payload of 13 tonnes but, when coupled to a four-axled drawbar trailer, it could legally run at 44 tonnes gtw. Some twin-steer tractor units were also built during the four years that OMT survived in production. The company then went back to trailer building. The OMT MF4 helped pioneer a breed of truck that soon dominated the Italian transport scene, but most were twin-steer models with proprietary fourth-axle conversions.

RUSSELSHEIM, GERMANY

OPEL

Adam Opel's history can be traced back to 1862. A 1-tonner was introduced in 1910. Opel was taken over in 1929 by General Motors. From 1931 the 2½-tonne Blitz appeared. A plant at Brandenburg was set up to build trucks. During World War II GM relinquished control as post-war Brandenburg was commandeered by East Germany. From 1948 GM re-established at Russelsheim, and production of light trucks continued to the mid 1970s.

OSHKOSH, WISCONSIN, USA

OSHKOSH

■ LEFT *A five-axled bonneted F series delivering to a construction site.*

■ BELOW *An E series 6×4 with drawbar trailer in New Zealand.*

The Oshkosh Motor Truck Manufacturing Co. was formed in 1917 and was originally called the Wisconsin Duplex Auto Company. The company built trucks using the front-wheel drive system invented by William Besserdich, who had earlier helped to develop the FWD. The first truck to enter full production was a 2-tonner. This was joined by a 3½-tonner in 1920 and a 5-tonner in 1924. Oshkosh went on to build heavier models during the 1930s with engines up to 200bhp. During World War II the company continued production of heavy all-wheel drive machines for the United States government.

After the war 6×6 models were introduced for oilfield and mining. Some 4×4s were characterized by their set-back front axles and long bonnets (hoods), designated the 50–50 series, launched in 1955. During the 1970s on-highway tractors were added, such as the cabover E series with its square cab and full-width grille. Oshkosh is synonymous with rugged trucks for construction, mining and military use. In the 1970s a South African plant was established at Paarl. Currently the range includes a variety of 8×8 military designs, some of which, such as the MK48, steer by pivoting in the middle.

RENTON, WASHINGTON, USA

PACIFIC

■ LEFT *A re-cabbed ex-army Pacific used on heavy haulage in the UK.*

The Pacific Car & Foundry Co., originally formed in 1905, were commanded by the United States government in 1942 to build 6×6 tank transporter tractive units. The Fruehauf Trailer Company built the 40-ton capacity transporter's low-loading trailer. The tractors were designated TR-1 and were powered by Hall-Scott 240bhp 6-cylinder gasoline engines. In the post-war years many of the Pacific tractors survived as heavy-haulage tractors but were largely re-engined with Cummins diesels and fitted with non-armoured civilian cabs.

VANCOUVER, CANADA

PACIFIC

In 1947 three former executives of the Hayes Mfg. Co. set up Pacific Truck & Trailer Ltd to build heavy-duty logging trucks suited to the tough Canadian lumber industry. Similar trucks were also built for construction and oilfield duties. In 1972 it became a part of International Harvester of Canada but was sold off in 1986. Pacific became a member of the Inchcape Group. During the 1980s it continued to build a wide range of heavy trucks and construction vehicles, such as the P500 and P.12.W series, using a variety of Cummins, Detroit Diesel and Caterpillar engines. Production was phased out in the early 1990s.

■ ABOVE *A dual-steer Pacific PLW-500PSA Constructor 14cu yd/10.7cu m cement mixer powered by Cummins L10-300 diesel.*

DETROIT, MICHIGAN, USA

PACKARD

■ LEFT *A standard Model E Packard truck of c.1918 for a payload of 4 to 5 tons.*

One of the oldest American motor manufacturers, Packard was building cars from the turn of the century and in 1905 began offering a 1½-ton truck with a horizontal twin-cylinder gasoline engine located beneath the driver. This was replaced by a new 3-ton bonneted truck in 1908 with a 4-cylinder vertical gasoline engine. Chain drive was used on the early trucks but in 1914 a worm drive was introduced on the lighter models. A 5-tonner that was announced in 1912 continued to feature chain drive, as did a 6-ton version but, from 1920, Packard switched to shaft drive. A new 2-tonner, the X, was the first to have pneumatic tyres in 1920. The range consisted of 2, 3, 5 and 7½-ton models during the three years up to when they finished production in 1923.

WIGAN, ENGLAND

PAGEFIELD

■ LEFT *A 1933 Pagefield Plantaganet rigid six-wheeler for 12-ton payload, powered by a Gardner 6LW oil engine.*

Pagefield Commercial Vehicles was set up in 1907. In 1911 a 2-ton truck appeared with 2-cylinder gasoline engine and chain drive. Four-ton and 5-ton trucks were added in the pre-World War I period, including a 5-ton dump truck with patent gearbox-driven screw-type rams. Subsidy type trucks were built during 1914–18 and in the early '20s a demountable body system for transporting horse-drawn dustcarts was introduced. This was the forerunner of today's swap-body container trucks.

In the 1930s the company developed chassis for garbage collection as well as a range of heavy trucks. The model types included the Pompian, Paladin, Pathfinder, Pegasix and Plantagenet, the latter two being six-wheelers. Gardner diesels and Kirkstall axles were fitted. Pagefield ceased trading in 1947. In 1948 Walkers & County Cars was formed to continue building municipal vehicles, and a Walker 5-ton truck was offered in the same period. Walkers & County Cars was disbanded in 1966.

PARIS, FRANCE

PANHARD

■ LEFT *A 1928 Panhard-Levassor 3-tonne payload truck with drawbar trailer.*

S.A. Etablissments Panhard & Levassor's history dates back to 1893. Light trucks were built during 1895 and by 1900 a 1½-tonne truck was entered in Military Trials. Heavier chain-drive trucks were added, as well as a military 4×4. By 1930 there were models up to 8 tonnes capacity. Trucks between 4 and 8 tonnes were Panhard's main products in the 1930s, and by 1939 there were forward-control models.

In 1954 Panhard joined Citroën and truck production was progressively cut back, ceasing altogether by 1959.

LYONS, OREGON, USA

PAYMASTER

■ RIGHT *The unique Paymaster P36 tractor later became the Ryder.*

Trucks do not come more unconventional than the Paymaster P36. It was the aim of designer Dean Hobgenseifken to shun all that had gone before and provide the owner, driver and mechanic with the ideal vehicle. It claimed to be quieter, safer and more comfortable, while minimizing costs and simplifying overhauls by having a removable engine, gearbox, axle and exhaust system in one "power module". It was the result of 10 years of design work. The engine was a Detroit Diesel 6V-92TTA two-stroke. Other engines were optional. The first trucks were completed in 1973 but the same year Ryder Systems of Miami, Florida, bought the design rights and the make was changed to Ryder. About 10 production vehicles were built by the Hendrickson Manufacturing Co. for Ryder's truck rental fleet.

MADRID, SPAIN

PEGASO

■ LEFT
The distinctively styled 1066 30-tonne gvw 8×2.

■ LEFT
The Pegaso II resembled its Hispano-Suiza forerunner.

Spain's state-owned Empresa Nacional de Autocamiones SA (ENASA) acquired the Hispano-Suiza truck-building operations in Barcelona in 1946 and relaunched the Hispano-Suiza 66G as the Pegaso I 7-tonner. An improved model, the Pegaso II, for 8 tonnes payload, was developed from 1947, still virtually identical to the old Hispano-Suiza. There was a choice of gasoline or diesel power. The gasoline-engined Z-203 had a 5.65 litre/345cu in 6-cylinder unit developing 110bhp, while the Z-202 had a 9.3 litre/567cu in 6-cylinder diesel rated at 125bhp, soon uprated to 140bhp. The trucks had a gtw rating of 26.5 tonnes. An articulated version, the Z-701, had a design gcw of 22.7 tonnes. The Hispano-Suiza-based models continued to be built up to 1958.

Meanwhile, development work on a completely new design of truck, the streamlined Barajas, was underway. A prototype of this was exhibited at the Salon del Automovil in Barcelona in 1955. It took its name from a new factory opened at Barajas, Madrid, in the same year. The Barajas truck featured very individualistic styling with its curved lines and heavily ribbed panels. The Z-207, as it was designated, was a 6-tonner powered by a V6 diesel of 120bhp.

■ BELOW LEFT
By the early 1980s eight-wheelers grossed 36.25 tonnes.

A heavier model, the Z-206 developed from the old 66G/66D, was powered by a big 9.3 litre/567cu in 4-cylinder diesel with a 140bhp output. A 165bhp horizontal diesel was used in a revolutionary new model in 1955 – the Z-210 twin-steer six-wheeler for 20 tonnes gvw and a 12-tonne payload. From the mid 1950s Pegaso collaborated closely with Leyland Motors of England in the development of new models. A double-drive six-wheeler, the Z-211 for 22.9 tonnes gvw appeared, followed by an even larger prototype model on four axles, the Z-212, which was built in the late 1950s and inspired by the Leyland Octopus. This was an 8×4 while the majority of rigid eight-wheelers, which became popular in Spain in the 1970s, were 8×2s – basically twin-steer six-wheelers with a self-steering fourth axle.

In 1960 Leyland Motors became a major shareholder in ENASA. This soon led to increasing use of Leyland running units and the development of the Pegaso Comet (a Leyland type name) for 8-tonne payloads powered by the Leyland 6.4 litre/390cu in 6-cylinder diesel and using an Albion gearbox and rear axle. In 1965 a lightweight 7-tonner, the 1100 Comet was added to the range.

■ LEFT *The 19-tonne gvw 1065 had a similar cab to the Comet 1090 but developed 170bhp as opposed to 125bhp. An Albion rear axle was fitted.*

This was powered by a 90bhp, 4.4 litre/268cu in 4-cylinder version of the 0.400.

Important new models were introduced in 1964, powered by Pegaso's own 10.5 litre/641cu in 200bhp diesel. These included twin-steer production vehicles, the 1063A 6×2 and 1066 8×2. The 1066 had a design weight of 34 tonnes and a payload capacity of 24 tonnes. In 1966 ENASA acquired a controlling interest in Sòciedad Anónima Véhiculos Automóviles (SAVA) which was mainly involved in the light to medium sector, although it assembled Berliet heavy vehicles as Berliet-SAVA. In 1968 ENASA took over SAVA and continued producing the BMC J4 vans which SAVA built under licence from the British Motor Corporation.

A completely new range of heavy trucks appeared in 1972. These featured a new, squarer design of full forward-control cab and new 10 and 12 litre/610 and 732cu in 6-cylinder diesel engines covering a horsepower range from 170 up to 310bhp and up to 352bhp in turbocharged form. The old Leyland-designed engine continued to be available on some lighter models and was turbo-charged to produce 155bhp. In 1975 a tilt version of the new cab was introduced.

During the late 1970s, in a declining market, Pegaso began making a loss. In 1981 the American International Harvester Company purchased a 35 per cent shareholding and took charge of the management. This arrangement was not to last long and International were forced to pull out of their European activities in 1983–84. International also had a large share in DAF and had bought Seddon Atkinson in the UK. In 1983 Pegaso acquired Seddon Atkinson for the token sum of one pound sterling from International.

Pegaso maintained its links with DAF, and the two companies formed Cabtec in 1984 to develop a new heavy truck cab. This went into production in 1987 on the new Troner model. It was also fitted to the DAF 95 series and the Seddon Atkinson Strato. The new Troner was launched at the 1987 Salon de Barcelona. The impressive new range was designed for gross weights up to 44 tonnes and featured a new 12 litre/732cu in, 24-valve 360bhp diesel. The Troner proved to be the last true Pegaso as ENASA was absorbed into the Italian Iveco Group in September 1990. By 1992 the Barajas factory was geared up to building the Iveco EuroTech and EuroStar.

■ LEFT *The 1972 1086/52 8×2 featured a new-style cab, 260bhp diesel and grossed 35.5 tonnes.*

■ BELOW *Pegaso's last new model was the 1987 Troner with Cabtec cab and 360bhp turbo-intercooled 12 litre/732cu in diesel.*

CLEVELAND, OHIO, USA, & SLOUGH, ENGLAND

PEERLESS

■ RIGHT ***A 1931 Peerless LA-type Gardner-engined, forward-control 7-ton dump truck.***

From 1911–18 the Peerless Motor Car Co. built a range of heavy trucks of conventional design. Up to 1915 they were mainly bonneted 3 to 6-ton payload models with Peerless' own 4-cylinder gasoline engine and chain drive. From 1916 these were joined by a shaft-drive 2-tonner. All were of rugged, workmanlike build and large numbers of the early 4 and 5-ton models were shipped to the UK following World War I.

Large numbers of reconditioned war-surplus Peerless trucks were sold in the UK following World War I through Slough Lorries and Components Ltd. From 1925 the Peerless Trading Company took over to build trucks from spare parts and British-made components. As supplies of war-surplus parts diminished the British content increased until the British Peerless was a vehicle in its own right. By 1930 an 8-tonner with strengthened chassis was available with optional pneumatic tyres and a Gardner 4-cylinder diesel. A fully fledged 8-tonner, the chain-drive Trader, also became available with a Meadows 6-cylinder engine. The following year an updated range, the 90 series, featured a protruding bonnet (hood) and set-back front axle, and an impressive 12-ton six-wheeler with trailing axle and shaft drive followed. There were plans to build a lighter 4 to 5-ton range with Gardner engine, Meadows gearbox and Kirkstall axle, but in 1933 truck production was discontinued, Peerless Motors being re-formed to distribute Studebaker trucks.

OAKLAND & NEWARK, CALIFORNIA, USA

PETERBILT

■ LEFT ***Peterbilt's 378 and 379 conventionals are the timeless classics of the United States highways.***

In 1932 the Fageol Motors Company of Oakland, California, was one of the casualties of the great depression, and was forced into bankruptcy after producing high-quality trucks for 17 years. The receivers, with support from the Waukesha Motor Company and the Central Bank of Oakland, kept the business going until 1939 when a buyer was found in the person of logger and plywood maker Theodore Alfred Peterman from Tacoma. Peterman had rebuilt army-surplus trucks and modified old logging trucks in the course of his own lumber business. As a man who did things his own way he bought the Fageol assets in order to build his own custom chain-drive logging trucks. From the outset Peterman put the emphasis on quality, not quantity. Finding a name for the new truck was easy. The Fageols had gained the nickname "Bill-built" after the company's president W. H. Bill, so the natural choice was Peterbilt. Over the years the name became synonymous with top quality and Peterbilts are often referred to as the Rolls Royce of trucks.

Soon after the start of production the company had to put all its resources into fulfilling government contracts for heavy trucks. The experience gained from this was invaluable in post-war development.

Following Peterman's death in 1945 the company passed into the hands of a group of employees, and in June 1958 it became a wholly owned subsidiary of Pacific Car & Foundry (Paccar). Early Peterbilts were all bonneted conventionals, but in 1950 the Model 350 cabover was introduced featuring a Kenworth cab. In 1959 the 90-degree tilt hood was introduced for easier servicing. From August 1960 production was moved to a new plant at Newark, California. Over 800 trucks were built in the first year at Newark and demand was such that a second plant at Madison, Tennessee, was opened. By 1973 an expansion

■ LEFT *This 1991 Cat-engined 357 transfer dump outfit operates around Vancouver and grosses 52 tons.*

■ RIGHT *Since Paccar took over Leyland-DAF, a new range of Peterbilt trucks uses Leyland's T45 cab.*

program doubled Madison's capacity. Another Peterbilt plant opened at Denton, Texas, in 1980. Meanwhile, in 1975 Peterbilt of Canada was set up to market the trucks throughout Canada. During the 1970s Peterbilt branched out into building more specialized trucks for municipal garbage collection. These were the CB300s that developed into the 310 and in 1987 the 320. These are now produced at the Denton plant.

In 1984 the 349 construction range appeared with such innovations as an engine rear-power take-off and self-steer lift axle. The Aerodynamic 377A/E models were introduced in 1986, as Peterbilt joined the trend towards greater fuel efficiency by reducing wind drag. The Unibilt sleeper cab was an important innovation in 1993, affording much-improved facilities. Meanwhile, the 379 with its classic lines remains the ultimate long-haul tractor for the image-conscious trucker.

SOCHAUX, FRANCE

PEUGEOT

While Peugeot is normally associated more with light vans than trucks, the old established company did once build heavy trucks around the time of World War I. Established in 1897, Peugeot, from its earliest days, offered lightweight, tiller-steered chain-drive vans. By 1913 it had introduced a range of seven truck models, the heaviest of which was a 5-tonner with a 4-cylinder side-valve gasoline engine and chain drive. Production continued during the war, but by 1917 only 3 and 4-tonne models were being built, these now having worm-drive axles. Only light commercial vehicles up to 1½ tonnes were built from then on, but Peugeot became involved in truck production once more as recently as 1978 when it acquired Chrysler's European operations which included the Dodge and Karrier marques. Shortly after, Peugeot's Dodge operations were acquired by Renault Véhicules Industriels.

BUFFALO, NEW YORK, USA

PIERCE ARROW

■ RIGHT *A 1915 Pierce Arrow 4-ton truck. It featured worm drive when most contemporaries were chain-driven.*

In 1910 Pierce Arrow Motor Car Co. entered the truck market with a 5-tonner. It had chain drive and a cab-over-engine layout, but it was not pursued. Instead a normal-control, worm-drive truck (the R model) was put into production. Worm drive was unusual and its choice was influenced by Pierce Arrow's design engineer, John Younger, who was formerly with Dennis Bros. in the UK. A model X 2-tonner appeared in 1914. During World War I the company supplied large numbers of military versions of their trucks as well as building Class B Liberty trucks. In 1928 the company was merged with Studebaker of Indiana and some trucks were badged as Studebaker Pierce Arrow.

PRAGUE, CZECH REPUBLIC

PRAGA

■ LEFT *The Praga S5T had a long production run from 1957–73 and was a rugged 5-tonner with air-cooled T912 6-cylinder diesel.*

The old established Praga factory dated back to 1907, established by an agreement between the First Czech-Moravian Machine Factory and the Frantisek Ringhoffer Co., the first Praga trucks under Dykomen licence appearing in 1910. They were shaft-drive models for payloads of $1\frac{1}{2}$ to 6 tonnes. The 4 to 5-tonne V type announced in 1911 became a war subsidy truck. During the 1920s models included the MW 2-tonner and RN $2\frac{1}{2}$-tonner. Diesel-engined versions appeared from 1930 using Deutz air-cooled engines. The heavy-duty Type T was developed into the TN and TND by the late 1930s. The RN was also built under licence in Yugoslavia, as the TAM.

In 1945 the factory was destroyed by bombing. In October the same year the company was nationalized. It became Letecke Zavody Narodni Podnik in 1946 and Auto-Praga Narodni Podnik in 1948. In the post-war period the RN truck continued to be built with a cab reminiscent of the International KB. In the 1950s Praga developed a new range, the V3S 6×6 powered by a Tatra air-cooled diesel. A 4×2 version became available as the S5T, continuing until the early 1970s. Between 1974 and 1984 Praga built only truck gearboxes and equipment, but prototypes of a new multi-purpose truck were built in 1985 and truck production was resumed in 1992 with the UV80 and NTS265, the latter being a 14-tonne gvw 4×4 powered by a turbocharged Deutz diesel engine.

BOMBAY, INDIA

PREMIER

■ LEFT *The Premier PST-118 7-tonner was basically an Indian-built Kew Dodge with Perkins 6.354 diesel.*

During the 1970s and '80s Indian-built Dodge and Fargo trucks were sold as Premier. Outwardly the normal-control models were almost identical to the British-built Kew Dodge of the 1950s, while forward-control models often had locally built cabs of square appearance typical of Indian trucks. Power units included locally built Chrysler gasoline engines or Perkins diesels.

NORWICH, ENGLAND

PROCTOR

Proctors were developed by an operator seeking to improve on performance and economy. Proctor Springwood Ltd of Mousehold, Norwich, were hauliers founded in the 1930s, and after World War II they built a prototype 6-ton truck with a Perkins P6. It featured a Moss gearbox and rear axle. A short-wheelbase dump truck and tractor unit were added to the range. Proctor's distributor, Praill's Motors, took over production in 1949 but by 1952 the marque was withdrawn.

■ LEFT *Proctor's lightweight 5/6-ton truck was built in small numbers from 1947–52.*

TELFORD, ENGLAND

QUEST

■ LEFT ***The highly unconventional Quest F1646 had a choice of Mercedes OM.352 or Perkins T6.354 diesel.***

Quest 80 was formed at Telford, Shropshire in 1979 as a design consultancy to develop trucks and buses for the South African Sigma Corporation. Technically the Quest F1646 truck was very innovative, having self-levelling air suspension and a very unusual design of cab with the instrument panel above the windscreen. Long and short-wheelbase versions were available. Of the few that were built, some had Perkins T6.354 and some Mercedes OM.352 diesels. ZF S6-36 gearboxes and Rockwell rear axles were used. In spite of having aluminium cabs, the trucks were very heavy, restricting payloads to 3 tons – 2 tons below average. This and the highly unconventional design features probably led to their demise. In 1984 the company was bought by the United Engineering Industries Group and only 18 months later production ceased. Currently the Quest Motor Corporation of Zimbabwe, owned by Leyland Overseas Holdings, assembles Leyland trucks.

GYÖR, HUNGARY

RÁBA

■ LEFT ***The Rába has a DAF cab, MAN diesel engine and Rába's own axles.***

Rába Magyar Vagon és Gépgyár of Györ has a long history. The company built its first truck in 1904. In 1912 a licence was acquired to build Praga 5-tonne trucks. Another agreement was formed with Fried Krupp of Essen in 1920 to build Krupp trucks under licence. By 1928 Rába had introduced its own 3-tonner. In the late 1930s Rába negotiated with MAN to licence-build its diesel engines. During the wartime occupation, the factory was dismantled. It wasn't until the late 1960s that truck production resumed.

Between 1968 and 1975 a large investment in the Hungarian motor industry saw Rába taking out a new licensing agreement with MAN to build diesel engines and, from 1970, complete trucks. From 1984, when MAN replaced the Saviem cab with the F90, Rába began fitting the DAF 2800 type cab but continued using Rába-MAN engines. Since then they have offered a wide range of heavy trucks.

JOHANNESBURG, SOUTH AFRICA

RALPH

■ LEFT ***Ralph, South Africa's only truck builder, survived in business for just four years. This 6×4 tractor had a Detroit Diesel 6V-71.***

Ralph were the only heavy trucks to be designed and built entirely in South Africa. The enterprise began in 1968 when Ralph Lewis and a small team of engineers built the first prototype. The company was registered as Rolway Enterprises (Pty) Ltd at Ophirton, Johannesburg, and the range included heavy-duty tractor units and rigids using proprietary units from Cummins, Detroit Diesel, Allison, Spicer, Fuller, Rockwell and Hendrickson. Ralph cab-over 6×4 tractors bore a close resemblance to contemporary Kenworths.

Ralph built a 105-tonne tank transporter for the South African Government, and a couple of 50-tonne ore dump trucks powered by 700bhp V12 Cummins diesels. Limited production led Ralph to seek outside investment in 1970, and the company was taken over by the International Development Corporation who acquired a 51 per cent shareholding. The company underwent expansion but ran into further financial problems, closing down in 1971.

BILLANCOURT, FRANCE

RENAULT

France's leading truck manufacturer built its first truck in 1903, a 1-tonner. The company was founded as Renault Frères to build cars in 1898. By 1909 it began building heavy-duty trucks, including a bonneted, 4-cylinder gasoline-engined 3-tonner, soon followed by a 5-tonner with a 6.1 litre/372cu in 4-cylinder gasoline engine with 4-speed gearbox and chain drive. A forward-control 3-tonne truck was introduced in 1910 and, just before World War I, an artillery tractor with four-wheel drive and four-wheel steering was developed. For the next few years production was concentrated on military vehicles, but in the early 1920s a full range of trucks for payloads up to 7 tonnes entered production. They were instantly recognizable by their dash radiators and "coal scuttle" bonnets (hoods).

In the late 1920s the characteristic "coal scuttle" front ends gave way to conventional front-mounted radiators, and as early as 1930 Renault were introducing heavy-duty diesel engines. These included a 7.25 litre/442cu in 4-cylinder and a 10.5 litre/641cu in 6-cylinder, both direct-injection. The 10.5 litre/641cu in became available in 1931. Another innovation of the early '30s was a 5-speed gearbox for the heavier models. By 1935 Renault's heavy trucks boasted a forward-control cab of very modern and handsome appearance, while mechanical improvements, including power-assisted braking and power steering, were becoming available. Just before the advent of World War II Renault was offering a comprehensive truck range, their largest models being for 15 tonnes payload and powered by 6-cylinder diesels of 12.5 litre/763cu in capacity.

After France was liberated from German occupation in 1945 Renault was nationalized, becoming Régie National des Usines Renault, and an impressive array of forward-control trucks was put on the market in the early 1950s. These were the full forward-control underfloor-engined models for payloads of 5 and 7 tonnes (as rigid 4×2s) and 12 tonnes in articulated form. These had the 105bhp, 6.23 litre/380cu in AAA6 horizontal diesel engine and 5-speed overdrive gearbox with steering-column gearshift. Heavier models of similar specification followed over the next couple of years, like the R4153/54/58 for 8.25 tonnes payload powered by an uprated engine, the 512, developing 120bhp.

A major landmark in Renault's history took place in 1955 with the formation of Saviem (Société Anonyme de Véhicules Industriels et Équipements Mécaniques) by the merger of Renault, Latil, Somua and Floirat. Very soon, the group vehicles were appearing with Saviem and Saviem-Renault badges. Some were also badged Saviem-LRS. The unmistakable underfloor-engined Renaults survived up to the mid 1960s, becoming the Saviem Tancarville TP-10 in 1962, by which time the engine was included in the new Fulgur family and had been bored out to a 6.84 litre/418cu in capacity and developed 150bhp. The TP-10s had floor-mounted gearshifts.

■ LEFT *This 1929 SG 5/6-tonner was among the last type of Renault to have the dash mounted radiator.*

■ BELOW LEFT *This Renault G290 artic has the Club of Four pattern cab in high roof sleeper form.*

■ BOTTOM LEFT *The Renault Magnum has one of the tallest cabs on the market.*

■ RIGHT *The C range bonneted Renaults are not as common as cabovers in Europe. This one is Dutch-registered.*

From 1965 the Renault name disappeared from heavy trucks although it was still used on lighter commercials. However, Renault was to re-emerge as a major truck marque in 1980 after some organizational changes. In 1975 Saviem acquired the Berliet truck business from Citroën, which had owned the company since 1967. Peugeot merged with Citroën in 1974 and disposed of Berliet to Saviem. This meant that Saviem had a new range of heavy trucks in the form of Berliet's TR first introduced in 1972. After Renault Véhicules Industriels (RVI) was established in 1977, the Berliet range was relaunched as the Renault R-series, becoming an important seller in the heavy-duty market. Renault was re-establishing itself on the truck scene and expanding its empire with the acquisition of Chrysler's former truck business in the UK in 1981. This had been owned by Peugeot since 1978. At the same time, RVI acquired Chrysler Espana, builders of Spanish Dodge trucks at the former Barreiros plant. Meanwhile it was acquiring an increasing share in Mack of America.

Trucks built after 1980 (at which time the Saviem name was dropped and Renault reinstated) inherited their cabs from two different sources. One was the Berliet Premier or KB, the other an updated version of the Club cab. The Berliet TR, originally launched in 1972 while the company was under Citroën ownership, became the R-series. Later still, in 1990, it was marketed as the Renault Major. The other cab, which was fitted both to medium and heavy trucks, was a legacy from the Club of Four project. The same basic design was fitted to Volvo's F6 and F7. In Renault's range it appeared on the Midliner medium trucks and on the G-series heavy tractor units. The latter were relaunched in 1991 as the Manager. The following year 6×4 and 8×4 rigids with the cab were named Maxter.

There was an important model launch in 1990, with the announcement of the new Magnum. This is Renault's long-haul flagship with its distinctive high datum, flat-floored cab. It has sufficient headroom for drivers to stand up and move around, making it popular for international transport where space and a comfortable sleeper are important. Power units include the 12 litre/732cu in Renault in-line-six with electronic control and power ratings from 390 to 470bhp. There is also the option of a 16.4 litre/1000cu in Mack V8 diesel developing 560bhp. In Australia the Magnum is marketed under the Mack badge, with Cummins Signature 565bhp 15 litre/914cu in diesel engine.

Another Renault launch took place in 1996 when a whole new family of trucks from 17 tonnes gvw up to 44 tonnes gcw was announced. This is the Premium range and features an elegant new cab design. The cab comes in two different heights – a low-profile version for short-haul distribution trucks and a high profile for long-distance operation. Completing the new range are rigid three and four-axled trucks, aimed mainly at the construction market and sold under the Renault Kerax name. The power unit for the Kerax is the Renault 9.8 litre/598cu in 6-cylinder turbo diesel with ratings of 260 to 400bhp. Other current models include the bonneted C range aimed at the worldwide market but mainly sold outside of Europe. They are the modern equivalent of the old Berliet-designed TLR model which was marketed as Renault from 1980 onwards. Catering for light to medium-weight operators is the new Midlum range that replaced the Midliner in 2000.

■ LEFT *Renault's stylish Kerax 8×4 built in 1997 has an exceptionally well-appointed cab for a truck aimed at the construction industry.*

LANCING, MICHIGAN, USA

REO

■ ABOVE ***A late 1930s Reo Speedwagon 3-ton dump truck powered by the 6-cylinder Gold Crown gasoline engine.***

The man who formed Reo, Ransome Eli Olds, was one of the pioneers of the American motor industry. Born in 1867, Olds built a steam car in 1886 and introduced a gasoline-engined car in 1897. Owing to a disagreement with the board, he left Olds in 1904 and founded the Reo Motor Car Co. The original company, Olds Motor Works, also survived and was absorbed into General Motors in November 1908. Olds Motor Works went on to build a variety of trucks under the Oldsmobile name up to 1939. The Reo company entered the truck market in 1913 with a 2-ton payload bonneted Model J which featured electric starting and lighting. The volume seller was Reo's legendary Speedwagon range, first introduced in 1915. It remained in production for about 10 years and was then modernized, continuing to be offered through to the late 1930s. From 1925 a 6-cylinder engine was available, and this was to become the main type of power unit. In 1928 heavier models for 3 and 4-ton payloads were available. Reo also built up a healthy export business and a UK assembly plant was set up in 1929.

A 4-tonner, introduced in 1932, had an 8-cylinder gasoline engine and in 1934 Reo offered their 6-cylinder Gold Crown gasoline engine across the range, which now included a heavier 6-ton model. After World War II their Model 30 and 31 bonneted trucks appeared, the heaviest being for 10-ton payloads and powered by Continental gasoline engines up to 200bhp. The first diesel-powered Reos were introduced in 1956 using turbocharged Cummins engines. In 1957 the company was acquired by the White Motor Co. The following year White also acquired Diamond T, and production of both Reo and Diamond T was concentrated in Reo's Lancing plant from 1960. By that time a new series of heavy-duty tilt-cab forward-control models, the DC range, was in production. In the final years of production a wide variety of heavy-duty trucks was offered, including 4×2, 6×4, 6×6 and 8×6 with, in some cases, diesel engines up to 335bhp. In 1967 Reo ceased to exist as an independent marque, the products becoming Diamond Reos.

CHESTER HILL, AUSTRALIA

RFW

■ LEFT ***RFW trucks were custom-built. This is an 8×4 site vehicle on test.***

Robert Frederick Whitehead founded his engineering company in the mid 1940s after serving as a fitter in the RAAF. A self-taught engineer, he turned to truck making in 1969, when he produced a Scania-engined twin-steer eight-wheeler fitted with a Bedford KM cab. RFW went on to offer a range of custom-built trucks in which quality and durability were more important than price. An almost endless choice of diesel engines was available, including Detroit Diesel, Cummins, Caterpillar, Scania, AEC, Rolls Royce and Nissan UD. Power ratings ranged from 190 to 550bhp. Later, as the range became established, RFW had their own composite fibreglass and steel cab of very functional design. Model types included 4×2, 4×4, 6×4, 8×4 and 8×8, plus individually designed machines. During the late 1980s on-highway trucks gave way entirely to low-volume, custom-built specials including fire-fighting vehicles and special road-rail trucks.

BRIDGEPORT, CONNECTICUT, USA

RIKER

The Riker name was adopted for Locomobile trucks from 1917 after the name of Locomobile's founder Andrew Riker. All were built on a 3.8m/12.5ft wheelbase and powered by a Locomobile 4-cylinder gasoline engine. Production of the 3 and 4-ton bonneted trucks continued until 1921, passing to Hares Motors in 1920.

BRASOV, ROMANIA

ROMAN

The Roman name was applied to a range of MAN-based trucks introduced by Autocamioane Brasov in 1971. The range was also marketed as DAC. Interprenderea de Autocamioane Brasov was originally the ROMLOC company, which built locomotives and rail wagons back in the early 1920s. It then became SR (Steagul Rosu, which means "Red Star") and began truck building, under the SR, Bucegi and Carpati names, from 1954. The new Roman range was based on MAN/Saviem technology and, in some cases, was sold through MAN dealers. The Saviem-designed MAN cabs were locally produced under licence and RÁBA-MAN diesels were used in the early models. Later, Roman produced MAN diesels under licence. A wide range of models, from 4×2 dump trucks for 16 tonnes gross up to maximum-weight 6×4 tractors, was offered. In 1990 the company changed its name to Roman SA, but the trucks are now marketed under the DAC badge.

■ ABOVE RIGHT *Roman trucks of the 1970s were basically MAN designs built under licence. This six-wheeler is UK-registered.*

■ RIGHT *The MAN origins are clearly evident in this 38-tonne artic with the MAN/Saviem pattern sleeper cab.*

COLNBROOK, ENGLAND

ROTINOFF

■ LEFT ***Very few Rotinoffs entered civilian operations. This one worked in the UK.***

Rotinoff Motors Ltd was formed at Colnbrook, near Slough in Buckinghamshire, in 1952 by George Rotinoff, a White Russian immigrant, to build heavy tractors suitable for military tank transport. After suitability trials, the 6×4 Rotinoff Atlantic GR.7 was approved by the Swiss Army. The first example appeared in 1955. It had a maximum gross train weight rating of 140 tons, was powered by a 12.17 litre/743cu in Rolls Royce C6.SFL Series 109 direct-injection supercharged diesel developing 250bhp, and had a David Brown 12-speed (four main, three auxiliary) transmission. Kirkstall axles were fitted. Later models had the 275bhp C6.TFL Rolls Royce turbocharged diesel and 15-speed transmission. A heavier Super Atlantic GR.7 took the C8.TFL 16.2 litre/988cu in "straight eight" Rolls Royce turbo diesel giving 335bhp. These were fitted with 15 or 18-speed transmissions and were capable of gross train weights up to 300 tons. As well as the Atlantic and Super Atlantic, Rotinoff built a 7.3m/24ft wheelbase Viscount GR.37/AU load-carrying drawbar tractor suitable for Australian roadtrain operations. This had the additional option of a Rolls Royce B.81.8P 8-cylinder gasoline engine rated at 220bhp, designated the Viscount 64.GKS. Also listed was a forward-control Viscount 84.BJS rigid eight drawbar tractor. An estimated 35 Rotinoffs were built. From 1960 onwards the company changed its name from Rotinoff Motors to Lomount Vehicle & Engineering Ltd. Later still, when Lomount ended production in 1962, the design rights were acquired by Atkinson Vehicles Ltd of Walton-le-Dale, Preston, who briefly marketed the trucks under the Atkinson name badge.

LISKEARD, ENGLAND

ROWE-HILLMASTER

■ BELOW ***The 1960 Rowe-Hillmaster tractor unit had a wide engine choice. This one was powered by an AEC AV470.***

Rowe's Garage Ltd of Dobwalls, Liskeard in Cornwall, were coach operators who turned to building a coach of their own design in 1953. A Meadows 4DC diesel engine was used. Only five coaches were built, but proprietor Maurice G. Rowe turned to truck building in 1954. The aim was to build a powerful, rugged truck which could master the steep hills in Rowe's native Cornwall. The appropriate name Rowe-Hillmaster was adopted, and the first model was a 6 to 7-ton payload forward-control four-wheeler powered by a 90bhp Meadows 4DC-330 diesel engine. An 8-ton version of this also became available but with an Eaton 2-speed axle as standard. In 1955 an underfloor-engined 7-tonner was available powered by a Meadows 4HDC-330 mounted amidships behind the front axle, a layout already tried in an earlier coach chassis. By this time Maurice Rowe had sold the garage and coaching business and set up a truck-manufacturing operation under the name M. G. Rowe (Motors) Doublebois Ltd. The company went on to offer an extensive range of trucks with payload ratings from 6 to 14 tons, plus an artic tractor for a 15-ton payload. A 10-ton four-wheeler, the M/10 at 14 tons gvw, announced in 1956, had a Meadows 5.4 litre/330cu in 4DC-330 but it was also available as a 9 to 10-tonner with a wide choice of power units. The L/9-10 had the Leyland

■ RIGHT *Most Rowe-Hillmasters were sold in their home territory. This livestock truck was based at Liskeard, Cornwall, where it was built.*

Comet O.350, the A/9-10 had the AEC AV470 and the G/9-10 had the Gardner 5LW. Others, for 6/7-ton payloads, were available with the Gardner 4LK or 4LW, according to model. No less than 14 basic models were listed by 1959, including a 14-ton six-wheeler with Hendrickson bogie and a choice of Meadows 6DC-500, AEC AV470, Gardner 5LW or 6LW.

For an extra charge – according to model – almost any Rowe-Hillmaster could be supplied with underfloor engines from Meadows, Gardner, AEC or Leyland. The trucks were fitted with coachbuilt cabs supplied by Jennings of Sandbach. Despite Rowe's high engineering standards and custom-build approach, sales were mainly limited to south-west England, and the company ceased trading in 1962 after nine years in business.

CROYDON, ENGLAND

RUTLAND

■ LEFT *Though a small company, Motor Traction offered a very wide range. This is a typical Rutland 6-tonner dating from 1957.*

Motor Traction Ltd was established in 1951 at New Addington, Surrey, to build Rutland trucks. These were sold as MTN in certain export markets. The origins of the company date back to 1946 when Frank Manton left the Royal Navy and set up Manton Motors at Tee Van Road, Addiscombe, Croydon, with a Commer distributorship. He began building his own design of truck called the Manton, powered by a Perkins P6 diesel and grossing 8 tons gvw. These sold well in Spain, and Frank Manton established an agency at the Mack Distributors, Sumassa, in Madrid. As there were restrictions on the number of vehicles one agent could sell, the name MTN was introduced to double the quotas. Those sold in the UK were usually badged Rutland.

To avoid clashing with Commer, Manton transferred his truck-manufacturing business to new premises, under the name of Motor Traction Ltd. In the five years the company survived, an amazingly diverse range of trucks was built. To keep costs down, items such as spring hanger brackets were fabricated rather than forged or cast. The range covered almost every conceivable type, from the 2 to 3-ton payload M4 up to a projected TH 10716 rigid eight-wheeler at 24 tons gvw. Both bonneted and forward-control models were built. Many had type names like the Toucan 5 to 6-tonner, the Albatross 6 to 7-tonner, and the Stuka and Eagle 7-tonners. Motor Traction could fit almost any engine and drive-line the customer wanted, and cabs were custom-built by almost any coachbuilder. There were well over 50 different types on offer, including 4×4s and special mobile-crane chassis. However, production figures were low, some even being one-offs. The firm folded in 1957. The name Rutland was derived from the county of Rutland where Frank's father, Arthur C. Manton, was born.

OTHER MAKES

■ RAMIREZ

MONTERREY, MEXICO

Grupo Industrial Ramirez built heavy-duty trailers at their subsidiary, Trailers de Monterrey SA, and in the late 1950s began building 4×2 and 6×4 bonneted highway tractors, typical of which is the R-22, powered by a Cummins NTC-350 diesel. Most components are licence-built in Mexico to American design, including Spicer transmissions and Rockwell axles. Gross train weight capabilities extend up to 54.5 tonnes.

■ LEFT ***The 1966 Ramirez 4×2 bonneted tractor features all-American drive components but these are locally produced under licence.***

■ RAPID

DETROIT & PONTIAC, MICHIGAN, USA

One of the United States' pioneer truck builders, the Rapid Motor Vehicle Co. was established in 1904 after brothers Max and Morris Grabowski had built their first truck back in 1900. That was a very basic single-cylinder affair capable of about 16kph/10mph. In 1905 production moved to Pontiac. By 1907 Rapid was building 1-ton and 1½-ton forward-control models with a driver-over-engine layout. In 1907 Max Grabowski pulled out of Rapid and set up the Grabowski Power Wagon Co., which survived until 1912. Meanwhile the newly formed General Motors Truck Co. showed an interest in Rapid, absorbing the company in 1911.

■ ABOVE LEFT ***Relay's massive Duo-Drive 300A 6×4 of 1931 had twin 8-cylinder gasoline engines producing 275bhp.***

■ LEFT ***The 1930 Relay 3/4-tonner featured a unique final drive referred to as the "Surmounting Principle".***

■ RELAY

LIMA, OHIO, USA

The Relay Motor Corporation was set up in 1927 with substantial financial backing. It was formed as a consortium of three existing manufacturers, namely the Commerce Motor Truck Co. of Ypsilanti, Michigan, the Service Motor Truck Co. of Wabash, Indiana, and the Garford Truck Co. of Lima, Ohio. Eventually all production was centred at the Lima plant. The three individual makes were retained and a separate Relay range was introduced. This included eight bonneted models for payloads in the 1 to 4 tons range. While the Commerce, Service and Garford trucks featured worm drive, Relay adopted a unique final-drive arrangement in which drive pinions engaged with toothed rings in the rear wheels, enabling it to "climb" over obstacles – Relay referred to it as their "Relay Surmounting Principle". In 1931 a 7-ton payload 6-cylinder truck was introduced.

Relay's last grand gesture before folding up in 1933 was their high-powered Duo Drive – a 6×4 monster powered by two Lycoming Type AEC straight-eight gasoline engines mounted side by side with combined output of 275bhp. Each engine drove one rear axle through its own air-shift Fuller 5-speed gearbox. Other features included power steering, hydraulic clutches and full air brakes. Cleco-Gruss air springs were mounted at the front, and the cab incorporated a sleeping bunk. Relay advertised it as the world's most powerful truck, but it attracted few sales.

■ REPUBLIC

ALMA, MICHIGAN, USA

Beginning in 1913 as the Alma Motor Truck Co., Republic built light to medium trucks from 1914 with payload capacities of around 1 ton. By 1917 heavier models for up to 3¼ tons were available, powered by Lycoming, Continental or Waukesha gasoline engines. These were marketed in the UK as Whiting by Whiting (1915) Ltd of North London. Early trucks had Torbensen drive, but this was soon abandoned in favour of Timken and Eaton worm drive. During the 1920s heavier models still were added, the biggest being a 5-ton payload machine. However, Republic were suffering financial difficulties. In 1928 they acquired the Linn Manufacturing Co. of Morris, New York, which built half-track tractors. The following year Republic merged with the American LaFrance Truck Co., forming the LaFrance Republic Corporation. This survived until 1932 when it was taken over by the Sterling Motor Truck Co. of West Allis, Wisconsin, production carrying on until 1942, but the latter-day LaFrance Republics were basically Sterlings under a different name.

ARBON, SWITZERLAND

SAURER

Adolph Saurer was experimenting with gasoline-engine design back in 1888, and by 1896 had produced his first motor car. This pioneer of the European motor industry entered the truck market as early as 1903 with a 5-tonner powered by a 25 to 30hp T-head gasoline engine. In 1905 lighter trucks for 1½, 2½ and 3 tonnes appeared, and the following year an improved 5-tonner on solid rubber tyres. Saurer vehicles scored many successes in international trials in Europe. In 1909 the Zurich-based Safir Co. took out a licence to build Saurers and it was there that Saurer's first high-speed diesel engine was built.

As early as 1910 truck factories were set up in Germany and France to assemble Saurers for these markets. Also, the International Motor Co. of Plainfield, New Jersey, began licensed assembly (see "Mack").

In 1918 Saurer introduced its A types for civilian customers, and by the early 1930s was building 2, 3, 4 and 5-tonners. The B type appeared in 1926. The first diesel appeared in the B types which, by 1930, included trucks for payloads of 2 to 6 tonnes.

In 1929 Saurer acquired its Swiss rival, Motorwagenfabrik Berna AG of Olten, but the Berna name was allowed to continue. During the late 1920s a British operation was established, and from 1931 Saurers were built in Newcastle-upon-Tyne under the Armstrong Saurer name. Diesel-engine development continued throughout the 1930s, the first direct-injection Saurer diesel appearing in 1934. Later that year the company introduced its famous C type which was of very modern appearance.

During World War II Saurer developed a highly innovative 8×8 military truck plus 4×4 and 6×6 versions. After the war the C type resumed production and a forward-control C type was also introduced, the heaviest being a 7-tonner. Heavier models, including the 10-tonne payload 6C, appeared in 1956 and the C range continued to 1963. By the late 1950s D type trucks were under development, consisting of two basic chassis, the 2D and 5D. These were offered in a variety of wheelbases, powered by diesel engines of 120 to 240bhp. All-wheel drive versions were also offered. From 1971 the 2D became the 4D while the 5D continued. The largest and most impressive 5D model, the 5DF 8×4 rigid eight-wheeler, was launched in 1974.

From 1976 the main models were the D180/D230 4×2 and the D290/D330 which were built in various configurations as 4×2, 6×2, 6×4 and 8×4s. Declining sales in the early 1980s saw the two leading Swiss truck makers, Saurer and FBW, forming a joint organization called NAW (Nutzfahrzeuggesellschaft Arbon & Wetzikon). In 1982 Daimler-Benz acquired a major shareholding in NAW and soon took full control.

■ LEFT *The Saurer C type truck was a great classic with its origins in the 1930s. This is an early '60s 7-tonner.*

■ BELOW LEFT *Saurer's first truck was this 1903 shaft and pinion drive 5-tonner.*

■ RIGHT *The D model designation covered the entire range from the 1970s onwards. This is the heavy-duty D290.*

■ LEFT *Successor to the C type was the D type, which bore a strong family likeness to its predecessor but had a facelifted cab with flush mounted headlights.*

SEINE, FRANCE

SAVIEM

Saviem, an acronym of Société Anonyme de Véhicules Industriels et Équipements Mécaniques, came into being in 1955 when Latil, Renault, Somua and Floirat merged. It was primarily a marketing organization, and for two years or so the various companies' trucks were marketed as Saviem Latil, Saviem Renault, Saviem Somua, Saviem LRS and Saviem Floirat. The widely differing model types led to a complex range. Renault's distinctive underfloor-engined models had little or nothing in common with Latil and Somua's vertical-engined types. Latil were still producing their unusual four-wheel steer timber tractors and Somua offered a choice of heavy-duty dump-truck chassis. Clearly there was room for rationalization in such a conglomeration of models, and by 1960 some simplification was taking place, notably in the range of diesel engines. Saviem Fulgur 4 and 6-cylinder diesel engines of 4.6 and 6.8 litre/281 and 415cu in capacity were introduced in 1961 and some of the older designs were phased out. A diesel engine plant was set up in the former French Government's Limoges armaments factory, which had been producing engines for military use. Also in 1961 Saviem entered a brief association with the German company Henschel, under which Henschels were to be marketed in France as Saviem Henschel. The arrangement was ended after only two years.

New models, badged Saviem, appeared in the early 1960s, including a medium-range, the S5, S7 and S8 for 5.5, 7.5 and 8.5-tonne payloads respectively. There was also an

■ ABOVE *After the formation of Saviem, Renault's old underfloor-engined models were given a new lease of life as the Tancarville.*

■ BELOW *The JM240 artic featured a stylish new cab and a 235bhp MAN diesel.*

■ RIGHT *Saviem's SM range had a lot in common with MAN, resulting from technical co-operation in the late 1960s and '70s.*

■ RIGHT *Later versions of the Saviem cab had this full-width black grille, giving them their own identity.*

■ BELOW RIGHT *The mid 1970s J range of medium trucks had the Club of Four cab.*

articulated model for up to 16.5 tonnes payload. Engine choice included the 3.0 litre/183cu in Renault 591 4-cylinder diesel and the 5.8 litre/355cu in Perkins 6.354 diesel. These models had a column-mounted gearshift, carrying on a Renault tradition. The 1962 heavy-duty range, featuring a stylish new cab with four headlights, consisted of the JL with payload ratings from 6.8 tonnes up to 12.75 tonnes. There were also seven heavy-duty tractor units ranging from the JL21 at 18 tonnes gcw up to the JL32 at 32 tonnes gcw, plus the JL20 and JL20/200 for 35 tonnes gcw. The latter featured a Henschel 520D6T 6-cylinder 204bhp direct-injection diesel and a 10-speed gearbox. Latil's 4×4 timber tractor continued to be available, marketed as the Saviem TL23. Certain models from the underfloor-engined Renault range were still marketed as the Saviem Tancarville TPIO, powered by the 150bhp F646 horizontal diesel and featuring a floor-mounted gearshift.

In 1971 Saviem became a member of the Euro Truck Development Group, otherwise known as the Club of Four. Along with DAF, Magirus-Deutz and Volvo, they developed a tilt-cab medium truck range, appearing in 1975 as the Saviem J models. These were powered by an MAN 5.5 litre/335cu in diesel licence-built by Saviem at their Limoges factory. Technical co-operation between Saviem and MAN of Germany, which had begun in the late 1960s, resulted in a new range of heavy-duty trucks, the SM models, with a new tilt cab of Saviem design. This became standard fitment on MANs as well as Saviems, while MAN engines were fitted in the Saviem versions. Many of these models also featured a steering-column gearshift.

A major development in 1974 was the acquisition of Berliet from the Citroën Group. This resulted in an even more complex range, with certain Berliet designs being marketed with Renault and Saviem badges. By 1978 the organization had undergone rationalization and became known as Renault Véhicules Industriels. The Berliet and Saviem names were replaced by Renault and by 1980 Saviem no longer existed as a make.

WATFORD, ENGLAND

SCAMMELL

Scammell's Articulated Six-wheeler of 1922 set the scene for the company's highly individual approach to truck design throughout its 66-year history. Scammell Lorries Ltd, which set up at Tolpits Lane, Watford, in 1922, was an offshoot of the coachbuilding and steam wagon repair company, G. Scammell & Nephew Ltd of Spitalfields, whose history dates back to 1837. In 1919 the company began experimenting with a matched three-axled articulated truck using a design closely based on the American Knox Martin. The weight of the trailer, or "carrier" as Scammell preferred to call it, was taken on semi-elliptic leaf springs attached to the tractor rear axle.

Shortly after setting up their Watford factory, Scammell took on a young engineer called Oliver D. North, who was responsible for a number of important designs at Scammell. However, his first project was less than successful. He tried a 3-cylinder radial engine in a light delivery Scammell called the Autovan. Only four were ever built, and the project was abandoned. The same year a decision was made to develop the legendary 6×4 and 6×6 Pioneer which was an unqualified success.

■ TOP ***From 1924, Scammell's articulated truck could have "four-wheels-in-line" twin rear axles enabling a payload of up to 12 tons.***

■ ABOVE ***Heavy tractors were Scammell's forte, like this Cummins-powered 240-ton Contractor of 1967.***

■ BELOW ***In the 1960s Scammell modernized its Rigid 8 concept by launching the Routeman. This is a Routeman III.***

North's next project was equally sensational. In 1929 plans were drawn up for what was claimed to be the world's largest truck – the Scammell "100-tonner". The heavily built chain-drive machine was matched to a massive "carrier" (trailer) with a steerable rear bogie. Only two were built. Initially they were fitted with Scammell's standard 4-cylinder 7 litre/427cu in gasoline engine, geared to a maximum road speed of 10kph/6mph. During their working lives they were both re-engined with Gardner diesels.

Scammell also began offering 6-ton four-wheelers, which were basically longer versions of their motive units. The first appeared in 1929. Then came a six-wheeled rigid in 1933. This, like all Scammells up to 1934, was fitted with the 4-cylinder gasoline and chain drive although, by then, pneumatic tyres were standard. Within a year, Scammell's technology had taken a leap forward with the introduction of a Gardner 6-cylinder diesel and shaft drive. Until 1933 the company had devoted all its

■ RIGHT *Scammell's Rigid 8 continued in production until 1958.*

attention to heavy-duty trucks, but then it launched its famous Mechanical Horse articulated lightweight truck for town deliveries.

Scammell's next significant design was their first rigid four-axled truck which they named the Rigid 8, presumably to distinguish it from their earlier Artic 8. It was powered by a Gardner 6LW and had a 6-speed overdrive gearbox. The first went into service in 1937.

Just after World War II Scammell designed and built a series of special heavy four-wheeled fairground generator trucks called Showtracs. Also, a modern-day equivalent to the Pioneer was built in the shape of the 6×6 Explorer. Other heavy tractors, often aimed at the overseas market, included the Mountaineer and Constructor.

In 1955 Scammell was absorbed into the Leyland Group, but because of the specialist nature of its products it was allowed to carry on as their Special Vehicles division.

■ RIGHT *The Scammell Highwayman kept alive Scammell's long tradition of bonneted artics.*

■ RIGHT *This 1973 Crusader represents Scammell's modernized range. The engine was a Rolls Royce 220 or 280 diesel.*

In 1958 the old Rigid 8 was due for updating, and Scammell launched the Routeman which had similar running units. A fibreglass cab was fitted. Shortly after, in 1962, the completely new Routeman II was launched with a striking fibreglass cab styled by Giovani Michelloti. During the 1950s the Artic 8 became the Highwayman tractor unit using a conventional fifth wheel in place of Scammell's patented Spherub semi-permanent coupling.

By 1968 new designs were appearing in the form of a heavy-duty Crusader 6×4 tractor and later a 4×2 version. The standard power unit for this was a Rolls Royce Eagle 6-cylinder diesel, but 6×4s were powered by 8V-71 Detroit Diesel two-stroke engines. A solitary eight-wheeled version called the Samson was built for Pickfords, the heavy-haulage contractors. Super heavy-haulage tractors, like the Contractor of 1966, were designed for gtws of 75 to 240 tons.

The Highwayman was phased out in the late 1960s, and the Routeman was replaced in 1980 by the new Leyland Constructor rigid eight which, though developed by Scammell, was badged Leyland. During the 1980s Scammell continued building heavy vehicles in the form of the S24 and the Commander tank transporter but, following the acquisition of Leyland by DAF Trucks in 1987, the plant closed in 1988.

SÖDERTÄLJE, SWEDEN

SCANIA

The Scania name appeared on trucks from 1903–11 and was not to reappear until 1969. Between 1911 and 1969 the trucks were marketed as Scania-Vabis. The first Scania truck, named the Tor, was built in 1903. The company's origins can be traced to 1891 when a Swedish agency was set up at Malmo by Danish-born Fredrik Petersen to assemble English-designed Humber bicycles. Svenska Aktiebolaget Humber & Co. manufactured the bicycles under licence. Bicycle production was discontinued from 1900 and a new company, under Petersen's directorship, was formed under the name Maskinfabriksaktiebolaget Scania.

Vagnfabriks Aktiebolaget i Södertälje (VABIS) was established even earlier, in 1892, building railway rolling stock and horse-drawn wagons. From 1897 Vabis began design work on internal combustion engines led by engineer Gustaf Erikson. From 1907 the company began to concentrate on automotive engines and passenger cars which were marketed under the Vabis name. After suffering financial difficulties during 1909–10, Vabis merged with Scania to form A.B. Scania-Vabis in 1917.

Prior to the merger, each company had begun developing its own designs of trucks. While Scania had produced the Tor in 1903, Vabis had already built its first truck, a 1½-tonner, in 1902. By 1908 there were Vabis trucks for 2 and 3 tonnes payload, powered by their own designs of gasoline engines. These included the E2V V-twin 12hp (later increased to 15 and 18hp) and the E4 four-in-line 5.4 litre/330cu in, producing up to 36hp. Shaft drive was used. Some 20 Vabis trucks were built prior to the merger. Scania's pre-merger truck production included a forward-control 1½-tonne chain-drive truck designed in 1902.

The first Scania-Vabis trucks were based on Scania chain-drive designs, but by 1913 a new range from 1½ to 6 tonnes payload capacity was launched. These were of bonneted layout with chain drive and gasoline engines with power ratings from 30 to 70hp. By the end of World War I Scania-Vabis had developed a four-wheel drive army truck which also found customers in the civilian market. This was unusual in having four independent drive shafts, one to each wheel, from a centrally mounted transfer box. A double-drive six-wheeler was launched in 1923. Other important developments of the era were a double-reduction drive axle and a patented design of progressive road spring.

Experiments with diesel power began in 1927, resulting in the Hesselman-Scania oil engine. This used gasoline for starting before being switched to diesel oil. It was some years before Scania's high-speed diesel engines actually entered production, the first appearing in 1936.

■ **LEFT** ***Vabis' first truck of 1903 carried 1½ tonnes and had a top speed of 12kph/7.5mph.***

■ **BELOW LEFT** ***A forward-control, chain-drive 1½-tonner with 12hp twin-cylinder gasoline engine.***

■ **BOTTOM LEFT** ***A 112M 32-ton artic with low datum P sleeper cab. The "M" signifies "medium duty".***

All pre-World War II Scanias were built with right-hand drive as Swedish traffic, like that of the UK, drove on the left and did not change over to the right until September 1967. Most Scania trucks were of bonneted layout, but as early as 1933 forward-control conversions were being built, inspired to some extent by the Bulldog buses that appeared in 1932. They were called Bulldogs because of their "flat-faced" design, which enabled the driver to sit beside the engine. The Bulldog principle was introduced on trucks in 1934, with the very functional-looking 34511 4½-tonner featuring a cab-ahead-of-axle layout with long doors and a low-entry step.

Major expansion plans were underway at the end of the 1930s and truck production was stepped up. During the war, fuel-oil shortages led to the wide use of producer gas, and civilian demand for trucks diminished as road fleets were laid up. Lack of civilian orders was compensated by demand for military trucks, and by 1943 Scania-Vabis production was entirely geared to the war effort. From the end of 1944 civilian production resumed. New bonneted heavy-duty trucks, the F10 and L10, were unveiled in 1944. The F10 was a four-wheel drive of 8.5 tonnes gvw while the L10, at the same design weight, was a 4×2. These were the first production Scania-Vabis to have left-hand drive. Large numbers of these trucks were fitted with third-axle conversions. A heavier version for 10/11 tonnes gvw, the L20 (4×2), soon followed and a factory-built 6×2 version, the LS20 for 15 tonnes gvw, was also introduced for 1946.

During the 1950s Scania-Vabis was seeking to increase its export sales to remain profitable. Many new models, mainly bonneted heavy-duty trucks, were launched and direct-injection diesels, based on Leyland technology, were introduced. To power the heaviest trucks, like the experimental LS85 6×2, the D815 8-cylinder in-line engine of 11.3 litres/689cu in was tried. This was turbocharged to boost the output from 180 up to 205bhp and was claimed to be the first-ever production turbo diesel. Bonneted 6×2 trucks up to 22 tonnes gvw and 4×2s of 13 to 15.5 tonnes gvw were Scania-Vabis' most common models of the 1950s and '60s, but in 1963 the forward-control LB76 ("B" standing for "Bulldog") entered the scene.

The company established a very important production plant in Brazil in

■ **ABOVE LEFT** ***The LB76, introduced in 1963, led to an expansion in sales, especially in the UK.***

■ **ABOVE RIGHT** ***Scanias, like this late 1970s 141, had reserves of strength and power to cope with their domestic weight limit of 52 tonnes.***

■ **RIGHT** ***In the 1990s Scania were trend-setters – this 124L with R sleeper cab is for fast international haulage.***

■ LEFT *A 1996 94C 32-tonne eight-wheeler. The "C" indicates heavy-duty specification for the construction industry.*

1962. To gain an improved share of the European market another plant was opened at Zwolle in The Netherlands in 1965. The LB76 played an important part in establishing Scania-Vabis as a major force in Europe and the UK. The replacements for the LB76, the LB80 and LB110 of 1968 consolidated the company's position as one of the market leaders. In 1968 Scania-Vabis, which was owned by the Swedish Wallenburg empire, was merged with another Wallenburg enterprise – the car and aircraft manufacturer SAAB – becoming SAAB-Scania. The name Vabis was dropped and the trucks were simply badged as Scania from 1969. The LB80/81, 110/111 and 140/141 cabs were replaced in 1980 by the 82 and 112/142 models. The first digits indicate the approximate engine capacity (8 , 11 or 14 litres/488, 671 or 854cu in, the latter being Scania's high-powered V8 engine), while the "2" indicates the development level (2-series). Hence the 1988 replacements for the 82/112 and 142 became the 93/113 and 143, which were visually similar. Next came the current 4 series with its striking new design of cab. A new family of low-emission diesels powers these models, including a 12 litre/714cu in. The range consists of the 94, 114, 124 and the 144. A prefix "P" indicates a low-profile cab, "R" a full-height cab and "T" a bonneted cab. Since 1995 Scania and SAAB have operated separately, the SAAB operations coming under General Motors ownership.

In 1999 it was announced that Scania was being taken over by Volvo, but the deal was blocked by the European Union.

LETCHWORTH, ENGLAND

SD

■ LEFT *T series municipals sometimes fulfilled other roles, like this tanker.*

■ BELOW LEFT *SD's most famous municipal model was the W type.*

Harry Shelvoke and James Drewry developed a unique concept in municipal chassis while employed at Lacre Lorries. In 1922 they left to start their own company, Shelvoke & Drewry, or SD. Their unusual transverse-engined low-loading truck, the Freighter, was a great success. The company also built the Latil tractor under licence, using the Traulier name. One of SD's most famous trucks was the W type. This had SD's own 3.9 litre/238cu in gasoline engine but, from 1954, a Perkins P4 diesel was offered. As the 1950s and '60s progressed, SD developed larger trucks, aimed at the municipal market. The TW of 1960 had a choice of SD gasoline or Perkins P6 diesel and grossed 11 tons, while the new fibreglass-cabbed TY of 1963 grossed 14 tons and featured a Leyland 0.350 diesel engine.

In 1975 the company launched its SPV (Special Purpose Vehicle) division and branched out into heavier-duty 4×4 and 6×4 crash tenders and fire trucks. In 1984 SD was taken over by the American-based Dempster Co. and then traded as Shelvoke-Dempster. The SPV range was discontinued and SD's share of the market declined until it was sold to a private investor in 1988. It was then to trade as Shelvoke, but the venture failed and the company had vanished from the scene by 1990.

OLDHAM, ENGLAND

SEDDON

Seddon was a relative latecomer to the truck industry compared with most of its rivals in the north-west of England. The company was formed as Foster & Seddon in 1938 at Salford, near Manchester in Lancashire. Foster & Seddon were hauliers and truck agents who realized the potential for a low-weight diesel truck that could weigh under 2½ tons unladen and was, therefore, exempt from the 32kph/20mph restrictions then in force. The object was to move a 6-ton payload over long distances at minimum cost. The higher 48kph/30mph legal speed meant faster turnaround and diesel power was more economical, giving more km/miles per gallon, on fuel that was half the cost. The formula was a sound one and the first Perkins P6-powered Seddon fulfilled all its promises. At first production was limited, owing to the cramped premises at Salford, but increasing demand justified a move to bigger premises at Oldham, where their Woodstock factory began full production in 1948.

There the Mk.5 forward-control four-wheelers were built in increasing numbers, and Seddon built up export business as well as healthy sales in the home market. In the 1950s Seddon, which was renamed Seddon Diesel Vehicles Ltd in 1951, began to widen the range with lighter and heavier models. The first was the Mk.7 3-tonner powered by a Perkins P4 diesel. An even lighter model, the bonneted Twenty Five 1¼-ton delivery vehicle, took the P3. By then Seddon was making extensive use of fibreglass in its cab and bodywork and was a pioneer of this technique. Cabs were built by a subsidiary called Pennine Coachcraft.

Seddon continued to generate increasing export business, selling into the Far East, Central and South America, Spain, Portugal and Europe. In the mid 1950s it began to move up the weight range, the UK weight limit having been increased to 14 tons and the 32kph/20mph limit having been abolished. A stylish new cab with curved screen appeared in 1956.

■ **TOP** ***Seddon built its reputation on its Perkins-engined Mk.5.***

■ **ABOVE** ***The Sirdar heavy-duty 30-ton 6×4 was aimed at the export market.***

■ **BELOW** ***The Cummins-engined 34:Four of the early 1970s era was Seddon's last tractor unit as an independent maker.***

■ LEFT *Seddon entered the maximum-weight sector in 1958 with their SD8 and DD8 rigid eight-wheelers.*

■ LEFT *A 1968 six-wheeled beer tanker grossed 22 tons and was available with an AEC AV470 diesel.*

■ BELOW LEFT *The 16:Four dump truck was powered by a Perkins V8-510 and features a Motor Panels cab.*

There was also a 14-ton gvw model, the Mk.14 with Gardner 6LW engine, and a Seven-tonner which was also available in artic and six-wheel form for up to 15 tons gvw. In 1958 the 14-ton gvw Mk.15/10 appeared with a choice of Perkins, Leyland and Gardner diesels.

In 1958 Seddon announced a completely new heavy-duty range, including a 24-ton gvw rigid eight-wheeler, the DD8 (8×4) and SD8 (8×2). This had a design weight of 28 tons in anticipation of increased weight limits. The new eight-wheeler had a choice of Gardner 6LW, 6LX or Cummins HF6, one of the first Cummins installations in a UK heavy truck. Another vehicle of interest in 1958 was the Sirdar 30-ton six-wheeled heavy tractor in bonneted or forward-control form, for up to 45 tons gtw. This was powered by a 198bhp Cummins NH.B.6.

Seddon benefited from being an assembler rather than manufacturer of its own components, and was able to offer a broad range of optional power units. In 1962 the range underwent some simplification and the rigid eight received a number of changes, becoming the 24DD8 or 24SD8. One was a very advanced design of tapered-leaf high-articulation rear bogie called the Maxartic. In 1964 the range was updated with a new model, the 13:Four, which featured a completely new steel cab bought in from Motor Panels. The 13:Four was powered by the Perkins 6.354 6-cylinder diesel. The following year a heavier model, the 16:Four (the first two digits indicated the gvw) with a 170bhp Perkins V8, was introduced. With an increase in demand for tractor units on the UK market, the eight-wheel range was dropped in 1964 and, by 1966–67, heavy-duty tractor units for 28 to 34 tons gcw were available, the heaviest being the 32:Four powered by Gardner 6LXB 180 or Rolls Royce 220bhp diesels.

There were few new models in the early 1970s, these being mostly heavy tractors, plus a 16-ton drawbar model for 32 tons gtw. A 34-ton tractor unit, the 34:Four with a choice of Rolls Royce Eagle 220, Cummins NH 220 or Gardner 8LXB 240bhp diesel became available. In 1970 Seddon acquired Atkinson Vehicles of Preston and by 1974 Seddon's and Atkinson's individual models were phased out, to be replaced by the new Seddon Atkinson range. (See "Seddon Atkinson".)

OLDHAM, ENGLAND

SEDDON ATKINSON

■ LEFT *The 400 tilt-cab range appeared in 1975, with a choice of Gardner, Cummins and Rolls Royce diesel engines.*

■ LEFT *From 1992 Stratos began appearing with the Iveco Group cab, as seen on this 44-ton drawbar outfit in New Zealand.*

Atkinson Vehicles of Preston was taken over by Seddon Diesel Vehicles Ltd of Oldham in 1970 but, for five years or so, each company retained its identity. A new joint product, the Seddon Atkinson 400, was under development when International Harvester purchased the company in 1974. The first Seddon Atkinson 400 came on the market in 1975. The next models to appear were the 200 and 300 series, which featured International diesels. Seddon Atkinsons were fitted with a Motor Panels steel tilt cab. From 1982 the range was updated with the 201, 301 and 401 series, recognizable by their black plastic grilles. At the same time Atkinson's famous circle "A" badge was reinstated at customers' request. Also, International engines were supplemented by Perkins and Cummins alternatives on certain models.

By 1986 the range was again updated, becoming the 2-11, 3-11 and 4-11, and International engines were deleted. By this time International had sold Seddon Atkinson to the Spanish ENASA Group. The Motor Panels cab was phased out after the introduction of a new long-haul truck, the Strato, which shared Cabtec design used by DAF and Pegaso. In 1992 ENASA was taken over by Iveco, and very soon Seddon Atkinsons began to be fitted with similar cabs to Iveco-Ford. At first these were customized by the addition of Seddon Atkinson's distinctive black grille but, during 1999, this was deleted. The "A" badge remains. Meanwhile fewer and fewer premium long-haul trucks are being built at Oldham as the plant becomes more involved in specialized municipal chassis.

■ ABOVE *The 200 series four-wheeler with International DH358 diesel engine was available from 1976–82.*

■ RIGHT *Between 1988 and 1992 the top-of-the-range Strato featured a version of the Cabtec cab developed by DAF and ENASA.*

SHREWSBURY, ENGLAND

SENTINEL

■ LEFT *Sentinel's legendary Super undertype steam lorry first appeared in 1923.*

■ BELOW LEFT *The S type steamer of 1934 was an advanced design but, even so, could not compete with diesel trucks.*

While Sentinel is synonymous with Shrewsbury, the company was originally established in 1906 as Alley & MacLellan Ltd based at Polmadie, Glasgow. Their Standard 5-ton steam wagon featured a vertical water-tube boiler incorporating a super-heater coil, an undertype 2-cylinder engine and single chain drive. So successful was that early wagon that it remained in production with relatively few changes through to the launch of Sentinel's famous Super of 1923. Alley & MacLellan had changed its name to the Sentinel Waggon Works Ltd when a new factory was opened at Shrewsbury, Shropshire, in 1915. In 1920, after being beset by financial problems, the company was reorganized as Sentinel Waggon Works (1920) Ltd. The highly successful Super wagon incorporated many advanced features, including a crankshaft differential and twin chain drive.

The DG series was a direct development of the Super, appearing in 1926. The DG4 had a payload rating of 6 to 7 tons, and had the benefit of 2-speed gearing for a better performance span between hill climbing and flat roads. The same year a six-wheeled version, the DG6, appeared for payloads of 12 tons. An even larger DG8 four-axled version was introduced in 1929. This has the distinction of being the first British rigid eight-wheeler but only a small number were built and, in practice, legal weight limits meant they could not carry any more than the DG6.

Sentinel and Foden dominated the steam market, but the 1930s were to see the demise of both ranges as new legislation forced the development of lighter trucks. Sentinel survived the longest. In 1934 they defied all odds and launched a new and very advanced steamer – the S type with a single-acting 4-cylinder underfloor engine with longitudinal crankshaft suited to cardan-shaft drive to an overhead worm-drive axle. It was lighter and featured a modernized driver's cab with a set-back boiler. It came in four, six and eight-wheel form, designated S4, S6 and S8. In spite of its sophisticated design, it could not compete with diesel trucks for all-round convenience and payload capacity, and it was phased out in the late 1930s. However, that was not the end of Sentinel's involvement with steam, since the company built about 100 wagons for export to Argentina as late as 1950.

By that time the company had become Sentinel (Shrewsbury) Ltd, and had developed a new range of diesel trucks. The first, the DV44, went into production in 1948 and was powered by Sentinel's own 4-cylinder horizontal indirect-injection engine, mounted in much the same location as that of the S4 steamer. David Brown gearboxes and Kirkstall overhead worm rear axles were standard. The all-steel 3-seater cab was of very handsome appearance and featured sliding doors. Prototypes of an underfloor gasoline-engined truck had been under development during the war, but the gasoline engine option was

■ RIGHT *From 1948 Sentinel Diesels entered full production. This is a 1955 Sentinel DV46T coal dump truck.*

soon abandoned. In late 1950 the DV46 light six-wheeler, basically a DV44 with trailing axle, became available, followed in 1952 by the DV66 heavy six-wheeler with a direct-injection 6-cylinder engine. The 4-cylinder was also revised to direct-injection design. Despite Sentinel's superbly engineered trucks, sales were diminishing during the 1950s, and by 1956 the company was forced to pull out of truck production. The factory was bought by Rolls Royce for diesel engine production, while the remaining stock of parts and vehicles was taken over by Sentinel's main dealer, North Cheshire Motors Ltd of Warrington, who formed a new company, Transport Vehicles (Warrington) Ltd in 1957 to build Sentinel-based designs under the TVW name.

SHEFFIELD, ENGLAND

SHEFFLEX

■ LEFT *This six-wheeler was one of Shefflex's largest trucks in the early 1930s.*

During World War I, when Commer Cars were working at full capacity to meet demands for their RC military trucks, the Sheffield Simplex Car Co., builders of luxury passenger cars, sub-contracted manufacture of lightweight 1½ to 2-ton Commers. When Commer returned to normal peacetime production, the contract with Sheffield Simplex was ended. Commers built at Sheffield were then marketed as Shefflex, but surplus stock was sold to R. A. Johnstone, an operator and motor dealer. Johnstone set up a production plant to build more, and production continued through to 1935. In 1930 heavier models were introduced, including a 5-ton payload 6×2 and a 6-ton articulated truck. Forward-control models were also offered. Engines used included Dorman, Meadows and Petter.

NANTERE, FRANCE

SIMCA

■ BELOW *During Simca's brief presence in the truck market it offered this Cargo 5-tonner.*

The history of Simca (Société Industrielle de Mécanique et Carroserie Automobile) is more concerned with cars than trucks, but in 1954 it acquired the French S.A. Ford operation at Poissy, which provided it with an established truck factory. A 5-tonne payload forward-control truck was marketed as the Cargo. A bonneted 5-tonner powered by a Ford V8 gasoline engine, the Caboteur, was also built briefly from 1957, but the following year truck production was transferred to Simca's associate company, UNIC.

HELSINKI, FINLAND

SISU

Sisu, built by OY Suomen Autoteollisuus AB, is Finland's leading truck make. Sisu began production in 1931 with a bonneted 3-tonner, the SH, powered by a 6-cylinder side-valve gasoline engine. In 1943, under a Finnish government nationalization plan, Sisu was merged with the newly formed Vanaja company, Vanajan Autotehdas OY, and production was concentrated on military vehicles that went under the Yhteissisu name. In 1948 Yhteissisu was de-merged, and Sisu and Vanaja became independent companies. Most Sisus built in the late 1940s ran on wood gas, wood being a plentiful commodity in Finland. Sisu's first diesel engines were available by the mid '50s. The 8.7 litre/531cu in 140bhp engines powered new bonneted trucks up to 13 tonnes gvw. By the late '50s Sisu had standardized on Leyland diesel engines, but continued to build its own axles. Its range now included 6×2s up to 20 tonnes gvw, with electro-hydraulic lifting devices on the trailing axle to transfer weight on to the drive axle. This system also became a universal feature of Scandinavian six-wheelers and was widely adopted in many other countries. In the mid 1960s, tilt-cab forward-control trucks appeared and in 1966 normal-control models were restyled using fibreglass bonnets (hoods). The K normal-control models covered 16-tonne 4×2 and 4×4 up to 24-tonne 6×2 and 6×4, while there were two KB cabover models – a 4×2 tractor and a 6×2, both for gcws of 38 to 45 tonnes. A lighter-bonneted range, the U models, covered the 15 to 22 tonnes gross bracket.

In 1967 Sisu took over Vanaja, reuniting the two manufacturers that had split up 20 years earlier. By the early '70s a complete range of 14 heavy trucks, in normal and forward control, was available, plus "half-cab" terminal tractors for yard shunting. The largest truck built by Sisu was a 180-tonne gcw bonneted 6×6. During the 1970s Leyland and Rolls Royce engines were the main fitment. The M-series appeared in 1971 with a new design of forward-control tilt cab. This was later used on Dennison trucks in Ireland. At that time Leyland and Saab-Scania both had a 10 per cent stake in Sisu, but by 1974 it had returned to Finnish state ownership. Leyland and Rolls Royce engines were phased out in favour of Cummins. Restyled bonneted SR and forward-control SM ranges appeared during the mid 1980s and, by now, Sisu were offering a wide range of multi-axle trucks, including 8×2, 8×4 and 10×4 with gtws up to 60 tonnes. Cummins became the main choice of engine, including the new M11 and the E14, during the 1990s. In 1997 Sisu updated their forward-control cab by using the new Renault Premium cab in place of the SM.

■ TOP *Hauling a 125-tonne trailer in the early 1970s is this Sisu K42 bonneted 6×6 tractor.*

■ ABOVE *The M series of the 1970s had a new design of tilt cab that Sisu also supplied to Dennison.*

■ LEFT *Sisu is a significant producer of special half-cab terminal tractors like this 1996 example.*

MNICHOVO HRADISTE, CZECH REPUBLIC

SKODA

Emil Skoda's engineering business originated in 1859 and grew to be one of the largest engineering companies in Europe. During World War I it was the largest arms manufacturer in the Austro-Hungarian Empire but, after the war when military production ended, new products had to be introduced. Skoda built locomotives, ships, aircraft, power stations and many other projects. In the mid 1920s it entered truck production, first building Sentinel DG steam wagons under licence from 1924 and, the following year, absorbing the old established truck builder Laurin & Clement AS of Mlada Boleslav to the north-east of Prague. Laurin & Clement had built trucks since 1907, a range from 2 to 6-tonne payload capacity being produced around the World War I period. Skoda-Sentinel steam wagons were phased out around 1932. Meanwhile, existing Laurin & Clement trucks were built under the Skoda name. New and improved trucks appeared in the late 1920s and early '30s. Skoda's first diesel truck appeared in 1932 as the 60D model for 5 tonnes. An 8-tonne payload six-wheeler, the 706N was introduced in the same year. By the mid '30s Skoda's largest trucks were bonneted 6×4s for up to 10-tonne payloads.

During World War II, while under German occupation, most Skoda companies were incorporated into the German war-related industries. The works was nationalized in 1945 and truck production was centred on Plzen at Liberecké Automobilové Závody (LiAZ). This was officially established as a Czechoslovakian state enterprise in 1951, and from then on the trucks were badged LiAZ. One of Skoda-LiAZ's best-known trucks, the forward-control 706 was launched in 1946 and built at the Avia factory in Letnany, Prague. Up to 1951 they carried the Skoda badge. The Mlada Boleslav plant concentrated on cars. Although the trucks were sold as LiAZ, they also carried the "winged arrow" trademark of Skoda. In 1974, when the 706 was phased out, the modernized 100 series made its debut.

In 1989 LiAZ truck production came under the Truck International AS division of Skoda. In 1992 LiAZ AS became a privatized stock company and in 1995 the privatization process was finalized when a majority share was acquired by Skoda Plzen. It now trades as Skoda Mnichovo Hradiste or Skoda-LiAZ AS, and the Skoda name has been reinstated on the recently introduced Xena 42 tonnes gcw long-haul tractor. The new model features a stylish tilt cab, and the power train consists of a Detroit Diesel 60 Series turbocharged and intercooled diesel, synchromesh Eaton RTSO 16-speed gearbox and a Meritor U180E rear axle. A Rába rear axle can also be specified.

■ ABOVE *The 706RT was one of Skoda's most memorable trucks.*

■ BELOW *Skoda's latest range includes this Detroit Diesel-powered Xena.*

ST OUEN, FRANCE

SOMUA

■ LEFT ***Mid 1950s Somua four-wheelers grossed up to 19 tons. This stylish example is Dutch-registered.***

The Société d'Outillege Mécanique et d'Usinage Artillerie was formed in 1914, combining three existing engineering companies, including the vehicle-building activities of Societé Schnieder of Le Havre. Somua chassis were built mainly for municipal use until the early 1930s, when a range of heavy-duty semi-forward-control diesel trucks for payloads of 10 to 13 tonnes, including six-wheelers, was introduced. A lighter range for 5 to 8 tonnes payload had gasoline engines. In the late '30s full forward-control trucks of two and three-axle type became available with a choice of gasoline or diesel. During World War II a large proportion of Somuas were converted to run on producer gas and production was suspended altogether between 1943 and 1946. Production of diesel-engined trucks resumed in 1946 with a new model, the JL15 11-tonner, being added. In 1955 Somua introduced the JL19 four and six-wheelers powered by a 9.3 litre/567cu in diesel of 150bhp output. A tractor-unit version was also available. In 1956 Saviem (Société Anonyme de Véhicules Industriels et Équipements Mécaniques) was formed, encompassing Latil, Renault, Somua and Floirat.

HAMBURG, PENNSYLVANIA, USA

SPANGLER

■ LEFT ***The unique Spangler Dual had twin Ford V8 engines and dual wheels on all four axles.***

The Spangler dual-engined 8×4 truck announced in 1947 was unusual in having front and rear bogies of equal capacity. They featured a walking-beam arrangement suspended on coil springs, and the front axles had dual-ratio steering, 25:1 for on-road use and 50:1 for low-speed manoeuvring, selected by a lever on the steering column. Running units were of Ford manufacture and servicing was through Ford agents. Power came from two 100bhp Ford V8 gasoline engines mounted side by side under the cab. Each drove one rear axle independently. Vacuum hydraulic braking operated on all wheels and each driveline had an emergency transmission brake. Three wheelbases were offered for bodywork of 4.9 to 8.2m/16 to 27ft.

Only a small number of the trucks were built up to 1949. They were built by Hahn Motors at Hamburg, Pennsylvania, and took their name from D. H. Spangler, Hahn's president. After 1949 Spangler carried out twin-steer conversions on various makes.

WOLVERHAMPTON, ENGLAND

STAR

The Star Engineering Co. built light vans from 1904 until 1907 when a heavier chain-drive truck for 4 tons was announced. By 1909 the range had been extended, and the heaviest 4-tonner had a 6.2 litre/378cu in 4-cylinder gasoline engine. After World War I a 2½-tonner and a 1½-tonner featured worm-drive rear axles, and pneumatic tyres became standard on the lighter model. Star had a reputation for quality engineering. From the mid 1920s front-wheel braking became standard. A new bus chassis that appeared in 1920 evolved into the 1927 Star Flyer, the company's best-remembered model. The VB-4 Flyer for truck or bus use was introduced in 1928. As a truck it was one of the fastest available, being capable of well over 80kph/50mph. After the Star Flyer there were no further truck models introduced, and the business was sold to Guy Motors in 1928 who kept production going on a small scale until 1931.

STARACHOWICE, POLAND

STAR

■ RIGHT ***The 1980 Star TRL38 5-tonne truck featured a forward-control cab by Chausson.***

Just after World War II Poland established its own truck industry. Fabryka Samochodów Ciezarowych began with the Star Model 20 3½-tonner powered by an 85bhp gasoline engine. Articulated and dump-truck versions followed. A 6×6 was introduced in 1958 and in 1961 diesel engines became available. The Series 28/29 launched in the late 1960s had a modern steel cab from the French company, Chausson. In the 1970s and '80s Star's principal models were the TRL38 5-tonne forward-control, the 200 series 6-tonner and the 266 6×6 powered by the 359-62 6.8 litre/415cu in 6-cylinder diesel of 150bhp. Current Star models are the 3-tonne payload 742 with Andoria power unit, the 12-155 7 to 8-tonner with MAN diesel and the 1142 available as a 12-tonne gross four-wheeler or lightweight 12-tonne gcw artic, both powered by Star's own 150bhp diesel engine. Star's plant is now Zaklady Starachowice Star SA which is part of Grupa Zasada.

MILWAUKEE, WISCONSIN, USA

STERLING

■ LEFT ***The Sterling chain-drive with end-dump bodywork dates from 1928.***

The Sterling Motor Truck Co. was formerly known as the Sternberg Motor Truck Co. The latter produced early designs of cabover trucks from 1 to 5 tons capacity between 1907 and 1915. In 1914 it had introduced a normal-control truck for up to 7 tons using chain drive. Concerned about anti-German feeling aroused by World War I, founder William Sternberg chose to rename the company Sterling in 1916. Wartime production included Class B Liberty trucks. In the 1920s chain-driven 5 and 7-tonners powered by Sterling's own 4-cylinder gasoline engines continued to be built, a distinctive feature being wooden inserts in the chassis frame. The mid '20s saw a 6-cylinder engine added to the range and heavier models appeared, including tractors for up to 12 and even 20 tons. The classic bonneted F series was launched in 1931 and, to expand production, the LaFrance Republic Corporation was taken over in 1932. Another development of the early 1930s was the introduction of Cummins diesels, Sterling being one of the first manufacturers to offer them as an alternative to their gasoline engines.

In the mid 1930s demand for cabover trucks was on the increase and Sterling designed an unusual tilt cab, part of which tilted backwards, leaving the front section, windscreen and wings undisturbed. By 1937 this had been abandoned and an orthodox forward-tilt cab had appeared as the G series, setting a trend that was eventually adopted throughout the industry. The Oakland-based Fageol Truck Co., established in 1916, ceased trading at the end of 1938 and Sterling stepped in and purchased its assets. Retaining ownership of the sales network, Sterling sold the manufacturing rights to T. A. Peterman, who formed Peterbilt Motors at the former Fageol plant. Sterling was a significant producer of heavy-duty military trucks during World War II. After the war Sterling specialized in extra-heavy-duty trucks but a downturn in the market led to the company being taken over by White Motor Co. of Cleveland, Ohio, in 1951. For a couple of years production continued as Sterling-White.

WILLOUGHBY, OHIO, USA

STERLING

In 1997 the Ford heavy truck operations in the United States were absorbed into the Freightliner Corporation, which is owned by DaimlerChrysler, and the products have since been marketed as Sterling. The model line-up can be divided into five basic groups. The Cargo series consists of medium-duty cabovers for city deliveries and features the former UK Ford Cargo tilt cab first introduced on the European market in 1981. The 7500 series is a conventional range for short-haul and urban duties. Then comes the heavy-duty conventional 8500, available with a choice of mid-range diesels as an all-round general-purpose range. The 9500 series is the long-haul range of conventionals, with performance and driver comfort for heavy-duty operation combined with powerful on/off-road models for construction work. The top-of-the-range tractor, for line-haul work, is the Sterling Silver Star, offering a combination of luxury, durability and performance.

■ RIGHT *The 1999 Sterling 7500 L-Line 6×4 has a choice of Cummins or Caterpillar diesels.*

BUFFALO, NEW YORK, USA

STEWART

The founders of the Lippard-Stewart Motor Co. of Buffalo, Thomas R. Lippard and R. G. Stewart, parted with the company in 1912, within one year of its formation, and set up the Stewart Motor Corporation also at Buffalo. Lippard-Stewarts were lightweights up to 2 tons and featured a "coal scuttle" bonnet (hood). They ceased production in 1919. Early Stewarts resembled their Lippard-Stewart counterparts, but in 1916 they launched the K model 1-tonner with a driver-over-engine layout. Heavier models, up to 3½ tons, appeared powered by engines from Buda, Continental and Milwaukee. By the early 1930s there was a range of six models up to 7 tons payload, Waukesha gasoline engines being the most common fitment. In 1938 Stewart offered their first cabover for payloads of 1½ to 3 tons. Stewart's president, Thomas R. Lippard, left to join Federal in 1939. Three years later Stewart ceased production.

VIENNA, AUSTRIA

STEYR

■ LEFT *This early 1990s 19S31 drawbar outfit was available with Steyr WD815 V8 turbo intercooled diesel of 355bhp.*

Steyr trucks began production in 1922 at the former weapons factory of Osterreichische Waffenfabriks-Gesselschaft AG situated at Steyr near Vienna. The company had been in arms production since 1864 and, following World War I, it turned to vehicle building to supplement its dwindling weapons activities. The first Typ III 2½-tonne truck was a shaft-drive machine on solid tyres, powered by a 34hp 6-cylinder gasoline engine. In 1926 the company was officially renamed Steyr-Werke AG and continued to offer a range of trucks, mainly in the light to medium-weight bracket.

■ RIGHT *This Steyr Typ III features street-sprinkling equipment.*

■ RIGHT *The 1965 Type S862 bonneted tanker had a Steyr 6-cylinder diesel.*

■ BELOW RIGHT *The Steyr Plus 1291 38-tonne artic had a choice of in-line-six or V8 diesel engine.*

In 1935 it joined forces with two other Austrian vehicle builders, Austro-Daimler of Vienna and bicycle manufacturer Puch Werke. Austro-Daimler was formed in 1900 as a subsidiary of the German Daimler company and had built trucks from 1900 through to 1920. The merged businesses became known as Steyr-Daimler-Puch AG. Until the post-World War II period Steyr-Daimler-Puch produced light and medium trucks, including military vehicles, but a new range of trucks, mainly of normal-control layout, appeared for payloads of 4 to 8 tonnes. These were designated the 380 (4-tonner), 480 (5-tonner), 480z (6-tonner), 586z (7-tonner) and the 780 (8-tonner).

From 1968 a new truck range, the forward-control Plus models, entered production. These featured a modernized cab design and spanned a wider payload range from 5 up to 16 tonnes. The heaviest were powered by Steyr's own 320bhp 6-cylinder diesel engine. A wide choice of drive configurations was offered, including 4×4 and 6×6 models. From 1975 the already comprehensive range was joined by rigid eight-wheel models that were becoming popular in Switzerland, following a change in weight legislation. An assembly plant for Steyr trucks was set up at Thessaloniki in Greece in 1974 and later another in Bauchi, Nigeria. During the 1980s Steyr-Daimler-Puch's truck divisions were in a loss-making situation despite bold export-marketing plans.

In 1990 the truck building activities were taken over by MAN of Germany. Steyr's last range before the takeover included the 17S18 and 17S21 4×2 17-tonne gvw models featuring a modern steel tilt cab (which Steyr also supplied to ERF in the UK for their ES models), and their 195 4×2 tractor powered by a choice of Steyr's WD615.63 6-cylinder 9.7 litre/592cu in diesel engine or their 12 litre/732cu in V8 providing up to 386bhp. Both were turbocharged and intercooled. The high-powered tractors were marketed as the Gottardo, named after the famous mountain pass. Similarly, their heavy V8-powered 8×4, aimed mainly at the Swiss market, was called the Simplon. The Steyr plant was eventually turned over to the production of medium-weight MAN trucks that still feature Steyr's design of tilt cab.

BRISTOL & TWICKENHAM, ENGLAND

STRAKER-SQUIRE

■ BELOW ***A Straker-Squire 5-ton chain-drive brewer's dray powered by a 4-cylinder gasoline engine.***

A steam-wagon builder from 1906, Sidney Straker & Squire Ltd of Bristol had a manufacturing agreement with Büssing of Germany to sell Büssing vehicles as Straker-Squire in the UK. The earliest models were 3-tonners with 4-cylinder gasoline engines. The arrangement with Büssing lasted until 1909, from which point Straker-Squire began building its own designs. A heavy 5-ton Colonial truck was produced in 1910 and a 3 to 4-ton truck was introduced in 1913 and was built in large numbers for military use during World War I. After the war the company suffered along with others from a slump in the market. A semi-forward-control 5-ton truck with 4-cylinder engine and worm-drive axle, the A type, was introduced in 1919. The Bristol factory closed in 1918, production moving to Twickenham and, later, Edmonton. Production ceased in 1926.

BRENTFORD, ENGLAND

STRAUSSLER

Hungarian-born Nikolas Straussler was a consulting engineer who specialized in designing military trucks during the 1930s. He set up Straussler Mechanization Ltd at Brentford, Middlesex, in 1935 to build specialist civilian trucks, the first of which was a highly unconventional one-off 8×4 chassis for the Anglo Iranian Oil Company. The short-wheelbase chassis marked a completely new approach to truck design, the drive going to the front two axles. A Straussler 7.2 litre/439cu in twin overhead camshaft V8 gasoline engine provided 150bhp and had two separate radiators side by side cooled by a fan on each bank. All eight wheels were independently sprung. The truck was built in Hungary by Nikolas Straussler's former employer, Manfred Weiss of Csepel, and originally carried the MW badge. It was shipped to England where it was fitted with a 16,820 litre/3700 gallon spirit tank body by Thompson Bros. of Bilston. Other Straussler products included a 7-ton payload 4×4 with a rear-mounted Ford V8 engine. Smaller military vehicles were also built, but the company ceased production in 1940.

■ ABOVE ***The unusual Straussler front-wheel drive 8×4 with V8 gasoline engine developing 150bhp.***

SOUTH BEND, INDIANA, USA

STUDEBAKER

■ LEFT *The 1962 Transtar had a 170bhp V8 gasoline engine.*

■ BELOW *The Studebaker 2R16A of 1950 with 3.7m/12ft stake-side body had a 102bhp L-head 6-cylinder Power Plus gasoline engine.*

The history of one of America's oldest truck manufacturers, Studebaker, dates from 1852 when the Studebaker family built horse-drawn wagons. In 1902 they began building electric vehicles. Their first gasoline-engined truck appeared in 1913. Heavier trucks did not enter the scene until 1927, with 3-tonners powered by a 5.9 litre/360cu in 6-cylinder gasoline engine. The following year Studebaker joined forces with Pierce Arrow, leading to the trucks being called Studebaker Pierce Arrow. During 1932 there was a brief tie-up with the White Motor Co. By the mid '30s Studebaker was independent again, with normal and forward-control models being listed for 1936. The heaviest of these was for 3 tons payload. Military 6×4 and 6×6 trucks were built during World War II, powered by Hercules engines. The post-war period saw updated light trucks for 1½ to 2 tons. It wasn't until 1962 that Studebaker really ventured into the heavy-duty market when the E45 19-ton gcw tractor unit, featuring the same cab as the lightweight 2-tonners, appeared. This had a 3.5 litre/213cu in 4-53 Detroit Diesel two-stroke engine delivering 130bhp. Gasoline-engined versions of these "heavies" were marketed as Studebaker Transtar, having the Power Star 4.2 litre/256cu in V8 delivering 170bhp at 4200rpm. The heavy-duty trucks were short-lived, the company ceasing truck production in 1964.

OTHER MAKES

■ SCOT

DEBERT, CANADA

The Atlantic Truck Manufacturing Company of Debert, Nova Scotia, entered the market in 1972 with the Scot conventional 6×4 tractor unit. It had a Cummins NTC335 engine and a Ford Louisville cab. By 1977 the company had developed its own cabs, including forward-control versions. Scot went on to diversify into specialist vehicles such as logging trucks, fire engines and aircraft refuellers. Some have gross train weights up to 180 tons, and power units include Detroit Diesel, Cummins and Caterpillar up to 600bhp.

■ SR

BRASOV, ROMANIA

Autocamioane Brasov began truck production in 1954 with the SR101 ("SR" is taken from Steagul Rosu or "Red Star" works at Brasov). Based on the Russian ZIL-150, the 101 was a ruggedly built 4-tonner powered by a 90bhp gasoline engine. The 101 was replaced by a more modern design in 1962 under the Bucegi and Carpati name. The emblem on the bonnets (hoods) of the new trucks was changed to AB (for "Autocamioane Brasov"). Since 1990 the company has been renamed Roman S.A. and currently manufactures DAC trucks. (See also "Bucegi", "DAC", and "Roman".)

■ BELOW *A 1950 SR 101 truck.*

MARIBOR, YUGOSLAVIA

TAM

■ LEFT *The Yugoslavian TAM 6½-ton dump truck is based on Magirus-Deutz technology.*

TAM (Tovarna Automobilov Maribor) trucks first appeared in 1947, being Czechoslovakian Pragas built under licence. Production of these carried on until the early 1960s but in the meantime, in 1957, an agreement was formed with Klockner Humboldt Deutz to manufacture Magirus-Deutz designs, including Deutz air-cooled diesels, under licence. Pragas were soon phased out. Models included 4×2, 4×4 and 6×6, the 4×4 and 6×6 being for both civilian and military use. In 1996 TAM became MPP Vozila d.o.o. after bankruptcy and a new group of 14 smaller companies owned by the Slovakian Government carries on the production of TAM trucks. The main selling truck is the TAM 90T-50 in both 4×2 and 4×4 form.

JAMSHEDPUR, INDIA

TATA

■ LEFT *The 1978 forward-control Tata LPT1210E grossed 12 tons and was powered by 4.8 litre/ 292cu in 6-cylinder diesel.*

■ BELOW *This hard-worked semi-forward-control 1210SK has similar mechanical specification to the LPT1210E above.*

The Tata Engineering & Locomotive Co. Ltd was established in 1945 to manufacture steam locomotives, but in 1954 the company entered into a collaborative agreement with Daimler-Benz of Germany to manufacture heavy commercial vehicles. By 1969 Telco had been fully established as a truck manufacturer in its own right, with an almost 100 per cent local content. Telco is the largest truck producer in India, building a complete range from 5 tonnes gvw up to 35 tonnes gcw. The company has plants at Pune, Lucknow and Dharwad, as well as its main plant at Jamshedpur. While Tata trucks are based largely on Mercedes designs, Telco has undertaken its own developments and also builds Cummins diesels under licence.

Tata trucks have used model designations similar to those of Mercedes-Benz. The LPS1516/32, for instance, was a forward-control tractor unit introduced in 1980. This had a tractor gvw of 15 tonnes and a 6-cylinder turbocharged diesel, designated the 697, developing 160bhp. The "32" indicates a gcw of 32 tonnes. Other popular models were the 1210SK, which featured an adaptation of Mercedes-Benz's semi-forward-control cab. Some models, like the LPT1210, have cabs of local design while others have adaptations of the Mercedes New Generation cab usually fitted with a two-piece windscreen. The current range hardly differs from that of the early 1980s, and consists of the LPT1613 (4×2), LPT2213 (6×4), LPT2416 (6×2), LPT2516 (6×4), LPS1616 tractor unit and the SK1613 and SE1613 semi-forward-control models. The heaviest six-wheeler is Cummins-powered.

KOPRIVNICE, CZECH REPUBLIC

TATRA

■ LEFT *The all-wheel drive Tatra T815 grosses 26 tonnes and has a choice of diesels up to 320bhp.*

■ BELOW *An 815 Jamal 6×6 36-tonne gvw dump truck with 360bhp V8 diesel.*

Tatra's origins lie in the Nesseldorfer Wagenbau-Fabriks-Gesellschaft formed in 1898 at Nesseldorf in Austria. The first Nesseldorfer or NW truck was built in 1899, a tiller-steered forward-control design with a rear-mounted Benz gasoline engine. NW's next truck, in 1915, was a 2-tonner featuring shaft drive. This was followed by a 4-tonner the following year. While both were to continue until the mid 1920s, those built after World War I were called Tatra. As a result of the war, Czechoslovakia had been formed, taking in the region of Austria where Nesseldorf stood. The town changed its name to Koprivnice.

A completely new concept in truck design came in 1925 with the introduction of Tatra's unique tubular "backbone" chassis with independently sprung, fully floating half axles. From 1935 these principles were applied to a heavy truck, the Type 24 six-wheeler for 10-tonne payloads.

In 1942 the first of Tatra's famous air-cooled V diesels was developed. These were built as V4, V6, V8 and V12. At the same time Tatra launched the legendary Type 111 six-wheeler that was to continue in production for 20 years. The 111 was designed for 20 tonnes gvw and took the 14.82 litre/904cu in V12 engine developing 150bhp. In 1957 it was joined by two new models with bold new styling, the 137 four-wheeler for 7 tonnes payload and the 138 6×4 for 12 tonnes. These both had the 11.75 litre/717cu in T928K V8 diesel with power ratings of 180 or 220bhp. All engines were air-cooled.

Tatra's next major launch was of the Type 813 all-wheel drive forward-control trucks. Currently Tatra offers a range of 75 models, including heavy tractors up to 85 tonnes. Also available are 4×4, 6×6 and 8×8 trucks with

gvws between 15 and 36 tonnes. In addition there are 4×2 and 6×4 trucks for on-highway use featuring day and sleeper cabs. Tatra-based Semex heavy trucks and crane chassis were also built in Dorsten, Germany, by Tatra's agents Semex, now called Tatra Deutschland GmbH.

BENSCHOP, THE NETHERLANDS

TERBERG

■ LEFT *A Terberg F2850 50-tonne gvw 10×4 concrete mixer with 12cu m/15.6cu yd drum.*

Automobielbedrijf en Machinenfabriek W.G. Terberg & Zn began by rebuilding ex-United States Army trucks, and from 1965 turned to building its own designs. As war-surplus parts diminished, Terberg began manufacturing some of its own units, such as axles, and then complete trucks. The first was a 6×6 dubbed the N800, and used a DAF diesel engine. This was followed by the 6×4 semi-forward-control SF1200 model featuring a Mercedes-Benz cab and diesel engine. The heavier SF1400 6×4 for 14-tonne payloads had a cab to Terberg's own design, but later models began to feature the Volvo N series cab. During the 1980s and '90s the company has offered a wide range of specialist trucks including 6×4, 8×4, 8×8, 10×4 and 10×8s. The company is now called Terberg Benschop BV.

BASINGSTOKE, ENGLAND

THORNYCROFT

One of the pioneers of the motor industry, John Isaac Thornycroft built his first steam van in 1896 at his Chiswick boatyard on the banks of the River Thames. It was powered by a lightweight marine engine with chain drive to the front wheels. Tiller-operated steering acted on the rear wheels. A new works was set up nearby to build road vehicles while Thornycroft's main business of boat-building continued. The Thornycroft Steam Wagon Co. of Chiswick soon outgrew itself, and a new factory was built at Basingstoke in 1898. In the meantime, improved designs of wagons for 3 and 4 tons had been developed and in 1898 Thornycroft built one of the world's first articulated goods vehicles.

■ RIGHT ***An 1899 Thornycroft 3-ton undertype steam wagon with vertical water tube boiler and a horizontal compound engine beneath the driver.***

■ RIGHT ***A 1935 Bulldog CE/GD4 4-ton truck powered by a 3.6 litre/219cu in 4-cylinder gasoline engine.***

■ BELOW ***This Trusty PF/NR6 eight-wheeler dates from 1953 and is powered by a 6-cylinder diesel engine.***

Their first gasoline-engined truck, a 4-tonner, appeared in 1902. By 1907 the company was pulling out of steam but a subsidiary, Stewart & Co. of Glasgow, continued to build some steamers up to 1910. World War I saw a significant increase in truck production when the firm's J type 3-ton War Office Subsidy models appeared. Some 5000 were built, powered by 40hp 4-cylinder gasoline engines. The X type 3-tonner of the 1920s was a derivative of the J type. A lighter model, the A type for 1½ to 2 tons, was introduced in 1923. This had pneumatic tyres and electric lighting.

From 1931 model identification was simplified by the use of names rather than letters. Among the truck models were the 2-ton Bulldog, the 2½-ton Speedy and the impressive 6½-ton Jupiter and Taurus with their long "snouted" bonnets (hoods) and set-back front axles. By 1933 diesel engines were becoming available on the heavier models.

One of Thornycroft's largest trucks of the mid 1930s was the 12-ton Stag six-wheeler. Officially designated the XE type, the Stag was a high-speed, long-distance 6×2 machine powered by a 100bhp 6-cylinder gasoline engine with 8-speed gearbox.

In 1934 the Trusty 7½ to 8-ton full forward-control four-wheeler was introduced, with a choice of a 4 or 6-cylinder Thornycroft diesel. Another significant model of the 1930s was the long-bonneted 6×4 Amazon used mainly as the basis for mobile cranes.

During World War II some 13,000 trucks were built for military service, as

■ LEFT *A 1960 Trident RG/CR6/1 for 12 tons gvw, powered by a 90bhp 6-cylinder diesel engine.*

■ BELOW *Dating from 1949, this Sturdy ZE/TR6 4-tonner has a 6-cylinder diesel engine.*

well as 2000 civilian models for essential users. Civilian production got going again from 1945, the main models being the Nippy 3-tonner, Sturdy 5/6-tonner and Trusty VF four, RF six and PF eight-wheelers for payloads of 8, 12 and 14 tons. The Sturdy, which had taken on a new look in the late 1930s, became available with a new indirect-injection 6-cylinder diesel. The Trusty also appeared in a new guise including an eight-wheeled version originally planned just before the war. This was powered by the NR6MV 7.88 litre/481cu in diesel engine developing 100bhp, but an alternative gasoline-injection power unit was also tried. This did not enter full production.

In 1948 the automotive side of John I. Thornycroft was renamed Transport Equipment (Thornycroft) Ltd to distinguish it from the boat-building division. An uprated Sturdy, the Sturdy Star, was announced in 1948, and over the next couple of years important new models included the Mighty Antar heavy tractor for up to 100 tons gtw. This was originally powered by an 18 litre/1098cu in Rover Meteorite Mk.101 V8 diesel developing 250bhp. It was fitted with twin radiators. Other models aimed at the export market were the bonneted Trident and Trusty.

Medium-weight vehicles like the Sturdy and Sturdy Star received a new-style Motor Panels Mk.1 cab in 1952. Along with their road-going trucks, Thornycroft offered a variety of heavy-duty specialized trucks mainly for the overseas market, such as the Nubian and Big Ben. The lightweight 4-ton Nippy Star of 1952 and the slightly heavier Sturdy Star were phased out in 1957 when the new Swift and Swiftsure were introduced.

Thornycroft vehicles were built almost entirely from in-house components, which meant that developing new models was costly. However, a new version of the Trusty eight-wheeler, the PK model with the higher powered 130bhp 9.8 litre/598cu in QR6MV diesel, was announced in 1956, entering production in 1957. Its cab resembled that of another new model, the Mastiff, which appeared shortly after in four and six-wheel form, plus a tractor unit. By 1960 Thornycroft were beginning to concentrate more on heavy-duty specialized trucks for military and export use, the main sellers in the UK being the Trusty eight-wheeler and Mastiff range.

In a declining market, Thornycroft were struggling to keep their large works productive, and in 1961 the company was taken over by the ACV Group which was the parent company of AEC. Very soon those models that competed with AECs were phased out and production turned to specialized trucks like the Nubian, Big Ben and Antar. ACV itself was taken over by Leyland. Leyland already owned Scammell, which they regarded as their special vehicles division, so it was almost inevitable that the Thornycroft and Scammell ranges would be rationalized. The last Thornycrofts were built not at the Basingstoke factory but at the Watford plant of Scammell, the Basingstoke plant having been sold off in 1969.

MAIDSTONE, ENGLAND

TILLING STEVENS

■ LEFT *A Tilling Stevens equipped with hand-operated tower wagon for overhead servicing.*

The old established Tilling Stevens company is probably remembered more for its buses than for its trucks. Beginning in 1897 as W. A. Stevens Electrical Engineers, they developed a gasoline-electric vehicle in 1906. In 1907 Stevens began an agreement with Hallford (J. & E. Hall of Dartford) to convert their gasoline trucks to gasoline electric. An important customer, Thomas Tilling, took over the Stevens company, ended the agreement with Hallford and renamed Stevens "Tilling Stevens Ltd". As well as buses, Tilling Stevens produced trucks for 2 and 4-ton payloads in both gasoline electric and conventional gasoline-engine form. These were based on the TS3 and TS4 chassis. Many TS3 models entered war service during World War I. Truck and bus production resumed after 1918, and during the 1920s a full range was on offer, payloads going up to 4 tons. The company sought new investment in 1930 and was refloated as T. S. Motors Ltd. In 1933 TSM acquired the Vulcan Motor & Engineering Co. of Southport, Lancashire, which was in receivership. This led to the production of Vulcan trucks at Maidstone from the late 1930s, using Vulcan's own gasoline engines or Perkins diesels. Although some Tilling Stevens trucks were built during World War II, the bulk of the company's production was concentrated on buses through to its takeover by the Rootes Group in 1949. Production of all models, including Vulcan, ceased in 1952.

MILWAUKEE, WISCONSIN, USA

TITAN

Between 1917 and about 1931 the Titan Truck & Trailer Co. built a variety of heavy trucks, the first being a 5-ton payload, solid-tyred model with a 4-cylinder gasoline engine. Lighter models appeared later for payloads of 1, 2 and 3 tons, powered by Buda engines. Production continued until the early 1930s.

APPENWEIER, GERMANY

TITAN

■ LEFT *Titan heavy-haulage tractors like this 8×8 are largely based on Mercedes engineering.*

Beginning in 1970, Titan GmbH has built heavy multi-axle crane chassis and special vehicles for logging, earthmoving and construction work. In 1977 a range of three and four-axled heavy tractors was launched mainly at the instigation of the German heavy-haulage concern, Schutz. The tractors, for train weights of up to 200 tonnes plus, are Mercedes-based. Titan re-engines standard Mercedes heavy trucks with 20 litre/1220cu in Mercedes OM 404N/A and 404A turbocharged V12 diesels of 420 to 525bhp and reinforces the chassis frames, suspension and axles. Titans are built in 6×6, 8×4, 8×6 and 8×8 drive configurations and carry the Mercedes "long" cab. MAN cabs are now used on certain models.

TOKYO, JAPAN

TOYOTA

■ BELOW ***The 1964 DA90 with gvw of 10.5 tonnes had a Toyota 2D 6-cylinder diesel developing 130bhp.***

■ BOTTOM ***The DA115 7-tonne truck grossed 11.5 tonnes and was powered by a 140bhp 6.5 litre/397cu in 6-cylinder diesel.***

While Toyota ranks among the world's largest motor manufacturers, its commercial vehicle range has, in recent years, been limited to light trucks. Production of medium to heavy trucks is left to its associate company, Hino. What was originally the Toyota Automatic Loom Works Ltd, based at Kariya City, began building light trucks in 1935. The first vehicle was a bonneted 1½-tonner. The company was re-formed into the Toyota Motor Co. Ltd in 1937, and production of lightweight trucks continued through to 1951 when their first medium-duty truck, the BX 4-tonner, appeared.

By the early 1960s larger normal and forward-control trucks for 5 to 6-tonne payloads were in production. These were available with a choice of gasoline or diesel power. The DA80 ("D" indicated "diesel") had a gvw of 9.5 tonnes, while the DA90 and DA95 grossed 10.5 tonnes. The power unit was Toyota's own 6.5 litre/397cu in 6-cylinder indirect-injection diesel with an output of 130bhp. The lighter DA80 had a 5.9 litre/360cu in version producing 110bhp. A 4.23 litre/258cu in 6-cylinder gasoline engine was available as an option on all models, and gasoline variants were the FA80, FA90 and FA95. A 4-tonner, the FC80, was only available with gasoline engine. A 6×6 truck, the ZDW15L, closely resembling a World War II United States Army design, was also available for a payload of 4.5 tonnes (on-highway) or 2.3 tonnes (off-highway).

From 1965 a new range with a completely restyled cab was available as the FA100 and FA115 (gasoline) and DA110, DA115 and DA116 (diesel). The DA range of diesel trucks had an increased gvw of 11.5 tonnes and a payload rating of 6.5 tonnes. The power output of the 6.5 litre/397cu in diesel was increased to 140bhp. A 5-speed synchromesh gearbox was standard and a 2-speed rear axle was optional. An unusual feature of Toyota trucks was the under-seat fuel tank that harked back to some American light trucks of the early 1930s. Production of the DA and FA continued into the mid 1980s, but since then Toyota have concentrated on light vans and pickups.

ST LOUIS, MISSOURI, USA

TRAFFIC

■ LEFT *This 1918 Traffic 2-ton forward-control truck used a Continental 4-cylinder gasoline engine and 3-speed gearbox.*

Formed in 1918, the Traffic Motor Corp. built a 1¾-ton four-wheel truck with a Continental 4-cylinder gasoline engine. Up to 1925 the appearance of the Traffic was quite distinctive, thanks to its rounded front and rear chassis crossmembers that served as bumpers. Solid tyres were standard, but pneumatics could be supplied to special order. In 1927 Traffic launched 2 and 3-ton models with more powerful 4.15 litre/253cu in Continental engines. By then the front and rear crossmembers were of conventional design. Production ended in 1929, and during that year a 4-tonner with 6-cylinder engine appeared briefly.

WARRINGTON, ENGLAND

TVW

■ LEFT *TVW trucks were developed from Sentinel designs.*

■ BELOW LEFT *This early TVW is a converted Sentinel fitted with a Gardner engine.*

Transport Vehicles (Warrington) Ltd was established in late 1957 to build a range of heavy-duty trucks largely based on Sentinel designs. Sentinel of Shrewsbury folded in 1957 and their main UK dealer, North Cheshire Motors Ltd, purchased the remaining vehicle and parts stocks to set up its own truck-building operation

under the TVW name. The range consisted of tractor units and six and eight-wheeled rigids in the 19 to 24 tons gvw bracket. Sentinel's practice of using horizontal diesel engines was abandoned and TVW offered a choice of Gardner, Meadows, Perkins, Leyland and Rootes diesels, the latter being the unusual 3-cylinder opposed-piston two-stroke used in Commer trucks. The trucks were fitted with proprietary cabs from Boalloy and a local coachbuilder, Williams of Grappenhall, Warrington. The best-selling TVWs were their rigid eight-wheeler and their 24-ton gcw tractor, but most sales were to associate companies that had helped raise finance for the venture. An estimated 100 trucks were built up to 1961 when the company closed.

PUTEAUX & TRAPPES, FRANCE

UNIC

The history of one of France's most famous truck manufacturers, Unic, began in 1905 when SA Etablissements Georges Richard was formed, but only light vehicles and taxi cabs were built through to the 1920s. It was then that a 3-tonne truck, the M5C, was introduced. By 1931 a range of heavier trucks for 6 to 11 tonnes payload was available. The largest model, the CD3, was a bonneted rigid six-wheeler powered by a licence-built Mercedes-Benz 6-cylinder 8.6 litre/525cu in diesel engine. "CD" stood for "Codra Diesel". CODRA was the Compagnie des Diesel Rapides, which held the licence for Mercedes diesels in France. In 1937 Unic introduced its own diesel engine – the first to be entirely designed and built in France. It was a 10.3 litre/629cu in indirect-injection 6-cylinder unit.

During World War II the company formed an association with Bernard, Delahaye, Laffly and Simca under a government-led plan called Groupement Français de l'Automobile (GFA). It was disbanded in 1951. From 1945 Unic offered their ZU range, which featured a stylish new semi-forward-control cab.

From 1952, faced with the need for new investment for modernization, Unic joined forces with Simca, which was formed in 1934. By 1958 Unic had become the Industrial Vehicle Division of Simca. Simca had also purchased the Ford France truck business. The Ford Cargo medium trucks were built alongside Unic heavy-duty trucks. In 1956 Unic, still under Simca ownership, was merged with Saurer France.

Four years later another administrative change took place when Simca de-merged their Automobile Division (which was assigned to Chrysler) and their Industrial Vehicle Division. From that point Unic only had

their heavy-duty range as Cargo production ceased. To fill the light to medium gap they marketed imported OM models from 4 to 7 tonnes gvw. The mid 1950s Unic range of heavies included their superbly designed "long-nosed" ZU94 Verdon and ZU122 Izoard of which there were many almost identical variants under other names like Auvergne and Tournalet. The

long-nosed cab was called the Longchamp while a new forward-control cab, introduced in 1960, was the Vincennes.

In 1966 Simca Industries was absorbed by Fiat France and there was increasing product exchange with the Italian parent. It was in 1960 that Unic introduced their M625 V8 diesel using Saurer fuel injection. In 1969 a higher-rated version, the 14.9 litre/909cu in V855 developing 340bhp, was announced. Between 1971 and 1973 production of Unic trucks was transferred from Puteaux to Trappes, and in 1975 it became part of the newly formed Iveco Group. The Unic name was phased out in the early 1980s.

■ TOP *An Izoard T270 38-tonne artic with 270bhp V8 diesel engine.*

■ ABOVE LEFT *The Unic Vercors dump truck grossed 17.8 to 18.2 tonnes with 5-cylinder or 6-cylinder diesel engine.*

■ LEFT *Latter-day Unics had the Iveco Group cab. This refrigerated van is virtually identical to a Fiat 110C.*

GAGGENAU, GERMANY

UNIMOG

■ LEFT *The 1998 Unimog 2540 artic is powered by a 240bhp Mercedes OM366-LA turbo diesel.*

Unimog's light 4×4 might be of marginal relevance in truck terms owing to its highly specialized nature, but it is worthy of mention in view of its legendary history. It has its origins in an all-terrain military design that was under development in the early part of World War II but finally emerged in 1948. In its more familiar guise it was developed by Gebr. Bohringer GmbH of Goppingen and was aimed at the agricultural industry. Unimog stands for Universal Motor Unit or UNIversat MOtor Gerat. It was powered by a Mercedes-Benz 1.7 litre/103cu in 4-cylinder diesel. In 1951 manufacturing rights passed to Daimler-Benz.

In 1954 a new model appeared as the Unimog S powered by a Mercedes 2.2 litre/134cu in 6-cylinder gasoline engine. The versatility of the Unimog was explored to the full during the 1970s and '80s with heavier models up to 9 tonnes gvw, powered by diesels up to 200bhp, capable of gross train weights of 50 tonnes plus. There were countless variants, such as road/rail shunters, long-wheelbase self-loaders and 6×6 fire appliances. Currently there is a heavy-duty Unimog 2540 articulated version for a gcw of 31 tonnes. This is powered by a 5.9 litre/360cu in OM366-LA turbocharged diesel developing 240bhp.

LONDON, ENGLAND

UNION

■ LEFT *Union ballast tractors were built and operated exclusively by the Union Cartage Company.*

In the late 1930s the Union Cartage Company of London required a rugged ballast tractor to haul meat-container trailers and, unable to find an off-the-shelf model, it decided to build its own. Some 42 tractors were built in total, all powered by Gardner 5LW diesel engines. Many Union tractors survived in operation well into the 1960s.

PERIVALE & WATFORD, ENGLAND

UNIPOWER

■ RIGHT *A 1972 Unipower 4×4 tractor unit with Motor Panels cab and Perkins V8 diesel engine.*

Universal Power Drives was formed in 1934 with its head office at Aldwych, London, and a factory in Perivale, Middlesex. It specialized in Unipower third-axle conversions. In 1937 Unipower introduced a 4×4 timber tractor which was produced in large numbers during World War II when the UK government stepped up timber production. The Forester tractor was built along similar lines to the French Latil. It had a 4-cylinder Gardner 4LW oil engine. In the late 1940s a 5LW-powered Hannibal was introduced. Production continued until 1968 and, in the meantime, a short-lived Centipede four-wheel steer version was introduced in 1956.

In 1972 Unipower switched to building a forward-control 4×4 called the Invader, powered by a choice of

■ LEFT *An Alvis-Unipower HET 8×8 heavy tank transporter powered by a Cummins SQK 19 litre/1158cu in 750bhp diesel.*

■ BELOW *A 1952 Unipower Hannibal 4×4 timber tractor powered by an 85bhp Gardner 5LW diesel.*

Perkins V8 or Cummins V8 diesel. This was aimed at on/off-road, fire-fighting, municipal and construction use. A heavier model with Motor Panels cab and a choice of Rolls Royce gasoline or Cummins NTF365 diesel was also offered. The company was taken over by AC Cars in 1977, and production moved to Thames Ditton in Surrey. With the closure of Scammell Lorries in May 1988, Unipower set up a new factory at Watford to carry on production and servicing of certain Scammell trucks. It soon introduced new models like the C series heavy-haulage tractor and a range of military trucks. In 1994 Unipower became part of Alvis PLC, and continues to build a range of specialist heavy trucks.

■ BELOW RIGHT *Ural 6×6 trucks can be supplied for both civilian and military duties.*

MIASS, RUSSIA

URAL

In 1942 part of the ZIS (Zavod Imieni Stalina) operations was relocated to a shadow factory at Miass in the Chelyabinsk Region of the Ural mountains to ensure continuity of production if the Moscow plant suffered war damage. The trucks were called Ural-ZIS, the Ural-ZIS 5 being a 3-tonner. Production carried on after the war. The trucks were now simply called Ural.

In 1961 the first of Ural's own designs appeared as the 375D 5-tonne 6×6. A ZIL 7 litre/427cu in V8 gasoline engine was fitted. In 1964 a heavier-duty 6×4 7-tonne 377 appeared with a V8 diesel. These trucks continued in production with little change, but recently Ural has developed its own engines and also uses Kamaz diesels. The heaviest Ural is the 9-tonne payload off-road 5323 8×8 military truck, which is available with a Kamaz or Ural's own air-cooled diesel with power ratings up to 320bhp.

PORTSMOUTH, ENGLAND

USG-PITT

■ LEFT *The rear end of the USG-Pitt front-wheel drive truck could be lowered to facilitate loading.*

The USG-Pitt R35 front-wheel drive low-loading truck was designed and built between 1964 and 1967. It was based on the Bedford RLC1 and had a gvw of 9.5 tons and a wheelbase of 5m/16.5ft. It had a 5.4 litre/330cu in, 107bhp 6-cylinder Bedford diesel and a 4-speed gearbox coupled to a transfer box that took the drive forward to a Bedford steer-drive axle. Only a small number were built, and the truck was aimed at operators such as electricity-generating companies. The rear end of the load platform could be lowered to form a ramp on to which cable drums or similar loads could easily be winched. It was a joint development of United Services Garages, a Bedford truck main dealer, and Pitt Trailers Ltd.

GOTHENBURG, SWEDEN

VOLVO

■ ABOVE *With Sweden's generous length limits, bonneted tractors like this N88 were popular in their home country.*

■ LEFT *Until the 1960s nearly all Volvos were bonneted, such as this early 1950s L220 4-tonner.*

The two men behind the formation of Volvo, economist Assar Gabrielsson and engineer Gustaf Larsen, both spent part of their careers at Svenska Kulgerfabriken, better known as SKF, the famous Swedish ball-bearing manufacturer. "Volvo" is Latin for "I roll", and a company of that name had been formed as a subsidiary of SKF in 1915. Assar Gabrielsson secured the rights to the dormant company in 1926.

Volvo avoided the high overheads of in-house component manufacture by sub-contracting their work to established firms like Pentaverken (the Penta Engineering Works) of Skövde. Penta produced Volvo's car and truck engines from the outset, and in 1931 Volvo took the company over, renaming it AB Volvo-Pentaverken in 1935. Likewise, gearbox and rear-axle gearing were farmed out to Köpings Mekaniska Verkstad at Köpings. When pressed-steel cabs became standard, Volvo turned to Olofströms Stålpressings AB (the Olofström Pressed Steel Co.).

Within a year of building its first car, Volvo introduced a 1½-tonne bonneted truck, the LV40 – the "LV" signified "Lastvagen" (or "Lorry"). In 1929 a larger LV60 2-tonner appeared, powered by a new 6-cylinder side-valve 3.0 litre/183cu in gasoline engine reminiscent of American designs. An even larger 4.1 litre/250cu in "six" was produced for the heavier-duty LV66/67 which, with a 6×2 layout, took the gvw up to 9 tonnes. A short-lived forward-control model (it was really a semi-forward), the L75 Bulldog, appeared in 1932 and about 250 were built before the model was withdrawn in 1935.

Several new truck models appeared during 1935. The LV81, 83 and 93, the heaviest being a 4-tonner, replaced the LV71, 73 and 68, and the new models took on a streamlined cab with a grille covering the radiator. The front axle was set back more giving them a more

■ BELOW *In the medium-weight class the L465 with a 4.7 litre/287cu in 6-cylinder diesel was an important seller in the 1960s.*

modern appearance and improved weight distribution. Around the same time a Hesselman type "diesel" engine was offered as an alternative power unit. The Hesselman principle, also tried out briefly by Scania, enabled a low-compression gasoline engine to run on cheap fuel oil by using a combination of fuel injection and spark ignition.

Wartime fuel shortages led to the development of producer gas units. While most had the gas equipment mounted behind the cab where it robbed load space, some had a peculiar contraption in the form of a trolley pushed along ahead of the front bumper. At a time when most British and European manufacturers were adopting austerity pattern wartime cabs, Volvo did the opposite, introducing a new rounded radiator grille and front-end pressings with more flowing lines in 1940. This was to become Volvo's new face of the post-war years on such models as the LV140 and LV150 5-tonners.

In the immediate post-war era Volvo began stepping up their exports and, during the early 1950s, had established outlets in Africa, South America, Cuba, the Middle East, Spain, Turkey, Greece and most of the European countries. Volvo were poised for even bigger expansion on the world stage. There were heavier-duty models under development. Heavier trucks, still of bonneted layout, appeared in 1951 as the L395 Titan. "L" now stood for "Lastbil", the commonly used Swedish word for "truck". A further styling improvement distinguished the new models – the bonnet (hood) was wider and the wider grille had vertical slats. Powering the L395 was the new D96AS, a 9.6 litre/588cu in, 130/150bhp 6-cylinder direct-injection diesel that bore some similarity to the British AEC 9.6. Gross weight in 4×2 form was 14 tonnes, while six-wheeler models grossed 19 tonnes. A turbocharged version appeared in 1954, providing 185bhp.

In 1953 came the L385 Viking of similar appearance but powered by the D67, 6.7 litre/409cu in diesel developing 115bhp. This had a gvw of 12.5 tonnes or 16 tonnes in three-axle form.

In the early 1960s Volvo stepped up its sales drive in Europe, but it was clear that most operators required forward-control trucks. Volvo had steered clear of cabovers, but in 1962 it set aside such reservations and launched its tilt-cab Tip Top models. Mechanically these were developed from the bonneted Raske, Viking and Titan, and had the designations L475, L485 and L495.

Just one year later Volvo unveiled its most famous range, the System 8. The prefix "F" for "forward control" or "N" for "normal control" was used, followed by "85", "86" or "88" according to the model. The System 8 concept was based on the eight components that underwent major renewal: engine, gearbox, rear axle, frame, steering, brakes, suspension

■ ABOVE LEFT *Rigid eight-wheelers such as this 1978 F731 were developed and built at Irvine in Scotland.*

■ ABOVE RIGHT *Tilt-cab forward-control System 8 trucks enabled Volvo to expand its European sales.*

■ RIGHT *This 1973 F88 artic with TIR tilt trailer was used on international service from the UK.*

and cab. The new range was an overwhelming success and really put Volvo on the world map. In 1964 Volvo acquired Gösta Nyström's Karosserifabrik at Umea, which became its cab plant. In 1969 the Volvo Truck Division was formed as an autonomous operation.

In the UK the F86 and F88 were received with great enthusiasm after an agent was appointed in the person of one-time haulage contractor Jim McKelvie of Glasgow. He set up Ailsa Trucks and within about three years Volvo held a commanding position in the UK heavy truck market. A Scottish assembly plant was set up in 1972 and was responsible for developing and building Volvo's first F86 rigid eight-wheelers, although similar models were being launched in Australia around the same time. By now Volvo was establishing other overseas assembly plants. Alsemberg in Belgium had started assembling in 1951 and the main Ghent plant opened in 1965. Assembly got underway in Peru in 1966. Brazilian assembly began in 1980, followed later by a plant in Morocco. The Volvo-White Truck Corporation was formed in 1981 when Volvo bought the ailing White business. In 1986 it took over the GM heavy truck division.

The N86 and N88 still featured the old-style bonneted cab dating back to the early 1950s, but in 1973 new normal-control models appeared as the N7, N10 and N12. In 1971 Volvo became part of the Euro Truck Development Group known as the Club of Four in association with Magirus-Deutz, DAF and Saviem. The result was a new cab that became familiar on the F4 and F6 range announced in 1975. The F7 followed in 1978. The next important new model range was the F10 and F12, the latter having the TD120 engine with power ratings from 330 to 385bhp. These appeared in 1977. Improvements in cab comfort took high priority over the coming years and the superbly equipped Globetrotter became a trendsetter in 1983.

Since then Volvo has maintained its pacesetting image with the FH in 1993 and, more recently, the FM that was launched in 1998. The FM features a lowered version of the FH cab. FH models have newly engineered low-emission diesels. Power outputs range from 240 to 520bhp. A bonneted adaptation of the new model, the NH, is produced in Brazil while another, the aerodynamically styled VN is marketed as a Class 8 truck in the United States where truck assembly is carried out in Dublin, Virginia. VN engine options include Volvo, Cummins, Caterpillar and Detroit Diesel.

In August 1999 Volvo announced a takeover bid for Scania, but the takeover was blocked by the European Union Competition Authorities.

■ ABOVE LEFT *The FH Globetrotter is Volvo's top-of-the-range European truck.*

■ ABOVE RIGHT *The FM is an important seller in the distribution vehicle market.*

■ LEFT *This VN-hauled B-train in Canada has a Caterpillar 525 diesel engine and grosses 63 tonnes.*

OTHER MAKES

■ VANAJA

HELSINKI, FINLAND

Vanajan Autotehdas Oy of Helsinki was once a body-building company and began building trucks around 1943 when it was merged into Sisu (Oy Suomen Autoteollisuus) to manufacture military trucks under the Yhteissisu name. After the war the two companies were de-merged and Vanaja became a make in its own right. Initially it produced medium-weight trucks with a 6-cylinder 5.0 litre/305cu in gasoline engine. During 1954 it began offering a diesel which then became standard.

As the range expanded, Vanaja formed an agreement with the British AEC company which supplied it with engines. Trucks included 4×2, 4×4 and 6×4 tractor units that offered extra traction to cope with Finland's severe road conditions. The 6×4s were driven on the front and the first rear axle – in effect a 4×4 with a trailing third axle. After AEC was absorbed into Leyland in 1962 some forward-control Vanaja trucks were fitted with the Leyland Ergomatic cab. One such model was the TTB 8×4 crane chassis. In 1967 Vanaja was taken over by its former partner Sisu.

■ VERHEUL

WADINXVEEN, THE NETHERLANDS

Verheul was originally a coachbuilder and in 1961 it acquired Kromhout of Amsterdam who were truck manufacturers. Verheul continued production of some Kromhout models, but introduced a new range of normal and forward-control cabs. These carried a large "V" motif on the grille. Both were taken over by the British ACV Group in 1960, and greater emphasis was placed on bus models. Truck sales were limited and the range was withdrawn in 1965.

■ VOMAG

PLAUEN, GERMANY

Vogtlandische Maschinenfabrik AG once specialized in printing and textile machinery, but in 1915 it began building chain-drive 3 and 4-tonne trucks. Some were also built with shaft drive. After the war a 1.5-tonne truck was the main production model until the mid 1920s when a comprehensive truck range for payloads of 3, 4, 5, 6 and 7 tonnes was offered. Four-cylinder gasoline engines were the standard, but from 1930 Vomag built diesel engines. Some impressive bonneted trucks appeared up to the outbreak of war, including a 9-tonne six-wheeler with 140bhp diesel. Production ceased in 1939.

■ VULCAN

MAIDSTONE, ENGLAND

Vulcan's history began at Southport, Lancashire in 1907, as the Vulcan Motor & Engineering Co. Ltd. It turned to building light trucks in 1914. In the early 1920s a variety of models ranging from 1½ to 4 tons payload was available. A light-weight articulated model appeared in 1922.

Financial difficulties, resulting from a couple of unsuccessful joint ventures, contributed to the company's collapse in 1931. In receivership, it continued to offer a small range in the 1½-ton to 4-ton payload bracket, while a 5/6-ton forward-control model was added in 1934. The option of a Dorman or Gardner diesel engine was also offered. Owing to persisting financial problems, the company was taken over in 1938 by Tilling Stevens Ltd. It was relocated to Maidstone in Kent and renamed Vulcan Motors Ltd.

From then on a new forward-control range appeared, but full production was interrupted by the war. Vulcan was allowed to build limited numbers of 6-tonners for essential civilian users. After the war it resumed full production, the range including the 6VF (gasoline) and 6PF (Perkins P6 diesel) 6-tonners in short and long-wheelbase form, plus a tractor unit. Tilling Stevens was taken over by the Rootes Group in 1950. The same year a new range for 7-ton payloads was launched, the 7GF with Gardner 4LW engine. These had a new cab design. However, under Rootes' ownership Vulcan was phased out in 1952.

■ TOP ***Finnish Vanaja trucks were generally powered by AEC diesel engines.***

■ ABOVE ***1927 Vulcan VSD 2-tonner powered by Vulcan's own design of 4-cylinder gasoline engine.***

■ ABOVE ***This Perkins P6-engined Vulcan 6PF dropside truck dates from 1948.***

VOORHEESVILLE, NEW YORK, USA

WALTER

■ BELOW *Cummins-engined Walter type ACU 4×4 Snow Fighter had unique drive system with automatic differential locks.*

Walter specialized from the outset in 4×4 trucks. Its founder was William Walter, a Swiss engineer who emigrated to New York in 1883. He began by making confectionery machinery, but in 1898 turned his talents to motor cars. The first Walter truck was made in 1909, and this formed the basis for his first 4×4 of 1911. The early trucks had a dashboard radiator and "coal scuttle" bonnet (hood) reminiscent of the old Renault and Latil designs. Some conventional rear-wheel drive versions were also built. Until 1920 Walter built its own gasoline engines, but later used Waukesha units. The heaviest truck went up to 7 tons payload. By the mid 1920s the trucks began to take on their distinctive snout with the front axle set back under the cab – a Walter trademark for much of its history. In 1929 the first Snow Fighter snow-clearance truck was launched, and during the '30s the company diversified into specialized fire appliances, concrete trucks, articulated dump trucks and logging outfits. Some 4×4 medium artillery tractors were supplied to the army during World War II. Over the past five decades Walter has remained a major force in the specialized all-wheel drive market, building a wide range of snowploughs, crash tenders and similar machines, some with power ratings up to 540bhp.

ELMIRA, NEW YORK, USA

WARD LAFRANCE

Although Ward LaFrance became a prominent manufacturer of fire appliances, it has no direct business connection with American LaFrance except that it was formed by a member of the same family in Elmira, New York. Ward LaFrance was set up in 1918, some 13 years after American LaFrance, and built trucks from 2½ to 7 tons payload capacity powered by 4-cylinder Waukesha gasoline engines. A 6-cylinder model was added in 1926. During the 1930s much heavier trucks entered the scene, many being custom-built bonneted heavy tractors. Ward LaFrance was among the earliest American companies to offer diesel power using Cummins engines.

During World War II the company specialized in building 6×6 heavy wreckers, as well as 6×4 and 6×6 Cargo trucks. A new range of on-highway trucks appeared in 1945, the handsome bonneted D series for up to 30 tons gcw. By the mid 1950s more emphasis was being put on fire appliances, which had first been available in the pre-war period. Trucks were discontinued from about 1956, production being given over entirely to fire vehicles and airport crash tenders. In the late 1970s heavy-duty 8×8 trucks were supplied to the United States Army, powered by 600bhp diesels. During the '80s the company continued building fire appliances but, after financial losses, it closed in 1993.

KELOWNA, CANADA

WESTERN STAR

Since 1981 Western Star has been a make in its own right, but it began as an offshoot of White Trucks in 1968 when that company launched a new model aimed at the West Coast market. White Western Star 4900 conventionals soon earned a reputation for ruggedness and reliability in the United States and in Canada where White had set up the production plant at Kelowna, British Columbia. When White collapsed in 1980 and was taken over by Volvo Trucks in 1981, the deal did not include Western Star and the division was re-formed into Western Star Trucks Inc, owned by two Calgary-based companies. As well as the familiar conventionals, some cabover Western Stars were built featuring the White Road Commander cab.

By 1990 the company was experiencing another downturn and it was bought by Australian, Terrence Peabody. Under new ownership, sweeping improvements were introduced plus new models for on/off-highway duties. More engine options were added, including the Detroit Diesel 60 Series. In the early 1990s Western Stars were assembled at a plant in Queensland, Australia, where new models were developed especially for the Australian and New Zealand markets. The company reached an agreement with DAF of The Netherlands to market Western Stars through DAF dealers, and some technical collaboration led to the production of a small number of Western Star 1000 Series rigid eight-wheelers with DAF 95 cabs when Western Star couldn't offer its own cabovers.

During the 1990s the company saw a remarkable turnaround, and in 1996 it acquired the British ERF concern as well as Orion Bus Industries of New York and Ontario. In the same year it launched its new Class 8 Constellation series. All manufacture is now located at Kelowna, apart from the British-built Western Star Commander cabovers based on the ERF EC that were launched in 1997. In February 2000 Western Star sold ERF to MAN of Germany. As well as its wide range of heavy-duty trucks, Western Star produces military trucks for the Canadian government.

■ ABOVE *Constellation 4964FX B-train for bulk cement transport in Canada.*

■ LEFT *The Commander 8×4 features an ERF EC cab.*

■ BELOW *5964 dump truck features aerodynamic cab styling.*

CLEVELAND, OHIO, USA

WHITE

■ LEFT *This 6×4 tractor is a good example of White's stylish WA and WB conventional models of the 1940s era.*

■ BELOW *Between 1932 and 1955 Labatt's Streamliners became legendary. This one is based on a 1948 WA122 with Mustang 6-cylinder gasoline engine.*

Under the curious title of the White Sewing Machine Co., this company built its first commercial in 1901, a light car-based van nicknamed the "Pie Wagon". Prototype steam trucks for 3 and 5 tons payload were built around 1906 but went no further than White's own transport fleet where they spent some years in service. The company's origins can be traced back to 1859 when Thomas Howard White formed his sewing machine company. His son, Rollin H. White, travelled to Europe to observe the developing car industry. He was particularly impressed by Leon Serpollet's flash tube boiler, and on his return home began work on a modified version which he installed in the first White steam car of 1898.

Production got underway in 1900, and by 1906 the White Co. was formed as a separate entity to build cars and trucks. In 1910 White turned from steam to gasoline power and built its first real heavy truck, the bonneted GTA 3-tonner with 30hp engine and chain drive. Lighter models for 1½ tons also appeared. In 1912 the TC 5-tonner was introduced. Both the GTA and TC continued in production until 1918.

During World War I the United States Army ordered 18,000 military trucks for the Allied Forces in Europe. Some organizational changes took place in this period and the name was changed to the White Motor Co.

The first 6-cylinder gasoline truck appeared in 1928 as the Model 59, and was for a 3 to 4-ton payload. Three-axle variants of the heaviest model were introduced in 1930 for a payload of 10 tons. In 1932 White purchased the Indiana Truck Corp. of Marion, Indiana, from the Brockway Motor Truck Co., and production was transferred to Cleveland. The same year White became involved with Studebaker Pierce Arrow, assembling Pierce Arrows at Cleveland until 1934.

The most striking model of the period was White's first cabover, the heavy-duty 730 of 1935, which was powered by a 7.6 litre/464cu in version of an 8.3 litre/506cu in opposed-piston horizontal 12-cylinder gasoline engine first tried in buses in 1932. The fully rated 8.3 litre/506cu in was offered later. Despite its impressive specification, the 730 series did not attract many sales due to poor economy and reliability. Subsequent forward-control vehicles, like the 800 series, used in-line-six engines. The 800s appeared in 1937 and were White's first truly competitive cabovers, some of which featured tilt cabs.

During World War II much of White's production was given over to military vehicles, including 6×4 and 6×6 trucks. A replacement for the 700 and 800 series appeared in 1940 as the WA in both normal and forward control. Normal-control WA models were succeeded by the WB just after the war, although these were of very similar specification. In 1949 a further development of the WA and WB appeared as the WC, and this bonneted range was to become one of White's best-sellers during the 1950s. White's next new model was the memorable 3000 with its futuristic styling. The bulbous set-forward cab was equipped with a motorized tilting system. These were built mainly as gasoline-engined trucks as those fitted with diesels suffered cooling problems owing to the design, which featured a flat cab floor and a set-back engine. The 3000s aerodynamic appearance was timeless, but it was an expensive cab to produce and repair. It was eventually replaced by the 1500 series which went to the other extreme, having a box-like appearance similar to that of the Mack MB.

In 1951 White formed an agreement with the Freightliner Corporation to sell and service its trucks as White Freightliner. This arrangement continued until 1977. White was very profitable in the 1950s and was able to take over a

number of other makes, the first of which was Sterling, in 1951. Some trucks were sold as Sterling-Whites up until 1953. The same year, White took over Autocar. Autocar survived as a make in its own right within the White organization.

Reo Motors was the next acquisition, in 1957. The following year Diamond T was acquired and was soon merged with Reo leading to the Diamond-Reo marque. New designs of White's own trucks continued to appear, like the fibreglass-cabbed forward-control 5000 series of 1959. This signified the continuing trend towards cabovers, to maximize trailer lengths under the prevailing United States limits. Diesel engines became standard on the 5000. With a 124cm/50in BBC, it could haul 12.2m/40ft semis.

Meanwhile, longer bonneted trucks were announced in 1966 as part of the 4000 series, and in 1968 White formed Western Star to serve the West Coast market. White Western Star conventionals were built in a new plant at Kelowna in British Columbia, Canada. In the early 1970s White started converting Cummins diesels to run on gasoline, calling them White Giesels, but they proved unsuccessful. Instead White bought in diesels from Detroit, Cummins and Caterpillar.

During the remainder of the 1970s White over-committed itself with big investments in new factories. Production was transferred to New River Valley, Virginia, in 1975 and only a year earlier a new plant at Ogden, Utah had been commissioned to build the Autocar. There was also heavy investment in a planned new model range. This level of commitment, combined with a downturn in the market, led the company into financial difficulties in 1980. White went into liquidation and in August 1981 became part of Volvo as the Volvo White Truck Corporation.

Volvo White continued to market White trucks and even introduced new models. In 1983 the successor to the Road Boss appeared as the White Conventional with a longer bonnet (hood). The Road Commander 2 was also revamped, becoming the White High Cabover. These now carried the Volvo diagonal stripe on their grilles. In 1987 came the droop-snoot Aero plus an extended sleeper for the long-nosed conventional. As Volvo's influence increased, its engines and drivelines were introduced, as they also were on Autocar. Eventually the White name disappeared, and from 1995 all the trucks were badged Volvo.

■ TOP *By the early 1990s White had become WhiteGMC, most models having an all-Volvo driveline.*

■ ABOVE *The tilt-cab 3000 series became a market leader in the 1950s.*

■ LEFT *Following a marketing agreement, Freightliner trucks were sold as White Freightliner from 1951–77.*

NANTERE, FRANCE

WILLÈME

■ BELOW ***During the 1970s Willème concentrated more on the production of heavy-haulage tractors like this 8×4. Engines included Detroit Diesel, Mercedes and Cummins.***

Etablissement Willème of Neuilly, Seine, was set up in 1919 to recondition ex-United States Army Class B Liberty trucks in the aftermath of World War I. There were large numbers of the 5-ton workhorses left over from the hostilities, and they were refurbished and sold to civilian customers as Liberty-Willème. Various improvements were later introduced, including pneumatic tyres and the fitment of more powerful engines. By 1930 there were Liberty-Willème 4×2 dump trucks for 7½-tonne payloads and 6×2 conversions for payloads up to 12 tonnes. Later, some models were fitted with CLM-built Junkers opposed-piston diesels.

From about 1930 Willème began manufacturing its own designs under the Willème name badge, the first being a 1-tonner. By 1935 heavier trucks appeared for payloads of 8 to 15 tonnes in both normal and forward control. After World War II Willème built some massive heavy-haulage tractors, including 8×4s for up to 150 tonnes gtw.

In 1962 Willème formed a joint agreement with AEC, under which AEC supplied it with diesel engines. Some models also featured a high degree of AEC technology in their chassis and running units. After AEC was absorbed into Leyland in 1962, Leyland curtailed AEC's technical collaboration with other manufacturers and, instead, Willème began producing BMC trucks under licence. These were badged Willème-BMC. In 1965 financial problems led to the closure of Willème but a manufacturing licence was granted to Pinez et Raimond, who developed a range of massive heavy-haulage tractors for gross train weights as high as 1000 tonnes. These were renamed PRP from 1978.

■ LEFT ***The early 1960s Willème 38-tonne gcw artic was powered by an AEC AV690. It featured a ZF gearbox and Willème's Horizon cab.***

OTHER MAKES

■ WABCO

PEORIA, ILLINOIS, USA

Though Wabco has not built on-highway trucks in the normally accepted sense, the company is worthy of mention as the builder of some of the world's largest dump trucks. Wabco was formed in 1956 by the Combustion Equipment Division of the Westinghouse Air Brake Company. In 1953 Westinghouse took over the Le Tourneau Co. which was an old established manufacturer of earth-moving equipment, forming the Le Tourneau-Westinghouse Co., which began building dump trucks under the Haulpak name. This became Wabco from 1958.

The colossal off-highway dump trucks, like the 320B, for the mining industry can carry up to 235 tons and are powered by GM EMD 127 litre/7620cu in V12 two-stroke diesels developing 2475bhp. The drive is transmitted to the ground by hub-mounted electric traction motors. The main engine has a compressed-air starter motor and the vehicle, which has an all-up weight of 393 tons, is carried on hydro-pneumatic suspension. Access to the cab is up a nine-rung ladder. Wabco has since become part of the Komatsu D Corp.

■ WICHITA

WICHITA FALLS, TEXAS, USA

Between 1911 and 1932 the Wichita Motor Co., later renamed the Wichita Falls Motor Co., built a range of trucks of between 1½ and 5 tons payload capacity powered by Waukesha gasoline engines and using their own axles as well as Timken's.

■ WOLSELEY

BIRMINGHAM, ENGLAND

Wolseley's early designs, from its formation in 1901 as the Wolseley Tool & Motor Car Co., were the work of Herbert Austin, who left in 1905 to set up the Austin Motor Co. A varied range appeared in the early years, the largest being a 4-ton army truck with a 4-cylinder horizontal engine. J. D. Siddeley took over in 1908 and a vertical-engined Wolseley-Siddeley was introduced. An X-type chain-drive 3½-tonner also went into production, but by 1908 Wolseley-Siddeley abandoned trucks. In 1912 J. D. Siddeley moved on and Wolseley resumed production. By the start of World War I, it was offering 1½ and 4-ton subsidy types for the War Office. Wolseley were no longer in the market from 1919.

■ **ABOVE RIGHT** ***A Wolseley 1½-ton truck from around 1912, with shaft drive and 4-cylinder gasoline engine.***

■ **RIGHT** ***Among the largest trucks in the world is this Wabco 3200B, with a 235-ton payload capacity powered by a GM EMD V12 of 2475bhp.***

YAROSLAVI, RUSSIA

YAZ

YAZ were the forerunners of KrAZ, their history dating back to 1925, when production began of their 3-tonne YA-3 powered by an AMO gasoline engine. In 1928 the YA-3 was replaced by the YA-4, powered by a Mercedes-Benz 6-cylinder gasoline engine. An even heavier truck, the YA-5 for 4.5 tonnes appeared in 1929. Between 1925 and 1945 YAZ were known simply as YA. After World War II they became YAZ or sometimes YAAZ. The range was extended to include trucks for payloads of 7 to 12 tonnes. The trucks were of simple but rugged construction and included all-wheel drive 6×6 variants popular as dump trucks. Power units were largely 6-cylinder diesels. From 1959 truck production was transferred to a new factory at Kremenchug and the trucks were renamed KrAZ (from Kremenchug Auto Zavod). The YAZ plant concentrated on diesel engine production for KrAZ and was renamed YAMZ (Yaroslaviski Motornoi Zavod).

LEEDS, ENGLAND

YORKSHIRE

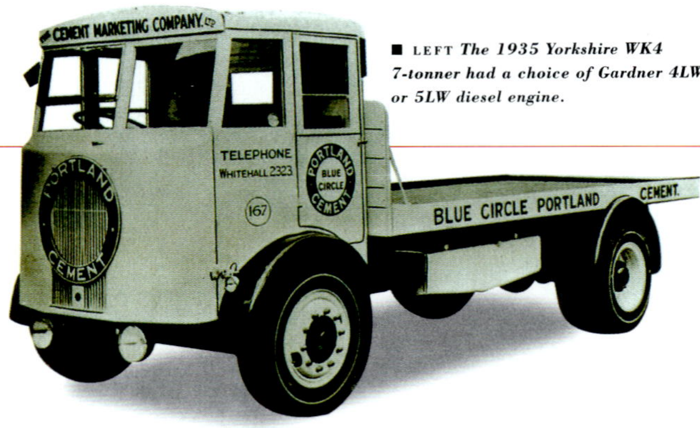

■ LEFT *The 1935 Yorkshire WK4 7-tonner had a choice of Gardner 4LW or 5LW diesel engine.*

As its name clearly implies, the Yorkshire Patent Steam Wagon Co. Ltd, formed in 1903, was concerned only with the building of steam wagons. Its speciality was the patented double-ended transverse locomotive boiler, which had a central fire-box. This unusual arrangement, which overcame the limited loadspace problem associated with locomotive boilers, was to be used by the company through to the end of steam-wagon production in 1937. Aware that steam was losing out, Yorkshire began considering a gasoline-engined truck as early as 1912.

In 1933 it built a forward-control 6-ton payload four-wheeler powered by a Dorman Ricardo 4-cylinder diesel. This was the first WK model, and Yorkshire offered it with a standard crash gearbox or a Wilson pre-selector. One of the problems that faced steamer drivers transferring to diesel trucks was their lack of gear-changing skills and the Wilson gearbox made a diesel easier in this respect. In 1935 a Gardner 6LW-engined six-wheeler for a 12-ton payload appeared, and the following year came an even larger 15-ton payload rigid eight-wheeler, the WK6. This had a Gardner 6LW, David Brown gearbox and Kirkstall rear axles. However, sales of Yorkshire diesels were limited and production ended in 1938. The company continued to trade after World War II, supplying municipal bodywork on various makes of chassis.

NANJING, CHINA

YUEJIN

■ RIGHT *A late 1970s Yuejin NJ23A 4×4 truck for 4.8-tonne gvw powered by a 6-cylinder gasoline engine.*

The Yuejin 2.6-tonner was a long-running make of Chinese truck built in 4×2 form for civilian duties and as a 4×4, restricted to 1.6 tonnes payload, for military and civilian use. Production of the 4×2 NJ130 began as long ago as 1958, the truck being a copy of the old Russian GAZ-51. The NJ230 entered production in 1965. An NJ230 with winch was also built as the NJ230-A.

TULSA, OKLAHOMA, USA

ZELIGSON

■ LEFT *A Zeligson 6×6 forms the basis for this recovery vehicle powered by a Cummins diesel.*

This company was formed in 1946 by ex-serviceman Samuel Zeligson and two colleagues to refurbish war-surplus trucks for civilian use. All-wheel drive conversions were also carried out on 4×2 and 6×2 trucks for off-road use. Zeligson's founder also formed CCC, the Crane Carrier Corporation, which built specialized construction and concrete mixers. In the 1960s and '70s Zeligson built special trucks for the oil and mining industries using a variety of military and proprietary components, including Detroit Diesel two-stroke engines. In 1980 the company was sold to a new owner, who carried on a similar business on a small scale until finally closing down in 1989.

MOSCOW, RUSSIA

ZIL

■ LEFT *A 1985 ZIL 4331 artic for a 14-tonne payload, powered by a 185bhp diesel engine.*

ZIL trucks were in fact ZIS trucks under a new name. As a development of the old AMO (Automobilnoe Moskowvoskoe Obshchestvo) company, which built Fiat trucks under licence from 1924, the ZIS plant was formed in 1933 in honour of the Russian leader Joseph Stalin. ZIS stood for Zavod Imieni Stalina, and the first ZIS trucks of 1934 were virtually identical to AMOs. Heavier 6×4 4-tonne versions were added in 1935. During World War II a shadow factory was built in the Ural mountains and trucks built there were known as URAL-ZIS. In the post-war era ZIS introduced its 150 4-tonner based loosely on the American International Harvester K series.

In 1957, during the de-Stalinization of the USSR, the ZIS name was changed to ZIL, the "L" being in homage to the company's manager, Mr Likhacheva. During the 1960s and beyond, ZIL developed its own models like the ZIL-130, probably one of the best-known Russian trucks. The bonneted 6½-tonner was produced in vast numbers and is still to be seen in most of the former Communist countries and Eastern Europe. Six-wheelers, like the 15-tonne gvw ZIL-131 6×6 are aimed mainly at military duties, being powered by 150bhp V8 gasoline engines. Heavier bonneted six-wheelers for up to 24 tonnes gvw, using an adaptation of the ZIL-130 cab, take a Kamaz-built V8 diesel providing 210bhp. These are designated 133VJA models.

SLOUGH, ENGLAND

ZWICKY

■ LEFT *Typical of Zwicky's products is this purpose-built airport runway sweeper powered by a Ford engine.*

Zwicky specialized in fire appliances, aircraft refuellers, runway sweepers and similar machines for airfield use. They were in production from 1910 until about 1970. Ford engines were used.

ACKNOWLEDGEMENTS

The publishers would like to thank the following picture libraries and photographers for the use of their pictures in the book (t=top; b=bottom; l=left; r=right; c=centre; u=upper; lo=lower).

TRACTORS

Agripicture: 30bl (Peter Dean); 81tl (Peter Dean); 133tl; 148br; 157tl (Peter Dean); 168t (Peter Dean); **Alpha Stock:** 19b, tl; 20tl, bl; 21bl; 32r; 84bl; 133r; **John Bolt:** 34bl; 35tr, cl, bl; 37bl; 39tr; 49tr, br; 51br; 54b; 60bl; 69br; 81cr; 88cr, bl; 92bl; 93tr, cr, br; 94tr, cr; 95br, bl; 99tl; 99tl, tr; 101 (all); 104tr; 105tc, tr, br; 110br; 111tr, b; 115bl, br; 117tl, tr, br; 118t, tr, b; 123t; 130b; 134b, tr; 136c, br, bl; 137bl; 142br; 145bl; 146t, bl, br; 149tr, br; 150cr, bl; 154b; 159bl; 164tl, tr; 165br, tr; 169t; 182c; 192; 193t; 197t, c, b; 184bl; 200b; 201bl, br; 206tl; 212t, c, b; 221tl, tr, c, b; 228t, c, b; 229tl; 231tl, tr; 232t; 252br; 253tc, tr, b; 255bl; **John Carroll:** 18 all; 20tr; 33bl; 64tr, bl; 66; 70tl; 83cr; 89cr, br, bl; 91cl; 92br; 96bl; 99b; 110t, bl; 120tr; 121t, b; 123c, b; 128b; 132t, bl, br; 133bl; 134tr; 135bl; 136tr, 137tr; 149tl; 151tl; 154c; 155b; 157tr; 158t, c; 165c; 166tl; 171b; 184br; 185t; 199t, c, b; 203bl; 206tr; 214t; 215tl, tr, b; 216t,; 217t, c, b; 232b; 233br; 235b; 238t, b; 239t, b; 241c; 242t; 247t; 252t; **CDC:** 28–9 (Orde Eliason); 50br (Orde Eliason); 61br (Judy Boyd); 62; 63tr (Orde Eliason), b (Orde Eliason); 92tr; 129t; **C.F.C.L:** 137tl; 241b; 246t; **Ian Clegg:** 69cr; 135t, cr; 142bl; 144t; 145t, br; 148bl; 157b; 201t, c; 203t, bl; 233bl; **Image Bank:** 244bl (Guido A. Rossi); **Impact:** 33cl (Alain le Garsmeur,), t (Alain le Garsmeur), cr (Alain le Garsmeur); 79cl (Erol Houssein); 82br (Tony Page); 130t (Colin Shaw); 138c (Tony Page); 166tr (Julian Calder); 244tl (Alain le Garsmeur), cl (Mark Henley), br (Michael Good); 246b (Anne-Marie Purkiss); **Imperial War Museum:** 39b; 40tr, br; 41br; 59b; 76cr; 85tr; 90cr, cl; **Massey Ferguson:** 93bl; **Andrew Morland:** 2; 10; 11b; 14 all; 15 all; 16tr, r; 17br: 22bl; 23br, tl; 24br, tl; 25b, tl; 26tl, br; 27t, bl; 31br; 36all; 37cr; 38bl; 39cl, bl, tl; 39; 40tl, cr; 41cl, tl, cr, tr; 48bl; 50tl; 56bl; 57bl, tr; 58 bl, tr; 59t; 71tl; 85b; 86b, c; 87t, bl, br; 90tr, bl; 91bl, cl; 96tr, br; 97t, b; 102bl, tr, br; 103t, b; 106tl; 108bl, tr; 109tr, c, br; 112t, br; 113; 119t, c, b; 120bl, br; 126; 127b; 129b; 140t; 141br; 142t; 143tl; 148t; 150t, cl; 151tr, br; 152t, c, b; 153tl, tr, bl, br; 155tr; 158b; 159t, br; 161t, c, bl, br; 169b; 194t, c, b; 195t, b; 196t; 206br; 207c, b; 210t, b: 211c, b; 213t, b; 214b; 218t; 219t; 220t; 222t, c, b; 223t, b; 224; 225t, c; 226t, b; 227tl, tr, b; 229tr, b; 235t; 236; 237bl, br; 240tr, tl, bl, br; 242c, bl, br; 243t, b; 245t, bl, br; 247b; 248t, b; 250bl, br; 251t, b; 254t; 258cr; **Public Record Office Image Library:** 91tr; **Ann Ronan Picture Library:** 16bl; 17tl, tr, r; 18tr; 21br; 78tr; **Royal Geographical Society:** 141t; **Rural History Centre, University of Reading:** 52c; **Spectrum Colour Library:** 42–43; 53t; 77tr; 78bl; 79cr; 93tr; 122b (E. Chalker), t; 128t; 131; 139t; 147t; 155tl; 156t; 168b; 181t; 185b; 186t; 204t; 205b; 206bl; 207t; 216b; 225b; 233t; 255cr; 258tl, b; 259tl, tr; **Still Pictures:** 68b; 81cl; 83br (Pierre Gleizes), bl (Jeff Greenberg); 95tl (Mark Edwards); 182b (Allan Morgan); 202t (Paul Harrison); 203br (Chris Caldicott); 241t (Pierre Gleizes); **Tony Stone Images:** 12–13 (Peter Dean); 51t (Colin Raw); 54tl (Gary Moon); 72–3 (Mitch Kezar); 74b (Peter Dean); 75cr (Arnulf Husmo); 76tl (Bruce Forster) 1/4 pg; 77tl (Kevin Horan); 79br (Bruce Forster); 82bl (Wayne Eastep); 83cr (Jerry Gay); 100 (Art Wolfe); 127t (Billy Nustace); 147b (Bertrand Rieger); 154t; 166bl (John & Eliza Forder); 167tl; 187t; 249t (Arnulf Husmo); 255br (Andrew Sacks); 257b (Andy Sacks); 259b (Bruce Hands); **Gary Stuart:** 30tr; 31t; 32tr, bl; 37tr; 38tr; 44r, bl; 45tl, tr, br; 46tl, br; 47t, bl, br; 48tr; 49bl; 52bl, cl, br; 53br; 54tr; 55br, t; 68 tr, c; 69tl; 70 br; 71br; 74cr; 75br, tl, tr; 76br, bl; 77br, bl, cr; 79tl, tr; 80tr, cr, bl; 81tr, cr, b; 82cr, tr; 83tr; 86t; 88tr, br; 94bl; 104bl; 106c, b; 107t, b; 114b, t; 115t; 116tl, c, br, bl; 124tl, t, b; 125t, b; 138t, b; 139cl, cr, b; 141b; 141bl; 143b; 144b; 149bl; 156tl; 160t, b; 162bl, br; 163t, cl, c, cr, b; 164bl, 1/4 pg; 165tl; 166c; 167tr, cr, b; 170b; 171t; 172t, c, b; 173t, c, b; 174t, cl, cr, b; 175c, b; 176t, bl, br; 177t, c, b; 178t, c, b; 179t, c, b; 180tr, c, tl, b; 181b; 182t; 183t, c, b; 184t; 185c; 186c, b; 187bl, br; 188t, b; 189t, c, b; 190t, b; 191t, c, b; 196 b; 197t, c, b; 200t; 202c, b; 203c; 204b; 205t, cl, cr; 208t, c, b; 209tr, tl, cl, b; 211t; 219b; 220b; 230t, c, b; 231b; 234; 249b; 250t; 252bl,; 254c, b; 255t; 256t, b; 257t, c; 259c; **Superstock:** 16tl; 22tr; 34tr; 60tr; 61tl; 74t; 78br; 151br; 162t; 165bl; 175t; 218b; **Tank Museum Collection:** 23tr; 56tr; 65; 67br; tl; 83tr; 84tr, cr; 85cl, cr; 89t.

TRUCKS

Peter J. Davies supplied the majority of the trucks photographs, together with the following picture libraries.

TB Scania: 277t; 470t, c; **Ashok Leyland:** 330br, lo, br; **N. Baldwin:** 351t; **Bering Truck Corp:** 336t; **BMC Sanayi ve Ticaret AS:** 339t, b; **DaimlerChrysler:** 270t; 273tl; 277b; 362c; 437t; 438 tl, b; **E.T. Davies:** 507c; **F. Gambut:** 347b; **A.J. Ingram:** 316bl; 331bl; 333c, b; 341br; 342c; 351t; 351c; 356b; 357b; 363t, cb, br; 379b; 382c; 392t, c; 393b; 409t; 411c, b; 426c; 434t; 444c; 445b; 451b; 455b; 457b; 464t; 480t; 482t; 484t; 490t; **Iveco:** 331cl; **N. Jansen:** 427cl; **P. Love:** 346bl; 426b; 445uc; 481c; 502t; **Mack Museum:** 428tc; **MOL n.v:** 444b; **National Motor Museum:** 268c; 269t; **Nicolas:** 446b; **Oshkosh Truck Corp:** 306b; 307tr; 449c; **R. Pearson:** 306t; **Peterbilt Motors Co:** 455tr; **M.D. Phippard:** 314br; 316lor; 331tr; 341t; 498b; **M. Platt:** 317br; **Roman SA:** 362t, 485b; **Skoda-LiAZ:** 479b; **P. Sposito:** 317tl; 345bc; 367b; 456c; 486b; **A. Syme:** 507t; **E. van Ingen-Sohenau:** 411u; 506b; **Tony Stone Images:** front cover; 264–5; 280–1; 292–3; 310–11.

INDEX